Why You Need This New Edition

Goode: Deviant Behavior, 9/e

- The new edition is thoroughly updated with the latest research.
- An all new chapter (7), discusses alcohol abuse as a form of deviance.
- New examples of deviant behavior are incorporated throughout the chapters. Here are just a few of the new examples discussed:
    - Eliot Spitzer, then governor of NY, was discovered by an IRS-FBI team to have engaged in liasons with call girls. He had to resign his position.
    - Derek Wolcott, a Nobel Prize-winning poet, is accused of sexual harassment; Ruth Padel, Wolcott's rival for an academic position, sent reporters email allegations of Mr. Wolcott's improprieties.
    - In the chapter on organizational behavior, the author discusses Bernard Madoff, an investment broker, who committed the largest fraud ever carried out by a single individual. He swindled his 4,800 clients of between $50 and $65 *billion*.
    - In the chapter on cognitive deviance, there is discussion of a fundamentalist Christian who accused Buzz Aldrin, an astronaut, of having lied about the moon landing. He waved a Bible in the astronaut's face, the two scuffled and Aldrin punched the moon-landing denier in the face. The police refused to press charges. Pollsters point out that atheism is declining with respect to the seriousness with which Americans regard it as a form of deviance. Americans are becoming more secular and the % self-identifying as Christian is declining.
    - In the chapter on alcohol consumption as a form of deviance, the author discusses whether there is a relationship between a country's consumption of alcohol and its rate of criminal homicide.

PEARSON

NINTH EDITION

DEVIANT BEHAVIOR

ERICH GOODE

State University of New York at Stony Brook

Prentice Hall

Boston Columbus Indianapolis New York San Francisco Upper Saddle River
Amsterdam Cape Town Dubai London Madrid Milan Munich Paris Montreal Toronto
Delhi Mexico City Sao Paulo Sydney Hong Kong Seoul Singapore Taipei Tokyo

Publisher: Karen Hanson
Editorial Assistant: Alyssa Levy
Executive Marketing Manager: Kelly May
Marketing Assistant: Gina Lavagna
Production Manager: Fran Russello
Associate Project Manager: Maggie Brobeck
Full Service Project Management/Composition: Shiny Rajesh/Integra Software Services Pvt. Ltd.
Creative Director: Jayne Conte
Cover Designer: Bruce Kenselaar
Cover Art: Jupiter images/Getty images, Inc.

Credits appear on page 328, which constitutes an extension of the copyright page.

Library of Congress Cataloging-in-Publication Data

Goode, Erich.
Deviant behavior/Erich Goode.—9th ed.
p. cm.
Includes bibliographical references and index.
ISBN-13: 978-0-205-74807-5 (alk. paper)
ISBN-10: 0-205-74807-4 (alk. paper)
1. Deviant behavior. 2. Criminal behavior. 3. Deviant behavior. 4. Criminal behavior. I. Title.
HM811.G66 2011
302.5'42—dc22

2010005275

10 9 8 7 6 5 4 3 2 1—DOH—14 13 12 11 10

Prentice Hall
is an imprint of

PEARSON

www.pearsonhighered.com

ISBN-10: 0-205-74807-4
ISBN-13: 978-0-205-74807-5

Brief Contents

Contents

Preface

In the pages of *Deviant Behavior*, the reader will meet a gay drunkard, a devotee of S&M sex, a computer pirate, an ex-convict, a transitioning transsexual, a believer in the reality of UFOs—and many other offbeat and interesting characters who depart from the mainstream norms of the society and deal with the fallout they'll likely experience for their actions, beliefs, or conditions. What makes them the way they are? How do they live their lives? Are they really that different from the rest of us? And why are such people ostracized and condemned by others? And how does such ostracism and condemnation shape a person's life?

Deviance and social control are basic and ineradicable features of social life. All societies define what's acceptable and unacceptable with regard to behavior, beliefs, and characteristics, and the manner in which they punish and condemn members who enact, promulgate, and possess them is socially and culturally patterned. In other words, humans are rule-making and rule-violating creatures. The central thesis of the study of deviance is that sociologists can study, understand, and explicate patterns of social control and departures from norms of acceptability; this book provides Exhibit A in support of that assertion.

Historically, the first two textbooks devoted to the sociology of deviance appeared in the 1950s: the first, written by Edwin Lemert, bore the strangely anachronistic title *Social Pathology: A Systematic Approach to the Theory of Sociopathic Behavior* (1951), which staked out the constructionist approach, and the second, a more traditional positivistic volume, was Marshall Clinard's *Sociology of Deviant Behavior* (1957). In effect, these two texts created the field—and the course—of deviance and, together, trailblazed the twin emphases or approaches that are still shared by contemporary instructors and researchers, which run like bright threads throughout this book. Howard Becker's *Outsiders: Studies in the Sociology of Deviance* (1963), the paradigmatic constructionist opus, further specified where a major sector of the field was going and would go, a direction that prevails to this day—though Becker's work reflected the usual biases of the 1960s, revealed by his choice of prototypical deviants: marijuana users and jazz musicians. Becker's slant, that deviants were "more sinned against that sinning" (1967), was mocked in doggerel a few years later by sociologist Don Martindale—who actually referred to Robert K. Merton: "Saints stink while whores smell good. . . . Before the stench of saints can clog our pores/Let us all embrace those fragrant whores" (*ASA Footnotes*, May 1976, p. 5). The charge of embracing "fragrant whores" applied even more emphatically to Becker's approach to deviance than to Merton's.

But this bias toward irony proves not so much wrong as overstated. People designated as deviants often, indeed, usually engage in benevolent or inoffensive actions; and in principle, conventional, law-abiding behavior, taken as a whole, is not infrequently destructive. The condemnation that rains down upon the head of the normative violator, when it does, may or may not be well earned; some condemnations are ignited by evil, harmful actions, while others are touched off by persons who don't deserve the stigma. One lesson that students should take away from a deviance course, if they haven't learned it by now, is that life often isn't fair. Conventional society doesn't necessarily play the role of the "bad guy," and the condemned, stigmatized party may be neither innocent nor benevolent. The relationship between wrongdoing and harm, and engaging in normative violations and being condemned, is an empirical question—although it'll probably never be answered to the satisfaction of all observers. Suffice it to say that, sometimes, more than a trickle of justice oozes out of the mechanism of social control.

In the present edition, the ninth, I have added Chapter 7, on alcohol abuse as a form of deviance, condensed the former Chapters 2, 3, and 4, which discussed theories of and approaches to deviance, into two chapters; and streamlined the remainder of the chapters, as well as updated the book's documentation and examples. The book retains the core assumption that the study of deviance is not an inquiry into marginal, exotic, subterranean activities and people, but represents an investigation into the nature of the human condition; again, the processes of rule-making, rule violation, and rule enforcement constitute the very foundation of human life everywhere and throughout the span of human existence. All of us engage in these processes, and all of us experience them as real or implied reactions from others. As Emile Durkheim said a century ago, the survival of all societies depends on some of us acting out normative imperatives, yet a too-strict enforcement of society's rules is stifling and sclerotic; it chokes off social change. All societies walk the tightrope of too little versus too much social control.

I am deeply indebted to the contributors of the accounts that appear at the end of the chapters of this book; some were the subject of a particular account, others interviewed or wrote about the subject of an account. They shared their time and experiences and observations with me—or with another interviewer—and now they are sharing them with the reader; I hope my presentation of their accounts will prove to be a worthwhile pedagogical device. Most of these contributors have chosen to remain anonymous; a few were willing to publicly reveal their names. I'd also like to thank my many students of deviance at SUNY/Stony Brook and the University of Maryland, who challenged me to clarify the ideas and findings of this most fascinating subject, the sociology of deviance. As usual, discussions with my wife, Barbara Weinstein, herself a social scientist and a historian of Brazil, and my good friend, Nachman Ben-Yehuda, a professor of sociology at The Hebrew University of Jerusalem, have proven fruitful and useful in my preparation of this edition. And, as always, I am eternally grateful to the practitioners and authors in the field of the sociology of deviance who have investigated and written about this lively and fascinating subject. I also owe a debt of gratitude to James Colliver of the National Survey on Drug Use and Health, Substance Abuse and Health Administration, and Patti Meyer of Monitoring the Future, for supplying me with the beautiful tables that appear in Chapter 7 on the relationship between alcohol (and tobacco) consumption and illicit drug use, Tables 7-4 and 7-5. These researchers' assistance was generous—they contributed their time and expertise to my endeavor—and I am grateful for their help.

The account that appears in Chapter 7, on alcohol abuse, was previously published in *Deviance in Everyday Life: Personal Accounts of Unconventional Lives*, Waveland Press, 2002. I am grateful to Waveland for permission to reprint this material. I also adapted a few pages from my essay, "The Stigma of Obesity," which originally appeared in my anthology, *Social Deviance*, Allyn & Bacon, 1996. Here's how I interpret the "fair use" of written copyrighted material. I have the right to reprint up to 500 words, if taken from a book or a book-length manuscript, and up to 250 words, if taken from an article or an article-length manuscript, without obtaining permission from the copyright holder. If the work is briefer than the usual article, I have the right to reprint up to 10 percent of said work, again, without obtaining permission from the author or publisher. For a "practical guide" to copyright, see William S. Strong, *The Copyright Book*, MIT Press, multiple editions. And I'd like to thank the Department of History at New York University for hiring my wife as a faculty member and the good people of Greenwich Village for being such fascinating, lively, and unconventional neighbors.

Erich Goode
New York, NY

CHAPTER 1

Introduction

At an Internal Revenue Service (IRS) office on Long Island, a routine examination of "suspicious transactions" reported by banks turned up records of large sums of money being transferred by Eliot Spitzer, governor of New York. Intriguing to the IRS auditors was the fact that the money ended up in, and was withdrawn from, dummy or "shell" corporations—fake companies that conducted no actual business. The auditors suspected that these transactions indicated possible bribery or political corruption of some kind, so they got in touch with officials at the FBI who specialized in political corruption. After obtaining permission from the U.S. attorney general to proceed with the case, the IRS–FBI team began tracing where the money was going. Prostitution, they said, "was the furthest thing" from their minds.

But soon into the search, investigators discovered that Governor Spitzer was in fact using the money to pay for liaisons with call girls. The Justice Department then authorized taps on relevant phones and computers, and the team contacted a woman who had previously worked for the Emperor's Club VIP, the service that they suspected Mr. Spitzer was using. She agreed to serve as a confidential informant to infiltrate the business to turn up incriminating evidence about its operations and its clients, including, possibly, Governor Spitzer. The team intercepted 5,000 telephone calls and text messages, along with 6,000 e-mail messages and bank, travel, and hotel records. This surveillance recorded Mr. Spitzer on wiretap discussing payments and arranging to meet "Kristen," a call girl, in a room at the Mayflower, in Washington, D.C. The club's code name for the governor was Client 9. Although he had made use of the club's services before, for one particular encounter the team gathered evidence that Spitzer had paid the young woman $4,300 (Rashbaum, 2008).

Two days after the story of the scandal broke, the governor held a news conference, with his wife at his side. "Over the course of my public life, I have insisted, I believe correctly, that people, regardless of their position or power, take responsibility for their conduct," Spitzer explained. "I can and will ask no less of myself. For this reason, I am resigning from the office of governor. . . . I cannot allow my private failings to disrupt the people's work" (Ross, 2008).

In Washington, the Justice Department, at the insistence of President Barack Obama, revealed memos spelling out "brutal" interrogation techniques by CIA operatives. The Justice Department of the administration of President George W. Bush (2001–2009) had authorized methods many observers considered cruel, inhumane, degrading, and in violation of conventions covering rules of warfare signed by representatives of the United States. The Bush administration's argument held that anti-American insurgents are not "enemy combatants" in the usual sense of the word; they do not fight for officially recognized armies and do not themselves observe the rules of conventional warfare. Hence, these officials reasoned, the harsh techniques used against such insurgents did not constitute torture. One Bush official declared that the criteria of "cruel and inhuman" punishment are met only if the detainee suffers organ failure or death. A CIA memo claimed that restrictions against torture "did not apply" to these techniques, and *even if they did,* they are justified because of the threat facing the country from insurgents. One official claimed that these modes of interrogation do not "shock the conscience"—whose conscience, the official did not say.

The harsh methods of interrogation that Bush-regime officials authorized, and which CIA operatives used against Muslim insurgents, included the following: "walling," or slamming the detainee against a wall; depriving the detainee of sleep for up to a week; cramped confinement in a small, dark box; cramped confinement in a small, dark box along with informing the detainee that interrogators are releasing stinging insects into the box (only caterpillars were actually released); slapping the detainee in the face and the abdomen; and dousing the detainee with icy cold water from a hose. The most controversial technique is referred to as "waterboarding": placing the suspect on a surface, usually a board, his head titled downward, thereby immobilizing him, putting a cloth over his face, and pouring water from a height of one or two feet for up to 40 seconds, making him unable to breathe, thus simulating the experience of drowning (Mazzetti and Shane, 2009).

President Obama, who has already banned waterboarding along with other unconventional and severe interrogation techniques, denounced these methods as harsh and cruel but initially stated that he would not authorize the Department of Justice to pursue criminal cases against the interrogators. "This is not a time for retribution," he stated, "this is a time for reflection." But a few days later, he seemed to reverse his position by stating, "With respect to those who formulated those legal decisions, that is going to be more of a decision for the Attorney General within the parameters of various laws, and I don't want to prejudge that" (van Wagtendonk, 2009). Some pundits suggested that the public's conscience was so shocked by these methods that if the president did not pursue prosecution of their architects, he could not be reelected.

In Boston, Jennifer Cacicio, curious about what had become of an ex-boyfriend, entered the man's name into MySpace. What she saw on the screen shocked her: a portfolio of pictures of him suspended in the air by hooks, "his skin stretched out like freshly pulled taffy." One picture in particular, she says, both repelled and fascinated her: a wide, pale human back "darkened only by a big black tattoo of skulls and ghostlike faces from a vintage cartoon shrouded in a kind of webbing." Trickles of blood trailed through the tattoo. Jenifer's eyes traced the blood upward, to its source: "four large silver hooks pierced the skin of his upper back, which was stretched far beyond what seemed safe or even possible."

She called her sister. "Turn on your computer," Jennifer commanded, directing her to the ex-boyfriend's MySpace site.

"Oh, my God," her sister said.

"Oh, my God," Jennifer agreed (Cacicio, 2007).

In Bangkok, a novelist, Harry Nicholaides, is sentenced to three years imprisonment for "insulting the Thai monarchy" (Mydans and McDonald, 2009). In the Middle East, much of the population clings to the belief that Muslims did not perpetrate the September 11, 2001, attack on the World Trade Towers in New York City. "Why is it on 9/11, the Jews didn't go to work in the building," the Cairo cabdriver declares. "Everybody knows this. I saw it on TV, and a lot of people talk about it" (Slackman, 2008). In Rwanda, John Rucyahana, an Anglican bishop who, as a teenager, had fled the country as it erupted in an orgy of ethnic cruelty and mass violence and slaughter, joins a team of clerics digging for the graves of victims: "In one home, we found 27 dead bodies, including a dog and a cat. . . . Some of the pastors couldn't sleep; they spent the night crying. . . . Two of them had to be taken back home" (Cose, 2009). In New York City, the police charge a 27-year-old Queens middle school teacher with the statutory rape of a 14-year-old student "after his mother searched his cell phone and found logs of hundreds of text messages and calls with the woman" (Buettner, 2009). In Arkansas, a white supremacist organization tries to recruit new members (Conant, 2009). In the United Kingdom, Derek Walcott, a Nobel Prize–winning poet, withdraws his candidacy for a position at Oxford University as a result of charges that, in the past, he was guilty of sexual harassment (Lyall, 2009). Less than two weeks later, Ruth Padel, his rival for the coveted position, withdraws her name because she had sent reporters e-mail allegations of Mr. Walcott's improprieties (Burns, 2009).

What do these things have in common? All, in one way or another, describe deviant behavior or beliefs. What is deviance?

Deviance is behavior, beliefs, or characteristics (or behavior, beliefs, or characteristics that are *imputed* to a particular person) *that many people in a society find or would find offensive and which excite, upon discovery, disapproval, punishment, condemnation, or hostility. Deviance is behavior, beliefs, or characteristics that are likely to generate a negative reaction in others. Deviance* refers to the process by which the actor's, the believer's, and the possessor's character is tainted, stigmatized, and *inferiorized.* The sociology of deviance looks at *informal* and *interpersonal* reactions to behavior, beliefs, and traits, just as criminology looks at formal and legal reactions to crime, the latter being possible arrest, conviction, and imprisonment. Examples of deviance: engaging in acts of prostitution, expressing a favorable opinion of the Ku Klux Klan, bribing a government official, using heroin to get high, robbing a bank, engaging in sadomasochistic sex, being hideously ugly, being an ex-convict, being diagnosed as—and manifesting the symptoms of—a schizophrenic, embezzling company funds, engaging in sex with a minor, and being hugely obese.

The study of deviance is about *making* rules, *breaking* rules, and reactions *to* breaking rules. Deviance is a *process,* not specific forms of behaviors. *Deviance* describes what is likely to happen when people break rules that are held in a society or among certain social circles within a society. Of course, some actions are predefined as deviance because of the meaning of specific words; for instance, if we use the term "murder," by definition, we regard the act to which the word refers as an unauthorized, deviant killing; *crime* is by definition an illegal, illicit act. But at certain times, in certain places, and to certain social circles or sectors of the society, acts that many people today regard as blameworthy—such as prostitution, torture, white supremacy, and genocide—are or were accepted, tolerated, and even encouraged.

If asked, almost anyone can come up with a number of examples of what he or she regards as "deviant." I'm sure you, the reader, could. From time to time, on the first day of class, I have asked the students in my deviance course to define the term and come up with some examples of deviance. The last time I did this, the students who were enrolled in this course were able to name an average of six examples each; well over 100 separate activities or conditions were named. However, it was much harder for these students to define deviance *generally;* in fact, many of them did not answer this question. Most of us find it difficult to locate the *general property or characteristic* that defines an act, a belief, or a condition *as* deviance.

Some people think that in today's world, agreement on what's right and wrong has vaporized; since "anything goes," deviance no longer exists. "Deviance should be defined by the departure from a clearly defined standard," says Sumner in his "obituary" for the concept (1994). If a strong consensus on rules does not prevail, then deviance doesn't exist. In the view of most sociologists, this is entirely false. Would the critics who hold such a position predict, for instance, that *no one* would react to Governor Spitzer's visits and payments to call girls? Or that there would be *no* consequences of the Justice Department's approval, and the CIA's practice, of the torture of terrorist suspects—or to the assorted beliefs and practices from around the world—mentioned earlier? Are these acts and beliefs perfectly acceptable because hardly anyone makes judgments of good and bad any more? And if certain beliefs and practices *do* generate punishment and widespread condemnation, what does that say about the denial of deviance?

These questions practically answer themselves. Denying the reality of deviance is entirely mistaken for three reasons: One, we *can* find widespread agreement that certain acts and beliefs are wrong. Two, what's regarded and reacted to as wrong is not *simply* about firm society-wide consensus, but also about how certain social circles of people feel and what they do *in specific situations and contexts.* And three, some disagreement prevails even about widely accepted norms, but far from denying the relevance of deviance, it affirms it, since much of what deviance is about is the "struggle over whose rules will prevail" (Marshall, Douglas, and McDonnell, 2007, p. 71).

DEVIANCE IN EVERYDAY LIFE

Just about everyone has done *something* that someone else disapproves of. Perhaps we've stolen something, or told a lie, or gossiped about another person in an especially nasty manner. Maybe more than once we've gotten drunk, or high, or driven too fast, or recklessly, or gone through a red light without bothering to stop. Have we ever worn clothes someone else thought were out of style, offensive, or ugly? Have we ever belched at the dinner table, broken wind, or picked our nose in public? Have we ever cut class or failed to read an assignment? Do we like a television program someone else finds stupid and boring? Didn't we once date someone our parents and friends didn't like? Maybe our religious beliefs and practices don't agree with those of some other members of society.

Humans are evaluative creatures. We continually make judgments about the behavior, beliefs, or appearance of others. And each one of us does exactly the same thing—evaluate others. Societies everywhere have rules or *norms* governing what we may and may not do, how we should think, what we should believe, and even how we should look, and those norms are so detailed and complex, and so dependent on the views of different evaluators, that what *everyone* does, believes, and is, is looked on negatively by *someone,* indeed, in all likelihood, by lots of other people. Believers in God look down on atheists; atheists think believers in God are misguided and mistaken. Fundamentalist Christians oppose the beliefs of fundamentalist Muslims, and vice versa. Liberals dislike the views of conservatives; to conservatives, the feeling is mutual. Many college campuses are divided into mutually exclusive ethnic and racial enclaves; in student unions, often, the whites sit together in their own area and African Americans in theirs. Jocks and druggies, brains and preppies, Greeks, geeks, and hippies—the number of possible ways that what we believe, or do, or are could be judged negatively by others is almost infinite.

There are four necessary ingredients for deviance to take place or exist: One, a rule or *norm* must exist. Two, someone must violate (or be thought to violate) that norm. Three, an "audience" must be present, someone who judges the normative violation to be wrong. Four, there must be a measurable likelihood of a negative reaction by that audience—criticism, condemnation, censure, stigma, disapproval, and so on. To qualify as deviance, it isn't even necessary to violate a norm that's serious, like the Ten Commandments. Norms are everywhere; they vary in seriousness, and different people have different norms. In other words, "deviance" is a matter of degree, from trivial to extremely serious. "I've never done anything seriously wrong," we might tell ourselves. "There's nothing deviant about me!" we add. But "wrong" according to *whose* standards? And "deviant" in what sense? To what degree? We might feel that our belief in God is a good thing, but, as we saw, an atheist is likely to disagree. Chances are that we think our political position is reasonable; many of our fellow citizens will disagree, finding our politics foolish and wrongheaded. Our friends are probably in sync with us with respect to lifestyle and taste in clothing, but unbeknownst to us, behind our backs, there are others who make fun of us because of the way we dress and act. The point is this: Nearly everything about every one of us—both the reader and the author of this book included—is a potential source of criticism, condemnation, or censure, in *some* social circles, from the point of view of *some* observers.

The point is, deviance is not a simple quality resting with a given action, belief, or trait inherent in, intrinsic to, or indwelling within them. An act, for example, is not regarded as deviant everywhere and at all times (though some acts are *more* widely condemned than others are). What makes a given act deviant is the way it is seen, regarded, judged, evaluated, and the way that others—audiences—treat the person who engages in that act. Deviance is that which is reacted to negatively, in a socially rejecting fashion. Acts, beliefs, and traits are deviant *to* certain persons or audiences or in certain social circles. What defines deviance are the actual or potential *reactions* that actions, beliefs, and traits generate or are likely to generate in audiences. It is this negative reaction that defines or constitutes a given act, belief, or trait as deviant. Without that reaction, actual or potential, we do not have a case of deviance on our hands. When that reaction takes place, or is "stored up" in someone, we do.

Humans are evaluative creatures: We create and enforce rules. But we also violate some of society's rules. We park in "No Parking" zones; behind their backs, we make fun of bosses, parents, and professors; we smoke where we're not supposed to; shoplift when we don't have enough money or don't feel like waiting in line; speed to get where we're going; and perhaps occasionally have sex with the wrong partner. Not one of us is passive, obeying all rules like a robot programmed to follow society's commands. The human animal is active, creative, and irrepressible. Even though all societies generate a multitude of rules, their violations, likewise, are multitudinous. In fact, the more numerous and detailed the rules, the more opportunities there are for normative violations.

Hardly anyone abides by *all* rules *all* the time. Indeed, this is a literal impossibility, since some of these rules contradict one another. None of these rules are considered valid by everyone in any society. As we saw, in every society on earth—in some far more than in others—there is a certain degree of variation in notions of right and wrong from one person to another, one group or category to another, one subculture to another. Especially in a large, complex, urban, multicultural, multiethnic, and multinational society such as the United States, this variation is considerable—indeed, immense. This means that almost any action, belief, or characteristic we could think of is approved in some social circles and condemned in others. Almost inevitably, we deviate from someone's rules simply by acting, believing, or being, since it is impossible to conform to all the rules that prevail.

SO, WHAT *IS* DEVIANCE?

Sociologically, deviance exists where we have the following: (1) something—an act, a belief, or a physical condition—that violates a social norm or rule; (2) a person or persons who engage in the act, express the belief, or possess the condition; (3) an audience or a group of persons who judges and evaluates the normative violation; and (4) the likelihood that negative social reactions will follow the discovery of that violation. Deviance exists when what one does, is, or believes is likely to generate in an audience a negative reaction: scorn, mockery, ridicule, censure, condemnation, punishment, hostility, stigma, social isolation, shunning, and/or denunciation.

Once again, in every human collectivity that has ever existed, rules for proper behavior are laid down; and again, all people violate the rules of one or another group, or of the society at large; likewise, again, in every human collectivity, reactions of some members of these collectivities express disapproval of such violations. In every society or social circle, no member perfectly conforms to every rule or norm, and hence, indeed, this is impossible, since some of these rules are contradictory. Over a lifetime, no one has escaped some ridicule, censure, or punishment from someone. Humanity is diverse; there's a huge variation in definitions of right and wrong, true and false; humans are fallible, that is, they are unable or unwilling to conform to all of the many rules of the society. Or, since every society is made up of subcategories—diverse social circles—some normative violations, and the negative reactions they touch off, are inevitable. Deviance occurs in every society on earth. Although what is regarded as deviant varies considerably—but not randomly—from society to society and from one social category to another, the condemnation and punishment of enactors, holders, and possessors of unacceptable behavior, beliefs, and traits are universal, a panhuman phenomenon. There has never been, nor will there ever be, a society of saints on earth, with everyone in a society following the Golden Rule or the Word of God in all respects.

Does saying that something is deviant in a certain social circle or a society mean that we agree that it should be condemned? Of course not! Everyone of us has his or her own views, and those views may agree or disagree with the audiences whose reactions we are looking at. Does this mean that when we use the term *deviant* we seek to denigrate, put down, or humiliate anyone to whom the term applies? Absolutely not! Again, we may agree or disagree with the judgment, but if we observe it, and it hits us like a pie in the face, we would be foolish and ignorant to pretend that it doesn't exist. If we say that a president's approval rating is high, or low, it does not mean that we approve, or disapprove, of that president. What it means is that we take note of public opinion. When we say that in American society, generally, prostitutes, political radicals, and atheists tend to be looked down upon and regarded as deviants, this does not mean that we necessarily agree with that judgment. It means that, as sociologists, we recognize that certain negative consequences are likely to result from announcing to a cross-section of American society that one is a prostitute, a radical, or an atheist. In other words, the terms *deviance* and *deviant* are absolutely *nonpejorative.* This means that they are descriptive terms that apply to what others think and how they are likely to react. You may hate a particular movie, but if it is number one at the box office, you can still say it is a "popular" movie—because popularity is *defined* by box office sales. You could be an atheist and still say that atheism is deviant. Even if you don't agree with that judgment, it is materially real in that it has consequences, and as sociologists, we must acknowledge the existence of those consequences.

In short, deviance is an analytic category: It applies in all spheres and areas of human life; it is a transhistorical, cross-cultural concept. The dynamics of deviance have taken place throughout recorded history and in every known society, anywhere humans interact with one another. Everywhere, people are evaluated on the basis of what they do, what they believe, and who they are—and they are thus reacted to accordingly.

Deviance takes place during a basketball game; during your professor's office hours; during "happy hour" in the local bar; during final exams; in department stores; on the street; in the church, synagogue, and mosque; and within the bosom of the family. Deviance is everywhere and anywhere people engage in behavior, hold and express beliefs, and possess traits that others regard as unacceptable. Normative violations, and reactions to normative violations, occur everywhere. They exist and have existed in all societies everywhere and for all time. They are central to who we are as human beings.

SOCIETAL AND SITUATIONAL DEVIANCE

So far, it seems that I've been arguing that *anything* can be deviant, that if a collectivity of people—a group, a social circle, a segment of the population, any assemblage of people, really—regard something as unacceptable, by our definition, it is deviant. This is true, but only half true. There are two sides to judgments of deviance. One is its vertical or *hierarchical* side, the side that says that people with more power (or the majority of a society) get to say what's deviant. The other is its horizontal or "grassroots" or *mosaic* side, the side that says deviance can be anything that *any* collectivity says it is, no matter how little power they have. In other words, according to Kenneth Plummer (1979, pp. 97–99), we must make a distinction between societal deviance and situational deviance.

Societal deviance is composed of those actions and conditions that are widely recognized, in advance and in general, to be deviant. There is a high degree of consensus on the identification of certain categories of deviance. In this sense, rape, robbery, corporate theft, terrorism, and transvestism are deviant because they are regarded as reprehensible *to* the majority of the members of this society. Even though specific individuals enacting or representing specific instances of these general categories may not be punished in specific situations, in general, the members of this society see them as serious normative violations. Certain acts, beliefs, and traits are deviant society-wide because they are condemned, both in practice and in principle, by the majority, or by the most powerful members of the society. This is the hierarchical side of deviance.

On the other hand, *situational deviance* does not exist as a general or society-wide quality, but in actual, concrete social gatherings, circles, or settings. A given individual may not have been regarded as a deviant situationally—for instance, in his or her specific community or group or collectivity or social circle—but may enact a category of behavior or possess a condition that is so widely condemned that it is societally deviant. For instance, in certain cities or communities in the United States (Greenwich Village in New York, for instance, or San Francisco generally), homosexuality is accepted by the majority; hence, in such cities or communities, homosexuality is not deviant. But in this country as a whole, the majority still condemns it.

Our distinction also recognizes the fact that certain acts, beliefs, and conditions may be situationally but not societally deviant. For instance, among ultra-Orthodox or *haredi* Jews, heterosexual dancing is not permitted. If a couple were to engage in it at a social gathering such as a wedding or a Bar Mitzvah, they would be chastised by the *haredi* community, and, if they persisted, they would be ejected from the gathering. In other words, situationally, among the *haredi,* heterosexual dancing is deviant. But in the United States, societally, as everyone knows, heterosexual dancing is not only not deviant, it is also accepted as conventional; indeed, to refuse to dance with a person of the opposite sex is likely to be regarded as deviant.

The distinction between societal deviance (acts, beliefs, and traits that are considered bad or wrong in a society generally) and situational deviance (acts, beliefs, and traits that are considered bad or wrong specifically within a particular group, social circle, setting, or context) frees us from having to make the silly, meaningless, and indefensible statement that "Everything is deviant." It is true that "everything is deviant"—to someone—but that is not a very useful statement, since, societally, certain things (murdering an infant in its crib) stand a much higher likelihood of being condemned than others do (chewing bubble gum). Understanding the dynamics of deviance demands that we make the distinction between societal and situational deviance. It also frees us from making the equally silly, meaningless, and indefensible statement that unless consensus exists about the rules, there's no such thing as deviance (Sumner, 1994).

Looking at deviance from a vertical (or hierarchical) perspective raises the question of the dominance of one category or society over another. That is, even though different groups, categories, social circles, and societies hold different views of what's deviant, some of them are more powerful, influential, and numerous than others. In addition to looking at variation from one setting to another, we also have to look at which categories or groups have the power to influence definitions of right and wrong in other categories, or in general. Social scientists say that a dominant belief or institution is *hegemonic:* It holds sway over beliefs held or institutions supported by less powerful social groupings in the society. The vertical conception of deviance is obviously compatible with the societal definition of deviance; it defines the hegemonic view of what's deviant as deviant, that is, what the majority or the most influential segments of the society regard as deviant. Acts, beliefs, and conditions that are societally deviant are those that are regarded as wrong nearly everywhere in a given society. Most of the time, they can be regarded as *high-consensus deviance:* There is widespread agreement as to their deviant character.

In contrast, the horizontal or "grassroots" property of deviance refers to the fact that a given act, belief, or trait can be a normative violation in one group, category, or society, but conformist in another. This quality of deviance allows us to see society, or different societies, as a kind of mosaic or a loose assemblage of separate and independent collectivities of people who do not influence one another. Here, we have a jumble of side-by-side audiences evaluating behavior, beliefs, and traits only within their own category, independent of what's going on in other categories. Enacting certain behavior, holding a certain belief, possessing a certain characteristic makes someone a conformist in one setting and a deviant in another. Such a view does not examine the impact of these settings, groups, or societies on one another. Clearly, the horizontal approach to deviance is compatible with the situational definition of deviance. Acts, beliefs, and conditions that are situationally, but not societally, deviant may be regarded as *low-consensus deviance,* in that public opinion is divided about their deviant status. What fetches condemnation in one social circle produces indifference or even praise in another.

THE ABCs OF DEVIANCE

To recapitulate: Sociologists refer to behavior, beliefs, or characteristics that violate, or depart or deviate from, a basic norm and that are likely to generate negative reactions in persons who observe or hear about that norm violation as *social deviance* or simply "deviance." Many courses and books on the subject (including the book you are reading at this very moment), as well as the major academic journal in the field, bear the title "deviant behavior." This isn't exactly accurate. *Deviant behavior* is a handy term that sociologists of deviance use to refer to the field. The field might better be referred to as "social deviance," but unfortunately, we are stuck with the handy term because it's easily recalled. But the field isn't only about deviant *behavior.* It's about deviant behavior, *and* a great deal more. It's also about deviant attitudes or beliefs, and about deviant traits or characteristics—in short, anything and everything that results in interpersonal or institutional rejection or punishment. Adler and Adler (2009, p. 13) use the term, the "ABCs of deviance—*Attitudes, Behavior,* and *Conditions.*" *Attitudes* refers to unpopular, unconventional beliefs that may or may not manifest themselves in overt actions. *Behavior* is made up of any overt action (which includes the failure to act) that is likely to attract condemnation, hostility, or punishment. *Conditions* includes physical characteristics or traits that, likewise, make someone a target of an audience's disapproval, avoidance, derision, or other types of negative social reactions. In short, to the sociologist, deviance encompasses all three of the "ABCs"—attitudes, behavior, and conditions. Let's look at each one in turn.

DEVIANT BEHAVIOR

Most people who encounter the study of social deviance imagine that the field is entirely and exclusively about behavior that is regarded as unacceptable and likely to generate negative reactions. It is true that most forms of deviance we're likely to think of—as well as most of those that tend to be punished—are behavioral in nature. The vast majority of people, when asked to provide examples of deviance, offer types of behavior. In addition, thumbing through deviance textbooks and anthologies tells us that most of the forms of deviance their authors discuss are, again, behavioral. In short, nonnormative behavior is an element of most people's stereotype of what's deviant.

It is true that often what we *do* is the basis on which we evaluate one another. "Actions speak louder than words," we say—and most of the time, to most of us, they do. A man says he loves his wife—and he may in fact love her very much—but if he is out every night, having affairs with other women, his behavior is likely to be weighed very heavily in his wife's assessment of him as a decent husband, not his protestations of love. A woman says she believes that cocaine is a harmful drug, that no one should or can play around with it, but if she uses it regularly, no one is likely to take what she claims her beliefs are very seriously. In other words—*even if we actually do believe something*—our behavior is weighed more heavily than our beliefs. We'll come back to the ideas of sociologist Erving Goffman (1922–1982) throughout this book because some of his ideas remain important, relevant, and insightful for students and researchers in the field of deviance. His book *Stigma* (1963) is a classic. The fact is, as Goffman says, most of us see behavior we regard as deviant as indicating "blemishes of individual character" (1963, p. 4). A dishonest character is revealed or manifested mainly by dishonest behavior; a weak will and an inability to resist temptation are revealed by drug abuse, alcoholism, adultery, gambling, and so on (see Chart 1.1).

CHART 1.1 GOFFMAN'S TYPOLOGY OF STIGMA/DEVIANCE

1) "Blemishes of Individual Character"
   - (a) deviant behavior: alcoholism; addiction; unemployment; imprisonment; radical political behavior; etc.
   - (b) deviant beliefs: "treacherous and rigid beliefs"; holding radical political views
   - (c) mental disorder: schizophrenia; clinical depression; Tourette's Syndrome; autism; antisocial disorder; sociopathy; etc.
2) "Abominations of the body . . ., the various physical deformities"
   - (a) violations of esthetic standards: obesity; being extremely ugly; having a harelip; being facially scarred, burned, or otherwise disfigured
   - (b) physical incapacitation: deafness; blindness; being unable to walk;
3) "Tribal stigma of race, nation, and religion": being Black (among white racists); being white (among Black nationalists); being Jewish (among anti-Semites); being an Arab (among some Israelis and some Americans and Europeans); being an Israeli (among some Arabs and some leftist academics); being an Indian (in the U.S. during and before the mid-twentieth century); being an Asian (in the U.S. during and before the mid-twentieth century); being a Muslim (among nationalist Indians in India); being a Hindu (among fundamentalist Muslims in India and Pakistan); etc.

Note: Adler and Adler's "A" (Attitudes) and "B" (Behavior) *together* make up Goffman's "blemishes of individual character." Their "C" (Conditions) includes physical characteristics as well as some forms of mental disorder. They do not deal with tribal stigma at all.

To repeat, while deviant behavior is a major type of social deviance, it is not the only type. In this book, we intend to look at several others as well.

DEVIANT ATTITUDES AND BELIEFS

Is simply expressing an unpopular belief a form of deviance? Of course! Behavior is not solely or exclusively a set of physical or mechanical motions. When someone expresses a point of view, it is not the physical act of talking or writing that counts but the content of what that person says, the *worldview* that those words express and what that worldview means to the people listening to or reading them. Holding unconventional, unorthodox, unpopular—or deviant—beliefs may be regarded as *cognitive deviance.* This category includes religious, political, and scientific beliefs that are regarded as unacceptable. The negative reactions toward the people who hold such beliefs are very similar to those that would be touched off by the discovery of participation in behavior that is regarded as unacceptable.

It is possible that, in the history of the world, *holders* of unacceptable beliefs have been attacked, criticized, condemned, arrested, even persecuted almost as often and almost as severely as *enactors* of unacceptable behavior. Consider, for example, the Spanish Inquisition (1480–1834), during which thousands of "heretics" were executed for their beliefs (or supposed beliefs); the Crusades, the attempt by Christians during the eleventh to the fourteenth centuries to wrest Jerusalem from "unbelievers," that is, Muslims; the current Islamic *jihad,* which, according to its architect, Osama bin Laden, targets "Crusaders," that is, Christians, as well as Jews; the violence following and death sentence for Salman Rushdie for writing *The Satanic Verses* (1988), considered blasphemous by many orthodox Muslims; and, in ancient times, the execution of Christians who refused to worship the Roman emperor as a god. These are the expression of certain beliefs by some people that others considered wrong—evil, heretical, blasphemous, and deviant. Clearly, beliefs *can* be deviant.

Could a self-proclaimed atheist be elected president of the United States? It is extremely unlikely; a majority of Americans would vote against such a candidate, simply because of his or her atheistic views. Hence, to much of the population, not believing in God is deviant in American society.

In a department of biology, would a graduate student who believes in creationism be looked upon or treated in the same way as one who accepts the evolution of the species as fact? Of course not! Indeed, some faculty members believe that there is no place for creationists in biology departments (Brulliard, 2003; Madigan, 2003). Hence, in biology departments in the United States, believing in creationism is deviant.

In universities throughout the Western world, expressing what are regarded as blatantly racist views often results in ostracism and social and academic isolation (Schneider, 1999)—in short, it is deviant.

One absolutely crucial point in any examination of cognitive deviance: Certain beliefs are *not* deviant simply because they are wrong. They are deviant because they violate the norms of a given society, or an institution, or among members of a social circle within a society, and, as a result, they are likely to elicit negative reactions. When we see these negative reactions, we know we have a case of deviance on our hands. Hence, cognitive deviance is a major type of deviance.

You, the reader, believe that racism is bad; so do I. But to the sociologist, racism is not deviant *because* it is bad, immoral, or wrong in some abstract sense. The expression of racist views is deviant in certain sectors of this society because it offends many, most, or certain, members of this society. Before the Civil War, if a white southerner were to argue in favor of the abolition of slavery in the South, among slaveowners and other whites, that view, and the person who expressed it, would have been regarded as deviant. Again, not because it was wrong—everyone today agrees that it was the correct position—but because at that time it was considered deviant to southern whites generally, and to slaveowners specifically. Once again, "deviant" does not mean "wrong," it means "offensive to audiences in certain social circles."

Nearly all biologists and geologists believe that creationism is scientifically and factually wrong. But to the sociologist, creationism is not deviant because it is scientifically wrong. Indeed, belief in evolution is deviant as well—to fundamentalist Christians and Muslims, and Orthodox Jews. The reason we know that certain beliefs are deviant is that their expression violates prevailing norms in certain social groups and generates negative reactions among the members of those groups.

Likewise, it is not clear that atheism is "wrong" or "right" in some abstract sense. Indeed, most scientists and philosophers believe that the factual matter of theism or atheism can't be empirically tested. What makes atheism deviant is that it violates a norm—theism, or a belief in God—held by roughly 90 percent of the American public. In many social contexts, atheists are not treated the same way that believers are; they are, in those contexts, looked down upon, vilified, and condemned. According to a Pew Global Attitude Survey (taken in 2007), a majority of the American public (57%) believe that "it is necessary to believe in God to be moral," a clear statement that atheism is not only deviant, but immoral as well. In contrast, in Western Europe, this is a minority view, ranging from 39 percent in Germany to 10 percent in Sweden.

It turns out that many beliefs thought to be false have been demonstrated to be true (Ben-Yehuda, 1985, pp. 106–167), and the scientists who held them then were ostracized just as much as those scientists who hold beliefs we now regard as false. In other words, *some* deviant beliefs may be correct! In the 1850s, the physician Ignaz Semmelweis (1818–1865) discovered that the patients of doctors who delivered babies after washing their hands had lower rates of maternal mortality than doctors whose hands were dirty. He was ridiculed for his theory and hounded out of the medical profession, eventually being driven to insanity and suicide. Semmelweis's discovery was not accepted until the 1890s, but, although scientifically true, for nearly half a century, his belief was deviant (Chart 1.1).

PHYSICAL CHARACTERISTICS

What about physical traits or characteristics? Can someone be regarded as deviant as a result of possessing certain undesirable, involuntarily acquired physical characteristics—such as being extremely ugly, short, obese, disabled, or deformed? Ask yourself: Is a disabled person treated the same way as the rest of us? Do many "abled" persons socially avoid or shun the disabled? Do some of them tease, humiliate, joke about, stereotype, or make fun of the handicapped? Do they pity or scorn them? Is a great deal of social interaction between persons with a "normal" appearance and one who is disfigured strained, awkward, distant, and difficult? Haven't obese children often become an object of taunts, ridicule, harassment, and condemnation? Aren't the possessors of certain undesirable physical characteristics excluded from full social participation? (These are rhetorical questions, of course. A writer or speaker uses them to convince an audience of a certain point of view. You, the reader, should be wary of such devices.) Hence, if we mean by "deviant" the fact that persons with certain physical traits are often treated in a condescending, pitying, scornful, and rejecting fashion, the answer is that of course possessing unconventional, unacceptable physical traits is deviant! If the disabled receive negative social reactions from the abled, they are deviant.

Is this fair? Of course not! Most people with an undesirable physical trait have not done anything wrong to acquire it. Hence, it is unfair for others to reject or otherwise treat them negatively. But notice: It is not the sociologist who is being unfair here, or who is rejecting the possessors of these traits. Rather, it is the social audience, that is, the majority, or a sector of the society, who rejects these people and, hence, treats them unfairly. Sociologists of deviance aren't rejecting the disabled, they are merely noticing that many abled members of the society do that. It doesn't matter whether behavior, beliefs, or physical characteristics are freely chosen or thrust upon us. If they result in social rejection of some kind, they are deviant, and may qualify their enactors, believers, or possessors as deviants. The fairness or justice of this rejection is a separate matter. We'll be looking more closely at deviant physical characteristics in a later chapter.

The fact that physical characteristics represent a major form of deviance points us to a distinction that has been a fixture in the field of sociology for practically its entire existence: that between *achieved status* and *ascribed status* (Adler and

Adler, 2009, p. 13). Some social statuses are "achieved" (although they may have been assisted by certain inborn characteristics). Being a college graduate is something that has to be *achieved* or accomplished: One has to do something—such as have a high school record good enough to be admitted, enroll in courses, study to pass the courses one takes, and complete all the graduation requirements—to graduate from college. But being born into a rich family or a poor one; a black, white, Asian, or Hispanic one; or one in which one's parents are themselves college graduates or high school dropouts—these are *ascribed* statuses. They are not achieved, but are thrust upon the infant at birth. There is nothing a child can do to achieve or choose his or her family or parents.

As with statuses in general, so it is with deviant statuses: They may be achieved or ascribed. Being a drug addict is a result of making certain choices in life: to use drugs or not, to use it to the point that one's life becomes consumed by drugs or not. Clearly, being a drug addict is an achieved status. In contrast, being a dwarf or an albino is ascribed. One is born with certain characteristics or traits that are evaluated in a certain fashion by the society in which one lives. It is these evaluations, and the reactions that embody them, that determine whether or not a given ascribed characteristic is deviant. To the extent that these evaluations and reactions are negative, derisive, rejecting, or hostile, we have an instance of deviance on our hands. Is this fair? Once again: Of course not. But the sociologist would be foolish and ignorant to pretend that these negative evaluations and reactions do not exist and do not have an important impact on people's lives. In fact, it is *only* when we understand them—their basis, their dynamics, and their consequences—that we can face and deal with society's many injustices (Chart 1.1).

TRIBE, RACE, RELIGION, AND NATION

Erving Goffman pinpointed a type of stigma he referred to as "tribal stigma of race, religion, and nation."

In February 2002, an angry mob of Muslims set fire to a train holding Hindu militants who, some observers said, were shouting anti-Muslim slogans; at least 57 were killed (Lakshmi, 2002a). A day later, a mob of Hindus looted and burned shops, offices, and homes in a Muslim neighborhood; at least 76 died (Lakshmi, 2002b). For years, Osama bin Laden, a militant Muslim, hostile to anything American, Western, Christian, and Jewish, has taught his followers, "Kill the Jew and the American, wherever you find them." On the 11th of September 2001, 19 of his acolytes followed his teachings by hijacking airliners and crashing them into the World Trade Towers and the Pentagon, killing 3,000 people. In response, in the year after the attacks of September 11, the number of hate crimes committed against persons of Middle Eastern descent, Muslims, and South Asian Sikhs—who are frequently mistaken for Muslims—increased 1,500 percent from the year before, from 28 to 481. A caller threatened to kill members of the family of James Zogby, director of the Arab American Institute (Fears, 2002). These incidents, too, point to the phenomenon of stigma of race and nation. They refer to the fact that the members of some categories of humanity stigmatize *all* the members of another category—simply on the basis of that membership alone.

Throughout recorded history, members of one ethnic group have stigmatized, "deviantized," or "demonized" members of another simply because of the category to which they belonged. Any exploration of deviance must take a look at Goffman's "tribal stigma of race, nation, and religion." It is a form of deviance that automatically discredits someone for belonging to a racial, national, ethnic, and religious category of humanity. It is every bit as important as deviance that is determined by behavior or beliefs.

RELATIVITY

Another absolutely crucial point: The sociology of deviance is *relativistic*. The concept of relativity has been grossly misunderstood. Some people think that accepting relativity means that we have no right to make our own moral judgments. This is completely false. Accepting relativity as a fact does not take away our right to make moral judgments. Relativity says this: Judgments of what is good and bad vary, and these judgments play a role in actors' and audiences' lives, depending on where they are located. We have the right to our own judgments about good and bad, but if we are studying deviance, we have to pay attention to how such judgments vary through time and space. How we—how I, the author; how you, the reader; and how any observer—feel about or react to an act, a belief, or a condition is completely separate from how members of a given society feel and act toward it. We may despise the injustice that we feel an act inflicts on its victims, or the injustice that punishing or condoning an act entails, but as sociologists of deviance we cannot permit ourselves to be so ignorant that we fail to recognize that the act is enacted, punished, or tolerated in certain places or at certain times.

In my view, accepting relativism poses no ethical dilemma, as some have argued (Henshel, 1990, p. 14). It does not advocate a "hands-off" policy toward practices we consider evil. It simply says that what we consider evil may be seen as good to others—that is a fact we have to face—and before we attack that evil, we have to understand how others come to view it as good and come to practice it. Relativism simply says that our personal view of things may be irrelevant to how beliefs are actually put into practice and what their reception is in a given context. Hang onto your own moral precepts, relativity says, but make sure you realize that others may not share yours, and that their moral precepts may guide them to do things you consider immoral.

A man, naked from the waist down, walks down the aisle of a meeting room, his penis fully erect. He invites members of the audience to touch his erection. Is this a deviant act? Before relativists answer this question, they would need to know more about the situational *context* of this act. The time is 1983, and the context is a meeting at which a physician, Giles Brindley, is showing off the results of his research—a drug-induced erection. The man with the erection was a medical scientist who developed a drug that was a precursor to Viagra, a pill that treats male sexual inadequacy. Brindley was simply dramatically demonstrating that his research produced a product that worked. In response to the distress people might feel at hearing about Dr. Brindley's seemingly exhibitionistic behavior, sex researcher Irwin Goldstein shrugged and commented to a reporter: "It was a bunch of urologists" (Hitt, 2000, p. 36). In other words, he was saying, to us that *in the context of that scientific meeting,* touching an erect penis is no big deal. Was Dr. Brindley's act deviant? Goldstein's statement says it all: In that situation, of course not.

In the Middle East, the murder of Arabs by Jews may be seen as heroic—not deviant—among some (but not most) Israeli Jews, while the murder of Jews by Arabs, likewise, may be praised, not condemned, among some Arabs (Cowell, 1994; Greenberg, 1995).

In addition, the relativist approach emphasizes variations in judgments of deviance from one group, subculture, social circle, or individual to another within the same society. For instance, some social circles approve of marijuana use, while others condemn it. Some individuals condemn homosexuality while, increasingly, others do not. We will *almost always* be able to locate certain circles of individuals who tolerate or accept forms of behavior that are widely or more typically condemned within a given society. Some of these circles are, of course, practitioners of deviance themselves. But others are made up of individuals who, although they do not practice the behavior in question, do not condemn those who do, either.

Variations in definitions of deviance over *historical time* are at least as important as variations from one society to another. In 1993, the then senator representing New York state, Daniel Patrick Moynihan, argued that deviance has been redefined over time to the point where a great deal of crime and other harmful behavior that once generated stigma, condemnation, even arrest, is now tolerated and normalized, its enactors exempt from punishment. The mentally ill have been released onto the street, no longer held behind the walls of mental institutions. Unwed mothers, whose lack of a stable relationship with a man produces conditions conducive to their children failing in the essential performances considered necessary to a functioning society, no longer bear the burden of social stigma. And levels of crime once considered alarming are now regarded as acceptable, tolerable—business as usual. Defenders of the old standards of decency are powerless to halt this process of "defining deviancy down," Moynihan argued.

In response, social and political commentator Charles Krauthammer (1993) asserted that, true, some forms of deviance have been defined "down," but a parallel and equally important process is taking place as well: "Defining deviancy up." Behaviors that once were tolerated have become targets of harsh condemnation. Just as the deviant has become normal, "once innocent behavior now stands condemned as deviant" (p. 20). Entirely new areas of deviance, such as date rape and politically incorrect speech, have been discovered, Krauthammer argued. And old areas, such as child abuse, have been "amplified," often to the point where groundless accusations are assumed to be true. While two out of three instances of ordinary street crime are never reported, "two out of three reported cases of child abuse are never shown to have occurred" (p. 21). Over-reporting of child abuse, Krauthammer claims, results from "a massive search to find cases." Where they cannot be found, they must be invented (p. 22). Date rape, Krauthammer claims, is so broadly defined as to encompass any and all sexual intercourse. In some social circles, he argues, the distinction between violence and consensual sex has been erased (p. 24). And the right to hold notions that differ from the mainstream has been taken away, Krauthammer claims. "Thought crimes" and "speech codes" have replaced differences of opinion and their expression.

It is possible that both Moynihan and Krauthammer have overstated their cases. Both were catastrophically wrong about the direction that crime was to take in the United States after the early 1990s. Both believed that the disintegration of the traditional family—more specifically, the increase in families without a father—would lead to significantly higher crime rates. Fatherless families increased, as Moynihan argued was happening, but correspondingly, the crime rate in the United States declined. Hence, we are led to ask this: If the intact father-and-mother family is so important to insulating children against crime, how is it possible that fatherless families increased, but the crime rate declined? In any case, Moynihan's and Krauthammer's point should be clear: Definitions of right and wrong vary over time. What is defined as wrong at one time may be tolerated in another; what is accepted during one era may be condemned in another.

In sum, relativity applies across societies and cultures and up and down through the corridors of time. In order to understand deviance, just as we must be relativistic from one society and social circle to another, we must also be relativistic from one time period to another. While for some behaviors consensus in judgments of wrongdoing may be widespread, as students of deviance, we find the variation just as significant. The concept of relativity will continue to appear throughout this book. It is one of the basic building blocks of the sociology of deviance.

DEVIANCE: ESSENTIALISM AND CONSTRUCTIONISM

So far, we've learned that *deviance* is that which violates the norms of a society, or a segment of the society, and is likely to call forth punishment, condemnation, or censure of the norm violator. Deviance can be *anything* the observers or audiences in a particular collectivity don't like and react against. In the next two chapters, I'd like to take a step further and suggest that the study of deviance is fundamentally two independent but interlocking enterprises. When sociologists look at normative violations and censure of the violator, they think along two tracks and investigate two separate types of questions. In other words, they are up to two entirely different endeavors.

When we think of deviance, the question we should ask ourselves are these: *What is to be explained?* And deviance is explained or addressed through the lens of two very different perspectives toward reality. Sociologists refer to these two perspectives as *essentialism* and *constructionism.* We can regard these two approaches as "master visions." They might seem contradictory, but in fact they complement one another; they are two halves of the same coin.

Essentialism sees deviance as a specific, concrete phenomenon in the material world, like oxygen, gravity, or a snapping turtle. It does not have to be defined to be real, it just *is;* it's just *there.* The essence or reality of deviance is taken for granted, indisputable, apparent and obvious to all observers, an objective fact. And because deviance is objective or real, we are led to the inevitable question: "Why?" In other words, essentialism implies *positivism,* the belief that we can answer a question scientifically, with empirical or observable data. "Why do some people engage in deviance, hold deviant beliefs, and possess deviant physical characteristics?" The answer to the "What is to be explained?" question is that it is the *deviant behavior, beliefs, or conditions themselves* that must be explained. What causes these things to happen or exist is our guiding concern. The ruling questions the positivist is likely to ask are these: What kind of person would do such things? What social arrangements or factors encourage such behavior? For example, why is the crime rate so much higher in some societies or countries than in others? What kinds of people violate the norms of their society? For instance, why are men so much more likely to engage in most forms of deviance than women? The young versus the old? Urban dwellers as opposed to people living in small towns? Which categories in the population are more likely to engage in violence? Who uses and abuses psychoactive substances and why? What causes some young people to engage in sex at an early age? What factors or variables encourage, cause, or influence white-collar crime? These are the sorts of questions positivists who study deviance and crime ask, and they center around the guiding question: *Why do they do it?* (The positivistic approach to deviance usually studies deviant behavior, rarely deviant beliefs, and almost never deviance conditions.) Once we decide that something is objectively real, as a scientist, it is our mission to explain its occurrence.

In contrast, the approach we call *constructionism* or *social constructionism* answers the "What is to be explained?" question by saying that it is *thinking about* and *reacting to* rule violators that is crucial. This approach argues that it is the rules, the norms, the reactions to, and the *cultural representations* of certain behavior, beliefs, or conditions that need to be looked at and illuminated. In other words, constructionism is curious about how and why something comes to be regarded as or judged to be deviant in the first place, and what is thought, made of, said about, and done about it. How are phenomena generally, and deviant phenomena specifically, conceptualized, defined, represented, reacted to, and dealt with? How do certain actions come to be regarded as "crime," "prostitution," "treachery," or "incest"? How are certain beliefs conceptualized *as* "heresy," "blasphemy," "godlessness," "disloyalty," and "ignorance"? Why are certain physical characteristics even *noticed* in the first place? Are the disabled stigmatized? Are they integrated into the mainstream or "abled" society—or are they, in some ways, excluded? Are the obese treated and reacted to differently in different societies? Why is a specific behavior, belief, or trait condemned in one society but not in another? Why does atheism cause the nonbeliever to be burned at the stake in one place, during one historical era, and ignored or tolerated elsewhere, at another time? Do the members of a society think of corporate crime as "real" crime? What does the treatment of the mentally disordered tell us about how they are viewed by the society at large? How do the media report news about drug abuse? What do the members of a society do to someone who engages in a given behavior, holds a particular belief, or bears a specific trait? In turn, how does the person who is designated as a deviant react *to,* handle, and deal with the deviant designation, the label, and the stigma? The constructionist is more interested in issues that have to do with thinking, talking, writing about, narrating, or reacting to such actions than in why deviant behavior, beliefs, or traits take place, occur, or exist in the first place. To the constructionist, deviant behavior, beliefs, and traits "exist"—*as a social category*—because they are conceptualized in a certain way. The constructionist does not take the "deviance" of what is regarded as deviance for granted; instead, it is how something is regarded and dealt with that must be explained, not the occurrence of the behavior, the beliefs, or the conditions. Chapters 2 and 3 will discuss these two radically different approaches to deviance.

SUMMARY

Humans evaluate one another according to a number of criteria, including beliefs, behavior, and physical traits. If, according to the judgment of a given audience doing the evaluation, someone holds the "wrong" attitudes, engages in the "wrong" behavior, or possesses the "wrong" traits or characteristics, he or she will be looked down upon, treated in a negative, punishing, and condemnatory fashion. Sociologists refer to beliefs, behavior, or traits that violate or depart or deviate from a basic norm or rule held by a collectivity of people, and are likely to generate negative reactions among the members of that collectivity who observe or hear about that norm violation, as *social deviance* or simply *deviance.*

There are four necessary ingredients for deviance to occur: one, a rule or a norm; two, someone who violates or is thought to violate that norm; three, an audience who judges the violation; and four, the likelihood of negative reactions from this audience. What define or constitute deviance are the actual or potential negative reactions that certain acts, beliefs, or traits are likely to elicit.

Defining deviance is not a mere matter of departing from just anyone's norms, however. The sociologist is interested in the likelihood that a given normative departure will result in punishment, condemnation, and stigma. Hence, we must focus on the *number* and the *power* of the people who define a given act, belief, and trait as "wrong." The greater the number and the power of the people who regard something as wrong, the greater the likelihood that its believers, enactors, and possessors will be punished, condemned, or stigmatized—and hence, the more deviant that something is.

The distinction between *societal deviance* and *situational deviance* is crucial here for understanding the likelihood of attracting condemnation, censure, punishment, scorn, and stigma. Societal deviance includes acts, beliefs, and conditions that are widely condemned pretty much throughout the society—in a phrase, "high-consensus" deviance. Looking at deviance as a societal or society-wide phenomenon adopts a "vertical" perspective: It sees judgments of right and wrong as being hierarchical in nature. Some judgments have more influence than others. In contrast, "situational" deviance is whatever attracts condemnation, censure, punishment, scorn, and stigma specifically in particular groups or social circles. This view of deviance looks "horizontally" or across the society and accepts the idea that different groups, circles, and categories have different judgments of right and wrong, and hence, different notions of deviance. Situational deviance is usually low-consensus deviance, since there is a low level of agreement throughout the society that such acts, beliefs, and traits are deviant.

Contrary to the stereotype, deviance includes more than behavior. Sociologists refer to the "ABCs" of deviance—*attitudes, behavior,* and *conditions.* True, behavior constitutes a major form of deviance, but so do beliefs and physical traits or conditions. Throughout history, people are judged to be normative violators for their beliefs almost as often, and almost as severely, as for their behavior. And judgments of physical appearance, likewise, are sharply judgmental, pervasive, and deeply determinative of society's rewards and punishments. In addition, racial, ethnic, religious, and "tribal" distinctions play a major role in judgments of deviance; Goffman analyzes such distinctions in his delineation of sources of stigma. I refer to tribal stigma as *collective deviance.* Some members of certain ethnic groups stigmatize every member of one or more other groups, regardless of what any given individual has done to deserve it. Please note that Goffman's "blemishes of individual character" stigma encompasses the Adlers' attitudes ("treacherous and rigid beliefs") *and* behavior ("addiction, alcoholism, homosexuality, unemployment, suicidal attempts, and radical political behavior"). Even though both typologies entail three types of deviance of stigma, they overlap imperfectly. The Adlers' typology does not discuss tribal stigma.

Deviance is a coat of many colors; it assumes myriad forms, varieties, and shapes. Deviance is a conceptual category that cuts through a diversity of acts, beliefs, and traits. Hence, it might seem that, on the surface, phenomena that sociologists refer to as deviant share very little in common. But the very fact that the concept points to such diversity is what gives it its power. The concept of deviance highlights or illuminates features of social life that we might not otherwise have noticed. In the struggle to attain respectability, members of one category may resent being categorized with a less respectable category. For instance, self-avowed homosexual spokespersons have written to me, criticizing earlier editions of this book for referring to homosexuality as a form of deviance along with murder, rape, and robbery. They feel the term "taints" them and their behavior. This is an example of what philosophers called the "fallacy of reification," that is, identifying the part with the whole. "Deviance" represents only one dimension, and *in some ways,* homosexuals and murderers do share important characteristics, that is, their behavior and their identity are discredited in the eyes of much of the public. When I ask these spokespersons, "Are homosexuals discriminated against and looked down upon by most Americans?" their answer is an immediate, "Of course!" My reply is, "That's exactly what I'm taking about!" In a similar vein, adultery, using cocaine, prostitution, being an atheist, and being autistic are also deviant.

Several criteria are used by the naïve, uninformed student to define deviance: absolute criteria, mental disorder, statistical departures from the norm, and harm to individuals and to the society. These are false criteria, naïve definitions of deviance. Sociologically, deviance is not defined by absolute criteria, mental disorder, unusualness, or harm. Indeed, many absolute definitions of wrongness or deviance have been proposed, but everyone has his or her own such definition, and none of them have anything to do with how the majority reacts to certain behavior, beliefs, or conditions. Most "deviants" are mentally normal, so clearly, mental disorder is separate and independent from deviance. Unusual behavior, beliefs, and conditions are not always deviant, and common ones are not always conventional. And lots of harmless acts are deviant, while many harmful ones are conventional. Clearly, these four definitions of deviance are misleading and naïve; sociologically, they are dead ends.

To the sociologist, deviance is *relative, contextual, contingent,* and *probabilistic.*

Saying that deviance is "relative" means that members of different societies and social circles, as well as periods of historical eras, define good and bad, true and false, in different ways, and reward or publish different behaviors, beliefs, and physical characteristics. We may not agree with these judgments, but the fact that they exist and determine reactions and interactions is an indisputable fact.

Saying that deviance is "contextual" means that people's definition of wrongdoing depends on the physical or social situation or context within which behavior takes place, beliefs are expressed, or characteristics appear. Nudity is acceptable in certain locales but not others; the taking of human life is tolerated in warfare but not under normal circumstances; a delinquent boy can express academic knowledge and interest to his teacher, with no one else around, but not among members of his gang; acting slightly drunk or tipsy may be encouraged and approved at a raucous party, but it is unacceptable in the classroom, at a board meeting, or in a house of worship. The same behavior, in the same society, at the same historical era, is not always judged in the same way under all circumstances: Context matters.

Saying that deviance is "contingent" means that whether someone is punished, rewarded, or ignored for engaging in an act, expressing a belief, or possessing a given trait is dependent on a variety of factors independent of the act, belief, or trait itself. One of these factors is who the person is. When Eliot Spitzer was governor of New York, he could not have sex with a call girl without being condemned for it; his resignation was almost certain. Most ordinary private citizens are not likely to lose their job as a result of such an indiscretion. And in Italy, when Prime Minister Berlusconi "consorted" with "young and chesty women," these indiscretions were met with a widespread shrug of the shoulders.

Saying that deviance is "probabalistic" means that condemnation and punishment do not inevitably follow discovery. We could draw a spectrum or continuum from acts, beliefs, and conditions that are extremely likely to draw negative reactions at one end, over to those that are unlikely. To each act, expression of belief, and physical condition, we can attach a certain likelihood of censure and punishment upon discovery. Picture a white supremacist with a Swastika tattooed on his bald head screaming out racist slogans at a church, synagogue, mosque, university, mainstream political gathering, or school. Most of us would say the likelihood is extremely high that he would be socially shunned, censured, or condemned in these groups. On the other hand, lots of acts, beliefs, and conditions are very *unlikely* to result in seriously negative reactions among most audiences: bird-watching, wearing glasses, driving an old car, eating beef tongue, reading poetry, growing pansies, listening to Muzak, keeping an iguana for a pet, believing that Pluto is a planet, or being an inch or two taller or shorter than the norm. It's important to recognize that deviance is a continuum that stretches from whatever others find extremely offensive all the way over to the norm—which most others regard as not at all offensive.

Some behaviors are so widely condemned that they have been condemned pretty much everywhere; with them, there is virtually no "relativity" at all. No society on earth accepts the unprovoked killing of an in-group member; robbery (the "Robin Hood" syndrome notwithstanding), rape, and serious or aggravated assault rarely result in widespread tolerance or approval. On the other hand, many behaviors, beliefs, and traits, vary enormously over time and cultural space with respect to the degree to which members of societies are condemned for committing, believing in, and possessing them. Affirming atheism during the Spanish Inquisition could result in torture and execution; today, the disbeliever meets mild but not savage disapproval. At one time, in some places, teaching evolution was illegal and deviant; today, evolution is taught in every nonreligious high school, college, and university in the country. As late as the 1960s, the distribution of hard-core pornography was a crime, and was prosecuted; today, graphic hard-core porn depicting almost every conceivable sex act is available, in almost unlimited quantity, to anyone with access to the Internet. These changes tell us that the study of deviance is about setting, enforcing and violating rules, as well as the degree to which rules vary or remain the same over time and from one society to another. Some rules apply pretty much everywhere (though the punishment of the perpetrator does vary). With others, the sociologist's job is to understand and explain the variation. This book accepts the challenge of that task.

Sociologists adopt one of two radically different approaches to deviance: essentialism and constructionism. *Essentialism* argues that deviance exists objectively, and hence, its occurrence, rate, and distribution can be explained scientifically. In other words, essentialism implies and even demands scientific positivism. In contrast, constructionism argues that what's deviant is a subjectively arrived-at phenomenon, dependent on time and place, society and culture, and observer and enactor. What's most important about deviance is how different audiences regard behavior, beliefs, and conditions, both conceptually and evaluatively. What something "is" and whether it is good, bad, or neutral are outcomes of judgments of social actors within specific contexts. Behavior, beliefs, and conditions exist, as deviance, only as a result of the actions and reactions of audiences.

Account: A Computer Pirate Tells His Story

The contributor of the following account, Steve, was a 21-year-old college senior at the time he wrote it. His story illustrates a number of interesting principles about deviance, one of which is that behavior that may be tolerated—even revered—in one category of people, while it may, at the same time, be considered not only deviance but also a crime in another. It also shows that committing deviance is not necessarily generalizable; someone who is fairly conventional in one sphere of life may engage in wrongdoing in another. And third, Steve's account illustrates the fact that there may be many rewards to engaging in deviance, some of them intrinsic (i.e., those that come from the fun of the activity itself) and some secondary (the respect the behavior generates from others).

I had heard all the speeches from my parents about staying away from drugs, alcohol, loose women, and fraternities, but the speeches had always been half-assed. In high school, I had always been a pretty good kid and I don't think my parents were all that worried about me. I graduated with honors and a 3.8 GPA, and I was the second leading tackler on the football team. I dated a cheerleader and hung out with what could be considered the preppy kids. For the most part, we stayed out of trouble, aside from the occasional party that got raided by the police. I spent most of my free time in the gym, and enjoyed playing computer games online. . . . I was an Eagle Scout. My parents knew they had raised a physically and mentally strong son. When they helped me move to college, I could tell they were proud of me. My Mom cried and my Dad smiled. Once again, I heard all those speeches I had heard over and over. "Stay away from drugs." "Don't drink." "For every hour you are in class, you should study for two hours." I had heard them so many times I stopped listening long ago. As much as they nagged and worried, I think my parents knew I would be OK. After all, I was your All-American average child.

I applied and was accepted into the University's Scholars Program. . . . We were assigned in 1 of 13 programs. I was in the Science, Technology, and Society Program. All of us in that program lived together in the same dorm and took a special seminar. Many of us shared the same majors—I was in computer science—and thus shared many of the same courses. Through classes, our similar interests, and the fact that we all lived together, it was really easy to make friends. The more people I met, the more I realized I was surrounded by nerds. However, it didn't take me long to adapt.

I began playing several computer games. . . . The university has an extremely fast connection to the Internet, which gave me an advantage over my opponents. It didn't take me long to find out I could also download music from the Internet. The idea of not having to purchase CDs absolutely delighted me. There I was, a few weeks into my first semester of college. I went to all my classes, sat in the front of the class, did all my homework, did all the reading for my courses, visiting my professors during their office hours, and got good grades. In my free time, I went to the gym, played football, and played on my computer. I spent most of my time on the computer playing games, downloading music, or chatting on Instant Messenger. For a month or so, my life pretty much followed this pattern. But before long, everything changed.

Her name was Tess. She was in one of my computer courses. She was cute and really funny. We usually sat together in class and even studied for our first exam together. At some point, I asked if she'd like to hang out during the coming weekend. She said she'd love to and there was a movie she really wanted to see but she didn't have any money to pay for it. Normally, I'd jump at the opportunity to pay but I didn't have any money either. I left that conversation feeling more than a little annoyed.

Later that night, I told a friend what had happened and he told me he had the movie on his computer. It was too good to be true. Not only could I watch the movie with Tess, we could lie down on my bed instead of sitting in those awful movie theater chairs. I had my friend send me the file right away. That weekend Tess came to my room and we watched the movie. The night was fantastic. I knew I had found something great. The next day I nagged my friend until he told me how he had gotten the movie. He introduced me to IRC, Instant Relay Chat, which is a program that allows you to meet people in chat rooms to talk and exchange files. To use IRC, you just need to choose a nickname and connect to a server. I chose the nickname "Bear" and I was off. I joined the chat room and tried to absorb everything that was going on. The chat room was run by a group of people called "Chimera." To download movies, you connect to people who are running servers, request the files you want, wait in line, then they send them to you. It was easy. It was awesome.

I became intrigued by this system of distributing movies. There were three types of people on the system—ops, the voiced, and peons. The "ops" (for "operators") ran and had total control of the chat room. If they didn't like you, they could kick you out or permanently ban you from the room. In the case of this particular chat room, the ops were the members of Chimera. Each one of them contributed to the process of distributing these movies. Below the ops were the "voiced people." They were either friends of the ops or people who ran the servers. The voiced had no actual power but when their nicknames were displayed, a plus sign appeared. I guess it's a little like the Queen of England—she doesn't have real power but people look up to her. Finally there are the "peons." These are the people who wander in to download movies for their own use. (Ops and voiced people call them "leeches.") Everyone starts as a peon. You

(*Continued*)

Account: A Computer Pirate Tells His Story Continued

stay there unless you do something special. This [is] where I began my journey, as a leech, just downloading and collecting movies.

My everyday life didn't change much. I still went to nearly all my classes and was on top of my work. Other people on my floor began finding out that I had newly released movies. Friday nights, students in my dorm began gathering in my room to watch whatever hot new movie I had. They'd comment on how cool it was I could download these movies and save everyone eight dollars. Pretty soon people I didn't know dropped by my room and said they heard from a friend I had a particular movie and asked if I could send it to them. I became a kind of mini-celebrity in my dorm. I was the man to go to for movies. I loved making new friends but more important, I loved the attention. I loved controlling access to what they all wanted. I was hooked.

So I sent a message to one of the ops asking how I could become more involved. He gave me instructions on how to serve. So I set up a little file server and let three people at a time download movies off me. Since my Internet connection was so fast, I quickly became one of the more popular servers. The ops took notice of my server, and they made me one of the voiced. It felt great. Peons said "Hi!" to me and asked about my day. People sent me messages begging me to let them skip to the front of the line for my sends. It felt great. People liked me, respected me, even looked up to me. It didn't matter that I would never meet most of them face-to-face, the feeling of power was addictive. I couldn't get enough of it. I wanted more. I began sending out more files and trading files with other voiced people to increase my collection. I had built up my reputation to the point where I believed I should join Chimera and become an op. Internal conflicts caused some members of Chimera to leave and form their own movie release group, and I went with them. We formed The Ghost Dimension, and I was made an op in that group.

Founding a new movie release group proved to be much more work than I could have imagined. In Chimera, ops simply sent me movies and I stored them and sent them to others. But now that I was an op, I had no new movies to send. The other founders of Ghost Dimension and I spent the next few weeks calling in favors and tracking down sources and contacts. Sources are people who get the movies straight from theaters or in prerelease and supply us with them. We were able to acquire several bootleggers in Singapore, the movie piracy capital of the world. What they did was they brought a digital camcorder into a theater and taped the movie off the screen. So, after about two weeks, we had enough sources to go public. The quality was pretty bad, but the movies were new and free so not too many people complained. We also acquired the cooperation of a theater manager local to one of our guys who let us set up a stationary camera to capture the video from the screen, and we recorded and mixed in the audio later. This method produced relatively good quality movies. Our real prize arrived when one of the founders of Ghost Dimension managed to convince a critic working for a TV station to join our group. He was able to supply us with screener tapes, which are movies sent by studios to critics before they are released to the public. The files we created from these tapes were nearly theater quality. We also got them ahead of time, so getting the critic was a huge break for us. It was the reason why we gained notoriety so quickly. Also, someone associated with our group was able to modify the way we created our files . . . [which] opened our products to a whole host of users who did not have broadband Internet.

The new demands of being an op began to significantly impact on my everyday life. Most nights I wouldn't get to sleep until four or five in the morning. I survived on naps and caffeine. My class attendance began to fade and my homework became second priority, which was reflected in my grades. My trips to the gym became less frequent, and the time I used to spend with my friends I spent napping so I could stay up all night and get the newest release out. I never felt lonely, though. I found all the friends I needed online. I was an op in a channel that had over 500 people in it at any given time. They all looked up to me. They all wanted what I had. They all wanted to be like me. The power went straight to my head. It was great. It was unbelievable what people would do to get the new release. Girls sent us naked pictures and videos of themselves. Guys sent us all kinds of software. We literally had access to whatever we wanted.

It was through one of these transactions that I furthered my online piracy career. A user offered to trade some software for the newest movie release. When he saw how fast my connection was, he told me he was a member of a group called "Russian Roulette," perhaps the most notorious software piracy group ever to exist. They were founded by Russian hackers in the mid-1990s, and since then spread all over the world. When my user told me Russian Roulette was looking for an East Coast dumpsite, I readily agreed to join. As a dumpsite, I would archive the releases and distribute them back to the other members of the group and a few select VIPs. Distributing pirated software turned out to be a lot riskier than stealing movies, though. At the time, movie piracy was relatively new, but software piracy had been around for a while and had proved to be a huge problem for software companies. They were already aggressively hunting down pirates.

A week after I joined Russian Roulette, a competing piracy group was busted and several members were charged with criminal offenses. So Russian Roulette recruited help from Snafu, one of the more elite group of hackers. Snafu provided us with a number of security programs to help us operate without detection by providing us with what's called a tracer. . . . So there I sat, on top of the online world. I obtained movies before they came out, I had any software I could possibly want, and I was an op in The Ghost Dimension and Russian Roulette, with power over 1,100 people every day. It was an incredible feeling, having all those people hang on my every word. This must be what people feel like when they get high on some really fabulous drug. I was insane and I was addicted. At this point, I had pretty much stopped going to nearly all of my classes. I did manage to make it to a few afternoon classes and my exams, but that was about it. My grades were horrible; I ended up with a 1.4 for that semester. My face-to-face interactions with my friends were becoming rare. I spent almost all of my time in front of a computer. Yet I was still on top of the world. I was a god to these people, and I loved it. . . .

In November of the following year, I received an email from Universal Studios ordering me to cease and desist from my pirating activities immediately. The message was accompanied by some evidence that I was distributing copyrighted materials. Upon a careful analysis of their evidence, I knew it was not sufficient to hold up in a court of law, but the point was made. I was no longer invincible. In the face of a criminal lawsuit, I decided to retire from the piracy scene. . . . I destroyed the hard drive on which I stored the movies and files. When I destroyed it, my 80-gigabyte hard drive was nearly totally full, with over 400 different programs and movies on it. Just recently, Russian Roulette made the headlines as the target of an international police sting operation. The FBI executed 100 search warrants against Russian Roulette in the United States. It claimed that at the time of the raids, Russian Roulette was responsible for 95 percent of all pirated software that was available online. . . .

To give you an idea of how active I was in the online piracy world, over the period of just one year, my server sent out over 15 terabytes of data. (A terabyte is 1,000 gigabytes, and one gigabyte is 1,000 megabytes.) On average, a movie runs about 200 megabytes and a full program is about the same. During my career as a computer pirate, I served around 75,000 programs and movies. The most downloaded file I had was Adobe Workshop, a graphic arts program, which cost then about $400. If all the files I sent out had been Adobe Workshop, I would have sent out roughly $30 million in

(*Continued*)

Account: A Computer Pirate Tells His Story Continued

illegal programs. Of course, nothing else I sent out was nearly this expensive. I probably sent out no more than between one and two million dollars worth of software, if it had been purchased legally.

Did I engage in deviance? Of course. I was engaged in an illegal operation that smuggled stolen merchandise across the world. How could that not be deviant? I kept my online activities from my family and friends because I was afraid of how they would react if they found out. I don't think I should be treated like a common thief who steals merchandise off the shelves of a store, but what I did was a crime nonetheless. . . . Stealing from the Internet is very impersonal. You never see whom you take stuff from and you never see how it affects them. . . . Still, the value of what I pushed greatly exceeded the value of anything I could have taken off a shelf. During the time I was actively pirating, I probably would have told you my behavior wasn't deviant at all. To the subculture of computer piracy with whom I interacted daily, this behavior was common and strongly encouraged. At that time, that subculture was basically my world, my reality, so I would have said no way was it deviant. Still, during nights when we created a new file, we sent out two or three gigabytes overnight, more than the average college user sends out over an entire semester. When I came back to my dorm room, before I entered the hallway, I always checked to see if there were police officers standing outside my door.

Yes, at that time, there was something different about my lifestyle, and I guess it might be seen as deviant, but I didn't think of it that way. I have no regrets about what I did. I'm still friends with some of the people I met online, I had a lot of fun, and in the end I think I learned a valuable lesson or two. The recent sentencing of a Russian Roulette member to 10 years in a federal prison helped hammer home the point to me that what I did was illegal. In the last analysis, I knew what I did was wrong. After that sentencing, the FBI announced it would be executing more warrants in the Russian Roulette case; I had to admit I didn't sleep at all for a few nights after that. Yet sometimes I miss the feeling of absolute power I had. Piracy isn't about money, it's about power and respect. Believe me, they're the most addicting things I know.

(From the author's files.)

QUESTIONS

In your estimation, was Steve committing a deviant act when he engaged in computer piracy? Do you regard what he did as stealing? If so, is it stealing in the same way that shoplifting is? If not, how is it different? Who is the victim here? And if it is not wrong, what is the motive of the FBI in prosecuting cases such as his? Do the creators, producers, manufacturers, and distributors of CDs, DVDs, and files lose money by having their copyrighted materials pirated? Should there be copyright laws protecting their intellectual property from piracy? Or should it all be free? If so, shouldn't supermarkets distribute free food, doctors dispense free medical care, and teachers work for free? What was Steve's motive in engaging in computer piracy? Do you picture Steve still engaging in a life of crime? Or do you figure he has reformed and is highly likely to lead a more or less conventional life?

CHAPTER 2

Explaining Deviant Behavior: Positivist Theories

As we saw in Chapter 1, the sociology of deviance is made up of two distinct but interlocking enterprises—essentialism and constructionism. Essentialism sees deviance as objectively real and hence, scientifically explainable; in contrast, constructionism argues that the most fundamental feature of deviance is the fact that rules, judgments of wrongdoing, and assigning offenders to deviant categories are rendered by specific audiences in specific contexts. As I explained in Chapter 1, essentialism *implies* positivism, or the scientific effort to account for why people engage in deviant behavior. Hence, here, we'll focus mainly on the nature of positivism in the study of deviance and the perspectives that make use of the essentialist/positivistic framework.

It must be said at once that even the most positivistic of criminologists and sociologists of deviance recognize that *all* crime and deviance is defined by laws and rules and hence they are relativistic and socially constructed. Gwynn Nettler states that crime, and by extension deviance, represents "an *evaluation* of acts or conditions." Definitions of crime and deviance rest on moral judgments and consequently, "*there is no essence of criminality* [or deviance] to be observed in an act or situation" (1984, p. 1). However, all positivists believe—and *must* believe, in order for their enterprise to be legitimate—that an objective common core or thread holds all deviance and crime together, otherwise there would be nothing to explain. No positivist believes that deviance and crime are just a matter of social convention or construction. To put the matter another way, positivists are more likely to stress the essential characteristics that all things called "deviance" and "crime" have in common, whereas constructionists are more likely to stress the process by which certain things come to be regarded and judged as crime and deviance.

What is positivism in the social sciences? *It is the application of the scientific method to the study of human behavior.* The practitioners of positivism maintain that sociology and criminology are not radically different from the natural sciences. They believe that deviance and crime can be studied in much the same way that natural phenomena, like stars, chemicals, and ocean tides can be studied—of course, making the necessary adjustments in research methods and questions asked for the subject matter under study.

Positivism is based on three fundamental assumptions: (1) *empiricism,* (2) *objectivism,* and (3) *determinism.*

Empiricism. Positivism assumes that the material world is real and that the scientist can know the world through the five senses; in other words, the positivist is an *empiricist.* Empiricism is the belief that seeing, feeling, hearing, tasting, and smelling convey information that gives the observer sense impressions of the way things are. Often, these senses must be aided by instruments (such as a microscope, a telescope, or an oscilloscope). In addition, many things can never be directly observed, such as historical and geological events that happened in the past; hence, reasoning about them entails inferring from the data available to the scientist. For example, it is impossible to see the process of evolution take place, so biologists and geologists infer its existence by means of fossil and DNA evidence.

The guiding principle of the empiricist is, "I trust my senses to tell me what's true." This is the guiding principle of all positivists. Most positivists believe that if phenomena are not directly—or indirectly—observable through the information provided by the five senses and cannot be integrated into existing or conceivable theoretical and conceptual perspectives, questions asked and issues raised are not scientifically meaningful. Not necessarily wrong, just nonscientific—outside the scientific framework. Hence, the question of whether a given work of art, poetry, form of behavior, belief, or political regime is good or bad, or whether or not a painting or a musical composition is beautiful, or whether or not God exists, are considered *nonempirical,* and hence, nonscientific, questions.

The fact that certain things cannot be directly observed by the scientist is especially crucial for the sociologist and the criminologist because *most* human behavior cannot be seen at the moment it is enacted. Instead, as I said, social scientists must infer what happened through a variety of *indirect* indicators, including the answers to questions about the behavior of subjects, informants, and interviewees. Researchers have developed a variety of methods to determine the validity of answers to questions about behavior, and some of them get very close to the reality they are attempting to describe. Some research methods *do* entail direct observation—participant observation as well as field and laboratory experiments, for instance. But *most* social science research methods rely on indirect indicators, and here, the researcher must be skeptical, clever, and resourceful. I'll have a great deal more to say about research methods in Chapter 4.

Objectivism. The second assumption of positivism, objectivism, means that phenomena in the material world are *objectively real* and possess certain objective or internally consistent characteristics that distinguish them from other phenomena. In line with our interests, the social scientist can distinguish deviant behavior from conventional, conforming behavior. In other words, the many forms of deviant behavior share a *common thread,* a *differentiating trait* that distinguishes them from conventional, conforming, legal behavior. Positivists *reject* the notion that definitions of right or wrong are really as relative as constructionist sociologists of deviance argue (Curra, 2000). Public perceptions of right and wrong do not vary much across societal lines; there *is* a "common core" from society to society to what's regarded as deviant (Newman, 1976). Some observers argued that that common core is *harm:* Behavior that is harmful to the society, they say, is highly likely to be defined as wrongdoing; hence, the central assumption of deviance specialists—relativism—is incorrect, and consequently, "deviance is dead" (Costello, 2006).

The same thing applies to crime. As we saw, while positivistic criminologists will warn that there is no "essence," no common core, to criminal behavior (Nettler, 1984, pp. 1, 16), most will nonetheless regard correlations between this phenomenon, this entity, this phenomenon or *thing*—crime—and key sociological characteristics as extremely important. If crime were not a real "thing" in the world, they say, then how could it possibly manifest statistical relationships with key variables such as race, socioeconomic status, gender, and residence? Crime is not a simple product of the process of social construction, they say. There *is* a material reality to crime above and beyond social and legal definitions. Crime is much more than a mere social construction; there is an identifiable behavior core (or essence) to criminal behavior.

At the very least, each specific type of deviance or crime (such as homosexuality, robbery, drug use, adultery, mental illness, alcoholism, or homicide) shares key characteristics in common. The characteristics of deviant behavior and crime *are contained within the actions themselves.* It is their possession of certain observable properties that makes them deviant in nature. All positivists know that deviance is defined by norms and that norms are relative to time and place. Still, they feel that there is enough internal consistency among deviant categories that an explanation for their existence is possible; *something* about them leads the scientist to examine them together as a category. If labels were not at least minimally internally consistent, there would be no point in studying them as an analytic category; they would have no coherence and possess nothing in common except their label.

For instance, are definitions of mental illness arbitrary? Is a person who is labeled mentally ill in one society considered sane in another? Is there a common thread in mental disorder? Or is the term *nothing but* a label applied by psychiatrists, or by the general public? Does the principle of relativity apply to conditions that are commonly referred to as mental disorder, as some claim (Curra, 2000, pp. 169–185)? Is the enterprise of psychiatry little more than an updated version of "witchcraft," as other observers have argued (Turner and Edgley, 1983)? Positivists say no. Mental disorder is an identifiable thing or condition in the world and not the mere imposition of a socially constructed definition (Spitzer, 1975, 1976). Says Gwynn Nettler, an outspoken advocate of the positivistic position in the study of deviance and crime: "Some people are more crazy than others; we can tell the difference and calling lunacy a name does not cause it" (Nettler, 1974, p. 894).

Determinism. The third assumption positivists make is determinism. They ask the following: What *causes* the deviant behavior, beliefs, or conditions?

For centuries, the question, "*why do they do it?*" has been asked about persons who stray beyond society's moral or legal boundaries. What is it that influences some people to violate society's norms—the Ten Commandments, for example—while others of us do not? Or, taking the question to a structural, society-wide, or categorical level, what is it about certain societies or categories of people that leads to higher rates of deviance among their ranks than other societies or other categories? Do specific social *conditions* encourage deviance? Do other conditions inhibit it? These sorts of questions ask for an explanation of deviance as a certain type of action or behavior.

Scientists seek *naturalistic* explanations, that is, the location of cause-and-effect can be found in the material world. They avoid spiritual, supernatural, or paranormal explanations for causality. For instance, parapsychologists claim that they have empirical evidence that shows the mind can influence the workings of the material world. But the problem with this claim for most scientists is that parapsychologists leave out the issue of the *mechanism* by which this influence takes place; they leave out the question of precisely *how* the mind influences the workings of the material world. In other words, scientists don't accept parapsychology as a scientific discipline because it doesn't fit in with a materialistic or scientific framework. The same is true of the so-called theory of "intelligent design": Evolution produced living species, including humans, as a result of "designs" by an intelligent entity. Scientists reject intelligent design as nonempirical because it cannot be integrated into a naturalistic framework of how the world works.

Positivism looks for cause-and-effect *explanations* for the acts and beliefs that are regarded as deviant. The belief that the world works in a cause-and-effect fashion is referred to as *determinism.* And an explanation for a general class of phenomena or events is called a *theory.* The positivist assumes that the phenomena and events of the world do not take place at random, by accident. In other words, there is a *reason* for their patterning. A theory addresses the question: Why are things the way they are? This means that we must seek the reasons for the regularities we observe. When we discover that men are more likely to violate society's norms than women, we want to find out *why* this is so. Urbanization increases rates of drug abuse; strong ties to conventional others decrease rates of deviance; anonymity increases the likelihood that nonconformity will take place. Conditions or factors such as these *cause* or *influence* specific forms of behavior, deviance included. It is the scientist's job to locate the dynamics of the cause-and-effect sequences that exist in the world.

Some positivistic approaches are *individualistic* (or "micro") in that they focus on the characteristics of categories of individuals who violate norms or break the law. They argue that deviants share a trait or characteristic in common—which nondeviants lack—that can be isolated, which will help provide an explanation for deviance. Other positivistic approaches are more *structural* (or "macro"). They look at the big picture and argue that certain *deviance-inducing conditions* share a common thread that can be discovered, which will lead to an explanation of deviance—such as urbanism, anomie, society-wide income distributions, and so on. Either way, whether individual or structural, deviance is produced by certain factors in a cause-and-effect fashion, which can be discovered and explicated by the scientifically inclined sociologist.

Positivists seek general explanations for why things are the way they are. Scientists are not satisfied with explanations of specific, particular, or unique events. The goal of every scientist is to explain as many observations in the material world as possible. This means that they all look for *patterns* or *regularities* in the material world. When criminologists study criminal violence in one delinquent gang, they are looking for patterns of criminal violence in delinquent gangs *in general.* To the positivist, a case study of one prostitute is meaningful only insofar as it sheds light on *all* prostitutes, or the institution of prostitution *as a whole.* A detailed examination of a case of corporate crime that takes place in *one* company is not enough; what we need to know is what the picture of corporate crime *generally* looks like. Positivists are not interested in particulars or specifics for their own sake. They want to know how and to what extent these particulars fall into recognizable *patterns* that will enable them to make generalizations about how the world as a whole works.

DEVIANT BEHAVIOR: WHY DO THEY DO IT?

The earliest theories of wrongdoing, what we now call deviance, typically concentrated on the question: *Why do they do it*? Why adultery, murder, witchcraft, thievery, disobedience to authority, insanity, and so on? And why deviant beliefs—atheism, unbelief, blasphemy, heresy, and so on? And since undesirable *physical characteristics* were thought to be a consequence or product of evil deeds or thoughts, people in the past asked questions such as the following: Why are some of us afflicted with the curse of leprosy? What causes birth defects? Why are some women "barren," or childless? What causes blindness, albinism, curvature of the spine, dwarfism, extreme ugliness, and any manner of undesirable traits? In short, members of societies in the past attempted to explain the deviant ABCs I mentioned in Chapter 1—actions, beliefs, and conditions (Adler and Adler, 2009, p. 13).

Although the explanations that were devised in earlier times were inadequate or fallacious from today's vantage point, they all centered on an effort to account for anomalous and inexplicable phenomena—undesirable differentness that needed explaining. They cannot be referred to as positivistic theories because they lacked the essential ingredients of scientific theories: They were not *empirical*—they could not be falsified by observable evidence of any kind. And they were not theoretical; they did not offer a satisfying, materialistic or scientific cause-and-effect account of how certain behavior, belief, or traits came to be. But the important point is that, however crude from today's vantage point, past theories of wrongdoing *did* ask "*Why do they do it?*" This question has ancient roots.

Historically, the oldest explanation for deviant behavior has been *demonic possession.* For many thousands of years, evil spirits, including the devil, were thought to cause men and women to engage in socially unacceptable behavior. A half-million years ago, Stone Age humans drilled holes into the skulls of individuals who engaged in wrongdoing of some kind—who, today, would be recognized as being mentally ill—so that evil spirits could escape. Indeed, this procedure was still practiced as late as the 1600s. The ancient Hebrews, Egyptians, Greeks, and Romans performed rites of exorcism to cast out demonic beings dwelling in the body and soul of transgressors. During the Renaissance in Europe (roughly, the early 1400s to the early 1600s), hundreds of thousands of women and men were burned at the stake for "consorting" with the devil and engaging in wicked deeds. Among both the well educated and much of the mass of society, the theory of demonic possession was a dominant explanation for wrongdoing in Europe almost half a millennium ago. But as I said, though demonic possession asked the "Why do they do it?" question, it cannot be regarded as scientific or positivistic because it is not empirical and it does not seek a naturalistic cause-and-effect explanation of wrongdoing.

According to our definition, *all* the following approaches I discuss in this chapter are positivistic because they share the assumptions of *empiricism*, *objectivism*, and cause-and-effect *determinism.* Gottfredson and Hirschi (1990) argue that the free will approach to crime, discussed first, is *not* a positivist theory, and their own theory, the general theory of crime, is something of a synthesis of positivism (which they critique) and the classical free will school. I put them all in the same category because they all share the scientific approach. In addition, none focuses on or emphasizes the social construction of crime and deviance.

FREE WILL, RATIONAL CALCULATION, AND ROUTINE ACTIVITIES THEORY

By the 1700s, intellectuals had abandoned the idea of the intervention of the devil and other evil, diabolical spirits to explain worldly phenomena and, instead, concentrated on material or worldly forces. Rather than being seen as a result of seduction by demons, the violations of rules, norms, and laws were thought to be caused by free will—a rational calculation of pleasure versus pain. The "*free will*" or "classical" school of criminology was the first sophisticated and academically respectable perspective or theory of criminal or deviant behavior. This theory argued that individuals choose among a number of alternative courses of action according to benefits they believe will accrue to them. This model sees people—criminals included—as free, rational, and hedonistic. Actions that bring pleasure are likely to be enacted and continued; those that are painful will be abandoned. Or so eighteenth-century rationalists believed. The way to ensure conformity to society's norms and laws is to apprehend and punish offenders with celerity (or certainty), swiftness, and with sufficient severity to make the pain following a violation greater than the pleasure the actor derived from it. The celerity, swiftness, and severity of punishment will deter crime, these theorists argued.

The classical school made several assumptions we now recognize as false. We see that people are not completely rational in their behavior; they engage in deviance and crime for several reasons aside from pursuing pleasure and avoiding pain. And what is pleasurable to one person may be painful to another, and vice versa. Moreover, most of the time when a rule or a law is violated, the offender is not caught, thereby nullifying one of the theory's major underpinnings—celerity or certainty—making the offender's calculation of pleasure and pain more complicated than these early thinkers imagined it to be. Overall, as it was originally formulated, the classical school of criminology held a faulty model of human behavior.

The most often cited and discussed of all the contemporary free-will or rationality theories is referred to as *routine activities theory* (Cohen and Felson, 1979; Clarke and Felson, 1993). Routine activities theory argues that criminal behavior will take place when and where there is a conjunction of three elements or factors: *the motivated offender*, a *suitable target*, and the *absence of a capable guardian*. The most remarkable feature of this theory is that it makes a radical break with nearly all the other rationality theories in that it dispenses with criminal motivation. The "motivated offender" is very much in the background, a given—simply *assumed* by the theory. There will always be an abundant supply of people who are motivated to break the law, if that action is profitable to them. Criminal behavior, the theory argues, is a *purposive* and *rational* means of attaining an end—that is, acquiring money more efficiently than by any other method. People tend to act according to the utility that the outcome of their actions have for them, this theory argues. If homeowners leave a house unoccupied and a door unlocked, the motivated offender is more likely to burglarize that house than if it were occupied, the doors were locked, burglar alarms were installed, and a large guard dog were inside. Many—no doubt most—people will not burglarize the house because their utility is not maximized by the burglary, but still, the likelihood that they will be caught and punished, and that they will not be able to steal anything of value to them, is increased by an occupied house, decreased if it is unoccupied.

This theory focuses mainly on *opportunities* for committing crime—and by extension, a great deal of deviant behavior as well. (In contrast, the theory does not address deviant beliefs or conditions at all.) A "suitable target" could be money, property, or even the opportunity to engage in a certain activity that might be deemed desirable by a motivated offender. And the "absence of a capable guardian" would refer to the fact that formal or informal agents of social control are not operative in a particular situation. Hence, for instance, if a potential rapist encountered a woman, alone, in a physical setting in which she could be threatened or overpowered, the likelihood that a rape will take place is greater than if she were accompanied. To the extent that corporate behavior is not monitored by or accountable to government or any other social control agencies, then corporate crime is more likely to take place than if these control systems were operative. The theory would predict that people are more likely to use illicit drugs if their access to them were greater than is currently the case; in the absence of video cameras, store guards, and the prying eye of sales clerks, customers are more likely to engage in shoplifting than they do now; and students are more likely to cheat on exams if watchful professors, teaching assistants, and honest fellow students were absent. In other words, many more of us would engage in nonnormative—or *deviant*—behavior if "capable guardians" were not watching over us and able to sanction our potential wrongdoing than if they were.

Rationalistic theories do not so much attempt to explain deviance and crime as take the "motivated offender" for granted and focus on the conditions that bring him or her out of the woodwork. Although rationality certainly enters into the crime and deviance equation, the fact that jails, prisons, and reform schools are full of young and not-so-young men (and women) who committed crimes impulsively, without planning, and got caught as a consequence, indicates that at the very least their calculation of whether one or more capable guardians were in the picture is flawed. The free will factor alone is not a totally viable explanation. People who engage in deviance and crime do not represent a cross-section of the society; they are not simply people who conducted an erroneous calculation of the likelihood of getting caught. The fact is *most* individuals who commit crimes to make money could have earned more, in the long run, by working at a low-paying drudge job. Clearly, some other explanation is necessary; apparently, the thrill, excitement, and self-righteousness that much criminal behavior entails is at least as powerfully motivating as the rational acquisition of money or the engaging in self-evidently satisfying acts (Katz, 1988).

At the same time—even for "irrational" actors who seek more than a concrete goal such as money—opportunity is related to the enactment of deviance. For *all* actors and *all* activities, the greater the perceived payoff and the lower the perceived likelihood of apprehension and punishment, the greater the likelihood that deviance will be enacted.

SOCIAL DISORGANIZATION AND THE CHICAGO SCHOOL

Just after World War I, a school of thought emerged out of research that was conducted in the city of Chicago by professors and graduate students at the University of Chicago. This school came to view the factors that explained deviance and crime as being located not in the person or the individual but in the social structure. The Chicago School argued that *entire neighborhoods* become so disorganized that merely living in them hugely increased the likelihood of engaging in certain forms of deviant behavior. As cities grew, their residents increasingly came into contact with strangers. This encouraged impersonality, social distance, and a decline in social harmony. People no longer shared the same values or cared about how others felt about them and what they did. As a city grows, its residents' sense of community declines. And as social disorganization in a given neighborhood or community increases, deviant behavior increases along with it (Park, 1926; Traub and Little, 1999, pp. 63–67).

Not all neighborhoods are equally disorganized, however; therefore, rates of deviance and crime vary from one area, neighborhood, and community to another. Certain neighborhoods of a city inadvertently encourage nonconforming behavior while others do not. Why? What is it about certain neighborhoods that make them more hospitable than others to delinquency, crime, and deviant behavior? Social disorganization theorists locate the mechanism influencing nonconforming behavior in *land values.* Dwelling units in neighborhoods with low rental and property value are regarded as undesirable and unattractive to live in. Hence, such dwelling units tend to attract residents with two characteristics.

First, they are geographically unstable. Proponents of the Chicago School referred to such neighborhoods as *zones of transition.* Residents of these areas invest little emotionally in the neighborhood, and move out as soon as they can. And second, such residents are socially, racially, and ethnically heterogeneous; hence, they do not cohere into a unified and organized community. Residents who do not sink roots into the community in which they live do not care about its fate or what happens in them. Residents who are very different from one another do not care about the evaluations that others make of their behavior.

Socially disorganized neighborhoods are unable to develop "strong formal and informal linkages" among their residents; hence residents find it difficult to "regulate the behavior of their fellow neighbors" and exercise the kind of social control that would discourage delinquency, crime, and deviant behavior (Bursik and Grasmick, 1993, pp. x, 7). In short, Chicago sociologists insisted that deviance varies systematically by physical and geographical *location.* Where somebody is located residentially determines the likelihood of that person committing deviant and criminal acts.

The most important factor in the social disorganization school is very closely related to one of routine activity's key explanatory variables: the absence of a capable guardian. Social disorganization is the "macro" equivalent of the many "micro" factors that do or do not guard a "suitable target." It is *entire neighborhoods* that have lost the ability, the will, or the power to monitor and sanction behavior their residents consider untoward and nonnormative. When drug dealers move into an abandoned building, the community does not root them out—or lacks the clout with the police department to have them displaced. Prostitutes are permitted to patrol the streets, harass residents, and engage in sex in cars, alleyways, or hallways without local interference. Junkies shoot up on front stoops, homeless men urinate in hallways, burglars routinely rip off apartments and clean out their contents—and little or nothing is done to stop them. For the criminal and the deviant, a socially disorganized neighborhood is their playground. Clearly, such a community is the "absence of a capable guardian" writ large.

It must be emphasized that the school's generalizations don't apply to many of the forms of deviance we'll be examining. For instance, does it explain homosexuality? Of course not; in fact, with homosexuality, in many ways, the causal process works in a fashion that is precisely the *opposite* of that which social disorganization theory would predict. That is, in many large cities of the world, a substantial number of homosexuals gravitate *to* certain neighborhoods whose residents are less likely to harass them than those that they left. Thus, here, in a sense, the dependent and independent variables are reversed. White-collar corporate crime receive no illumination whatsoever from social disorganization theory. In fact, it is in the more affluent and *least* disorganized communities that the corporate offender is most likely to live! And while the most virulent forms of drug abuse and addiction can almost certainly be accounted for by a revamped version of social disorganization theory—that is, one that takes into account power and external political and economic factors—the more casual, recreational forms of drug use that were so common from the 1970s on remain unexplained by the Chicago School's approach. Are any of the forms of deviance that fall under the umbrella of "cognitive" deviance, such as belief that UFOs are "something real," explained by social disorganization? It seems unlikely.

The social disorganization school of deviance, with its emphasis on social disorganization, had its heyday between the two world wars, roughly from 1920 to 1940. By the end of World War II, it was widely regarded as obsolete. In 1987, a sociologist claimed that the social disorganization school "has been soundly dismissed" (Unnever, 1987, p. 845).

However, in the late 1980s and early 1990s, the social disorganization school made a comeback; a substantial volume of contemporary research and writing on deviance is making use of the Chicago school's approach, concepts, and theories. Although it will never regain its former dominant status in the field, social disorganization theory is experiencing a renaissance. However, to reenergize this approach, some theoretical reformulations were necessary.

What the early social disorganization theorists did not entirely grasp was the dimension of power and its relevance for their analysis. They never figured out how important decisions made at the top of the power structure impacted on the life of the community. Decisions made by the powerful can divide communities in two by approving the construction of a highway, or the destruction of small-unit housing and building a huge housing project, or the creation of a shopping mall. These dramatic disruptions of community life reflect the exercise of power. The fact is the fate of communities and the behavior of their residents are tied to political and economic realities. Contemporary theorists are looking at deviance, crime, and other phenomena in part through the lens of the social disorganization perspective; social disorganization is being revived, but with a sharper, tougher, power-oriented edge. The idea of community control of deviance is being given a political thrust, which it did not have in the 1930s (Feagin and Parker, 1990; Currie, 1993).

A major contribution of the social disorganization or Chicago school, however, was *empathy:* It asked readers to imagine that deviants, delinquents, and criminals were people much like themselves (Pfohl, 1994, p. 209). Since it located the cause of deviance not in individual characteristics but in neighborhood dislocation, the social disorganization school forced us all to realize that, in the shifting tide and fortune of an evolving society, we, too, could have been caught up in the process of ecological transition. Deviants are the way they are as a result of the fact that they are "disproportionally exposed to the disruptive forces of rapid social change" (p. 209). If the rest of us were to be exposed to the same forces, we might very well have ended up doing or being the same thing. This enables persons not living in such neighborhoods, and not caught up in a life of crime, to understand the plight of those who are.

ANOMIE OR STRAIN THEORY

Anomie theory was born in 1938 with the publication of Robert Merton's article, "Social Structure and Anomie" (1938). Influenced by the nineteenth-century study *Suicide* by French sociologist Emile Durkheim (1897/1951), Merton was struck by the insight that deviant behavior could be caused by a disturbance in the social order, which Durkheim called *anomie*. Major social changes generate *disruptions in the traditional social order,* resulting in a state of anomie, followed by a form of deviance—suicide.

After reading Durkheim, Merton agreed that states of anomie influenced the frequency of deviant behavior. He argued that anomie must vary from one society to another and from one group or category in the same society; consequently, rates of deviant behavior must also vary correspondingly. Merton reasoned that "*social structures exert a definite pressure upon certain persons in the society to engage in non-conforming rather than conforming conduct*" (1957, p. 132). Certain pressures, he concluded, could produce very *unconventional* behavior from very *conventional* origins and motives. Anomie theory is also referred to as *strain* theory, because it hypothesizes that a certain kind of strain, or pressure, produces deviant behavior.

In fashioning his argument, Merton completely reconceptualized anomie. To Durkheim, anomie was a disruption of the social order. It was characterized by a state of normlessness, where norms no longer grip the populace or hold them in check. It is the social order that restrains our behavior and our desires and keeps us from engaging in deviant behavior. The norms keep deviance in check and an *absence* of the norms—anomie—results in deviance. When periods of anomie prevail, the populace is no longer guided by culturally approved appetites. Unlimited greed is the rule; human desires run rampant. People no longer have any guidelines as to what is permissible and what is not, what is possible and what is not. Their lust for anything imaginable is unleashed.

Merton's conception of anomie is entirely different. In his view, deviance results not from a *too weak* hold of society's norms on actors, as Durkheim's did, but, in a sense, a *too-strong* hold—that is, from actors *following* society's norms. In addition, Merton's conception of anomie is far more specific than Durkheim's. Merton conceptualizes anomie as a disjunction between *culturally defined goals* and *structurally available opportunities*. Culturally defined goals are "held out as legitimate objectives for all or for diversely located members of the society" (1957, p. 132). These goals, Merton claims, are widely shared; more or less everyone in the society wishes to attain them. Merton shares Durkheim's view that anomie is instrumental in unleashing greedy behavior—behavior directed at attaining goals that, under different circumstances, would not be sought. Still, behind both Durkheim's and Merton's conceptions of anomie is a loud and vehement voice clamoring, "I want! I want!" For Durkheim, what unleashed this voice is a *disruption* of the social order. But for Merton, *it is the social order itself* that releases this voice. Our greedy desires are actually *created* by our culture. And it is the gap or *lack of congruence* between the cultural order (that says we must become materially successful) and the social and economic order (which won't give us what we have been socialized to want and expect) that causes deviant behavior.

What are Merton's culturally defined goals? In Western society, including the United States, they are, of course, primarily monetary and material success. "Making it," within the scope of the American Dream, means being affluent—rich, if possible. Everyone in this society is bombarded on all sides by messages to succeed. And success, for the most part, means only one thing: being able to buy the best that money can buy. This is an almost universal American value, a basic goal toward which nearly everyone aspires and by which nearly everyone is evaluated.

Every society places certain limitations on how to achieve culturally defined goals. While nearly everyone in our society may value wealth, it is a separate question as to how we are permitted to acquire that wealth. Some societies place a heavy emphasis on attaining a given goal but remain fairly tolerant about just *how* one goes about attaining it. Here we have a case of "winning at any cost." Merton maintains that we have such a situation in contemporary America. Contemporary culture "continues to be characterized by a heavy emphasis on wealth as a basic symbol of success, without a corresponding emphasis on the legitimate avenues on which to march toward this goal" (1957, p. 139). We have an acquisitive society, in which "considerations of technical expediency" rule supreme. It is less important just *how* one makes it; the important thing, above all, is *making* it.

In contemporary America, we have a conflict between the *culture* (what people are taught to aspire to) and the *social and economic structure* (the opportunities they have to succeed). We have, in other words, a *malintegrated* society. Aspirations cannot possibly be met by the available material resources. While the aspirations of the population are unlimited, their actual chances of success are quite limited. This creates pressure to commit deviance. "It is only when a system of cultural values extols [or praises], virtually above all else, certain *common* success-goals *for the population at large* while the social structure rigorously restricts or completely closes access to approved modes of reaching these goals *for a considerable part of that same population,* that deviant behavior ensures on a large scale" (Merton, 1957, p. 134). "It is . . . my central hypothesis," Merton wrote, "that aberrant behavior may be regarded sociologically as a symptom of disassociation between culturally prescribed aspirations and socially structured avenues for realizing these aspirations" (1957, p. 134). By itself, an ambitious monetary goal for the population will not produce a high rate of crime; by itself, the lack of opportunities to achieve that goal, likewise, does not produce a great deal of crime. It is their *combination* or *conjunction* that imparts American society with an almost uniquely high predatory crime rate among Western societies.

It should be noted that anomie theory is based on very nearly the *opposite* explanatory factor from that offered by the routine activities and social disorganization theories. Anomie theory tries to explain the *motives* for nonnormative behavior. It is based on the notion that the desire for material success must be *socialized into us* for deviance to take place. In other words, we need to be given a "push" to deviate. Without the desire to become—and the expectation of becoming—materially successful, our failure to succeed would not produce the necessary deviant "adaptations." In contrast, routine activities and social disorganization theories do *not* assume that we need to be "pushed" into deviance. Instead, they assume that some offenders will always be in sufficient supply to take advantage of the absence of social control by deviating from the rules or laws. What some of us lack is opportunity. In short, anomie theory assumes that it is *deviant behavior* that needs to be explained, while routine activities and social disorganization theories assume that deviance and crime don't need to be explained; instead, it is the *monitoring and sanctioning of illicit behavior* that needs to be explained. Everyone would deviate if given a sufficiently golden opportunity, but some social conditions offer that opportunity while others do not. For the latter, the absence of social control explains deviant behavior.

Another important point: Merton's theory is "macro" in scope, that is, it looks at differences between and among *large social units* such as entire societies in explaining and predicting deviant behavior. The theory does *not* focus on individual or "micro" differences in levels of anomie and hence, deviant behavior. Merton's theory, for instance, would argue that American society is more anomic than, for example, Portuguese society, since expectations of high levels of material success tend to be much more the rule in the United States. Because of this, the theory would predict that America's rates of deviant behavior would correspondingly be higher. The theory does *not* explain why one person in the same society deviates while another does not.

Merton drew up a typology of different responses to goal attainment and legitimate versus illegitimate means of attaining these goals. People subject to these conflicting pressures adapt to or react to them in different ways. What types of deviance should we predict for success-hungry Americans?

Conformity, or the *conformist* mode of adaptation, accepts both cultural values of success and the institutionalized, legitimate, or conventional means for reaching these goals. The conformist both strives for material success and chooses law-abiding ways of achieving success. This mode of adaptation is not of interest to the student of deviance except as a negative case since it is not characterized by violations of the norms. It is in the typology simply for the purpose of comparing it with various forms of deviance. Becoming an accountant, a physician, a lawyer, and striving for material success by becoming successful in one's profession—becoming affluent through a legal, legitimate profession, performed in a law-abiding, respectable fashion—is an example of the most common mode of adaptation: *conformity.* Conformity is not, in any case, deviance.

The mode of adaptation Merton called *innovation* involves accepting the goal of success but choosing to achieve it in an illegal, illegitimate, or deviant fashion. This adaptation is clearly the most interesting of all modes to Merton; he devoted more space to describing it than all the other modes put together. An innovative mode of adaptation to the pressures of American culture and society would encompass most types of money-making criminal activities; for example, white-collar crime, embezzlement, pickpocketing, running a confidence game, bank robbery, burglary, prostitution, and pimping. Innovators want success, but they attempt to achieve it by seeking a deviant or criminal route.

In contrast, *ritualism* entails "the abandoning or scaling down of the lofty cultural goals of great pecuniary success and rapid social mobility," but abiding "almost compulsively by institutionalized norms" (Merton, 1957, pp. 149–150). The ritualist plays it safe, plays by the book, doesn't take chances. Ritualism as an adaptation to American society's heavy emphasis on success is a kind of *partial* withdrawal—an abandonment of the goal of success, but a *retention* of the *form* of doing things properly, following all the rules to the letter. In many ways, ritualism is a kind of *overconformity.* A petty bureaucrat, who insists that all rules and regulations be followed in every detail, would exemplify this mode of adaptation. In this case, actors adhere to the rules, but their purpose—presumably, serving the public—has been forgotten, in fact, *subverted* by a rigid adherence to the rules.

Retreatism is a rejection of both goals and institutionalized means. It is a total cop-out, a "retreat" from the things that the society values most. They give up both the goal of success and any and all avenues of achieving it. Retreatists are "true aliens." In this category Merton places "some of the adaptive activities of psychotics, autists, pariahs, outcasts, vagrants, vagabonds, tramps, chronic drunkards, and drug addicts" (1957, p. 153). Retreatism is brought on by repeated failure, such failure causing severe personal conflict and a withdrawal from valuing success and routes to attain it. Merton feels that this mode of adaptation is the least frequently resorted to of those discussed so far.

Rebellion "involves a genuine transvaluation." It is an attempt to deal with the dominant goals and means by overthrowing them altogether. While the retreatist merely rejects them and puts nothing in their place, the rebel renounces prevailing values and introduces an alternative social, political, and economic structure, one in which the current stresses and strains presumably would not exist. The act of launching a revolution dedicated to the overthrow of the political and economic order would be a clear-cut case of rebellion. Merton devotes the least attention to this mode.

The anomie theory of Robert K. Merton exerted an enormous impact on the field of the sociology of deviance for decades after its initial publication in 1938. In fact, half a century after its publication, it was measurably the most cited work ever written by a sociologist. (Recently, depending on the year, others have supplanted it in that category.) Anomie theory has attracted considerable criticism.

Middle-Class Bias. Anomie theory, some critics say, suffers from the same middle-class bias that skewed all earlier theories of deviance: It made the assumption that lower- and working-class people commit acts of crime and deviance *in* general significantly more frequently than is true of the members of the middle class. Today, most observers readily admit that "street" crime is committed more often by individuals at or toward the bottom of the class structure than is true of those at or near the top. Yet—and here is where the problem enters—there are many criminal and deviant actions that are equally likely, or even more likely, to be engaged in by the more affluent, prestigious, well-educated, and powerful members of society. Although official police statistics on who commits crimes show that crime is a predominantly lower-class phenomenon, it is now clear that the specific crimes that upper-middle-class people commit are those that are far less likely to result in police scrutiny and action than those that lower- and working-class individuals commit. This is especially the case for white-collar and corporate crimes, the crimes of the rich and the powerful, which, its critics argue, anomie theory does not address.

Irrelevance of anomie for most forms of deviance. At one point, Merton claims that anomie theory "is designed to account for some, not all, forms of deviant behavior, customarily described as criminal or delinquent" (1957, p. 178). Yet in other places, he makes a case for anomie being the major cause of deviance in general. Deviance, he says, "is a symptom of disassociation between culturally prescribed aspirations and socially structured avenues for realizing these aspirations" (p. 134). Again, Merton writes, "It is *only* when" goals and means are disjunctive, "*deviant behavior ensues on a large scale*" (p. 146; my emphasis). Though Merton "is vague as to which behavior is covered by this explanation and which is not" (Clinard, 1964, p. 19), he clearly believes that *rates* of deviance vary by degree of anomie. Consequently, though some forms of deviance may be exempt from the theory (Merton never explains which ones are, however), deviance *in general* is supposedly explained by it.

Although the malintegration between means and goals that characterizes contemporary American society will typically put pressure on many members to engage in certain forms of deviance, *most forms of deviant behavior will not be produced by the pressure of such malintegration.* Merton's theory is not an explanation of deviant behavior in general, as he claims, but a delineation of some of the possible outcomes of a certain kind of strain induced by specific social and economic factors. The anomie approach turns out to be largely *irrelevant* to *most* forms of deviant behavior. Activities such as nonaddicting recreational drug use, assault, criminal homicide, petty gambling, adultery, homosexuality, child molestation, the consumption of pornography, holding unconventional beliefs, and so on, *are completely unexplained by the anomie theory.*

ANOMIE THEORY INTO THE 1990s AND BEYOND

In the 1950s and 1960s, anomie theory was the most frequently used theoretical tradition in the study of deviance and crime (Cole, 1975). But by the early 1970s, the anomie perspective underwent a sharp decline in influence, and from the mid-1970s and the mid-1980s, it seemed as if it would disappear from the field altogether, tossed onto the "dustbin of history." In 1978, in a detailed appraisal of theories of deviance, crime, and delinquency, Ruth Kornhauser stated: "Strain models are disconfirmed" (p. 253). She advised that sociologists seeking an explanation of delinquency, crime, and deviance forget anomie theory and turn their attention elsewhere.

But, as with social disorganization theory, some time in the late 1980s to the early 1990s, anomie theory experienced a renaissance. As with the social disorganization framework, anomie or strain theory will never recapture its former glory as the field's preeminent approach to the study of deviance. However, judging by a recent rebirth in research and writing adopting the theory as a lens with which to examine deviant phenomena, it remains as vital as ever (Adler and Laufer, 1995; Messner and Rosenfeld, 1997).

According to the *Social Science Citation Index,* which lists articles that refer to or cite a particular work. Merton's "Social Structure and Anomie," which appeared nearly seven decades ago, is actually cited more frequently today, in the 2000s, than it was in the 1970s and 1980s. It has helped countless researchers illuminate dozens of deviant, delinquent, and criminal activities. For instance, one recent research endeavor that has made use of anomie theory is the study of drug dealing. Bourgeois (1995, p. 326, 2003) argues that drug dealers should be accorded "their rightful place within the mainstream of American society. These deviant actors are," he states, "made in America. . . . Highly motivated, ambitious innercity youths have been attracted to the rapidly expanding, multibillion-dollar drug economy . . . precisely because they believe in Horatio Alger's version of the American Dream." Again, Merton's theory continues to be relevant. Duneier (1999, pp. 60–62, 364) describes Merton's retreatism adaptation, which he refers as "The 'Fuck It!' Mentality." This takes place when a homeless person has given up on both goals and means. It is, he explains, a pervasive state of resignation that affects "most major aspects of his life," when he "becomes indifferent to behavior that he once thought of as basic, such as sleeping in a bed or defecating in a toilet" (p. 61). It is, in Merton's "brilliant scheme" (Duneier's term), "an extreme form of retreatism" (p. 61), the end point along a continuum of an "I don't care" attitude. Clearly, in the sociology of deviance and crime, Merton's anomie theory remains influential. It is not likely to go away any time soon.

DIFFERENTIAL ASSOCIATION AND LEARNING THEORY

In 1939, a major theory of deviance was propounded for the first time (Sutherland, 1939). It was called the theory of *differential association,* and it has become one of a small number of important perspectives in the field. Sutherland set for himself two somewhat different but overlapping tasks. The first was to explain what he referred to as *differential group organization:* why crime rates vary among different groups of people, why a criminal tradition was endemic in certain social circles. The second task was to explain why some *individuals* engage in crime more than other individuals. Unfortunately, Sutherland did not develop his ideas on differential group organization in detail.

The first and most fundamental proposition of the theory of differential association states that criminal behavior, and, by extension, deviance as well, is *learned.* This proposition was directed against biological theories that assert that crime is caused by genetic, metabolic, or anatomical defects, and against the view that criminal behavior is hit upon accidentally or through independent invention. Hardly anyone, Sutherland asserted, stumbles upon or dreams up a way to break the law; this must be passed on from one person to another in a genuine learning process. The theory of differential association also opposed the view that mental illness or an abnormal, pathological personality is a major causal factor in the commission of criminal behavior. Rather, Sutherland argued, crime is learned in a straightforward, essentially normal fashion, no different from the way in which members of American society learn to speak English or brush their teeth.

A second proposition of the theory of differential association is that criminal behavior, and, again, by extension, deviance as well, must be learned through face-to-face interaction between people who are close or intimate with one another. People are not persuaded to engage in criminal behavior as a result of reading a book or a newspaper, seeing a movie, or (today, as opposed to 1939) watching television. Criminal knowledge, skills, sentiments, values, traditions, and motives are all passed down as a result of *interpersonal*—not impersonal—means. Two major factors that intensify this process are *priority* and *intensity.* The earlier in one's life one is exposed to attitudes and values ("definitions") favorable to committing crimes, the greater the likelihood that one will in fact commit crime. And the closer and more intimate the friends, relatives, and acquaintances that endorse committing crime, likewise, the more swayed one will be to break the law.

Sutherland's theory, then, argued that people who embark upon engaging in criminal behavior *differentially associate* with individuals who endorse violations of the law. Notice that the theory does not say that one needs to associate with actual criminals to break the law oneself—only that one should be more heavily exposed to *definitions* favorable to criminal actions. One can be exposed to law-abiding definitions emanating from criminals and criminal definitions emanating from law-abiding individuals (though, of course, it usually works the other way round). Still, as most of us know, "actions speak louder than words," and one wonders how much more of an impact the example of criminal actions has than criminal words.

In sum, Sutherland's theory of differential association holds that a person becomes delinquent or criminal because of an excess of definitions favorable to the violation of the law over definitions unfavorable to the violation of the law. The key to this process is the *ratio* between definitions favorable to the violation of the law to definitions that are unfavorable. When favorable definitions exceed unfavorable ones, an individual will turn to crime.

The theory of differential association has been criticized for being vague and untestable. Later efforts to refine and operationalize the theory (Burgess and Akers, 1966) have not been entirely successful in rescuing it from imprecision. Exactly how would a researcher measure this ratio of favorable to unfavorable definitions of violations of the law? And exactly how could "favorable" and "unfavorable" be indicated or measured? Even one of the theory's staunchest defenders admits that Sutherland's formulation of the differential association process "is not precise enough to stimulate rigorous empirical test" (Cressey, 1960, p. 57). Some conceptualizations of learning theory attempt to address these and other objections by incorporating additional factors and variables into their framework (for instance, Akers, 1998). In so doing, they depart radically from Sutherland's original formulation and become eclectic rather than instances of learning theory.

A great deal of research and anecdotal evidence demonstrates that much crime is, indeed, learned in intimate social settings. However, it seems at least as overly ambitious to assume that all criminal behavior is learned in a straightforward fashion as it is to assume that all noncriminal behavior is learned. Many actions, criminal and noncriminal alike, are invented anew by individuals in similar situations. All behavior is not learned, at least not directly. Much of it, deviant or otherwise, may be devised in relative isolation. There is a great deal of independent invention of certain forms of deviance, delinquency, and crime. The human mind is, after all, almost infinitely creative. The idea to do something, and its eventual enactment, almost always has a cultural or learning *foundation,* but it was not necessarily learned in detail. One can, either by oneself or in the company of an equally untutored individual, "put the pieces together." One can enact certain behaviors *in the absence of learning or learning about those behaviors themselves;* learning may take one to a certain point, after which creativity and imagination take over. Any learning theory that requires that one learn positive values *about the precise behavior itself* must therefore be incomplete and deficient. Any learning theory that includes all the other factors that go into human behavior, such as biological drives, the pleasure principle, and so on, is likely to be so vague as to be a tautology—true by definition.

Many criminal activities do not fit the differential association model at all: check forgery (Lemert, 1953, 1958, 1972, pp. 150–182), embezzlement (Cressey, 1953), child molestation (McCaghy, 1967, 1968), wartime black market violations (Clinard, 1952), as well as certain crimes of passion (Katz, 1988), and crimes involving psychiatric compulsion (such as kleptomania). While, for many deviant and criminal activities, learning may assist their enactment, they do not cause them. Some observers (Gottfredson and Hirschi, 1990) have gone so far as to argue that one does not have to learn anything to enact deviant or criminal behavior; it is simply "doing what comes naturally." In addition, many forms of crime are not even approved of by a majority of the people who engage in them—such as child molestation and murder. Consequently, they could not be learned in anything like the fashion that Sutherland suggests. That is, one may learn *about* certain crimes, but one hardly ever learns that they are activities or states one should emulate. In short, while it is true that much criminal behavior is learned, much of it is not. As a partial theory, differential association is valuable. As a complete or general theory, it is overly ambitious. Rather than a theory that explains all crime and deviance, differential association should be regarded as a concept that helps us to understand a particular process that some rule breakers go through and some do not.

SOCIAL CONTROL THEORY

Control theory is a major explanatory paradigm in the fields of deviance behavior and criminology. Control theorists see their perspective as a critique of and a replacement for both anomie theory and the subcultural or learning approaches. While most theories ask, "Why do they do it?"—that is, what processes *encourage* deviant behavior—control theory turns the question around and asks, "Why *don't* they do it?" In other words, control theory assumes that engaging in deviance is not problematic, that, if *left to our own devices,* all of us would deviate from the rules of society. In fact, control theorists believe that deviance is *inherently attractive.* Under most circumstances, we are encouraged to break the rules; deviance-making processes are strong and obvious and commonsensical. Why *shouldn't* we lie and steal, if they are what get us what we want? *Why not* hang out on street corners and get drunk and throw bottles through windows—it's so much fun! This approach takes for granted the allure of deviance, crime, and delinquency. What has to be explained, control theorists argue, is why most people *don't* engage in deviance, why are they discouraged from engaging in delinquent behavior, why don't they break the law and engage in a life of crime.

What causes deviant behavior, they say, is the *absence* of the social control that causes conformity and conventional behavior. Most of us do not engage in deviant or criminal acts because of strong bonds with or ties to conventional, mainstream social institutions. If these bonds are weak or broken, we will be released from society's rules and will be free to deviate. It is not so much deviants' ties to an unconventional group or subculture that attract them to deviant behavior, but their *lack* of ties with the conforming, mainstream, law-abiding culture; this frees them to engage in deviance.

Control theory would predict that, to the extent that a person has a *stake in conformity,* he or she will tend not to break the law and risk losing that stake; to the extent that a person lacks that stake in conformity, he or she will be willing to violate the law. Thus, jobs, especially satisfying, high-paying jobs, may act as something of a deterrent to crime. Attending college, likewise, represents a stake or investment that many students are not willing to risk losing. Being married and having a family, too, will discourage criminal behavior to the extent that arrest may undermine their stability. Everyone knows that *some* crime is committed by the employed, by college students, by married persons with a family. But control theory would predict that there are *major differences* in the crime rates of the employed versus the unemployed, college students versus their non-college-age peers, and married parents versus the unmarried. To the extent that a society or a neighborhood is able to invest its citizens or residents with a stake worth protecting, it will have lower rates of crime; to the extent that it is unable to invest that stake in its citizens or residents, its crime rate will be correspondingly higher. Home ownership, for instance, can act as a deterrent to crime, as can organizational and community involvement. A society with many citizens who have nothing to lose is a society with a high crime rate.

Control theory does not state that individuals with strong ties to conventional society are absolutely *insulated* from deviance, that they will *never* engage in *any* deviant or criminal action, regardless of how mildly unconventional it is. It does, however, assert that both deviance and social control are matters of degree: The more attached we are to conventional society, the lower the likelihood of engaging in behavior that violates its values and norms. A strong bond to conventionality does not insulate us from mildly deviant behavior, but it does make it less likely.

The theory works a great deal better for some behaviors than others. Many of the activities control theory sees as natural, recreational, and requiring no special explanation are part and parcel of relatively minor delinquencies. But then what about more seriously aggressive and violent behavior, such as murder, robbery, and rape? Are they part of the same constellation of acts that, if left to our own devices and in the absence of simple societal controls, we would engage in? It's difficult to envision that the same logic applies. In fact, there may be a very good reason why the vast majority of the research applying control theory has been self-report surveys of relatively minor delinquencies among youths: It works best for them. As we saw, such studies run into a serious roadblock. Hirschi's 1969 study found few class differences in rates of delinquency. There is a good reason why. The most important crimes, those that criminologists are most interested in (murder, robbery, and rape), tend to be relatively rare. The least important crimes are sufficiently common to make a self-report possible. The less common the behavior, the more difficult it is to study by means of self-report surveys, since so few of the sample will have engaged in them, especially within a recent time frame. Hence, control theorists are a bit like the drunk who is searching for his keys, not in the dark, where he lost them, but in the light, where he can see better. In spite of this restriction, control theory represents one of the more powerful and insightful approaches we have to explain crime, deviance, and especially delinquency.

A GENERAL THEORY OF CRIME: SELF-CONTROL THEORY

In 1990, Michael Gottfredson and Travis Hirschi devised what they refer to as *a general theory of crime,* that is, force or fraud in pursuit of self-interest (p. 15). The field of criminology refers to it as self-control theory, and it shares with social control theory the idea that deviance is self-evident and inherently attractive. The authors claim that their theory applies to any and all crimes, regardless of type: white-collar and corporate crime, embezzlement, murder, robbery, rape, the illegal sale of drugs, underage drinking, burglary, shoplifting—indeed, any and all illegal actions. In fact, in their view, their theory is even more general than that, since it is an explanation of actions that may not even be against the law or entail inflicting force or fraud against a victim. More properly, it is a general theory of deviance and includes, besides crime, a variety of self-indulgent actions (like smoking, getting high or drunk, and, one might suppose, even being a couch potato), and reckless behavior that has a high likelihood of resulting in accidents (such as driving dangerously fast or preferring a motorcycle to a car). Their theory, they say, stresses both the factors present in the immediate or "proximate" situation of the criminal action, which determine or influence its *enactment* (which they refer to as "crime"), *and* those background or "distant" factors, which determine or influence the *tendency* or *propensity* to commit crime (which they term *criminality*).

The origin of crime, Gottfredson and Hirschi say, is *low self-control,* which, in turn, results from inadequate, ineffective, and inconsistent socialization by parents early in childhood. Parents who raise delinquent and criminal offspring lack affection for them, fail to monitor their behavior, fail to recognize when they are committing deviant acts, and fail to control wrongdoing. What makes crime especially attractive to people who lack self-control? Criminal acts, Gottfredson and Hirschi say, are characterized by the fact that they provide *immediate* and *easy* or *simple* gratification of desires (p. 89). "They provide money without work, sex without courtship, revenge without court delays" (p. 89). People who lack self control "tend to lack diligence, tenacity, or persistence in a course of action" (p. 89). In addition, criminal acts are "*exciting, risky, or thrilling*"; crime provides, in the typical case, "*few or meager long-term benefits*"; it requires "*little skill or planning*"; and often results in "*pain or discomfort for the victim*" (p. 89; the emphasis is theirs). As a result of the last of these characteristics, people with low self-control, and hence, frequent enactors of criminal behavior, tend to be "self-centered, indifferent, or insensitive to the suffering and needs of others" (p. 89), although they may also "discover the immediate and easy rewards of charm and generosity" (p. 90).

Since crime entails "the pursuit of immediate pleasure," it follows that "people lacking in self-control will also tend to pursue immediate pleasures that are *not* criminal: they will tend to smoke, drink, use drugs, gamble, have children out of wedlock, and engage in illicit sex" (p. 90). Some crimes entail not so much pleasure but an attempt at relief from irritation or discomfort, such as physically abusing a crying child or beating up an annoying stranger in a bar. People with low self-control have little tolerance for frustration and little skill at dealing with difficult circumstances verbally or by applying complex, difficult-to-master solutions. "In short, people who lack self-control will tend to be impulsive, insensitive, physical (as opposed to mental), risk-taking, short-sighted, and nonverbal, and they will therefore tend to engage in criminal and analogous acts" (p. 90).

Their general theory of crime, Gottfredson and Hirschi argue, is both consistent with the facts of criminal behavior and contradicts the bulk of mainstream criminological theories. The authors are not modest either about the reach of their theory or its devastating implications for competing explanations. They insist that their general theory of crime *cannot* be reconciled with other theories; instead, they insist, it must of necessity *annihilate* them. In fact, Gottfredson and Hirschi abandon even Hirschi's own social control theory (discussed earlier), formulated some 40 years ago. The *social* controls that Hirschi saw previously as central he and his coauthor now view as secondary to the *internal* controls, which, they argue, are developed in childhood. Now, life circumstances such as marriage, employment, and home ownership, so crucial to control theory, are presumably rejected as irrelevant, having little or no independent impact on crime. After all, how can someone with low self-control maintain a marriage, keep a job, or buy a house? They lack emotional and psychic wherewithal—the self-control—to do what has to be done, to be *subject* to external or social controls. It is self-control that determines social control, not the other way around, Hirschi and Gottfredson now argue.

The problem with the theories of crime that are now dominant in criminology, Gottfredson and Hirschi claim, is that they are inconsistent with the evidence.

Strain or anomie theory "predicts that offenders will have high long-term aspirations and low long-term expectations," but that turns out to be false; "people committing criminal acts tend to have lower aspirations than others," while, among offenders, "expectations for future success tend to be unrealistically high" (p. 162). In anomie theory, crime is a long-term, indirect solution to current life circumstances, whereas, in reality, Gottfredson and Hirschi say, crime is an impulsive act which provides immediate, short-term, and rather skimpy rewards. Criminals lack the skills, diligence, and persistence necessary for the deviant adaptations spelled out by Merton. Strain does not explain the incidence or rate of criminal behavior as a whole, since most of it is petty, impulsive, and immediate.

Likewise, the many varieties of learning theory should be rejected as being inconsistent with the facts, Gottfredson and Hirschi argue. All such theories make the assumption that deviants engage in deviance as a result of a positive learning experience, that is, *they learn the value* of engaging in deviance and crime. In fact, one does *not* learn to engage in crime, since no learning is required. Criminal acts are simple, commonsensical, immediate, concrete, and result in immediate gratification. Neither the motivation nor the skill to commit them are problematic; everybody has them. What causes such behavior is not the *presence* of something—learning—but the *absence* of something—self-control. Learning theories simply fail utterly and completely to explain criminal, deviant, and delinquent behavior, Gottfredson and Hirschi argue.

More generally, they reject the idea that crime is *social* behavior (in fact, it is more accurate to refer to it as *asocial* in nature), that it is *learned* behavior ("when in fact no learning is required"), that the tendency to commit it can be an *inherited* trait (when it is clearly acquired, through childhood experiences), and that it is *economic* behavior (when, in fact, "it is uneconomical behavior outside the labor force"). To be plain about it, they reject all other explanations of criminal behavior except their own (p. 75); only a lack of self-control is truly consistent with the facts of crime. Gottfredson and Hirschi contemptuously reject any effort to integrate their own theory with the explanations they so roundly destroyed.

With two exceptions. Not all persons who exhibit low self-control commit crime; low self-control merely *predisposes* someone to commit crime. What determines which persons who are predisposed to commit crime will actually do so? In a word, opportunity. Hence, any explanation that focuses on the *patterning* and *distribution* of criminal opportunities—although incomplete—is consistent with the facts, Gottfredson and Hirschi argue. Their approach is an attempt to revitalize classical, free-will, or rational choice theory, mentioned early in this chapter, as half the crime equation. The contemporary version of the classic approach to crime, referred to as opportunity theory, the routine activity approach, or rational choice theory, argues that crime can take place to the extent that a *motivated offender* has access to a "suitable target" (such as money and valuables), which lacks a capable guardian. Routine activity theorists emphasize the factors of *proximity, accessibility*, and *reward* (Hough, 1987). They *assume* or *take for granted* a motivated offender—the criminal—since there will always be an abundant supply of them to go around; instead, they focus on the necessary preconditions for the commission of the crime. The assumption that crime is the most rational means to acquire property is abandoned, however, since Gottfredson and Hirschi argue that most crimes do not net the offender much in the way of goods or cash. Nonetheless, they say, opportunity is a crucial element in the crime equation. (Not in *criminality,* or the individual *propensity* to commit crime, but in *crime,* in the likelihood that criminal *actions* will take place.) While incomplete, Gottfredson and Hirschi say, a theory that focuses on opportunity is consistent with self-control theory. Moreover, they say, both are necessary for a complete explanation of criminal behavior (1987, 1990).

In addition, they argue, social disorganization theory is consistent with both classical theory and the facts of crime; the inability of a community to monitor the behavior of its residents complements, and is similar to, parallel parental incompetence (Gottfredson and Hirschi, 1990). As we saw, social disorganization theory is a form of control theory writ large.

As might be expected, self-control theory has met with mixed reactions. Strain theorists argue that social strain and anomie are indeed significant causal precursors to criminal behavior. For instance, the aggressiveness and anger that many criminals exhibit when committing their crimes is far more than a lack of self-restraint; only strain theory explains it, they say (Agnew, 1995, p. 125). Some learning theorists argue that a lack of self-control is a basic component or element of the deviant learning process (Akers, 1991)—hence, they say, learning theory *subsumes,* or swallows up, self-control theory. Certainly the reductionistic, mechanistic, either-or logic Gottfredson and Hirschi display in their theorizing has led some observers to believe that they may have missed crucial subtleties in characterizing and explaining human behavior (Lynch and Groves, 1995, pp. 372–378). One critic takes Gottfredson and Hirschi to task for selectively reading the data, focusing on those that seem to confirm their theory and ignoring those that would damage it (Polk, 1991). Gottfredson and Hirschi's theory clearly applies much more to the antisocial personality disorder (Black, 1999) than to deviance in general. It is too early to assess the validity of self-control theory in anything like a definitive fashion. Chances are, contrary to its claims, bits and pieces of it will be incorporated into mainstream criminology and deviance theory, while its global, overall—and perhaps overblown—critiques of rival theories will be taken far less seriously. The fact is that it is likely that Gottfredson and Hirschi have not offered a general theory of crime and deviance, but a plausible account of bits and pieces of the phenomenon they purport to explain (Goode, 2008b).

SUMMARY

Whenever some members of a society engage in what others regard as wrongdoing, the latter wonder why the former do it. Explanations for violating society's rules are as ancient as human existence. Historically, the most ancient of such explanations was demonic possession—the influence of the devil or evil spirits.

By the 1700s, intellectuals and the educated sectors of Western society no longer believed that the intervention of evil spirits caused people to violate the norms or the law. The eighteenth century in Europe was referred to as the Age of Reason. Hence, it makes sense that it was in this era that an explanation for crime arose that focused on humans as reasonable and rational actors, exercising their free will and guided by the pursuit of pleasure and the avoidance of pain. The contemporary version of a rationalistic explanation of normative violations is referred to as *routine activities theory*. It stresses that crime and deviance take place to the extent that a motivated offender and a suitable target are present, and a suitable guardian is lacking.

During the 1920s, sociologists came to see the community rather than the individual as the source of norm violations. Some neighborhoods are unstable by virtue of their undesirability. As a result, residents are heterogeneous (and hence, often strangers to one another) and do not sink roots into the community. In such neighborhoods, wrongdoing is common, since residents cannot or do not monitor or control normative and legal violations. In sum, deviance varies systematically by ecological location. The social disorganization school was the dominant perspective in academic sociology between the 1920s and the 1940s. After World War II, it suffered a serious decline in importance and influence. Although it never regained its former glory, roughly by 1990, the social disorganization school experienced a dramatic renaissance. Today, numerous researchers are conducting studies that are guided or inspired by the social disorganization perspective.

Anomie theory is distinctive by virtue of the fact that it had its origin (except for the work of Emile Durkheim, who had something different in mind) in a single article by a single sociologist: Robert K. Merton's *Social Structure and Anomie,* published in 1938. Merton argued that, in the United States, deviance was a product of a disjunction or contradiction between the culture, whose norms urged material and financial success for all members of the society, and the social and economic structure, which granted high levels of success only to some. This condition produces a state of stress or *anomie*. As a result of failing in the traditional sectors of the society, those who were left behind were forced into one of an array of deviant adaptations. During the 1950s and 1960s, the anomie perspective was the most often-used approach in the study of deviance. But in the 1970s, the theory underwent a sharp decline in influence. However, as with other perspectives in this field, anomie theory experienced a strong rebirth, roughly beginning in 1990. Today, once again, it is the focus of vigorous commentary and research.

Learning theories encompass a variety of perspectives, all of which center around the idea that deviance, delinquency, and crime are learned in a fairly straightforward fashion. By being isolated from mainstream society and its definition of deviance, and integrated into unconventional groups, one learns deviant values, beliefs, and norms and, thus, engages in deviant behavior. The most prominent of learning theories is differential association, devised by Edwin Sutherland in 1939. As with all other perspectives in the field, learning theory has been attacked, defended, amended, and added to.

Social control theory takes strong issue with both anomie and learning theory. Deviants do not have to be stressed into committing deviance, nor does anyone have to learn to become a deviant. Indeed, what requires explaining, say the social control theorists, is conformity. Deviance is readily understandable, commonsensical, and inherently appealing. Left to their own devices, everyone would deviate from the norms: It's easier, more fun, and more effective in getting the actor what is desired than is true of conformity. The important question is not, why do we commit deviance? Instead it is, why *don't* we commit deviance? The factor or variable that social control theorists have isolated as the explanation is that people engage in conventional behavior to the extent that they are involved with and attached to conventional others, activities, and beliefs. To the extent that we have an investment or stake in conventionality, we will engage in conventional behavior. To the extent that we don't, we will engage in deviance.

In 1990, the fully articulated version of a major control theory of deviance made its appearance—a general theory of crime. It is based on several tenets of control theory (as well as classic, free will, or rationalistic theory), but it breaks with it in its lack of stress on *current* conventional attachments. People violate norms and the law because they lack self-control; they tend to be insensitive, self-centered, impulsive, relatively unintelligent; they lack a long-range perspective, can't deal with frustration, and require immediate gratification. And they lack self-control because they were subject to inadequate, inconsistent, and ineffective socialization by their parents or other caregivers. Self-control theory is one of the few perspectives whose advocates argue that all other perspectives (except for rational choice and social disorganization) are completely incompatible with the facts of crime. Its advocates set out to destroy all now-dominant approaches to deviance and crime. As might be expected, self-control theory has met with a mixed reception.

Today, no single perspective or approach is dominant in the study of deviance. Moreover, contrary to what its advocates claim, the theories I discussed in this chapter are not, for the most part, contradictory or mutually exclusive; each of them contains a grain of truth. It is likely that all of them are valid explanations for some aspects of deviance and crime. And, as we can see, all the approaches discussed in this chapter are concerned entirely with *an explanation of deviant behavior.* In this sense, they are all positivistic or scientific in their general approach. In the next chapter, we'll look at theories that are up to a very different task, in a sense, looking at the opposite side of the deviance coin. Instead of attempting to explain why deviant behavior is enacted, for the most part, they ask about the nature and operation of *definitions* of deviance and the exercise of *social control.* Instead of asking why deviance is enacted, they wonder about why deviance is conceptualized and defined a certain way, and how and why certain behaviors, traits, and persons are caught up in the web of punishment and condemnation. No examination of deviance is complete without an investigation of the nature, social roots, and the exercise of social control.

Before we proceed to the next chapter, however, I must issue a most emphatic warning. The perspectives we are about to examine are largely focused on how the society or segments of the society *define* and *deal with* deviance and deviants. Theories or perspectives that focus on social control constitute the *constructionist* approach to deviance. Unfortunately, two of the theories we looked at in this chapter share names that are very similar to this social control emphasis—social control theory and self-control theory. I must emphasize that they are *not* theories of social control in the sense that I'll be using the term in Chapter 3—that is, they are not constructionist in their approach. The social control and self-control theories are etiological, explanatory, causal, or positivist theories of deviance. They ask, "*Why do some persons engage in deviant behavior*?" Or, to be a bit more precise, they ask, "Why do some people *not* engage in deviant behavior?" To repeat, they attempt to account for the behavior itself, *not* why it is defined in a certain way or why it is condemned. Proponents of these theories do not examine social control as problematic, that is, as the subject to be investigated. They do *not* ask, "*Why social control*?" Don't be confused by the similarity in their names. Their approaches are completely different; they share little else with the perspectives discussed in this chapter *aside from* their names.

Account: Clinical Depression

The contributor of the following account is Robert, a 26-year-old college student. "Recently," he explains, referring to himself in the third person, "he was involved in an altercation that led to five felony charges being set against him and [being] committed to a psychiatric ward for 55 hours. He has no prior [criminal] record. In most aspects of his existence, Robert leads a conventional lifestyle. Yet he has been plagued by depression since he was 16. He has only recently sought treatment and is in the process of finding a cure to what he now knows is a physical ailment related to [a disorder of the] thyroid."

Whatever disadvantage I had as a youth in the parenting department, it did not affect me. Even if it is argued that it in fact did affect me, this was not realized until much later. I do not believe that differential association [explains my condition or my behavior] in the first phase of my life. My youth was filled with situations that, according to differential association theory, should have affected me at an early age. Here I will stress only my activities and not my parents' raising me.

I can't remember when my parents didn't fight. They had heated arguments at least once a week. This often led to my father destroying various of my mother's possessions or just things that belonged to the house. They divorced for the first time when I was 6 years old. My mother went into the Army and my father took custody of me. I spent the next 10 months living with my father as he cohabited with various girlfriends while I stayed at my grandmother's house. When we were together, he took me to parties or friends' houses. There, I looked at pornographic magazines and hung out with my father's friends while they drank and smoked marijuana. I'd gamble with them; we played a type of game with quarters where you tossed them from a distance and attempted to get your quarter closest to a wall. I also made his friends mixed drinks and poured beer from the kegs they kept iced. They thought it was really amusing to see this little kid look up at them from the bar area and ask what they wanted. They tipped me a dollar a drink. After a while, I went back to gambling. Sometimes I won and sometimes I lost. When I got bored with these activities, I went back to the pornographic magazines. Every now and then he'd come up to me and ask how I was making out. I showed him the money and he'd smile. If I had anything left, we went out and got some food and maybe I'd buy a toy.

I hardly ever talked to anyone about the activities I had with my father. I didn't know it was out of the ordinary. To me, it was just my life. One time, when I was with my grandmother, I said something about these activities with my aunt, who then told my grandmother about what I had said. My grandmother interrogated my father about what I had told my aunt and later, he told me never to mention "shit" like that again to anyone. My aunt didn't look at me the same way for many months. I figured it was because she was a Baptist. These activities continued regularly until my parents remarried 10 months later, when my mother went AWOL from the Army.

These activities tapered off and stopped altogether when my mother became pregnant with my brother. This is when my parents had their most intense arguments and began destroying property. When I was 11, in the middle of a screaming argument with my mother, my father picked up the microwave we owned and smashed it on the floor. My mom once took a crowbar and smashed up my dad's 550 Kawasaki motorcycle. She also stuck a steak knife into the tires of his Ford pickup. He also punched holes in the wall and shattered my mom's dresser mirror. On two or three occasions, he walked out to the barn with a 30/30 lever-action rifle and threatened to shoot and eat my mom's horse. It was with this same rifle that he also almost killed himself with. In one of my parents' countless heated arguments, he said that he wanted to die and placed the gun barrel under his chin. Hysterically, my mother tried to stop him and in the struggle, the gun fired a round into the ceiling. These were the encounters at which I was present, and they would always bring me to tears. I yelled, I screamed, I begged them to stop. I told them to leave each other, to let me leave and go anywhere but where they were. Altercations like this happened frequently from the time I was 7 to the time I was 15. I believe that my parents were, and still are, mentally ill because of organic causes, just as, I believe, my own mental illness is due to an organic condition. Without the medication I'm now taking, I'd be dangerous both to others and to myself.

When I was 16, my parents finally divorced for good. It involved a bitter custody battle which left me emotionally damaged from the trauma. After my parents split up, they both left the area; my father went to the Philippines and my mother went to California. I was left to stay with my grandparents in Florida. I felt abandoned. It seems I was a remnant of the past he wanted to forget. Yet he could never erase it, he could only run away. Shortly after my dad left, I went to California to visit my mother for a two-week stay. Soon after I arrived, she told me she had plans to be with her boyfriend. She handed me $400 and told me she'd be back in nine days. So I spent the time alone in an apartment complex. I spent my time eating at restaurants, buying music, playing videogames at a local arcade, and going to a club nearby. I felt alone, strange not having anyone around to look after me. I did my best to keep preoccupied. This is when I became severely depressed. I left soon after my mother returned with her escapade with her boyfriend. When I returned to Florida, my depression continued to get worse. Within a week or so, I was at the point when I wanted to die. My great-grandmother, whom I often visited when she was alive, had died recently, and I went through her house trying to

(*Continued*)

Account: Clinical Depression Continued

absorb the life she had lived and left behind. On one of these explorations, I found her gun, tucked in the back of a dresser drawer. It was loaded. I took it in my hand, cocked the firing hammer, put the barrel in my mouth, and thought for a moment about the world I would not miss, the world that had rejected me. I pulled the trigger.

The gun was still in my trembling hand, the barrel was still rattling against my teeth, but obviously I was still alive. I pulled the gun out of my mouth, took the bullets out of the chamber, and held the one with the firing pin perforated into it. It was a dud. I stared at it for a few minutes, then put the other bullets back in the gun and nestled the gun back into the dresser drawer. I realized I didn't really want to die. I stuck the dud into my pocket, walked out of my great-grandmother's house, threw the bullet into the creek behind the house, and went home. No one ever found out about my attempt. The event left me traumatized even more; my mental health deteriorated. Even so, in the 10 years since then, I never attempted suicide again. I somehow managed to pull myself together enough afterwards to function and pass as "normal," but I was never the same. That's the time my rage cycles began. In my senior year of high school, halfway through the year, I stopped attending class and holed myself up in my room for two months straight. By this time, my grandfather had died and my grandmother didn't know what to do with me. She had unfaltering compassion but meager parenting skills. The resulting combination enabled me to survive, but not much else. After the two-month period, my depression receded and I managed to finish high school. I transferred to a different school in an adjacent district where no one knew me, and graduated six months later.

When I went to a different high school, I wasn't leaving any friends behind—I didn't have any friends. I wanted friends, but most people avoided me like a leper. My adolescent years were, for the most part, spent alone. My depression must have turned fellow students away from me. I didn't understand how my personality was related to my depression and to my outbursts. I guess no one else did either. Back then, I had less self-control than I do now. To help deal with my rage, in my first high school, I joined the wrestling team, but it didn't give me any friends. I later found out that the other guys on the team had nicknamed me "time bomb" because they thought that one day, I'd come to practice with a handgun and open fire on them all. I thought they were all assholes. I was just serious about practice, that's all. Actually, when I found out later about the nickname, I was glad they were all afraid of me. That just made me want to stay home even more.

After that bout of depression, my aunts and uncles on my father's side never treated me the same again. I was always the black sheep. I was considered the troubled child of a father and mother who were themselves considered of poor character.

I enrolled in a local community college. I didn't have wrestling any more, so I needed another outlet for my volatile and depressive emotions, so I turned to martial arts training. That allowed me to function without attracting attention. My grades were spotty, leaving my academic counselors confused. Yet I managed to find a girlfriend. I stayed in a relationship with her for two years, but ultimately my dysfunctional emotions got the better of me and I assaulted her. We only had one argument. She was ridiculing me for acting so depressed. It made me explode into a violent rage. I grabbed her by the shoulders and threw her off the bed she was lying on. She told me later that the look on my face was what scared her the most. She ended our relationship; that left me an emotional wreck because I thought I had become my father. I hated my father for the life I had to endure as a result of my parents' emotional state, their behavior, their violence. I was distraught because I could not stop the violent episode. Only after it was over did I realize what I had done. I was angry at myself, angry at my parents, angry at everything around me that didn't help. My outburst left my girlfriend curled up in a ball in the corner of the room, crying. I spent the next hour trying to calm her down, calm myself down. I began crying myself. I apologized for what I had done over and over again. Even though she became calm, she never forgave me for that outburst. Shortly after that, she said she could never trust me again and she didn't want to go out with me. I was also distraught because I didn't know if I could trust myself either.

After the break-up of my relationship with my girlfriend, I started to teach myself to hide my emotional dysfunction. Through weightlifting and martial arts, I could sap my body of energy and fill my brain with mind-numbing endorphins. When I felt I was in an unstable state, I avoided people I normally interacted with. I didn't return phone calls and I stood people up. I found that the more I mastered this act, the more people wanted to be around me. I found another girlfriend. The trick was to balance these two parts of my life, one, the normal, nice, upstanding, cool persona, and the other the tortured, angry, volatile, severely depressed alter ego. Ultimately, my relationship with my girlfriend turned sour; she started to see the "Mr. Hyde" in my "Dr. Jekyll." Yet I was able to hold the friendships together because they were at a distance, I could manipulate them. I even managed to stay friends with my former girlfriend and am still friends with her to this day. My "Mr. Hyde" tormented me for over a year about the end of that intimate relationship, and my torment affected my relationships with other women I had at that time.

I decided to move to New York City. I lived in a dormitory at a school for the martial arts. It was the perfect place to remedy my emotional dysfunction. I had all the opportunities I needed to focus my aggression and anger on martial arts training under the eye of the person I called "the old Japanese guy," my martial arts teacher. Yet this training didn't fully eliminate my depression. So, with the other guys in the school, I started using marijuana heavily on weekends and occasionally on weekdays. I also began drinking heavily on weekends with them as well. "The old Japanese guy" provided us with most of the alcohol; he was an alcoholic himself, though he didn't know about the marijuana. If he had, he would have kicked us out and replaced, even though we were "prodigy martial artists." He had two rules for his students: no sex in the dojo and no drugs. We constantly broke both rules. It was our home, so we did what we did at home, which for us included sex and drugs.

I am torn between differential association theory and social control theory to explain my use of alcohol and my sexual promiscuity at the time. In one sense, the camaraderie of my peers in the school made me want to join in. Yet at the same time, I felt alienated from conventional society due to my emotional dysfunction, therefore I didn't feel bound by society's rules.

I continued in this way for a year, at which time I moved to Washington, D.C. I had maintained a long-distance friendship with the girl I had dated in community college, and so she let me stay on her couch until I could find my own place. I wanted to have an intimate relationship with her again—I wanted her to be my girlfriend—but she rejected my advances and soon after, I moved into my own apartment and got a job at a bar-coffee house-lounge. At the time, I no longer had my martial arts to help with my emotional dysfunction, so I turned even more heavily toward alcohol and marijuana as a remedy. And once I started working at the bar, alcohol was plentiful and most of the time it didn't cost me anything.

After the place closed for the night, I sat with the shift manager, the bartender, and the other coworkers and drank whatever I wanted on the house and got high. Almost every night I left work drunk unless I had a date with a girl I had picked up across the bar the night before. We usually went to my place for some sex. The girls really liked this, they felt like VIPs. Honestly, I felt better half-numb than being sober and straight and in emotional anguish. I

(*Continued*)

Account: Clinical Depression Continued

made a lot of friends and acquaintances at the time. No one ever saw the violent, anguished, depressed side of me. It was still there—as it always was—but the "animal" was sedated almost all the time. I liked it that way. There were a lot of people around me and I knew that if I showed my problems, they wouldn't want to be around me. In most ways, this era of my life is an example of deviant socialization. I could have dealt with my emotional dysfunction in another way, try to find out what was causing it, but instead I just followed the crowd I was exposed to. It was a remedy to my problems, and I took it. I even began stealing from work because I saw how easily many of the other employees, who were my friends, did it. I started to feel overworked, working hard for not enough money, so that's where the thievery came in. I made drinks without paying for them or used code numbers to order food from the kitchen on the house. Eventually, I had many drinks while I was working. It helped me loosen up. I felt everybody who was stealing was in a conspiracy to screw the wealthy owner of the place for whatever we could get. Only when I returned to college did I start to deal with my dysfunction in a different way.

QUESTIONS

Positivists attempt to answer the question, "Why?" When it comes to deviant behavior, they usually set in the background the process by which societies decide that an action should be regarded as deviant, and foreground or highlight the question of the *cause* or *causes* of the behavior in question. What do you think is an adequate explanation of Robert's behavior? Was it his experiences growing up in a particular family setting? Did his parents' socialization of him cause the behavior that led to the authorities taking action against him? Or was it the experiences he had as a teenager and young man in unconventional social groups? Do you accept Robert's explanation that a chemical or hormonal imbalance caused his aberrant behavior? Which of the theories discussed in this chapter best accounts for Robert's behavior? Do you feel that constructionist theories of deviance have any purchase in analyzing Robert's behavior? That is, would his behavior be regarded as deviant everywhere? Or would it be accepted and tolerated in some social circles, groups, or societies? Is there something distinct and specific to our society that led to Robert being sanctioned here for his untoward behavior?

CHAPTER

3

Constructionist Perspectives of Deviance

PLEASE NOTICE
1 NO DRINKING OR SMOKING ON THE MATS
2 COUPLES ONLY NO THREESOMES AT ANYTIME
3 WE ASK YOU NOT TO STAND IN FRONT OF ENTRANCE.
4 NO ONE ADMITTED FULLY DRESSED.
5 WHEN THE FEMALE LEAVES THE MATS, HER MATE WILL BE ASKED TO LEAVE TWO MINS
FANTASIES IN FUR
at
PLATO'S RETREAT

The theories in Chapter 2 see deviance as a type of action that needs to be explained. In contrast, constructionist approaches ask about *the conceptualization of behavior, beliefs,* and *traits; definitions of deviance; what the rules are; how they are enforced; and what the consequences of enforcement are.* Rather than seeing deviance as an action, these perspectives see the violation of rules as an *infraction:* What *makes* certain actions (and beliefs and conditions) infractions? Why are rules made in the first place? Who makes the rules? Why are *certain kinds* of rules made? Why are certain *persons* or *types of persons* apprehended and punished? What *consequences* do rule making and rule enforcement have? This approach turns the focus of attention around. Now, the spotlight is not on the rule violator or the conditions that make for rule violation, but on the society and the groups in the society that *make and enforce the rules.*

CONSTRUCTIONIST APPROACHES TO DEVIANCE: AN INTRODUCTION

Constructionism focuses on the creation of social categories, the imputation of deviance to those categories, why certain rules exist, how they work, what their consequences are, and what the dynamics of enforcement are. Constructionists do not ask the "Why do they do it?" question; the causes for deviant behavior, beliefs, and conditions are very much in the background. How members of the society think and talk about and react to behavior, beliefs, and conditions they regard as unacceptable becomes the central focus. In short, the constructionist looks at *how deviance is defined, conceptualized, and represented,* and how those definitions, conceptualizations, and representations are *enacted.*

The social constructionist approach permits inquiry into *false accusations;* it is secondary (although far from irrelevant) that the accused person didn't do it. Why were hundreds of thousands of women persecuted in Renaissance Europe for witchcraft? The positivist sociologist is powerless to ask this question because, in all likelihood, the women accused of witchcraft *didn't* engage in the crimes of which they were accused. In contrast, the constructionist is very comfortable about asking why the witch-craze arose (Ben-Yehuda, 1980) and why mainly women were accused and punished for a nonexistent crime. The fact that the crime was nonexistent is crucial for the positivist, because you can't offer an explanation for the enactment of a behavior that somebody didn't do. To the sociologists looking only at the causes of behavior, the witches didn't engage in deviance because they didn't *do* anything to attract the condemnation. To the constructionist, the enterprise of persecution and condemnation is *independent* of the enactment of the behavior of which deviants are accused.

To the social constructionist, the distinctions between voluntary behavior, beliefs, and involuntary conditions are irrelevant. What counts is how people who are seen as violating the law are *thought of* and *treated* in a particular society. Are blind people more likely to be socially accepted by the sighted today as compared with centuries past? Does acceptance or rejection of blind people vary from one society to another? Does acceptance or rejection vary in the same society at the same time by social category or group? How do blind people regard their condition? How do they relate to the sighted? Do they interact mainly with one another or do they integrate into the world of the sighted? We can ask similar questions about a variety of social conditions, including obesity, dwarfism, albinism, physical disfigurement or disability, and extreme ugliness. To the constructionist the fact that the conditions are involuntary is not the issue; that persons in such categories are treated in a certain fashion *is* the issue. For instance, the Greeks and other ancient peoples abandoned deformed children to the elements to die, believing that a stigma adhered to such imperfect creatures; in some societies, adulterers and presumed adulterers have been stoned to death, so serious is the stigma of the sin of adultery. Both the conditions—physical deformity and, the voluntary behavior, adultery—are deviant in that they generate stigma and punishment. Regardless of what caused them, from a constructionist perspective, both are deviant.

These two intellectual enterprises, the study of causes and the study of the social construction of deviance, are not contradictory but complementary. On the one hand, there are reasons why some people violate society's rules and why some societies experience more deviance than others, and these reasons can be discovered and explained. But these norms are also created and enforced as a result of systematic, identifiable sociological processes. While the sociological positivist takes the norms and their enforcement *as if* they were a given, the fact is they are not; they are every bit a social product and every bit in need of an explanation as deviant behavior itself.

DEVIANCE AND SOCIAL CONTROL

Sociologists define social control as *efforts to ensure conformity to a norm.* Every time people do something to induce someone to engage in behavior they believe is right, they are engaged in social control. When a mother yanks her child's hand out of the cookie jar, she is exercising social control. When a police officer arrests a burglar for breaking and entering an apartment, that officer is engaging in social control. When a professor gives a grade of zero to a student caught cheating on an exam, she is practicing social control. Social control includes "all of the processes by which people define and respond to deviant behavior" (Black, 1984, p. xi). Social control is formal and informal, governmental and interpersonal, and internal as well as external.

To the constructionist who studies deviance, social control is a central—perhaps *the* central—concept. Now and throughout human history, all societies everywhere have set and enforced norms—rules about what their members should and should not do. We encounter norms everywhere. As we cast our gaze up and down the annals of time, across the world's many nations and societies, we notice that, though rules and norms differ and so do the nature and severity of the punishments for violating them, nonetheless, *rules and norms themselves are universal.* All societies have rules, and some members of all societies attempt to enforce them. There is not now and never been any country, society, or collectivity where anything goes. If any such once existed, it could not long survive, for rules are the cornerstone of human survival.

A "norm" is simply a rule that calls for proper behavior, a kind of blueprint for action. Implied in a norm is the expectation that violators are punished or sanctioned when they violate it. Some norms apply in specific contexts, settings, or situations. For instance, one must *not* laugh at a funeral, but one is *expected* to laugh at a comedy routine. (If it's funny.) The injunction against laughing is specific to certain settings, and the expectation of laughter, likewise, applies to specific settings.

Other norms apply to the behavior of members of certain groups or collectivities but not others. Members of a tough street gang are expected to meet the challenge of an insult, a taunt, or a shove, with verbal and physical aggression. The failure to do so would result in chastisement from other gang members. However, if the faculty members at a university or the medical staff of a hospital were to respond as aggressively to a perceived verbal insult, it is their behavior that would be condemned. Such a response would be regarded as undignified, unprofessional, and unacceptable—in a word, deviant.

Still other norms apply across the board, that is, to everyone in a given society. For instance, no one is permitted to kill a baby in its crib simply because its crying is annoying. There is no person in any society who is exempt from that norm, and there exists practically no situation or context when such behavior is allowed.

Regardless of whether a given norm applies to all situations or only some, to *certain* people or all of them, the fact is this: *Everyone everywhere* is subject to norms. Being human means being subject to the norms of the groups to which one belongs and the society in which one lives.

As we saw, some minimal level of punishment for wrongdoing is necessary to ensure a minimal level of social order. At some point, the lack of norms in a given society would result in a state of collapse into a "war of all against all," in which life would be, in the words of seventeenth-century English philosopher Thomas Hobbes, author of *Leviathan,* "poor, solitary, nasty, brutish, and short." The central question for the functionalist sociologists is, given the natural human tendency to be selfish, *How is social order possible*? If there were no rules and we were permitted to obtain anything by any conceivable effective means—rape, murder, robbery, or assault—then how is it possible for societies to survive and even prosper? Why *don't* we collapse into a state of chaos, disorder, and disintegration? For the functionalists, a partial answer to this question is that *social control,* through both learning the acceptable norms and punishing unacceptable and rewarding acceptable behavior, operates to ensure a society's survival. The Sixth Commandment, "Thou shalt not murder" (*not* "kill," since the ancient Hebrews *did* kill a substantial number of their enemies—for instance, in warfare), is an obvious example of such a norm.

Actually, it is surprising how *few* norms are designed to condemn, punish, or protect a society or its members from injurious or predatory actions, such as murder, rape, robbery, or serious assault. Most norms attempt to discourage behavior that neither directly harms anyone nor threatens the society with chaos and disintegration. Most norms are intended to make a statement about what is considered—by some, many, or most members of a society—to be right, good, and proper. They embody certain principles of moral correctness—separate and independent of what they do for the society's physical survival. Norms such as the Sixth Commandment are in the minority of rules that members of a society learn and, for the most part, abide by. No one would be injured nor would society be threatened with disintegration if some of us were to wear our clothes backwards, speak every word twice, or eat steak by grabbing it with our hands and tearing at it with our teeth. But if any of us were to engage in these acts, others would greet us with disapproval, condemnation, and derision. Clearly, protecting the society from actions that are so harmful as to threaten the society's and our survival is not the sole purpose of the norms or the punishment of their violators. There is implicit in norms and their enforcement a version of moral correctness—an ethos, a way of life that is *an end in itself.* We are expected to do certain things because they are *right,* because *that's the way things are done.*

As I said, there are several distinctly different varieties of social control. *Internal* social control operates through the process of *socialization,* by learning and adopting the norms of the society or a particular group or collectivity within the society. All people are socialized by identifiable *agents.* The family is, of course, the earliest agent of socialization, one of whose primary functions is attempting to internalize into children the norms of the society in which they live. If the family fails to do so, children are more likely to engage in behavior regarded by the society as deviant. Later on, schools, peers, and the mass media represent influential agents of socialization. Much of their socialization also represents efforts at internal social control.

When the norms of the society are accepted as valid, they can be said to be *internalized.* To the extent that internalization is successful, persons feel guilty if they were to engage in the behavior the society or their collectivity considers wrong. When they refuse to do so, it is in part as a consequence of the fact that the relevant norm was successfully internalized. We do not kill or assault people who make us angry only because we will be punished for doing so, but in large part because we have come to accept that murder and assault are wrong.

Socialization is only one weapon in society's arsenal of social control. In one way or another, society is usually only partly successful in instilling its version of the norms into us. There are always some people—for the most important norms, the minority—who don't accept the legitimacy of the norms. Moreover, even people who are usually conformist and law abiding will find situations that call for exceptions to a rule or norm. (If we are faced with an especially tempting reward, or potentially deadly harm, many of us reevaluate our rigid adherence to the norm.) The fact is most of us are incompletely and to some degree partly *unsuccessfully* socialized. As a consequence, another form of social control is necessary; society moves to exercise *external* social control. A great deal of social control is coercive and repressive; it relies on punishment and force. Many of us wish to violate society's norms, to move "outside the lines." When we do so, certain agents of social control may detect our behavior and use some sort of punishment, coercion, or *external* social control to attempt to bring us back into line. Though rewards also make up a form of external social control, usually, we are not rewarded for things we are expected to do, we are simply not punished.

Most sociologists of deviance focus on external social control rather than internal. External social control is made up of the system of rewards and punishments that persons, parties, and agents use to induce others to conform to a norm. Rewards and punishments are referred to as *sanctions*. Obviously, a positive sanction is a reward, and a negative sanction is a punishment. Slapping, screaming at, ignoring, snubbing, ridiculing, insulting, taunting, gossiping about, humiliating, frowning at, denouncing, reprimanding, berating, criticizing, nagging, arresting, dissing, mocking, stigmatizing, showing contempt toward, acting in a condescending fashion toward, laughing at, booing, jeering—these and a host of others are negative reactions to someone, in the estimation of a particular audience, whose behavior, beliefs, and physical traits fail to measure up. They are all *negative* and *external* forms of social control. And social control is the very foundation stone of the sociologist's definition of deviance. *Deviance is that which calls forth efforts at social control.*

FORMAL AND INFORMAL SOCIAL CONTROL

Sociologists distinguish between *formal* and *informal* social control. In between, we find what might be referred to as "semiformal" social control.

Informal social control takes place in interpersonal interaction between and among people who are acting on their own, in an unofficial capacity. As we saw, reactions such as a frown or a smile, criticism or praise, and shunning or being warm toward someone are ways we have of exercising *informal* social control. They act to remind someone that his or her behavior upsets or annoys us. Since most people seek the approval of others whom they care about, they tend to adjust their behavior to avoid the disapproval of significant others by discontinuing the offensive behavior or at least hiding it from public view.

However, in large, complex societies, especially with a substantial volume of contact between and among strangers, informal social control is usually no longer sufficient to bring about conformity to the norms. In such societies, it becomes easy to ignore the disapproval of others if you do not care enough about them to be concerned about how they feel about you. So, *formal* social control becomes necessary. "Formal social control" is made up of efforts to bring about conformity to the law by agents of the criminal justice system: the police, the courts, and jails and prisons. In principle, agents of formal social control act not as individuals with their own personal feelings about whether behavior is wrong or right, but as occupants of specific statuses in a specific bureaucratic organization, that is, the criminal justice system. The sanctions they apply to wrongdoers flow from their offices or positions, not from their personal relationship with the rule violator. It is the job or function of such agents to act, when transgressions occur, to bring about conformity to the formal code, that is, the law.

Both formal and informal social control may operate at the same time. A drug dealer may simultaneously be arrested by the police *and* shunned by his neighbors. A child molester may serve a 10-year sentence for his crime and, after he is released, be shunned and humiliated by members of the community in which he lives.

Somewhere in between informal social control, which is based on personal and interpersonal reactions between and among interacting parties, and the formal social control of the criminal justice system—the police, the courts, and the correctional institutions—we find semiformal social control. Here we have a huge territory of noncriminal, nonpenal bureaucratic social control, administered by the government, which attempts to deal with the troublesome behavior of persons under their authority. If a person's behavior becomes extremely troublesome to others, an array of agencies, bureaucracies, and organizations may step in to handle or control that person, to punish or bring him or her into line with the rules. In other words, persons deemed difficult or problematic by members of a community come under "the purview of professional controllers" (Hawkins and Tiedeman, 1975, p. 111). These professional controllers do not have the power of arrest or incarceration, but they can make recommendations to agents of the criminal justice system that may have bearing on arrest and incarceration. Such agents include social workers; psychiatrists; truant officers; and representatives, functionaries, and officers of mental hospitals, civil courts, the Internal Revenue Service and other official tax agencies, social welfare offices, unemployment offices, departments of motor vehicles, and the educational system.

Some sociologists of deviance equate "social control" with formal and semiformal social control. They ignore the private, informal, and interpersonal reactions to behavior and beliefs by individuals as a means of keeping people in line with the rules and norms of the society (Cohen, 1985; Horwitz, 1990). The reason is that such a focus is consistent with their theory that social control is centralized and repressive (Meier, 1982). On the other hand, if you broaden your conception of social control to include informal social control as well, you have to recognize the fact that interpersonal relations are messy, untidy, less likely to conform to a pattern, far less centralized and far less subject to elite control. These social control thinkers (Foucault, 1979; Cohen, 1985; Lowman, Menzies, and Palys, 1987; Scull, 1988) equate state or statelike control, assuming that state control, much like an octopus, reaches out and grabs people who are administered by agencies and organizations spread throughout the society.

But contrary to such social control theorists, *most of the time* that social control is exercised, it is informal. Most of the time deviance is sanctioned, the actor is punished or condemned interpersonally, by individuals, not formally by representatives of a bureaucratic organization. Informal social control is the "meat and potatoes," the "nuts and bolts," of the labeling process. Relatively speaking, formal social control tends to be much less common and fitfully applied. The vast majority of rule-breaking behavior—such as making unwanted sexual passes at parties, breaking wind at the dinner table, or insulting one's peers—is *ignored* by the apparatus of formal and semiformal social control. Informal social control is the foundation of social life.

PERSPECTIVES THAT FOCUS ON DEFINING DEVIANCE

The constructionist approaches include labeling or interactionist theory, conflict theory, feminist theory, and controlology or the new sociology of social control. As with all perspectives, constructionists deal mainly with behavior rather than beliefs and conditions. But *unlike* the essentialist, causal, and positivistic perspectives we looked at in Chapter 2, constructionists—especially labeling and feminist approaches—look at beliefs and conditions *in addition to* behavior.

The labeling or *interactionist* theory or school focuses on rule making and, especially, *reactions* to rule breaking (Becker, 1963; Lofland, 1969; Schur, 1971). This school shifts attention away from the circumstances that produced the deviant act to "the important role of social definitions and negative sanctions" as well as "what happens to people *after* they have been singled out, identified, and defined as deviants" (Traub and Little, 1999, pp. 375, 376).

Conflict theory deals with the question of making the rules, especially the criminal law. Why is certain behavior outlawed? And why is other, often even more damaging behavior, *not* outlawed? Conflict theory focuses its attention on the role of powerful groups and classes in the formation and enforcement of the criminal law. The powerful are able to ensure that laws favorable to their own interests, and possibly detrimental to the interests of other, less powerful groups and classes, are passed and enforced (Turk, 1969; Quinney, 1970).

Feminist theory is a variety of conflict theory focusing specifically on the role of sex and gender in deviance and crime: How do men express and maintain their dominance by defining and enforcing certain actions as deviant and criminal? Why does patriarchy exist, whose functions does it serve, and what impact does it have on deviance and social control? (Schur, 1984; Daly and Chesney-Lind, 1988).

Controlology or the new sociology of social control is a perspective that grew out of the work of French philosopher Michel Foucault. It argues that social control is not only the central issue for the sociologist of deviance, but for the sociologist generally. Contemporary society has devised a system for the control of deviance that appears to be humane and scientific, but is far more thoroughgoing, systematic, efficient, and *repressive* than older, more barbarous forms of control that entailed torture and public execution. "Knowledge is power," it asserts, and the powerful strata use scientific knowledge to control the unruly, threatening masses (Foucault, 1979, 2003; Cohen, 1985).

LABELING OR INTERACTIONIST THEORY

In the 1960s, a small group of researchers produced a small body of work that exerted an enormous influence on the sociological approach to deviance; it came to be looked upon as a more or less unified perspective that is widely referred to as *labeling theory* (Schur, 1971). Labeling theory grew out of a more general perspective in sociology called *symbolic interactionism.* This approach is based on three simple premises. First, people act on the basis of the *meaning* that things have for them. Second, this meaning grows out of *interaction* with others, especially intimate others. And third, meaning is continually modified by *interpretation* (Blumer, 1969, p. 2). These three principles—meaning, interaction, and interpretation—form the core of symbolic interactionism and likewise of labeling theory as well. People are not robots, interactionists argued; they are active and creative in how they see and act on things in the world. People are not simple products of their upbringing or socialization, or of their environment, but arrive at what they think, how they feel, and what they do through a dynamic, creative process. All behavior, deviance included, is an interactional product; its properties and impact cannot be known until we understand how it is defined, conceptualized, interpreted, apprehended, and evaluated—in short, what it *means* to participants and relevant observers alike. Labeling theory is not a separate theory but an application of symbolic interactionism to deviant phenomena.

The year 1938 marked the publication of a book written by Frank Tannenbaum, a professor of history and a Latin American specialist; it was entitled *Crime and the Community.* Tannenbaum argued that in a slum area, nearly all boys engage in a wide range of mischievous, sometimes illegal behavior—getting into fights, skipping school, stealing apples, or throwing rocks at windows. These actions, perfectly normal and taken for granted by the boys themselves, are often regarded as deviant and criminal by the authorities—by teachers, the police, and the courts. In an effort to curtail this behavior, the police apprehend and punish some of these boys. If the boys persist in this behavior, they will be sent to reform school. However, punishment often has the ironic effect of escalating the seriousness of the deeds that these boys commit. Arrest and incarceration often results in the community regarding a boy as incorrigible—a budding criminal in the flesh. By being treated as a delinquent and forced to associate with slightly older and more experienced young criminals in reform schools, the troublemaker comes to see himself as a true delinquent. This escalates his deviant career, increasing the chance that he will go on to a life of crime.

About a dozen years later, Edwin Lemert published a textbook with the anachronistic title *Social Pathology* (1951). Lemert distinguished between *primary* and *secondary* deviation. Primary deviation is simply the enactment of deviant behavior itself—any form of it. Lemert argued that primary deviation is *polygenetic* (1951, pp. 75–76, 1972, pp. 62–63)—caused by a wide range of factors. For instance, someone may drink heavily for a variety of reasons—the death of a loved one, a business failure, belonging to a group whose members call for heavy drinking, and so on. In fact, Lemert asserted, the original cause or causes of a particular form of deviance is not especially important. What counts is the social reaction *to* the behavior from others.

Secondary deviation occurs when the individual who enacts deviant behavior deals with the problems created by social reactions to his or her primary deviations (Lemert, 1951, p. 76). "The secondary deviant, as opposed to his [or her] actions, is a person whose life and identity are organized around the facts of deviance" (Lemert, 1972, p. 63). When someone is singled out, stigmatized, condemned, or isolated for engaging in deviant behavior, it becomes necessary to *deal with* and *manage* this social reaction in certain ways. One comes to see oneself in a certain way, defines oneself in different terms, adopts different roles, and associates with different individuals. Being stigmatized forces one to become a deviant—to engage in secondary deviation. "Secondary deviation" does not *necessarily* mean that labeling causes more frequent enactment of the behavior that generated the label, but it is more likely than the absence of labeling.

It should be said that Lemert recognized that not all primary deviation results in punishment or condemnation. Some communities or social circles display more tolerance for rule breaking behavior than others (1951, pp. 57–58). When primary deviation results in punishment, however, the individuals engaging in it tend to be stigmatized, shunned, and socially isolated. They are forced into social groups or circles of other individuals who are also stigmatized. This isolation from mainstream, conventional society reinforces the individual's commitment to these unconventional, deviant groups and circles and the individual's commitment to the deviant behavior itself.

According to Becker (1973, pp. 177–208) and Kitsuse (1972, 1980), labeling theory is not so much an explanation for why certain individuals engage in deviant behavior as it is a perspective whose main insight tells us that the labeling process is crucial and cannot be ignored. Labeling theory is not so much a theory as it is an orientation, the discussion of a "useful set of problems" centered on the origins and consequences of labeling (Plummer, 1979, pp. 88, 90). The labeling approach shifts attention away from the traditional question of "Why do they do it?" to a focus on how and why judgments of deviance come to be made and what their consequences are. Why are certain acts condemned at one time and in one place but tolerated at another time, in another place? Why does one person do something and get away scott-free, while another does the same thing and is severely punished for it? What happens when someone is caught violating a rule and is stigmatized for it? What consequences does labeling have for stigmatization? What is the difference between enacting rule-breaking behavior which does not result in getting caught and enacting that same behavior and being publicly denounced for it? These are some of the major issues labeling theorists have been concerned with.

In many ways, labeling theory is a model or quintessential example of the constructionist approach. It addresses issues such as the creation of deviant categories, the social construction of moral meanings and definitions, social and cultural relativity, the how and why of social control, the politics of deviance, the criminalization of behavior, and the role of contingency in the labeling process. Together, these issues constitute the foundation stone of constructionism. Several issues represent the hallmark of the labeling theory's central concerns: *audiences, labeling and stigma, reflexivity, the inner world of deviance,* and *the "stickiness" of labels* and *the self-fulfilling prophecy.*

Audiences. An audience is an individual or any number of individuals who observe and evaluate an act, a condition, or an individual. An audience could be one's friends, relatives, or neighbors, coworkers, the police, teachers, a psychiatrist, bystanders, or observers—even oneself, for you can be an observer and an evaluator of your own behavior or condition (Becker, 1963, p. 31). *Audiences* determine whether something or someone is deviant: no audience, no labeling, therefore, no deviance. However, an audience need not *directly* view an act, condition, or person; audiences can witness behavior or conditions indirectly, that is, they can hear or be told about someone's behavior or condition, or they can simply have a negative or condemnatory attitude toward a class or category of behavior: "The critical variable in the study of deviance . . . is the social audience rather than the individual actor, since it is the audience which eventually determines whether or not any episode of behavior *or any class of episodes* is labeled deviant" (Erikson, 1964, p. 11; my emphasis). In other words, audiences can evaluate *categories* of deviance and stand ready to condemn them, even before they have actually witnessed specific, concrete cases of these categories. As we've seen in Chapter 1, audiences are absolutely central in the sociological definition of deviance. Whether an act, a belief, or a trait is deviant or not depends on the audience who does or would evaluate and react to the actor, the believer, or the possessor accordingly. Without specifying real-life audiences, the question of an act's, a belief's, or a trait's deviance is meaningless. Audiences include the society at large, official agents of social control, and the significant others of the actor, such as intimates. These audiences may or may not evaluate or react to the actor's behavior in the same way.

Labeling and Stigma. The key elements in becoming deviant are labeling and stigma. The processes of labeling and stigmatizing are done by a relevant audience. The audience is relevant according to the circumstances or context. Gang members can label the behavior of a fellow member of the gang, for instance, the refusal to fight, as deviant *within the gang context;* the police can label an action of a gang member, for instance, fighting, as deviant, wrong, or illegal by arresting or harassing him. Each and every audience or person can label each and every action, belief, or condition of each and every person as deviant—but the weight or *consequences* of that labeling process vary according to the context.

The labeling or stigmatization process entails two steps. First, an audience labels an *activity* (or belief or condition) deviant, and second, it labels a specific *individual* as *a* deviant. In these two labeling processes, if no audience labels something or someone deviant, *no deviance exists.* An act, belief, condition, or person cannot be deviant *in the abstract,* that is, without reference to how an audience does or would label it. Something or someone must be defined as such by the members of a society or group *as* deviant—it must be *labeled* as reprehensible or wrong. Likewise, a person cannot be regarded as a deviant until this labeling process takes place. An act, belief, or condition need not be *actually* or *concretely* labeled to be regarded as deviant, however, but it is deviant if it belongs to a category of similar actions, beliefs, or conditions. In other words, *we already know* that the public regards shooting the proprietor of a store and taking the contents of that store's cash register as deviant. Even if the robber gets away with the crime, we know that *if known about,* it would be regarded as deviant in the society at large—that is, it is an instance of "societal deviance."

Labeling involves attaching a *stigmatizing* definition to an activity, a belief, or a condition. Stigma is a stain, a sign of reproach or social undesirability, an indication to the world that one has been singled out as a shameful, morally discredited human being. Someone who has been stigmatized is a marked person; he or she has a spoiled identity. A stigmatized person is one who has been labeled a deviant. Once someone has been so discredited, relations with conventional, respectable others become difficult, strained, and problematic. In other words, "being caught and branded as a deviant has important consequences for one's further participation and self-image. . . . Committing the improper act and being publicly caught at it places [the individual] in a new status. He [or she] has been revealed as a different kind of person from the kind he [or she] was supposed to be. He [or she] is labeled a 'fairy,' 'dope fiend,' 'nut,' or 'lunatic,' and treated accordingly" (Becker, 1963, pp. 31–32).

So crucial is this labeling process that, in some respects, it does not necessarily matter whether or not someone who has been stigmatized has actually engaged in the behavior of which he or she is accused. As we saw, according to the logic of labeling theory, *falsely accused* deviants—if the accusation sticks—are still deviants (Becker, 1963, p. 20). In many important respects, they resemble individuals who really *do* commit acts that violate the rules. For example, women and men burned at the stake for the crime of witchcraft in the fifteenth and sixteenth centuries were deviants in the eyes of the authorities and the community (Ben-Yehuda, 1980), even though they clearly did not engage in a pact with the devil. Two individuals, one who engaged in a deviant act and the second of whom is falsely accused, will share important experiences and characteristics in common, *by virtue of the labeling process alone,* even though they are poles apart with respect to having committed the behavior of which they were accused. While their lives are unlikely to be *identical* simply because both are seen by the community as deviants, the similarities they share are likely to be revealing. Is this fair? Of course not! Is this the way the world works? Of course it is.

Reflexivity. Reflexivity means looking at ourselves in part through the eyes of others. It is what is widely referred to, although too mechanistically, as the "looking glass self." Labeling theory is based on a seemingly simple but fundamental observation: "We see ourselves through the eyes of others, and when others see us in a certain way, at least for long enough or sufficiently powerfully, their views are sure to have some effect" (Glassner, 1982, p. 71).

In other words, both direct *and* indirect, or concrete *and* symbolic, labeling operate in the world of deviance (Warren and Johnson, 1972, pp. 76–77). Indirect or symbolic labeling is the awareness by an enactor of deviant behavior that his or her acts are saturated with public scorn, his or her identity is potentially discreditable, and he or she *would be* stigmatized if discovered. People who violate norms have to deal with the probable and potential, as well as the actual and concrete, reactions of the respectable, conventional, and law-abiding majority. All violators of major norms must at least ask themselves, "How would others react to me and my behavior?" If the answer is "They will punish me," then the rule breaker must try to avoid detection, remain within deviant or minority circles, or be prepared to be punished, condemned, and stigmatized.

The Inner World of Deviance. One major endeavor of the labeling theorist is the attempt to understand the *inner world* of deviance. Interactionism stresses the ethnographic, anthropological, or participant observation research method: hanging around the individuals under study, observing them in their natural habitat, and getting as close to the activity of interest as possible. This means attempting an understanding of the deviant world *as the deviant lives and understands it.* For instance, how do homosexuals see and define their behavior? What is their attitude about being gay? How do they experience being homosexual? How do they look upon the "straight" world? What is the construction of *their* moral meaning like? How do they define right and wrong with respect to sexuality? What does it feel like to be a member of a minority whose members are looked down upon by the straight majority? To know how the world of homosexuality is lived, it is necessary to enter that world and listen to and observe those who actually live it. Interactionists are *fascinated* by the details of the lives of individuals and groups defined as deviant. It emphasizes how *creative* and *diverse* reactions to being so defined are, how incapable powerful deviance definers are in imposing their will and conceptions on deviants, how *active* deviants are in creating their own definitions and conceptions, and how truly *complex* the lives of deviants are.

The "Stickiness" of Labels and the Self-Fulfilling Prophecy. Labeling theorists argue that stigmatizing someone as a socially and morally undesirable character has important consequences for that person's further rule breaking. Under certain circumstances, being labeled may intensify one's commitment to a deviant identity and contribute to further deviant behavior. Some conventional, law-abiding citizens believe, "once a deviant, always a deviant." Someone who has been stigmatized and labeled "is ushered into the deviant position by a decisive and often dramatic ceremony, yet is retired from it with hardly a word of public notice." As a result, the deviant is given "no proper license to resume a normal life in the community. Nothing has happened to cancel out the stigma imposed upon him" or her. The original judgment "is still in effect." The conforming members of a society tend to be "reluctant to accept the returning deviant on an entirely equal footing" (Erikson, 1964, pp. 16–17).

Deviant labels tend to be sticky. The community tends to stereotype someone as, above all and most importantly, a deviant. When someone is identified as a deviant, the community asks, "What kind of person would break such an important rule?" The answer that is given is "one who is different from the rest of us, who cannot or will not act as a moral being and therefore might break other important rules" (Becker, 1963, p. 34). Deviant labeling is widely regarded as a quality that is in the person, an attribute that is carried wherever he or she goes; therefore, it is permanent or at least long lasting. Deviant behavior is said to be caused by an indwelling, essentialistic trait; it is not seen as accidental or trivial, but a fixture of the individual. Once a deviant label has been attached, it is difficult to shake. Ex-convicts find it difficult to find legitimate employment upon their release from prison; once psychiatrists make a diagnosis of mental illness, hardly any amount of contrary evidence can dislodge their faith in it; ex-mental patients are carefully scrutinized for odd, eccentric, or bizarre behavior.

Such stigmatizing tends to deny to deviants "the ordinary means of carrying on the routines of everyday life open to most people. Because of this denial, the deviant must of necessity develop illegitimate routines" (Becker, 1963, p. 35). As a consequence, the labeling process may actually increase the deviant's further commitment to deviant behavior. It may limit conventional options and opportunities, strengthen a deviant identity, and maximize participation in a deviant group. Labeling someone, thus, may become "a self-fulfilling prophecy" (Becker, 1963, p. 34) in that *someone becomes what he or she is accused of being*—even though that original accusation may have been false (Merton, 1948, 1957, pp. 421–436; Jones, 1977, 1986)

Labeling Theory Today. Labeling theory left two legacies to the contemporary study of deviance. The first, its major mode, was its constructionist vision. Other, earlier approaches were careful to point out that deviance and crime were a matter of violating rules, norms, and laws, which are socially constructed and vary somewhat historically and culturally. But labeling theory stressed and highlighted this point more forcefully. Indeed, it went further and emphasized that definitions of wrongdoing vary not only from society to society but from one *category* or *social context* to another. This remains a basic and crucial assumption in all sociological work on deviance. The second legacy of labeling theory, its minor mode (which, unfortunately, critics stress as its main point), is its argument about the causal mechanism of deviance: being labeled as engaging in wrongdoing inevitably or usually leads to a strengthening of a deviant identity and, hence, an escalation in the seriousness and frequency of deviant behavior. This argument is as often wrong as it is right; its lack of empirical verification should not negate the perspective's major mode or constructionist legacy.

Labeling theory's influence has declined sharply since its heyday roughly from the mid-1960s to the mid-1970s. At that time, it was the most influential, most frequently cited perspective in the study of deviance. This was especially so among the field's younger scholars and researchers, who yearned for a fresh, unconventional, and radically different way of looking at deviance. The perspective was widely and vigorously attacked, and many of these criticisms stuck. Eventually, much of the field recognized its inadequacies, and moved on to other perspectives, or sharply modified or adapted interactionist or labeling insights. Today, no single approach or paradigm dominates the field in the way that the Chicago School did in the 1920s or labeling theory circa 1970. What we see today is diversity, fragmentation, and theoretical dissensus. While the practitioners of a variety of perspectives attacked labeling theory for its inadequacies, no single perspective has managed to succeed in attracting a majority following in the field. In spite of the criticisms, the labeling school left a legacy to the field that even its critics make use of, albeit, for the most part, implicitly. Today it is clear that while, as a total approach to deviance, labeling *theory* is incomplete, labeling *processes* take place in all deviance, and deserve a prominent place in its study.

CONFLICT THEORY

Social scientists can be divided according to how much *consensus* or *conflict* they see in contemporary society. Many of the early sociologists viewed the social order through the lens of the *functionalist* perspective (Parsons, 1951; Coser, 1956; Merton, 1957). Functionalism adopts a consensus paradigm: Harmony is the rule, and a disruption of that harmony calls for steps to reestablish peace and tranquility. The members of a society are socialized to behave properly; most of them accept the central values and norms of their society and act accordingly; a few are improperly or inadequately socialized, or, for some reason, the components of the social system are improperly integrated; deviance ensues, disrupting the social order; and the forces of equilibrium act to restore society to its former state of balance, harmony, and cohesion.

In contrast, conflict theorists do not believe that consensus, harmony, or cohesion prevail in contemporary society. They see groups with competing and clashing interests and values. They see struggles between and among categories, sectors, groups, and classes in the society, with winners and losers resulting from the outcome of these struggles. Most social institutions, they argue, do not benefit the society as a whole. Rather, they benefit some groups *at the expense of* others. Conflict theorists envision the resources of the society as being distributed according to a "zero sum game," that is, they are of a fixed size, and whatever is distributed to one faction or category is taken away from another. For instance, they challenge the functionalists' analysis of stratification as benefiting the society as a whole (Davis and Moore, 1945). In contrast, the conflict theorists argue, stratification benefits the rich and the powerful *at the expense of* the poor and the weak. Moreover, it is to the advantage of the rich and the powerful to have the disadvantaged *believe* that stratification is for the good of the entire society; that way, the disadvantaged will be less likely to threaten the interests and privileges of the rich. Likewise, in contrast to the functional analysis of prostitution as benefitting the society as a whole (Davis, 1937), conflict theorists argue that prostitution benefits the more powerful members of the society—mainly men—who profit from society's patriarchal institutions.

Groups struggle to have their own definitions of right and wrong enacted into law. The key word here is *hegemony,* or dominance: Groups struggle to legitimate their own special interests and views and to discredit and nullify the influence of those of competing groups. Societies are made up of factions struggling for dominance or hegemony, struggling to have their own views translated into law and public opinion. The conflict theorist sees a constant struggle between and among competing groups and categories in contemporary society, with the most powerful strata usually winning out.

Perhaps the most conflict oriented of all the conflict theorists are the Marxists. (Of course, come the institutionalization of the socialist revolution, society's major conflicts will dissolve and harmony, peace, and equilibrium will prevail.) Their ideas are somewhat distinct and different from that of the non-Marxist conflict theorists. Since the 1980s, Marxism has plummeted in intellectual and theoretical influence—in the study of deviance, and more broadly, among sociologists, and, even more generally, among academics and intellectuals as a whole.

The central issue for all conflict-oriented criminologists is the emergence and enforcement of norms, rules, and, especially, laws. How do laws get passed? Which groups manage to get their own special interests and views enacted into laws? Who profits by the passage of laws? Which laws are enforced, and which are passed but never enforced—and why? Why are certain activities regarded as deviant while others are regarded as conventional by the members of a given society? The answer provided by the conflict approach is that laws, rules, and norms grow out of a power struggle between and among interests groups, factions, and social classes. The most powerful group or groups in society are those that are successful in having their own views of right and wrong accepted by the society as a whole and formulated into the criminal law. Likewise, the enforcement of the law represents the application of power against the powerless by the powerful.

Conflict theorists explicitly *reject* two commonly held views concerning the law. The first is the *consensus* view that the law is a "reflection of the social consciousness of a society," that laws make up a "barometer of the moral and social thinking of a community" (Friedman, 1964, p. 143) and reflect "the will of the people." Instead, conflict theorists argue that public views on what is regarded as conventional or deviant, law abiding or criminal, vary strikingly from group to group in a large, complex society. Even where consensus exists on a given issue as to what should be against the law, the conflict theorist asks *how* and *why* that consensus is achieved. For most issues, there is no majority consensus—only different views held by different social groups. The point of view held by the most powerful of these groups tends to be the one that becomes law.

The second widely held view that conflict theory rejects is that laws are passed and enforced to protect the society as a whole, to protect all classes and groups more or less equally. The conflict theorist argues that laws do not protect the rights, interests, and well-being of the many, but the interests of the few. There is no such thing as the society as a whole, the conflict theorist would argue. Societies are broken up into segments, sectors, classes, groups, or categories that have very different interests. Very few laws have an impact on all segments of society equally. For instance, the earliest laws of vagrancy in England were passed to protect the interests of the wealthiest and most powerful members of English society—the landowners in the 1300s and the merchant class in the 1500s (Chambliss, 1964). The laws of theft in England, again, were interpreted by the courts in the 1400s as a means of protecting the property of merchants, the emerging powerful class at that time, a class the Crown needed to protect and curry favor with (Hall, 1952).

Conflict theorists do not see laws as an expression of a broad consensus or as an altruistic desire to protect a large number of the members of a society from objective, clear, and present danger. Rather, they are the embodiment of the beliefs, lifestyle, and/or economic interests of certain sectors of the society. Thus, the law is a means of forcing one group's beliefs and way of life onto the rest of the society. Laws are passed and enforced not because they protect society in general or because many people believe in their moral correctness but because they uphold the ideological or material interests of a certain sector of society. This serves to stop certain people from doing what others consider evil, undesirable, or unprofitable—or to make them do something that others consider good, desirable, or profitable. The passage of a law represents the triumph of a point of view or an ideology held by the members of a particular group, social category, or organization—even if that law is not enforced.

Conflict theorists also emphasize the role that power and status play in the enforcement process. Even for the same offense, apprehension is more likely to lead to more serious punishment if the law is upheld by the person who commands more power and a higher ranking in the socioeconomic status system; for juveniles, especially, this extends to the parents of offenders. The members of two juvenile gangs, the "Saints" and the "Roughnecks," were accorded very different treatment at the hands of local law enforcement. The Saints, whose parents had respectable, relatively powerful upper-middle-class occupational positions, were treated far more leniently by law enforcement than the Roughnecks, whose parents were lower and working class. None of the "Saints" had ever been arrested, while all of the Roughnecks had been, and most of them, on numerous occasions; yet, their offenses, and the frequency with which they had been committed, were quite comparable (Chambliss, 1973). A tenet of the conflict perspective is that not only does the *law* define actions as illegal in conformity with the interests of the most powerful segments of the society, but the *enforcement* of the law is also unequal in that, in any society, it reflects the distribution of power.

In addition to being interested in the passage and enforcement of criminal laws, conflict theorists also examine—although to a far lesser extent—the question of the *causes* of criminal behavior. These are the etiological concerns discussed in Chapter 2. What causes criminal behavior according to the conflict perspective? To be succinct about it, conflict theorists answer this question by pointing to the *nature of the society* we are focusing on and the classes or categories in them. Conflict theorists generally would argue that inequalities in power and income cause certain types of criminal behavior; Marxists, for instance, would say that *capitalist society is criminogenic*—that the exploitation of the working class by the capitalist class or ruling elite causes certain kinds of crime to take place.

The conflict theorist is careful to point out that the issue is not explaining criminal behavior as such, but explaining forms of behavior that have *a high likelihood of being defined as criminal.* What forms of behavior are these? The behavior of the poor and the powerless stand a higher likelihood of being defined as crimes, while the behavior of the rich and the powerful stand a considerably lower likelihood. Thus, the predatory actions that the poorer strata are more likely to commit are actions that tend to be criminalized and enforced, while the harmful, unethical corporate actions of the wealthier strata are not as likely to be defined as crimes, and, even if they are, tend not to lead to arrest, and are not as often studied by the criminologist. Thus, when someone asks, "What causes criminal behavior?" he or she almost invariably means, "What causes people to engage in a particular *type* of illegal behavior—namely, street crimes such as robbery, rape, and murder?"

FEMINISM

Until a generation or two ago, most Western intellectuals viewed the world through the perspective of *androcentrism. Androcentrism* is a male-centered bias. It is the view that men are the center of the universe and women are at the periphery of the action. Women take on relevance only insofar as they relate to men and their activities. The androcentric bias in the study of deviance and crime began to be subject to criticism only in the late 1960s, and these critiques are having an impact on the way sociologists view the phenomenon of deviance. And it was *feminism* that launched this assault on androcentrism.

There is no single universally agreed-upon definition of feminism. However, perhaps the definition that might win the broadest acceptance is this one: Feminism is the perspective that stresses that "women experience subordination on the basis of their sex" (Gelsthorpe and Morris, 1988, p. 224). Feminism argues that men and women are typically treated as *representatives* or *embodiments* of sexual categories and that men attempt to keep women subordinate to men. Feminists are concerned with uncovering the origins and functions of this unequal treatment and seek to bring about a more sexually equalitarian society. For feminists, the enemy is *patriarchy*—institutions of male dominance. Patriarchy is responsible for the oppression of women, and hence, patriarchy must be analyzed, critiqued, and eliminated. Feminists often begin their analysis with an examination of how a given field has studied a phenomenon in the past, because past theories typically justified patriarchy. Such an analysis usually entails uncovering the sexist biases of more traditional approaches.

In 1968, Frances Heidensohn noted that the "deviance of women" was one area that has been "most notably ignored in [the] sociological literature." At first glance, she said, this seems understandable; after all, in comparison with men, women "have low rates of participation in deviant activities." Such a defense might seem to be a reasonable explanation for the field's concentration on men, Heidensohn writes, "but not the almost total *exclusion*" of studies on female deviance and crime (1968, pp. 160–162). The exceptions to this rule, she argues, show that women are not only virtually invisible in the field of criminology and deviance studies, but they hold peculiar and skewed place in its literature as well. Feminists argue that traditional analyses of women as enactors solely of deviant behavior that embodies their gender—which has usually meant prostitution and sexual delinquency (Cohen, 1955, pp. 44–48, 137–147; Heidensohn, 1968, pp. 166–168)—should be replaced with a more balanced approach.

The neglect of women in the field of criminology and deviance studies, feminists argue, is not only characteristic of the traditional approaches; it also marked the more contemporary perspectives, such as labeling or interactionist theory and radical or Marxist theory. Marcia Millman (1975) argues that, in much of the writings by labeling theorists, men appeared as interesting, adventurous deviants who lead exciting lives, while women were depicted as boring, conventional, and nagging drudges who attempt to rein in the wilder side of the men in their lives. While deviants were depicted with understanding and empathy in interactionist research, it was almost always *men* who are engaged in the deviance that was focused on, while *women* play a passive, inhibitory role. It was not until the 1980s that the implications of labeling theory were fully spelled out for the involvement of women in deviance (Schur, 1984).

Critical, radical, or Marxist criminology was no better in its analysis of women's role in deviance and crime than the more conventional perspectives. As one feminist analysis of criminological theory pointed out: There is *not one word* about women in Taylor, Walton, and Young's radical treatise on the new criminology, and Quinney, a major self-designated Marxist of the 1970s, "is all but blind to the distinctions between conditions of males and females in capitalist society." These authors "thoroughly scrutinize and criticize theoretical criminology, yet they never notice the limited applicability of these theories to women" (Leonard, 1982, p. 176). The sexism lurking in earlier writings can be illustrated by a male-centered aside made by Alvin Gouldner (1968), critic of traditional sociology, especially functionalism, and author of a well-known critique of the interactionist approach to deviance, who, in arguing that the sexual lives of sociologists may influence their work, remarks, "For example, it is my strong but undocumented impression that when some sociologists change their work interests, problems, or styles, they also change mistresses or wives" (Gouldner, 1970, p. 57). Are all sociologists men? The answer to this question is obvious, and betrays Gouldner's androcentric bias.

Three main points can be made about the depiction of women in writings on deviance prior to the 1960s and 1970s. (These generalizations apply even today, although to a far lesser extent.) The first is, as we saw, that women represented a minor theme in these writings. They were studied less, appeared less often as subjects of attention, and remained marginal, secondary, and almost invisible. The study of women and deviance suffers from "a problem of omission"; women have been "largely overlooked in the literature" (Millman, 1975, p. 265).

Second, as we saw, the study of deviance reflects an androcentric or "a male-biased view" (Millman, 1975, p. 265). Not only was the deviance of women less often studied, when it was, it was also nearly always *specialized* deviance; the deviance of men was deviance *in general,* the deviance of women was *women's* deviance. In a chapter entitled "The Criminality of Women," which appeared in a textbook that was eventually published in multiple editions, Walter Reckless (1950, p. 116) argued that the criminal behavior of women should not be considered "in the same order of phenomena as crime in general"—meaning the criminal behavior of men. Unlike men, in committing crimes, women are deceitful (p. 122), kill by administering poison (p. 121), throw acid in the face of a victim, "usually an unfaithful lover" (p. 122), and are prone to "make false accusations of a sexual nature" (p. 123). In short, the *forms* of deviance and crime women engage in are said to be very different from those that men commit. The three specific forms of deviance that have attracted attention from the field are shoplifting, mental illness, and prostitution. While women do play a majority role in the first of these, at least an equal role in the second, and the overwhelmingly dominant role in the last of them, they *do* commit a far wider range of deviant actions than these, their participation in deviance *has* been stereotyped in the literature, and men's deviance is not equivalent to deviance in general, as some observers have claimed.

And third, until recently, the role of women *as victims* of crime and deviance was underplayed. This was especially the case with respect to rape, domestic assault, and sexual harassment. It was not until the 1970s, when feminist scholars began a systematic examination of the ways women are brutalized and exploited by men that deviant and criminal actions such as rape (Brownmiller, 1975), wife battering (Martin, 1976), and sexual harassment (MacKinnon, 1979) found a significant place in the literature on deviance and crime, and the suffering inflicted on women at the hands of men given sufficient attention. In the 1980s, a number of radicals recognized that the question of women as victims of crime created "enormous theoretical problems for the radical paradigm in criminology" (Jones, MacLean, and Young, 1986, p. 3; Gelsthorpe and Morris, 1988, p. 233). Specifically, feminist research on female victims of crime has brought home to certain radicals "the limits of the romantic conception of crime and the criminal" (Matthews and Young, 1986, p. 2; Gelsthorpe and Morris, 1988, pp. 232–233). While it is true that men are significantly more likely to be the victims of crime than women, for some crimes (such as the three I just mentioned), the sex ratio is *overwhelmingly* in the other direction. Moreover, women suffer certain crimes *specifically* because of their powerless position relative to that of men. In short, women victims of crime have been "hidden from history" (Summers, 1981).

No approach that treats the behavior of less than half the population as if it were behavior in general can claim to be adequate or valid. The fields of criminology and deviance studies still have a long way to go before they fully incorporate the insights of feminism into the way they look at their subject matter. It is possible that feminism may have a more revolutionary impact on the field than that of any other perspective we've examined. Feminism forces us to think about sex biases and how they distort our views of deviance, crime, the law, and the criminal justice system. These biases are deep and pervasive. Confronting and overcoming them makes us better sociologists, criminologists, and students of deviance, and, just perhaps, more capable of changing society for the better.

CONTROLOLOGY OR THE NEW SOCIOLOGY OF SOCIAL CONTROL

All constructionist theorists of deviance are interested in the dynamics of social control. The perspective that gives social control a central place and views social control as almost exclusively oppressive, centralized, and state sponsored is referred to as "controlology" or the "new sociology of social control." Perhaps the most dramatic image of this school's perspective was captured by Stanley Cohen, one of controlology's central thinkers, in the following quote: "Imagine that the entrance to the deviancy control system is something like a gigantic fishing net. Strange and complex in its appearance and movements, the net is cast by an army of different fishermen and fisherwomen working all day and even into the night according to more or less known rules and routines, subject to more or less authority and control from above, knowing more or less what the other is doing. Society is the ocean—vast, troubled and full of uncharted currents, rocks, and other hazards. Deviants are the fish" (Cohen, 1985, pp. 41–42).

The spiritual father of the school of thought known as the new sociology of social control is Michel Foucault (pronounced "foo-COH"), a French philosopher. Foucault's ideas have been extremely influential; he may be the most frequently cited intellectual in the world. For the controlologist, the field of deviance is about a "struggle over whose rules prevail" (Marshall, Douglas, and McDonnell, 2007, p. 71). This emphasis has been the foundation stone of the field at least since Howard Becker's *Outsiders,* published in 1963.

In *Discipline and Punish* (1979), Foucault elaborated the idea of enlightened but repressive social control. The centerpiece of traditional social control was torture and execution. Its goal was the mutilation or destruction of the offender's (or supposed offender's) body. Traditional means of punishment were fitful and sporadic rather than continual and ongoing. Public confessions, torture, and execution created spectacle but, increasingly, they were ineffective. Eventually, crowds came not to be seized by the terror of the scaffold but instead began protesting the injustice of harsh punishment. In the end, public executions produced disorder and mob violence, not fear and compliance.

With the growing importance of portable property in the 1700s, the merchant class needed a stable, predictable means of protecting their investments from the predatory activities of the lower classes. The traditional means of punishment had to be replaced by a system of control that was more effective, certain, comprehensive, and which operated all the time. The traditional prison was used almost exclusively to detain suspected offenders before trial or execution. It was only in the second half of the eighteenth century that the modern prison became a location specifically for the incarceration and punishment of the offender. The new prison, Foucault believed, revealed the special character of the new age.

Jeremy Bentham (1748–1832), British philosopher, reformer, and utilitarian, came up with a plan for the modern prison. It was designed so that a small number of guards could observe a large number of inmates. He called this arrangement the *panopticon.* It was Foucault's belief that the central thrust in the history of Western society was the evolution away from traditional society where the many observe the few (as was true in spectacles such as execution) to modern society, where the few observe the many (as in the modern prison, with its panopticon). According to Foucault, Bentham's panopticon was typical, characteristic, or paradigmatic of modern society in general. The panoptic principle, Foucault believed, had become generalized and imitated throughout the entire society. We live, he said, in a society in which state and statelike agents are bent on observing and controlling its citizens in a wide range of contexts. In a sense, then, Foucault believed, modern society had become one gigantic, monstrous panopticon.

Foucault's argument is more a literary and philosophical formulation than a sociological one. To describe historical changes, Foucault uses clever analogies and metaphors that may or may not fit empirically. He takes *thought* and *discourse* as concretely realized reality, as indicative of the way things are—in a sense, as even more real than actions. In fact, modern prisons are not even remotely like Bentham's panopticon. In real-life prisons, surveillance and control require a substantial ratio of guards to prisoners. As a general rule, Foucault takes consequences, including unintended consequences, as if they were a direct outcome of the motives of the powerful actors on the scene. He ignores all countervailing forces that operate to control its exercise of power. In his scheme, there is no political opposition (Garland, 1990, p. 167). He nearly always presents the control potential of the powers that be as the reality (p. 168). And, for all its claims to being a political understanding of modern society, *Discipline and Punish* presents a "strangely apolitical" analysis of the exercise of power (p. 170). There is no "motive to power"—only more power, discipline, and control. Why and for what purpose the power is wielded is never fully explained. Foucault writes as if a society without the exercise of power is possible; he seems to be against power per se (pp. 173–174). He never presents an alternative system, one that could operate through the humane, enlightened exercise. In fact, to Foucault, in the context of modern society, humane and enlightened mean only one thing: insidious attempts at greater and more effective control, that is to say, *repression.*

Foucault died in 1984, of AIDS, before the emergence of the drug "cocktails"—developed, ironically, by the very oppressively scientific, state-sponsored agencies he denounced—that could have prolonged his life. His ideas have become the inspiration for later generations of controlologists. These are the central points of this school.

First, *social control is problematic; it should not be taken for granted.* By that, controlologists mean it does not emerge naturally and spontaneously by the "invisible hand" of society but is "consciously fashioned by the visible hand of definable organizations, groups, and classes" (Scull, 1988, p. 686). We cannot assume, as the functionalists seemed to have done, that society will be wise enough to preserve institutions and practices that serve the whole in the best possible way by sanctioning what is harmful and encouraging what is beneficial. Social control, as it is practiced, is not a product of a broad, widely shared social need or the workings of basic functional prerequisites, to use functionalist terminology. Instead, the controlologists say, social control is imposed by specific, and powerful, social entities, for their own benefit, and at the expense of those individuals and groups who are controlled.

Second, *social control is typically coercive, repressive, and far from benign.* Agents of social control typically try to make control seem benevolent, or at least enlightened, but this is a façade; control appears as a "velvet glove" rather than an "iron fist." Traditional criminologists have looked upon social control generally, and the criminal justice system specifically, as society's natural, inevitable, and beneficial means of self-protection against harmful behavior. As viewed by controlologists, social control takes on a more sinister coloration; its purpose: to repress and contain troublesome populations. Hence, the purpose of psychiatry is not to heal but to control; the purpose of the welfare system is not to provide a safety net for the poor but to control; the purpose of education is not to teach but to control; the purpose of the mass media is not to inform or entertain but to control—or rather, the mass media entertain *in order to* control. And when segments of the population under institutional control are perceived as no longer threatening, they are dumped out of the system (Scull, 1984).

Third, *social control is coterminous with state or statelike control.* The government is made up of a virtual alphabet soup of agencies of social control, including the DEA (the Drug Enforcement Agency), the ATF (Bureau of Alcohol, Tobacco, Firearms, and Explosives), the FDA (Food and Drug Administration), NIDA (the National Institute on Drug Abuse), NIMH (the National Institute of Mental Health), and the INS (the Immigration and Naturalization Service), all of which have one aim—to monitor and control the behavior of troublesome populations. In addition, a number of organizations, agencies, and institutions are performing the function of social control *on behalf of* or *in the service of* the state. These include private social welfare agencies; psychiatrists and psychiatric agencies; professional organizations such as the American Medical association, hospitals, clinics, mental health organizations, treatment facilities, educational institutions, and so on. It is the contention of controlologists that state control is increasingly being assumed by civil society. Troublesome populations can now be controlled on a wide range of fronts by a wide range of agencies. The same clients are circulated and recirculated between and among them. Even institutions that would appear to have little or nothing to do with the control of deviance as such—such as the mass media of communications—are involved in social control through shaping public opinion about deviants (Ericson, Baranek, and Chan, 1991).

Fourth, *the social control apparatus is unified and coherent.* The subsystems fit together into interrelated, functionally equivalent parts. Interlocking agencies and overarching institutions that work together to control troublesome populations may be referred to as the phenomenon of *transcarceration* (Lowman, Menzies, and Palys, 1987)—institutions of incarceration and control that reach across institutional boundaries. Foucault refers to this "transcarceral" system as the "carceral archipelago" (1979, p. 298), a reference to Aleksander Solzhenetisyn's description of the Soviet prison camps, *The Gulag Archipelago* (1974). The carceral archipelago transported the punitive approach "from the penal institution to the entire social body" (Foucault, 1979, p. 298). Controlologists point to a "peno-juridical, mental health, welfare and tutelage complex" in which "power structures can be examined only by appreciating cross-institutional arrangements and dynamics" (Lowman, Menzies, and Palys, 1987, p. 9). In other words, more or less all the organized entities in society have become a massive network dedicated to the surveillance and punishment of deviance.

One must be impressed with the variety and range of people-processing institutions and agencies in modern society, many of them designed to deal with or handle the behavior of troublesome individuals and groups (Hawkins and Tiedeman, 1975). No one can doubt that some of the functionaries who work for these agencies are often uncaring and insensitive. Especially in the inner cities, these agencies are overwhelmed with the sheer volume of clients, and the community is shortchanged. But most of these problems stem not from too much control but too few resources. Modern society is unprecedented in the number, variety, and near-ubiquitousness of organizations, agencies, and institutions that perform statelike functions and operate in place of and on behalf of the government. Social control is certainly one of their functions; how could it not be? If people who make use of their services engage in unruly, troublesome, disruptive behavior, representatives of these agencies will predictably attempt to control that behavior. In most cases, from the clients' perspective, that may not even be their main function. Such service and welfare service institutions are neither primarily nor exclusively agencies of social control. Clients themselves seek out the services of these organizations, institutions, and agencies and are more likely to see them as a shield to protect them than a net to catch them.

Controlology or the new sociology of social control is not interested in social control per se. It is interested in how the state and its allied organizations and institutions control, or attempt to control, deviant behavior. In fact, it is not interested in deviant behavior per se, either; it is interested more or less exclusively in the populations whom the elites consider troublesome and against whom the elites take action. What this perspective turns out to be is an exaggerated caricature of labeling theory, but with social control equated with formal (or semiformal) social control. It turns out to be an extremely narrow view of both deviance and social control.

SUMMARY

The other side of the coin, the "flip side," so to speak, of the positivist or etiological quest ("Why do they do it?") is the focus on the structure and dynamics of *social control:* definitions of deviance and rules and their enforcement. The rules and their enforcement cannot be assumed or taken for granted. A variety of perspectives has taken this side of the equation as problematic and worthy of study. Less concerned with etiology or the causes of deviance itself, labeling theory, control theory, feminism, and controlology have tried to understand why certain definitions of deviance emerge and why they are enforced.

The labeling or interactionist perspective had its roots in the work of two precursors, Frank Tannenbaum and Edwin Lemert, who shifted their attention away from the etiology or causes of deviance, crime, and delinquency to an examination of what implications punishment has on the deviators' identity and the enactment of their further deviance. The labeling theorists of the 1960s (who never approved of the title "labeling theory" to apply to their approach, preferring instead the term, "the interactionist perspective") stressed the relativity of deviance from one time and place to another; the social construction of moral meanings and definitions; the inner or subjective world of the deviant; the impact of labeling and stigma on the person so labeled; the role of audiences in defining deviance; the role of contingencies, such as ancillary characteristics in influencing the labeling process; the reflexive or the looking glass self; the stickiness of labels; and the self-fulfilling prophecy. Although a number of its insights have been incorporated into the mainstream of the field as a whole, the labeling approach to deviance nonetheless remains controversial.

Conflict theory overlaps with the labeling approach but contrasts with functionalism on a number of key points. Conflict theory sees struggles between and among classes and categories in society, with winners and losers resulting from the outcome of these struggles. Advocates of this perspective stress the fact that (contrary to functionalists) the interests of one faction or segment of the society often conflict with or contradict those of another; what helps one may hurt another, and vice versa. For instance, the institution of prostitution may reinforce male power and help to oppress women; social stratification may be good for the rich and harmful to the poor. Classes and categories attempt to establish dominance or hegemony over others to maintain their interests. The criminal law, for instance, may help to reinforce the rule of the ruling elite and assist in exploiting or oppressing the poorest segments of the society.

Feminists hold that women are subordinated as a result of their sex; it is their intention to eliminate *androcentrism* (a male-centered bias), *patriarchy* (male supremacy), and *sexism* (prejudice and discrimination against women). Feminist sociologists argue that earlier researchers displayed male biases in neglecting the deviance and crime of women; they looked at the few crimes that they did examine in a distinctly skewed, biased fashion; and they neglected the victimization of women by male-initiated acts of deviance and crime. Moreover, feminists stress, the issue of the social control of female versus male deviance and crime is a neglected topic and should be examined.

Contrology, or the new sociology of social control, received its primary inspiration from the writings of the French philosopher Michel Foucault. This perspective centers on how psychiatric and medical expertise has been used to control troublesome populations in ways that are more enlightened and sophisticated than was true in the past. "Knowledge is power," Foucault said, and power translates into more repressive means of control (the "velvet glove") than the naked brutality that characterized law enforcement in past centuries (the "iron fist"). The major social control agencies in modern society have become woven into a huge net to monitor and control deviants, contrologists claim. Some critics argue that this perspective neglects informal social control and pretends that the more benign features of modern bureaucracies do not exist.

Account: Cody, The Identity-Constructing Homosexual

The following account was written by, and the following interview was conducted by, Shawna Stoltenberg, a student at the University of Maryland who was enrolled in my course on deviant behavior. It highlights some issues that are central to constructing certain categories of behavior, and categories of humanity, as deviant. As we'll see, in American culture, homosexuality is gradually but unmistakably "departing from deviance." Nonetheless, young men and women feel the stigma directed at their identity and have to struggle with it for much, if not the rest, of their lives. It is this transition that dominates the discussion of homosexuality in Chapter 10, on sexual deviance.

What makes Cody deviant? In our society—one that prides itself on accepting all walks of life, people of all backgrounds—what makes homosexuality deviant? [Recently]

(*Continued*)

Account: Cody, The Identity-Constructing Homosexual Continued

I saw a picture in the newspaper of a man wearing a leather thong riding a bicycle. In the basket of his bicycle was a dog, and attached to the basket was a sign that read "Ass-Sniffers Anonymous." If this can be printed in the newspaper without millions of complaints, how can homosexuality be considered deviant? [What makes homosexuality deviant] is the stigma that society still places on homosexuals. It is the gay jokes and the hatred and the stereotypes. It is [caused by] the ignorance of society [toward homosexuality].

For Cody, it is a matter of situational deviance. Cody is a very intelligent, white, Jewish male who is 20 years old; he was raised in suburbia. He is of medium build, has shaggy, dirty blonde hair, and wears glasses. I have known Cody since the 7th grade. We all assumed he was gay, but we never mentioned that to him. We inferred that from the stereotypical signs. His room was filled with Playbills from Broadway shows, whereas his twin brother's room was filled with covers from *Sports Illustrated*. Cody was into Sheryl Crowe and folk music. And his name was Cody, a name that was androgynous—that seemed feminine in and of itself. We just knew. It was one of those things that was understood among my friends. We were just waiting for him to come to terms with it because we all had. But the rest of our classmates [outside of our little circle of friends] were not so accepting. We attended a high school where the vast majority of the students were white, middle-class snobs who wouldn't know diversity if it smacked them in the face. The parking lot was filled with Lexuses, Mercedes-Benzes, and Acuras the students had gotten on their 16th birthdays. For the most part, the parents who gave these cars to their children did not preach diversity at home. We looked through the yearbook and counted how many Black students were in our school: 33. It was an appalling number, considering that our graduating class alone was 340 students.

I can remember getting comments about Cody being gay from people since I was in the 7th grade. Kids 11 years old would ask me, "You're friends with Cody and Zeke. Isn't one of them gay?" I would respond that Cody was just effeminate. Sometimes they would be okay with it, sometimes they'd push it further. . . . Granted, Cody wore jeans that were tighter than the ones most of the girls in my school wore, but that does not warrant blatant ignorance. . . . No one in my high school ever said anything to his face. They were all cowards. We knew they talked to one another, though—they talked to us about it and we were his friends—which was reason enough not to come out.

If there was little diversity based on race, there was even less based on sexual orientation. Only in my senior year was there any semblance of a gay and lesbian organization. I went to their first meeting to take pictures for the school newspaper, at which a speaker told of his first coming out. He was a high school student who, apparently, toured the area speaking about homosexuality and his experiences with it. He . . . did not look any less "normal" than you [that is, the author of this book and the instructor of the deviance course in which Ms. Stoltenberg was enrolled] or I [that is, Ms. Stoltenberg]. He did not speak with a lisp or a stereotypical gay voice. If it were not for the content of his speech, you would never know he was gay.

It is here that my account of Cody as a homosexual really begins. In the months before I heard this speaker, Cody had been hinting at his homosexuality, but he never really came out. It was more as if he had opened the closet door, but he was peering rather than stepping out. After the speaker talked, I approached him and . . . told him that I had a friend who was hesitating to come out and wondered if he could give me contact information so that my friend could ask him questions. I figured Cody would be more comfortable with someone he could relate to [on that level]. . . . Little did I know that I was opening a door to a whole different experience.

"What happened after I gave you that boy's contact information?" I asked Cody. . . .

"I emailed him and we kept in touch this way for a week or so. It was nice to finally be able to talk about my feelings with someone who could relate and who wouldn't judge. I felt more able to tell him things that I would not be able to tell you guys. It's different when someone is in the same shoes. So we kept in touch through email and decided we should meet in person. . . . We met at the house of [another speaker] at the meeting I attended. I felt some sort of intense connection to him, which, looking back, was probably just that he was the first gay man my age I had come into contact with. We began kissing. Which led to more than kissing. I'd rather not go into detail, but just know that a hot tub was involved." His voice began trailing off and he had a reminiscent look in his eye.

"This was your first sexual encounter with another man, right?" I asked.

"Yes it was," he answered. "And it was intense. It left me with so many unanswered questions. And feeling so overwhelmed. It's very hard to go from 'Maybe I'm gay' to 'I'm having oral sex with a stranger.' "

"Had you ever kissed a girl before your encounter with this man?" I asked.

"No, this was my first sexual encounter of any kind," he replied, tossing his hair, which had gotten extremely long since I last saw him. . . .

"Did you continue to keep in touch with him?" I asked.

"For a little while. He decided that he couldn't have a relationship with someone who isn't out of the closet," Cody replied, almost embarrassed.

"How did that make you feel?"

"I don't know. On the one hand, I knew he was right. Here he is, touring local high schools and speaking about how open he is with his sexuality, and at the time, I had told maybe two or three close friends. On the other hand, though, it was my first experience with rejection, which was tough."

"How many people have you come out to now?" I asked.

"All of my friends from high school and mostly everyone at [the university he attends]," he responds.

"What about your parents?" I asked.

"I haven't come out to them yet. Or Zeke," he responds.

In high school, we were also friends with Zeke, his twin brother, who was teased many times for having a gay brother, even though Cody never really came out. I changed the topic and asked, "How did your identity as a homosexual continue to develop?"

"I kept hooking up with people. It was a whole new world for me and I felt the only way to find my place in it was to keep exploring it. The problem was, though, that there were not that many people to explore it with. There was no one at school and there was really nowhere else for me to turn, so I turned to the Internet. I began going to chat rooms and meeting men online. I started off just talking to them about themselves and being gay, but that led to mutual curiosity, which led to engaging in cyber sex. I'd meet these men online and act out sexual fantasies with them. But after a while, that too wasn't enough. I needed to meet them. So I did. I started to arrange face-to-face meetings with people I had been meeting online. Part of me knew it was dangerous and wrong, but the other part just didn't see any other way of exploring this new identity. I met these men and sometimes we just talked, sometimes we hooked up [had sex]. It was a matter of clicking with them."

"How did this help to develop your identity?" I asked, unclear of what his rationale was. . . .

Once you have that "ah-hah! I'm gay" moment, "you have to learn to get used to yourself as gay. You need to build up a lifestyle based on your identity. And certain things don't change. My personality isn't any different. I still have the same sense of humor, I still love my family. But now I have a gay identity, too."

"If I may get back to your sexual escapades in forming your identity," I asked, "what happened after meeting people online?"

"That summer I worked in [a well-known retail store chain] and a man came into the store every day to flirt with me. I liked the attention, especially from a stranger I met in person. This was different from cybering with someone who had never seen you. He thought

(*Continued*)

Account: Cody, The Identity-Constructing Homosexual Continued

I was cute. One day he asked me to go with him on my break to the lake by our house. I went with him in his car to the lake, where we engaged in sexual acts."

"Didn't you realize how dangerous that was?" I asked, shocked at his lack of concern [for his safety].

"Yes and no. Looking back, I'm lucky I didn't get killed. But at the time I felt that my newfound sexuality made me invincible. Jess realized it was not such a good idea, and essentially told my parents on me."

[*Shawna explains:* Jess is Cody's best and she also happens to be one of my closest friends. Cody tells her everything, including his homosexual escapades. She saw his behavior as not only deviant but dangerous. It wasn't even that he was homosexual, or even that he was being promiscuous, but it was the fact that he was doing it with strangers that she saw as being so dangerous. She felt for his own safety she had no choice but to step in and tell his parents. She believed that his judgment was blurred by the whirlwind surrounding his new identity.]

"What did your parents do?" I ask, confused because he told me that he has not yet come out to them.

"They sent me to counseling. I met with a therapist once a week to discuss my feelings and what not. My parents did not know I was gay per se. Jesse didn't exactly say, 'Cody went to the lake and went down on some guy.' She was more vague than that. She just told them that I was putting myself in dangerous situations. It was never once mentioned that I was gay."

"Why haven't you come out to your parents? Why not just come out to them?" I asked, knowing the family he comes from.

[*Shawna explains:* His family is very loving and supportive. His father is an ear, nose, and throat specialist, and his mother is a librarian. Their home is filled with unconditional love, and I am almost certain that his parents would not judge him or be upset if he came out to them. They already know. They have to. I think they have come to terms with it and are just waiting for Cody to come to terms with it himself.]

He thinks for a minute. I can see how he is trying to figure out how to explain it. "Then, the time just wasn't right. It's like for you, you're not going to just tell your parents, 'I like boys, I'm sexually active.' That would be weird. Instead you'd wait until you had a boyfriend to bring home to tell them or show them. Well, I don't want to just say, 'I'm gay.' I want there to be someone there for me to show them. Maybe that doesn't make sense to you."

[*Shawna explains:* It makes sense, but to me it's just further proof that Cody is not totally comfortable with his identity as a homosexual. The fact that he has not come out to his twin brother or his parents shows how he is still constructing his identity, and does not want to present it to the people most important to him until he feels he has completed this process.]

"It makes sense," I responded. "What about when you went away to school? How did that affect your identity?"

"Wow! When I first got to school, things were crazy. It was a chance to start over and create my identity from scratch. No one knew me or who I had been in the past. I came out totally at school."

[*Shawna explains:* It is important to note that Cody attends . . . an Ivy League school, which has more diversity, and more accepting students, than most universities. These students are also affluent and posh, and interested in the same things Cody is.]

"Did you make out with people there, too?" I continued to question.

"Oh, God, yes! That's all I did when I got to school. It was sort of a re-birth for me. All new people, and so much of a selection! If you think there's not much of a selection of [heterosexual] boys in high school, try being gay. But in college, yeah, there were a ton of boys, and at first, I had to make the right friends, but eventually, I just started having random hookups. I even had a threesome with two other boys."

"How do you think most people would react to all this? The promiscuity, the randomness, the homosexuality?" I asked.

"I don't really care. I don't really know. They don't know me and they don't really know what I do. Or understand it for that matter."

"What do your friends at school think?" I asked.

"Well, first of all," he answered, "I don't tell them every detail of my sexual exploits, so it's not a huge deal. But the ones I do tell don't care. They accept me for who I am."

"Who are you friends with at school? Boys, girls, gays, lesbians?"

"I am friends mostly with gay guys and straight girls," he responds.

[*Shawna explains:* It has become obvious to me that Cody deals with stigma by avoiding it. In high school, no one ever said anything to his face about being gay. We—his friends—had to field the gay jokes and comments and defend him since the seventh grade. He knew people made comments, I'm sure, but he didn't let that bother him. He always thought he was better than everyone else. That's how he got by. He threw himself into his schoolwork and the newspaper, and just went along thinking he was smarter than everyone else. In addition, he has always surrounded himself with people who would be accepting of who he was. He sometimes takes for granted how accepting we were. When he came out, we were all very supportive. He even confronted a straight friend of mine that he had a crush on him. Instead of panicking and telling Cody off, he talked it through with him and told him that he was going to be there for him. In high school, we were the smart kids, so I guess we were more accepting and tolerant than other groups. He has managed to find more accepting friends in college. His friends are accepting of him as he is, and he feels comfortable around them, so he does not have to deal with the stigma that many homosexuals attract. His tactic for dealing with stigma neutralization involves avoidance of people who would stigmatize him and concentrating on people who don't.]

"Tell me about the gay culture at school," I asked him. "Are you really involved?"

"Uh—I'm not really involved. I'm not in any of the LGBT [Lesbian-Gay-Bisexual-Transgender] clubs at school. A bunch of my friends are. Basically, the gay subculture is really into hooking up and placing these ridiculous ideals on the perfect partner. I said, 'screw it!' I've given up on finding the perfect partner right now, and I'm sick of hooking up just to hook up. I don't really hook up at school any more. I'm very concentrated on my work."

[*Shawna explains:* His resistance against the gay subculture says two things to me. One, that he is becoming more comfortable with himself in that he does not feel the need to subscribe to the ideals of the subculture of the new identity. And two, he is not comfortable enough with himself as a homosexual yet to really embrace the subculture beyond the sexual aspects of it.]

"One a random note," I asked, almost randomly, "what do you think of the words, 'queer' and 'fag'?"

"I use them sometimes. I feel like it's an acceptance thing. Being part of the group. Like how Black people can use the 'N' word—I can use the 'Q' word. I only use it to describe really gay guys, though," he replied with a sense of pride.

[*Shawna replies:* The fact that he uses derogatory words to describe the people he is the same as is another obvious sign to me that Cody is not yet comfortable with his identity. He feels cool because he can use these words, but then he uses them to describe "really gay guys," who he is clearly uncomfortable around. This is evidence that although he has taken great strides toward creating a homosexual identity for himself, he hasn't completed this process, and he is not yet fully comfortable with the one he has created. Like many homosexuals, Cody has found comfort in surrounding himself by other gays and by accepting straight people, mainly women. He doesn't feel deviant in this situation, whereas in high school, he had no choice. Although he is not completely comfortable with himself, what 20-year-old is? He is building an identity for himself; he just got a late start. Every time I see him, he's more and more flamboyant, demonstrating

(*Continued*)

Account: Cody, The Identity-Constructing Homosexual Continued

that as time passes, he is becoming more comfortable with his homosexuality. He needs to come to terms with himself first, create an identity that he finds acceptable, and be comfortable with himself before he presents that identity to his parents and his brother.]

"I've really turned my life around," Cody said, "and gotten it together now. I stopped the promiscuous hooking up and I am focused on what matters now. Sooner or later, I'll have it all figured out, but anyway, who has it all figured out?"

QUESTIONS

As Shawna Stoltenberg says, to the constructionist, what is most interesting about Cody's account is the situational aspect of his homosexuality, that is, its acceptance in certain social settings and rejection in others. In other words, homosexuality is *socially constructed* as deviance here, and is acceptable there. In addition, *Cody's* construction of his own behavior and identity as a gay man and—during a time in his life—as a promiscuous gay man is also crucial. Do you feel that constructionism is a productive way of looking at deviance? Does it lead us to make insightful observations about normative violations? With respect to Cody's behavior, is constructionism a more interesting perspective to use—or is positivism? Is the *cause* of Cody's behavior the most interesting question you'd want to raise?

CHAPTER

4

Studying Deviance: Research Methods

The researcher of deviance and crime faces special problems and challenges. At the same time, studying these topics is rewarding in ways that more conventional research is not. It is difficult to imagine a research endeavor that offers as much excitement or drama.

Since deviance entails behavior, beliefs, and conditions that are widely regarded as discrediting, shameful, or stigmatizing, the researcher necessarily enters a world that is partly shrouded in secrecy and deception; the subject is frequently the "skeleton in the closet." In addition, a certain proportion of deviant acts is illegal, and hence, when subjects, informants, or interviewees reveal their participation in them to anyone, those persons risk arrest. And when people who talk to researchers are punished as a consequence of talking to sociologists or journalists—for instance, by being arrested—this is bad for the business of social research and journalism. Others will learn that they are also likely to be punished for being honest about what they've done. After a while, no one who has something to lose by being honest will talk to researchers. As a result, research on deviance will have become impossible; the only research that can be conducted will be on polite, inoffensive topics. Hence, if only to protect their own interests, social researchers, like physicians, should live by the maxim "First, do no harm" (Humphreys, 1975, p. 169): No one should be harmed for revealing information to the sociologist, and that harm includes arrest. Sociologists should do everything they can to minimize potential harmful, unanticipated consequences to informants, respondents, and subjects.

In addition to exposing informants to arrest, simply by being around illegal activity and criminal actors, the researcher may expose himself or herself to arrest (Adler, 1985, pp. 23–24). Moreover, some deviant and criminal actors are violent and hence, by being around them, likewise, sociologists may themselves risk becoming victims of violence. Lastly, researchers of deviance face what's called "courtesy stigma" (Goffman, 1963, pp. 28–31): Because they interact with deviants, their academic colleagues may regard them as deviants. Such are the risks of doing research on our chosen topic.

Here, we'll look at a variety of methods sociologists use to obtain information, and assess their strengths and weaknesses with respect to unconventional and illegal behavior. Perhaps the broadest, crudest categorization of research techniques divides them into quantitative and qualitative methods. "Quantitative" methods are those whose data can be measured and rendered into precise numbers or statistics. In contrast, "qualitative" methods are those that do not produce information that is easily measured or expressed in numbers; instead, the researcher renders them in the form of relevant and revealing illustrations, quotations, sense impressions, metaphors, observations, and descriptions of behavior.

Survey methods—a quantitative methodology—is the most popular research technique among sociologists; reports based on it tend to dominate the pages of the most prestigious journals. Other quantitative research methods include laboratory and field experiments and the use of official data. Qualitative research encompasses what is known as participant observation, field methods, or ethnography, as well as unstructured interviews, and the use of personal accounts. Content analysis, a research method for analyzing written or pictorial material, yields data that are both quantitative and qualitative, depending on how it is done.

THE USE OF OFFICIAL DATA

Federal, regional, state, county, and municipal governments everywhere gather, record, and publish information. (This category is separate and distinct from surveys that are sponsored or conducted by the government.) Births and deaths, marriages and divorces, hospitalizations, employment and unemployment, the purchase of property, and the registration of everything from peddler's licenses to corporate mergers—these and thousands of other social facts are on official government records. Some of these records entail activities or characteristics that are of interest to the sociologist of deviance. Crimes reported to the police, arrests, convictions, and imprisonments are collected, recorded, tabulated, and published by the FBI. Drug overdoses, likewise, are recorded by hospitals and county coroners and entered into the federal record by a program called DAWN (the Drug Abuse Warning Network), under the umbrella of the Substance Abuse and Mental

Health Administration Services (SAMHSA). Arrestees are drug tested in select cities around the country, and this information is put together by a program that is referred to as ADAM (Arrestee Drug Abuse Monitoring Program), and is available to anyone interested in the connection between drugs and crime. These and dozens of other deviance, crime, and drug-related realms of data are gathered, recorded, and published by government agencies. These data can be tabulated in quantitative terms, in the form of numbers.

The Uniform Crime Reports (UCR)

Each year, the FBI gathers data on arrests and crimes known to the police from the jurisdictions containing nearly the entire population (93%) of the United States. And the FBI issues *Crime in the United States*, a yearly report that publishes the findings of these tabulations, which focuses largely on seven Part I or Index Crimes, that is, those offenses it considers emblematic or characteristic of street crime in general. These are murder (or criminal homicide), robbery, forcible rape, aggravated (or serious) assault, burglary, motor vehicle theft, and the grab-bag category of larceny theft. These are crimes known to the police, that is, reported by citizens to the police, then "founded" or verified by the police to have occurred, and hence, entered into the official record. I'll have more to say about this data source in Chapters 6 and 7.

In addition—not included in the Index Crimes or Part I offenses—the UCR also records arrests for a variety of other offenses, including some in which a researcher of deviance is likely to be interested, for instance, drug and alcohol offenses and prostitution. However, it is clear that neither crimes reported to the police nor arrests represent a valid measure of the total number of crimes committed in the United States each year. Many, indeed, more than half, of the crimes that are committed are not reported to the police. With nonvictim crimes, the percentage of unreported offenses is even higher. How do we know this? We know because of what's referred to as triangulation: using multiple and independent measures and data sources. For instance, we can compare crimes reported to the police, as tabulated by the FBI's Uniform Report, with the data collected by victimization surveys, which entails asking a sample of the population if they have been victims of certain crimes within a specific period of time (Rand, 2008). Of course, whether or not a crime is reported depends on its seriousness: The more serious the crime, the higher the likelihood the victim (or bystanders) will report it to the police.

In spite of the fact that the UCR's figures on the absolute number of crimes that take place—and hence, their rates—are extremely inaccurate, they are useful for some purposes. What these figures are good for is relative or comparative rates. If we were to arrange social categories in the population (males versus females, young versus old, etc.), states or regions of the country, as well as year by year by their rate for each crime, their ranking is approximately correct. For instance, the UCR indicates that the robbery rate is enormously higher (along the order of 20 times) in big cities than in smaller communities; independent data such as victimization surveys tell us that is indeed the case. Another example: The UCR data indicate that the crime rate has sharply declined since the late 1990s; again, independent data tell us that is decidedly true.

DAWN (The Drug Abuse Warning Network)

The federal government, through a program called DAWN, collects information on the incidence of two crucial drug abuse indicators in the United States. These are, first, emergency department (ED) episodes and, second, death or mortality figures based on medical examiner/coroner (ME/C) reports. The first tallies drugs that were reported by sampled hospitals to have been involved in an ED visit; and in the second, those that, in the estimation of the medical examiner or county coroner, was involved in the death of the deceased in a drug-related mortality.

Emergency department episodes include panic reactions, hallucinations, any other undesirable (and undesired) psychic effects, and overdose reactions requiring medical care, such as suicide attempts, unconsciousness, extreme pathological allergic reactions; EDs also count patients who present requesting detoxification, withdrawal, or "drying out." More than one drug can be counted in a single nonlethal emergency-department episode; each year, in roughly half of all ED episodes, more than one drug was recorded. The drugs that are recorded are those either mentioned by the patient or those whose use can be inferred from a result of a variety of objective indicators (DAWN, 2008a).

The second drug-related measured tabulated by DAWN is its tabulation of drug-related mortalities, as determined by ME/C reports. The area's ME/C conducts autopsies on nonroutine deaths and deems whether drugs played a significant role in that mortality. If drugs are determined by the medical examiner to have been a factor in the death, it is counted as an ME episode. Again, more than one drug can be counted in a single fatal overdose or ME report; about three-quarters of all drug-related mortality incidents (lethal overdoses) entailed more than one drug (DAWN, 2008b).

DAWN's data are valuable to the researcher of deviance. If the methods by which its data are drawn are standardized as to the areas that contribute data and procedures by which overdose events are classified, we have a moving picture of drug abuse: in some areas versus others, over time, and among different categories in the population. In addition, DAWN can yield information on the rise and decline over time of the abuse of specific drugs. (In 2003, DAWN revamped its data-gathering procedures; hence, data before that date are not comparable to those after.) It is from DAWN that we learn, for instance, that among older drug users (those 35 and older), death by overdose is much more likely to occur than among younger users, and that many legal prescription drugs (such as antidepressants and antipsychotics)—which are practically never used recreationally—cause far more deaths than many illicit drugs (such as PCP and LSD); that heroin is mentioned in most drug-related deaths (70%); and that methamphetamine, much-touted as an extremely dangerous drug, almost never appears among the top five drugs contributing to mortality statistics (DAWN, 2008b). These findings are valuable for the deviance researcher because they point to possible discrepancies in the use of types of drugs that are condemned, and hence, suggest some possible reasons as to why this might be the case. In short, DAWN's data address the concerns of both positivists and constructionists.

ADAM (The Arrestee Drug Abuse Monitoring Program)

If you want to know about the relationship between drugs and crime, what better place to begin than the drug use of people who have been arrested for criminal behavior? Each year, a sample of persons who are arrested for violence, property, drug crimes, DWI/DUI, and domestic violence crimes in the counties in which most of the nation's largest cities are located is drawn. Arrestees are asked if they would be willing to be interviewed and supply urine samples. Responses are confidential, and neither testing positive for drugs nor giving information about illegal activities results in any legal consequences. About 85 percent of the arrestees approached agree to an interview, and of these, more than 90 percent agree to provide a urine specimen. Adult male samples are made up of nearly 40,000 in about 35 sites, and adult female samples number roughly 30,000. The Arrestee Drug Abuse Monitoring Program also draws juvenile samples, of both male and female.

ADAM accesses populations that are inaccessible by means of more conventional research methods, such as surveys. Very few of ADAM's respondents would be drawn by the samples collected by the two major government-sponsored drug surveys, the National Survey on Drug Use and Health (NSDUH), which draws a sample of the general population, because many of them do not live in locatable households, and Monitoring the Future, which studies schoolchildren, because practically none of them are in school. For anyone interested in the relationship of drug use and crime, ADAM is the best place to start.

ADAM tells us that the relationship between drug use and criminal behavior is very close indeed. In 2008, in 10 cities across the country, at the time of their arrest, arrestees tested drug positive between 49 (in Washington, D.C.) and 87 percent (in Chicago). Since only 6 percent of the population says that they used one or more illicit drugs during the past month, ADAM shows the researcher that criminals (and arrestees are unquestionably criminals) are many times more likely to use drugs than does the public at large. (Of course, drug tests are much more reliable than responses to a survey.) In addition, ADAM shows us that the use of certain drugs (methamphetamine is the best example) is very unevenly spread around the country; that among arrestees in the last decade or two, the use of cocaine has declined, while the use of marijuana has remained more or less stable; and that a minority of arrestees test positive for heroin—many times more than for the population as a whole, true, but less than the stereotype has it (ADAM, 2009). Among other things, the story of the extremely strong connection between illicit drug use (a type of deviance) and criminal behavior (another type of deviance) speaks to the possible validity of one or more theories of deviant behavior (for instance, Gottfredson and Hirschi, 1990).

SURVEY RESEARCH

Survey research is the methodology of choice among positivist or explanatory sociologists; it is also likely to be employed by criminologists, as opposed to deviance specialists. This is not to say that in the field of deviance, researchers never make use of survey research. But most sociologists who study deviance do not conduct survey research as their main methodology, though it is important to know what surveys are and what their uses and limitations are for deviance researchers.

Survey research entails asking a sample of respondents formal, standardized, structured, and uniform questions about their past, current, or future behavior, beliefs, attitudes, and/or characteristics. Ideally, surveys are based on a large number of respondents, preferably thousands, who were selected in such a way that everyone in the target population (or "universe") has an equal chance of appearing in the sample. Many surveys select such a huge sample that a small number of researchers cannot conduct the interviews themselves. Consequently, researchers of most large surveys "farm out" or subcontract their interviews, and sometimes even the data analysis, to an organization that conducts such studies for a fee. Public opinion polls are the surveys with which the public is most likely to be familiar. For instance, every few months, polling organizations, such as the Roper Center or the Gallup Poll, conduct surveys on a variety of subjects; many of them include public attitudes toward controversial topics, such as abortion and homosexual marriage.

Survey researchers are interested in finding out about three things.

First, what is the number or percentage of people in the population who engage in certain activities, hold certain beliefs, or possess certain characteristics? For instance, what's the percentage (and the total number) of people who used one or more illicit drugs during the past month? The percent of the population who report having been robbed during the previous year? Support marijuana legalization?

Second, what's the relationship between key factors or variables and certain behaviors, beliefs, and characteristics? For instance, are men more likely to have engaged in adulterous sex than women? Which categories in the population are most likely to approve of homosexual marriage? Is drug use related to socioeconomic status? Are the members of certain ethnic categories more likely to use alcohol than those of others?

And third, what's the cause or causes of the behavior, beliefs, or traits asked about, as well as their condemnation? Who favors the death penalty, and why? What causes greater hostility toward certain less harmful behaviors as opposed to lesser hostility toward more harmful activities? Is religious conservativism the explanation for hostility toward certain unconventional beliefs or activities? Do people change their definition of and feelings toward deviance when they move from small towns to large cities?

Representativeness

In surveys, the selection of the sample is extremely important. Except for the U.S. Census, which is conducted only once every 10 years, no survey is based on the entire population. It would be prohibitively expensive to do so. Instead, researchers must select a subset or sample of the population to represent the entire population. For a sample to give answers that reflect the ones that would be given by the population at large, it must be a cross-section of or look like the population at large (or universe) in crucial respects. A sample can represent or be a cross-section of the population as a whole only if it is drawn in a random fashion, that is, if every person in the population has an equal chance of appearing in the sample. If a study oversamples specific groups or categories in the population (for instance, too many men and too few women, too many young people and too few older ones, and so on), it produces what's called a biased or "skewed" sample, which means that the answers we get may not reflect reality. The sample of one of the most famous of all surveys, the studies on sexual behavior by Alfred Kinsey and his associates (1948, 1953), was so unrepresentative as to render their conclusions questionable.

It must be said that not all—or even most—surveys are based on representative samples. In fact, a very substantial proportion is based on "convenience" samples: the students in a particular course at a particular university; the residents of a particular city or community; the members of a particular organization or work site; or what's called a "snowball" sample, that is, people known to a researcher supply the names of additional interviewees, who in turn supply others, and so on. Such samples are generally small—a few dozen or a few hundred respondents. And they do not represent any known universe or population except themselves. And surveys based on such surveys cannot give us an accurate picture of the number or percentage of people in the population at large who engage in certain activities, hold certain beliefs, or possess certain traits, or who do or do not condemn people who do. What such surveys are better at doing is giving us an idea of which categories in the population do, and why this is so.

The fact is that most of the things that sociologists of deviance are interested in cannot be studied by means of direct questions in a large-scale survey with a random population. Most of us need an inside look at, rather than a formal interview with, our subjects of investigation. Still, some deviance-related matters can be investigated by means of a formal survey.

Truthful Answers?

Surveys usually ask questions in one of three different ways: one, face-to-face interviews; two, telephone interviews; and three, self-administered questionnaires. Recently, surveys have adopted interviewing via computer. (Some surveys have used a combination of these methods.) Which of these a given survey uses depends in part on budgetary restrictions and the nature of the questions asked. Obviously, one major problem facing researchers who conduct surveys—especially those that deal with touchy or deviant topics—is whether respondents are answering truthfully.

Surveys are based on the assumption that if the researcher asks direct questions, even about sensitive, controversial, deviant, and criminal subjects, people will give more or less truthful answers. It is something of a popular cliché that nobody will give truthful answers when asked about shameful or illegal behavior. This isn't entirely true. In fact, it is remarkable how honest—up to a point—people are when they are convinced that they are anonymous, the answers they give will not be traced back to them personally, and they will not get into trouble for revealing information about illicit behavior.

How do we know this? Through a process I referred to earlier as triangulation. "Triangulation" means getting a fix on something by looking at it from several different angles. If we use multiple and independent sources of data that say the same thing, we have more confidence that the respondent is telling the truth. On the other hand, if what the respondent says is different from what we learn from hard or very reliable data sources, chances are what the respondent says is likely to be inaccurate or invalid. For instance, we can compare answers to the question "Have you used an illicit drug in the past 24 hours?" with the results of a drug test. As we saw, ADAM both drug tests and asks questions about drug use. Or we can compare answers to the question "Have you ever been arrested?" with official arrest data. Answers to questions about deviant behavior are more truthful than the stereotype claims, but less truthful than researchers would like.

Still, there are many places we cannot go with formal questions asked in a large-scale survey. Imagine the answers you'd get by asking a respondent, "Are you an alcoholic?" "Did you ever murder someone?" "How big is your heroin habit?" or "Do you practice sexual sadism or masochism?" The mind reels at the possibilities. Surveys are useful for certain purposes, but of limited utility for the deviance specialist, even one who is a creative and imaginative researcher.

The Response Rate

The response rate is just as much of a problem as the issue of truthful answers. The response rate of a survey is important because of the issue of representativeness. A sample may have been drawn in a random fashion, but if there is a very high nonresponse rate, then the respondents may not represent the total universe. A response rate of 90 percent or higher is excellent; 75 percent is adequate; and much below 75 percent is poor.

Sample Size

The size of the sample may or may not be a problem, depending on the purposes of the researcher. For polls that predict the outcome of an election, a nationally representative sample of only two thousand respondents may be adequate. Why? Because what the pollster is interested in is fairly clear-cut and common: The respondent intends, or does not intend, to vote; the respondent is going to vote for one candidate or the other. (Or not vote at all.) In the United States, roughly half of the adult population votes, and roughly half of the likely voters are likely to vote for a given candidate. (Of course, predicting which candidate has the edge among voters can be a tricky proposition because the margin between victory and defeat is often razor thin.) But for other purposes, a sample of two thousand is far too small to be of any value. For studies on extremely rare behavior, beliefs, or traits, such a sample may be worthless.

For instance, if we're interested in heroin addiction, a survey would be a poor choice of a research method. In the United States, heroin addicts number roughly a million, or less than half of 1 percent in the adult population. Hence, in a survey with a sample of two thousand—even if addicts could be located on a random basis—only 10 addicts would appear. This number is too small a number on which to base firm statistical conclusions. In another hypothetical sample of two thousand, even if it were representative of the population at large, how many have committed serious crimes, such as murder? The number will be minuscule, again, not large enough to draw meaningful conclusions from. For rape, the number would be considerably larger—although too small to be viable in a survey—and for female victims of rape, the figure may be accurate, but for male offenders, we run into the phenomenological problem: whether a respondent interpreted his action as a rape. As a general rule, the more serious the crime, the less common it is in the population; the more trivial it is, the more common it is. Very serious crimes are not asked about in most surveys because sample size of such surveys is too small to reflect their incidence. Depending on the purpose of the study, sample size can be a serious issue in conducting a survey.

Descriptive Versus Explanatory Statistics

Surveys seek to produce, as I said, quantitative data, that is, information that can be expressed in the form of precise numbers, either absolute numbers (how much or many of something) or percentages (what proportion of something). Most of us call these numbers statistics. There are two kinds of statistics: descriptive statistics and explanatory statistics. The number of people who were diagnosed with HIV in the United States during 2009 is a descriptive statistic. The murder or criminal homicide rate for that year is a descriptive statistic. The percentage of 18-year-olds who said they drank an alcoholic beverage during the previous year is a descriptive statistic. Descriptive statistics say, "This is the way things are at this time," no more, no less. For descriptive statistics to be considered valid and reliable, it is absolutely essential that randomized samples of respondents be drawn, the number of respondents be sufficiently large, the questions be worded properly, the respondent's anonymity be assured, and the interview or questionnaire situation be conducive to honesty. These are formidable and exacting requirements.

Explanatory statistics are more ambitious, more theoretical, even a bit speculative. They argue that this is the cause of the way things are. For explanatory statistics to be considered valid by researchers, the matter is different from but more complicated than for descriptive statistics. For the quantitative social scientist, devising a theory and convincing the practitioners of a field of study that it is valid is the prize, the king's ransom, the goal of all research. But statistically based explanations are difficult and require methodological rigor. And rigor requires the researcher to think seriously about variables, correlations, and controls.

Variables

Social scientists are interested in the influence of one variable on another. A variable is anything that varies or changes, whether from one time period to the next, one condition to another, or one person to another. Age is a variable. Looking from one person to another, or at the same person over time, we notice variations in age, stretching from infancy to old age. Sex is a variable: Some people are male, some are female. Race, geographical residence, household income, education, and marital status—all of them are variables, as are drug use, sexual identity and orientation, criminal behavior, and any and all beliefs.

When positivists reason in cause-and-effect terms, they distinguish the independent from the dependent variable. The "independent" variable is the causal variable, the factor that influences or causes or has an effect on the "dependent" variable. Age causes or has an effect on drug use: Younger people are much more likely to use illicit drugs than older people. Hence, in this case, age is the independent variable and drug use is the dependent variable. Sex causes or has an effect on criminal behavior: Men are significantly and usually strikingly more likely to commit most serious illegal acts than women. In this case, sex is the independent variable, and criminal behavior is the dependent variable. Not all cause-and-effect relationships are this easy to untangle. It is the job of the positivist social scientist who studies deviance and crime to trace out the cause-and-effect relationships between and among the many variables under study.

Does drug use cause criminal behavior or the other way around? Is homosexuality caused by inborn, genetic, hormonal, or neurological factors, or is it caused by environment, socialization, and experience? Is the higher rate of arrest among African Americans as compared with whites a product of a biased criminal justice system or higher rates of crime? Is white-collar crime a product of individual predilection or institutional environment? These are the sorts of questions positivists looking at deviance and crime attempt to answer.

The lion's share of these researchers' efforts involves determining which independent variables have what kind of an impact on specific dependent variables. In all (or nearly all) positivistic studies of deviance and crime, enacting deviant and criminal behavior is the dependent variable—the factor on which independent variables have an effect. By definition, the independent variable is always the "explanatory" factor—the variable that causes or influences the deviant or criminal behavior. Positivist theories ask the following: What causes deviant behavior? What causes criminal behavior? All positivistic theories of deviance have this same basic logic: Variable X (the factor on which the theory is based, the independent variable) causes variable Y (deviant or criminal behavior, the dependent variable). And usually, the name of the theory constitutes what is variable X or the independent variable: social disorganization theory (social disorganization causes deviance and crime), anomie theory (anomie causes deviance and crime), social control and self-control theory (a lack of self control causes deviance and crime), differential association theory (differentially associating with persons who express positive definitions of deviance and crime causes engaging in deviance and crime), and so on.

Correlations

Quantitative social scientists pay close attention to what statisticians call correlations. A "correlation" is a statistical relationship between two or more variables. Some correlations can be expressed in linear terms, that is, as one variable increases, another also increases, or when one increases, the other decreases. For instance, the correlation between size of community of residence and the per population robbery rate is a positive relationship: As we saw, as the size of the residence increases, the likelihood that robberies take place will also increase. On the other hand, some correlations are negative: As one variable goes up, the other goes down. When we say younger people are more likely to use illicit drugs, we mean that there is a negative correlation between age and drug use: As age goes up, drug use declines. The same thing applies to the relationship between household income and criminal homicide victimization: As household income increases, the likelihood that a member of the household will be a victim of homicide decreases. Not all correlations are linear, however. For instance, men are more likely to engage in homosexual behavior than women, and to have such experiences earlier in their lives. For our independent variable—sex—there is no such thing as an increase or a decrease, only statistical differences between men and women.

A correlation does not demonstrate causality—it only suggests it. Just because two variables are correlated with one another does not demonstrate that one causes the other. Both could be caused by a third or common variable. We know there is an extremely strong correlation between the use of psychoactive drugs (both legal and illegal—but especially illegal) and criminal behavior. But, as we just asked, does drug use cause criminal behavior? Does engaging in criminal behavior cause drug use? Or are they both the effects of a common cause, for example, poor parenting, leading to low self-control (Gottfredson and Hirschi, 1990)? Using marijuana in the midteens is very strongly correlated with using hard drugs such as cocaine, methamphetamine, and heroin in the late teenage years. This is an indisputable fact. But does the use of marijuana per se cause the use of more dangerous drugs, as some claim (O'Donnell and Clayton, 1982)? Or is the relationship an artifact of some third variable, such as the kind of person who uses marijuana, or the friends and acquaintances one makes when using marijuana (Earleywine, 2002, pp. 49–65)? It is essential to understand that in tracing out cause-and-effect sequences, correlations are only a first, not a final step.

Controls

The way that social scientists determine cause-and-effect relationships by separating correlation from causality is by applying what they call controls. To apply a control is to hold things constant. Every generalization a scientist makes is qualified by the implicit qualification, other things being equal. This means that when we look at the causal relationship between two variables, it is in a kind of pure state, with all other variables taken out of the picture. In research, by controlling for other factors or variables, we make them the same, even if it is only theoretically or on paper. Eating ice cream is correlated with the rate of rape. This correlation is true—but is it meaningful? Does this mean eating ice cream causes men to rape women? Of course not! Ice cream is eaten more in the summer than in other seasons, and it is in the summer when rates of rape are the highest. If we looked at each season separately, there is no relationship between ice cream consumption and rates of rape. In this case, we have controlled or held constant the effect of the season of the year. When we apply one or more controls and a relationship that previously existed disappears, we say that our original explanation that one variable caused the other is spurious, or false. If a correlation between two variables holds constant whenever the relevant controls are applied, social scientists feel confident that there is a cause-and-effect relationship between them.

Survey Research: A Major Sex Survey

Although nineteenth-century physicians and psychiatrists investigated and wrote about the "abnormal" sex lives of their patients, it was not until the 1930s that researchers carried out surveys on "normal" sexual behavior in the general population. As a faculty member at Indiana University, Alfred Kinsey, an entomologist specializing in the gall wasp, was asked to teach the unit on sex in a course on marriage. Surprised that virtually no information was available on the subject, he decided to conduct research on human sexual behavior. He located respondents wherever he could find them—in classes, student groups, fraternities and sororities, parent–teacher associations, clubs, hospitals, prisons, rooming houses, circles of friends, people who just stepped forward and volunteered to be interviewed, and even hitchhikers he picked up on the road. Kinsey's sample was huge—18,000, almost unheard of at the time. Kinsey's findings indicated that Americans engaged in a great deal more deviant sexual behavior than most people imagined at the time. The problem was Kinsey's sample was not representative, and hence, his findings may have been flawed. His rationale for this odd and patchwork sample? At the time, he explained, very few respondents in a randomly selected sample would give honest answers about private matters, such as their sexual behavior. It wasn't until the 1990s that a sex survey employing a large, representative sample was conducted in the United States. And at almost exactly the same time, similar surveys were also conducted in other countries.

Early in the 1990s, goaded by the AIDS crisis, four sociologists affiliated with the University of Chicago—each with expertise in a particular area—decided to conduct a survey on sexual behavior, based on a nationally representative, randomized sample. Because of conservative opposition, the study's government sponsorship was cancelled and the researchers had to seek private funding. The sample, nonetheless nationally representative, was scaled back from the original goal of 20,000 to only 3,500 respondents. Its response rate was 80 percent, which is considered quite adequate for a study of this sort. Respondents were assured that their answers would be held in the strictest confidence, their privacy would be protected, and their answers would be reported either as part of a statistical pattern or, if they were quoted, there would be no way that they could be personally identified. The sexual behavior of the American public, according to the survey published in 1994, took place less frequently and is substantially less adventurous, more conservative, more conventional, less deviant, and more "vanilla," than the results of the Kinsey Report indicated (Laumann et al., 1994; Michael et al., 1994): less homosexual behavior, less heterosexual promiscuity, less frequent heterosexual behavior, more marital fidelity, and more traditional, conventional sexual activities. The conservatives who managed to get public funding for the survey canceled would have loved the findings of this study.

How much confidence can we have in the findings of this survey? Some observers have criticized the study because they assumed that respondents would lie about their sex lives—for instance, that men would exaggerate the extent of their sexual behavior, while women would minimize it. Some critics claimed that many people simply forget about a great deal of what they have done sexually, and hence leave it out of their answers to an interviewer. It is too early to tell whether the results of this study can be taken as definitive; it will be a while before its validity will be sorted out by later researchers. Nonetheless, it is certainly the best survey ever conducted on sexual behavior in the United States. Its answers are probably as close to what we'll get to the true picture of sexual behavior for some time to come. The fact that the researchers used a variety of techniques to cross-check the answers respondents gave (asking the same question twice, in different parts of the survey, in different ways, or having respondents fill out a questionnaire for especially touchy and sensitive subjects) gives us more confidence that the answers they received are accurate. And the fact that similar surveys were conducted elsewhere—for instance, in Britain (Wellings et al., 1994) and France (Spira et al., 1992, 1993)—and reached similar conclusions for a number of behaviors, again, imparts confidence to the study's conclusions.

Survey Research: The National Crime Victimization Survey

The National Crime Victimization Survey (NCVS) is an ongoing survey on crime victimization conducted yearly by the U.S. Bureau of the Census in cooperation with the Bureau of Justice Statistics of the U.S. Department of Justice. It began in 1972 with the intention of generating much more valid crime statistics than the Uniform Crime Reports, with its huge rates of underreporting, could provide, in short, to measure what criminologists call the "dark figure of unreported crime." Originally, its target sample was 50,000 households comprising a total of 100,000 respondents, but in the 1990s, budget cuts reduced the sample by about 20 percent. The NCVS asks questions about personal crimes, or crimes of violence and property crimes, both against the individuals living in them (such as theft) and against the household as a whole (for instance, burglary). It does not ask a question about criminal homicide, because in that case, the victim is dead and cannot respond to a survey! The response rate is excellent: Roughly 90 percent of the households that are contacted and asked to participate do so. It is because of the findings of the NCVS that criminologist are able to state with confidence that crime victimization is considerably higher than the data in the UCR indicate.

For instance, in 2007, fewer than 100,000 rapes (90,427, to be exact) were reported to the police and recorded in the UCR. But the NCVS victimization survey, based on interviews with its respondents, estimated that 248,300 rapes took place in the United States in 2007, more than twice as many. (The NCVS counts the rape of males, the UCR does not, but too few such rapes were recorded to influence this difference.) The UCR posted 445,125 robberies for 2007; the NCVS, 597,300, an underreporting of nearly a third. The UCR recorded roughly 2.2 million burglaries; the NCVS, 3.2 million. Larceny thefts were underreported by half: UCR, 6.6 million; NCVS, 13 million. Most criminologists believe that the NCVS's figures are more valid, closer to the actual crime rate, were that known, than the one the UCR tallies. The fact is a higher proportion of the victims of a number of crimes, especially rape and simple theft, do not report these crimes to the police (Rand, 2008, p. 7). These two data sources do, however, reflect the same trends that have been taking place in criminal behavior over time: Both show a peak in the seventies and a decline during the 1990s and into the 2000s.

Since the NCVS entails interviewing respondents, the criminologist has information on who the victims of crime are. (Moreover, if the crime entails face-to-face confrontation between perpetrator and victim—rape, robbery, and aggravated assault—the victim can, approximately, identify key characteristics of the perpetrator, such as age, sex, and race.) So we know that persons living in low-income households are more than twice as likely to be victimized by violent crime than persons living in more affluent households; that males are somewhat more likely to be victimized than females; that blacks are more likely to be victimized than whites; and that the young are more likely to be victimized than the old (Rand, 2008, p. 4). We also know that women are twice as likely to be raped by someone they know (in 2007, a total of 150,000 rapes) than someone who is a stranger to them (72,780), an important fact (p. 6). And while males are more likely to be robbed and assaulted by a stranger, females are more likely to be robbed and assaulted by someone they know (p. 6). All in all, the NCVS imparts valuable data to the criminologist, data that has crucial theoretical and policy implications.

Surveys on Deviant Behavior: An Overall Assessment

Researchers have conducted an uncountable number of surveys and polls, one or more of whose questions have asked about deviant behavior, beliefs, or traits, and/or criminal behavior. Most of them have been mainly concerned about conventional matters, and they have devoted only a small number of questions to issues directly of interest to the deviance specialist. Of those that have been focused on matters deviant, only a minuscule percentage was based on large, randomized samples. Though the samples of most surveys cannot accurately produce descriptive data, they are probably adequate—though not ideal—for testing relationships between key factors or variables and inquiring about the cause of deviance and crime.

Probably the most useful function of survey research is to investigate attitudes about deviant behavior, beliefs, and conditions. Indeed, this is what many public opinion polls do. Surveys have also been conducted on the public's attitudes regarding the seriousness of a range of crimes, a phenomenon that is very closely related to the concept of deviance. Crime victimization surveys produce very useful information about the likelihood that Americans will become victims of a variety of criminal acts during a given period of time. From such surveys, estimates can be made about the national crime rate, and such estimates can be compared with official information about crimes reported to the police. Drug use surveys are useful if the samples are large and researchers recognize that estimates of the use of relatively rare, exotic drugs are likely to be off the mark, especially if we are interested in rates of addiction and dependence (SAMHSA, 2008; Johnston et al., 2009). Surveys on sexual behavior are probably useful, since most of the questions in such a survey will be asked about fairly conventional acts; determining the extent of deviant sexual expressions are a by-product of such surveys, not its explicit aim (Laumann et al., 1994; Michael et al., 1994). Estimates of the extent of crime in the population drawn from self-report surveys decline in accuracy as the seriousness, and hence the rarity, of the acts asked about increases. Surveys on criminal and delinquent behavior are much better for examining relationships between and among variables than for determining the extent of offenses in the population.

Surveys are also useful for learning about a variety of unconventional, unacceptable acts, beliefs, or traits that take place within more or less conventional settings, such as school and college, marriage and the family, community and neighborhood, hospitals, and work settings. Some examples include student cheating during exams; violence within the family; levels of alcohol consumption; holding unconventional—for example, paranormal—beliefs; Internet-related or cyber deviance, for instance, the consumption of cyberporn; automobile-related deviance (speeding, driving without a license, etc.); legal and illegal gambling; and mental health and disorder in the noninstitutionalized population at large.

Still, some activities, organized belief systems, or collectivities of possessors of undesirable traits and characteristics need to be studied from the inside, in situ as it were—on the ground, on the site where their participants, believers, or possessors are located. We need to live the lives they lead; eat meals with them; find out what they do on a day-to-day basis; and listen to them explain and justify what they do, what they believe, and who they are. In short, we may need to engage in a particular type of qualitative research—participant observation.

PARTICIPANT OBSERVATION

Unlike sociologists in general, most deviance specialists make use of some form of participant observation as their primary research tool. The pages of the journal most centrally devoted to the study of deviance, *Deviant Behavior*, are filled with participant observational studies of strip clubs, tattoo parlors, biker gangs, racist skinhead gangs, methamphetamine manufacturers, rodeo groupies, participants in "flesh hook suspension," prisons, homosexual bathhouses, meetings of Alcoholics Anonymous, and dozens of other less-than-respectable scenes. What is this research method sociologists refer to as participant observation?

Some kinds of behavior can only be studied by direct, firsthand, face-to-face, natural observation. Imagine conducting not just one interview but many. Imagine that these interviews are very much like ordinary conversations: spontaneous, free flowing, informal. Imagine too that you not only converse with the people you are studying but that you also do just about everything else that goes along with them as well: go bowling, play cards, attend weddings, visit families, go out drinking—and many other activities as well. Participant observation thrusts researchers into the day-to-day, minute-by-minute behavior they are studying. They examine social life in the field, in its natural habitat, observing behavior as it takes place, more or less around the clock, over a period of many months or even years. Studying behavior in its natural setting is referred to as participant observation, fieldwork, or ethnography.

This methodology entails that the researcher acquire a huge mass of information and write down his or her observations in the form of what's called field notes. There is no need to rely on a single question or two or three questions to find out about behavior or attitudes, as is true of surveys. The many observations the researcher makes cross-verify one another and ensure the validity of conclusions that are drawn. The participant observer also profits from the richness of this mode of research. Any idea or hypothesis may be confirmed and reconfirmed with many different indicators, questions, and observations.

Another advantage of participant observation is that it maximizes the chances that what the researcher hears and sees will reflect real-life behavior and beliefs. All other research methods are several steps removed from the actual behavior itself. By going into the streets, factories, and homes—into the lives of informants—sociologists remove many of the barriers between what they want to know and what they can—and do—observe. More than almost any other research technique, participant observation gives access to the insider's point of view.

In addition to its strengths, participant observation has a number of drawbacks as well. One such drawback is that it forces us to rely on a case study. If you rely on only one street gang, bar, corporation, or house of prostitution, how do you know what gangs, bars, corporations, or houses of prostitution are like in general? How can you be sure that the group, scene, community, or organization you study is typical? Answer: You can't. Unlike survey research, participant observation does not employ formal sampling procedures, so the issue of nonrepresentativeness is an even more serious problem. You can never really know if what you have seen in your research site is a cross-section of the whole picture or merely a very narrow and unusual slice of it.

Second, fieldwork tends to yield qualitative rather than quantitative data. Qualitative data cannot be measured precisely, while quantitative data can be. Usually, the results of participant observation cannot be worked up into numbers or statistics, tables, charts, or graphs. Data from questionnaires and formal interviews can be systematized and standardized, and the results can be analyzed statistically. This is typically not the case with quotes from informants or observations of people's everyday lives.

In addition, participant observation cannot resolve questions of cause-and-effect. In general, it suits description better than explanation. Participant observers are not likely to answer the question "Why?" definitively. They are, however, able to accurately describe the details of a particular social setting.

One important distinction among participant observers is the matter of the actual participation of the researcher in the behavior under study. The roles the researcher may adopt while engaging in this method of study range from a complete participant to a complete observer (Adler and Adler, 1994). Some observers believe that actual participation in deviant and even illegal behavior by the researcher is not only desirable but also necessary (Ferrell and Hamm, 1998). Others believe that observation alone is not only sufficient but the wisest and most productive strategy; the researcher, they say, should most decidedly not engage in deviant or illegal behavior (Williams, 1996). As I said earlier, all researchers strongly believe that no one should be harmed by their research. But most deviant and illegal activities entail no direct harm to anyone.

If one is conducting a participant observational study of the homosexual community, does one engage in homosexual sex to get closer to one's informants? Some researchers think so (Styles, 1979; Bolton, 1995, 1996). If one is studying strippers firsthand, does it help to become a stripper oneself? Some researchers would nod assent to that question (Ronai and Ellis, 1989; Ronai, 1992). If one is studying drug dealers in their natural habitat, in the field, is it wise to use drugs oneself? It is not only wise, it may also be necessary, say some researchers (Adler, 1985, 1994). What about dealing drugs? Should the researcher also sell drugs to best understand what drug dealing is all about? These researchers don't say. There is probably no definitive or cut-and-dried answer to the question of researcher participation. Certainly no participant observer believes it is necessary to murder someone in order to study murder. Where does one draw the line? It's not clear. Engaging in deviance in order to study it, however, is extremely risky and may result in endangering the research one is conducting.

Researching Drug Dealers: Conducting a High-Risk Participant Observation Study

For many behaviors or scenes, a survey of the general population is not feasible. Most of us recognize the difficulty of obtaining truthful and complete answers when the behavior asked about is as deviant, supersensitive, and illegal as drug dealing. Patricia Adler (1985, 1994) argues that the only way to acquire accurate, valid knowledge about deviant behavior is to interact with informants on a face-to-face, day-to-day basis in real-life or naturalistic situations, that is, to engage in participant observation research. That way, she argues, we get an insider's perspective. This is especially the case with drug dealing; given the "highly illegal nature of their occupation," dealers have become "secretive, mistrustful, and paranoid. To insulate themselves from the straight world, they construct false fronts, offer lies and misinformation, and withdraw into their group" (Adler, 1985, p. 11). The reason why sociologists have so little information on how drug dealing is conducted is that they have had such a difficult time "penetrating into their midst" (p. 11). Only by entering the social circle of drug dealers, becoming friendly with them, and adopting a "peripheral" role in that circle, was Adler able to conduct her research on drug dealing.

Patricia Adler and her husband, Peter, both at the time graduate students at the University of California at San Diego, became friendly with a neighbor, Dave, who had an abundant supply of drugs, including cocaine, which was (and still is) extremely expensive for graduate students. This neighbor also seemed to be very knowledgeable about drugs and their prices. And his apartment seemed to attract a large number of well-to-do visitors, yet he and his friends didn't seem to have what could be called a job or a visible means of support. When the Adlers asked him what he did for a living, he was vague and evasive. It soon became clear to them that the man sold drugs for a living. On the advice of their graduate advisor, they decided to study their neighbor's drug-dealing activities. One day, in a casual conversation, one of Dave's companions let it slip that they were engaged in drug selling and were part of a smuggling crew. After some embarrassment, Dave finally agreed to allow the Adlers observe his world. The research that ensued is an example of serendipity—a fortunate or "happy accident."

So, for six years, they conducted detailed interviews, which were tape-recorded, and observed interactions and transactions in Dave's world. Day by day, year by year, the Adlers' circle of informants "snowballed" into an expanded study, with more and more dealers and customers, and more and more dealing operations. With new people in the study, Patricia and Peter took a "covert" or hidden research role, not informing them initially that they were engaged in research, waiting until they were accepted as peers, at which time, they informed them of their role. In general, they were accepted as cool friends of dealers who could be friendly with other dealers. When they built up the trust of new acquaintance-dealers, they could inform them about what they were up to, then ask them more detailed, probing questions. After the Adlers had children, their involvement with the research diminished considerably. The study culminated in a Ph.D. dissertation and later, a book for Patricia Adler, *Wheeling and Dealing: An Ethnography of an Upper-Level Drug Dealing and Smuggling Community* (1985, 1994). It is considered something of a classic in participant observation research on deviance.

Obviously, research of this type is more difficult and stressful than constructing and administering a questionnaire or interview schedule and then analyzing the data it generates. The problems the Adlers faced in conducting their research were myriad. Here are a few.

The Effect of Drug Use on the Research Process. Under the influence of marijuana, respondents became sleepy, disoriented, distracted, and uninterested in being interviewed. The authors believe, in contrast, that under the influence of cocaine, their interviews were superior to those that were conducted when their informants were not under the influence of any drug. Interviewees under the influence of cocaine were alert, sharp, and focused.

Assuming Risks While Doing Research. The research posed special dangers for the researchers. Dealers were not infrequently moody and erratic; the Adlers' fear was that they might have become dangerous and violent. Dealers also became paranoid about the Adlers' use of the tape recorder during interviews. And the Adlers were also fearful of being arrested by the police or subpoenaed by the authorities. Obviously, by observing crimes and not reporting them to the police, the Adlers were committing crimes themselves. Drug deals took place in their house, and thus, they were aiding and abetting crimes—which was itself a crime. And of course, they possessed and consumed drugs with their informants. All of which created concerns for the researchers.

Ethical Problems. The Adlers also found that there were ethical problems in conducting their research, which I alluded to earlier, and will discuss in more detail later. Is deception of informants ethical? Some researchers do not believe it is (Erikson, 1967). How much deception is necessary? How much should they lie to some of their informants to protect others? And which ones? How much detail should they go into in writing up their research report, which would inevitably reveal intimacies to others on the scene they studied? Would their informants feel they had been exploited by the Adlers' research? And was violating the law really necessary to gather the information they got? As we've already seen, some researchers feel it is unacceptable (Williams, 1996); clearly, the Adlers disagreed.

Participant Observation: An Assessment

As I said earlier, the Adlers strongly believe that participant observation is not only the best but is also the only methodology that should be used to study deviance. Survey methods are preferred by researchers with a more positivistic or natural science bent; participant observation or field methods are favored by social constructionists. I do not regard either method as superior overall. Each has strengths and weaknesses for certain purposes. Participant observation is stronger on the basis of validity—that is, researchers can be confident that what they say is true. Field-workers get into the intimate, day-to-day lives of their informants in a way that no other technique can. And participant observation can study phenomena that survey methods cannot hope to approach—dangerous scenes, extremely illegal or deviant behavior, and activities in which a very small proportion engages. In contrast, survey methods are superior on the basis of reliability—that is, they can be confident that their findings will be reproduced or replicated by other researchers using the same methodology. Certainly the survey method gets a good cross-sectional view, that is, they are based on a randomized sample that reflects the population as a whole. But survey methods cannot study many, perhaps most, of the issues that participant observers study. Neither can be said to be better as a whole; the question of which is superior depends on what the researcher is attempting to find out.

AUTOBIOGRAPHIES, LIFE HISTORIES, AND PERSONAL ACCOUNTS

The use of personal or autobiographical narrative or accounts has been both embraced and rejected by sociologists for a century. A classic work by W.I. Thomas and Florian Znanieki, *The Polish Peasant in Europe and America* (1918–1920), a five-volume work of 2,500 pages, devoted 800 pages to personal life histories from informants. But with the growing emphasis in sociological research on quantitative, statistical methods, biographical accounts fell out of favor in the field. It has only been in the last decade or two that the use of narrative and biographical materials has once again come into its own as a legitimate research method.

The narrative method encompasses a range of research modes, stretching all the way from the detailed, informal interview, conducted by the sociologist, to the formal, detailed autobiography, written by the subject. As a general rule, narratives are accounts rendered by informants about their own lives. They give minimum control over the content of the material to the researcher and maximum control to the subject. Moreover, of all research methods, the narrative technique is the most democratic, in that it gives subjects who have traditionally remained marginal and powerless their own voice, a forum, the means of expressing themselves in ways that, to a major degree, they have chosen themselves. In a sense, unlike all other research methods, in the biographical method, the subject is the "star of the show." The narrative technique is probably the prime example of constructionist reasoning, one in which the subject defines or constructs his or her own reality. Of course, that reality is always filtered through the researcher's slant or perspective; moreover, the researcher selects specific autobiographical material to publish—material that the informant/autobiographer might not have chosen.

Four decades ago, overwhelmingly, personal accounts were examined by researchers and scholars more or less exclusively with respect to their factual accuracy. The issue that guided such investigations was whether accounts could be used to determine what happened in the literal, concrete sense. Good accounts were empirically accurate; bad accounts were those that were factually false or distorted. But researchers eventually recognized that accounts informants give are historical data worth investigating. Instead of simply being factually accurate or inaccurate, accounts are also social and historical creations in their own right. They represent testimonies that are organized according to principles that convey cultural, social, and personal truths. This recent stress on subjectivity does not mean that the issue of empirical or concrete facticity be abandoned. But it does mean the value of an account does not lie solely in its factual accuracy.

All contemporary observers who study the subject of personal accounts agree on at least one basic assumption: Narratives are not a simple reflection of or a window on material reality, that is, the events that are narrated. All students of narrative argue that "Just the facts, ma'am" is quite literally an impossibility—in effect, a fiction. Events and experiences do not simply imprint themselves on our brains and come out in the telling—intact and identical for all narrators. The meaning of events and experiences is unstable, liable to interpretations that vary from one teller to another. Stories get told in particular ways, both with respect to a particular cultural and social setting and with respect to individual predilection.

Why do we tell stories in a particular way? Why do we include these events in our narrative and leave those events out? Which events get recalled? Which ones are forgotten? Everyone who studies narrative assumes that a great deal of variation prevails from one teller to another in the stories that are told. Even the same set of events will be narrated in radically different ways. For instance, if we were to ask Alan and Sarah, a divorced couple, about their marriage and why it broke up, we would receive two very different accounts of supposedly more or less identical events. Yet, those two accounts are not necessarily contradictory. Both may be literally and factually true; if we had videotaped the events each describes, chances are we would have seen more or less what one said and more or less what the other said. But Alan's account left out much of what Sarah's account included, and vice versa. Again, their accounts are factually true—but highly selective, a particular spin or interpretation on the events that took place.

In the words of Jerome Bruner (1993, p. 46), all autobiographical accounts possess "both verisimilitude and negotiability." As for verisimilitude, there are the "bare bones" of the events themselves, not subject to interpretation. Did these events take place or didn't they? For certain purposes, the verisimilitude of these bare bones matters. In autobiography, explains Bruner, there are "matters of consensual public record to be taken into account" (p. 46). Certain versions of a life are constrained by the events that take place in the material world. Just as ignoring matters of record makes bad history, subverting the factual record makes bad autobiography. Setting aside or falsifying the bare bones of a life lends an aura of unbelievability to autobiographical accounts.

Thus, an autobiographical account by a supposed alcoholic would make no sense whatsoever if he or she had really been drinking grape juice all those years rather than bourbon. (An interesting tall tale—but not the account of an alcoholic!) One account by a man claiming to be a devotee of homosexual S&M "leather" sex would be utter nonsense as autobiography if he were actually a happily married heterosexual who engaged only in "missionary" intercourse with his wife. (Imagination, yes; verisimilitude, no.) And if a woman weighing a svelte

120 pounds wrote about her life as an obese woman, her account would make no autobiographical sense as a rendition of her lived experiences. We would be forced to say, as Bruner does when the autobiographer's account is alienated from the bare bones of his or her life: "It just doesn't make sense" (1993, p. 47).

Many of the assertions contained in autobiographical accounts can be checked against the documentary record: photographs; hospital records; employment records; school records; college transcripts; physicians', psychiatrists' and psychologists' diagnoses; arrest records; prison records; DNA tests; blood and urine tests; and so on. In addition, we are free to consult coparticipants in the events being described to seek independent confirmation. Many autobiographical claims are unmasked as false after the historical record is checked. And for many autobiographical accounts, the question of whether the narrated events actually took place is important and interesting. After all, if some people really were abducted by extraterrestrials (Mack, 1995), the world would be a very different place from the way it is had those stories been imagined or invented. But for most narratives, literal facticity is not the most interesting issue. Once again, the reader assumes a core of verisimilitude.

There is negotiability in autobiographical accounts as well as verisimilitude. What explains the "same events, different accounts" phenomenon? Here again, slant, emphasis, and focus loom large. People's experience and narration of the same set of events vary one from the other. In other words, there are personal, idiosyncratic reasons why we select certain features of our experience to recall and tell others about. In addition, there are cultural reasons why events are rendered in a certain way. For instance, during the nineteenth century or Victorian era, matters dealing with sex were much less likely to be narrated in autobiographies than is true today. Certain features of one's past are considered more, versus less, appropriate to recollect and tell others about, again, depending on the cultural norms of one's social group and historical time period.

How do people define and experience unconventionality? What is the experience of being stigmatized? How do conventionals regard, think about, and act toward persons whom they define as socially unacceptable? And how do such experiences shape the content of the accounts that these persons contribute? These and other questions can be addressed in deviance accounts.

ETHICAL ISSUES IN THE STUDY OF DEVIANCE: TEAROOM SEX, A CASE STUDY

In the 1960s, sociology graduate student (and Episcopal priest) Laud Humphreys decided to conduct a participant observation study of sexual transactions in "tearooms." A tearoom is a public urinal where anonymous male homosexual contact is common. Humphreys was acquainted with an inside informant, a man who frequented tearooms—"David." Humphreys assumed a nonsexual role in his study, that of "watchqueen"—or a lookout who observes when the police or strangers approach a restroom, then warns the persons inside who are participating in sexual activities. During the course of his study, Humphreys observed 134 sexual encounters in urinals and recorded and wrote up his observations in the form of a doctoral dissertation and a classic book, *Tearoom Trade* (Humphreys, 1970). As we might expect, the research on which the book was based was extremely controversial; among other things, by conducting his research in the way he did it, Humphreys was accused of violating the sociologist's code of ethics. One faculty member at Washington University was so outraged by Humphreys' research that a verbal altercation between them escalated into a fistfight.

Most sociologists who commented on the research regarded Humphreys' research unethical, less because of his observation of homosexual encounters in public toilets than because of the deception he used in his follow-up interview study. He wrote down the license plates of cars parked near the urinal he studied (it was located in a public park accessible to vehicular traffic) and convinced a police officer that he was conducting market research and needed to obtain the addresses of the owners of these cars. A year after his observational study, he interviewed 50 of the men who had participated in the sexual acts he observed. (None remembered him.) Why was this unethical? Because Humphreys lied to his interviewees. He told them he was conducting an innocuous social health survey, not a survey about homosexual behavior. (Remember, this study took place in the 1960s, when rules about such matters were more lax than they are today.) In fact, in the interview, he did not deal with the topic of homosexual behavior at all. Many sociologists believe that deceiving one's interviewees, informants, or subjects is seriously unethical and should not be done in any study social scientists conduct. Says Kai Erikson, "it is unethical for a sociologists to deliberately misrepresent the character of the research in which he [or she] is engaged" (1967, p. 373). Nonsociologists, including journalists and university administrators, were also distressed by the fact that Humphreys hung around public toilets and watched homosexuals engage in oral copulation. The book received a torrent of criticism for its supposed unethical research methods. Five years after Humphreys' study was published, a new edition appeared (1975) which reprinted a few of the criticisms it received. These comments summarize much of the opposition to the deception in which the researcher engaged.

Donald Warwick, a social scientist writing in an academic journal devoted to discussions of "ethics and the life sciences" (1973), accused Humphreys of "deception, invasions of privacy, and harmful uses" of his research findings. The researcher, he says, was guilty of a "concatenance of misrepresentation and disguises [that] . . . must surely hold the world record for field research." Humphreys lied to his respondents about a half-dozen matters, including deceiving them about the reason he was conducting his survey, the fact that he had tracked down their names and addresses as a result of obtaining confidential records, and, implicitly, the fact that he already knew that they had engaged in homosexual acts in a public urinal. All in all, says Warwick, the costs of Humphreys' deception to human freedom, to privacy, to his informants and interviewees, and to social science as a whole were too great; the study should never have been conducted in the way it was done. Arlene Kaplan Daniels claims that "no one in the society deserves to be trusted with hot, incriminating data. Let me repeat, no one" (quoted in Glazer, 1975, p. 219). And in a textbook on research methods, sociologist Myron Glazer states that he would "attempt to dissuade others" from the research path that Humphreys followed.

> The dangers to respondents, to the researcher, and to the precious sense of respect for the privacy of others seem too great for the returns. Had Humphreys faltered, had his data been secured by police officials or unscrupulous blackmailers, Humphreys would have been branded a rogue and a fool. (Glazer, 1975, p. 220)

Are these critics correct? In 1968 and again in 1997, the American Sociological Association (ASA) issued policy statements stipulating that sociologists should not conduct research "without the informed consent of subjects." It also issued qualifications; "waivers" may be obtained under certain circumstances. Institutional Review Boards (IRBs) pass judgments concerning the "protection of human subjects," including the matter of deception. Had there been an IRB in place in Washington University when Humphreys conducted his study (1965–1968), its committee most decidedly would not have permitted him to do it the way he did. On the other hand, the actual membership of the ASA is more divided on the issue. Two sociologists (Long and Dorn, 1983) conducted a survey of ASA members and found that 6 out of 10 agreed with the statement: "It is ethically acceptable for sociologists to deceive research subjects and to expose them to temporary 'harm' so long as care is taken to eliminate long-term post-research effects" (1983, p. 293). According to Long and Dorn, sociologists favored neither "restrictions in research in the name of ethics, nor did they favor unrestricted research—an apparent inconsistency" (1983, p. 293). What are sociologists willing to do about unethical research? Long and Dorn's data suggest "not too much"—except write and talk about the subject (1983, p. 297).

Many sociologists, including the Adlers (Adler, Adler, and Rochford, 1986), Jack Douglas (1976), and myself (Goode, 1996), are not as distressed about these ethical issues as Humpreys' critics are. It is true that Humphreys did not debrief his informants and interviewees about the true nature of his research. However, he did take extreme measures to ensure their anonymity, to make sure that their names would not fall into anyone's hands. Von Hoffman, a journalist, compares "sociological snoopers" to police undercover agents, but he ignores the fact that the police do take names and have one purpose in mind—to make arrests—whereas sociologist keep identities anonymous and names a secret, and are dedicated to ensuring that no one is ever arrested as a result of their research. As we saw, Daniels claims that no one in our society should be entrusted with "hot, incriminating evidence," but in fact, journalists, psychiatrists and psychologists, physicians, and the clergy (not to mention inadvertent observers and bystanders) do have such information. And sociologists are the only profession among this list whose practitioners are not involved in pinning such evidence to specific persons. Instead, they are more or less exclusively involved in depicting patterns and drawing generalizations from such "evidence"—without the names of specific persons.

In my view, a democratic society can afford to tolerate a little snooping from a tiny number of researchers engaging in controversial research methods for the purpose of disseminating findings about unconventional behavior. To close down such behavior would have a chilling effect on the freedom of expression guaranteed by the Constitution. It would in fact make this society a more repressive, boring, and stultifying—and less free—place in which to live. And yet, I must emphasize, all human behavior should be guided by a sense of moral conviction, and this behavior includes social research. The researcher of deviance and crime is faced with moral and ethical dilemmas. Once we admit that IRBs typically protect the interests of the university at the expense of the interests of social researchers, and once we agree that if researchers were to follow the law to the letter of the law, a great deal of controversial research would be prohibited and we'd be restricted to the study of polite, inoffensive, namby-pamby, and distinctly nondeviant behavior.

SUMMARY

Deviance is a subject whose study poses special problems but, at the same time, yields special rewards. The subject has been studied by means of a variety of research methodologies. Some are quantitative, that is, they generate data that are easily measured, that can be reduced to numbers and statistics. Others are by their very nature qualitative, that is, they produce data that are not easily reduced to numbers but reside in the form of apposite and revealing quotes, metaphors, and examples. Survey methods, laboratory experiments, and the use of official data tend to be quantitative. In contrast, participant observation or field methods and autobiographical accounts tend to be qualitative. A method that entails the close examination of texts or cultural documents—content analysis—can be conducted in such a way that the researcher generates both quantitative and qualitative data.

Information generated by government agencies for administrative purposes is referred to as "official" data. Sociologists often use such data for theoretical, descriptive, and analytic purposes. Three major sources of data used by sociologists of deviance, crime, and drug use are the Uniform Crime Reports (UCR), DAWN, and ADAM. The Uniform Crime Reports are tabulations made by the FBI of crimes reported to the police and arrests that take place each year in nearly all the police jurisdictions in the United States. Clearly, neither crimes reported to the police nor arrests accurately reflect the actual commission of crime, and so sociologists and criminologists have figured out limited ways of using these flawed data. DAWN examines both nonlethal and lethal drug overdoses in urban areas around the country; such tabulation tell us a thing or two about changes in drug abuse over time as well as how dangerous and widely abused different drugs are. ADAM looks at drug use among arrestees. It tells us about the strong relationship between drug abuse and criminal behavior as well as regional differences in the use of various drugs.

The survey method represents the most important and prominent methodology for sociologists in general as well as for many positivistic criminologists, but it is not as important for the sociologists who study deviance. Ideally, surveys are conducted on large, randomized samples that represent a cross-section of the country as a whole. Researchers have attempted to ensure that the answers of their respondents are honest and that the response rate of their surveys is high. The National Crime Victimization Survey (NCVS), the NSDUH, and Monitoring the Future are three of the most important government surveys that sociologists rely on to understand deviant behavior. Most survey researchers go beyond a simple description of the social world; they want to explain why things are the way they are. They establish cause-and-effect explanations by controlling for or holding constant the relevant variables. However, survey methods are not ideal for the study of all, and possibly most, deviant phenomena. Attitudes held by the general public about deviant behavior are one possible subject that is amenable to the survey method, as is the study of crime victimization, sexual behavior, and drug use. Still, many other subjects require too large a sample or involve too touchy a subject to be amenable to survey methods.

Participant observation entails the direct, face-to-face observation of the intimate, day-to-day lives of informants in their natural habitat. It is a method that is based on getting as close to the people one is studying as possible, being with them around the clock, and engaging in as much of their behavior as ethics and legality will allow. This method generates mountains of rich descriptive data, called field notes. The many observations by the researcher, and behavior and statements by the informants, maximize validity, or the confidence that what the sociologist observes is true. But the scene, the group, or the social circle selected by the researcher may not be typical or representative of such scenes, groups, or circles in general. Some field-workers prefer to be observers only and do not participate in the behavior under study; others prefer to participate in the behavior under study.

Narratives, autobiographies, life histories, and personal accounts represent a major means of studying deviant scenes. In the past, personal statements by subjects were looked at as valuable only insofar as they were factually truthful. However, more recent researchers have focused on the social construction of life stories—what is included and what is left out, the slant of a particular narrator. Contrary to what some commentators have argued, literal facticity cannot be dismissed as irrelevant. Nonetheless, it is not the only issue; indeed, how life histories are told has been the central focus of most researchers who use this research method. The study of vocabularies of motive or techniques of deviance neutralization probably represents the most interesting line of inquiry of this particular methodology.

Since the 1960s, researchers and university administrators have been increasingly interested in the matter of research ethics. (Actually, IRBs are more concerned about preventing their parent institution from being sued than the rights of human subjects, but that is another matter.) Central to the official interpretation of research ethics are the twin matters of informed consent and deception. A strict interpretation of ethics requires that all subjects, informants, and interviewees be informed as to exactly what the researcher is doing, what his or her aims are: The strict ethicist regards any deception or disguised observation as unacceptable. Not all researchers agree. A survey of the members of the ASA revealed that most sociologists regard deception as acceptable under certain circumstances. According to the strictest interpretation of research ethics, as interpreted by most IRBs, the majority of participant observation studies on deviance would be quite literally impossible since researchers cannot inform each and every person they observe from moment to moment what they are up to. Indeed, had they been operative at the time, university IRBs would not have permitted most of the classic participant observation studies discussed in this chapter to have been conducted, and that includes Patricia Adler's study of drug dealers and Laud Humphreys' study of tearoom sex. Many conservative university administrations—and not a few sociologists—do not feel this would represent a great loss to scholarship. I do not agree, and have argued that IRB regulations are too restrictive to accommodate much valuable research on deviance (Goode, 1996).

Account: Public Reactions to Norm Violations

Field experiments represent a rarely used method of social research in the sociology of deviance. Nonetheless, they can be an interesting and productive means of studying normative violations. One technique is to engage in behavior openly and publicly and observe and then record the reactions of witnesses or audiences. Whenever actions consistently elicit negative reactions, we know we have a case of deviance on our hands. By varying the conditions of the experiment, we can test the factors that elicit, versus those that do not elicit, negative reactions. Are onlookers more likely to chastise a man, as opposed to a woman, for a given normative violation? Do they chastise women more for certain violations? Are the residents of cities more likely to chastise norm violators than residents of small towns? These and other questions can be addressed by the field experiment. I got the idea of assigning the following field experiment from R. H. Potter, who assigned it to the students in his deviance courses at the University of New England, Australia (1999).

Here are the instructions I gave to my students:

> *You will commit a deviant act in a public place, or have someone else commit a deviant act in a public place. You will observe, record, and write in detail the reactions you observed to the deviant act. Engage in the act again, in another public place, varying systematically from the first in some meaningful way. For instance, do the same thing—same act, two different settings—on a college campus versus in a shopping mall; in a very public place versus only in the presence of a few friends who do not know you are engaging in an experiment; indoors versus outdoors; in a city (D.C. or Baltimore) versus a small town; etc. Interview people who have observed or reacted to your unconventional behavior and ask them why they reacted as they did, or how they feel about your behavior if they did not react, or why they didn't react at all. Analyze these reactions by using the theoretical, analytic, or conceptual perspective(s) you believe best explain(s) or illuminate(s) the act. Possible issues to discuss: Why did you expect this act to be deviant in this particular setting? Why did the people react as they did? Any interesting observations? Deviant reactions? Did these reactions and/or your analysis give you any insight into the processes of deviance and social control? Did the settings you chose make any difference? Be as detailed in your descriptions as you can. Possible deviant behaviors: eating at the dinner table with your hands; wearing bizarre clothes; attempting to haggle over price in a store that sells items for a fixed price; standing in a particular spot and reading aloud from a book; standing in a particular spot and staring intently at nothing in particular; ostentatiously picking your nose; swearing repeatedly; drinking water out of a vodka bottle or tea out of a whiskey bottle; standing in front of a class in which you are not enrolled as the lecture is about to begin and staring vacantly into space; smoking in a non-smoking area; constantly interrupting someone in an ordinary conversation or asking for clarification for simple, commonplace words; walk backwards through the campus; etc. I'm sure you can think of others.*
>
> *Under no circumstances are you to do, or ask someone to do, anything that could be construed as dangerous or criminal. I will not bail you out if you are arrested, or serve as a character witness at your trial. (Potter, 1999)*

At the University of Maryland, during one semester, I received a half-dozen papers from students who chose this option. An example of one of these papers follows.

Field Experiment: Two Guys Holding Hands in Public

Steven M. Clayton

Randy, my best friend, and I conducted our field experiment in New York City. My study centered on the notion that we were homosexual partners. My goal was to demonstrate that fact to the people who saw us in the public places where we carried out our project, and to observe

(Continued)

Account: Public Reactions to Norm Violations Continued

their reaction and interview them about how they felt about what we did. We conducted this study in two locations. One was in public on 42nd Street, in Times Square in midtown Manhattan. The other site was in a restaurant in Greenwich Village in downtown Manhattan. In a city as diverse as New York, we were eager to observe and understand the reactions of people on the street when they saw what was depicted as homosexual tendencies and behavior.

We hit the streets on November 3rd. We began by walking along 42nd Street, holding hands—holding one another more closely than friends hold one another. Throughout that day, we were never more than a few feet from each other. We also drank from the same soda cup and shared food from a hot dog vendor on the street. It was our hope that these actions showed to the people around us that we were homosexual partners. Our aim was to determine what their naturalistic reactions would be to our (perceived) acts of homosexuality.

Throughout the day we got many different reactions from different people. Some of them seemed unfazed by our behavior. We even had a few people come up and wish us good luck in our relationship. However, the great majority of the people we observed reacted negatively. One reaction that stands out above the rest was when we saw a mother pull her children away from us, yelling "Didn't I tell you to stay away from these type of people!" A substantial number of others didn't say a word to us but gave us dirty looks and stares.

One middle-aged man came up to us and stated, "You know what you are doing is wrong." When I asked him if I could ask a few questions, I was pleasantly surprised when he accepted the offer. The first question I asked was, "Do you find homosexual acts to be deviant?" The man replied, "To be frankly honest, yes I do. Well, at least in public areas such as this. What you do behind your bedroom doors is none of my damn business, but don't come out here to corrupt the straight, moral ones in our society!" Then I asked him a follow-up question: "By engaging in such actions in public how do you feel we are corrupting society?" The man replied: "History will teach you that every action people engage in is done for copycat reasons. Heck, the reason why you and your buddy over there are gay is probably because of some fucked up stuff you saw in your childhood. At least have the morals not to do the same stuff to the millions of people walking every day in this congested area."

I also had the opportunity to interview one of the women who wished us good luck in our relationship. I asked her the same question as I asked the gentleman: "Do you find homosexual acts to be deviant?" Her response was very interesting. She said: "I would have to say yes, I do believe that homosexuality and homosexual actions are indeed deviant, from my perspective. However, who am I to tell you what you can and can't do. It's your life, so I wish you the best of luck in whatever endeavors you choose to pursue, whether I may personally approve of them or not."

I expected the perceived homosexual acts that Randy and I were engaging in to be deviant, in Times Square particularly, because of the very large crowd of people there. By sheer probability alone, there being a range of different perspectives on homosexuality, chances were that someone would react in almost any imaginable way. Still, the majority in our society in the present day view homosexual acts in public as deviant. I felt comfortable that in a crowd or a space that large, we would have little trouble drawing reactions from people who thought the perceived homosexual acts we supposedly engaged in were deviant. . . .

Our second day of the project brought us downtown to Greenwich Village. This time, instead of being on the street, we did our study in a restaurant that was about six blocks from New York University. We engaged in many of the same activities that we had on the street in Times Square, such as holding hands, being physically close to one another, drinking out of the same cup, and so on. However, we did add a few activities.

Part of the reason why we were drawn to Greenwich Village was that we understood that the area had a high percentage of homosexuals and that overt homosexual acts in public were accepted much more than they would be had they taken place in other locations in New York. We were curious to see if this theory was correct. For the most part, it was. We received many fewer dirty looks or stares than we did on 42nd Street and more people communicated feely regarding homosexual issues and asked questions on the supposed homosexual relationship that my friend and I were having. However, it should be noted that we did receive some negative reactions, especially from one tourist in particular. In fact, we experienced something of an altercation. I'll describe his reaction momentarily.

The first person I interviewed happened to be a gay male who lived in the Village. I was intrigued to have at least one of my interviews to be with a homosexual, since I felt it vital and necessary to get their perspective in my study. I asked him, "Did many people who are regular customers of this restaurant regard public acts of homosexuality as deviant?" He responded: "Most people in the area don't give it a second thought, since it [homosexuality] has become such an important and vibrant part of the Village community." He went on to say: "You [referring to homosexuals] will always be safe here." I then asked him: "Do you believe that is why the Village has such a high population of homosexuals—because of the established success of homosexuals in the past and possible support networks here that wouldn't be found in other places?" The man answered: "To be honest, that is why I came here. I'm from Toronto, so I wasn't even an American at birth. The Village, however, can honestly be viewed . . . as a Disney World for gays and lesbians."

Not all reactions we received were quite as positive, however. A tourist from Oklahoma approached us and yelled at us, "This is hell and you fools are the Devil's servants! Burn in hell, you cocksuckers!" Somehow, I summoned up the courage to ask this gentleman if I could ask him a few questions in an attempt to understand his perspective. He agreed, his hope being for him to save us, to convert us to moral and productive heterosexuals. That way, he said, we could be "one of God's loving children." The first question I asked him was: "What is your reason for your feelings toward homosexuals?" He responded: "Well, the truth is that those of you, who are different from the result of us, started off as God's children, but you fell along the path. You are not to blame—it is because of your stupid culture. From where I am from [Oklahoma], we have such things as values and morals that will not allow one of us to stray such as you folks have." The second question I asked him was, "Saying that New York culture is to blame, would that prevent you from doing anything more than simply to visit as a tourist?" His answer was: "Most definitely yes. Come on, honestly, how am I supposed to raise my family and try to teach them what is right and moral in God's eyes, when all of this [homosexuality] is going on around us? That would fight the good my wife and I instill in our children."

Negative reactions to our actions gave Randy and me an inside look into the workings of social control. Like many forms of deviance, homosexuality and homosexual behavior for the most part are perfectly legal. They are in New York State. So, forms of social control other than the police and the courts are used to effect social control. Homosexual acts are controlled by informal means, such as receiving the negative reactions we observed and even threats from individuals. This certainly operates in public areas, as we found out.

But on the other hand, the proportion of people who don't seem bothered at all by homosexuality, or those who respond positively, has increased because of the influence of gay liberation in the 1990s. We expected that in Greenwich Village, but to be honest, we were surprised that we found some similar feedback in Times Square as well. Before the gay liberation movement, you would rarely if ever see anyone engaging in homosexual acts in public. Today, one can go to almost any major city and observe the kind of behavior that Randy and I exhibited on those November days in New York City. It can be that exposure of homosexuality to the majority is beginning to overcome the preconceived stereotypes and produced more favorable reactions toward homosexuality and homosexual behavior.

(*Continued*)

Account: Public Reactions to Norm Violations Continued

There are also sociological reasons why some people gave us bad looks or stares as well as the negative feedback we received to our supposed homosexual behavior. There are still many who view homosexuality as a major sin. Thus, when they see such behavior, it causes them to condemn such acts and even speak against or abuse persons who engage in those acts. A significant proportion of this country, especially those living in rural areas of the South and the Midwest, view homosexuality in a very negative and very deviant light. This prompts them to openly condemn the people they perceive as homosexuals. The belief that homosexuality is the ultimate sin has been spurred on by fundamentalist Christians such as Jerry Falwell, who said: "What was considered a deviant lifestyle is now considered by many Americans to be an alternatively lifestyle. . . . The entire homosexual movement is an indictment against America and is contributing to its ultimate downfall" (1996, p. 13). It is no wonder that some people condemned us openly and publicly.

Another reason we elicited the negative reactions we received was that there is a great deal of negative, anti-homosexual literature out there in American society, educating the way the public thinks about the matter. For instance, as Mary McIntosh said of the male homosexual, as of the 1960s, in American culture, there is "the expectation that sexuality will play a part of some kind in all his relations with other men, and the expectation that that he will be attracted to boys and very young men, and probably willing to seduce them" (1968, p. 185). It is through such beliefs, which are passed on through the media, that express negative images of the homosexual lifestyle and thus in turn this influences how they would react to us engaging in perceived homosexual acts on the street. Such media and religious influences that cast a negative light on homosexuals and homosexuality combine to produce a negative and sustained stigma. Many of the negative reactions we got were as a result of this stigma that people have entrenched in their minds. They don't even have to think about it before coming to a negative judgment on the actions they saw my friend and me supposedly engage in. . . . The tourist from Oklahoma felt we were deliberately offending God and heaven by engaging in our supposed homosexual acts. . . .

With respect to the question, "What makes our actions deviant?" the answer is that the majority perceives the actions as deviant and reacts to them negatively. If the act were not deviant, people would not have condemned us for what they thought we were doing. From both a normative and a reactive perspective, what we were doing was deviant. We violated the majority's norms about proper sexuality and many condemned us for it. That makes what we did deviant.

In conclusion, this study was very compelling for Randy and me. Being straight men who are not personally bothered by seeing homosexual acts, we were given a unique and inside view on how overt homosexuals are treated on a daily basis. We found that while there were some positive reactions, and some places were better suited for our activities than others, it is difficult to engage in those activities and not face a harsh backlash. . . . Should homosexual acts be considered deviant? We don't think it should, but clearly others disagree. All the different opinions we got to that question were extremely interesting.

QUESTIONS

Do you think that Steve Clayton's experiment is an interesting method of investigating whether and to what extent homosexuality is deviant? What other methods might be used? Of the methods discussed in this chapter, which one is most productive? Or is any one most productive in the abstract? Are some methods more productive for certain purposes, and others more productive in different ways? Can you imagine yourself conducting research on deviance by using one or more of the research methods we looked at here? Which one might be the most enjoyable and interesting to conduct? Of the many forms of deviance you can think of, which one would you most like to study? Which research method would you use?

CHAPTER

5

Criminal Behavior: An Introduction

Two men, drinking in a bar, begin an argument that escalates to mutual shoving and shouting. Outside, on the sidewalk, one pulls out a knife, the other smashes a whiskey bottle against a lamppost; within minutes, one of them lies dead in the gutter. At a party, a dozen people in their twenties sit in a circle and snort cocaine, brought by one of the guests. A waiter uses the credit card number of a customer to charge tens of thousands dollars worth of merchandise against the cardholder's account. A man meets a woman in a bar and she agrees to go home with him; in the car, he parks, holds a knife to her throat, and sexually assaults her. At a meeting, the executives of a factory discuss and then agree to violate the state's antipollution laws; over the following months, their factory releases toxic chemicals into a nearby stream.

Are these crimes? How do we know? Who decides? And what's the relationship between crime and deviance?

In the study of crime and deviance, for the most part, American sociologists have followed a rough division of labor. In most American college and university curricula, courses designated with "deviance" or "deviant" in the title tend to examine a subject matter that's different from yet overlaps with courses the department lists on crime. In contrast, for British sociologists, the two subjects overlap much more heavily; there, not infrequently, the words "crime" and "deviance" appear together in a book's title (Downes and Rock, 2007).

If we were to look at the study of deviance and crime, taken as a whole, we'd notice three distinctive emphases.

First, we'd see the emphasis of the positivist criminologists. The majority of criminologists focus on "hard" or "high consensus" deviance—those activities the enactment of which is likely to result in arrest and imprisonment, such as robbery, rape, murder, and burglary. In the United States, criminology has been dubbed the Eastern school of deviance (Ben-Yehuda, 1985, pp. 3–4) because many of its practitioners received their training, or much of its research has been conducted, or many of its researchers have been located, on the East Coast of the United States, at such institutions as the University of Pennsylvania, the State University of New York at Albany, the University of Maryland, and the University of Delaware. Most practitioners of this school are positivists; they generally adopt a natural science model and study criminal behavior by means of official police statistics, formal interviews, questionnaire studies of crime victims, and self-report crime surveys. As we learned in the first two chapters, the central issue in the natural science model adopted by criminology is *etiology,* or the cause or causes of criminal behavior. "Why do they do it?" is the central concern of its practitioners; *explanation* is their game. This field is very large. Over 4,000 criminologists subscribe to the field's flagship journal *Criminology,* and in the United States each year, more than a quarter of a million students enroll in introductory criminology.

A second emphasis of researchers of deviance and crime is that adopted by Marxists, radicals, and critical theorists. In the language of Chapter 3, they are constructionists, but of a certain sort. They are mainly interested not so much in criminal behavior as the processes adopted by the ruling elite to control persons and behavior the elite's members regard as troublesome. This perspective is a top-down approach: Rules and laws issue from the most powerful strata of the society, they say, because that strata's representatives aim to protect their own material and ideological interests. National alcohol prohibition (1920–1933) was instituted because the capitalist elite wished to maintain an efficient, hard-working labor force; Prohibition failed because the capitalist elite was fearful that widespread violations of the liquor laws would create disrespect for the law and, hence, subvert the capitalist system (Rumbarger, 1989). The vagrancy laws passed in England in the 1300s and the 1500s were designed, in the earlier era, to protect the interests of the powerful landowning class by keeping peasants on the land, and in the latter era, to protect the growing merchant class by keeping rogues and idlers who might rob carriers of goods on the highways (Chambliss, 1964). Even academic *theories* of crime and deviance are designed to protect the interests of the rich and the powerful (Quinney, 1979; Sumner, 1994). Or so these radical criminologists have argued. This radical and Marxist school of deviance and crime studies has declined in importance since the 1970s; many of its previous advocates have given up their original approach and adopted a very different one (such as contrology, discussed in Chapter 3, and postmodernism, a perspective in the humanities), while others have died or retired.

A third emphasis in research on deviance and crime is adopted by sociologists who study deviance *as opposed to crime.* Some have referred to this emphasis as the Western (Ben-Yehuda, 1985, pp. 3–4) or the Chicago/California school (Petrunik, 1980) because many of its practitioners teach or taught at the University of Chicago, Northwestern, and the University of California. It is mainly inhabited by social constructionists, and its researchers usually focus on "soft" or "low-consensus" deviance, that is, behavior that may (or may not) be technically against the law but is unlikely to lead to arrest, being punished mainly informally, unofficially, and interpersonally. Examples of such behavior include alcoholism, marijuana use, homosexuality, being tattooed, nude dancing, and prostitution. In addition to deviant *behavior,* members of this school have examined unconventional beliefs, mental disorder, and undesirable physical characteristics. Even when its practitioners look at criminal behavior, they mainly do so not from the perspective of what causes it, but at its social definitions, meanings, and interpretations. More generally, regardless of what generates it, practitioners of this, the Western or Chicago/California, school tend to investigate the creation of deviant categories, deviant stereotypes, deviant identities; being socialized into deviant subcultures and deviant careers; deviants' justifications, explanations, or accounts of their behavior; and their adjustment to labeling and stigma. And they usually conduct their research by means of participant observation (or anthropological, ethnographic methods) and qualitative interviews. Adler and Adler's book, *Constructions of Deviance* (2009), offers examples here, as do the essays in Rubington and Weinberg's *Deviance: The Interactionist Perspective* (2007) and (though decreasingly) most of the articles in the journal *Deviant Behavior.*

I have followed this division of labor by focusing mainly on deviance and only secondarily on crime. In the study of deviance, we are more interested in the exercise of *informal* sanctions than formal: How deviant categories are created, how persons are classified and reacted to as deviants, how they cope and deal with those social reactions, and how they experience what they do. To the extent that the study of crime focuses on the etiology of crime and the machinery of the criminal justice system, the fact is there is another field that studies these matters—criminology—and dozens of textbooks that discuss them. The sociology of deviance is not coterminous with the field of criminology. The two fields study different although overlapping phenomena. Hence, the approach I adopt in this book and the topics I cover will more resemble the landscape laid out by the Western or Chicago/California school of deviance (the constructionists) than the Eastern school of criminology (the criminological positivists).

Some critics claim that the topics covered by deviance texts are too repetitive with the topics that are covered in criminology texts (Bader, Becker, and Desmond, 1996). Approximately half the behavioral topics discussed in many such texts, these critics say, deal with criminal acts. The instructor of deviance should ensure that students do not receive the same information in both courses (p. 319). They suggest that a discussion of the usual crimes be dropped and propose a wider range of noncriminal but deviant phenomena be substituted, including unconventional political and religious beliefs, a variety of conditions, both psychic (mental illness) and physical (obesity, physical disability, AIDS, etc.), nudism, homelessness, and suicide.

One reason why all crime cannot be dropped out of deviance texts is that certain concepts that center on defining deviance—deviant labeling, stigma, acquiring an unconventional identity, the neutralization of deviant definitions, deviant careers, and exiting from deviance—are as relevant for legal violations (that is, crimes) as for normative violations (deviance). In making a point about a *concept,* it may be necessary to refer to its relevance to certain types of criminal *behavior.* Benson's "Denying the Guilty Mind" (1985) discusses how white-collar criminals explain or justify their involvement in the behavior for which they were convicted and imprisoned. Hence, that article is *primarily* about deviance neutralization, and only technically and *secondarily* about white-collar crime. The same applies to Scully and Marolla's "Convicted Rapists' Vocabulary of Motive" (1984): The *subject* is rape—a criminal act—but the relevant analytic *concept* is deviance neutralization. Excising the deviance curriculum from the criminology curriculum cannot be achieved at the expense of cutting out major conceptual and theoretical tissue (Kunkel, 1999).

When the focus is on theoretical and analytical concepts, the subjects' deviance and crime only superficially discuss the same topics. They discuss the same topics *from a different point of view.* Crime can be discussed *as a form of deviance,* which is different from discussing it *as crime.* The etiological and criminal justice adjudication of cases of rape are topics that belong to the field of criminology; the social construction of rape and the stigma that attaches to the rapist—and the rape victim—are more likely to be investigated by sociologists of deviance. Moreover, crime is a form of deviance—a specific *type* of deviance—because it generates condemnation and punishment. Crime elicits both formal and informal condemnation, and so, it deserves at least some discussion in any deviance text. A study of conventional crime—that is, the kinds of criminal acts that come to mind when the word crime is encountered—is instructive for both the positivist and the constructionist. Crime is both an objective reality whose causes and consequences can be investigated *and* a concept that people have in their heads, a subject about which people talk and try to do something. At once, crime is both objectively (that is, essentialistically) and conceptually real. Hence, it is of interest both to the positivist and the constructionist.

CRIME AND DEVIANCE: A CONCEPTUAL DISTINCTION

A substantial number of deviant acts are also criminal. In the United States, however, deviant beliefs and conditions are not crimes. In addition, many deviant acts are not against the law. For instance, obesity, being a creep, a loser, a geek, a dweeb, an eccentric, an atheist, and an alcoholic are all deviant—but they are not crimes. In other words, crime is not a precondition for deviance.

What about the other way around? Are all crimes deviant? Most of the conventional or mainstream public regards having been convicted of and, even more so, imprisoned for a crime, as stigmatizing. True, in some social circles, being an ex-convict brings a certain measure of hip, edgy, romantic cachet. But the more conventional the audience, the more discrediting someone having been imprisoned is likely to be regarded. In that sense, yes—though, again, crime is not a defining criterion of deviance—criminality is one specific *type* of deviance. By itself, *being* a criminal is deviant because it can stigmatize a person in the eyes of some others.

But *independent* of its stigmatizing character, is violating the criminal code a form of deviance? Are laws a type of norm the violation of which constitutes deviance? Sociologists answer this question in two different ways.

First, a broad definition of deviance sees *any and all* punishing or condemnatory reactions—regardless of whether it comes from a friend or the criminal justice system—as the defining criterion of deviance. According to this definition, a crime is a violation of one *specific* kind of norm—a law—which generates formal sanctions, state-supported sanctions, including prosecution, conviction, and imprisonment. Clearly then, according to this definition, *all* crime is deviant. (Of course, some laws are not enforced; hence, they are not actionable crimes in the sense that their violation does not generate formal sanctions.) But again, the reverse does not hold: Crime does not define deviance. Instead, this definition sees laws as a *type* of norm, and criminal punishment a type of condemnation or punishment. Hence, crime is a *form* or *subtype* of deviance. Crime is *sufficient* for deviance to exist, but it is not *necessary.*

A second, somewhat different, definition of deviance is offered by other observers. By this definition, deviance is *solely and exclusively* informal and interpersonal in nature, while crime is *specifically* the violation of formal norms and, hence, is conceptually *separate* and *distinct* from deviance. According to this definition, crime is *not* deviance. Crime and deviance are two different and separate phenomena. Of course, once again, the *informal* stigma that the status of being a criminal tends to generate is a separate matter; to the extent that criminality is stigmatizing, crime is a form of deviance by any definition.

To sum up, then: *One,* criminality is not a *necessary* defining criterion of deviance according to *any* definition. *Two:* To the extent that crime is stigmatizing, it is a form of deviance by *all* definitions. And *three:* According to *some* definitions of deviance, crime is a form or variety of deviance, and according to *others,* crime is separate and distinct from deviance. Clearly, then, deviance and crime intertwine in interesting and important ways. They overlap but imperfectly.

The *analytic* or *theoretical* concepts that run through any course on deviance—and which will run through this book—may also apply to any number of illegal actions. As I've said, such concepts include the social construction of reality, deviance neutralization, vocabularies of motive, stigma, stigma management, condemnation, identity, subculture, moral entrepreneurs, power, social conflict, and contingency. In addition, many theories of deviance are *also* theories of crime, for example, those I discussed in Chapters 2 and 3. The most important thing about both deviance and crime is not the specific details of each activity—important though they be—but the insight that studying them give us concerning how society works. What the study of both deviance and crime is about is primarily the dynamics of normative violations and, ultimately, the glue of social life generally. The details about each form of behavior should serve the concepts, not the other way around.

In short, there is a kind of rough division of labor between the fields of the sociology of crime and the sociology of deviance. By that I mean that different sets of scholars focus on somewhat different subject matters. Specialists in crime, often referred to as criminologists, tend to focus on behavior (almost never beliefs, and *never* physical conditions) that generate *formal* sanctioning, as well as the origin, dynamics, and consequences of the formal sanctioning itself. (Examples: Adler, Laufer, and Mueller, 2006; Siegel, 2008.) In contrast, deviance specialists tend to focus on behavior, beliefs, and conditions that generate *informal* sanctioning, as well as the origin, dynamics, and consequences of the informal sanctioning itself. (Examples: Rubington and Weinberg, 2007; Adler and Adler, 2009.)

COMMON LAW AND STATUTORY LAW

Western society distinguishes two different types of laws—common law (sometimes called "primal" law) and statutory law. Common law stems from ancient custom, tradition, and precedent. Most legal experts regard common law as a set of rules that defines acts as crimes that violate norms that have existed for thousands of years. Common law existed even before societies enacted norms into written statutes. These laws are based on the *unwritten* law (or, later, court decisions *based* on these norms, which were decided on by a courtroom judge rather than adjudicated by a legislature). Laws against murder, robbery, and rape are examples of common or primal law. Their violations are referred to as high-consensus crimes because practically everyone in a given society agrees that laws against them should exist and are valid and legitimate. The implication of common law is that it does not come into being as a result of the pressure of special interest groups, but has the force of tradition behind it. In the United States, nearly all common law has been enacted into statutes enacted by a legislature—a formal body of elected or appointed officials. Nonetheless, violations of these laws had already been punished, with the force of sanction of the society as a whole, long before they were inscribed on paper, parchment, or stone.

The history of common law, then, was a three-step process. First, such laws *began* as tradition (the violations of which were primal crimes); then (at least in England) were codified judicially, in the courtroom, by legal precedent; and finally (at least in the United States), they were enacted into statutory form.

In contrast, laws whose existence *began* as statutes (known collectively as "statutory law") have a history that is completely different from laws that began in the common-law tradition. Most statutory laws refer to crimes for which there are *no* roots in historical or cultural tradition. Most also tend to have less than complete public consensus concerning their legal status. Statutory laws arose because technological change made certain controls necessary (those regulating computer crimes, for instance); because conflict between social categories in the population resulted in the triumph of a more restrictive or moralistic group's views over those of more permissive groups (for instance, the liquor laws); or because social change or innovations or discoveries generate new situations, activities, or substances (such as laws criminalizing the possession and sale of psychoactive substances).

Consider gambling. While many societies developed informal norms concerning gambling, even where they existed, they were often ignored and rarely mobilized the sentiment of the entire community. Our current gambling laws, such as they are, are statutory laws. Only a small percentage of the population feels that gambling should be a crime; in effect, their struggle has been lost. The government permits many forms of gambling, which substantially undermines the possibility of extending the scope and force of any proposed gambling statutes. And gambling laws do not have the reach of thousands of years of tradition behind them. Unlike murder, forcible rape, and robbery, gambling was not always considered a crime; for the past couple of thousand years, gambling was considered a vice that some members of the society engaged in while others didn't, or objected to.

Corporate and white-collar crimes, likewise, do not carry the authority of historical tradition. For the most part, they came to be defined *as crimes* only in the twentieth century and only as a consequence of statutes, that is, the decisions of a legislature. In fact, many of the very activities proscribed by the laws against white-collar crime *did not even exist* three or four decades ago. Many statutes addressing corporate malfeasance are extremely technical, and a violation of them can be understood only as a result of knowledge not available to the general public.

The drug laws, likewise, are statutory in nature. In the United States, except for some local ordinances, most of the drug laws did not exist before the twentieth century. And, although nine out of ten Americans believe that possession and sale of the hard drugs (such as heroin and cocaine) should remain a crime, nearly three-quarters of the public believes that marijuana possessors and users should not be imprisoned. And a majority (about 80%) of the voters believe that the *medical* use of marijuana—by federal law, a crime—should be legal. In short, there is a certain measure of disagreement over the criminal status of many statutory crimes.

Unlike the primal or common law that has come down to us after thousands of years, most illegal behavior defined by a set of statutes (statutory law) is often subject to change over time and may vary from one jurisdiction to another. Prior to 1973, abortion was illegal in the United States; today it is legal. The prolife movement challenges its legitimacy, aiming to return to some form of criminalization. Before the 1930s, the possession and sale of marijuana was legal; after that decade, it became illegal in every jurisdiction in the country. Then, beginning in the 1970s, more than a dozen states decriminalized small-quantity marijuana possession (no arrest, no imprisonment, and no criminal record), and a dozen have made medical marijuana legal. In the early 1960s, homosexual acts between consenting adults were against the law; today, the majority of the states have abolished their laws against such behavior. (Sexual solicitation in a public place, however, is illegal in many jurisdictions.) The legislative status of the sale of alcohol has come full circle over the years, from legal to illegal to legal. Moreover, in each jurisdiction, the absence or presence of a law addressing each of these behaviors is under attack; each one could change at some time in the future. Not possessing the force of tradition behind them, most statutory laws sway with the shifting winds of public opinion or legislative mutations.

However, even for the primal or common-law crimes, a measure of relativity exists (Curra, 2000), not so much with respect to whether the actions are against the law or whether they are considered wrong, but judgments dependent on *when, by whom,* and *under what circumstances* such crimes were presumably committed. By that I mean that ancient societies often permitted one party to inflict harmful actions against another, but punished that same action if inflicted against a different party. For instance, if a man committed forcible or violent intercourse upon a woman, the judgment of the members of a given society as to whether or not it was rape depended on a variety of factors, including the power, social standing, and tribal affiliation of the family of both the man and the woman. Likewise, the killing of the member of a society other than one's own was often considered acceptable—indeed, it may even have been encouraged—but if it involved a member of one's own society, the offender was punished. Moreover, during periods of turmoil and widespread bloodshed—for instance, in Vietnam in the 1960s and early 1970s; Cambodia in the 1970s; Rwanda, Kosovo, Somalia, and Ethiopia in the 1990s; and Liberia in the early part of the twenty-first century—killings on a mass scale have been condoned by the regimes in power or by some sectors of the local populace.

Hence, while primal crimes have existed for thousands of years, the judgment that such a crime took place has varied according to local custom and tradition. Even today, the taking of human life is condoned under certain conditions—for instance, legal execution, warfare, and in some jurisdictions, euthanasia. On one side of a border between Israel and the West Bank and Gaza, a killing is regarded as an act of heroism, and on the other, murder. In Iraq and Afghanistan, is a suicide bomber a murderer? To the relatives of the people he or she killed, and to the authorities in the jurisdiction where the act took place, the answer to this question is obvious: *absolutely!* To many of the bomber's friends, compatriots, political allies, coreligionists, and like-minded conspirators, the answer is equally clear-cut: The act was justified and the actor is a martyr, not a murderer. Murder may be a primal crime, condemned everywhere and at all times, but *what murder is,* is socially constructed.

WHAT IS OUR MISSION? CONSTRUCTIONISM VERSUS POSITIVISM

The fact that even common law crimes are interpreted differently according to who the perpetrator and who the actor are tells us that we can view crime *as* a social construct. It is constructed by definitions—called laws—and interpretations *of* those laws that regard certain actions as unlawful, worthy of punishment, and other actions as acceptable and noncriminal. And, as we saw, even the same action may be regarded as a crime or not a crime because of the circumstances of the act; the constructionist is interested in these circumstances. What makes an act a crime *here,* but a law-abiding action *there?* For certain criminal statutes, consensus does not exist, and the laws change from one decade to another. Looked at as a social construction, legislation is not simply a product of abstract right or wrong but the outcome of conflict, with different segment of the society attempting to gain the upper hand and pass a law favorable to its views and interests. If circumstances were to change, matters could reverse, and the law would be rewritten to reflect that fact. How the laws change, how they are interpreted, how they vary from one jurisdiction and society to another, and how the circumstances of the act and the characteristics of the actor influence arrest, conviction, and incarceration: Answering these questions is the social constructionist's mission.

There is a big *but,* however. Sometimes we hear the phrase, "Everything is relative." With regard to crime, this platitude is not completely true. *In addition* to the relativity we see in what's a crime from one time period to another and from one society to another, there is also a *common core* to crime. As we already know, some crimes have existed—*as punishable offenses*—nearly everywhere and for many thousands of years. Hence, crime remains a mixed bag. Many crimes look very similar the world over, in all societies that exist now or that have ever existed. (But again, just which specific *actions* committed by which specific *actors* against which specific *victims* is highly variable.) Murder is illegal and is prosecuted the world over, just as it has been from the dawn of humanity. But, as I said before, the word *murder* is a loaded term; it refers specifically to a *deviant* and *unlawful* killing. Taking property not one's own by force is regarded as an offense everywhere. (Warfare and violent ethnic conflict often provide an exception; many observers or audiences do not regard such actions against outsiders as criminal.) Having sex by force with a woman, likewise, is criminal behavior in all jurisdictions known to criminologists, though it is not equally vigorously prosecuted everywhere, and whether or not sufficient force or sexual provocation took place is often disputed by an array of audiences. It is true that it is possible to find small, exotic locales or circumstances where these and other such generalizations do not hold, nonetheless, *as a general rule,* there is a set of statutes that exists everywhere, and if violated, arrest, prosecution, and imprisonment are likely to follow. In contrast, consider the fact that such acts as blasphemy, heresy, professing atheism, and practicing a variety of minority religions were crimes during certain times, and remain so in some locales, but have been tolerated at other times and places, and are virtually never prosecuted in the Western world. One of the positivist's missions is the study of the cause of widely criminally prosecuted acts. Behavior that is regarded as criminal just about everywhere is the principal subject matter of the field of criminology. Common core crimes also form the common core of the subject matter of criminology; nearly all criminology textbooks contain one or more chapters on what the Federal Bureau of Investigation (FBI) calls the Index Crimes, in the sections that follow: murder, rape, serious or aggravated assault, robbery, burglary, larceny, and motor vehicle theft.

The majority of criminologists study the causes, consequences, and control of common law or street crimes, acts that are defined as criminal throughout history and in most or nearly all places of human habitation. The FBI collects and publishes information on crimes known to the police, and on arrests. The data on crimes known to the police are collected only for what are referred to as Part I offenses, that is, Index Crimes. The study of the classic street crimes is the meat and potatoes of the positivist's mission, and it makes up the bulk of the field's introductory textbooks. To repeat, most criminologists investigate the causes, consequences, and control of street crimes, principally Index Crimes. In addition, a high proportion of incarcerated offenders have been convicted of, and are serving a sentence for, one or more Index Crimes; moreover, the vast majority of those who were convicted of non-Index Crimes have *also* committed one or more Index Crimes. There is a measure of consistency the world over in what is regarded as street or Index-type Crimes. There is a common core to what's considered criminal behavior; what's regarded as a legally punishable offense is not random, not entirely dependent on the characteristics of the offender, and not completely relative from one time and place to another.

Criminologists *also* study non-Index Crimes. Just because statutes came into existence only in the past century or the past few decades does not mean that their violation is not harmful to the society, or that their understanding is not important for the criminologist's mission. As we saw, drug laws are statutory laws, and understanding the whys and wherefores of substance abuse is just as crucial as understanding why the drug laws came into existence and how they are enforced. Laws governing white-collar and corporate crime are of an even greater impact on the society than the violation of street crime. One of the more interesting facts about the relationship of deviance and crime is that while corporate crime steals more money from, and inflicts more bodily harm on, the public, committing such offenses is not as stigmatizing as engaging in street crime. In a like fashion, organized crime, political crime (such as treason), offenses against children, violations of the laws against weapons possession, driving under the influence, the sale of alcohol to minors, and fraud—none of which are Index Crimes—all have important consequences for the society and are studied by criminologists.

In this and the next chapter, I'll discuss the Index Crimes, the seven crimes the FBI uses to measure crime in general (excluding arson, which very few criminologists consider characteristic enough to be included among the Index Crimes). In the next chapter, I'll discuss three of the four of the violent Index Crimes—these are rape, murder, or criminal homicide, robbery, and aggravated assault—but will briefly summarize them here. We'll look at the three property crimes that are included among the Index Crimes—burglary, motor vehicle theft, and theft—here as well. I'll discuss the so-called public order or moral crimes, mainly drug and alcohol offenses and sex crimes, throughout this book. Each type of crime, in its own way, highlights the relationship between deviance and crime.

THE UNIFORM CRIME REPORTS

We've already been introduced to the FBI's Uniform Crime Reports, in the chapter on research methods. The criminological positivist is usually most interested in studying street crime.

And a substantial proportion of street crime is encapsulated by the seven Index Crimes. The FBI chose seven offenses—Part I offenses or Index Crimes—to represent or indicate crime in general; four violent crimes: murder and "nonnegligent manslaughter," or criminal homicide, forcible rape, robbery, and aggravated assault; and three property crimes: burglary, larceny theft, and motor vehicle theft. (As I said, in 1979, Congress added arson to the list, but also as I said, criminologists do not consider arson indicative of crime in general. They rarely include it in their discussion of Index Crimes, and don't include it in their property crime tabulations.) The seven Index Crimes are *predatory* crimes: They entail one or more parties *victimizing* one or more other parties. Most of the behaviors discussed in this book are not predatory; they are either "crimes without victims" or are not crimes at all.

The FBI's annual *Crime in the United States* is based on the population's reporting of crimes *to the police.* So let's be clear about this: Some Index Crimes are *hugely* underreported. When criminologists compare other data sources with the figures in the UCR, they find that crime is considerably higher than is indicated by police reports, and the discrepancies are systematic, not random. Criminologists believe that statistics on murder and motor vehicle theft are fairly complete. But judging from victimization surveys—which, as we saw in the chapter on research methods, is a major data source on crime for criminologists—assault and rape are two or three times as common as the police data indicate.

The FBI has collected the data reported in the UCR's *Crime in the United States* since 1930. Every year, over 17,000 law enforcement agencies, making up over 90 percent of the population, send to Washington such vital information as crimes reported (or "known") to law enforcement, the characteristics of victims, the geographic locale of the offense, offenses solved (or "cleared") by arrest, the demographic characteristics of arrestees, and information about law enforcement personnel.

In each jurisdiction, when Part I offenses are reported to the police, they are "founded" (established as valid), recorded, and tabulated by each jurisdiction; then, yearly, the totals are sent to the FBI, which adds up their incidence nationwide. The FBI adds the number of murders, rapes, robberies, and aggravated assaults together to produce a *violent crime rate;* in 2007, this rate was 466.9 per 100,000 in the population, sharply down since the 1990s: In 1991, this figure was 758.2. Burglary, larceny theft, and motor vehicle theft are added together to obtain a *property crime index;* in 2007, it stood at 3,263.5, again, a substantial drop from the early 1990s; and in 1991, the figure clocked in at 5,140.2. Table 5.1 summarizes Index Crime in the United States between 1991 and 2007, as reported to the FBI's Uniform Crime

TABLE 5.1 THE FBI'S INDEX CRIMES, 1991–2007

	1991		*2007*	
	NUMBER	**RATE**	**NUMBER**	**RATE**
Violent Crime:	1,911,767	785.2	1,408,337	466.9
Murder	24,703	9.8	16,929	5.6
Forcible Rape	106,593	42.3	90,427	30.0
Robbery	687,732	272.7	445,125	147.6
Aggravated Assault	1,092,739	433.4	855,856	283.8
Property Crime:	12,961,116	5,140.2	9,843,481	3,263.5
Burglary	3,157,150	1,252.1	2,179,140	722.5
Larceny-theft	8,142,228	3,229.1	6,568,572	2,177.8
Motor Vehicle Theft	1,661,738	659.0	1,095,769	363.3

Source: FBI, Uniform Crime Reports, Crime in the United States 2007 (2008); rate is number per 100,000 in the population.

Report. Property crime is much more common than violent crime. Non-Index or Part II offenses include drug abuse violations, weapons possession, drunk and disorderly, embezzlement, prostitution, and receiving stolen property; they are recorded in the UCR only when they result in arrest. The data in the Uniform Crime Reports are referred to as official crime statistics.

VIOLENT CRIME

The FBI defines murder and nonnegligent manslaughter as the "willful . . . killing of one human being by another." Deaths caused by negligence, suicide, or accident, justifiable homicide (an officer of the law willfully killing a felon in pursuit of his or her legal duty), and attempted murder are not included. In addition, the killing of a felon, "during the commission of a felony, by a private citizen" (if so determined by law enforcement investigation) is not considered murder. But a nonintentional "felony murder," a death that occurs during the course of a felony, *is* murder. For instance, if a little old lady dies when someone commits burglary, that's a felony murder, and therefore, murder; the intent to harm someone is irrelevant. Murder is, *by far,* the least common Index Crime, and one of the rarest crimes on the books. According to the FBI's "crime clock," one murder occurred in the United States every 31.0 minutes during 2007. In that year, the police recorded slightly fewer than 17,000 murders (16,929), a decline of 31 percent since 1991 (when the figure was 24,703).

The FBI defines forcible rape as "the carnal knowledge of a female forcibly and against her will. Assaults and attempts to commit rape by force or threat of force are also included; however statutory rape (without force) and other sex offenses are excluded." Sexual attacks on males "are counted as aggravated assaults or sex offenses, depending on the circumstances." Forcible rape is the most underreported of the violent crimes. In the United States, one was reported to law enforcement during 2007 every 5.8 minutes. Again, remember that other data sources indicate that the rate of rape as indicated by victimization surveys is twice as common as the FBI figures suggest. In any case, *reported* rapes declined sharply between the early 1990s (42.3 in 1991) and the 2000s (30.0 in 2007).

The FBI defines robbery as "the taking or attempting to take anything of value from the care, custody, or control of a person or persons by force or threat of force or violence and/or putting the victim in fear." Robbery is, by definition, a face-to-face crime. It always entails force, violence, or the threat of violence. Simple theft and burglary are not robbery. Robbery entails both the theft of property and violence, but its violent character is much more interesting to criminologists, and more significant to the general public, than the fact that it involves theft; hence, it is classified as a crime of violence. Robbery is a very serious crime and, compared to simple theft, is relatively rare. One robbery was reported every 1.2 minutes in the United States during 2007; roughly a quarter of all robberies are not reported to the police. The decline of the robbery rate in the U.S. has been more spectacular than for any other violent Index Crime; in 1991, it stood at 272.7 per 100,000, while by 2007, it had dropped to 147.6, a decline of about 46 percent. The FBI estimates that roughly $588 million was stolen in the latter year through acts of robbery, an average of $1,321 per offense. Obviously, the emotional impact of robbery far outweighs its relatively small monetary weight.

Aggravated assault is defined as "an unlawful attack by one person upon another for the purpose of inflicting severe or aggravated bodily injury." The crime, according to the FBI, is "usually" (but not always) "accompanied by the use of a weapon or by other means likely to produce death or great bodily harm." The line between "aggravated" (or serious) and "simple" (less serious) assault is not always easy to draw; it is a matter of degree. A punch in the nose is not usually aggravated assault, though it is (simple) assault; a blow over the head with a baseball bat, resulting in a fractured skull, a concussion, and a trip to the hospital, is aggravated assault. Many (perhaps most) serious assaults that take place in a domestic situation, most commonly, between a husband and wife, are not reported to law enforcement. In 2007, the FBI recorded one aggravated assault every 36.8 seconds.

PROPERTY CRIME

As all data everywhere around the world indicate, property crime is *much* more common than violent crime; nearly nine out of 10 (88%) of Index Crimes are property crimes. Burglary, a property crime, is "the unlawful entry of a structure to commit a felony or theft. The use of force to gain entry ['breaking and entering'] is not required to classify an offense as a burglary," although degrees of seriousness are determined by whether the entry is forcible or not. And nothing need be stolen for an act to qualify as a burglary. The FBI's crime clock recorded one burglary per 14.5 seconds in 2007, though most burglaries are not reported. That year, the country racked up a total of just over two million reported burglaries, down from over three million per year in the early 1990s. (See Table 5.1.)

Larceny theft is a grab-bag category; it includes acts of stealing that are not robbery, not burglary, not the theft of a motor vehicle, and not "embezzlement, confidence games, forgery, and [writing and attempting to pass] worthless checks." The FBI defines larceny theft as "the unlawful taking, carrying, leading, or riding away of property from the possession or constructive possession of another; attempts to do these acts are included in this definition. This crime category includes pocket-picking, purse-snatching, thefts from motor vehicles, thefts of motor vehicle parts and accessories, bicycle thefts, and so forth." More larceny thefts are reported to the police than all other Index Crimes put together; even so, larceny theft is the most underreported of all serious crimes. In 2007, one larceny theft was recorded every 4.8 seconds. Proportionally speaking, the vast majority of larceny thefts go unreported, although in absolute terms, more larceny thefts are reported than any other crime; two-thirds of all property crimes reported to the police are larceny thefts; six and a half million larceny thefts were reported in the U.S. in 2007, down from eight million in 1991. Obviously, the greater the amount stolen, the greater the likelihood that the victim will report the theft to the police. According to the FBI, in 2007, larceny theft offenses cost victims $5.8 billion, for an average of $886 per offense.

And lastly, there is motor vehicle theft, "the theft or attempted theft of a motor vehicle. This offense includes the stealing of automobiles, trucks, busses, motorcycles, snowmobiles, etc." For 2007, the crime clock recorded one motor vehicle theft every 28.8 seconds. As the country with the greatest number of motor vehicles, the United States has the world's highest rate of motor vehicle theft. Still, today, the rate is fairly low (363.3/100,000), and considerably lower than it was in 1991 (659.0), a 46 percent decrease, a sharper decline than for any other property crime. To judge by victimization surveys, among Index Crimes, motor vehicle theft is most likely to be fully reported (81%).

PROPERTY CRIME AS DEVIANCE

Injunctions against property crime have ancient roots. Two of the Ten Commandments prohibit taking something of value not one's own: the Eighth, which says "Thou shalt not steal," and the Tenth, which says "Thou shalt not covet thy neighbor's house . . ., his ox or donkey, or anything that belongs to thy neighbor." Indeed, the taboo against theft can be traced back thousands of years before the Bible was written, back before settled communities, agriculture, or the fashioning of metals, to hunting and gathering societies the world over, back to when the concept of movable property was institutionalized. In societies everywhere and throughout the span of human existence, whenever anything of value could be owned by individuals, some other individuals coveted, and stole, whatever it was, and societies promulgated rules that prohibited such theft.

Larceny, it has been said, is "in the American heart" (McCaghy et al., 2006, pp. 159–162). It is and has been in the hearts of the people of many societies the world over and throughout human history as well, since stealing is extremely widespread, practically universal. Polls as far back as the 1940s indicate that most people have stolen something of value at least once in their lives. But the popularity of property crime does not mean that we are all thieves. One study (Tracy, Wolfgang, and Figlio, 1990) found that, in the United States, roughly 5 percent of the population commits 70 percent of the serious property crime.

Most of us steal very little and very infrequently, while very few of us steal a great deal, and steal frequently. Hence, there are significant differences between someone who says he or she has stolen something of value at least once and someone who steals routinely, as a living. Saying "we are all thieves," therefore, is misleading because, while hardly anyone is completely honest, relatively few of us make a *habit* of stealing.

Theft flourishes in societies in which some members do not care a great deal about the deprivations they cause to their fellow citizens, or where members of different societies come into contact with one another and the wants and needs of the members of the other society are deemed of no significance. Stealing is high in societies in which the collective conscience has broken down, in which the social community has become a fiction. Theft is common because some among us want certain things and how we acquire those things matters less than having them. We steal because we are successful at convincing ourselves "it isn't really so bad," or "no one will miss it," or "it's covered by insurance," or "I need it more than they do," or "they're bigger crooks than I am." Basically, people are able to steal because persons from whom they steal have become impersonal, faceless, almost nonhuman to them. And stealing is particularly common in societies in which inequities in income and other resources are sharp, stark, and publicized, and, as anomie theory argues, where persons at the bottom of the hierarchy learn to *want* the things that the more affluent have.

The street thieves whose acts are tabulated in the pages of the Uniform Crime Reports run the gamut from the rankest amateur who shoplifts to obtain items he or she sees others enjoying to the professional who earns a comfortable livelihood exclusively from larceny. For both, stealing seems to be a rational activity: It is a means to an end that many of us seek, although the means used are somewhat unconventional. Other benefits that may be derived from stealing ("kicks," fun, excitement, and so on) tend to be secondary to the monetary ones. A nation with high rates of theft, as Merton argues, is one that

1. emphasizes material values
2. manifests great material differences between rich and poor
3. prominently displays the possessions of the affluent
4. portrays the possessions of the affluent as attainable for everyone
5. deemphasizes the means of attaining these possessions
6. makes it difficult, if not nearly impossible, for a substantial number of a society's members to obtain these possessions legally

It is these features that almost guarantee that a society or nation will have a high rate of theft. They make for a "rip-off" society, a "society organized for crime" (Messner and Rosenfeld, 1997, pp. 1–14).

Among the tugs and pulls inducing people to attempt thievery as a means of earning money, two stand out most prominently. The first would be the gap between poverty and having cash. In a nation with high unemployment rates in many neighborhoods, with a black unemployment rate twice that of whites, and an unemployment rate for teenagers three times that for adults, many people are induced to steal because they literally have no other means of earning money. In the neighborhood studied by anthropologist Philippe Bourgeois, "El Barrio" or East Harlem in New York, 40 percent of all households earned no legally declared wages or salary at all. It is Bourgeois's contention that its residents had no choice but to resort to a variety of activities in the underground economy, among them, stealing (1995, p. 8). Even if a family receives government benefits or one or more members work at a minimum wage job, there is no possibility of moving about in the world with physical dignity or comfort. Indeed, many minimum wage jobs put substantially less in one's pocket than many illegal activities. Clearly, poverty has to be counted as a major inducement to engage in property crime.

We experience a great deal of theft in this society because the economy does not guarantee enough people a decent livelihood and because our economy is incapable of distributing income in an equitable fashion. Many poor countries, likewise, experience high rates of theft as well, but this is far from an absolute rule. It is not poverty alone that guarantees high rates of property crime; theft tends to be rare in some nations of the world in which people are the most impoverished. This may be because the rule of the rich is far more tyrannical than is true here, or because the poor do not dream that they could, through simple acts of theft, acquire some of what the rich have.

In principle, a cross-national comparison of property crime should enrich our understanding of the factors that contribute to theft and why it is so much more common in some societies than in others. However, many of the poorest countries of the world have unreliable crime statistics, especially for property crimes. Moreover, property crime takes place most in the wealthier countries of the world, largely because more wealth means more property to steal. For instance, auto theft is common in rich countries and less common in poor countries, because the rate of auto theft is computed on a per population, not on a per auto, basis; hence, countries with few cars have few auto thefts. The United Nations' figures on burglary, reported by nationmaster.com, produce a mixed bag. In any case, the report ranks Australia (with 21.7 per 1,000 in the population for a given year in the 1990s) as the country with the world's highest rate of burglary, followed by Dominica (18.8), Denmark (18.3), Estonia (17.5), Finland (16.8), New Zealand (16.3), the United Kingdom (13.8), Poland (9.5), Canada (8.9), and South Africa (8.9). The United States ranks seventeenth in the world. The world's lowest rate of burglary is recorded by Saudi Arabia (0.0004 per 1,000 people), followed by Yemen (0.01), Armenia (0.03), South Korea (0.1), India (0.1), Thailand (0.2), Colombia (0.3), Qatar (0.3), Georgia (0.4), and Papua New Guinea (0.5). Here, the severity of punishment (Saudi Arabia's laws call for the amputation of a hand in the case of theft), as well as what proportion of the time dwellings are occupied, may explain a major part of the difference. It almost seems as if burglary is inversely correlated with affluence, with many of the wealthiest countries having the highest rates of burglary and some of the poorest having the lowest. Hence, international statistics provide a complex picture on the whys and wherefores of property crime.

The second factor that many thieves claim caused them to steal is that most jobs available to a poor, uneducated young person are not interesting or rewarding. Most are boring, tedious, alienating, and demeaning. So the choice for some of us is not between poverty and having cash but between working at a legal job that pays little and that one despises and doing something that is illegal but is less humiliating, or at least that doesn't consume eight or ten hours a day. Stealing for a living involves being one's own boss, choosing one's working hours, and doing jobs one decides to do. It is difficult to imagine more persuasive inducements. Of course, the down side is arrest and penal confinement, but some young people have a sense of bravado and invulnerability that insulates them from seriously considering the down side.

Richard Wright and Scott Decker (1994) argue that, for the burglar, the "pressing need for cash" is the primary factor in committing a crime. Most of Wright and Decker's interviewees "regarded money as providing them with the means to solve an immediate problem. In their view, burglary was a matter of day-to-day survival" (p. 37). Says "Mark," one of their informants: "I didn't have the luxury of laying back in no damn pin-striped [suit]. I'm poor and I'm raggedy and I need some food and I need some shoes. . . . So I got to have some money some kind of way. If it's got to be the wrong way, then so be it" (p. 37). For most of Wright and Decker's sample, the decision to go out on a job "was governed largely by the amount of money in their pockets. Many of them would not offend so long as they had sufficient cash to meet current expenses. Explains "Dan," another of their interviewees, "a burglary . . . will get me over the rough spot until I can get my shit straightened out. Once I get it straightened out, I just go with the flow until I hit that rough spot where I need the money again. . . . [The] only time I would go and commit a burglary is if I needed the money at that point in time. That would be strictly to pay [the] light bill, gas bill, rent" (p. 37).

Wright and Decker also explain that burglars' accounts are to be taken with a grain of salt. That is, their justification for stealing to put food on the table is true as far as it goes, but many are clearly motivated by other reasons as well. Nearly three-quarters admit that they used their ill-gotten gains for "high living." Wright and Decker call this motive "keeping the party going" (pp. 38–42), that is, "pleasure-seeking pursuits." For most, this entailed purchasing illicit drugs. "Getting and using drugs were major preoccupations for a majority of the offenders, not just a small cadre of addicts." Even the burglars who said they stole to put food on the table, explain Wright and Decker, "ended up spending a portion of the profits [they earned from their thefts] on drugs" (p. 41). In short, these researchers explain, "among the major purposes for which the offenders used the money derived from burglary was the maintenance of a lifestyle that centered on illicit drugs, but frequently incorporating alcohol and sexual conquests as well. This lifestyle reflects the values of the street culture, a culture characterized by an openness to illicit action, to which most of our subjects were strongly committed" (p. 42).

In addition to simple survival and "keeping the party going," roughly half of Wright and Decker's burglars said that they used the money they stole to purchase "status" items; "keeping up appearances" was a major motive for them. Mainly this entailed buying chic, expensive, fashionable clothing. Dressing "in the latest status symbol clothing is virtually mandatory for those who want to be seen as hip on the street." Most wanted to impress others with their sartorial splendor, to be seen as a "better class of person" than they actually were. "I think every crook likes the life of thieving and then going and being somebody better. Really, you are deceiving people, letting them think that you are well off. . . . It takes money to buy that kind of life" (p. 44).

Why did these individuals choose burglary over a legal job? For these men, say Wright and Decker, "legitimate work did not represent a viable solution for most of the offenders in our sample. These subjects . . . wanted money there and then, and, in such circumstances, even day labor was irrelevant because it did not respond to the immediacy of their desire for cash. Moreover, the jobs available to most of the offenders were poorly-paid and could not sustain their desired lifestyles" (p. 48). In fact, roughly a fifth of Wright and Decker's sample was employed; as one explained, he had a job but, he said, "I got tired of waiting on that money. I can get money like that. I got talent, I can do me a burg [burglary], man, and get me five or six hundred dollars in less than an hour. Working eight hours a day and waiting for a whole week for a check, and it ain't even about shit" (p. 48).

As we saw, according to both victimization surveys and the Uniform Crime Reports, property crime has declined *very* sharply since the 1970s. In 1973, according to the National Crime Victimization Survey (NCVS), the total property crime rate in the United States was nearly 550 per thousand households. In other words, during that year, more than half of all American households were victimized by at least one property crime. In 1993, the figure was 319, a decline of nearly 40 percent. By 2006, this was 159, less than a third of the 1973 figure and only half of what it had been just a dozen years before (Rand and Catalano, 2007). This decline is remarkable, even startling, unexpected, and very possibly unprecedented. Theories of why the decline took place abound (Blumstein and Wallman, 2000; Zimring, 2007), including an improvement in the economy, the aging of the American population, the imposition of longer prison terms, and declines in drug use. An economist (Levitt, 2004; Levitt and Dubner, 2005, pp. 117–144) even argues the drop came about as a result of the legalization of abortion and the disappearance of unwanted and therefore poorly supervised, troubled children who, chances are, would have been born and gone on to high rates of juvenile, criminal behavior. Whatever the cause, the decline in rates of crime, especially rates of property crime, in the United States is perhaps the most remarkable development in criminal behavior during the past 30 or 40 years.

SHOPLIFTING AND EMPLOYEE THEFT

Shoplifting falls under the FBI's classification as a form of larceny theft. However, it possesses several features that make it distinctly different from some of the other crimes that also fall under that classification, such as burglary. Roughly 15 percent of all larceny thefts reported to the police are incidents of shoplifting. However, most larceny thefts are not reported to the police, and most incidents of shoplifting are likewise not reported to the police. Moreover, since shoplifting is typically not an offense against a specific victim, we don't have more accurate figures on their incidence from victimization surveys. Hence, a substantial sector of the shoplifting picture remains in the dark.

To the sociologist of deviance, what makes shoplifting most interesting is that, despite the fact that it is a crime—a type of property crime—a substantial proportion of its perpetrators are "respectable," very different from the burglar and the motor vehicle thief. To most Americans, burglary is deviant yet shoplifting is, if not respectable, then at least *less* deviant than burglary. Moreover, a high proportion of shoplifters are respectable men and women; the shame and ridicule comes in getting caught and exposed as a thief and less in the act itself. Many Americans do not regard shoplifting as real crime and would object if someone received a long prison term for it. The majority of shoplifters do not regard themselves as criminals, and they are not so regarded by their nonshoplifting peers. Shoplifters tend to take low-value items. Although some may do it often, they do not make a career out of shoplifting and do not earn enough to support themselves. They generally have no connections with people who steal for a living and hold no values, beliefs, or practices that contrast sharply with those of the rest of us, other than engaging in shoplifting. The kind of stealing that most retail store thieves engage in requires little or no skill. Shoplifters stem from all walks of life. They are teenagers and the elderly, homemakers, stable, working-class men and women, professionals—in short, shoplifters could be just about anyone. For the most part, as I said, shoplifters are respectable folks, and shoplifting borders on respectable behavior. Serious stigma does not adhere to persons who steal low-value items once in a while from stores. "Everybody does it," we say to ourselves, and hold ourselves blameless; "it's covered by insurance," we say, neutralizing any potential stigma that might come our way. "Just don't get caught," we add.

In addition to being almost, but not-quite respectable, shoplifting has group support. This is especially the case among teenagers. Some join one another on shoplifting expeditions, ripping off items of value for amusement and personal gain. There is often peer pressure for others to join in, should someone express reluctance to do so. Moreover, the activity is an adjunct to other pleasurable activities—socializing, fantasizing, hanging out, and meeting and interacting with members of the opposite sex. In this respect it is not unlike going to a movie, going to the beach, driving around in a car, or standing around on street corners. For many teenagers, meeting friends to go to stores and steal—particularly in large shopping centers such as suburban malls—does not appear to be a form of deviant behavior. This is one of the aspects of shoplifting that is so fascinating to the researcher of deviance. More than anything else, it manifests adherence to several basic, conventional, mainstream values, such as sociability, materialism, and hedonism. When adults steal from stores, for the most part, they are much less likely to do so in the company of others, and, in all likelihood, derive less excitement from it, but as for teenagers, it is driven by conventional values.

Shoplifting is far from being small potatoes when it comes to the total monetary value that is stolen. When we compare rates of larceny theft recorded in the Uniform Crime Reports by the FBI with rates of theft from persons and households in victimization surveys, we see that the overwhelming majority of simple thefts are not reported to the police. Moreover, shoplifting from retails stores is *very* rarely reported to the police. The FBI calculates that victims of larceny theft lost a total of $5.8 billion in 2007, of which 14.5 percent was from shoplifting, which means that victims of shoplifting, nearly all of which are retail stores, lost $841 million. This figure is so undercounted as to be totally worthless. A team of criminologists at the University of Florida headed by Richard Hollinger conducts the National Retail Security Survey, asking a sample of retail stores about "inventory shrinkage," that is, the loss of goods or money during a given time period. Its 2007 survey is the latest at this writing (Hollinger and Langton, 2008). The total amount of inventory shrinkage in the United States from retail stores for that year, tabulated by extrapolating from the sample, was calculated at $35 *billion*, "a staggering monetary loss to come from a single crime type." A shade under half of this figure (44%) was from employee theft, or about $15.2 billion; a third (34%) came from shoplifting, a total of $11.3 billion; and the remainder resulted from paper and administrative error (15%) and vendor fraud (4%). This study, a kind of victimization survey of retail stores, reveals that the FBI understates the loss to shoplifting *by over 30 times!* In other words, if Hollinger's survey is accurate, the actual value of inventory stolen via shoplifting is more than 30 times greater than what is reported to the police.

Shoplifters come in two basic varieties: the *booster* and the *snitch* (Cameron, 1964). Boosters steal primarily for the purpose of resale, to earn a living or augment what they already earn. They take expensive items, those that can readily be converted to cash. Obviously, they are more likely to steal repeatedly and figure out ways of circumventing the security measures stores put in place to deter theft. In contrast, snitches are amateurs and steal mainly for the personal use of the items they take. They are more likely to steal impulsively and to be less aware of the store's security devices. Representatives of stores make a clear distinction between professionals and amateurs.

The greater the value of the items taken, the greater the likelihood that the thief will be reported to the police. In one study of over 6,000 cases of shoplifters who were apprehended in drug stores and supermarkets, only 13 percent of those who had taken small-value items were reported to the police, but 40 percent of those who had taken large-value items were reported. In addition, items that can be readily resold—especially meat, liquor, and cigarettes (Hindelang, 1974)—tend to be stolen. This action is clearly designed to punish the habitual professional thief, the "booster." According to the author, "the characteristics of the offense, more than the characteristics of the offender, are associated with decisions to take official action" (p. 592).

As we saw, the National Retail Security Survey conducted by criminologist Richard Hollinger estimated that nearly half of the inventory shrinkage that retail stores lost was due to employee pilferage; the total loss came to $15.2 billion for 2007. In addition, employees steal not only from retail stores but also from all workplace locales: hospitals, factories, ships and docks, airlines, construction sites, trucking companies, business offices, the armed services and other government agencies, and even schools, colleges, and universities. Aside from corporate and other white-collar crime, employee pilferage is probably the costliest offense committed in the United States.

In spite of the huge monetary loss from employee theft, this type of crime attracts relatively little attention from criminologists and sociologists. Judging from the articles that appear in *Criminology,* criminological studies on money-making street crimes probably outnumber those on employee pilferage by a ratio of 100–1. Employees rationalize and justify their theft on the job—that is, they use techniques of stigma neutralization—by saying: "It's a corporation—it's not like taking from an individual," "Nobody cares," "They expect it," "Everyone's doing it," "The insurance company pays for it," and "The company doesn't pay me enough—I'm just taking what's rightfully mine." The general public doesn't feel threatened by employee pilferage because organizations, retail stores, and corporations are impersonal, faceless entities. And the perpetrators of employee pilferage *are* the general public.

DISCREPANCIES

To the constructionist, perhaps the most endlessly fascinating feature of social life is what can be called *perturbations,* or unexpected discrepancies between different realms of social life. That is, when we compare likelihood of certain outcomes, based on measurable fact versus culturally constructed expectations, we find systematic differences. People rely on biases that lead them to expect certain outcomes that are not true. An entire field of psychology called judgmental heuristics has grown up around just an observation. Most people reach conclusions about what's going on around them on the basis of "rules of thumb" or mental tools that rely heavily on stereotypes and cultural conventions that are usually right, but often wrong, and in important ways. Consistently and overwhelmingly, both in experiments and in real life, people tend to think in stereotypes, discount evidence that disconfirms their biases, ignore sample size, poorly estimate probability, and recall instances that incorrectly validate their biases (Gilovich, 1991; Kahneman, 1982; Piatelli-Palmarini, 1994). For instance, 90 percent of people believe in the "hot hand" phenomenon; they'll say that if a basketball player has made three shots in a row, he or she is more likely to make the next one than if he or she had missed the last three. In fact, the likelihood is close to the player's season average, regardless of whether he or she made or missed the last three shots (Gilovich, 1991, p. 12). If we are told that a person possesses certain characteristics and then asked to guess his or her profession, we tend to guess according to how we mentally "fit" the characteristics together with stereotypes we hold of the sort of person who works at such a profession, rather than the real-world likelihood of people working in that profession. Contrary to what most people guess, an outgoing, adventurous man who takes risks is *far* more likely to be a teacher than an astronaut, simply because there are very few astronauts and many teachers.

Perhaps the greatest of such discrepancies we find is that between fear and risk: Often, what we fear most is the least likely to happen, while what we fear least is far more likely. *What accounts* for the fact that people often believe things that are not factually correct? For instance, if people are concerned about and fear a given condition much more than is warranted by that condition's objective threat (Glassner, 1999), we are alerted to the fact that *something is going on* that we should find out about. When the discrepancy between such parameters is huge, the inquiring sociologist wants to know why.

Most people are concerned about and fear "street" crime, especially violent crime, far more than other sources of danger. But the fact is, in the United States, we are far less likely to be murdered (about 17,000 victims in 2007) than to die of tobacco-related causes (440,000 yearly). Our chances of being robbed are minuscule (445,000 in 2007) compared with being a victim of a corporate crime (which includes pretty much the entire population, considering the fact that the public has to pay for corporate schemes that are subsidized by the tax dollar). And the classic stranger rapes that are stereotypically thought of as rape and reported to the police are less common than date or acquaintance rape that is often not regarded as rape and is reported in only a minority of cases. Yet most of us are much more concerned about, and fear, murder, robbery, and stranger rape far more than these other, far more common, sources of victimization. In a noncriminal sphere, people fear dying in an airplane crash more than in a car crash, but mile-for-mile, hour-for-hour, driving or riding in a car is much more likely to result in death.

The public fears violence at the hands of a stranger far more than violence at the hands of intimates. Yet, statistically speaking, intimates are *far more* likely to inflict violence on us than strangers. For instance, studies show that family violence—wife battering and child abuse, including sexual abuse—is extremely common. All incidents of serious family violence, most of which are not reported, are many times greater than all the cases of aggravated (or serious) assault that are reported to the police. Where the police know the relationship between victim and killer, about a quarter of all murder victims are killed by a family member, and less than one in 10 entail a killing by a boyfriend or girlfriend. (When the killing involves a husband and wife or a boyfriend and girlfriend, in three-quarters of the cases, it is the male who kills the female.) Family members are small in number but make up a *huge* source of the total picture of violence. Of all the violence that takes place, a substantial proportion stems from the very people we are closest to—and yet, for most of us, they are the very people we fear the least. In contrast, there are many millions of people who are strangers to us, but their contribution to criminal homicide is the same as family members, a quarter, whose numbers in the population are minuscule. Again, to the sociologist of deviance, paradoxes such as these are interesting and very much in need of investigation.

SUMMARY

Deviance and crime overlap, but imperfectly. Many forms of deviance are not crimes—witness eccentricity and obesity. Some forms of crime are not deviant in the narrow sense, at least, they do not generate a great deal of informal condemnation, even though they may lead to arrest; many white-collar offenses qualify here. The field of criminology focuses on criminal behavior. Rather than repeat what's in such courses, in this book I will devote my discussion mainly to acts and beliefs (and traits) that are interesting mainly because they generate *informal* negative reactions. However, it should be kept in mind that *conceptually* and *theoretically,* deviance and crime share much of the same territory; hence they cannot be cleanly separated.

Both deviance and criminal behavior cover a diverse collection of activities and phenomenon, though deviance, as we might expect, is *vastly* more varied than crime, including, as it does, not only behavior but beliefs and conditions as well. Still, as with deviance, what is a crime—what is a *violation of the law*—is determined by judgments of specific audience. A crime is not a "thing" in the material world but a *decision* made by specific parties, from a victim or a private citizen to a police officer and a judge, that a punishable offense has been committed. After a report of untoward activity has been lodged with the police by a complainant, the audience that decides what a crime is is made up of *agents of formal social control*—the police and the courts, including prosecutors, judges, and juries.

Some acts have been punished by the judgments of agents of the society or tribe for thousands of years, even before such a thing as a formal written legal code or a law-making body existed. It was custom, not legislatures, that determined their criminal status. These are the *common law* or primal crimes, which have existed pretty much everywhere and throughout human history. They include murder, rape, robbery, and theft. It is difficult to refer to such offenses as being relative to time and place, since there is a *common core* of such offenses that exists everywhere and has always existed. Even so, even for the common law crimes, judgments of *who* commits *what* offense against *what* party is variable, relative to time and place.

Legislature-created law is called statutory law; it rarely has the force of sentiment that is as strong as that behind common law, which is based on the force of tradition and custom.

As with deviance, crime can be studied both from the essentialist, or *positivist,* or causal perspective, and the *constructionist* perspective. The constructionist agrees with the positivist's argument that, worldwide and over historical time, there has been and continues to be a common thread to or "common core" of a great deal of crime, the common law or so-called primal crimes. Still, in the past, and even today, in certain locales, who the perpetrator and the victim are makes a difference with respect to public judgments of whether or not a crime has taken place. Most criminologists are positivists, and most are interested in the objective causes and consequences of crime. Moreover, most criminologists focus on certain crimes as characteristic of crime in general; they are taken as a measure or *index* of criminality. For the most part, they correspond to the public's notion of street crime, which is entirely predatory in nature—they have victims who are harmed by the criminal act. The FBI refers to them as Index Crimes, and tabulates the incidence of seven of them, in the form of "crimes known to the police," in detail in a yearly volume entitled *Crime in the United States.* These crimes are murder and nonnegligent manslaughter, rape, robbery, and aggravated assault (the violent crimes); and burglary, motor vehicle theft, and larceny theft (the property crimes). Some criminologists (a minority) study non-Index Crimes, for instance, illicit drug possession and sale, prostitution, unauthorized gambling, and public intoxication.

The taboo against stealing goes as far back in historical time as the ownership of private property; two of the Ten Commandments prohibit the faithful from thievery. It has been said that the United States, in comparison with other industrialized societies, is a particularly larcenous society. Merton's anomie theory predicts that any society, such as the United States, that prominently displays symbols of affluence, suggests that the poor can acquire the affluence enjoyed by the rich, and denies access to that affluence is likely to have a great deal of crime. However, the property crime rate in the United States has declined sharply in the past two decades, while in parts of Western Europe, it has increased. Moreover, most of the crime, including property crime, is committed by a very small percentage of the population, indicating that we are *not* "all criminals." Although, in a given society, certain property crimes are more likely to be committed by the poor, interestingly, the wealthiest countries have the highest rates of certain property crimes, such as auto theft and burglary. This is because there is a greater abundance of material goods to steal in the first place.

Shoplifting and employee theft are two crimes that tend to be committed by the full spectrum of the society, and not predominantly the poor. Most of their offenders are respectable people who do not steal for a living, do not have a criminal identity, do not associate with people who steal as a way of life, and have a more or less respectable style of life. They are crimes that are not regarded as seriously deviant in this society and do not, for the most part, stigmatize the offender. Of course, getting caught and publicly labeled as a shoplifter does stigmatize the offender. Boosters are shoplifters who steal a great deal, steal for resale, and steal to earn a living. Representatives of retail stores tend not to turn the apprehended amateur thief over to the police; they are more likely to do so with shoplifters who are thought to be professionals. The total dollar value of goods and money stolen by shoplifting and employee theft is vastly greater than the figures tabulated by the FBI in its Uniform Crime Reports. This is because these crimes are rarely reported to the police, since, individually, they are not considered important, even though, collectively, their total sums are enormous, greater than for any other form of outright theft, and because retail and office establishments do not want to foment a public relations embarrassment.

Some of the findings of criminologists and sociologists of deviance should remind us that conventional assumptions and biases do not offer a valid guide to the way things are in the world of crime. To put the matter another way, popular misconceptions are a type of social construction that may *become* valid by being believed and acted upon. Fear is an essential ingredient in the study of criminal behavior. The contrast between the findings of positivist criminology and the constructionist's perspective provides an interesting paradox: The classic crimes of violence, which we fear the most, tend to be relatively rare, while other, more common sources of harm tend to be feared far less. The sociologist of deviance is interested in paradoxes such as these.

Account: Crime: Omar's Story

At the time of this interview, Omar was an ex-convict in his late twenties, and a recent college graduate. His illegal activities spanned the gamut of crimes, from drug possession and sale and simple larceny theft to armed robbery.

It seems a life of deviance was predestined for me. From conception, I was out to beat the odds. I was born out of wedlock from parents who had sex only once. My father stumbled upon me on the street, as my mother was pushing my stroller, when I was two years old. He immediately recognized the resemblance. When he showed my mother a picture of himself at two, she realized that he was my biological father. Unfortunately, my father lived in the Caribbean and was unable to guide my life as he wished. . . .

Looking back, I can recall being involved in deviant behavior at a young age. Once, in nursery school, I was caught in the girl's bathroom. . . . In the second grade, I stole some money; I walked into an empty classroom and saw a purse lying on the desk with the corner of two $20 bills sticking out. . . . I went home and put the money in an envelope and wrote the words "From the Devil" on the envelope. After my mom got home, I got the envelope where I had stashed it and took it to my mom and said, "Look what I found!" That was a mistake. She spanked me with a belt until I confessed where I had gotten the money. I was so stupid. I should have just kept the money and had a ball at the candy store for two weeks.

I went to a predominantly white middle school in Capitol Hill. I took the Metro to get there. Outside the station, I bummed money. I realize that I was exploiting my attractiveness, innocence, and youth. I used the money I received to purchase a Metro ride, a pepperoni sub, and an ice cream. From a young age, I believed I could

(*Continued*)

Account: Crime: Omar's Story Continued

find a way to get what I wanted. I always found a way to sidestep conventional ways of obtaining things. Sometimes the conventional ways simply weren't available. Once, I heard my mom tell me she had to steal food to eat. Maybe I learned something from this, I can't say for sure. Anyway, my tendency to get what I wanted by however means I could increased as I got older.

When I was 11 and 12, I got caught twice for stealing, once at 7/Eleven and once at Toys 'R' Us. At the 7/Eleven, I was even arrested. Stealing wasn't the only way I could earn money. One time, a thirty-something Spanish guy solicited me to take a ride with him. He told me if I took a ride with him, he would give me money. I took the ride, he touched my leg, and I walked away with $40. In high school, I worked at the school store. A girl who worked there taught me how to embezzle money. She'd steal $30 a day from the store. I took more modest amounts, knowing she was already ripping them off. Still, I got pretty good money by embezzling from the store, considering I was only a ninth grader.

It was in the ninth grade that I started dealing drugs. . . . This involved being away from home a lot of the time. Still, I did abide by some of my family's rules—I just couldn't stay out all night, every night. Believe it or not, through all this, I was a pretty good student, I just missed a lot of classes. . . . In my senior year, I missed 48 days of school. Can you imagine how independent I felt? I was making my own money—and good money at that. And the girls that came along with my deviant behavior! Don't get me wrong, I know I am a little attractive, but I think the money attracted girls, too. I'd flash a wad of money in front of the girls, buy breakfast and school lunches for them. It was cool. Hell, I began having sex at 12 or 13. By the time I graduated from high school, I am sorry to say I contributed to three abortions. I threw a party once to raise money for an abortion. Sex was a huge part of my high school years. My best friend and I skipped school a lot to find action with some girls. I did it alone, too. Looking back, I was moving pretty fast. I used to keep a few girlfriends. Once I had sex with three different girls, one after the other, in the same day. I really don't know how I got the attitudes and beliefs that allowed me to act the way I did. I know now that my behavior wasn't that normal compared with the other kids at my school. I also know that my behavior led to a lot of unfortunate situations.

By the time I graduated from high school I had sold drugs, stolen cars, committed an armed robbery (it was a carjacking), and had a baby on the way. Soon after I graduated from high school, I was incarcerated for a robbery that I committed earlier that year. Looking back, it seems that I had grown up in a rebellious era in which Black males, including myself, followed along with the rebellion. I mean, "gangsta rap" was born and the crack epidemic was at its peak. Instead of following the examples laid out by my parents, I wanted to follow the social trend and be one of the thugs on the street. I don't understand why I didn't go along with being at home at a certain time. The fact is, I respected the street life and the people in it. And it was fun. I felt a sense of exhilaration. Breaking the rules provided an edge to my life. I felt I wasn't your average "Joe." I gained respect for taking risks. Ironically, my dad used to tell me not to compare myself with people who had less than me, always compare myself with those who had better. My problem was that I didn't look at street people as having less than I did. They showed me love, and they had culture and spirit.

I had been stealing cars off and on for about eight months. Accura Legends. I'd break in, use an instrument to pop the ignition out, then start it up with a screw driver. Here's how it started. I had a girlfriend. I promised to take her to King's Dominion. I was 17 at the time. However, I couldn't get a rented car. A couple of friends sold me a stolen Accura Legend for $100, so we drove to King's Dominion in this stolen Accura Legend. I thought, "Wow!" So I started stealing Accura Legends for the people who sold me the one I bought. I used to have a couple of friends in DC, drug dealers, who bought parts from stolen cars, radios, CD players, tires, stuff like that. But it was a lot of trouble to steal it the way we did it [popping the ignition and starting it up with a screwdriver], it was risky, and it took several minutes to do all this. Then I sold cocaine for a while. But that involved standing outside in the cold with a couple of schoolmates of mine. We were in the 12th grade. We decided it was taking too long, standing out in the cold. We decided we'd make more money and take a less time stealing cars. We went to Tyson's Corner with the intention of stealing late model Lexuses. We figured we'd take a gun and threaten somebody with it, take the keys, and it would be a lot quicker. So we went to a garage in Tyson's Corner, we got out of the car, and walked around. We saw a couple walking toward a Lexus sedan. I was in front, my two friends were in back, and one of them had a gun. The one with the gun brandished the weapon at the couple. I shouted, "*Gimme the motherfuckin' keys!*" The man gave me the keys, my friends went to the car we came in, I got in and started up the car and drove away. I got to DC, went north on 14th Street, and a cab changed lanes right in front of me without signaling, so I had to swerve to avoid hitting him, and I jumped the curb and ran into a bus stop. I didn't know for a minute or two how to get out of the car—I wasn't familiar with the seat belt and I hesitated—and at that moment, a police paddy wagon was at a red light. Finally, I freed myself and jumped out of the car and ran away, but two cops from the paddy wagon pursued me. I ran into an alleyway, but it was a dead-end and I was apprehended. They ran the tags and found out the car was stolen. I was arrested, booked, and released for trial.

After that, I hooked up with the same guys. These guys would break into the key box of car dealerships and drive the cars off the lot. We were staking out a Mitsubishi dealership in a stolen Caravan. We were parked in an alleyway near the dealer, and a cop was making his routine rounds. They saw us in the Caravan and he called for backup. The tags on the Caravan were fictitious—the other guys had gotten the van off that same lot. Backup comes, they searched the car, and they found a gun under the driver's seat. The guy sitting in the driver's seat didn't have a license. They pull their guns on us and yelled, "*Don't motherfuckin' move!*" We could see them trembling. They were very excited. My hands were up in the air. I thought, damn! The second charge in a month! I ended up staying in county jail for three weeks. I never got officially charged with anything—the other charges took precedence. I was arrested in February for the stolen Accura and I was incarcerated in June. We were just dumb criminals. It wasn't as if we had guidance or anything. I served two years on the Youth Offender Act. But after the other case, I was charged as an adult and sent to a medium security prison.

My deviant behavior continued after my two-year incarceration. Before long, I began peddling drugs again. In the year after my release, I was arrested twice for cocaine distribution. I also caught a maiming charge that was dropped. I worked for a while in a job my mom hooked me up with, a day treatment center for the mentally retarded. That was an experience in itself. Those employees really used to beat up on their clients. I guess they just got frustrated sometimes. While I worked there, I managed to engage in unconventional activities. For a month, I operated a strip club out of my apartment. It was a big party where I got to control and interact with the women as I wished. I saw some wild things! I also sold drugs as a kind of side job.

I began college at the age of 22. I started at a small Black college in the South. I only stayed there for a year, but the drug dealing followed me there. I used to transport weed and crack from DC to South Carolina. Once, when I was traveling south, the bus stopped at a town in North Carolina and was searched by the police. I had a quarter pound of weed on me, and it had a strong smell. Luckily, I was seated in the middle of the bus and I had time to see what was going on. I got the weed out of my bag and put it on my body, so when the police checked my bag, I had nothing but books in it. That was a close call!

(*Continued*)

Account: Crime: Omar's Story Continued

I believe if it hadn't been for my unconventional behavior, I wouldn't have been able to reach the goals I've reached. I managed to graduate from college at a very good university and I'll be applying to law school. Maybe that is backwards, maybe if I had followed the rules more my life would have been simpler. However, I cherish my experiences and believe that they have given me valuable insights about human behavior and the ways of the world. After interacting with drug addicts, dealers, inmates, prostitutes, the police, and being arrested, as well as being acquainted with the world of violence, going to college and finding out why these things exist gives me a dynamic spin on the way I look at them. I wouldn't say I am cynical, but many things don't surprise me. I'm glad I deviated as a youngster. I'm glad I didn't have certain constraints that would have keep me narrow-minded, which would have given me a fictitious understanding of the world. After coming to college, I realized that there was a reason why I broke society's rules. . . . I realize, though I had no business doing the things I did, my deviance allowed me to connect with underprivileged people, people I would have had little sympathy for if I hadn't lived their reality and shared experiences with them. I am glad I was deviant and I had the courage to break the rules. Still I'm fully aware of the consequences. Now I am able to make calculated risks that give me high rewards. I am a risk-taker. I pray that God continues to lead me in the right direction. I give Him and my parents all the credit for the successes I've had.

Questions

In many ways, Omar is an unusual criminal. Both parents are college graduates, and during some of his childhood, he grew up in a middle-class household. Moreover, he attended college after his incarceration, graduated, and applied to law school. In other words, he seems to have shed his "gangsta" image. Why did he find life on the streets initially alluring? Do you have faith that Omar will "go straight"? Do you sense a feeling of remorse in him for his criminal behavior? Does Omar's case tell us anything about the process of "exiting" from deviance? Will Omar's earlier involvement with crime and his ex-con status work for him or against him? What does his case tell us about criminal behavior? About deviance?

CHAPTER 6

Violence

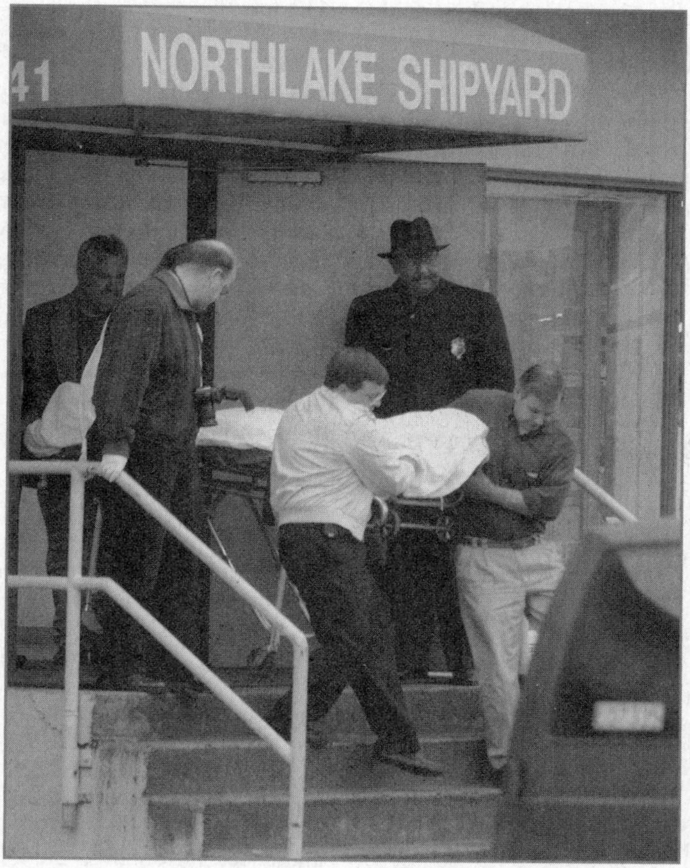

It might seem that everyone knows what violence is and nobody likes it. But this isn't completely true. Violence, as with every other concept in this book, is a social and cultural construct. What different observers *mean* by violence varies from one to another. When a police officer shoots and kills a struggling suspect, many observers would say that that killing is justified, and hence not a legitimate instance of violence—yet the suspect is still dead. Most people would argue that a punch thrown in the boxing ring or a block that levels a would-be tackler on the football field is not violent, even though both involve a great deal of force, and the man on the receiving end of each may experience pain for a while. When intergroup conflict breaks out and members of a group kill or beat members of another, they rarely see the violent acts their own group inflicts on the other as violence; violence is what is done to a member of their own group. At least one observer has argued that racism, classism, warmongering, and exploitation constitute a class of violence that he referred to as "covert, institutional" violence, that which inflicts harm to victims' body, dignity, autonomy, and freedom (Liazos, 1972). Labeling an act as violence is not solely dependent on the harm inflicted but on what the audiences consider illegitimate, unjustified, inexcusable motives.

MURDER

Paramount among the primal crimes is murder. Of all prohibitions, we might expect that the prohibition against murder is the one that is completely universal. Every society on earth—every single one, and at all times—has had a taboo against murder. If a primal crime can be said to exist, surely this is it. In other words, it might seem that, for murder, the constructionist's mission is irrelevant, and that only the essentialist and the positivist would have something to say about the subject. But the matter is not quite this simple. To understand what I mean, we have to make a distinction between "murder" and "killing."

The Social Construction of Murder

It is true that *murder* is universally condemned. But as we saw, the word murder is a loaded, evaluative term. It is a predefined category and *implies* a negative judgment. *By definition,* murder is a deviant, criminal killing. To say that murder is universally a crime is like saying a dog is a mammal. Since that is how murder is defined, murder is *always and by definition* deviant, as well as a crime. Saying that murder universally is a crime is a *definitional* not a descriptive or an empirical statement. *Of course,* murder is always and everywhere considered wrong, deviant, and a crime—that is how it is defined. But is the taking of human life—that is to say, *killing*—always and everywhere a crime? And the answer is this: "Of course not."

Presumably, the Sixth Commandment says, "Thou shalt not kill." Or so the commandment reads, in English, in the King James Version of the *Holy Bible.* This is a serious mistranslation. The original text of the Hebrew Bible actually read, "thou shalt not murder," which specifically refers to an unauthorized, illegitimate, and *criminal* form of killing. The verb "to kill" is objective and descriptive. It simply refers to the taking of human life, regardless of motive or circumstances. In contrast, the use of the term "to murder" is subjective, a judgment that a particular killing belongs to a category of deviant acts. King David, who was unquestionably aware of the Sixth Commandment, killed in battle; he was a warrior, he took human life—he *killed.* And he did so, according to Jewish tradition (and, as later interpreted by Christian theologians), not *in violation* of God's law but *in pursuit* of it. To the ancient Hebrews, David's slaying of Goliath, the Philistine, was a righteous killing, most certainly *not* one prohibited by the Sixth Commandment. David *killed,* but he did not *murder* Goliath. (I would like to thank Nachman Ben-Yehuda, an Israeli sociologist, for making this distinction clear to me.)

All societies accept, tolerate, authorize, legitimate, and even encourage certain sorts of killing. In other words, a very hard, concrete, and seemingly indisputable fact—the taking of human life, the death of a human being—is judged very differently, is subjectively evaluated and placed into vastly different categories, according to how it is seen by observers and audiences surrounding the killer and the victim. The legal status of a killing is determined by the law, the criminal justice system, and the courts. But in addition, we all have our own opinions on the matter. And whatever that opinion is, it is the result of a certain *judgment* that is made about the termination of human life. Making a judgment one way or another will transform a given act, in the blink of an eye, from criminal to noncriminal behavior, and vice versa. The point should be clear: *The taking of human life is tolerated, even encouraged, under certain circumstances. Some* killings are not seen by certain observers or audiences as murder, criminal, or deviant. Human life has never been an absolute value in this or in any society in human history. What is evaluated as murder, criminal homicide, or a deviant form of killing is the result of a socially and culturally based judgment. In other words, what is or is not murder is *socially constructed.*

The statistical majority of Americans do not consider human zygotes (newly fertilized eggs), embryos (developing organisms roughly eight weeks or less following conception), or fetuses (developing organisms more than eight weeks following conception) as full-fledged human beings. Therefore, the majority of the population does not regard abortions—which *kill* zygotes, embryos, and fetuses—as murder. Yes, most would say, an abortion destroys human *tissue,* but it does not kill *a human being.* Hence, to the "pro-choice" advocates, abortion is not murder. To "pro-lifers," in principle, since the instant a human sperm penetrates and fertilizes an egg, beginning with the zygote, a full-fledged human being exists; it is a "baby" or an "unborn child." Therefore, to the pro-life advocate, the abortion of zygotes, embryos, and fetuses is murder. Which position is correct? This cannot be determined empirically, with the tools of science. Whether abortion is or is not murder is socially constructed by the contestants in the abortion controversy. To say that one or the other position is correct is to adopt the essentialist perspective, which argues that socially constructed judgments are in fact based on an objective reality. I should note that the FBI's Uniform Crime Reports' *Crime in the United States* does *not* include abortions in its tally on murder and nonnegligent homicide.

When someone jumps in front of a car and is run over and killed, the law usually considers the killing an accident. However, during times of intergroup tension, if the driver belongs to one group and the deceased, another, unruly mobs have deemed such seemingly accidental killings as murder, and have attacked, even killed the driver. Justifiable homicide is a killing that results from the dictates of a legal demand, such as a police officer shooting a felon "in the line of duty" or a citizen taking action against a felon, presumably to protect his or her life or that of another. But until the 1970s, shooting a fleeing suspect was legal; today, it is not, and the officer who engages in such a killing could be prosecuted. Are assisted suicides criminal or noncriminal—acts of murder or mercy? In Switzerland and the Netherlands, such actions are legal; in the United States (except for Oregon), they are not. An absolute pacifist would see *all* killings, including those that take place in warfare, as murder. Again, the same objective fact, the termination of human life, results in differing subjective judgments.

These examples illustrate the fact that we should keep in mind *how* homicides are categorized and *why.* A basic question we have to ask here is this: *What sorts of killings are judged as criminal—and deviant?* And which ones are tolerated, accepted, and condoned—*not* considered criminal or deviant? These are some of the issues that a constructionist would deal with in studying murder as a social construct.

Murder: The Positivist's Mission

In spite of the importance of the social construction of murder, many killings *are* legally classified as murder. And there is a social *patterning* to illegal killings. As we saw in the previous chapter, according to the FBI, 16,929 criminal homicides took place in the United States in 2007, a rate of 5.6 per 100,000 in the population for that year. The FBI refers to criminal homicide as "murder and non-negligent manslaughter" and defines it as the *willful* killing of one or more human beings by one or more others. Not included in the classification "are deaths caused by negligence, suicide, or accident; justifiable homicides; and [unsuccessful] attempts to murder or assaults." Although legally, the terms "murder" and "criminal homicide" refer to somewhat different phenomena, from here on I'll use them interchangeably.

The murder rate in the United States has fluctuated substantially over time. The country's murder rate was high in the 1930s (in the 1933–1934 period, 9.5 per 100,000 in the population). Part of that high rate was caused by poor medical care. Victims of violent incidents (who would have been saved today) died in the street, because medical care arrived too slowly, or on the operating table, because medical care was inadequate; what would have been aggravated assault today turned into murder then simply because the victim died. The murder rate declined throughout World War II, partly because a substantial segment of the population most likely to engage in violent incidents—young men—were not in the United States but away, fighting a war in Europe or the Pacific. In the 1943–1944 period, the murder rate was only 5 per 100,000, slightly more than half of what it had been a decade before. But starting roughly in 1960, criminal homicide began to increase, from under 5 between 1953 and 1964 to roughly 10 per 100,000 during the 1970s. It stayed high during the 1980s. In 1991, the U.S. murder rate stood at 9.8. But between the early to the late 1990s, it dropped, and in the 2000s, it has held more or less steady between 5.5 and 5.7 per 100,000 (Lane, 1997, p. 308; FBI, 2008).

Agreed, the category, criminal homicide, is a social construct, but once we've agreed on a definition and we've encompassed the actions included within that definition, we notice that these actions are *socially patterned* (Beeghley, 2003). The willful taking of human life is not a random event; it follows a set of sociological generalizations. These generalizations can be boiled down to 11.

One: *The public and media image of murder is extremely distorted.* The image of criminal homicide that is conveyed in the news, television crime dramas, and in murder mysteries, as well as the image most people have of the typical or modal murder, bears a loose relationship to the real thing. The public and media image exaggerate the role of mass and serial murders, murders committed during the course of a felony, such as a robbery or a rape, intentional or premeditated murder, murder for hire, murder for material gain, gangland slayings, and murders committed either by deranged, psychotic killers or truly evil human beings. These tend to be rare; they do not describe the modal or most common murder. Most murders take place during the course of an altercation between two uneducated males with low impulse control.

Two: *Most murders take place in the heat of the moment.* Very few killings are planned or premeditated. Explosive altercations or escalating interpersonal disputes represent the circumstances of the vast majority of all criminal killings: an argument between husband and wife or boyfriend and girlfriend; a fight between friends or acquaintances in a bar; or a dispute between neighbors.

Three: *Most murders are justified by killers as a form of vindication, a way out of an intolerable situation.* Assailants usually feel that in the killing they are obliterating, or defending themselves against hostile circumstances. They have defined the source of their oppression or humiliation as an evil that *demands* retaliation. ("He was in my face," "She slept with every guy in town," "He was my best friend—how could he *do* that to me?" "What the hell makes you think you can say that to *me?*" "You think you can get away with *that?*" or "Wadda think—you can dis *me?*") Only through a violent expression of rage are these killers capable of wiping away the disgrace of stigma, shame, and humiliation. In the words of Jack Katz (1988, pp. 12–51), murder is often "righteous slaughter."

Four: *The more intimate the relationship, the greater the likelihood that one person will kill another.* On a person-for-person basis, intimates—friends, acquaintances, neighbors, relatives, spouses, and lovers—are much more likely to kill one another than strangers are. Statistically speaking, murder is an *exceedingly* rare event; it very, very rarely happens; the vast majority of intimates do *not* kill one another. But of the willful killings that *do* take place, intimates figure in them extremely prominently. There are only a few dozen or a few hundred intimates in our lives, and many millions of strangers. However, only a quarter of all criminal homicides take place between and among strangers. Two plausible explanations: One, we are in the company of, or *with,* intimates, on an hour-by-hour basis, much more than we are with strangers, and two, though intimates are much more capable of stimulating positive emotions in us, they also stimulate our negative emotions, including rage.

Five—and this is an extension of our fourth generalization: *Murderers and victims look remarkably alike*. The stereotype is that the murderer selects a totally innocent victim and inflicts undeserved violence on him or her. Of course, no one *deserves* to be a murder victim, but the fact is, given the circumstances and interpersonal dynamics of murder as well as the social circles in which people who kill travel, in the majority of cases, the person who kills and the person who is killed are often difficult to distinguish—with respect to age, race, social class, residence, prior criminal record and background, the use of drugs and alcohol, the locales they frequent, and lifestyle. There are exceptions, of course, but the majority of homicide victims resemble their killers in most important ways.

Six—and this is also an extension of both our fourth and our fifth generalizations: *Murders tend to be overwhelmingly intraracial*. This means that blacks tend to kill blacks, whites tend to kill whites. There are many exceptions to this rule, of course, but in the United States, roughly 90 percent of all intentional killings by both blacks and whites conform to this rule. It is true that the intraracial factor is weaker in large cities than in smaller communities, and it is also true that interracial killings—those that take place between persons of different races—are on the rise. But in all communities and even today, intra-racial killings remain in the vast majority. The reason makes a great deal of sense: People who know one another stand a higher likelihood of killing one another than people who are more socially, emotionally, and physically distant. And people tend to be more intimate with persons of the same race and more distant from persons of different races. People of the same race interact more with one another, they spend more time with one another, they are emotionally more significant to one another, they tend to marry one another—and they tend to kill one another.

Seven: *African Americans are both more likely to kill and to be the victims of criminal homicide than whites are*. In the United States, each year (where the race of both victim and killer were known, where both were either white or black, and the killing was a single-victim, single-killer homicide), about half of all murderers are black and just under half of all murder victims are black. This means that, relative to their numbers in the population, African Americans are overrepresented as both killers and victims by a factor of four. Most criminologists argue that the reasons are demographic, that is, poverty, urban residence, and residence in more socially disorganized neighborhoods are the explanatory factors, not race per se.

Eight: *Murder is related to social class*. Socioeconomic status (or SES)—that is, occupational prestige, income, and education—is *very* strongly correlated with criminal violence generally and homicide specifically. Murders are *typically* committed by people toward the bottom of the SES ladder, that is, men who are relatively uneducated and unemployed or who work at poorly paid, low-prestige jobs. (Let's keep in mind, however, that murder is an extremely rare event, and so very, very few members of the lower class ever commit murder—but even fewer members of the middle classes do so.) When a murder is committed, it is extremely uncommon for someone at the upper end of the SES continuum—a successful lawyer, corporate executive, or physician—to have committed it. Just about every study that has ever been conducted on this relationship finds the same correlation. It is one of the most robust findings in the field of criminology (Beeghley, 2003, pp. 73–74). Researchers cite a number of factors to explain the relationship: being at the bottom of the heap; experiencing sharp social and economic inequality and its attendant deprivations; inadequate parental socialization, the relative absence of fathers or, more generally, intact families; having poor impulse control; living in neighborhoods and communities with high levels of disorganization and disintegration; being socialized into a subculture of violence; and living in an environment that combines continual challenges to one's manhood with physical prowess, strength, daring, and a resort to violence as tests of one's manhood.

Nine: Everywhere, *men are much more likely to kill than women*. In the United States, roughly nine out of ten killers are men; in 2007, the figure was almost exactly 90 percent. And men tend to kill men (in the United States, over seven out of ten of the criminal homicides that men commit are committed against another man); likewise, women tend to kill men (again, over 70% of the time that women kill, they kill a man). And when men *are* killed, they tend to *have been killed* by a man (this is true 90% of the time); when women are killed, they tend to have been killed by a man (again, this is true 90% of the time).

In other words, men loom much larger in the criminal homicide picture, both as killers and as victims. Whenever the exceptional woman kills, it is usually a man whom she kills; whenever the exceptional woman is killed, it is usually a man who kills her. The explanation? Men tend to be more directly governed by matters of dominance, hierarchy, competition, rivalry, rank, altercation, confrontation, and physical risk than women. And it tends to be other men with whom these rivalries and confrontations are involved. In contrast, when women kill men, they are most often defending themselves, whether directly or indirectly, in a physically abusive relationship.

Ten: *Rates of criminal homicide vary enormously from country to country, from one society to another.* Admittedly, the crime data from many countries are not very reliable. And legal definitions of criminal homicide are somewhat different the world over. Still, official statistics on murder are better than for any other crime, and so a few generalizations can be formulated. A number of Latin American countries, such as Guatemala (36.4 per 100,000 in the population), El Salvador (57.5/100,000), Colombia (61.1), and Brazil (30.8), have extremely high rates of criminal homicide. In general, the murder rate is also very high in African countries south of the Sahara; currently, Sierra Leone (34.0), Angola (36.0), and, especially, South Africa (69.0) have high rates as well. Murder tends to be extremely rare in Arab Muslim countries such as Egypt (1.3), Morocco (1.1), Kuwait (1.4), and the United Arab Emirates (0.7), which have rates that are one-fortieth to one-fiftieth those of countries with the world's highest half-dozen rates. Poverty is *related* to high rates of criminal homicide, but Bulgaria (3.1), Romania (3.3), Hungary (2.2), and Portugal (1.8), European countries that are substantially less affluent than the United States, have rates that are half that of the United States. As a general rule, the murder rate is strikingly lower among fully industrialized, especially those in northern and western Europe, than in industrializing Third World nations. The United States (5.9 in these data) has the highest rate of criminal homicide among the industrialized countries of the world. Some experts attribute this distinction to the ready availability of guns, but guns are also readily available in Canada (2.0), Switzerland (2.9), and Australia (1.5), countries with much lower murder rates. (These data are available from the United Nations, Office on Drugs and Crime, "International Homicide Statistics," which are based on the World Health Organization's statistics; I have taken the WHO's higher estimates.) Among all industrialized societies, the United States has the strongest tradition of resolving conflicts with violence. Still, as we saw, the rate of criminal homicide in the United States, along with crime in general, has been declining for two decades.

And eleven: *In the Western world, violence, especially lethal violence, has dropped enormously since the Middle Ages* (Johnson and Monkkonen, 1996; Pinker, 2009). Europe prior to industrialization was an extremely dangerous place in which to live; violent death at the hand of another was a common event. One estimate has it that medieval Europe's homicide rate was 10 to 20 times higher than it is today (Gurr, 1989). Nearly everyone at the time went about armed with a knife, a staff, a sword, or a club. Violence as a solution to disputes was routine; "murderous brawls and violent deaths . . . were everyday occurrences" (Givens, 1977, pp. 28, 34). Historians argue that the reasons for the decline in the homicide rate over the past half-millennium or so include the growing power of a central authority, that is, the monarchy; the expanded role of courts of law to settle disputes; and what's called the "civilizing process" (Elias, 1994), that is, as a result of socialization through the educational process, learning manners, civility toward others, propriety, and restraining the expression of one's emotions through physical actions (Beeghley, 2003). In addition, the higher the level of economic development, the lower the rates of criminal violence. The United States is, as we saw, a partial exception to that rule, since it is both affluent and more violent than many less economically developed countries. Muslim countries, likewise, offer an exception, since most are not wealthy but have very low rates of criminal homicide.

Positivists take the constructed nature of murder for granted—they put it on the back burner, so to speak—and examine criminal homicide as a consistent, coherent, materially real form of behavior rather than a socially defined and judged phenomenon. However, as we've just seen, murder possesses enough internal consistency to reveal social patterning; certain categories of people in the population, certain types of societies, and certain eras in history exhibit higher rates of criminal homicide than others. As a result, positivists argue, specific conditions are consistently and causally related to the likelihood of committing violence. It is the job of the positivist social scientist to locate those conditions, establish relevant generalizations, and explain *why* murder breaks out.

FORCIBLE RAPE

The FBI defines forcible rape as "carnal knowledge of a female forcibly and against her will." Statutes regard any forced penetration of a woman's mouth, vagina, or anus by a man's penis as rape. Men can be raped by men, and it does take place frequently in prison, but it is far less often studied, and is less likely to be taken seriously by the public. Male-to-male rape is not *defined* by the FBI as rape; hence, legally, it does not exist, at least not as rape. Currently, among criminologists and other social scientists, forcible rape is regarded primarily as a violent rather than a sexual act. (Forcible may be distinguished from statutory rape, or consensual sex with an underage female; legally, an underage female is not capable of granting sexual access.) Rape is an *assault.* It employs force, violence, or the threat of violence. This is not to say that sex is not involved in any way—after all, there is a difference between beating a woman and sexually assaulting her. If there were no difference, acts of rape would be classified exclusively as assault, and rape would not exist as a separate category. In rape, there is, to be technical about it, genital contact, or an attempt to effect genital contact, while there is no such element in simple assault by itself. But what defines an act as rape is that it is nonconsensual, a sexual act *forced on,* or *against,* a woman, against her will. *In this respect,* it is no different from aggravated or serious assault. Legally and by definition, forcible rape entails the use of force, violence, or the threat of violence. Thus, rape is *always* and *by definition* a violent act. Rape is *never* free of its violent character. Even if the victim, the offender, the general public, or law enforcement did not regard a specific rape as violent, legally, *if it is forced,* it is rape. What *defines* or *constitutes* it *as* a rape is that it is, *by definition and by its very nature,* against the victim's will—and therefore violent, and therefore rape. As we might expect, however, even this clear-cut and emphatic formulation hides a swarming host of social constructions.

The Social Construction of Rape

As Diana Scully says, the arguments that emphasize the violent and aggressive character of rape often "disclaim that sex plays any part in rape at all" (Scully, 1990, p. 142). The fact that rape is—always, by definition, and by its very nature—violent, does not mean that it cannot be *other* things as well. The "rape isn't about sex—it's about violence" cliché is a bit too simplistic for sociological purposes. It sets up a false dichotomy, which assumes that rape is about *either* violence *or* sex—it cannot be about both. This formulation assumes that there is one and only one way of looking at rape, that there is an inner concrete or objective "essence" contained by rape—which is violence—that manifests itself to all reasonable and unbiased observers under any and all circumstances. *And* that this essence precludes other, very different, essences, such as sex—whose essence is mutual consent. Since rape lacks the latter essence, it cannot, by definition, be true or real sex. But, as we've already seen, the same phenomenon can be regarded, defined, or experienced in different ways. What is rape to the woman and to the law *may* be sex to the man. This does not mean that it is any the less violent—and therefore not rape. What it does mean is that it may be experienced differently by the rapist. It may be both sex (to the man) *and* a violent assault (to the law, much of the public, and the female victim).

Scully argues that rape can be sex *in addition to* being violence. First, for some men, violence and sex are fused. For them, violence against women has become sexualized. There is something erotic and sexually exciting about inflicting violence upon women. To these men, sex and violence do not exist in separate worlds. To the contrary, they are coterminous. Rape is sexual *because* it is violent. Of course, for their female victims, there is nothing erotic at all about rape. And second, for many men, rape is instrumental—to gain sexual access to otherwise unattainable women (Scully,

1990). For many men, rape represents a means of attaining sexual access to women who are otherwise unattainable to them. For these men, rape is not about violence because they do not imagine that what they do is particularly violent. "When a woman is unwilling or seems unavailable for sex, men can use rape to seize what is not offered" (Scully, 1990, p. 143).

The social construction of rape is relative (Curra, 2000). Different audiences define it in different ways. Two persons or audiences could watch a videotape or hear a description of exactly the same act—both of which qualify by the FBI's definition *as* rape—and one would regard it as an instance of rape and the other wouldn't. This does not mean that we cannot settle the issue of what rape is according to the law. In fact, the law is quite specific concerning its definition of rape. What it means is that social, cultural, group, and individual conceptions vary as to just what constitutes rape (Estrich, 1987; Bourque, 1989). What rape *is thought to be* is partly a matter of definition. What we have here is a striking contradiction between how the law defines rape ("the carnal knowledge of a female forcibly and against her will") and how many people judge concrete cases *that actually qualify as rape* according to the law. As a result, it is absolutely necessary to examine *how rape is seen, defined, and judged by audiences.* The central importance of these varying judgments becomes clear when we examine their role in subjective judgments of rape made by three crucial audiences: *the general public, the criminal justice system,* including the police and the courts, and *victims of rape.*

The general public can be divided according to a *spectrum* or *continuum* of judgments of what's rape. At one end, we have those that are *exclusive,* that is, the definition is very *narrow,* which judge *very few* acts of sexual aggression by men against women as rape. At the other end, we have judgments that are *inclusive*—that is, they are extremely generous, very broad—which include *many* acts as rape.

Perhaps the most extremely exclusive definition would be held by rapists, many of whom believe, in effect, that rape does not exist, and that all or nearly all charges of rape are false. One convicted rapist expressed this view when he denied the existence of rape on the grounds that "if a woman don't want to be raped, you are not going to rape her." Said another, rape is when a woman says, "No, you're not going to get it and you're going to have to beat me senseless to where I can't fight you" (Williams and Nielson, 1979, p. 131). A minuscule number of acts of intercourse against a woman's will would qualify as rape by the exclusivistic or narrow definition, which sees men as having nearly unlimited sexual access to women, regardless of their resistance, and women as having no rights at all—only the choice between death or being beaten unconscious on the one hand and being assaulted on the other. In one study of convicted, incarcerated rapists (Scully and Marolla, 1984), nearly a third said that they had sex with their victims but denied that it was rape. "As long as the victim survived without major physical injury," these men believed, "a rape had not taken place" (p. 535).

At the other end of the spectrum, equally as extreme, is the *inclusive* definition, held by some radical, militant, lesbian feminist separatists, who believe that *all* intercourse between men and women, however consensual it may appear on the surface, represents an assault, an act of aggression, an invasion, a violation—in a word, rape. Men exercise power over women—*every* man has power over *every* woman—and consequently, *no* sexual relationship between any man and any woman can be freely chosen by the woman. *All* heterosexual sex is coerced—that is, is not freely chosen by the woman—and hence, qualifies as rape. Heterosexual sex is, *by its very nature, tainted* by patriarchy, *saturated* with its sexist essence. In a patriarchal society, women are brainwashed to think they want male companionship and all that goes with it. In a truly equalitarian society, no woman would want to have sex with any man. Hence, *all* heterosexual sex is rape (Dworkin, 1981, 1987).

Both the extremely *exclusive* view, held by most rapists, and the extremely *inclusive* view, held by a few (and dwindling number of) radical feminist separatists, represent tiny minority views. Very few Americans would agree with them. Between these two extremes, we will find the *moderately exclusive* and the *moderately inclusive* definitions, which, together, encompass the views of the overwhelming majority of the American public.

The moderately exclusive definition tends to be held by sexual and sex and gender-role *traditionalists* and *conservatives.* Persons who hold to the moderately exclusive definition believe that a woman's place is in the home and that she must have a man to protect her from the advances of other men. If she puts herself in a vulnerable position, this view holds, such as going to bars, acting flirtatiously or seductively, going alone to a man's apartment and allowing one in hers, wearing "provocative" clothing, dating a number of men, hitchhiking, or walking on the street alone at night, or even remaining single too long, perhaps she is responsible for provoking men's sexually aggressive behavior, maybe she provoked men into forcing intercourse on her. Maybe she wanted it all along—maybe it wasn't force at all. This definition does not see a great many acts of coercive intercourse as rape because it does not accept the view that women should have the freedom, especially the sexual freedom, that is granted to men. This view is summed up in the saying, "Nice girls don't get raped." In other words, if women don't engage in all these sexually provocative activities, they won't bring on men's sexual attention in the first place. The corollary of this saying is that if a woman is raped, maybe she wasn't so nice after all. It is possible that some version of this definition is held by a majority of the American public. It is possible, in other words, that most Americans hold a moderately exclusive definition of rape. Many, perhaps most, Americans—to a degree, and under a number of circumstances—will blame a woman for certain kinds of sexual attacks against her. They restrict their notion of what rape is to a relatively narrow or exclusivistic set of acts.

In contrast, the *moderately inclusive* definition tends to be held by sexual and sex and gender-role *liberals.* They believe that a woman has the right of sexual determination, the right to choose where and with whom she wants to go. Thus, she cannot be blamed for an attack against her. If a woman makes it clear she is not interested in a man's advances, and he persists, then he is forcing himself on her; she is being coerced, the act takes place against her will, and it is a case of rape. Moderate inclusionists feel women should not have to be protected by a man to live a life free of sexual assault. She has the same rights to go where and when she wants as a man has. And she has the right of control over her own body, whom she chooses to go to bed with, and whom she refuses to bed down with. Men have no right to force her to do anything sexual; if they do, it's rape. Men do not have the right to threaten to harm, or pin a woman's shoulders down, twist her arm, force her legs open, physically restrain her, or jam an elbow into her windpipe—or do *anything* to physically overpower or coerce her—in order to have intercourse with her. If they do, it's rape. The moderately inclusive definition is probably held by a minority, albeit a substantial minority, of the American public.

Judgments made by the criminal justice system—the police, prosecutors, and the courts—reflect the same discrepancy between what rape is legally (or objectively) and how it is defined by various audiences. Each year in the United States, hundreds of thousands of women are victims of coerced intercourse—they are raped, according to the legal definition—who are not *regarded* as having been raped by the criminal justice system. Sexual violence inflicted against women is tolerated by the criminal justice system under certain circumstances. To understand how this happens, it is necessary to grasp the distinction between two kinds of rape—*simple* and *aggravated* rape. These categories correspond roughly, but not perfectly, with *acquaintance* and *stranger* rape (Estrich, 1987).

Simple rape is forced sexual intercourse in which there is little overt, clear-cut violence (i.e., there is no weapon and no beating), there is a single assailant, and he has some prior relationship with the victim. Aggravated rape—to the law, "aggravated" means serious—is defined by overt violence (a weapon and/or a beating), or multiple assailants, or no prior relationship between victim and assailant. The American criminal justice system is schizophrenic about rape. Even though, by law, there is only one kind of rape, the way that sexual violence is prosecuted—or not prosecuted—makes us realize that, in fact, there seem to be two kinds of rape: simple and aggravated rape, as spelled out earlier.

If our definition of rape is limited to aggravated cases, then rape "is a relatively rare event, is reported to the police more than most crimes, and is addressed aggressively by the police." On the other hand, if the cases of simple rape are included, "then rape emerges as a far more common, vastly underreported, and dramatically ignored problem" (Estrich, 1987, p. 10).

Almost no one "has any difficulty recognizing the classic, traditional rape—the stranger with a gun at the throat of his victim forcing intercourse on pain of death—as just that" (Estrich, 1987, p. 13). In such cases, victims usually report the crime to the police, who record it as a crime, and undertake an investigation to discover and apprehend the perpetrator. If the offender is caught and the evidence against him is compelling, he will be indicted and prosecuted. Chances are he will be convicted. Given our system of plea bargaining, the likelihood is high that he will be convicted on a less serious charge than rape; nonetheless, there is a better than even chance that he will serve jail or prison time for the offense.

On the other hand, when the case is one of simple rape—say, when a man has forced himself on a woman he knows, especially in a dating situation, when he is in her apartment, or she in his, willingly and voluntarily, and when there is no overt violence and no weapon—the criminal justice outcome is almost always different. Women who are victims of such attacks rarely report them to the police. If they do, the police are not likely to pursue the case, even to officially record it as a rape. And if the suspect, by some accident, is arrested, he is unlikely to be indicted. If he is, the case is unlikely to go to trial. If it does, he is not likely to be convicted. And if he is, he is unlikely to go to jail or prison.

The crucial importance of the subjective dimension becomes even clearer when we look at definitions of rape *used by the victims themselves.* Research indicates that the *majority* of women who are victims of forced intercourse *do not see themselves as having been raped! Any* time a man coerces, forces, or threatens violence against a woman to have sex with her, it is rape. But most women who are so coerced, forced, or threatened do not define themselves as the victims of rape. One study asked 595 undergraduates at a large Eastern university several questions about rape and forced intercourse. One question read: "Have you ever been forced to have sexual intercourse when you did not want to because some degree of physical force was used (e.g., twisting your arm, holding you down, etc.)?" Sixteen percent of the sample answered this question in the affirmative. But when they were asked, "Have you ever been raped?" only *2 percent* said yes. (In addition, not all of those who said yes to the second question also said yes to the first.) In other words, only about one out of seven of the women (or 15%) who said that they had been forced to have intercourse saw themselves as having been raped! For most of them, there was a failure to perceive forced sex *as* rape. "There seems to be a tremendous confusion among these victims regarding their experiences and their legal rights. They were legally raped but they do not understand this behavior to be rape, or they are not willing to define it as such" (Parrot and Allen, 1984, p. 18).

Explanations of Rape: The Positivist Approach

The FBI recorded a total of just over 90,400 rapes in 2007, for a rate of 30.0 per 100,000 in the population. (Or roughly twice that for the females in the population.) All criminologists recognize that this figure substantially underreports the frequency of sexual assault in the United States, since most rape victims do not report the crime, or even, as we just saw, recognize forced sex, when it occurs, *as* rape. Victimization surveys find that of all serious violent crimes (rape, robbery, and aggravated assault), rape is *least* likely to be reported. The 2006 National Crime Victimization Survey (NCVS) estimates the number of rapes or sexual assaults to females age 12 and older in the population at 272,000, substantially higher than the official FBI figures (Rand and Catalano, 2007, p. 3), which means that most rape victims (59%) do not report the offense to the police. Rates of reporting are *higher* when the offender was a stranger to the victim, is armed, and when the victim is physically injured, and *lower* when the offender is known to the victim, is not armed, and when the offender is not physically injured (Rennison and Rand, 2003, p. 1). Hence, from official police statistics, we receive not only a distorted view of the *frequency* of rape, we also receive a distorted view of its *nature* as well. *Unreported* forced sex—in comparison with *reported* forced sex—is much more likely to be acquaintance or date rape, and much less likely to involve a weapon, and to result in serious physical injury. With information on rape, as with all other social phenomena, we must pay close attention to *how* researchers gather that information and thus, what *aspect* of reality is included—and excluded.

Perhaps the three major types or broad categories of theories of rape causation are *individual, sociocultural,* and *situational.* Individual explanations of rape are those that argue that some men have a higher *tendency* or *proclivity* to sexually assault women than others do. Rapists are different from nonrapists, and men who rape have different personalities or a different upbringing from those who don't. Sociocultural explanations of rape are those that argue that the content of certain *cultures* or *subcultures* influence men to be sexually aggressive toward women; men influenced by these cultural messages are more likely to force women to have sex than is true of men who learn to treat women in a more equalitarian and less aggressive manner. And situational explanations are those that focus on factors that place women in vulnerable situations. A certain proportion of the men in those situations will sexually aggress against these women because the women are available and there is nothing to prevent them from committing the act.

The most *extreme* form of the individual explanation of rape is the *psychopathology* theory. It holds that rapists are disordered, mentally ill, or "sick." (Groth, 1979.) It is clear that this perspective cannot explain the actions of *most* rapists. Most are, in fact, depressingly normal. Most are able to function in the everyday world—attend school, hold down jobs, interact with others in a conventional fashion. As an explanation for the typical or most common rapist, the psychopathology theory is clearly wrong. This does not mean that no rapist is mentally disordered. In fact, the more violent and brutal the rape, the greater the likelihood that a mental disorder comes into play. And the further from conventional male–female courtship a given rape is, the greater the likelihood than it was motivated by psychopathology.

More moderate individual explanations argue that the personalities and backgrounds are not so much sick or disordered as they are *different* from the men who do not rape women. Psychologist Neil Malamuth more or less conclusively demonstrated that rapists are different from nonrapists. He asked a group of undergraduates to fill out questionnaires and say whether there was "some" (on a sliding scale) or "no" chance that they would rape a woman, if they could get away with it. Then he played (fictional) audiotapes of a variety of sexual encounters, including sexual aggression by men against women without the woman's sexual consent. The men who said that there was some chance that they would rape a woman were significantly more sexually aroused (as measured by a monitoring device) by the sexual aggression tapes than the men who said that there was no chance. Then Malamuth played these tapes to convicted, incarcerated rapists—who presumably actually *had* raped women. The college men who said that there was some chance that they would rape a woman and the rapists had similar arousal patterns, while the arousal patterns of the "no chance" men were very different. In addition to looking at arousal patterns, Malamuth found that, like the convicted rapists, the "some chance" men were also more likely to believe in rape myths (women enjoy rape, that women who were raped were "asking for it," etc.), and more likely to have admitted to actually having used force women to have intercourse with them. In short, there is a cluster of individual or personal factors that indicate that some men have a higher proclivity to rape women, and that men characterized by these factors have in fact raped women (Malamuth, 1981).

Gottfredson and Hirschi (1990) agree that rapists are a particular type of individual. (They *also* support the situational or opportunity theory, which I elaborate later.) As we saw, their "general theory of crime" argues that crime is a product of poor parental socialization, which in turn leads to low self-control. Recall from Chapter 2 that Gottfredson and Hirschi argue that criminal acts "provide immediate gratification of desires . . ., *easy* or *significant* gratification of desires," including "sex without courtship." In addition, such behavior is "*exciting, risky, or thrilling.*" Moreover, crime "often results in pain or discomfort for the victim." People who lack self-control and who commit predatory crimes against others "tend to be self-centered, indifferent, or insensitive to the suffering and needs of others" (p. 89). In other words, Gottfredson and Hirschi's general theory of crime is an example of an individualistic explanation of rape. They argue that it is the early childhood experience of males growing up in an inadequate parental or supporting only child-care environment that determines their likelihood of sexually aggressing against women (and a great deal more as well). Their rape proclivity is an *aspect* or a *feature* of their more general tendency to grab, take, steal, exploit, and satisfy themselves at the expense of others—regardless of the consequences. The gratification that Gottfredson and Hirschi see as motivating the rapist is primarily sexual rather than political or ideological. That is, they do not seek to subdue or humiliate women, as feminists claim. Instead, they correspond to one of Scully's rape characterizations, they "seize what is not offered" (Gottfredson and Hirschi, 1990, p. 143). And they do this because they lack impulse control, and they lack impulse control because their parents or caretakers did not monitor or sanction their deviant behavior when they were growing up. In short, they rape because they are different kinds of individuals from conventional, law-abiding, nonrapist males.

Sociocultural theories argue that the norms, values, and beliefs held by the members of a given society, or social group, circle, or category, are *conducive* to men raping women. In other words, men *learn* to rape in much the way that, in our society, they learn to play football or eat pizza. According to this perspective, rape is *conventional* behavior. Sanday (1981) analyzed ethnographic data from 95 small, tribal societies and found a substantial proportion in which rape was extremely uncommon or unknown (which she called "rape-free"), while in a few, rape was a much more likely event ("rape-prone"). The norms of the rape-free societies discourage sexual aggression and encourage sexual equality, while those of the rape-prone society encourage sexual aggression and male dominance. Similarly, Sanday (1996) believes that different campuses also vary with respect to how rape-free or rape-prone they are. Some college campuses (the relatively rape-free ones) urge norms that are conducive to female equality, friendship between men and women, and acceptance of homosexuality, discourage heavy fraternity drinking, and severely punish sexual assault. In contrast, other campuses (the comparatively rape-prone ones) are characterized by male dominance, heavy drinking, taking advantage of intoxicated women, male sexual promiscuity, the ridicule of homosexuals, and ignoring or "slap-on-the-wrist" penalties for sexual assault. On the former campuses, we can expect low, and on the latter, high incidences of rape. Sanday also argues that, in general, the majority of college fraternities teach their members values and norms that are conducive to rape: drinking heavily, sexual inequality, exploiting and taking advantage of women, and sexual promiscuity (Sanday, 1990). Sanday's explanation for rape is sociocultural; she argues that the factor explaining sexual aggression by men against women is the socialization process. In some collectivities, men *learn* to rape women; in others, they do not.

In spite of what some observers have argued, the sociocultural explanation is not mutually exclusive or contradictory with the individual explanation. Neither can be expected to explain all or most rapes. In fact, in the vast majority of rapes, neither is the only valid explanation; both operate simultaneously. Feminist proponents of the sociocultural model argue that in American society, rape is common because rape-positive values are an essential component of American culture. We live, it is said, in a patriarchal culture in which men are dominant, a sexist culture in which women are devalued and relegated to an inferior status, and an androcentric culture in which men are center stage and women occupy a secondary, servile, and marginal status. Men learn that they deserve to be served and gratified by women; women exist to cater to men's needs. It is inevitable that in a society, men would be imbued with a culture that fosters rape. In fact, some feminists argued, not only are women systematically victimized by rape, rape is also a political instrument for keeping women servile, subservient, and submissive (Brownmiller, 1975; Russell, 1975). To cite one spokesperson for this view: "All men are socialized towards an aggressive masculinity and encouraged to see women as inferior to themselves." Thus, she says, all men are capable of rape, the only missing element being an "individual man's decision to become a rapist" (Roberts, 1989, p. 28).

This simplistic model of rape holds a mistaken conception of culture. No culture is ever a seamless, unified, coherent whole. All members of all cultures are exposed to, and learn, different strands of an elaborate, complex mix of teachings. There is practically no value or norm that is swallowed whole by all members of any society. While the eroticization of dominance and subordination exists in our society, as it does in many others, this is not necessarily a cultural strand that is picked up and adopted by all, or even most, of its male members.

We live in a society, it is true, in which many, and very likely the majority of, men learn that women are inferior and should be expected to serve them. There is a sexual double standard, which accords men more sexual freedom than women, which dictates that men are free to come and go as they wish, but that if a woman takes on the same freedoms, well, she should expect the consequences, rape being one of them. A society that discourages women from seeking their own destiny, freedom, and autonomy, from wanting to have some of the mobility and privileges that men enjoy, will be one that will excuse certain forms of rape as justified or provoked by the woman.

But conventional, mainstream cultural values do not *directly* encourage men to rape women. They may (for some men) provide the raw material, which some men use to justify hostile, exploitative attitudes and behavior against women. By themselves, they dictate no rape-related behavior. To repeat: There is no doubt whatsoever sociocultural factors influence rape. But since *most* men, even in a society with sexist values, never rape women, clearly, this theory is not a complete explanation. You cannot explain a variable (some men rape and some don't) with a constant (American society is sexist, and hence, encourages rape). Mainstream American values do not support, condone, or encourage violence against women to the point of rape. What they do support, in varying degrees, is masculine dominance over women, which, *if taken to a behavioral extreme,* can find an outlet in rape. The key to an adequate explanation is finding what causes some men to push such values to their behavioral extreme. Saying that rape has a cultural component does not imply that there is no difference between conventional and deviant sexual aggression, or that "all men are rapists," or that there are no detectable differences between men who rape and those who do not, or that mainstream American values directly encourage the rape of women by men. Just as violence is a cultural value for some American males, not all men are violent to the point of homicide, or even assault. Cultural values are adapted, shaped, and transformed—or ignored—by each person living in every society.

Situational theories argue that the key to rape is *opportunity.* Clearly, routine activities theory fits in here. To the extent that a "motivated offender" (the potential rapist), a "suitable target" (i.e., a vulnerable, available woman), and the "absence of a capable guardian" (a locked door, a snarling dog, the police, or others who would protect the woman from attack) are in conjunction, rape is more likely to take place. To the extent that these three do not come into conjunction with one another, it is less likely (Cohen and Felson, 1979). Malamuth's research, which supports the individualistic theory of rape, also suggests the importance of opportunity, since 35 percent of his male subjects said that there was some chance they would rape *if they could get away with it.* In fact, this figure rose to 50 percent if they were asked about the likelihood of "forcing a woman to have sex" (Malamuth, 1981). In other words, the chances are a lot more men would rape if they had the chance. The fact that many are deterred by the fear of arrest or other sanctions keeps the incidence of sexual assault lower than it would otherwise be. In short, men are deterred from rape as a result of the *cost* to them, and that cost includes both arrest and social stigma. If both are low, the likelihood that a certain proportion of men will rape women is increased; if both are high, that proportion is correspondingly higher.

Tedeschi and Felson (1994) argue that women who date a number of different men, and who spend a substantial amount of time outside the home, especially at night, especially in cars, and especially in situations that are not supervised or monitored, are more likely to be rape victims than those who date no, or only one, man, and spend more time at home. Of course, as we know, some women are raped by dates, boyfriends, and even husbands, and being at home is no protection from sexual assault (Johnson, 2002). Moreover, focusing on women's behavior as an explanation for the rapes that are committed against them can be construed as *blaming the victim* (Ryan, 1976).

But some observers have argued that there is a clear-cut distinction between blame, which is a *moral* concept, and cause, which is a *scientific* or explanatory concept (Felson, 1991). Saying that women who date different men and go out a lot at night *do* have a higher than average statistical likelihood of being sexually assaulted is completely different, Felson says, from saying that they should be *blamed* for their behavior. If I take a plane to Los Angeles and the plane crashes and I die, my taking that plane is one *cause* of my death—but I should not be *blamed* for my death. In a society based on equal rights for all, women should have the right to come and go as they please. Opportunity is one cause of crime, and to the extent that women place themselves in situations in which motivated offenders face an absence of capable guardians, rape is more likely to take place. One way of cutting down on the odds is for women to become *their own* "capable guardians," that is, by carrying a weapon or learning karate.

These three factors—sociocultural, individual, and situational—have to be taken into account to explain a phenomenon as complex as rape. After summarizing the available literature as well as their own research, a team of psychologists (Malamuth, Heavey, and Linz, 1992) presents a perspective they refer to as the "interactional" model. It argues that for a male to commit an act of sexual aggression against a woman, several factors must converge in the same man: (1) becoming sexually aroused at the sexual assault of women; (2) being angry or hostile toward women; (3) holding attitudes that support violence against women; and (4) engaging in impersonal, promiscuous sex. These factors, the authors say, "interact" with one another. When presented with an available opportunity, a male who ranks high on a scale consisting of these four dimensions is substantially more likely to force a woman to have sex than the male who ranks low on it.

These four factors may be regarded as *proximate* causes of sexual aggression against women, that is, they stand near, next to, or immediately prior to the physical act of rape. They motivate or disinhibit some men to inflict sexual violence or aggressive actions against women. But what factors or forces encourage these orientations? Malamuth and his collaborators locate a number of earlier, prior, or more *distal* factors that stand out as crucial: being abused, especially sexually, as a child; experiencing poor, conflictual, violence-ridden parent-child interactions; and observing violence between parents.

Malamuth and colleagues also argue that a specific subculture—the delinquent subculture—acts as an intermediary between early conflictual experiences and the later, four-part constellation discussed earlier. A subculture of delinquent peers may contribute to the development of these attitudes and values. Youngsters are socialized by the delinquent subculture; it may exaggerate incipient attitudes they already have, as a result of their childhood experiences. "Subcultures and societies that regard qualities such as power, risk-taking, toughness, dominance, aggressiveness, 'honor defending,' and competitiveness as 'masculine' may breed individuals hostile to qualities associated with 'femininity.' For these men 'aggressive courtship' and sexual conquest may be a critical component of 'being good at being a man.' Men who have internalized these characteristics are more likely to be controlling and aggressive toward women in sexual and non-sexual situations" (Malamuth, Heavey, and Linz, 1992). Sanday (1990) argues that college fraternities facilitate much the same socialization process.

ROBBERY

Most people use the term "robbery" very loosely. They say, for example, "My apartment was robbed yesterday." To criminologists, robbery has a very specific meaning. Robbery entails *victim confrontation;* it is a theft involving force, violence, or the threat of violence. There is some controversy among criminologists as to whether robbery is a property crime or a crime of violence; clearly, it has some elements of both. In fact, it is the one crime that is *both* a property crime—since the perpetrator takes money or goods from the victim—*and* a crime of violence—since the perpetrator uses force, violence, or the threat of violence. About four out of ten of all robberies entail the use of firearms, about one out of eight entails the use of a knife, and about four out of ten are strong-arm or weaponless robberies.

Because of the confrontational nature of the offense and because both robber and victim might be injured in the course of the offense, robberies are much less common than other property offenses. Few who contemplate the crime have the daring and recklessness to face a victim and demand property or cash; most thieves prefer stealth and secrecy. One need only compare the 445,000 robberies tabulated in 2007 by the FBI with the 2.2 million burglaries and 6.6 million simple thefts (or "larceny thefts") to appreciate that robbery is a *vastly* less common offense than the other forms of stealing property. Most offenders simply do not wish to engage in robbery. It is a dangerous, high-risk activity. Robbers are very atypical of property crime offenders, since their crime is both a property and a violent crime; they are statistically more likely than property offenders to rape, commit aggravated assault, and murder. And, perhaps equally as important, robbery, like murder and rape, is one of those crimes most highly feared by the citizenry.

The total financial take for all robberies reported to the police in the United States in 2007 was $588 million—a minuscule haul for such a high-profile, well-publicized crime. (Remember, as we saw in the previous chapter, during that same year, retail stores were ripped off to the tune of $35 *billion*—mostly by shoplifters and employees—and not a single offender had to lift a gun to commit the crime.) Cash or property worth an average of $1,321 per incident was taken, although bank robbers ($4,201 per incident) did better than robbers of gas or service stations, convenience stores, or private residences. In 2007, about a quarter of all robberies were "cleared by arrest." Although this might seem low, consider that, if a typical robber steals only $1,300 per offense, and assuming his crime is reported half the time, and he is arrested only a quarter of the time his crime is reported, he will earn under $10,000 for each arrest. (Of course, consider two additional facts: One, the more that is stolen, the greater the likelihood that the incident will be reported, and two, commercial robberies are *almost always* reported.) Stated this way, robbery doesn't seem like a very promising way to make a living. Naturally, the FBI's statistics include a great many young, inept, unprofessional robbers who do not plan their jobs and who are very likely to get caught, and relatively few older, professional robbers who do plan their jobs carefully. Robbery may very well be a lucrative career for a small professional elite, but for the average robber, it represents a distinctly risky and unlucrative means of earning a decent income. Its appeal for those so motivated is that it yields a quick buck.

Robbery is overwhelmingly a big-city offense. The likelihood of being a victim of a robbery in a big city is *stupendously* greater than in a small town or a rural area. In 2007, according to the FBI, the robbery rate in counties with no cities of any size was 16.4 per 100,000 in the population; in cities with a population of a million or more, the robbery rate was 374.2 per 100,000—*almost 23 times higher.* Moreover, the robbery rate for nearly every category increased as community size increased; mid-sized cities were also in-between with respect to their robbery rates. No major crime increases as sharply in concert with community size as robbery. The reason should be obvious: Since robbery is a crime that entails victim confrontation, the victim typically sees—and can identify—the perpetrator. In a smaller community, the likelihood of identification is vastly greater than in a larger one. What big cities offer to the robber is *anonymity.* The two other offenses, both crimes of violence that entail victim confrontation—rape and aggravated assault—also increase with community size, but not nearly so sharply. The lack of anonymity in violent crimes is indicated by arrest rates: 44 percent for violent crimes versus 16 percent for property crimes. Assault is usually a crime that takes place between intimates, and it is almost never planned; the arrest rate for aggravated assault was over half, 54 percent, in 2007. Thus, anonymity rarely figures into the perpetrator's calculations as to when, where, and with whom to commit the offense. Rapists rely on the victim not to report the offense to the police, an assumption to some degree valid for acquaintance rape, but increasingly less so for stranger rapes. (The clearance or arrest rate for forcible rape in 2007 was 40%.) Clearly, anyone who wants to understand robbery must understand big-city life. In most cases, then, the robbery victim is confronted by a stranger. In a victimization survey of robbery victims (Harlow, 1987), this was true in just under seven out of ten cases of robbery by a single offender (69%) and just over eight of ten cases involving multiple offenders (82%).

Who is victimized by robbery? In the 1940s, Hans von Hentig (1948), a German criminologist, launched the study of the relationship between criminals and their victims. Hentig argued that much of what victims *do* or *are* leads to their victimization; crime is a product of an *interaction* between offender and victim, he said. The field of victimization was born. The earliest victimization studies were heavily influenced by Freudian psychology, which argued that victims *yearned,* and were in some way *responsible,* for their victimization. As we saw, such an assumption came to be dubbed "blaming the victim" (Ryan, 1976). But, again, as I've noted, current criminologists are much more careful to make a distinction between *blame* and *cause* (Felson, 1991). Victims may be selected by offenders in part because of what they do or who they are, but they should not be *blamed* for their victimization. *Blame* is a heavily value-laden term, whereas *cause* is a more objective, readily determinable sequence of events. For instance, young women are more likely to be the victim of a sexual assault than older women—this is a causal, not a moral, statement—but younger women cannot be *blamed* for being raped. Poorer households are more likely to be burglarized than more affluent households, but, again, to assign blame to their criminal victimization is both causally suspect and a confusion of analytically separate dimensions.

Members of what categories in the population are most likely to be victimized by robberies? Males are twice as likely as females to be robbery victims—2.9 per 1,000 versus 1.3 per 1,000 (Catalano, 2005, p. 7). Of all age categories, older teenagers (age 16 to 19) are most likely to be robbery victims, 4.8 per 1,000, while the elderly, age 65 and older, are least likely—in fact, less than one-tenth as likely as teenagers, 0.3 per 1,000 (p. 7). The rate of robbery victimization for African Americans, 3.8 per 1,000, is twice as high as for whites, which is 1.8 per 1,000 (p. 7). Lower-income persons are between four and five times more likely to be robbed than are the more affluent—6.4 versus 1.3 per 1,000 (p. 8). Street crime victimizes the poor and weak more than the affluent.

One of the reasons robbery is so important to criminologists is that it is a much more serious crime than the FBI's property offenses, and hence, a far better predictor of an offender's overall rate of involvement in crime. Given its relative rarity and the reluctance of most potential offenders have against forcing, or attempting to force, a person to hand over money or property, it tells us a great deal about someone who overcomes those inhibitions and does the deed. An offender who robs is highly likely to have previously engaged in a number of other types of offenses. In contrast, someone who engages in larceny theft or even burglary is significantly less likely to have engaged in other offenses. In other words, robbery is a very powerful *indicator* or *measure* of someone's involvement in or commitment to criminal behavior; it is a good predictor of future criminal activity.

Although robbery is technically a property crime *and* a crime of violence, most of the time, the concrete violence is more potential than actual. Usually the robber *threatens* his victims with harm rather than actually harming them. However, victims are harmed a fair proportion of the time—a minority, but a significant minority nonetheless. In a summary of a number of victimization surveys, victims were injured in 33 percent of all robberies; of these, they required hospital care in 15 percent of the cases, and in 2 percent, robbery victims required hospitalization at least overnight (Harlow, 1987, p. 7). In 2007, according to the FBI, more than 2,000 murders (2,184) were committed while the offender was committing a felony, such as a rape, burglary, or robbery, of which just under a thousand (924) were committed in the course of a robbery. In other words, of all the murders that took place in the United States in 2007 whose circumstances could be determined by the police, robbery-murders made up 1 out of 16 of the total (924 out of 14,831).

The likelihood of being injured during a robbery varies with the nature of the weapon. As a general rule, robberies committed with a gun are the *least* likely to result in injury, and strong-arm or weaponless robberies are the *most* likely to result in injury. Though the victim is unlikely to be killed during the course of a robbery (out of roughly 550,000 personal robberies and perhaps 150,000 robberies of commercial and financial establishments in the United States in 2007, as we saw, a bit less than a thousand resulted in the death of a victim, or less than one out of a thousand of all robberies), it is also true that, if the perpetrator uses a gun, death is more likely than for any other type of robbery, strong-arm included (Wright, Rossi, and Daly, 1983, p. 208). The use of a weapon and the occurrence of injury strongly influence whether a robbery will be reported to the police. In one victimization study, 45 percent of all strong-arm robberies, 54 percent of all robberies in which a knife was used, and 73 percent of those in which a gun was used, were reported to the police. And only 49 percent of noninjury, 61 percent of minor injury, and 76 percent of serious injury robberies were reported (Harlow, 1987, p. 9).

Who is the robber? The statistics on arrest compiled by the Uniform Crime Reports paint the following portrait of the robber—at least, the *arrested* robber. He is overwhelmingly male—90 percent, according to the Uniform Crime Reports. Just over half of all arrested robbers (54%) were black; only four out of ten (45%) were white. For no other Index Crime are African Americans so overrepresented. And he is young: 60 percent were under the age of 25, and 23 percent were under the age of 18. The problem with these statistics, as anyone might guess, is that they represent *arrested* robbers, not robbers in general. Robbers who aren't caught are likely to differ in important ways from those who are. For instance, almost certainly the younger, less experienced robber is more likely to be caught than the older, wiser, more cautious, more professional, and more experienced robber.

One way of verifying this suspicion is to compare the FBI's arrest figures with the *perceived offender characteristics* supplied by robbery victims in the victimization surveys of the National Crime Victimizations Surveys. The two sources of data generally agree with one another on robbers' characteristics, with some minor inconsistencies.

In nine out of ten robbery victimizations (89%), the offenders were male; in 5 percent of all cases, they were female; and in 4 percent, the victim was robbed by both male and female offenders—that is, victims said that at least one male and at least one female committed the crime. Clearly, then, there is nearly perfect agreement between the FBI's statistics on arrest and victims' reports with respect to sex. In about half of all robbery victimizations, the offenders were identified as black (51%); in a third, they were white (36%); in 4 percent, they were members of some other racial category; in 4 percent, the offenders formed a salt-and-pepper team of mixed race offenders; and the rest of the victims weren't sure of the race of the offenders. Here, there is close but less than perfect agreement: Nearly 10 percent more *arrested* robbers were black than robbers identified in victimization surveys.

In four out of ten of all cases of robbery (41%), offenders were described as 20 years old or younger; in another four out of ten, they were identified as 21 or older; and in not quite one in ten, they were described as being of mixed ages (Harlow, 1987, p. 2). Here, the correspondence between arrest and victimization figures is fairly close.

In a nutshell, then, the portrait we received from the FBI's figures on arrest and the characteristics as identified in victimization surveys is that, relative to their numbers in the population, robbers tend to be young, male, and black—and, of course, overwhelmingly urban.

Clearly, any explanation of robbery focusing on the offender must make use of at least two factors: *daring* and *poverty*. Robbery is not a crime for the fainthearted; it entails a great deal of risk, both to the victim and to the perpetrator. Robbers, therefore, tend to be (unrealistically) confident that they won't be injured or caught. Such misplaced confidence is more characteristic of males than females, the young than the older.

The race of robbery offenders is probably largely a function of a combination of the economic position of blacks in the United States and the fact that African Americans live in large cities. Black family income is roughly 60 percent of that of whites, and black unemployment is twice as high. Moreover, although a growing proportion of blacks earn incomes that, increasingly, approximate those of whites, a substantial proportion of the African American population is seemingly permanently stuck in the "underclass." In addition, since 1973, the poor have been getting poorer and the rich have been getting richer; hence over the past two decades or more, the economic situation of the underclass, of whom a disproportion are inner-city minority members, is not only stagnating, but deteriorating (Cassidy, 1995; Krugman, 2003). Added to the economic picture is the demographic factor: African Americans are much more urban than whites. Nearly three out of ten whites live in a rural area, whereas only 15 percent of blacks, half the white figure, live in rural areas. At the other end of the scale, a quarter of all whites in the United States live in central cities (25%); for African Americans, this is more than twice as high—between 50 and 60 percent. The combination of a lower per capita income and a far more urban residence makes it almost predictable that blacks will have a higher rate of robbery than whites. In addition, there is the factor of age; while only 30 percent of the white population is under the age of 20, 40 percent of the black population is that young. And as we saw, robbery-murders made up one out of 14 percent of all murders. Since the African American population is so much younger than the white population, this factor alone would tend to boost its robbery rate.

SUMMARY

The Index Crime lists murder and "nonnegligent homicide," rape, and robbery as its three violent Index Crimes. They form the "common core" of crimes all humanity punishes—although this is tempered or relativized by contingent factors such as who commits the act, against whom, and under what circumstances.

Murder has been a primal crime since the dawn of humanity. Even though there has been a common core to the acts that are judged murder nearly everywhere and at all times, exactly what specific acts are deemed murder has varied from one time and place to another. In many societies, if a member of a society killed an acceptable victim (a member of an "out-group"), the act was not deemed murder. If that same member of the society willfully and without reason or sufficient provocation killed an *unacceptable* victim (a member of the "in-group"), this was generally deemed murder, a deviant, unauthorized, and criminal offense. In this sense, cultural relativity exists even for the most reprehensible and heinous of acts.

Even though it is condemned in one form or another pretty much everywhere, rape exhibits even more relativity than murder. In the contemporary United States, a distinction is made between "aggravated" and "simple" rape. The law, the general public, and the courts distinguish two types of forced intercourse, one of which is regarded as reprehensible, criminal, and deviant, the other of which is regarded simply as a somewhat aggressive form of sex. Audiences vary with respect to how "inclusive" (or broad) versus "exclusive" (or narrow) their definitions of rape are; the variation is sociologically patterned.

Robbery is both a property and a violent crime. It entails victim confrontation, putting the victim in fear, or forcing the victim to relinquish money, property, or other things of value. Since it is dangerous both for the perpetrator and the victim, in comparison with theft and the other strictly property crimes, robbery is relative rare. In addition, the fact that a given perpetrator has committed robbery is more predictive of extensive involvement in crime than is true of property crimes. The *victims* of robbery, in comparison with the population at large, are more likely to be male, young, urban, poor, and African American. The perpetrators of robbery *also* tend to be male, young, urban, poor, and African American. The positivist criminologist attempts to explain the whys and wherefores of robbery.

Account: Having a Deviant Father

The following account was written by Danielle Fritze, when she wrote it, a 21-year-old college senior at the University of Maryland. She describes her life with her father, Arnold. In the following account, Danielle explains, "I aim to recollect the deviant life of my father through the experiences I have had with him, and from what I have been told by others whose recollections precede my memories of him."

My parents' . . . marriage was rocky from the start. About a year into the relationship, my father became physically abusive. I have seen a picture of my mother with a black eye my father gave her. . . . During the three years after my birth, life was relatively stable for my mother and father. . . . [Then] my little sister, Jeannie, was born. My mother told me that my father was very upset that he did not have a son. . . . To support his family of four, my father picked up a second job. . . . With the added stress of a second job, and a second child, my father's [previous] drug habit resurfaced. Although his drug use had basically [just] been marijuana from the time he and my mother were married, [after my sister was born] he started doing PCP and LSD again. My mother was extremely disapproving of my father's drug habit. This was often the subject of many fights between them. One fight in particular I remember being told about resulted from an incident when my father neglected my sister. One day, while my father was off from work, he and his friend did drugs in the basement of our house. My father left the house, abandoning my two-year-old sister for a few hours.

I recall many confrontations during which my father became violent towards my mother. The worst fight I witnessed between my parents happened when I was about six years old and my sister was about three. My sister and I were on the first floor of our house playing with toys when we heard our parents yelling upstairs. We went upstairs to find my father, a two-hundred pound man, sitting on top of my mother, a one-hundred pound woman, strangling her against the headboard of their bed. Despite the pleas of my sister and me for my father to stop choking my mother, he did not stop. This incident of abuse ended when I crawled up onto the bed and bit my father until he bled. Additional episodes of abuse I remember witnessing include my father threatening to throw my mother down the basement stairs, him holding her up by her hair and shaking her, and throwing a dining room chair on top of her after knocking her down. Despite my father's constant abuse of my mother, he never abused my sister or me. . . .

After twelve years of abuse, my mother and father separated. My father moved out of our house into an apartment. At first, it was hard for my sister and me to deal with the separation, but my mother explained to us that it wasn't safe for her and my father to remain married. My sister and I saw our father on Tuesdays and Thursdays after school and spent the night at his apartment every other weekend. During my visits with my father, he often sat me and my sister down and had long conversations with us. For the most part, these conversations were about the fact that my father thought my mother was trying to brainwash us into hating him. Although she never did anything of the sort, my father was convinced that because she had ended their marriage, my mother would try to end his relationship with his children. For about four years, my sister and I were having steady visits with my father, and he held those "brainwashing" conversations with us.

The first time I remember my father being admitted into a mental institution was when I was in the fifth grade. My mother received a call from my father's sister, Becky, and she told her that my father was unable to see my sister and me for a while, explaining the events leading to my father's hospitalization. Apparently, one day after work, Aunt Becky stopped by my father's apartment to give him something. When she entered his apartment, she found him, heavily armed, hunched behind his sofa, wearing a helmet. When my aunt asked my father what he was doing, he explained to her that it was Armageddon and he was preparing himself to fight for his life. He also revealed delusions that his mother was the Virgin Mary and that his father was Joseph, implying that he thought himself to be Jesus Christ. After seeing my father in this state, my aunt had him committed to a mental hospital. . . . There, he was diagnosed as bipolar, or manic depressive. During this time, my father maintained a correspondence with his work supervisor, who was very forgiving of his leave of absence, promising him his job back once he was mentally stable. Finally, my father was discharged from the facility after his condition was stabilized with lithium.

For a few months after my father left [the psychiatric facility], my mother supervised his visits with my sister and me. During the first

(*Continued*)

Account: Having a Deviant Father Continued

few weeks after my father was out of the hospital, he was a wreck. He had random crying spells. His voice was very high-pitched and he gave very long, inspirational life-lesson speeches. A few weeks after being discharged, he went back to work. Shortly after his return to work, because he felt normal, my father stopped taking his medicine. This led to his first relapse. At the time of my father's first relapse, I was in the sixth grade. His superiors at work were on the lookout for symptoms of mental irregularity. After seeing some signs that he was no longer on his medication, they made him recommit himself in order to keep his job. He was readmitted, this time for a longer stay than the first. My mother took my sister and me to visit him a couple times during his stay, thinking it might help get his spirits up and encourage him to stay on his medication. Shortly after leaving [the hospital the second time], my father returned to work, and once again he stopped taking his medicine, feeling his condition was regulated.

After stopping his medication for the second time, my father stopped working as well. My mother received no child support payments for over a year. Because my mother earned very little, my father's child support payments were necessary to make ends meet. Finally, my mother went to court. Since my father was not in any condition to work and since symptoms of a mental illness were apparent, my mother convinced him to file for disability payments from the government. That way, she would receive payments from social security in place of child support. My mother had realized that my father would never get better. She revoked his right to unsupervised visits with my sister and me. He was unhappy with this arrangement. Because of the return of income to his life [in the form of disability payments], my father started doing drugs again. Because he did not keep track of his spending habits—including indulgences in drugs, stereo equipment, and lottery tickets—he filed for bankruptcy and moved in with his parents. Eventually, he stopped seeing my sister and me. At some point, my grandmother, thinking that the beach would help my father get well, moved them into a trailer near the beach.

My mother, sister, and I heard nothing from my father for two or three years. The first news we got of him came late September when I was in the ninth grade. . . . The phone rang at six in the morning. . . . My sister answered the line and eavesdropped. [I didn't hear this until she got home from school when] she told me that our aunt called to tell our mom that there had been a murder. I insisted that my sister was mistaken, but she was persistent in her claim that she had heard correctly. When I asked for details, my sister told me to ask our mom because she wanted to go outside and play. . . . When my mom got home from work, I told her that my sister claimed that there had been a murder. After I told her that Jeannie was playing at a friend's house, my mother explained what happened. My aunt had called that morning to explain that my father had killed his mother and then attempted to kill himself. She did not elaborate and in fact she did not know the details, so she was unable to answer many of my questions. When my mom explained the contents of the phone call, I began having a panic attack.

It was extremely difficult for me to accept what my father had done and what had happened to my grandmother. After about a month, my aunt came to our house to explain the situation. Sparing no detail, my aunt told me the complete story leading to my grandmother's murder. Apparently, my father's mental health had drastically deteriorated. Although he was still receiving disability checks, his mother controlled the money, and this was often the cause of arguments. A few weeks before the murder, my grandmother called my Aunt Becky and explained to her that she was becoming increasingly afraid of my father. She often saw him sharpening knives and witnessed him talking to someone when there was no one in the room but himself. My aunt told my grandmother to have my father committed [to a mental institution] but she didn't listen. On the day of the murder, once again, my father and grandmother had been arguing about money. My grandmother was afraid of my dad, and she walked out of the trailer, but my father chased her and knocked her to the ground and threw a heavy metal object, a ring to contain campfires, on top of her. My father went back into the trailer and when he came back, wielding the knives he had been sharpening, he repeatedly stabbed my grandmother in the chest and abdomen. My grandmother's cries for help attracted an audience of concerned neighbors, fellow residents of the trailer park who had come outside to see what was going on. My father sat on the hood of his car, smoked a cigarette, then stabbed himself in the abdomen.

My father and grandmother were taken to a local hospital. My grandmother died shortly after arriving at the hospital and my father was treated for his wound and sent to the infirmary at the nearest hospital. Tests revealed that my father had some kind of foreign substance in his body which turned out to be medicine for his fish, which he was using to get high. When Aunt Becky asked my father why he had murdered their mother, he said that "The voices told me to" and "She is out of this horrible world now." My aunt told him not to think he did anyone any favors. After the incident, my grandfather was approached by the district attorney as to whether or not he wanted to pursue the death penalty against my father, but he refused their offer. My grandfather then went to live with my Aunt Becky because he was unable to deal on his own with the shock of what had happened.

About a year after my father was sent to jail, he began communicating with my sister and me both by mail and by phone. He was never particularly interested in talking to my sister because he thought my mom had successfully brainwashed her. . . . Nonetheless, they engaged in meaningless chit-chat. In my conversations with him, my father and I didn't mention his crime very much. The subject matter of our correspondence revolved around his trial—whether he was competent to stand trial, his lawyer, his lawyer's defense strategy, and other aspects related to his trial. At the time, the prison system held him in a psychiatric ward. He was more or less coherent, although he still heard voices. He was diagnosed as having a drug-induced condition characterized by symptoms similar to paranoid schizophrenia. At his trial, my father pled not guilty by reason of insanity.

The trial returned a verdict of guilty but insane; he was sentenced to life in prison without parole. When he could, he called or wrote and asked us to come and visit him in prison. My sister and I haven't gone to visit him since he has been incarcerated because, for the most part, he still isn't sane. He talks about creating a perpetual motion machine, and thinks his ticket out of prison is his invention of a magnet-powered automobile engine. My father thinks that if he can get someone to build his invention and get it patented, he will win the Nobel Prize for science and receive a presidential pardon from his prison sentence. He also believes that because he saw a cloud that looked like a human face, he is a spiritual messenger, with three half-brothers in heaven. Until last year, my sister and I indulged my father by listening to what he had to say without voicing our doubt about his delusions. The last few times my dad called, when he started speaking about his ideas, we just changed the subject. My father's calls have recently become few and far between, and he rarely writes us any more.

QUESTIONS

What's your reaction to reading this account? Clearly, the behavior and the condition of Danielle's father, Arnold, exemplify what is defined as deviance in this chapter. His drug use—to the point where its effects interfered in the conventional demands of his life—his violence toward his wife, and his delusions all violate the norms of this society. In addition, societal reactions toward him as a result of his behavior and his delusions point to its deviant character. His behavior and delusions generated both *official* reactions—Arnold was arrested, convicted, and incarcerated—and unofficial or *interpersonal* reactions, that is, his daughters have become increasingly estranged from him. In other words, what Arnold did and how he thought are both deviant and criminal. Has Arnold been labeled as *a* deviant? How do you feel about his daughter writing an account of her father's deviant behavior?

CHAPTER 7

Alcohol Abuse

What makes drinking alcohol deviant? The majority of adult Americans consume alcoholic beverages. According to SAMHSA's 2007 survey, roughly 8 out of 10 in the population age 12 and older has had an alcoholic drink once or more in their lives, and more than half (51%) said that they had had one in the past 30 days (2008). And 50 percent of high school seniors (all of whom are seriously underage) said that they had done so as well (Johnston et al., 2009). So, what's *deviant* about drinking alcohol? Shouldn't we acknowledge that the widespread consumption of a legal substance—in the United States, the basis of a more than $150 billion-a-year industry—and a perfectly conventional, mainstream activity is decidedly *not* a form of deviance? Isn't the consumption of a glass of wine or two at dinner well within the normative framework of nearly all the social circles in America? Shouldn't sports fans be allowed to enjoy a brew or two while watching a ball game? Indeed, isn't the *refusal* to drink considered a bit odd, eccentric, and unconventional—in a word, *deviant?* One sociologist even wrote his PhD thesis on the *under*consumption of alcohol as a form of deviance (Paton-Simpson, 1995). So, why should a sociologist of deviance study alcohol use?

FIVE REASONS DRIVE OUR INTEREST

First, the excessive consumption of alcohol makes it difficult for most people to effectively perform their expected institutional roles—marital, familial, economic, and educational. Swill down five or six drinks during lunch, stagger around your office, slur your words, appear dazed and confused while wandering the halls, fall asleep at your desk—and you're likely to be told to stop drinking or lose your job. Drink too much before class or when you should be doing your homework and you'll find you can't learn as much and you may flunk out of school. All societies depend on adequate performance in its fundamental institutions; an overly generous consumption of alcohol imperils that performance. No doubt about it: Failing to perform expected roles as a result of intoxication is a form of deviance.

Second, the effects of alcohol *facilitate* or *are associated with* the enactment of many forms of deviance, including crime, violence, sexual misbehavior, and needless and avoidable accidents. Epidemiologists find that the greater the amount of alcohol someone consumes, the greater the likelihood that he or she will engage in most deviant and criminal activities. Even being a *victim* of rape, robbery, murder, as well as a range of other predatory crimes is associated with drinking. Here, the deviant is not the victim but perpetrator; the victim is *forcibly* and *causally implicated* in the act by being victimized. Some critics have referred to this line of reasoning as "blaming the victim" (Ryan, 1976), but factually, the researcher can separate *blame* from the concept of *cause* (Felson, 1991). More on this later.

The third reason that drinking is interesting to the student of deviance is that, at certain times and in certain circumstances and social circles, the mere consumption of alcohol—*regardless* of its consequences—has been or is regarded as both legally and informally nonnormative. For instance, the distribution of alcohol was banned in the United States during Prohibition (1920–1933); it continues to be banned in a number of "dry" counties in the United States, and it is banned in certain jurisdictions around the world, mainly in Muslim nations. It is also regarded as unacceptable and untoward behavior among most evangelical Christians.

Fourth, while very few sociologists *define* deviance by harm (but see Costello, 2006), harm and deviance are not randomly related to one another; many of the most harmful activities are condemned. (In addition, condemnation sometimes makes an activity even more harmful.) Still, the relationship between harm and condemnation is an empirical question, testable with the use of systematic evidence. So our fourth concern is the flip side of our first one. The fact that alcohol causes, generates, or is implicated in, as much harm as it has, mostly without being banned or strongly condemned everywhere, is an interesting fact, one worth exploring. The enterprising sociologist of deviance wants to know *why* alcohol has received such fitful and mild, "slap-on-the-wrist" condemnation, while many less harmful activities are illicit, illegal, and strongly condemned. Certainly proponents of marijuana legalization have made this observation in advocating their cause. (For instance, click on NORML.org and SAFERchoice.org.) There may be a cultural or historical explanation, and perhaps the facts support a more rationalistic explanation. In any case, to the student of deviance, the issue is worth discussing.

And fifth, there's a concern that practically all adult members of the society harbor when it comes to drinking: alcohol consumption among minors. The majority of adults consider drinking *at all* among young people as nonnormative, because they don't believe that young people can handle their liquor. Among adolescents, intoxication is more likely to lead to problematic behavior, they believe, than among the mature. Even if *most* episodes of teen drinking result in unproblematic consequences, factually speaking, enough teens get into sufficiently serious trouble for adults to regard youthful alcohol consumption as unacceptable, nonnormative, and deviant.

ALCOHOL: AN INTRODUCTION

Fermentation is one of the most ancient of human discovering, dating to the Stone Age. Alcohol emerges spontaneously from the fermented sugar in overripe fruit; the starch in grains and other food substances also readily converts to sugar and from sugar to alcohol. Because this process is so simple and basic, the discovery of alcohol by humans was inevitable and early. Alcohol consumption, in all probability, began when a prehistoric human consumed fermented fruit and experienced its effects, enjoyed them, and communicated his or her discovery to others. Alcohol can induce pleasure, euphoria, intoxication, a sense of well-being, a state of relaxation, a relief from tension, a feeling of goodwill toward others, the alleviation from pain, drowsiness, and sleep. Unpleasant effects occur at higher doses, but nearly everywhere, such levels of use tend to be the exception rather than the rule. As a result, it is an almost universally accepted beverage. Consequently, as paleontologists and anthropologists tell us, alcohol's use tends to be both ancient and nearly universal: Humans have been ingesting alcohol for at least 10,000 years, and it is the most widely imbibed psychoactive substance in the world, ubiquitous, almost omnipresent the world over.

In spite of its universality around the globe, societies differ vastly in their average level of alcohol consumption. Every society that has some acquaintance with alcohol has devised and institutionalized rules for the proper and improper consumption of alcohol. These rules vary from one society to another and from one social category to another. Although alcohol does have objective biochemical effects, both short-term and over the long run, these effects can be influenced, mitigated, or altered by the observance of cultural rules for consumption. For instance, if alcohol is consumed on an empty stomach, its effects will be more drastic and debilitating than if taken in conjunction with the consumption of food. If male drinkers are surrounded by intimates, especially women and children—who usually control or mitigate their behavior—their tendency to take harmful risks will be diminished. In most societies, the vast majority of episodes of alcohol consumption pose little or no problem to the society. The drug is consumed in moderation and associated with very little untoward behavior. But in other societies, drinking, whether on multiple occasions or taken as a whole, has been catastrophic. The impact of alcohol consumption is not determined solely by the biochemical effects of the drug but by the relationship of those effects to the characteristics of the people drinking it, constrained by the culture and the society in which it is used.

WHO DRINKS? WHO DOESN'T?

Who drinks and who doesn't? Are certain groups or social categories significantly and consistently more likely to drink than others? Do the social origins of drinkers influence the tendency to label their behavior as deviant?

There are at least two crucial measures of alcohol consumption: first, drinking versus abstention, and second, among drinkers, drinking to excess. Drinking varies dramatically from one category in the population to another; likewise, drinking heavily, compulsively, and abusively—that is, to excess—varies along sociological lines. We might expect that categories in the population that have a high proportion of drinkers (and, contrarily, a low proportion of abstainers) would also rank high in the likelihood that their members are alcoholics, that is, those who drink to excess. The opposite side of the coin should be expected as well: The lower the proportion of drinkers in a given social category, the lower the likelihood that the members of that category will be abusive drinkers. This is not always the case, however; some groups in the population have extraordinarily high proportions of drinkers but low proportions of alcoholics, while other groups are more likely to abstain, but its drinkers are more likely to drink compulsively and abusively. For instance, persons of Jewish and Italian ancestry are highly likely to drink, but their rates of alcoholism are extremely low. In contrast, men over the age of 60 have higher than average rates of alcohol abstention but also higher than average rates of alcoholism.

Social class or socioeconomic status (SES), which is usually measured by income, occupation, and/or education, correlates strongly and consistently with the consumption of alcohol. As a general rule, in the Western world, the United States included, the higher the social class or SES, the greater the likelihood of drinking at all; members of the lower and working class are much more likely to be abstainers. This generalization is confirmed by the 2007 National Survey on Drug Use and Health, which found a remarkably strong correlation between education and drinking during the previous year. Among respondents 18 and older, only 37 percent with less than a completed high school education drank at all during the prior year, but 69 percent of college graduates had done so. But when the NSDUH researcher used measures indicating *binge* (having five drinks on the same occasion at least once in the prior 30 days) and *heavy* drinking (having five drinks on the same occasion five or more times in the prior 30 days), this pattern was reversed. Among respondents 26 or older, 23 percent of high school dropouts were binge drinkers versus 20 percent for college grads; and for heavy drinkers, these figures were 7 versus 5 percent (SAMHSA, 2008, p. 34). High school dropout drinkers were two-and-a-half times more likely to be "heavy" drinkers (about 18%) than college graduate drinkers (7%). In short, the lower the SES, the greater the likelihood of *abstaining* from alcohol use but, among drinkers, the higher the likelihood of binge and heavy drinking.

Gender, too, correlates strongly with drinking. Of all variables (except age), perhaps gender correlates most strongly with alcohol consumption. Men are consistently more likely to drink than are women, and they drink more when they do drink. The 2007 National Survey on Drug Use and Health found a sizeable male–female difference in drinking: 57 percent of the males but only 46 percent of the females in the study had drunk alcohol during the past month. And men were twice as likely as women to be binge drinkers and three times as likely to be heavy drinkers. The interesting thing about gender, though, is that the use of alcohol in the prior month among male and female youths age 12–17 was identical: 16 percent for both. Is the female's tendency to drink catching up with the male's? Possibly. The Monitoring the Future's 2007 survey found that, among high school seniors, a 9 percentage point difference between males and females in the likelihood of having had five or more drinks in a row during the past two weeks (22% for females, 31% for males), but in 1975, it found a 23 percentage point gap. In other words, the gender gap in drinking had closed by more than half (Johnston et al., 2008, p. 27).

Age is also strongly correlated with drinking. Drinking tends to be extremely low in early adolescence, shoots up in the middle-to-late teenage years, reaches a peak between 19 and the early 20s, and declines slowly after that. In the 2001 National Survey on Drug Use and Health, drinking in the past month increased from 2.6 percent among 12-year-olds to a peak of 67.5 percent among 21-year-olds, remained at something of a plateau after that, diminishing only very slightly into middle age: 53 percent among 50- to 54-year-olds, then 46 percent between the ages of 55 and 64, then to 33 percent at the age of 65 and older. This pattern differs from that drug use, which peaks more sharply at the younger ages and drops off more sharply with age. Of course, drinking during the past month is not as "deviant" as illicit drug use; in moderation, it is conventional, very much in the mainstream.

But consider this: Heavier drinkers are more likely to be drawn from the social sectors of the population who contribute the highest proportion of participants in deviant behavior: less-well educated, lower-SES young males. While drinking once or more in the past month is hardly a form of deviance, drinking five or more alcoholic beverages on repeated occasions, month after month, is certainly nonnormative. Moreover, such an activity opens the door to other deviant activities. Not only are the people who engage in such drinking patterns also likely to get into other kinds of trouble, but intoxication may contribute to that tendency. The social characteristics of binge and heavy drinkers may facilitate further and related deviant behavior.

ALCOHOL: ESSENTIALISM VERSUS CONSTRUCTIONISM

In our consideration of alcohol consumption as deviance, which makes more sense: essentialism (with its stress on positivism, or the naturalistic, scientific approach) or constructionism (with its stress on norms, social and cultural definitions, and the exercise of social control)? In other words, what determines alcohol's place in the society—the objectivistic effects of the substance itself, or the particular features of a society or subculture that leads its members to tolerate, encourage, or condemn drinking? Is it even possible to separate the two? Why is drinking accepted at one time and place and rejected in another? Is the answer related to alcohol's effects, or the unique and distinctive history and culture of a particular society in relation to alcohol?

The answer is this: Alcohol's objectively harmful effects, though formidable, can be and are mitigated or softened and rerouted by society's norms. The same substance is used in strikingly different ways in societies around the world—and with strikingly different consequences. There are two keys to alcohol's consequences, and only one is the pharmacological effects of this psychoactive drug; the other is the normative culture that lays down rules about drinking.

Consider the fact that more than a hundred epidemiologists and biostatisticians from the World Health Organization (WHO) surveyed the available data and isolated roughly 20 leading risk factors for premature death in countries around the world. The risk factors were somewhat different in developing (or less fully industrialized) countries as compared with the more economically developed countries. In the developing or Third World countries such as Bolivia, Nigeria, and Indonesia, factors such as malnutrition and poor sanitation were the leading causes of premature death. But in the more fully industrialized countries of the world, such as France, Japan, and the United States, tobacco consumption accounted for 12.2 percent of the years of life lost (YLL) to risk factors, while excessive alcohol consumption contributed to 9.2 percent. For these countries, tobacco and alcohol were the number one and three factors in this respect. In contrast, the use of illicit drugs only accounted for 1.8 percent of YLL. In other words, in the industrialized world, the legal drugs, taken together, contribute over five times more to premature death than the use of illicit drugs. Clearly, then, objectively, legal drug use is a far more serious social problem than illegal drug use. Yet illegal drug use is *socially constructed* as a more serious problem. Subjectively, in the way that the public regards it and the government deals with it, the consumption of illicit substances is the more serious social problem. An interesting question is why?

How do societies tame this "raging tiger" of a social problem? Is creating and enforcing inappropriate drinking as a form of deviance one avenue to minimizing the damage that alcohol consumption inflicts on populations everywhere? Or does *deviantizing* excessive and inappropriate drinking simply add fuel to the fire?

ACUTE EFFECTS OF ALCOHOL: A (MAINLY) ESSENTIALISTIC INTRODUCTION

Chemically, alcohol is known as "ethyl alcohol" or *ethanol;* it is one of dozens of other substances chemists call "alcohol." (Methyl alcohol, a poison, is another.) Scientists measure the potency of alcoholic beverages by the percentage of alcohol (often referred to as "absolute" or *pure* alcohol) they contain. Pure ethyl alcohol is 100 percent absolute alcohol. Beer contains 4 or 5 percent alcohol; wine is 10–13 percent alcohol. "Fortified" wine, wine to which alcohol or brandy is added, is legally set at 20 percent. Sherry is a fortified wine to which brandy has been added. Wine "coolers" contain roughly the same percentage of alcohol as beer, 4 or 5 percent. The process of distillation (boiling, condensing, and recovering the more volatile, alcohol-potent vapor from the original fluid and adding an appropriate quantity of water) produces drinks such as Scotch, vodka, gin, and tequila, that are 40 or 50 percent alcohol, or 80 to 100 proof. Consequently, in order to consume one ounce of alcohol, one consumes two 12-ounce cans of beer, *or* one 8-ounce glass of wine, *or* a mixed drink containing about 2 or 2½ ounces of Scotch or gin.

The rule of equivalency states that, other factors being equal, the effects of alcohol are determined by the volume of alcohol that is consumed, rather than the type of drink itself. Hence, if consumed in the same period of time by the same person under the same conditions, two 12-ounce cans of beer, one 8-ounce glass of wine, and a mixed drink containing 2 to 2½ ounces of Scotch or gin would have the *same* effects. With respect to the drink that is consumed, nothing else except the quantity of alcohol, consumed within the same period of time, makes a difference. (Of course, it generally takes longer to guzzle two cans of beer than to sip one mixed drink.) In other words, alcohol is alcohol is alcohol; nothing else makes a significant difference in its impact, except of course the usual mitigating physiological factors. Drinking lore has it that different *kinds* of drinks—wine versus Scotch; gin versus beer; and tequila versus vodka—have different capacities to make drinkers drunk. This is false; aside from mitigating factors (which I discuss later), how much pure or absolute alcohol one has consumed is the *only* factor that matters in determining level of intoxication. But this is a crucial point: Level of alcohol intoxication does *not* automatically translate into behavior under the influence. Two people with the same *measurable* level of intoxication may exhibit very different behaviors; people in the same society but drinking in two different locales or situations may reach a given level of intoxication but behave substantially differently; people in different societies may react differently to the same level of intoxication. Here's where our story gets really interesting: Alcohol is both a drug, with objective, measureable effects, and a social phenomenon, the impact of which is shaped by culture, society, and social context.

But the objective level of alcohol in the body is crucial as well; beyond a certain level of intoxication, it is practically the only thing that matters. Alcohol is "the only addictive drug that dangerously alters behavior that at the same time is freely and legally available without a prescription" (Goldstein, 2001, p. 137). When it enters the body, a given quantity of alcohol translates into what pharmacologists call *blood-alcohol concentration* (BAC). This corresponds to the percent of the volume of one's blood that is made up of alcohol. Goldstein describes a given BAC as "bathing the brain" in a given alcohol concentration (p. 137). A close relationship exists between BAC and behavior. The effects of alcohol are drug related: As a general rule, the greater the amount one consumes, the more intoxicated one becomes, and the more extreme is any given effect.

The effects of alcohol are contingent on, or influenced or mitigated by, a number of crucial physiological factors in addition to the total volume of alcohol in the drinker's body. Women are more sensitive to the effects of alcohol than men; the smaller the person (and therefore the less blood someone has to dilute the effects of alcohol), the more substantial the effect; the less body fat someone has, likewise, the more substantial the effect. And the less food (and water) one has in one's stomach, the more substantial the effect that the same quality of alcohol has. And, as with practically all drugs, alcohol builds up pharmacological tolerance: It takes more alcohol to achieve a given effect in a regular, experienced, or frequent drinker than in an abstainer or infrequent drinker.

Alcohol is a depressant, much like sedatives, such as barbiturates. Ethyl alcohol depresses, slows down, retards, or *obtunds* many functions and activities of organs of the body, such as heartbeat rate and neurological response time. Organs become more sluggish, slower to respond to stimuli. This is especially true of the central nervous system. If the dose is too high, the body's organs will shut down, and death will ensue. Alcohol also disorganizes and decreases the ability of the brain to process and use information, and hence, impairs most perceptual cognitive and motor skills needed for coordination and decision making. One ounce of alcohol, or roughly two mixed drinks, consumed in less than an hour will result in a BAC of roughly .05 percent in a man roughly 150 pounds. This BAC produces in most people a mild euphoria; a diminution of anxiety, fear, and tension; a corresponding increase in self-confidence; and, usually, what is called a "release" of inhibitions. Decreased fear also typically results in a greater willingness to take risks; this effect has been observed in laboratory animals. Alcohol is, for most people, a mild sedative, anxiety agent, and tranquilizer. This is not universally the case, however; in many people, alcohol ingestion results in paranoia, fear, distrust, and heightened anxiety, even hostility. These effects typically occur, when they do, at moderate to higher doses.

Alcohol's effects on motor performance are familiar to us all: clumsiness, an unsteady gait, the inability to stand or walk straight, and slurred speech. One's accuracy and consistency at performing mechanical activities dramatically decline as one's BAC increases. And the more complex, abstract, and unfamiliar the task, the steeper the decline. The most noteworthy instance of such a decline is one's decreasing ability to drive an automobile. It is clear that drinking, even moderately, impairs the ability to drive, and contributes to highway fatalities. How intoxicated does one have to be to lose the ability to perform highway tasks? What does one's BAC have to be to produce a significant decline in motor coordination? And how many drinks does that represent? All drinkers experience a loss of motor skills at a certain point, and it occurs at a fairly low BAC. At about the .025 blood-alcohol level, that is, after finishing an average drink, some very inexperienced and particularly susceptible individuals will display a significant decline in the ability to perform a wide range of tasks. At the .10 level, even experienced drinkers will exhibit measurable impairment in coordination; this is the consumption of roughly four drinks, each containing a half-ounce of alcohol, that is, an ounce of Scotch, rum, or tequila. And many drivers seem to be willing to get behind the wheel while intoxicated: According to the FBI's Uniform Crime Reports, in 2007, the police made 1.4 million arrests for driving under the influence, and 589,000 for "drunkenness."

THE CO-OCCURRENCE OF ALCOHOL ABUSE AND RISKY, DEVIANT BEHAVIORS

To understand the relationship between the use of alcohol and other forms of deviance, it is essential to define our terms. Here, we have two terms that refer to concepts that point to things in the real world. The first is alcohol "abuse" and the second, "risky and deviant behavior." It's important to define terms in such a way that they are independent of one another. By that I mean if we want to establish an empirical or factual relationship—in such a way that we can argue that one has an impact on the other—between two things in the world, we have to make sure we don't *define* one by the other. If we were to define alcohol abuse as problem alcohol consumption, that is, drinking to the point where one gets into trouble (DUI/DWI, arrest, divorce, alienation of friendship, accident, etc.), that would mix up cause with consequence. It is only by defining our terms along separate dimensions that we can determine what their co-occurrence or empirical relationship is.

Thousands of studies have investigated the relationship between alcohol consumption and untoward, risky, criminal, violent, and deviant behavior. Of course, different researchers or research teams have measured different aspects of these phenomena and have used somewhat different definitions of their key concepts. How does the researcher define alcohol abuse? And what is untoward, risky, criminal, violent, and deviant behavior? Most researchers regard *binge* and/or *heavy* drinking as a form of alcohol abuse. One common operationalization of "binge" drinking is the consumption of five or more alcoholic drinks three times during the prior month (some researchers set this figure at two, others, four; some track such drinking over a month, others, two weeks; and so on), and "heavy" drinking (one way of defining this is consuming more than three drinks per day during the past month; another is five or more episodes of five or more drinks on a single occasion). And by risky, deviant behavior, researchers tend to be interested mainly in behaviors that society regards, likewise, as nonnormative, or those that physicians and epidemiologists regard as actually or potentially harmful. Risky, deviant behavior includes the following: driving under the influence; smoking; engaging in criminal and violent behavior; putting oneself into a situation in which becoming a *victim* of criminal and violent behavior is likely; engaging in risky sexual behavior (multiple partners, unprotected sex, sex with strangers, etc.); using and abusing illicit drugs; and suicide.

Not every study of drinking in the United States specifically and the Western world generally have produced findings confirming the co-occurrence of alcohol abuse and risky, deviant behavior—but most have. Empirically, drinkers, taken as a category, are more likely to engage in risky, deviant behavior than nondrinkers, and the more they drink, the greater is this tendency; and people who are intoxicated are more likely to engage in risky, deviant behavior than persons who are not intoxicated, and the more intoxicated they are, the greater this tendency is. One study even found that the *sale* of alcohol in an area was strongly correlated with the likelihood that local residents will be hospitalized for assault. If you live near a place that sells a lot of alcohol, you're more likely to be seriously injured by a heavy drinker than if you live near a place that sells very little alcohol (Ray et al., 2008). In this case, the victim isn't the deviant, the victimizer is.

Here's a sociologically important qualification: The relationship between alcohol abuse and risky, deviant behavior is strongly *contingent* on drinking locales or contexts, that is, the social and physical circumstances or situations within which drinking takes place. Here are a few examples of social and physical drinking locales: a bar, a restaurant, a beach, a park, in the drinker's own home, in the home of friends, in a moving car, at a party, among intimates, among relatives, and among strangers. For instance, aggressive and other problematic behaviors, such as arguments, fighting, and drunk driving, are more likely to occur in or follow after drinking in a bar than at home (Nyaronga, Greenfield, and McDaniel, 2009). And *where* people drink and *what they are doing* determine how, and how seriously, they get injured. Compared with other locales, a relatively low proportion of people drink on the job; hence, again, relatively speaking, few show up at an emergency room (ER) as a result of an alcohol-impaired injury. On the other hand, again, a very high proportion of people in bars (and restaurants) drink, and hence, by that factor alone, a great many people show up in ERs, injured in those locales as a result of alcohol impairment. In fact, in a summary of data from dozens of studies gathered in 16 countries, a team of researchers (Macdonald et al., 2006) found that injuries in bars were significantly more likely to involve alcohol impairment than any other setting. Of all injuries that took place in a bar in which the party injured was taken to an ER, nearly 35 percent entailed alcohol impairment; this was true of only 2 percent where the injured person was in a school or workplace, 5 percent in a park or beach, just under 10 percent in a house, and just under 15 percent in a vehicle on the street or highway (Macdonald et al., 2006).

Broadening our conception of context or locale, and addressing violence specifically, we could include the society or country in which drinking takes place. In some countries, such as France, Italy, Portugal, and Spain, a high proportion of regular drinkers consume alcohol, usually in the form of wine, in a convivial setting with family and other intimates copresent, often during eating occasions, such as dinner. Such societies tend to have low rates of violence, especially criminal homicide, following drinking, and the relationship between alcohol consumption and violence is weak. In other countries, such as Russia and the other countries of Eastern Europe and the former Soviet Union, a high proportion of drinkers are single men who consume alcohol, mainly in the form of distilled spirits and mainly for the purpose of getting drunk, in the presence of other single men, often in a public place, such as a bar, with few females or family members to restrain their aggressive, argumentative behavior. Such societies manifest higher rates of violence and a closer relationship between heavy drinking and violent behavior. Hence, it is not *only* heavy alcohol consumption that counts in this relationship, but the social, cultural, and local contexts of drinking behavior, as well as the specific alcoholic substance (wine versus distilled spirits) that is consumed.

Here, the 64 million dollar question is *why*. What *causes* higher (and nonnormative) levels of alcohol to covary with risk, deviant behavior? Hypotheses differ somewhat among one another, and hence, the mechanism by which this relationship occurs differs according to the hypothesis. For instance, some hypotheses argue that *being under the influence* is the key mechanism causing this relationship. Other hypotheses argue that it is the *kind of person* who drinks, and drinks heavily, that is the key explanatory factor here; hence, it doesn't matter whether the drinker is under the influence at the moment the act is committed, what counts is that he is the *kind of person* who drinks, especially in substantial amounts. In any case, three possible explanations of our relationship come to mind (Young, Sweeting, and West, 2008, pp. 204–205).

First, we have the *disinhibition* hypothesis: Alcohol *causes* risky, deviant behavior. Because one of alcohol's effects is a release from the inhibition that result from normative constraints on dangerous acts, under the influence, the drinker is more likely to engage in those acts. Sober, we do not engage in these behaviors; intoxicated, we do because of this "release of inhibitions" effect. A variation on the disinhibition hypothesis is the "alcohol-myopia" model: Alcohol disorganizes the brain's capacity to pay attention and process information, and hence, "do the right thing" (George and Norris, 1991).

Second, there's the *susceptibility* hypothesis: Alcohol abuse and engaging in risky, deviant behavior are related because they are *effects of a common cause*. The abusive drinker is more likely to engage in risky, deviant behavior because the person who drinks heavily is *also* the sort of antisocial person who engages in behavior that either harms others or himself or herself. These are people who are unable to regulate or control their own behavior: impulsive, sensation seeking, aggressive, and highly risk tolerant. Neither factor causes the other; they are both caused by the configuration of the antisocial proclivity of the drinker.

Third, there's the *reciprocal* hypothesis: Alcohol abuse and risky-antisocial behavior feed back into and fuel one another. True, a certain type of individual seeks out certain types of risky behaviors; but getting intoxicated also disrupts one's judgment and further behavior, and contributes to further both heavy and binge drinking and impulsive, risky, deviant behavior (Young, Sweeting, and West, 2008).

Which of these three hypotheses fits the facts most faithfully? Are they even mutually exclusive? If one is right, are the others wrong? Or do we need more information?

ALCOHOL CONSUMPTION: DEATH ON THE HIGHWAY

Driving while intoxicated is both a deviant and dangerous act. Alcohol consumption substantially increases the likelihood of a fatal automobile accident. In fact, the likelihood of fatalities increases in proportion to the BAC of the driver: The greater the BAC, the greater the chance that the driver will get into an accident that kills someone. For young, and particularly male, drivers, this likelihood begins to increase at an extremely low level of BAC. Among 16-to-20-year-old male drivers, a BAC level of 0.02 *doubles* the likelihood of a fatal accident. Remember, that's about two-thirds of what's considered one drink. In the 0.08 to 0.10 range, 35-year-old and older drivers increase their likelihood of having a fatal accident by 11.4 times; for 16- to-20 year-olds, the increase is 51.9 times (Zador, Krawchuk, and Voas, 2000). Compton and his colleagues (Compton et al., 2002) calculate a "relative risk estimate" in the form of a curve that rises slowly at first, then very steeply, and then less steeply at the top of a very high curve. In earlier decades, before such precise calculations had been made, most states defined a 0.15 BAC as drunk driving; the Compton research team estimated that, controlling for demographic factors for age, gender, and SES, at the 0.15 BAC, drivers are 22 times more likely to get into a fatal car crash. At the 0.20 level, this likelihood was estimated to be 82 times, and at the 0.25 level, 154 times.

All of this is true—but something else is true as well. Over the past quarter century, a great many changes have taken place on the American highway: Roads are safer, cars are safer (more "crashworthy"), passengers are more likely to wear seat belts, motorists drive more slowly and more safely, alcohol consumption is down, and, specifically, drivers are less likely to drink and get behind the wheel of a car. Thus, for a variety of reasons, traffic fatalities have substantially declined. When automobile fatalities are expressed per 100 million miles driven, the decrease is impressive: In 2006, this rate was 1.42; in 2007, it was 1.36; and in 2008, 1.28—the lowest ever recorded in the history of the automobile. According to the National Institute on Alcohol Abuse and Alcoholism (NIAAA), between the early 1980s and today, the number of deaths in alcohol-related car crashes declined by half, from 26,000 (in 1982) to 13,000 (in 2007). The years of potential life lost (YPLL) has declined from over 880,000 to about 500,000, or about 40 percent. The decline among youths under the age of 21 is especially precipitous: In 1982, 5,215 alcohol-impaired youths died in fatal car crashes, a rate of 6.9 per 100,000; in 2007, 1,840 died, at a rate of 2.1 per 100,000 (Century Council, "2007 State of Drunk Driving Fatalities in America"). Nonetheless, alcohol remains related to death on the highway. Today, about a third of all fatal car crashes are alcohol related. Moreover, the *more serious* the crash, the greater the likelihood that alcohol played a role in it. According to the National Highway Safety Administration, one-quarter (24%) of drivers who died in a car crash tested out at a BAC of 0.10 or higher; in one out of 10 (9%) of crashes that were nonfatal was the driver this impaired; and in only 6 percent of crashes, which caused *no* personal injury did the driver register a 0.10. Clearly, the intoxication of the driver *substantially* increases the odds of dying in an accident. Drinking and driving is itself a deviant act. And driving while intoxicated increases the driver's likelihood of taking chances not usually taken when sober—in other words, drinking increases the likelihood of engaging in *deviant* driving.

ALCOHOL AND VIOLENCE: AN INTRODUCTION

As we saw, alcohol consumption is extremely widespread; more than half the U.S. population drinks monthly or more. Wine, beer, and liquor are very much an established fixture of mainstream American society and culture. Hence, the assertion that alcohol is related to violence is likely to sound strange. Such a statement might seem equivalent to saying that consuming tea, chocolate, and Pepperidge Farm cookies are related to violence. Common sense rejects the idea that alcohol has anything to do with committing violent behavior. What could possibly be wrong with drinking a glass of wine with dinner, a beer while watching a ball game, or a sherry nightcap before retiring? Most Americans drink, and the vast majority of those who do so experience no untoward consequences.

However, let's keep in mind what criminologists and drug and alcohol researchers mean when they say that alcohol is related to violence. They do not mean that alcohol—and alcohol alone—arouses the impulse to inflict harm upon others. They do not mean that most episodes of drinking lead to violence. They do not mean that most people who drink have committed one or more criminally violent acts during the past week, month, or year. Of the many millions of daily instances of alcohol consumption, very, very few have anything to do with violence. Violence *extremely rarely* accompanies alcohol consumption.

Criminologists mean two things when they say that alcohol and violence are related. One, drinkers have higher *rates* of violence than nondrinkers. And two: The more that someone drinks, the greater the likelihood that he or she will inflict violence on another person. Alcohol is also related to being a *victim* of violence: Drinkers are more likely to be victimized by violence than nondrinkers, and the more one drinks, the greater that likelihood is. This relationship is especially strong if one or more of one's companions are drinking, and even more especially so if one is a female and one's companion is a male.

These statements are statistical, not absolute; again, they refer to *likelihoods*—not certain outcomes. They are based on a comparison of the rate of violence of drinkers versus nondrinkers, and heavy versus light drinkers, and people who are under the influence versus those who are sober. Granted that violence is an extremely rare event, the fact that it is more common among drinkers in comparison with nondrinkers, and more common among heavy than light drinkers, and more common among the intoxicated than the sober, means that the statement, "Alcohol is related to violence" is true. While most of the time alcohol is consumed violence does not take place, it is also true that, with respect to the total number of drinking episodes, alcohol consumption is an *extremely frequent* accompaniment of violence, when it does take place. *Most* cases of criminal violence are accompanied by the consumption of alcohol. It's just that alcohol consumption is hugely more common than acts of criminal violence.

Remember, for a relationship between two things to exist it is not necessary to always or usually find these things together. What is necessary is that when the first thing is present, the second is *more likely* to be found than is the case when the first is absent. Even if alcohol were associated with violence in only one out of ten thousand instances of drinking, if that frequency is *higher* than when alcohol is *absent,* we can say that a relationship between alcohol and violence exists.

The generalization that alcohol and violence are related is so well established that it seems almost redundant to document it. But since it contradicts common sense, establishing this relationship empirically seems to be in order. The epidemiologist—the specialist who studies the social and geographical distribution of diseases, disorders, or harmful behaviors—looks at data across societies, time periods, and individuals. Hence, we have three types of information that we might use to determine the relationship between alcohol and violence: a country-by-country international comparison, a year-by-year comparison in one country, and an individual-by-individual comparison. Let's begin with the international comparison.

ALCOHOL AND VIOLENCE: THE INTERNATIONAL PICTURE

For decades, researchers of the "big picture" of alcohol consumption accepted the validity of the *Ledermann hypothesis.* Sully Ledermann was a French demographer who, in the 1950s and 1960s, argued that all countries followed the same statistical distribution for alcohol consumption: The higher a country's per capita alcohol consumption, the greater its medical and behavioral problems, and the higher its alcohol-related mortality and morbidity. Ledermann would have approved of the quest to empirically support the alcohol–violence link by comparing countries around the world with respect to the conjunction of their per capita alcohol consumption and homicide rates.

Following the Ledermann hypothesis, we might assume that per capita alcohol consumption is closely correlated with alcohol-related or alcohol-caused behavior and murder. Hence, the greater the amount of alcohol a society or nation drinks, the greater the likelihood that its most inebriated members will enter a physiological state in which they are lacking in sound judgment, mentally incapacitated, disinhibited or released from the norms telling them not to engage in aggressive, violent behavior, and disorganized in their capacity to process information as to the proper line of action. As a consequence, we'd further reason, the top alcohol-consuming countries would also be the top countries with respect to committing violent acts, including murder. We'd use alcohol *sales* because that's an officially recorded statistic, and the rate of criminal homicide, because that is the most reliable crime statistic the police have.

An examination of the evidence at once disproves this intuitively appealing empirical test of alcohol's impact on violence. For one thing, the task isn't as easy as we might think, since different countries define homicide in different ways, and the statistics that certain countries collect are, sadly, incomplete. Still, as I said, homicide statistics are the best that criminologists have; hence, a gross, big-picture snapshot using official data sources on murder might yield some inkling of the relationship between our key variables. The second inconvenient fact for our test is that, a huge volume—some experts (Haworth and Simpson, 2004) believe, as much as *half,* of all alcohol consumed globally—is moonshine or home brew, and thus, does not appear in official sales or statistics. And this statistic varies by economic development: In economically industrialized countries like the United States, official sales are close to the actual rate of consumption; in poor countries such as India, as much as 90 percent of the alcohol consumed never appears on the official record. But perhaps the most important flaw in our simple alcohol–violence equation is the fact that the *pattern* of drinking is more important than the *quantity* consumed. Here's where the Ledermann hypothesis completely breaks down.

Let's find out why. According to data compiled by the WHO's report, *Global Status Report on Alcohol,* more than half of the top 20 countries with respect to alcohol consumption are western European countries with low homicide rates, such as Luxembourg, Germany, Denmark, France, and Spain. In contrast, according to the data collected by the United Nations, all but one of the 20 countries with the highest rates of criminal homicide (with rates between 28.6 and 69.0, roughly 5 to 10 times that of the United States) are in Latin America (Honduras, Guatemala, El Salvador, Venezuela, Colombia, and Brazil), the Caribbean (Jamaica, Belize, and Haiti) or Africa (Sudan, the Central African Republic, Zimbabwe, Sierra Leone, the Democratic Republic of the Congo, Burundi, Angola, Lesotho, the Ivory Coast, and South Africa). These figures give us only a glimmer of the alcohol–violence picture, however, since the data on both ends of the equation are flawed. The alcohol data are flawed because, as we saw, they are based on sales (with WHO estimates for home brew) rather than actual use. In countries wracked by war and civil insurrection, such as Iraq and Angola, the homicide figure is distorted by artificial and temporary conditions. In addition, criminal homicide is defined differently in different countries; for instance, some may not include infanticide, some may include warfare deaths.

Nonetheless, as I said, with the flawed data that we do have, we see a glimmer of the relationship, on an international scale, of the dynamic between alcohol consumption and violence, and what we see is that there is almost *no* correspondence between the two sets of figures. If we were to construct a list of the 20 countries with the highest rate of alcohol consumption and lay that alongside the countries with the 20 highest rates of homicide, only one country appears on both lists, that is, that has *both* a top-20 level of alcohol consumption *and* a top-20 level of criminal homicide—Russia. Most of the Latin American and sub-Saharan African countries on these lists have very high rates of criminal homicide but only moderate rates of alcohol consumption (again, taking into account the home-brew issue). Countries within the ambit of the former Soviet Union, including those in Central Asia, have relatively high rates of criminal homicide and moderate-to-high rates of alcohol consumption—Russia itself being the prime example. The United States has the highest criminal homicide rate in the fully industrialized world, although lower than many nonindustrialized countries, but a lower level of alcohol consumption in comparison with Western Europe.

Clearly, the factors that cause violence generally and criminal homicide specifically are too varied to draw a direct causal arrow from high per capita levels of alcohol consumption to violence. The statistics (admittedly flawed) for both indicate that a high society-wide level of consumption of alcohol does *not* automatically or inevitably—or even usually—lead to a high society-wide level of violence. In some society's pattern of use, high levels of alcohol consumption indicate that drinking is widespread throughout the country and common in mainstream settings, including family gatherings and restaurants, and not distinctive to the social sectors of the society whose consumption is likely, under certain circumstances, to trigger an altercation leading to a lethal struggle between two combatants. (Of course, it is always possible that if these countries had no alcohol consumption, they would have lower rates of criminal violence.) Moreover, as Barbara Leigh points out (1999, p. 374), when we compare alcohol-related outcomes, such as injury or other harms, from one country, society, or population to another, we do not know that the individuals who manifest these outcomes are specifically the ones with the highest levels of alcohol consumption.

In a given country or society, the pattern of drinking is, as I said, much more important than quantity of alcohol consumed. Included in the patterning of drinking are the following: the quantity of alcohol consumed on a single occasion (at the higher end, binge drinking); duration and frequency of drinking; *who* drinks; the setting in which drinking takes place; and the roles and significance of alcohol in the culture, the society, and the lives of drinkers (Grant and Litvak, 1998; Stimpson et al., 2007, p. 14). Are drinkers men or women? Adolescents or mature adults? Well educated or not so well educated? Rich or poor, middle class or working class? Does drinking take place in bars? Predominantly among single-sex gatherings of men? In restaurants or at home among families? Is the alcohol product commercial or noncommercial (home-brew wines or beers)? Are the drinks high in alcohol content (50%) or low (5 to 10%)? Do workers get paid on

TABLE 7.1 TOP 20 COUNTRIES, ALCOHOL CONSUMPTION, BY TOP 20 COUNTRIES, CRIMINAL HOMICIDE

	Top 20 Countries			*Top 20 Countries*	
Country	**Per Capita Alcohol Consumption**	**Rate of Criminal Homicide**	**Country**	**Rate of Criminal Homicide**	**Per Capita Rate of Alcohol Consumption**
Uganda	19.47	25.2	South Africa	69.0	7.81
Luxembourg	17.54	1.1	Colombia	61.1	5.92
Czech Republic	16.21	2.2	El Salvador	57.5	3.45
Ireland	14.45	1.1	Jamaica	55.2	3.37
Moldova	13.88	8.2	Ivory Coast	45.7	1.71
France	13.54	1.6	Lesotho	37.3	1.83
Germany	12.89	1.0	Venezuela	37.0	8.78
Croatia	12.66	2.0	Guatemala	36.4	1.64
Austria	12.58	0.8	Angola	36.0	2.91
Portugal	12.49	1.8	Burundi	35.4	9.33
Slovakia	12.41	2.3	Congo, D.R. of	35.2	2.01
Lithuania	12.32	10.3	Sierra Leone	34.0	6.64
Spain	12.25	1.4	Haiti	33.9	6.51
Denmark	11.94	1.1	Zimbabwe	32.9	6.51
Hungary	11.92	2.2	Honduras	32.2	2.28
Switzerland	11.53	2.9	Brazil	30.8	5.32
Russia	10.58	29.7	Belize	30.1	4.50
Finland	10.43	2.8	Russia	29.7	10.58
United Kingdom*	10.39	1.6	Central African Rep.	29.1	1.66
Belgium	10.06	2.1	Sudan	28.6	0.27
United States	8.51	5.9	*United States*	5.9	8.51

*UK, England and Wales only.

Sources: World Health Organization (WHO), 2004, Global State Report on Alcohol, and United Nations, Office on Drugs and Crime, "International Homicide Statistics" (high estimates appear above).

Notes: Alcohol consumption is per capita sales, age 15 and older, of specified number of liters of "absolute" or "pure" alcohol per year, latest figures. (A liter is 1.75 pints, or 40% of a quart; time period is per year.)

Note that the United States is not in the top 20 of either category.

Friday at 5 o'clock, go to their local bar, get "blasted" on two dozen drinks, blow their paycheck, and stagger home, penniless, to the admonishment of their wives? Or are bottles of wine passed around to the whole family, children included, at a Sunday feast once a week?

In short, the most important facts about a given per capita level of alcohol consumption are buried in a misleading overall statistic. *How* alcohol is drunk is at least as important as *how much*—at least, if we are comparing one culturally different country with another. The facts of sociology and anthropology are crucial in explaining *why* we see a lack of correspondence between the alcohol–violence link—*at the international level.* But what if we stay within the same country and look at alcohol consumption over time? Is it legitimate to expect an alcohol–violence link along a time line?

ALCOHOL AND MURDER: THE CRIME DROP IN AMERICA?

Though our international comparison does not yield much pay dirt, perhaps a second data source might establish the alcohol–violence link: year-by-year comparisons within the same country. As we saw in Chapters 5 and 6 on crime and criminal violence, during the past two decades, criminal behavior, especially violent behavior, has been declining sharply in the United States, and criminologists don't know why. Table 7.2 suggests one factor: Over time, there's been a decline in the use of alcohol. This table focuses on two factors or variables: per capita alcohol consumption and criminal homicide, or murder. Look at the table

TABLE 7.2 HOMICIDE RATE BY ALCOHOL CONSUMPTION, 1950–2007, UNITED STATES

YEAR	*PER CAPITA ALCOHOL CONSUMPTION (IN GALLONS)*	*HOMICIDE RATE*	*YEAR*	*PER CAPITA ALCOHOL CONSUMPTION (IN GALLONS)*	*HOMICIDE RATE*
1950	2.04	4.6	1972	2.56	9.0
1951	2.01	4.4	1973	2.62	9.4
1952	1.98	4.6	1974	2.67	9.8
1953	2.01	4.5	1975	2.69	9.6
1954	1.96	4.2	1976	2.69	8.8
1955	2.00	4.1	1977	2.64	8.8
1956	2.03	4.1	1978	2.71	9.0
1957	1.99	4.0	1979	2.75	9.7
1958	1.98	4.8	1980	2.76	10.2
1959	2.06	4.9	1981	2.76	9.8
1960	2.07	5.1	1982	2.72	9.1
1961	2.06	4.8	1983	2.69	8.3
1962	2.11	4.6	1984	2.65	7.9
1963	2.15	4.6	1985	2.62	7.9
1964	2.23	4.9	1986	2.58	8.6
1965	2.27	5.1	1987	2.54	8.3
1966	2.32	5.6	1988	2.48	8.5
1967	2.37	6.2	1989	2.42	8.7
1968	2.45	6.9	1990	2.45	9.4
1969	2.51	7.3	1991	2.30	9.8
1970	2.52	7.9	1992	2.30	9.3
1971	2.59	8.6	1993	2.23	9.5

(*continued*)

TABLE 7.2 CONTINUED

YEAR	PER CAPITA ALCOHOL CONSUMPTION (IN GALLONS)	HOMICIDE RATE	YEAR	PER CAPITA ALCOHOL CONSUMPTION (IN GALLONS)	HOMICIDE RATE
1994	2.18	9.0	2001	2.18	5.6
1995	2.15	8.2	2002	2.20	5.6
1996	2.16	7.4	2003	2.22	5.7
1997	2.14	6.8	2004	2.23	5.5
1998	2.14	6.3	2005	2.24	5.6
1999	2.16	5.7	2006	2.27	5.7
2000	2.18	5.5	2007	*	5.6

Sources: National Institute on Alcohol Abuse and Alcoholism (NIAAA), "Apparent per capita ethanol consumption for the United States, 1970–2006" (based on population age 14 and older); FBI, Uniform Crime Reports, Crime in the United States, 1950–2007.

Rate: number per 100,000 in the population.

*Figure not available at this writing.

closely. Between the early 1950s to the early 1960s, the per capita alcohol consumption remained fairly stable at about two gallons of ethanol (pure or absolute alcohol) per year, and the murder rate remained more or less stable at just under 5 per 100,000 in the population. But beginning with 1962, there is an uninterrupted stretch of 14 years during which the population increased its alcohol consumption, from 2.11 gallons in 1962 to 2.69 in 1976, after which the rate wobbled around in the 2.76 to 2.45 territory (1977–1990). Correspondingly, the homicide rate almost doubled between 1965 (5.1) and 1974 (9.8), and remained high for two decades. In 1991, it stood at 9.8, after which it declined for about five years, then remained relatively low (in the 5.5 to 6.3 range) until toward the end of the first decade of the 2000s.

Since the relationship between alcohol consumption and the rate of criminal homicide is complex and probably far from direct, I'd like to direct the reader's attention to five more or less distinct eras during this stretch of time. Let's take a median figure for both alcohol consumption (2.31 gallons per year) and the homicide rate (6.95) and look at the years when the figures were above and below that figure. Between 1950 and 1965, both alcohol consumption and homicide were lower than this median. Between 1966 and 1968, a transitional period, alcohol consumption rose above the median and the homicide rate remained below the median. During the period between 1969 and 1990, both alcohol consumption and the homicide rate were above our median. During a second transitional period, 1991 to 1996, alcohol consumption dropped below the median but the homicide rate remained high. And between 1997 and today, both alcohol consumption and the homicide rate were below the median. In 47 of the designated 56 years, alcohol consumption and the homicide rate were consistent with one another; in only 9 of these 56 years, they were inconsistent with one another. In other words, typically, when Americans drink more, they are more likely to engage in murder; when they drink less, they are less likely to engage in murder.

Because the causal links are so complex and diverse, it is impossible to definitively argue that this link is causal or direct. Chances are the conjunction of these two trends is the effect of a common cause, that is, the departure from and then the return to moderation and conventionality. Alcohol consumption follows a normal or bell-shaped curve; this means that as per capita consumption increases, the consumption at the upper end of the curve likewise increases and hence, during periods of greater use, the heavier user is drinking more. Likewise, murder represents the *extreme end point* along a continuum of lack of control and the tendency to engage in violence—that began with shoving, slapping, and punching. In the United States, at least as indicated along a time line, the consumption of alcohol is more than moderately related to violence, in this case, murder. Is alcohol one cause of the "crime drop in America" since 1990? It seems likely.

Early on, Parker and Cartmill (1998) noticed this up-and-down tendency, arguing that alcohol played a major role in this roller coaster ride. However, while the conjunction of alcohol and criminal violence is close and intimate, level of alcohol consumption is neither the only nor the most important factor in a given level of violence. Still, holding all other relevant variables constant, there is a "verified causal link between alcohol and violence" (p. 1374). Parker and Cartmill's measure of alcohol consumption is slightly different from that of most researchers, however. They concentrate on the concentration of "outlets" for alcohol distribution—bars, restaurants, and liquor stories. The greater the concentration of alcohol outlets in a given area, the greater the number of violent incidents, on a per population basis, and hence, the greater the homicide rate, near those outlets. They offer two explanations for this strong relationship: *selective disinhibition* and *great attractors.* By selective disihibition, the authors refer to the role that alcohol plays in the drinker's decline in individual and social restraints; by "great attractors" they mean that the areas with a high density of bars, restaurants, and liquor stores are more likely to attract people who are seeking nonnormative recreation (prostitution, drug use and sale, and conflict-related gang activities), "all of which would lead to greater rates of violence around those social attractor locations" (p. 1380). Hence, in these locales we find, first, a high concentration of people who are intoxicated, and hence, who are less restrained with respect to social norms, and whose judgment is impaired, and second, a high concentration of people seeking, and finding, activities that violate the usual normative constraints. The evidence is overwhelming that alcohol both causes and encourages violent behavior. In other words, deviant *places* attract deviant *actors,* who in turn engage in deviant *behavior* as a result of the effects of deviant *alcohol consumption.*

Although one of their explanations operates at the individual level, the data that Parker and Cartmill offer operate at the neighborhood level. Do we have data on the individual, person-by-person level?

ALCOHOL AND MURDER: INDIVIDUAL COMPARISONS

In 1998, the U.S. Department of Justice released a report surveying its own data on crime; its publication, *Alcohol and Crime,* established that in an extraordinarily high proportion of criminal offenses, the perpetrator had been drinking prior to the offense. In about a third of all violent offenses committed yearly (35%) in the United States, the victim reported that the offender had been drinking prior to the offense. Two-thirds of all victims who suffered a violent act at the hands of an intimate (current or former spouse, boyfriend, or girlfriend) reported that alcohol had been a factor in the violence; the figure was three-quarters for spouse violent victimization. For rape and sexual assault, roughly four offenders in 10 were perceived by victims to have been drinking prior to the offense; for victims of robbery, the figure was less than half of that (16%); and for aggravated or serious assault, the figure was three in 10. Of the five million convicted offenders on parole or probation, nearly two million (36%) were drinking at the time of their offense. In other words, no, by itself, alcohol intoxication does not promiscuously cause crime. The type of crime in which intoxicated offenders engage varies enormously from crime to crime. For violent offenses, the connection is strong; for crimes involving an economic motive, it is comparatively weak. The one bright spot in the panoply of alcohol-crime connections is in DUI offenses: Although this has leveled off in the past decade or so, in comparison with the 1990s, over time, the offense of driving under the influence is becoming less and less common (Greenfield, 1998).

In *Alcohol and Health,* the review of the worldwide research literature conducted by the U.S. Department of Health and Human Services (the last of which, the 10th, was published in 2000), consistently, an average of 50–60 percent of the perpetrators of criminal homicide were under the influence of alcohol when they killed their victims. True, government sponsored, authorized killings—in warfare, for instance—rarely involve alcohol intoxication. (Although if armies were under the influence in battle, the carnage would almost certainly be even higher than it is.) But alcohol is implicated in the majority criminal killings, and criminologists regard this fact as causally significant.

As I said, an important aspect of the alcohol–crime picture is the huge contribution that *being under the influence* makes to being victimized by criminal acts, especially violence. The proportion of homicide victims who had been intoxicated at the time of their demise is usually very similar to the figure of offenders under the influence. Intoxication interferes with judgment and self-protection, increases the likelihood of risky behavior, and places the weaker party in a position of profound vulnerability. Hence, its causal connection with violent victimization. More on this later. Also interesting is the fact that the role of alcohol varies according to the sex of the perpetrator and the victim. In one study, alcohol was present in 62 percent of cases involving a male assailant and male victim, in 53 percent of those involving a male assailant and a female victim, but in only 27 percent of all cases involving any female assailant (Pernanen, 1991). This study indicates that norms play a role in the contexts within which alcohol-related violence occurs. The role of alcohol in episodes of violence generally and homicide specifically is one of the most robust, well-established, and empirically grounded generalizations in the entire criminological literature. Any challenge to it would be a fool's errand.

Once again, after we've established the empirical regularity, the question becomes: Why? What *causes* higher rates of violence among drinkers versus nondrinkers, and higher rates of heavy versus lighter drinkers? As we know, establishing a correlation or statistical relationship between two variables is one thing; determining a causal relationship is quite another.

For centuries, folk wisdom held that alcohol caused violence because drinking releases inhibitions. What is alcohol's role in causing violence? The commonsensical answer has traditionally been that the inhibitions that normally prevent most of us from striking out at others are released. It seemed a reasonable explanation for such a long time that few questioned its validity. The proposition that alcohol more or less automatically released inhibitions and caused violent behavior in the violently inclined is referred to, as we saw, as the *disinhibition* or pharmacological theory. This theory assumes that it is the effects of alcohol, and that factor alone, that causes what drinkers do under the influence, violence included. Describing the effects of alcohol, one expert wrote: "Progressively the centers of basic emotional control are depressed, and the inhibitory functions of the centers are lost with an alteration in the conduct of the individual moving towards [being] 'miserable, mean, nasty and brutish' " (Paul, 1975, p. 16).

A different perspective is presented by anthropologists Craig MacAndrew and Robert Edgerton, in their book, *Drunken Comportment,* whose central thesis directly challenges the "release of inhibitions" claim (1969). MacAndrew emphasizes the factor of cultural context. Alcohol does not act on the human animal in a standardized fashion, they argue. Instead, alcohol's effects are influenced or mediated by cultural norms that dictate that specific forms of behavior are appropriate under the influence, while other forms are defined as completely unacceptable. In other words, drinkers are not simply under the influence of alcohol; instead, the effects of alcohol are under the influence of the culture in which drinkers live and grow up. Alcohol alone cannot account for the variation in alcohol-related behavior since alcohol is the same everywhere it is consumed. In short, "drunken comportment"—behavior under the influence—is as much a cultural as a pharmacological product. Drinking does not simply release inhibitions and stimulate the drinker's assaultive and homicidal tendencies. Instead, the alcohol–violence link is culturally determined and usually takes place within circumscribed, normatively governed limits.

This perspective is referred to as the *cognitive guidedness approach.* So marginal are alcohol's effects to this approach that one researcher was led to comment with reference to two anthropological studies of barroom behavior, "as far as one can judge from their description, the patrons might as well have been drinking orange juice."

In such studies, said this researcher, "the role of the physiological and psychological effects of alcohol is downplayed almost to the vanishing point" (Pernanen, 1991, pp. 18, 211).

Which perspective is correct—the pharmacological (disinhibition) or the cultural guidedness perspective? Is it the effects of the alcohol or the norms of the society that create the link between drinking and engaging in violent behavior? Which of these two "explanatory master frames" (Pernanen, 1991, p. 215) offers the best explanation of why the heavy consumption of alcohol so often leads to assault, rape, and criminal homicide? As is frequently the case, the best explanation borrows a bit of both frames.

It is clear that the norms do not provide a ready justification for the most seriously untoward behavior that takes place under the influence of alcohol *that would not happen when the actors are sober.* Pernanen (1991, p. 211) cites the case of drunken passengers of jet planes who attempt to enter the cockpit to convince the pilot that they should fly the plane. Examples could be multiplied endlessly. Such extremely dangerous behavior is fairly rare under the influence—but it is also vastly rarer when sober. "Why is alcohol used in this way and not coffee, tea, or milk?" Pernanen asks (p. 212). The obvious answer is that alcohol has certain "natural" effects that these other substances do not.

Arguing that alcohol has natural or pharmacological effects does not deny the fact that, in being socialized into the rules and norms of drinking, the drinker learns culturally approved behavior under the influence. In learning the appropriate norms of drinking, drinkers also learn that drinking puts them in a position where they are able to do things that they would not ordinarily do. Part of learning the drinking process involves learning *what the effects of alcohol are*—which is itself largely a product of the natural, pharmacological effects of this drug (p. 213).

For instance, the social setting in which drinking takes place influences how much one drinks—the amount consumed in one sitting, the speed of drinking, and the length of drinking occasions (Pernanen, 1991, p. 193). Of course, once the drinking begins—socially occasioned though it be—the effects of the alcohol begin kicking in. In other words, yes, the pharmacology of alcohol *does* disinhibit behavior, and yes, this disinhibition sometimes *does* result in violent behavior. But that violence clearly has limits, at least statistically speaking; it is selective as to time, place, and target.

And yes, there are other "causal agents" in violent behavior aside from alcohol (Parker, 1995, p. 28). But given the fact that violence is such a statistically rare event, some situations involving heavy alcohol consumption are much more likely to result in violence than other situations, identical except for the presence of alcohol. Acknowledging that alcohol is selective in producing disinhibition, we are nonetheless forced to accept the fact that alcohol disinhibits, that this disinhibition is a product of the drug's pharmacological effects, and that one consequence of disinhibition is the hugely higher incidence of violent behavior. Does alcohol cause violence? Stripped of qualifications and reservations, most contemporary researchers would answer this question with an affirmative answer. In Goldstein's vocabulary (1985), the alcohol–violence link seems—in large part—to be *psychopharmacological* in origin.

ALCOHOL CONSUMPTION AND SEXUAL VICTIMIZATION

As I've indicated, the reader might regard the inclusion of victimization in the relationship between alcohol abuse and deviance as an example of "blaming the victim" (Ryan, 1976). But, as I've noted several times before, *all* researchers of this topic distinguish "blame" from "cause" (Felson, 1991). Or, even more specifically, refer to a cause as a *factor,* even further removing the victim's drinking from blame in the dynamics of violence victimization. In the area of alcohol-related violence victimization, more research has been conducted on *sexual* victimization than any other type. A woman who is intoxicated is substantially and significantly more likely to be sexually victimized than a woman who is sober. Students of deviance are curious to know why. Is it spurious, that is, an artifact of the situation? Are women more likely to drink on *dates,* and hence, more likely to be in situations in which they are confronted by men who may force them to have sex? Are dates who offer women drinks more likely to be sexually aggressive than men who do not? Do men who offer women a drink on a date more likely to *perceive* women who accept drinks as sexual victims than they would women who refuse drinks? Do the physiological effects of alcohol render the intoxicated woman more sexually helpless than a woman would be if sober? Many causal explanations present themselves to account for this relationship. Which one is—or which ones are—valid?

Maria Testa (2004) surveyed four bodies of research on the role of substance use, alcohol included, when men commit violence against women: nonsexual physical violence perpetration, sexual violence perpetration, nonsexual violence victimization, and sexual violence victimization. We already know that men under the influence are more likely to commit violence, including sexual violence, against women than men who are sober. The weakest relationship of the four, Testa concludes, is that between alcohol (and drug) consumption and nonsexual violence victimization. However, the evidence supporting the relationship between substance use and a woman's experience of sexual victimization is substantially stronger. This is especially the case at the "proximal" or *event* level—that is, in the immediate context of the victimization. Sexually aggressive dates are more likely to include alcohol (and drugs) in their dating agenda and attempt to inflict sexual violence on their dates than is true of nonaggressive dates (Testa, 2004, p. 1497). Nonetheless, Testa concludes that women who have consumed alcohol "show impairment in their ability to recognize and respond to sexually aggressive risk" than women who are sober (2004, p. 1497). While Testa qualifies her literature summary by stating that the substance use–violence relationship is not universal for all people, all circumstances, or all measures of use, the pattern is strong enough to merit the generalization: Alcohol (and drug) intoxication increases the likelihood that women will be sexually victimized by men.

Muehlenhard and Linton (1987) report that when college women describe their alcohol consumption on a date as heavy, they are four times as likely to experience sexual aggression from the male than if it is light or none at all. About 15 percent of the women say they engaged in "unwanted sexual intercourse" (p. 186). Clearly, along with other factors, alcohol is strongly related to, and seems to facilitate, sexual aggression and tacit victimization in a college dating situation. In another study (Parks and Fals-Stewart, 2004), during a six-week period, college women were nine times more likely to experience sexual aggression on days when they are drinking heavily and three times more likely when it was lighter than when they are not drinking at all. Of course, these could be days specifically when they are out on a date, and hence, vulnerable to men's aggressive sexual advances. As the authors say, the "temporal association" between college women's alcohol consumption hugely increases their risk for sexual victimization (p. 625). Finally, in another study (Ullman, Karabatsos, and Koss, 1999), drinking by victims (and offenders as well) was associated with riskier, unplanned situations in which the victims did not know their offenders well prior to the assault. In addition, victim (and attacker) drinking was associated with more severe levels of sexual victimization (coercion, force, hitting, slapping, choking, etc.), though if she was drunk, her resistance was more easily overcome than if she was sober. In short, the study suggests that "alcohol use plays both direct and indirect roles in the outcomes of sexual abuse," including completed rape (p. 603).

Again, researchers do not blame the victim when they document that intoxication makes sexual victimization more likely. Victimizers, exploiters, and brutalizers are more likely to seek out vulnerable targets, and their perception that an intoxicated woman is more vulnerable to sexual victimization results in her actual sexual victimization. Here, women are unwillingly coerced into victimization partly as a result of their excessive use of alcohol.

The tendency of women to be victimized while intoxicated frequently leads to another victimization, some critics say. In a study using mock rape trials (Finch and Munro, 2007), juries regard complainants as *more* responsible than their sober attackers—a true case of "blaming the victim"—while their attackers are held to be *less* responsible than the sober defendants. In effect, if a woman who is drunk when she is raped is regarded as guiltier than a sober victim, but a drunk rapist is seen as less guilty than a sober rapist.

The social construction of the intoxicated woman's vulnerability is twofold: First, there is the men's construction of intoxicated women's vulnerability as well as their belief that taking advantage of such women is permissible and nonculpable. And second, there is society's after-the-fact interpretation or construction of the meaning of such assaults. Objectively, intoxication lowers the woman's "awareness of risky situations and impairs the ability to resist assault" (p. 592). The woman's involvement of intoxication in sexual consent scenarios "often influences the way in which observers assign responsibility to the parties involved" (p. 592). When the female is intoxicated, "audiences regard her drunkenness as her responsibility. But when the male perpetrator is intoxicated, his drunkenness is a partial exoneration for his crimes" (Stormo, Lang, and Strizke, 1997; Finch and Munro, 2007, p. 593).

Audiences regard alcohol intoxication "as a culturally sanctioned masculine activity" (p. 593), whereas when the female drinks too much, audiences regard her as deviating from gender-role norms. Hence, in a rape case, observers "tend to hold a voluntarily intoxicated complainant more responsible than her sober counterpart" (p. 594). She "has exhibited a reckless disregard for her own safety by sending out a message of sexual interest through her intoxication and by placing herself in a position in which she is vulnerable to the inevitable sexual aggression of an intoxicated male companion" (pp. 594–595). These stereotypes tend to govern the way that juries or potential juries think about the culpability of a rape defendant. A member of a mock jury assigned less responsibility toward the intoxicated defendant if he had sex with the woman when she was drunk than he or she did to her attacker because she accepted the drinks. Even if the defendant spiked her drinks with alcohol, the jury were unwilling to charge him with rape. It was only when his motive was to render the woman helpless and force her to have sex that they were willing to convict him of rape. In addition, this study showed, if the drug was Rohypnol rather than alcohol, in contrast, the mock jury attributed less responsibility to the female victim and were more willing to convict the perpetrator with rape. In other words, alcohol is "heavily normalized," and hence, not regarded as a "demon" substance instrumental in the heinous crime of rape. It was apparent, say the authors, that jurors "were often prepared to attribute responsibility for the rape to the defendant but are reluctant to translate this into an attribution of blame [to the defendant] in the form of a guilty verdict, possibly because they were simultaneously attributing some responsibility for the subsequent sexual events to the intoxicated complainant" (p. 603).

ALCOHOL AND DRUG USE

The consumption of alcohol and the use of illicit psychoactive drugs are related in revealing and important ways. But since fewer people use illicit drugs than alcohol, the relationship is far from perfect. Let's express their relationship in the following two generalizations. First: *People who drink alcohol are more likely to use illegal drugs than people who don't drink.* And second: *Most people who drink don't use illegal drugs.*

The data on the relationship between alcohol consumption and drug use are instructive. Drinking alcoholic beverages is significantly related to the use of *all* psychoactive recreational drugs. Drinkers consume alcohol *mainly* for its effects; illicit drug users take illicit substances *mainly* for their effects. Drinkers are more likely to know the users of illicit drugs than nondrinkers are, and hence, become socialized to accept the desirability of drug use as well as have access to illicit drugs. Statistically speaking, people who drink are more unconventional and more willing to take risks than people who do not drink; as a result, they tend to be more open to the experience of getting high on illegal drugs. In a nutshell, these are the most informative explanations for why we observe such a strong and irrefutable relationship between alcohol consumption and use of illegal drugs. To repeat: Not all drinkers take illegal drugs; most don't. But they are a lot *more likely* to use drugs than nondrinkers. In fact, as the 2007 NSDUH report indicates, drinkers are roughly *10 times* more likely to use illicit drugs than nondrinkers. But let's also keep in mind the following truism in the world of consumption of illicit substances: *Most illegal drug use is with marijuana.*

TABLE 7.3 ILLICIT DRUG USE IN PAST MONTH BY ALCOHOL USE IN PAST MONTH

		Alcohol Use in Past Month			
		No Use	Use but Not Binge Use	Binge Use but Not Heavy Use	Heavy Use
Illicit Drug Use in Past Month	Marijuana	1.9	4.0	12.4	25.1
	Cocaine	0.2	0.4	1.5	5.5
	Hallucinogens	0.1	0.2	0.9	2.2
	*Nonmedical Prescription Use	1.6	1.9	4.6	10.5
	**Illicit Drug Other than Marijuana	2.0	2.4	6.5	15.4
	ANY/ALL DRUG USE	3.4	5.5	16.1	31.3

Source: SAMHSA, NSDUH 2007, "Detailed Tables" (not in NSDUH, 2008). I would like to thank James Colliver for supplying me with these tables and helping me interpret their significance.

Note: Use of drugs whose numbers of past month users are too small to be meaningly presented in this table do not appear in this table.

*Nonmedical prescription use indicates the use of at least one prescription drug without a physician's prescription; includes the following: pain relievers, tranquilizers, stimulants, and sedatives.

**Illicit Drug Other than Marijuana refers to the use in the past month of at least one illegal drug in addition to or aside from marijuana.

About three-quarters of all episodes of illicit drugs are with marijuana alone. When anyone refers to illicit drug use, they are talking *mainly* about marijuana use. Let's look at Tables 7.3 and 7.4.

Tables 7.3 and 7.4 convey a simple message with a complex explanation: The consumption of alcohol and the use of illegal drugs are strongly related; not only are users of alcohol more likely to also use illegal drugs, but the more alcohol the drinker consumes, the greater the likelihood that he or she will *regularly* use psychoactive drugs. There is a stepwise and linear relationship between

TABLE 7.4 USE OF ILLICIT DRUGS IN PAST MONTH BY USE OF ALCOHOL AND CIGARETTES IN PAST MONTH

		Use of Alcohol and Cigarettes in Past Month			
		Neither Cigarettes nor Alcohol	Alcohol, No Cigarettes	Cigarettes, No Alcohol	Cigarettes and Alcohol
Use of Illicit Drugs in Past Month	Marijuana	0.9	4.6	7.0	20.3
	Cocaine	0.0	0.3	1.1	3.8
	Hallucinogens	0.1	0.2	0.4	1.7
	*Nonmedical Prescription Use	1.2	2.1	3.4	7.9
	**Illicit Drug Other than Marijuana	1.4	2.6	4.6	11.5
	ANY/ALL DRUG USE	2.2	6.4	9.7	25.3

For explanations, note, and source, see Table 7.3.

alcohol and illicit drug use; the heavy drinker is between 6.5 and 27.5 times as likely to regularly use certain drugs, depending on the drug, than the nondrinker, and moving up in use also moves up the likelihood of using one or more illicit drugs. We refine the relationship even further when we introduce smoking cigarettes into the picture, which is remarkable because Table 7.4 compares alcohol use during the past month with nonuse, whereas Table 7.3 compares degrees of alcohol use and has no category for simple use during the past month. In any case, smoking cigarettes seems to correlate even more strongly with illicit drug use than drinking (compare the figures in the "alcohol, no cigarettes" column with the "cigarettes, no alcohol" column). This may be because monthly or more cigarette smokers are less numerous and more committed substance users than the mainstream of monthly-or-more drinkers—and, very possibly, a bit more unconventional. But of course, using *both* tobacco and alcohol is even more compatible with psychoactive drug use than is using one but not the other. This is especially the case with smoking marijuana: Consumers of alcohol and cigarettes are *22 and-a-half times* more likely to have used marijuana in the prior month than nonsmokers *and* nondrinkers.

As we can see in Table 7.5, with the population at large, adolescents in the 8th, 10th, and 12th grades who drink alcohol are much more likely to use illicit drugs than those who do not drink; this pattern is true of drugs in general as well as with marijuana specifically, and it is true of each grade level separately. Moreover, the more that secondary school students drink (1–19 versus 20 or more occasions), the greater the likelihood that they also used drugs during the prior 30 days. Among 8th graders, the nondrinker was 27 times as likely to use any illicit drugs as the more frequent drinker; for 10th graders, this figure was 10 times, and for 12th graders, 11 and-a-half times. Clearly, a strong relationship exists between alcohol consumption and illicit drug use. Of course, for teenagers, the purchase and possession of both alcohol and illicit drugs are illegal.

The question is why? Do we have a *direct* cause-and-effect relationship on our hands, that is, is the relationship the result of feeling the *effects* of drinking alcohol that impels the drinker to want to seek the effects of a cognate psychoactive substance? Is it that heavy drinkers are the kinds of unconventional people who are likely to do other unconventional things, like getting high on marijuana or taking a "toot" of cocaine? Or, alternatively, are the social networks that heavy drinkers, and regular drinkers *and* cigarette smokers, hang out with and among *also* the kinds of social networks whose members encourage and

TABLE 7.5 ALCOHOL AND ILLICIT DRUG USE, 8TH, 10TH, AND 12TH GRADERS

	30-DAY ALCOHOL USE	% OF N	ANY ILLICIT DRUG	ANY ILLICIT DRUG OTHER THAN MARIJUANA	MARIJUANA
8th Grade	0 Occasions	84.3	2.7	1.3	1.7
$N = 15{,}260$	1–19 Occasions	15.2	31.0	14.9	25.0
	20+ Occasions	0.6	73.9	53.3	62.1
10th Grade	0 Occasions	66.8	6.1	2.3	4.5
$N = 15{,}423$	1–19 Occasions	31.8	37.8	16.0	32.5
	20+ Occasions	1.4	62.2	27.6	57.7
12th Grade	0 Occasions	55.7	6.2	2.6	4.6
$N = 14{,}116$	1–19 Occasions	41.2	39.4	16.1	34.7
	20+ Occasions	3.1	71.5	41.3	63.1

Source: Tabulations of the 2007 Monitoring the Future data, not in published report; I would like to thank Patti Meyer for supplying me with these figures.

practice the use of one or more illicit drugs? My guess is that it's all three; many deviant behaviors "cluster" together in the same social circles, and attitudes toward unconventional behaviors in one sphere of life tend to "spill out" into other areas of life. The generalizability of deviance is one more of the more firmly established patterns in crime and deviance, and may be taken as something of a truism (Gottfredson and Hirschi, 1990; Hirschi and Gottfredson, 1994).

SUMMARY

Humans are probably hard-wired to enjoy the low-to-moderate effects of alcohol; hence the use of this substance is both ancient and nearly universal. But at higher doses, drinking exacts a heavy toll: discoordination, mental confusion, risky behaviors, and, in the long run, mental and physical maladies. All societies regard excessive drinking as deviant and condemn the heavy drinker. Patterns of drinking are probably more influential in determining social problems and deviant behavior than the quantity consumed: who drinks it, why, how much during a single occasion, and socially where.

Men tend to drink more than women and the young drink more than older adults. Socioeconomic status displays a complex relationship with drinking: The higher the SES, the greater the likelihood of drinking; lower SES members of the society are more likely to abstain from alcohol than those higher up in the class ladder. However, among persons who drink, lower SES individuals are more likely to engage in deviant drinking and get into trouble as a result of their intoxication.

As with all forms of deviance we've considered in this book, alcohol consumption can be looked at both through the lens of essentialism and constructionism. Essentialism examines the objective properties of alcohol: its effects, the consequences of use, and the causes of excessive consumption. Alcohol is a sedative with complex, even contradictory properties, and some individuals react to it idiosyncratically. But as a general rule, the greater the amount of alcohol consumed, that is, the greater the degree of intoxication, the greater the likelihood that the drinker will engage in risky, deviant behavior, including fatal automobile accidents, risky sex, violence, and the greater the likelihood that one will be a victim of violence, including sexual violence.

Some alcohol researchers argue that alcohol "releases inhibitions" from normative constraint and disorganizes and diminishes the mind's capacity to reason effectively, making certain deviant behaviors more likely. In addition, the people who engage in deviant drinking are also the kinds of people who are more likely to engage in risky behavior in the first place, alcohol or no alcohol. And third, the occasions and locales of drinking are also the kinds of times and places when untoward events take place; alcohol may be little more than an accompaniment of risky, deviant settings.

Perhaps lethal violence is the most significant of the accompaniments of heavy drinking. But this relationship does not show up in a ranking of countries with respect to alcohol consumption and criminal violence because the causes of murder are complex, culturally determined, caused by far more than a release from inhibitions. However, if we track alcohol consumption over time in one country, we do see the co-occurrence of alcohol and criminal violence, indicating that perhaps a decline in alcohol consumption in the United States after 1990 had something to do with its decline in the murder rate. And looking at the individual level, people who drink in a deviant fashion are more likely to engage in violence than those who do not, and people who are under the influence, likewise, are more likely to do so than those who are sober. The same is true of engaging in risky sex and being a victim of sexual aggression. Sociologists and criminologists argue that the two preceding statements do not blame the victim but state an objectively true generalization.

Drinking alcohol (in moderation, a conventional act) is strongly correlated with the use of illicit drugs (not only an illegal but, in many social circles, a deviant act). Perhaps many of the intersections of these two activities that researchers observe explain many of the correlations they also see between the most common form of drug use, marijuana smoking, and a substantial number of deviant activities.

A WHO Report On Alcohol Use and Unsafe Sex

In 2005, the WHO published a literature review and research monograph investigating the co-occurrence of alcohol consumption and engaging in risky sex in eight countries, three in Eastern Europe (Russia, Belarus, and Romania), three in Africa (Kenya, South Africa, and Zambia), one in Asia (India), and one in Latin America (Mexico). All of these countries are less economically developed than North America and western Europe, and all have high or increasing levels of HIV infection, and in most of them, HIV is spread mainly through heterosexual sex. In all of them, alcohol is consumed vastly more by men than women, and home brew makes up a substantial proportion of the alcohol drunk, which means that its consumption is not recorded in official sales, indicating that their alcohol consumption is much greater than researchers realize.

The WHO study reports that alcohol use before unprotected sex is common among sex workers and among their nonpaying sex partners. (Sex workers are more likely to insist that their paying customers use condoms.) Moreover, the prevalence of alcohol dependence in men with HIV is high in all the countries studied. And the conjunction of drinking alcohol and visiting commercial sex workers is common among transportation workers, mainly truck drivers, and migrant workers; by frequenting sex workers, these mobile laborers spread sexually transmitted diseases from place to place and from high-risk groups to the general population (p. 8). In addition, alcohol use is associated with casual sex among adolescents: "Early sexual experience, a high level of risk taking, and alcohol use" increase the likelihood of sexually transmitted diseases, including HIV.

The WHO report focuses on key mechanisms in the relationship between alcohol use and risky sex: the cultural construction of maleness as defined by the consumption of alcohol; a denial of risk among certain sectors of the population; the empirical conjunction of alcohol use in certain locales in which sexual encounters take place (such as bars, nightclubs, "dark houses," highway eating joints, and brothels); and the use of alcohol before initial, adolescent encounters. In most studies conducted in the Western world, the attribution of responsibility in the alcohol-risky sex equation is placed mainly on the woman; in the less economically developed world, it is the man who is charged with the locus of responsibility in this equation (WHO, 2005).

Account: Harry, the Debonair Drinker

At the time of this interview, Harry was 39 years old, received a BA degree from a state university ("on the 12-year plan," as he explains), and took graduate courses in a variety of departments. Currently, he does not have a job; he is enrolled in a computer course. For years, Harry drank heavily, and his drinking significantly contributed to his inability to achieve many of his life goals. He is also gay, a subject to which in this account he makes only occasional reference. Harry's interview is so interesting, revealing, and insightful that I decided to reproduce it more or less exactly as I transcribed it. I began by asking him to elaborate on his life of heavy drinking.

HARRY: This is a pretty standard story, a typical drunkalogue. I started drinking at about [the age of] 13. And right from the start, I began drinking alcoholically. Whereas some people [I drank with] were drinking to get happy, to get loose, I was almost immediately drinking to get drunk.

ERICH: I wonder if you might go over a little bit about this early period of your drinking. First of

(*Continued*)

Account: Harry, the Debonair Drinker Continued

all, how does a 13-year-old get his hands on alcohol? Why don't you tell me about your early period of drinking?

HARRY: At the age of 13, it was once or twice a week. Thirteen seems to be a very common year for people to start drinking and doing drugs, for some reason. We would stand outside the 7-Eleven or the liquor store and wait for somebody to buy us some. Or we would get about a quart of vodka a week [which] would mysteriously appear in my friend's hands. He was at first kind of non-committal about where he got it from. Since he was a year and a half older and he was my best friend, I didn't push him [about it].

ERICH: What did he say?

HARRY: There was a guy who lived down the block who we hung out with sometimes who said his uncle got it for him. He had an uncle who was 18, and at 18 at the time, you could buy alcohol. So we would get drunk once or twice a week. And right from the start, I *absolutely loved* the stuff. When you are in high school, there were more opportunities to procure. And, unfortunately or fortunately, there's more drinking in high school. Also, I was in high school in the seventies. There was *a lot* of marijuana in high school [then].

ERICH: The seventies was the high point [in the recreational use of illegal drugs].

HARRY: Yeah. Now [at that time, in the 1970s, in high school], we're drinking maybe *four* times a week. And it becomes important in the rituals. Especially in the mating dance, the mating rituals. One of those unspoken contract things. You know, it's acknowledged, it's there. . . . What's a football game without some beers? Especially for me because I never liked sports. I hung out a lot. Outdoors. We used to have a lot of woods in our area, and we'd hang out there. Some people would hang out at the 7-Eleven parking lot, but they were the less savory [types]—they were the gang fighters, the rough guys. I was more with the heads, which was the more numerous group. Having alcohol always made sex a little easier, because you're young and you're insecure. Guys started going out on a date [and said to themselves]—"I've got to have some alcohol, I've gotta have some vodka." *There were no consequences to getting drunk in high school!* There were *none!* Maybe you would throw up! That was it! Our parents were *remarkably* lenient in that respect. It was the seventies. It was a remarkable time to be young. OK, then there was the eighties. I went to college in the eighties [laughs] and into the nineties. I would go to college for a semester or two, [drop out,] go back to college, go to tech school, go back to college.

ERICH: You stretched it out.

HARRY: Oh, my God! I was on the 12-year plan! It was terrible! They kept sending me checks and I kept going [to college]. It was wonderful. I think I'm pretty well educated for somebody who's only got a BA, though. That's one good thing I have to say about it.

ERICH: When did you realize you had a problem and what was the nature of this problem?

HARRY: They say that alcoholics are like people whose hair is on fire, who end up drowning when they run into the sea. And you could tell right from the start, I'm sure, if there were an objective observer, that I was an alcoholic. Part of that whole alcoholism thing is that the alcoholic is the *last* person in the world who recognizes that he is an alcoholic. Often, his family, friends—everyone—will recognize that he is an alcoholic. Bill Moyers did a special [which was broadcast on public television] on addiction called "The Hijacked Brain." And I thought that was the best description I've heard so far. It really is like your brain itself has been hijacked. Sometimes I was known to have said, "My brain is *broken.* It's trying to *kill* me!"

ERICH: So far, it's very abstract. Hijacked brain, hair's on fire, rushing into the sea. The generalizations are important and interesting, but what I'm interested *in addition* is how this manifested itself on an everyday basis. In other words, what *quantities* are we talking about, what *kinds* of disruption in your life are we talking about, how did you *manage* your day-to-day affairs, how did you get through *school*—you were talking about [drinking heavily] from, what, eighth grade until fairly recently, you said—so, there's a long period of time during which you had to *cope* with the realities of everyday life [while you were drinking heavily], so maybe you can fill this out a little bit.

HARRY: I never drove a car into a school bus full of nuns. But that doesn't mean that I didn't make a lot of things crash and burn.

ERICH: Like what?

HARRY: Relationships. I have never made a relationship, you know, the standard boyfriend-boyfriend, running-through-the-field-of-daisies-hand-in-hand kind of relationship, work for more than six weeks. I'm now 39. But it's always traceable to something I said or did, or decided to say or do while I was drunk. I can be brutally honest, still. I did everything while I was drunk. [Laughs.] I did all my eating while I was drunk, my sleeping, my watching TV. So it's difficult to separate life's mistakes from life's *drunken* mistakes. . . . [Long pause.] Why don't I couch it in general terms? I was insulting, overly honest—brutally honest—with people at times when I shouldn't have been. I've walked away from relationships or potential relationships that I shouldn't have. Or maybe walked into things I *wouldn't* have if I had been sober at the time. . . . However, realizing that you had sex with somebody you *really* wish you hadn't is worse than having to apologize for making rude suggestions to somebody that you shouldn't have the night before. Of course, you can't drive a car, or fly a plane, or work heavy machinery with the same aptitude or finesse when you're drunk, so of course, you're not going to be able to maneuver delicate situations, interpersonal conflicts or relationships as well when you're drinking. I'm sure of it.

ERICH: That makes sense.

HARRY: Why don't I recall my last year or two, because every day will be full of alcoholic coping mechanisms and dysfunctions. Some people [who drink heavily] become bartenders. Me, I *owned the bar.* I rented a house as a grad student. I was living on student loans, and I ended up $100,000 in debt. And it was wonderful. As an undergraduate, they [the university] would send me loans, and once a semester, they would send me a check, once a year, I would have to fill out loan forms and do an interview. And once a semester, they kept sending me this blue slip, telling me to register for graduation. And as long as I *didn't* turn in the blue slip, they kept giving me the loans. [Laughs.] And I thought that this was the most wonderful thing in the world. They're paying me to socialize, read books, and learn stuff. And alcohol was, as they say, the organizing principle of my life, even though I didn't realize it. Everything revolved around alcohol. Some people become terribly irresponsible, they lose everything, but there's a *need* to keep your supply, your pipeline. That is the last thing that you want to lose. I'm racking up $100,000 in debts. But I'm drinking bourbon that I was budgeting for *six months* earlier. And I really, really thought that I was being responsible [laughs], that I was managing my life great. Look at that! Oh, my God, he's got a budget made up six months in advance. I didn't take many classes that started before 10 in the morning. This is one thing that you learn early. Towards the end, I simply rented a house. And I became the agent. And once again, I was being responsible. I painted this house, I did little minor repairs here and there. And I rented it out, the other rooms. My nickname was "Tigger" [after the Winnie-the-Pooh character]. I used to have long hair and a short beard and moustache and it made me look a bit leonine. I also had a certain spring to my step when I walked, so some of my friends came up with "Tigger," because "Tigger's a wonderful thing. Their tops are made out of rubber and their bottoms are made out of springs." And so it [my apartment] became "Tigger's Place." It was like Rick's "Cafe American" [after the nightclub in the film, *Casablanca*]. Five nights out of the week, the place was *packed* with people. And I *liked* it. I was like a tiny, little Hugh Hefner. I swear to God. I had my room upstairs, I had this *smoking*

(*Continued*)

Account: Harry, the Debonair Drinker Continued

jacket, which I wore as a bathrobe [laughs]. It was wonderful. It was either that or a cardigan. But I would walk around constantly with a glass of bourbon in my hand, mingling and having fun. Mostly the people I rented to were younger than I was. I did a quick check once, before I left campus [and before "Tigger's Place"]. I and another guy were the *oldest* people in my dorm. At this point, I had spent about five or six years in Room 106 Wagner D. [Laughs.] And I had never thought of myself as being particular socially adept. A typical alcoholic has a very low opinion of himself. I'm an egomaniac with an inferiority complex. Never thought I was particularly socially adept. And yet, to speak to people, it seems that I really *was*. People *liked* me. People would gravitate towards my room [chuckles] when I lived on campus. Off campus, it was already an established pattern. One night a week, we would play "Risk." I would have a group of people playing "Risk." I surrounded myself with younger people, I think, largely because when you're drinking [heavily], you don't develop emotionally. You really don't grow. I had a Peter Pan Syndrome [aging, but inappropriately attempting to act like a younger person] to the point where my mother would refer to the guys that I had in the house as "The Lost Boys." Also, being gay, I liked having good-looking young men around. [Laughs.] This is not an uncommon thing. Also, it was nice that I could jokingly—I *demanded virgin sacrifice!* [Laughs.] And I'll be damned! They [my friends] started *bringing* it! [Laughs.] What more could I ask for? [Laughs.] And the interesting thing is, if you see photos of me during this period, in *every single photo,* I have a glass of bourbon either in my hand or next to me. Which is an indicator I should have picked up on. [Laughs.] At this point, I knew I was an alcoholic, but I figured that I was a *functioning* alcoholic. And, you know, that's OK. If I ever need to, I'll just dry out. [Sighs.] So, one day a week, we would have "Risk." Either the stereo or the TV was always on in the TV room. We would have "Risk" going on in the kitchen. People would come by—first they would call, I like that. There was lots of drinking [laughs] because I liked to drink and, interestingly enough, so did the people who gravitated towards me. There was always alcohol around. I tended to take in strays. And I ended up being the cook. It's like I had one duty. [Chuckles.] And people would come. And they would [be appreciative; they'd say], "Oh, my God, have you had his basil cream sauce?" I liked when people appreciated that [my cooking]. There were drinking games. There was a whole generation who didn't know about "Think While You Drink," [a game] which I liked. You've gotta play it with beer, though. And this was all right with me, but not my favorite because I was a bourbon drinker.

ERICH: Wait, what's "Think While You Drink"?

HARRY: Well, the purpose of drinking games usually is to get people very drunk very quickly. "Think While You Drink" is a game where you would sit in a circle and you have to chug beer, slowly, while you thought of a name of somebody. And if you said, "Albert Einstein," the next person would have to come up with the name of a person whose *first* name started with the *last* letter of the *last* name of the person that the person *before* gave. So, Albert Einstein would lead to *Norm Abrams,* who would lead to Sally Struthers. If you got a *double,* where the first name and the last name started with the same letter, the direction of play reversed. I was pretty good at "Think While You Drink." [Laughs.] For some reason I have a large storehouse of useless information. I spent a lot of time on campus. [Laughs.] Racking up a huge debt, learning about people. So, towards the end of the last few years, I started to get *nervous* about things like getting *too* drunk and getting sloppy. . . . So what I would do is I would buy my bourbon, and instead of buying it in fifths, or half-gallons, I would buy my bourbon in *pints.* [Chuckles.] So that I would only drink *one pint a day.* Which I thought was a very good strategy. You have to worry about things like, again, not getting too drunk and sloppy. And people were *absolutely amazed* at my ability to hold on a rational conversation after downing a pint of bourbon. I only weigh 125 pounds. And I would always have a little juicer in my hand. . . . I was never a big fan of orange juice, unless it was for making vodka go down smoothly, but those little six-ounce glasses were easier to keep a firm grasp on than a big, old Scotch tumbler. Basically, as the evening wore on, drinking, you know, halfway through the night, I would be two-thirds through a bottle of bourbon, and people would comment, "Oh, my God." Because you can't see how much someone is drinking when they just re-fill that little juicer once in a while. It's because I was drinking for so long that I used to joke that, "It's because I've had my liver in training for a decade. [Laughs.] Next year off to the Olympics in Japan!" This is not an uncommon thing. I'm good at getting drunk and talking shit. I mean, *bizarre* conversations. Pro and cons on the existence of God, *vis à vis* particle physics versus cross-cultural comparative religions, you know, wonderful, *wonderful* conversations. That's a real example. The funny thing was the person speaking *for* the existence of God was a particle physicist. [Laughs]. He was a born-again physics grad student. And I really miss that about not being drunk.

ERICH: You mean you would have these conversations when you were drunk but you *wouldn't* have them when you *weren't* drunk?

HARRY: Yeah, I think so. Because once Tigger's was cookin', you know, [at] one o'clock in the morning, that's the sort of conversation [laughs] that might be goin' on.

ERICH: In an average or typical evening, how many guys might be there?

HARRY: I threw a lot of what were called "sausage parties." [Laughs.] Indeed, the ratio of men to women was *way* the hell off. There were mostly guys. On an average night, [there] would be, if it wasn't, like, a Friday or Saturday, 12, 15 [men there]. You know, not a *party.* Relatively small.

ERICH: And then on Friday and Saturday nights?

HARRY: On a night when people were actually coming over, 25. That's a big night.

ERICH: If it's not too indelicate, could you tell me what a sausage party is?

HARRY: A sausage party? That's when you get a lot of guys. And no women.

ERICH: I see. I get the idea.

HARRY: It was a lot of getting drunk and talking shit. Which is what people *like to do* when there's a lot of alcohol in the room. I was never much of a *bar* drinker. I much preferred—and this is why the campus life suited me so well—to have a group of people that I knew and not have to mingle with a bunch of strangers at a bar. Or to mingle with strangers at least at a party. Something that wasn't so bar-like. I'm one of the [few] gay people who has a genuine, very negative feeling about the bars and the bar life. For some economic-cultural reason, gay bars seem to be the absolute *hub* of gay life. And it's very shallow, and it's very predatory, and it *looks* friendly, but it's not as friendly as it looks. I think the sexual tension and the predatory aspect of it [contributes to its unfriendly aspect]. And, unless you go to a leather bar, the music is always *disco,* and the music is always too loud. . . .

Anyway, one night [at our house], we had the police come to the door. And I have no idea what's going on. I answer the door, glass of bourbon in hand, smoking jacket on. It's the police. People with a *cell phone,* driving by, called to complain. And I'm [laughs] absolutely *clueless* [about why the police were there]. But sort of impressed and worried [laughs] that people on a *cell phone,* driving by, called to complain. [Supposedly] it was a sort of *rumble,* a *gang* fight, or something like that, was going on outside of my house. No, the Lost Boys were outside, doing professional wrestling moves up against the chain link fence, across the street [laughs], on Main Street, which is a fairly busy road for a suburban area. And people on the cell phone thought it was some kind of gang fight. The police stopped by to tell us, stop that. We didn't have many neighbors, the [few] neighbors [we did have] did not complain. . . .

(*Continued*)

Account: Harry, the Debonair Drinker Continued

To give you an example—I didn't rent the house all at once, first I had to settle in. And decide that I liked the arrangement, I had the apartment downstairs, it was a studio apartment. My second day of living there, I'm moving in, my friends are coming by, helping me carry boxes. And the other guys who had moved in upstairs a week earlier, are four guys from the football team. I show up [laughs] that night, there are people sitting on the roof, and somebody is pissing into the bushes. [Laughs.] The neighbors *do not* complain. Later on, I'm walking people out, there's someone curled up on the front lawn behind the hedges that kind of separate our house from the street, *throwing up.* And, you know, I was never *at* that level. I was never *that kind* of drunk. As my first sponsor [in an alcohol self-help program] said, I drank like a lady. I didn't start to drink until five or six [o'clock in the afternoon]. After dinner was usually my rule. Of course, by three in the morning, I had downed an entire pint, maybe a beer or two. [I said to myself,] I wasn't drinking, I was just havin' a couple a' beers. Who was [it that said] that? Some comedian. But that was a good tag line. As I said, I didn't drink early in the day. However, *getting to class* could often be a problem. Well, I wouldn't schedule my classes until, the *earliest,* was 12 noon, 11:30 class. So I had time to down some ice tea, shower, clear my head, and drive to campus.

And the alcoholism impacted my ability to function, because in the last couple of years [of my drinking], I would buffalo my way into classes that I didn't really belong in, like a [graduate] sociology course with students who had taken *real* sociology. I was in a comparative primatology class with students who had amusing stories about picking fleas off of Jane Goodall [an important, well-known primatologist]. So I always felt that I was faking it and people would call me on it. To the point where, in a couple of classes, I simply did not turn in the final projects. Because I felt that I had *no business* writing a paper in this discipline. In retrospect, that was kind of wrong. But that's how you think when you're an alcoholic. And I was constantly living in fear that people were going to discover that I was a faker. And I actually didn't attend some classes toward the end. [At the time,] I didn't know what this was. I was worried that I was getting agoraphobia [fear of open spaces, fear of going outside]. I could not leave the house. I had a panic attack and I was just in such fear that I could not bring myself to leave the house and go out on campus and function. I later found out that this is a phenomenon that happens to alcoholics, called "the terrors." I had no idea. I should have read a couple of books on alcoholism [laughs], to know what I had to expect.

I thought that Korsakoff's Syndrome was the big thing I had to worry about. Korsakoff's Syndrome is where the part of the brain that sorts emotion and memory becomes damaged. And you can get Parkinson's symptoms, where you get shaking, tremors. But it also makes it more difficult for you to assimilate new information. And as the years wore on, it was true, I used to just be able to read a textbook or sit in a class, towards the end [of my period of drinking], I used to have to read and take notes on the reading and then read the notes again, because [it would be necessary for me to do that to have] the same memory and the same ability to retain information as I did five years earlier by putting in a minimal effort. [Pause.] I think, intuitively, I knew early on, that I had a problem. It became a joke and a part of my persona for the last—I was drinking for about 20 years—I was a heavy drinker, in retrospect, for about 20 years. A friend of mine used to say, "You know, for a little guy, you toss your body a big man's beatin'." But you rationalize. And I rationalized. And it just became a part of my persona.

OK, so, I'm Harry, the lovable—sometimes not so lovable—drunk. I took on a Hugh Hefner, party-guy, with sophistication, a sophisticated—for an undergraduate crowd—drunk, with a party-guy kind of persona. Some people thought I was lovable. Especially younger people thought I was interesting. As someone said, "You know, most people, when you speak to them, you sort of know what they're going to say next. I never know what's going to come out of your mouth next!" Again, I didn't think I was all that interesting. But people did. The trauma for me was having to admit to myself that I was no longer going to be for very long a functioning alcoholic. Things fell apart.

The last six months was so. . . . I had a little "boy toy" jump ship on me. [Laughs.] He kind of deserted me. [In addition,] I had someone move in who was a recovering alcoholic—a dry drunk. Who I thought might be good to have around. He dragged me to a couple of AA meetings. I wasn't ready to quit, but it sort of opened my eyes a bit. And then he started drinking. I have this effect on people. Even in my sobriety. I've only been sober for a little under two years. The other newcomers that I've latched onto. People that I affiliated with all went out [and drank]. I'm just a rotten influence on people. So this guy, let's call him "Butt-Wipe," he started drinking heavily. And he was a serious alcoholic. His morals went out the window, he started stealing, he lost his job, he flunked out of school, and he made no attempt to do anything aside from male prostitution. And towards the end, it was fairly obvious that he wasn't going to be able to come up with his share of the rent. He was bad. Then, Fred, the stray that I took in, bailed on me.

See, what happened was, it was kind of my house. So I had to maintain the standards. Such that they were. And believe it or not, I actually, I had to stomp my tiny, little foot a couple of times. Like, this guy, one of the last people to move in, there was a hooker, a prostitute in the neighborhood [chuckles], he started to hang out with her. I think he identified—I met his mom once for a few seconds—I'm pretty sure she was a hooker, too. And he decided he was going to be a part-time male prostitute. And I had to put my foot down. And [I said to him,] "No more! She can't come to the house!" I never had to bar anyone from the house before. "No crack whores in the house! New house rule!" I had responsibilities. Collecting the rent. All kinds of stupid upkeep. The plumbing needed work, the painting, the yard work. And more than that, I had Fred, my stray. I had to help him get his life together. I had to be sure that somebody's car was working. There was always something. If you give me enough time, I will become responsible for the sunrise. And it got to the point where I was absolutely pulling my hair out. And the house and everything was dragging me down. I bombed out of school. Which I've done before. They put you on a six-month's probationary period, you get your grades up, and you take care of incompletes, and they take you back. But something told me that it wasn't gonna happen this time.

I needed help. And my parents had been begging me for the last couple of years, "Come home, get your life together, get sober, get on with your life." So I finally took them up on it. I am very, very fortunate to have had this family, insane as they are, dysfunctional as they are, offer me that opportunity. So I came home. I severed my ties with [my former friends]. I kind of became a hermit. With the intention of getting my life together. Gave up my responsibilities [in the house I rented]. I went home. What I did was, I said, I'm fine, I've got a BA in psych under my belt, I'm four years into a master's in liberal arts—that should have taken only two years—I'll put myself on a behavioral extinction program. I'll go from a pint of bourbon a night [each day of the week] to a pint of bourbon a night six nights a week. After a couple of months, I'll go to five nights a week, to four nights a week. That was relatively easy. Then to three nights, then to two nights. And every month I would ratchet it down. I got to the point where I was drinking only one night a week. And reality struck. I could not get down to less than one night a week. In fact, I had difficulty, I only made a couple of weeks where I was drinking one night a week. I would find myself drinking two nights a week.

Erich: Why was that a problem for you? I mean, you would think that you had cut it down to the point where it was moderate drinking.

Harry: Well, you hear a lot of people say, "Oh, my God, I drank because everyone in my family

(*Continued*)

Account: Harry, the Debonair Drinker Continued

was an alcoholic, and I was abused. Oh, I drank because I had such low self-esteem and it was the only way I could face myself and other people." I drank because I was an alcoholic. And I didn't realize until that point really, really, down in my heart, what being an alcoholic meant. But I found that I could not drink one night a week. And I put myself on a schedule. I had to be sober very soon. So, I tried and I found out that, deep in my heart that I was an alcoholic.

ERICH: When you say you couldn't drink one night a week, in what specific way?

HARRY: I've been wrestling with this since that time. I cannot tell you. It's so difficult to put into words. I would rationalize my drinking. I would be crawling out of my skin. And I would be miserable. And I would say, "All right, I'm not ready yet! Next week I'll be ready! I drank once last week. This week, I'll drink twice, next week I'll drink once! And the next week, maybe, maybe not, I would drink once. Maybe I would drink twice. And all this time, I would be overlapping into the time when I'm only supposed to be drinking every other week.

ERICH: But aren't these, like, artificial rules? I mean, if you set a rule for yourself that's so stringent, then you can't follow it. But if you say, well, why have these rules, why can't you live with once a week? Or twice a week?

HARRY: Because I knew that I was an alcoholic.

ERICH: Maybe it's just the product of somebody brainwashing you into thinking that you are an alcoholic.

HARRY: Right. Part of alcoholism is the denial. You're the last person to know, to really know [that you're an alcoholic]. In the back of my mind, as I'm drying out, I'm saying to myself, "Well, you know, I used to take that test in the back of the "Is AA For You?" pamphlet. And I would laugh because I was getting eight out of nine. [Laughs.] And the only reason I'm not hiding alcohol in the house [one of the AA questions asks if you hide alcohol in the house, a sign of alcoholism] is because [giggles] because it's OK not to hide alcohol in the house. And the other one [question to determine if you are an alcoholic] that I didn't answer "yes" to was only because there were no barnyard animals in my neighborhood.

But in the back of my mind, there is the doubt, well, just because I drank every day for the last 20 years doesn't mean I'm an alcoholic. But as it got to crunch time, and it became more and more difficult for me not to drink, the certainty that I was an alcoholic grew and grew as the realization that the depth of my problem was deeper [than I had originally thought]. It became like an inverse relationship: The harder it was to quit, the more and more I was convinced that I really, really had an alcohol problem. Which made it more and more important that I stick to the extinction schedule and that I do quit. So, it was a bit of a conundrum. And finally, I was still drinking one or two days a week, when I hit the calendar day when I was supposed to be dry—yah! OOOhhh! Panic!

But I did exactly what I was supposed to do. The Friday before I was supposed to completely quit, I enrolled myself a professional treatment program in my local area. And that next Monday, I started going for individual counseling, group therapy, and by the end of that week, I was already finding myself [self-help meetings] in the area to attend. Drying out was harder than I thought it was going to be. Even with this extinction schedule that I was on for six or seven months. The first week was just really, really annoying. Going out of my skin, being angry, feeling sorry for myself, running the whole range of emotions, like I was 14 again. And I got through and I didn't drink. After a couple of weeks, though, I was walking around in the undersea world of Jacques Cousteau. It was like I was surrounded with a very light Jello, and like I had the flu and a head cold at the same time. There were three instances when I almost had serious car accidents. But other people swerved, other people [chuckles] got out of my way, thank God.

I found out very quickly that you're not supposed to listen to the people—anyone—who ever gave you advice while you were drinking. And the last people in the world you want to listen to are your family. They'll be well-meaning, but they are the ones, and it's true, they are the ones who know how to sabotage you most effectively. And they will! With the best of intentions. People say, why is it that my parents know how to push buttons I don't even know I have? And the answer is, because they installed them.

I made it through. Thank God for a certain self-help group that's had a lot of success with a lot of people. It's been almost two years. It's a constant struggle, but as they say—and you want to whack them when they do—in the first few months, "Don't drink, go to meetings, and it gets better." It doesn't get better—you get better. [Laughs.] And then if you get better, hopefully, it gets better. But two of the groups that I attend, they call them "specialty" groups, that I attend are exclusively gay. Who have a much higher rate of alcoholism [than in the straight population] because of the pressure and the stress. Straight people don't realize how much pressure there is growing up gay in this culture. It's nice to see that in the last 20 years, it's lightened up a bit.

ERICH: Why did you think there was a necessity for you to stop drinking? You mentioned that you had flunked out of school a couple of times and you had to be re-instated, and you started worrying that you might not get another chance, so, problems with school are obviously one major [problem] area, a couple of close calls as far as driving is concerned—I know that was after you quit—but what were some other areas of your life that became problematic as a result of your drinking?

HARRY: I knew intellectually that I was an alcoholic. You rationalize some of the problems. Like being hung over. Well, when you're young, it's not so bad to be hung over. I also liked to drink alone. Because I drank every night. I was perfectly happy on those nights when the Lost Boys went out and I stayed home alone, sitting in front of the cable or the VCR.

ERICH: There are some theories that argue that alcoholism is a progressive disease and that people [who are alcoholics] drink more and more until at a certain point they become self-destructive, or at least, there are certain types or varieties of alcoholics who are like that. And I notice that you kind of plateaued out at a pint [a day]. Now, that doesn't seem like an outrageous amount. What do you think accounts for the fact that you didn't escalate to, say, a quart a day?

HARRY: Well, the thing was, I was drinking a fifth [of a gallon, or four-fifths of a quart; a quart equals two pints] a day for a while, and then I finally said, whoa, whoa, whoa! It was about five years ago, maybe. It did seem like my consumption was progressively going up. 'Cause I could drink a fifth, easily. Well, maybe not easily, but I could drink a fifth. [Laughs.] It had been known to happen. So, I just made a conscious intellectual decision. And I'm not saying that I always stuck to it.

ERICH: It's interesting, because I've gone to a few [alcoholic self-help] meetings, you know, as a visitor—open meetings. And you often hear war stories. A couple staggering around after buying a pizza, dropping the pizza in the driveway, picking it up and putting it back in the box, you know, and being so woozy that they ended up eating it. Or somebody smashing up a car and not even remembering driving a car. Or getting thrown out of the army. All these war stories—horror stories—about what happened when they were too drunk to even function. Where, you know, the wife left the husband. Or creditors were coming to their house, repossessing their furniture and this sort of thing. It doesn't seem like you have had that kind of litany of war stories. [Compared to the people who told these stories,] it sounds like you were in fact able to function reasonably well.

I like to read biographies [and autobiographies], and there are a number of writers who call themselves functioning alcoholics. Or filmmakers. Sam Peckinpah, the guy who did *The Wild Bunch,* called himself a functioning alcoholic. John Houston, who did *Treasure of the Sierra Madre,* called himself a functioning alcoholic. And they put away a fifth or more a day. But somehow, they were able to do the job. They

(*Continued*)

Account: Harry, the Debonair Drinker Continued

had unusual experiences [related to drinking], but they weren't necessarily destructive drunks. I mean, they got diseases and they died early [laughs], but, you know, they didn't crash up cars, they didn't fink out on their jobs, they made movies, they wrote books, this sort of thing. On the other hand, someone like Truman Capote drank so much that he was a falling-down drunk. Or Ernest Hemingway ended up blowing his brains out.

So, I'm not sure where that line is between the functioning alcoholic and the destructive alcoholic. I mean, I know what it means behaviorally, but in other respects, I'm not too sure.

Harry: The alcohol becomes the organizing principle. And if I had continued escalating my drinking, well, then I could not have continued to drink. Things would have fallen apart. And I think I knew that. Somewhere [in my mind], I'm pretty sure that was a fact [for me]. I mean, I did know that I couldn't keep escalating the amount [I drank]. I only weighed 125 pounds, 130 pounds. I've put on a little weight [laughs, grabs his belly] recently. But a friend of mine said, "I've never got into bar fights because they don't serve drinks in prison." [Laughs.]

Erich: You felt if you escalated the amount you drank. . . .

Harry: I know that I made a conscious decision that if I keep escalating the physical amount of alcohol that I drank, I'm gonna end up being non-functional. And I'm sure, now, in retrospect, in the back of my mind, I was thinking, "Oh, my God, then I won't be able to drink."

Questions

Do you find Harry's justifications for heavy drinking persuasive? Harry has made a decision to cut back on his drinking; do you think he will continue to drink moderately? Why or why not? Or do you believe that the theory, held by Alcoholic Anonymous, that alcoholics can't drink at all, but instead must abstain altogether, is valid? Harry considers himself a "functioning alcoholic," but he hasn't been able to establish an intimate, long-term relationship, doesn't have a job, took more than a decade to complete his college education, and has failed in several programs to receive a master's degree; so, do you accept his definition of "functioning"? Harry partly explains his alcoholism by the stress he suffers as a result of the stigma of homosexuality; do you accept his reasoning? Or is this yet another rationalization? Do you think Harry uses his charm and intelligence and sense of humor as a way of explaining away his heavy drinking?

CHAPTER

8

Illicit Drug Use

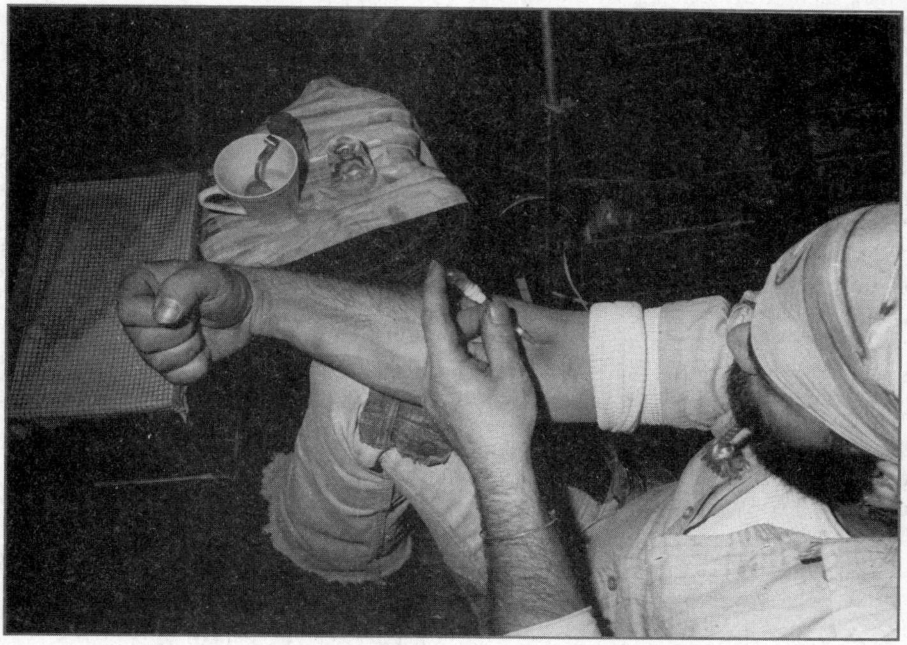

We can look at drug use as deviant behavior from both the positivist and the constructionist perspectives. With both, when looking at drugs, we must ask the same two questions I raised earlier: *What is our mission? What is to be explained?*

From a positivistic perspective, the issue that needs explaining is *why some people use illegal substances.* This perspective places the deviant nature of drug use in the background, of only secondary interest. To positivists, the issue of why the use of certain drugs is regarded as deviant does not need to be answered; it is irrelevant to their mission. In contrast, they believe, "Why do they do it?" *is* the question that needs to be answered.

Of course, each positivistic theory attempts to answer the "Why do they do it?" question in its own way. Some focus on individualistic explanations—such as biological or personality factors. Others examine differences between and among people living in certain types of social and economic structures, such as different types of neighborhoods, different societies and social structures, cities versus small towns, and so on. And some positivist theories ask, "Why *don't* they do it?"—which is simply the flip side of exactly the same question. But *all* positivistic explanations seek to reveal the causes of drug use; all take drug use as the *dependent* variable, as the variable that needs to be explained. And the factor they isolate as the cause, usually their theory's name, is the *independent* or explanatory variable. All positivistic theories have the same structure or form: Factor A (the explanatory or independent variable) causes outcome B (drug use, the dependent variable).

In addition, positivists examine the *consequences* of actions such as drug use. This is important to someone with a scientific or empirical approach to the consumption of psychoactive substances because it helps explain *why* these substances are used. The appeal of drugs is partly a result of their effects. For instance, certain drugs are highly reinforcing; they activate and "hijack" pleasure centers in the brain. They are so rewarding, some scientists argue, that the user takes them again and again, becoming dependent, abandoning what was previously valued, such as family, school, a job, and a home (DuPont, 1997). There is also an unstated or background assumption in the positivist's approach to drug use that the objective consequences of the use of certain substances are so harmful that society wisely attempts to control or limit their use through law enforcement. In other words, the condemnation of illicit use is a rational response to the very real and present danger such use poses, and hence, so commonsensical as not to require detailed, systematic study. Moreover, drug use could *covary* with other variables but not necessarily cause them. Hence, drug use and grades in school could be related to one another, but both caused a third or prior factor, such as the susceptibility to engage in deviant behavior, as we saw with Gottfredson and Hirschi's social control theory or "general theory of crime" (1990).

In contrast, for the constructionist, the very issue that for the positivist is theoretically unproblematic and taken for granted becomes central. This issue is this: *Why is the use of certain substances regarded as deviant?* For the constructionist, it is the "Why do they do it?" question that is assumed or is in the background. The constructionist raises questions such as the following: Why are certain substances regarded as "drugs" while others aren't? Why are the possession and sale of some drugs legal while those of others are illegal? What are the processes through which influential segments of the society mount an antidrug campaign to convince the public that substance abuse is wrong, more dangerous than other threats that are ignored? Why does so much of the public believe that the drug war should be fought with such ferocity? How did the drug "war" get started in the first place? Why are the use and distribution of heroin and cocaine widely seen as evil while the use of alcohol and tobacco is regarded as acceptable, respectable, recreational—or, at worst, a bad habit, or an illness? Is it solely a product of the former drugs' objective dangers and the latter drugs' safety? These are not ideological or rhetorical questions, but ones that demand serious investigation (Duster, 1970; Reinarman and Levine, 1997).

The constructionist does not assume that social constructions of drug use are "irrational," illogical, or unreasonable, that all crusades to stamp out the consumption of illicit psychoactive substances are "moral panics." For the most part, societies do not condemn or criminalize the possession and sale of drugs out of prejudice, ignorance, or perversity, simply because their culture or history or religion or sense of morality told them to do it. It would be wrong to trace the society's condemnation of drug use and the drug laws *exclusively* to politics, ideology, economics, or religious edicts. All of these factors and processes may play a role. The simple fact is most forms of drug use *are* harmful, and in varying degrees, according to the drug in question, the dose, and the frequency of use. But so are many activities that are not widely condemned or banned—scuba diving, hang gliding, NASCAR racing, hunting, possessing handguns, rock climbing, boxing, and playing football. Each of these activities has its supporters (and detractors) who are willing to offer a justification explaining how and why drug use is different. But all of these activities, drug use included, share several characteristics in common: All result in some harm, even the loss of human life, all are pursued because some people find them enjoyable, and all become an obsession for many participants. Activities involving excitement and danger tend to trigger chemicals in the body (endorphins) that are analogous to the dependency-producing substances we refer to as drugs. Hence, the question becomes this: Why condemn and outlaw one type of dangerous behavior but accept and permit another? Again, this is not a rhetorical or argumentative question but one that should be seriously considered.

Moreover, many activities, whether harmful or benign, are legal in some jurisdictions and at certain times but illegal in others. Gay marriage is legal in several states of the United States, in Canada, and several countries of Europe, but not permitted by law in most of the United States. Marijuana can be sold in the Netherlands, not in America. The age of sexual consent is, variously and depending on the jurisdiction, 15, 16, 17, 18, and even, in some places, 21. In Iran, China, Saudi Arabia, Pakistan, and Syria, the government blocks access to politically and sexually sensitive Web sites; in most other countries, such access is free, open, and unlimited. Before 1920, the sale of alcohol was legal in most of the United States. Between 1920 and 1933, it was illegal everywhere, and after 1933, again, it became legal in most places. In other words, arresting and prosecuting for, and condemning, certain behavior is not a simple product of that behavior's objective negative consequences. It's an obvious point but one worth making: The difference in the law of these many jurisdictions is not solely the threat or the harm or danger posed by the activity—that is pretty much the same everywhere—but political, ideological, economic, and cultural factors. In short, these laws are *social constructions.* What the constructionist is interested in is how these factors influence the law and the condemnation of certain activities. The harm of an activity is not the only factor influencing its illegality and its condemnation—it is one among many. Even the laws against and prosecution of murder, rape, and robbery, unarguably harmful acts with genuine victims, are constructed in a certain way for certain reasons.

THE SOCIAL CONSTRUCTION OF A SOCIAL PROBLEM

Humans have been ingesting drugs for thousands of years. And throughout recorded time, significant numbers of the members of nearly every society on earth have used one or more drugs to achieve certain desired physical or mental states. Drug use comes close to being a universal, both worldwide and throughout history. It is possible that the Inuit (or Eskimos), prior to the arrival of Europeans, are the only society on earth whose members did not use mind-altering substances (Weil, 1972).

Drugs are most often used in a culturally appropriate and approved manner (Edgerton, 1976, p. 57). Sometimes drug use is regarded as unacceptable to the society's more conventional members: The wrong drug is taken; it is taken too often, or under the wrong circumstances; or it is taken with undesirable consequences. In such cases, we have instances of deviant behavior.

"Execute Drug Dealers, Mayor Says," "Brutal Gangs Wage War of Terror," "Flood of Drugs—A Losing Battle," "Surge of Violence Linked to Narcotics," "War on Drugs Shifting to Street," "Drug Violence Erodes a Neighborhood," and "Drug Production Soars"—these and similar headlines fairly scream out the public's anxiety over the drug abuse issue.

These headlines tap a certain fear and *concern* felt by the public about drug abuse. (More specifically, they tap the fear and concern that journalists, editors, and newspaper publishers believe the public feels—a belief that is often justified.) Drug use, like every other existing endeavor or social condition, has a socially constructed or *subjective* dimension: the public's feeling or attitude about it; what is believed about it; what the public's, or segments of the public's, feelings, attitudes, and beliefs about the individuals who engage in it are.

Likewise, drug use and abuse have an *objective* side: What drugs actually do to humans who use them, how widely and frequently they are used, and what kind of impact they have on the society.

As with most other behaviors, conditions, and issues, the constructed and the objective sides of drug use overlap, but extremely imperfectly. We may be concerned about behavior and conditions that, objectively speaking, are not threatening or damaging at all; and we may be unconcerned about behavior and conditions that are objectively *very* threatening or damaging. Moreover, these two dimensions—the subjective and the objective—may be out of sync with one another over time, with concern rising when damage from drug abuse is dropping, and declining when it rises. It is wise, when investigating deviant behavior and conditions, to keep the subjective and the objective dimensions separate in one's mind (even though in real life, they influence one another). *Regarding* a given condition or behavior as threatening, damaging, or deviant, or as a social problem (the subjective or socially constructed dimension) may be completely unrelated to the *actual* physical or psychological damage it does (the objective or positivist dimension). The connection between these two dimensions cannot be assumed; it has to be investigated empirically.

Fear of and concern about the threat of drug use and abuse have waxed and waned over the years in the United States. One measure of that fear and concern is the number and content of news stories on the subject. In the 1930s in the United States, newspapers and magazines published hundreds of sensationalistic articles that detailed the supposed horrors of marijuana use. In the 1940s and 1950s, such stories declined sharply in number and stridency. In the second half of the 1960s, literally thousands of news accounts were published and broadcast on LSD's capacity to make users go crazy and do terrible things to themselves and others. By the early 1970s, LSD had ceased to be news, and heroin stormed into the headlines. By the mid-1970s, the media had quieted down on the drug front. But the mid-to-late 1980s witnessed a rebirth—indeed, something of an explosion—of public concern over the use and abuse of illegal drugs.

For instance, between the early and mid-1980s, the number of articles on the subject of drug abuse published in all the popular national magazines that are indexed by *The Readers' Guide to Periodical Literature* increased by some eight times. In the single year between 1985 and 1986, the number increased more than two and a half times. Clearly, although it had been building up in the prior two or three years, 1986 was the year that drug use and abuse fairly *exploded* as a social problem in the United States, subjectively speaking. However, into the 1990s, this concern, although it remained high, had declined significantly. And into the twenty-first century, drug use remains a focus of media attention, but that attention is only moderate compared with the peak years of the mid-to-late-1980s. Other concerns—such as the economy, the war in Iraq, and "the war on terrorism"—shoved drug abuse off the center stage of media attention.

Another measure of the subjective dimension is the public's designation of a given condition or behavior as a serious problem. Each year, and several times during some years, the Gallup Poll asks a sample of the public what they regard as the "number one problem facing the nation today." As with the articles published in *The Readers' Guide,* the Gallup Poll provides a very rough measure of subjective public concern over a given condition at a particular time. The public's concern over drug abuse rose and fell, and rose and fell again, between the early 1970s and the early 1990s. In February 1973, 20 percent of the respondents in the Gallup Poll felt that drug abuse was the nation's number one problem. However, between that date and 1985, the percentage mentioning drug abuse as the country's most serious problem was so low it did not even appear among the top half-dozen problems. During 1985 and into January 1986, between 2 and 3 percent of the American public mentioned drug abuse as the country's most important problem; in April 1986, in a set of parallel polls conducted by *The New York Times* and CBS

News, again, 2 percent mentioned drugs as the country's number one problem. In a July Gallup Poll, the figure was 8 percent; in an August *Times*/CBS poll, it was 13 percent. The figure continued to rise throughout the remainder of the 1980s until September 1989, when a whopping *64 percent* of respondents in a *Times*/CBS poll said that drugs constituted the most important issue facing the country at that time. This response represents one of the most intense preoccupations by the American public on the drug issue in polling history.

The September 1989 figure proved to be the pinnacle of public concern about drugs; it is unlikely that a figure of such magnitude will ever be achieved for drug abuse again. After that, said one media expert, intense public concern simply "went away" (Oreskes, 1990). By November 1989, according to a *Times*/CBS poll, the figure had slipped to 38 percent; in July 1990, to 18 percent; and in August 1990, to only 10 percent (Kagay, 1990; Oreskes, 1990; Shenon, 1990). Between November 1990 and December 1991, the figure remained in the 8–12 percent range; between March 1992 and August 1994, it had dipped slightly into the 6–8 percent range. According to the Gallup Polls, today, in the early 2000s, only 1 percent of the American public considers drug abuse the nation's number one problem. Drugs are currently hugely overshadowed by the war in Iraq (30%), the economy (25%), and health care (12%), along with a host of other issues such as unemployment, dissatisfaction with the government, and illegal immigration.

What we saw during late 1980s, then, was a period of *intense* public fear of and concern about drug use and abuse. It was so intense that observers referred to it as a drug "scare" or "moral panic" (Ben-Yehuda, 1985; Goode and Ben-Yehuda, 1994, 2009). A moral panic is an intense, widespread, explosively upsurging feeling on the part of the public that something is terribly wrong in their society because of the moral failure of a specific group of individuals, a subpopulation that has been defined as the enemy, a "folk devil" (Cohen, 1972, 2002). A category of people was *deviantized* (Schur, 1980). This is precisely what happened with drug use and abuse between 1986 and 1989. During this period, American society was undergoing something of a moral panic about drug use; drug abusers were defined, even more intensely than was true in the past, as deviants. Of course, illegal drug use was seen as deviant before 1986, and continues to be so regarded today, but the *intensity* of this feeling reached an apex during that relatively brief three- or four-year period.

This does not necessarily mean that, objectively speaking, by the late 1980s and early 1990s drug use had ceased to be a problem in the United States. In fact, by some indicators, such as drug overdoses, in the late 1980s the drug problem actually increased in seriousness. But the important point is this: Moral panics and the fear of and concern about a given behavior or condition do not emerge solely as a result of public awareness of an objective threat. There are usually far more serious conditions or more dangerous behaviors that attract little or no concern compared with those that generate fear during a given moral panic. As a rule, the public has an extremely hazy notion of how threatening or damaging certain conditions or forms of behavior are, and the world of drug abuse is no exception.

As I've asked before, why is illegal drug use, including the illicit use of prescription drugs, a source of far more public concern than the use of legal drugs (alcohol and tobacco cigarettes), when the former kills no more than 20,000–25,000 or so Americans each year, while the latter kills over 600,000 (Horgan, Skwara, and Strickler, 2001)? Why are illegal drug users deviant while legal drug users are not? There may be concrete reasons for this greater concern that relate to the objective or real-world impact of illegal drugs as opposed to legal drugs. Perhaps it is based, in part, on the fact that the victims of illegal drugs are *younger* than the victims of alcohol and tobacco, and hence, far more years of life are lost per death. Perhaps the public has the (objectively true) feeling that drugs such as cocaine and the narcotics are vastly more harmful *on a dose-by-dose basis* than is true of alcohol and tobacco. Perhaps there is the feeling that drug dealers destroy communities and corrupt law enforcement in a way that is quite unlike the way that purveyors of legal drugs work. (Of course, the very illegal status of some drugs may contribute to the harm they cause.) There may very well be a wide range of objectivistic factors influencing this relationship. But the fact remains, legal drugs kill 30 times as many Americans as illegal drugs, yet Americans are far more concerned about illegal drug abuse than about legal drugs. This paradox is central to any examination of drug use as a form of deviance. As a general rule, the public formulates judgments about the seriousness of certain conditions, behavior, and issues, and regards certain behaviors as deviant, on the basis of criteria that are to some degree *independent* of estimates of their objective harm. In fact, the public's estimates of the objective harm of specific conditions, behaviors, and issues are extremely faulty and are influenced by a wide range of extraneous factors (Slovic, Fischoff, and Lichtenstein 1980; Erikson, 1990; Slovic, Layman, and Flynn, 1991).

WHAT IS DRUG USE?

Drugs are defined in different ways, according to different criteria and different contexts of use; the use of drug substances according to some of these definitions are *themselves* forms of deviance, while the use of others may *cause* or be *associated* with deviance. Dictionaries define a drug as a medicine or any other substance used in the treatment of diseases. In addition, a drug is a substance with a significant effect on the functioning of the mind. And to the general public, a drug is an illegal or illicit substance taken for the purpose of getting high or intoxicated. Within this definitional context, taking drugs is illegal and, to most of the public, deviant. Hence, drugs are medicinal, and/or psychoactive, and/or illegal. LSD, for instance, is not used in medicine, is psychoactive, and is illegal. Penicillin is medicinal, is not psychoactive, and is legal, via prescription. The use of penicillin is deviant to practically no one. Some drugs (like antipsychotics or antidepressives) are psychoactive but are not used on the street to get high; the people who take them have a mental disorder that is treated with the drug substance.

Constructionist definitions of drugs assume a certain measure of *independence* between objective properties and how substances are defined, seen, and dealt with. These definitions would argue that it is not *only* the most harmful drugs whose possession and sale are against the law, it is not *only* the most medically efficacious that are used by physicians to heal the body and the mind, and it is not only substances that have drug-like effects that are *regarded* as drugs by the general public. It is this independence between the objective properties of substances—that is, their *effects*—and the way that substances and their users are thought about, dealt with, and treated by the medical fraternity, law enforcement, and the general public that is the central issue for sociologists of deviant behavior.

Using substances not authorized as medicine is regarded by physicians as deviant, a violation of the norms of the medical profession. Using substances whose possession and sale are a violation of the law is clearly a deviant act. Therefore, when contemplating drug use, the sociologist of deviance is confronted with a golden opportunity.

The drugs in which we are interested are psychoactive. However, psychoactive drugs have a vast range of different effects. The drugs in which we, as observers of deviant behavior, are interested fall into five broad types: stimulants, narcotics (also know as opiates and opioids), general depressants (or "sedative-hypnotics"), disassociative anesthetics, and two oddball substances—Ecstasy or MDMA, and marijuana—that don't fall into any general category.

A CLASSIFICATION OF DRUGS AND THEIR EFFECTS

Stimulants speed up signals passing through the central nervous system (CNS), that is, the brain and spinal column. They enable the user to feel more alert and awake. Strong stimulants include cocaine, amphetamine, and Ritalin. Caffeine is a stimulant so weak that most of us do not think of it as a drug at all.

Narcotics, or "narcotic analgesics," diminish the brain's perception of pain. This category includes the opiates—opium and its derivatives: morphine, heroin, and codeine. This category also includes the various synthetic and semisynthetic narcotics, called opioids (or opiumlike drugs), such as Percodan, Dilaudid, methadone, and meperidine (or Demerol), and oxycodone (including OxyContin). In addition to their painkilling property, all narcotics are also physically addicting, that is, they generate a physical dependency on regular, long-term use. In addition to dependence, their effects include mental clouding and euphoria. It is their euphoria-generating property that causes many people to use narcotics recreationally, that is, for the purpose of getting high.

Unlike the narcotics, which have a depressive effect principally on one bodily function—the perception of pain—*sedatives* or *general depressants,* while not effective painkillers, have a depressive effect on a wide range of body organs and functions. They tend to induce relaxation, inhibit anxiety, and, at higher doses, result in eventually, sleep. The most well known of the general depressants is alcohol, which scientists refer to as ethyl alcohol or ethanol. Other examples include sedative-hypnotics such as barbiturates, methaqualone (once sold under brand names like Quaalude and Sopor) and GHB; and tranquilizers, such as Valium, Xanax, Librium, lorazepam, and Rohypnol ("roofies"). In sufficiently high doses, general depressants induce mental clouding, drowsiness, and physical dependence; an overdose can produce unconsciousness, coma, and even death. Some users seek the woozy, cloudy, drowsy feeling that depressants or "downers" generate. Since such a psychic state is potentially dangerous, such drugs are controlled. Still, let's recognize that alcohol has many of the same effects as the other sedatives, and it is available to anyone over the age of 21.

Hallucinogens (once referred to as psychedelics) have effects on the CNS that cannot be reduced to a simple stimulation–depression continuum. These are the drugs that induce profound sensory alterations. They occupy their own unique and distinct category and include LSD, peyote and mescaline, and psilocybin or "magic mushrooms" ("shrooms"). The principal effect of the hallucinogens is not, as might be expected from their name, the inducement of hallucinations, but extreme psychoactivity, a loosening of the imagination and an intensification of emotional states.

Most recent classifications include a drug called PCP or Sernyl, once referred to as "angel dust," as a hallucinogen. Originally used as an animal tranquilizer, this drug has almost none of the properties associated with hallucinogens, such as dramatic sensory transformations. More sophisticated classification schemes see it as a disassociative anesthetic. Ketamine ("special K") is a milder version of PCP. These drugs produce drowsiness, discoordination, a distorted sense of the reality of one's physical surroundings, and a feeling of invulnerability.

MDMA or Ecstasy is sometimes referred to as a hallucinogen, but it does not produce sensory alterations; a more accurate term to describe it would be "empathogen," that is, capable of inducing empathy, or an emotional identification with others. In animals, research indicates, the drug causes brain damage.

Marijuana has, at different times, been classified as a depressant, a stimulant, and, as late as the 1970s, a hallucinogen. Most observers nowadays feel that it belongs in a category by itself.

According to the 2007 National Survey on Drug Use and Health, conducted in the general population, sponsored by the Substance Abuse and Mental Health Services Administration (SAMHSA), slightly over half (51%) of the sample said that they drank alcohol within the past month, and were therefore defined as "current" drinkers. Alcohol is by far the society's most popular recreational drug. A bit more than a quarter (29%) said they used at least one tobacco product, mostly cigarettes, in the past month. We can use these two benchmark figures against which to measure illicit drug use.

It is in the realm of illegal recreational use that we encounter our most harshly condemned instances of deviant drug use. The illegal drug trade is an enormous economic enterprise, variously estimated to represent a $65-billion-a-year business in the United States (Rhodes et al., 2001, p. 3). Other estimates vary somewhat from this one. In 2005, the United Nations estimated the illicit *global* drug market at 285 billion euros (at the current rate of exchange, about $400 billion). But in 2009, a team of RAND social scientists scaled this down by half (Reuter and Trautmann, 2009). Most observers argue that drug expenditures have declined since the 1990s. Clearly a great deal of money is spent on illegal drugs in the United States and worldwide—certainly tens of billions of dollars a year; and in worldwide, possibly hundreds of billions. And these sums represent a corresponding *immense* demand for illicit drugs.

Roughly a third of the American population has used one or more illicit drugs at least once during their lifetimes. The National Survey on Drug Use and Health cited earlier found that, in 2007, 8 percent, or 20 million, people, had used an illicit drug within the past 30 days and were defined as current users. As we might expect, of all age categories, young adults were most likely to have used illegal drugs: In 2007, for use in the past month, a fifth (20%) of 18- to-25-year-olds did so at least once; over half (57%) had at least one lifetime experience with illicit drugs (SAMHSA, 2008, p. 257).

The most frequently used illegal drug in America is, again as we might expect, marijuana; in 2007, 5.8 percent of the population age 12 and older were current users, that is, had used marijuana during the past month—a figure nearly six times as high as for cocaine (0.8%) and almost 15 times as great as for hallucinogens (0.4%). In fact, almost three-quarters (73%) of current illicit use was with marijuana specifically, and over half of current drug users took *only* marijuana (SAMHSA, 2008). Allow me to reiterate that *most illegal drug use is marijuana use.* About 2.5 percent of Americans had used one or more of the psychoactive pharmaceuticals—stimulants, analgesics, tranquilizers, and sedatives—nonmedically in the past month. According to this survey, crack cocaine, a highly publicized drug, had been used by only 0.2 percent of Americans during the past 30 days—about 600,000 people. Heroin, like crack, a well-known and highly publicized illegal drug, was used by only 0.1 percent, or 153,000, people. Just over half a million (529,000) were current users of methamphetamine (SAMHSA, 2008, pp. 254–255). However, the National Survey on Drug Use and Health is almost certainly least useful for estimating the drug consumption of heavy users of crack, heroin, and meth, because of the problem of locating them. Hence, these figures for the hard drugs are almost certainly substantial underestimates.

A study of drug use among high school seniors, college students, and young adults not in high school or college (the "Monitoring the Future" survey) found much the same picture with respect to illegal drug use, except that their level of use was slightly higher than is true for the population as a whole (Johnston et al., 2009). In 2008, just over a fifth of high school seniors (22%) had used one or more illicit drugs at least once in the past 30 days, a sixth of tenth graders (16%), and less than a tenth of eighth graders had done so (8%). For students in all grades, as with the population as a whole, again, marijuana was by far the most popular illicit drug. All of these figures represent slight but significant declines since 2000.

Whatever the drug, as a source of illegal and deviant behavior, drug use is substantial. But three qualifications are in order at this point: One, the use of nearly all illegal drugs declined *substantially* after the late 1970s. Two, illegal drug use is not nearly as high as many sensational media stories claim. Three, illicit drug use is considerably less widespread than the use of alcohol and tobacco.

Both legal and illegal drugs vary considerably in user loyalty or continued use. Users are much more likely to "stick with" or be "loyal to" certain drugs, while with other drugs, users are much more likely to take them episodically or infrequently, or to abandon them after a brief period of experimentation.

As a general rule, *legal* drugs tend to be used much more often on a continued basis, while *illegal* drugs tend to be used more infrequently, and are more likely to be given up after a period of time. Of all drugs, legal or illegal, alcohol attracts the greatest user loyalty: Roughly 6 persons in 10 who say that they ever drank, even once, did so in the past month. For cigarettes, 4 in 10 of all at least one-time smokers are still smoking. For illegal drugs, marijuana tends to be stuck with the longest—15 percent of all Americans who have tried it remain users. In other words, *the more legal the drug, the more loyal users are to it,* the more they stick with it, the more likely they are to *continue* using it over time, and the less likely they are to give up its use. Turning the equation around, the more illegal or illicit the drug, the less likely it is that one-time users will stick with it or continue to use it. Marijuana, the least illicit of the illicit drugs, is the one that one-time users are most likely to continue using. For cocaine and methamphetamine, the figure is 6 percent and 4 percent, respectively, and for heroin, it is 4 percent; only six-tenths of 1 percent of at least one-time users have taken PCP in the past month (SAMHSA, 2008).

MARIJUANA USE IN THE UNITED STATES, 1960–2007

We already know that widespread behavior, beliefs, and conditions are not necessarily conventional or normative, and that rare behavior, beliefs, and conditions are not necessarily deviant. In other words, infrequency of occurrence is not a *defining* characteristic of deviance. Still, knowing how rare or widespread something is is a relevant piece of information in any investigation of deviance.

At the beginning of the 1960s, very, very few Americans used illegal drugs. Even the use of marijuana, by far the most widely consumed illicit substance, was at an extremely low level. In 1960, less than 1 percent of youths age 12–17, and less than 5 percent of young adults age 18–25, had even tried marijuana. By 1967, these figures had nearly quadrupled, to over 5 percent for youths and over 15 percent for young adults (Miller and Cisin, 1980, pp. 13–16). The percent trying and using marijuana increased throughout the decade from the late 1960s to the late 1970s, and reached its peak roughly in 1979, when nearly a third of youths age 12–17 (31%) and two-thirds of young adults age 18–25 (68%) had tried marijuana. The use of marijuana declined during the 1980s but then rose again after the early 1990s. In 2007, in the most recent National Survey on Drug Use and Health available at this writing, only 6.7 percent of 12-to-17-year-olds and 16.4 percent of 18-to-25-year-olds said that they had used marijuana in the past month. For the population as a whole, this figure was 5.8 percent (SAMHSA, 2008, pp. 255–257). This up-and-down pattern was also revealed by surveys conducted by the Monitoring the Future study; an almost identical arc was traced by college students during this same era.

During the 1980s, after the all-time high figures for the late seventies and early eighties, it seemed as if the use of marijuana among young people was diminishing. Many commentators argued that marijuana specifically, and illegal drug use generally, would decline to the point at which they would cease to be a problem in the United States. But after the early 1990s, for both high school seniors and college students, the percent who used marijuana had increased to the point where well over a third had used it during the past year (Johnston et al., 2009). Among high school seniors and college students, during the decade of the 1990s, the use of marijuana had become more widespread, more common. (In 1991, the Monitoring the Future study began surveying eighth and tenth graders, and exactly the same increases prevailed in these younger age brackets.) While the prevalence of marijuana use today does not reach the late 1970s to early 1980s levels, it is significantly higher than it was in the early 1990s and much, *much* higher than it was in the late 1960s. Marijuana use would have to decline drastically to reach the vastly lower figures that prevailed in the 1960s. This is unlikely to take place within the first decade or two of the twenty-first century.

MARIJUANA USE AS DEVIANCE AND CRIME

In the United States, the use and criminal status of marijuana have had a remarkable and complicated history. In the 1920s, very few Americans had even heard of marijuana or even knew anyone who used it and, consequently, very few thought of it as deviant. Until well into the twentieth century, the few who did know of the drug thought of it as a kind of medicinal herb. In the eighteenth century, George Washington grew marijuana plants on his plantation, probably for that very purpose. By the decade of the 1930s, however, marijuana had become the subject of hundreds of sensationalist newspaper and magazine articles. The drug was dubbed the "killer weed," the "weed of madness," a "sex-crazing drug menace," the "burning weed of hell," a "gloomy monster of destruction," and the "green monster." Journalists and propagandist gave almost unlimited reign to the lurid side of their imaginations on the marijuana question. Every conceivable evil was concocted concerning the effects of this drug, the principal ones being insanity, sexual promiscuity, and violence (Rowell and Rowell, 1937). A popular film distributed in the 1930s, *Reefer Madness,* illustrates this "marijuana causes you to go crazy, become promiscuous, and want to kill people" theme. But in the 1960s, this movie had begun to be shown to pro-marijuana audiences, who found it so ludicrous as to be hilarious—evidence that confirmed their view that the drug was in fact harmless.

By 1937, partly as a result of the hysterical publicity surrounding the use of marijuana, laws criminalizing its possession and sale were passed in every state and at the federal level as well. Several observers argue that racism against Mexican Americans was one of the principal reasons for the white majority's belief in the drug's evil effects, as well as for the swiftness with which these laws were passed (Musto, 1987, pp. 219, 245, 1999). The majority of states that passed the earliest antimarijuana laws were Western states with the largest concentration of Mexican American populations. At times, an activity can be condemned, even criminalized, less as a result of a sober assessment of its objective impact than because of the majority feeling about the group that is thought to practice it.

Marijuana remained completely illegal and deviant throughout the remainder of the 1930s, and during the 1940s and 1950s; consensus has it that during this stretch, use was extremely low. During the course of the 1960s, however, the popularity of this drug dramatically increased. Along with this increase in use came the widespread awareness that it was not simply the poor or members of minority groups but also the sons and daughters of affluent, influential, middle-class folk who used it. Marijuana acquired a mantle, if not of respectability or conventionality, at least not of complete deviance. Attitudes began to soften; in the 1970s, 11 states comprising one-third of the U.S. population decriminalized the possession of small quantities of marijuana. Then, beginning roughly with the election of Ronald Reagan as president in 1980, the tolerant sentiment toward marijuana that had been growing during the 1960s and 1970s began to dissipate and a more condemnatory mood set in. The tide had been reversed: Marijuana, its possession, use, and sale, had become deviant once again.

One measure or indicator of the deviant status of marijuana use is the growing percentage of high school students who say that marijuana use should be illegal, that the regular use of marijuana is harmful, and that they disapprove of regular marijuana use. As with use, the late 1970s represented an era when tolerance and acceptance of marijuana were at their peak. After the late 1970s, a growing percentage of Americans said that the drug's use should be against the law, that the use of the drug is harmful, and that they disapproved of its use. In 1979, the Monitoring the Future survey showed that only a quarter (24%) believed that using marijuana should be a crime; only an eighth (14%) believed that people who smoked marijuana occasionally risked harming themselves; and under half (45%) said that they disapproved of the occasional use of marijuana.

What happened roughly after the late 1970s and throughout the 1980s was truly remarkable. Tolerance of marijuana use among high school seniors evaporated and a far more condemnatory attitude replaced it. By 1991, high school seniors' belief that marijuana use should be a crime doubled to 49 percent; the belief that one risks harming oneself by smoking marijuana occasionally more than doubled, to 41 percent; and the percent saying that they disapproved of the occasional use of marijuana increased to 79 percent (Johnston et al., 2005, pp. 354–363). In short, over the decade of the 1980s, marijuana use came to be seen as *more* deviant. In the sense of supporting the arrest and imprisonment of users, believing that use is medically dangerous, and disapproving of use, American's high school seniors *moved* away from seeing marijuana use as conventional, acceptable, safe, and ordinary *toward* seeing it as unconventional, unacceptable, dangerous, and out of the ordinary—in short, as deviant.

As with use itself, after the early 1990s, a significant (though far from complete) reversal in attitudes toward marijuana occurred. The 1990s and the early years of the new century witnessed a growing tolerance and acceptance of the drug. Between 1991 and 2008, the proportion of high school students saying that smoking marijuana should be a crime declined from 49 to 29 percent; those saying that people who smoked marijuana occasionally risked harming themselves declined in 1991 from 41 to 26 percent in 2008; and those who disapproved of people who smoke marijuana occasionally declined from 79 to 67 percent. Acceptance and tolerance of marijuana at the beginning of the twenty-first century was not as great as it was during the late 1970s to the early 1980s, but clearly, it is significantly—and strikingly—greater than it was just a bit more than a decade ago. We can assume that this pattern is not confined to high school seniors because, after 1980, the same questions were posed to college students and young adults not in college and precisely the same results were obtained. In short, the deviant status of marijuana use reached an all-time low in the late 1970s but grew throughout the 1980s, then retreated again during the 1990s and into the first few years of the twenty-first century. One indication: The decriminalization movement is back on track, energized by the issue of medical marijuana. Today, more than a dozen states permit small-quantity marijuana possession without arrest. The decline in the deviant status of marijuana consumption among teenagers and young adults will probably continue throughout the first two decades of the new century.

Among adults, the polls indicate complicated attitudes toward marijuana legalization. During April 2009, *The Washington Post* and ABC News conducted a poll that indicated qualified attitudes both for and against legalization. When asked about the legalization of small amounts of marijuana for personal use, the opposed response was a bare majority, 51 percent, while those in favor stood at 46. But when respondents were asked if people should be jailed for the possession of small amounts or pay a small fine but without serving any jail time, only 19 percent favored jail time. And 80 percent of the respondents in a CNN/*Time* magazine favored legal marijuana for medical purposes. Pretty much the same findings were obtained by 20 other surveys conducted after 2000. Today, the possession of marijuana, although not quite legal, isn't entirely deviant, either. Again, though illegality is not a defining criterion of deviance, when a growing and substantial proportion of the population favors the decriminalization of a previously illegal act, that act is losing its deviant status.

These shifts show that the deviant and criminal status of some activities, as well as their incidence, is a dynamic, labile affair. And just as activities can become more, or less, common, they can become more, as well as less, deviant and criminal over time. We witness historical fluctuations in the deviant and criminal status of marijuana use, possession, and sale. During the 1990s and the early 2000s, both the hostile attitudes that prevailed in the 1930s and beyond, and, on the other side, during the late 1970s and early 1980s, the blatant openness and tolerance that dominated, as well as the extremely widespread use, have all dissipated, replaced with more moderate feelings and behavior on both sides. This historic shift may continue well into the first decades of the new millennium.

HALLUCINOGENIC DRUGS

Hallucinogenic drugs are substances that produce severe dislocations of consciousness, those that act on the nervous system to produce significant perceptual changes. While all psychoactive drugs, by definition, influence the workings of the mind, hallucinogens are specifically, powerfully, and exquisitely psychoactive in their effects. They are the preeminent example of a category of psychoactive drugs. In the 1960s, hallucinogens were commonly referred to as "psychedelics," a tern that implied that the mind is "made manifest"—or is more perceptive than ordinarily—under the influence. In those days, substances such as mescaline (the major ingredient in the peyote cactus) and psilocybin (the major ingredient in the "magic mushroom") were much discussed but relatively little used. Today, the term "psychedelic" is used less frequently among drug experts than "hallucinogen." And virtually the only representative of this category that is currently used with any frequency is LSD. (I do not consider Ecstasy or PCP as hallucinogenic drugs; neither have the vision-inducing properties of LSD, mescaline, and psilocybin.)

It is in the mental, psychic, and subjective realm that the effects of LSD and the other hallucinogens have their most profound, dramatic, and interesting effects. Experiences take on an exaggerated emotional significance under the influence. Moreover, huge emotional mood swings tend to dominate an "acid" trip. On the other hand, in spite of their name, hallucinogens typically do not generate full-blown hallucinations, that is, cause users to see things in the concrete world they know "aren't really there." More often they will have experiences or visions they know are a product of the drug, that is, that are in their minds rather than a reality that is located "out there" in the material world. (These visions are sometimes revered to as "virtual" hallucinations.) Many users will experience synesthesia, or the translation of one sense into another—that is, "hearing" color and "seeing" sounds. Many LSD users, under the influence, experience the world as in flux—fluid, dynamic, wobbling, and flowing. The effects of LSD are experienced as vastly more incapacitating than those of marijuana (depending on the dose, of course); many users imagine that they can cope (drive a car, converse, and interact with others, especially parents and the police) on marijuana, whereas very few will say that they can do so at the peak of the LSD trip. Very few users of hallucinogens experience a psychotic outbreak sufficiently serious as to require hospitalization. Such reports reached their peak in the 1960s (when use was actually quite low) and declined sharply after that.

Psychedelic drugs have been used for thousands of years: psilocybin, or the so-called magic mushrooms, by Indians in Mexico and Central America; the peyote cactus by the Indians of northern Mexico; the Amanita (or "fly agaric") mushroom among the indigenous Siberian population; and the mandrake root among pre-Christian Europeans, to name only a few (Schultes and Hofmann, 1979). In 1938, a Swiss chemist named Albert Hofmann discovered the chemical that was later to be called LSD. Hofmann did not experiment with it until 1943, when he ingested a minuscule quality of the substance himself. He experienced an extraordinary and intense "play of colors," a sense of timelessness, depersonalization, a loss of control, and fears of "going crazy." The early researchers on LSD thought the drug might be the key to unlock the secrets of mental illness, especially schizophrenia. Later they found that the differences outweighed the similarities, and this line of research was abandoned. In the 1950s, the English writer Aldous Huxley, author of the classic novel *Brave New World,* took mescaline (the psychoactive ingredient in the peyote cactus) and wrote about his experiences in a slim, poetic volume, *The Doors of Perception.* Huxley drew the parallel with insanity, but he added a new dimension not previously discussed. Psychedelic drugs, he claimed, could bring about a view of reality that washes away the encrustation of years of rigid socialization and programming. These drugs, Huxley argues, enable us to see reality without culture's blinders—reality "as it really is." Taking psychedelic drugs could bring about a kind of transcendence, much like religious insight.

Huxley's book was read by Timothy Leary, holder of a PhD in psychology and lecturer at Harvard University. Leary took a dose of psilocybin and had a "visionary voyage." Soon after, he began a series of experiments that entailed administering the drug to convicts, theology students, and undergraduates; he claimed the drug "changed their lives for the better." Authorities at Harvard felt the experiments were casually administered, lacked sufficient safeguards, and were aimed mainly at proselytizing. Leary brushed off such concerns as so much hysteria that was hampering his research. In the spring of 1963, Leary was fired from his job, an event that touched off national headlines. In the decade prior to Leary's firing, a total of fewer than a dozen articles on LSD had ever been published in the national magazines indexed by *The Readers' Guide to Periodical Literature* (excluding *Science,* which is not really a popular magazine). These articles exploded in number after the Leary incident; publicity surrounding his firing focused an intense public glare on the use of LSD and the hallucinogens.

Prior to 1967, nearly all the articles discussed the drug's supposedly bizarre effects, especially those that seemed to indicate that it caused users to go insane. The effects of LSD were described as "nightmarish"; "terror and indescribable fear" were considered common, even typical experiences under the influence. *Life* magazine ran a cover story in its March 25, 1966, issue entitled "The Exploding Threat of the Mind Drug that Got Out of Control." *Time* ran a feature essay on LSD emphasizing the "freaking out" angle. "Under the influence of LSD," the story declared,

> nonswimmers think they can swim, and others think they can fly. One young man tried to stop a car . . . and was killed. A magazine salesman became convinced he was the Messiah. A college dropout committed suicide by slashing his arm and bleeding to death in a field of lilies.

Psychic terror, uncontrollable impulses, violence, an unconcern for one's own safety, psychotic episodes, delusions, and hallucinations filled the bulk of the early news stories on the use of LSD.

On March 17, 1967, the prestigious journal *Science* published an article that indicated that LSD damaged chromosomes (Cohen, Marinello, and Back, 1967). The media immediately surmised that the drug would cause birth defects; this wave of media hysteria was not quite as intense or as long lasting as that touched off by the insanity angle, but it did convince much of the public—some users included—that the drug was uniquely and powerfully damaging and dangerous. An article that appeared in *The Saturday Evening Post* (Davison, 1967) was typical. It explained that "if you take LSD even once, your children may be born malformed or retarded" and that "new research find it's causing genetic damage that poses a threat of havoc now and appalling abnormalities for generations yet unborn." Scientists learned soon after that the whole issue was a false alarm; in the doses taken on the street, LSD is an extremely weak mutagen or gene-altering agent, extremely unlikely to cause birth defects (Dishotsky et al., 1971).

In the 1960s, many critics and observers believed that LSD posed a major threat to American young people and possessed a uniquely deviant potential. In 1966, the New Jersey Narcotic Drug Study Commission declared LSD to be "the greatest threat facing the country today" (Brecher et al., 1972, p. 369). And yet this hysteria and fear evaporated in what was probably record time. Today, the use of the hallucinogen is no longer a public issue, at least not apart from the use of illegal drugs generally. LSD has been absorbed into the morass of drug taking in general—less seriously regarded than crack and heroin use, but more so than that of marijuana. LSD never really materialized into the threat to the society that many observers and critics (or, for that matter, its supporters) claimed it would. The drastic, dramatic, cosmic, philosophical, and religious claims originally made for the LSD experience now seem an artifact of an antiquated age. The psychedelic movement—whose members glorified the drug as a superhighway to an astounding new vision, perhaps a new way of life for the society as a whole, but who never made up a majority of even regular users in the 1960s—simply disappeared. The fear of the conventional majority that users would go crazy, drop out, or overturn the social order never came to pass. LSD became simply another drug taken on occasion by multiple drug users for the same hedonistic, recreational reasons they take other drugs—to get high.

One of the most remarkable aspects of the use of LSD and the other hallucinogens is how episodically and sporadically it takes place. In fact, of all drugs or drug types ingested currently in the United States (with the possible exception of PCP), it is possible that, among the universe of everyone who has taken the drug at least once, the lowest percentage is made up of current or recent users. Recall that alcohol generates very high continuance or loyalty rates: About six out of ten of at-least-one-time drinkers consumed one or more alcoholic beverages in the past month. But only one out of 20 persons who ever used LSD had taken it within the past month—one-twelfth the figure for alcohol and one-tenth that for cigarettes. LSD is simply not a drug that is taken very often or regularly—even among users. Psychopharmacologists rank the dependence potential of the hallucinogens as extremely low—in fact, close to dead last among all drugs and drug types.

There is a perception of the 1960s as a psychedelic era, a period of history when the use of LSD was not only widespread but characteristic of the period. Evidence points to the fact that the incidence of LSD use was extremely low (although climbing) in the 1960s; it reached something of a peak in the 1970s; it declined into the 1980s; and it has remained at a fairly stable level for the past 20 years or so. In 1967, according to a Gallup Poll, only 1 percent of American college students (in all likelihood, the category that was most likely to have taken the drug at that time) said that they had tried LSD, even once; by 1969, this figure had grown to 4 percent, and by 1971, 18 percent. In other words, precisely at a time when use was mushrooming, media attention to LSD dropped off. But in the past 30 years, the drug's use has declined; in 1980, the *lifetime* prevalence figure among high school seniors for LSD was 9 percent; by 1985, this had declined slightly to 7.5 percent; in 1990, it was 8 percent. In 2007, the latest year for which we have data at this writing, it was only 4 percent (Johnston et al., 2009). For college students and noncollege young adults, the trend lines are similar. Thus, although again, LSD and the psychedelics are used extremely episodically by those who use it, its use has not entirely disappeared, though its slope has been tilted downward.

The use of LSD in the United States should teach us some very important lessons about the perception of social problems and the imputation of deviance to an activity. *First,* the public hysteria generated over an activity, a belief, or a condition may be totally disproportionate to its objective threat to the society; some activities or conditions attract considerably more than their fair share of public hysteria, while others attract far less. *Second,* media attention does not necessarily reflect how common or frequent an activity is; some commonly enacted behaviors receive little or no media attention, while some rare or infrequent activities receive a great deal. Media attention to an activity could very well increase at a time when it is declining in frequency, or decline when its frequency is increasing. *Third,* it is likely that people base their notions of the frequency or commonness of behaviors, beliefs, and conditions and the threat they pose to the society more on how well known they are than on the objective, concrete facts of the matter. A study of LSD is more instructive for what it tells us about deviance in general than for what it tells us specifically about drug use. LSD use moved from an unknown phenomenon to a moral panic to "ho-hum" in what may be record time (Goode, 2008a, 2008c).

COCAINE AND CRACK

Cocaine is a stimulant. Its most commonly described effect is exhilaration, elation, euphoria, and a voluptuous, joyous feeling. Probably the second most frequently described effect by users is a sensation of mastery and confidence in what one is and does. And third, users most commonly report a burst of increased energy, the suppression of fatigue, a stimulation of the capacity to continue physical and mental activity more intensely and for a longer than normal period of time.

In the nineteenth century, before its effects were fully understood, cocaine was used by physicians for a variety of ills, ailments, and complaints—first, to offset fatigue and depression; later, to cure morphine addiction. Today, one of its very few medical uses is as a local anesthetic, that is, to kill pain when applied topically to delicate tissues and organs, such as the eye or gums. The earliest papers of Sigmund Freud were devoted to singing the praises of this drug; when he became a dependent on it, he realized his mistake (Byck, 1974; Andrews and Solomon, 1975; Ashley, 1975, pp. 21–28). At the end of the nineteenth and the beginning of the twentieth centuries, cocaine, like morphine and opium, was an ingredient in many patent medicines. Cocaine was even contained in many soft drinks, including Coca-Cola, until 1903, when it was removed because of pressure applied by "Southerners who feared blacks getting cocaine in any form" (Ashley, 1975, p. 46).

A major reason for the criminalization of cocaine after the turn of the century, many observers feel, was racism. Although there is no evidence whatsoever that African Americans were any more likely to use cocaine than whites, or that those who did were any more likely to become dangerous or violent under the influence, the fear among many whites that both were true may have been responsible for bringing the drug under state and federal control. Numerous articles published in the early 1900s made the claim that cocaine stimulated violence among blacks.

In 1903, *The New York Tribune* quoted one Colonel J. W. Watson of Georgia to the effect that "many of the horrible crimes committed in the southern states by the colored people can be traced to the cocaine habit." A Dr. Christopher Koch, in an article that appeared in the *Literary Digest* in 1914, asserted that "most of the attacks upon white women of the South are a direct result of a cocaine-crazed Negro brain." *The New York Times* published an article in 1914 entitled "Negro Cocaine Fiends Are a Southern Menace," which detailed the "race menace" and "hitherto inoffensive" blacks "running amuck in a cocaine frenzy" (Ashley, 1975, pp. 66–73; Grinspoon and Bakalar, 1976, pp. 38–40).

> All the elements needed to ensure cocaine's outlaw status were present by the first years of the twentieth century: It had become widely used as a pleasure drug . . . ; it had become identified with [groups that were] despised or poorly

> regarded [by middle-class whites] . . . [that is], blacks, lower-class whites, and criminals; and it had not . . . become identified with the elite, thus losing what little chance it had of weathering the storm. (Ashley, 1975, p. 74)

By the time of the passage of the Harrison Act in 1914, which included cocaine as a "narcotic," 46 states had already passed state laws attempting to control cocaine. This indicates that cocaine was seen at the time as a serious drug problem. And a reason for the criminalization of cocaine was, in all likelihood, racial hostility toward African Americans on the part of the white majority.

Most experts argue that the use of cocaine declined sharply during the 1920s and remained at an extremely low level until the 1960s (Ashley, 1975; Spillane, 2000). The increase in cocaine use during that decade and into the 1970s paralleled that of marijuana use, though on a much smaller scale. Although no systematic, nationally representative surveys were conducted on drug use in the United States until 1972, a 1979 study "reconstructed" estimates for the 1960s based on dates interviewees gave for when they began drug use (Miller and Cisin, 1980). This study estimated that only 1 percent of all Americans who were 18–25 in 1960—the category most likely to use the drug—had used cocaine even once in their lifetime; by 1967, this had doubled. In 1972, when a full-scale survey was conducted, lifetime prevalence figure for young adults stood at 8 percent, and by 1979, it had shot up to 27 percent (1980, p. 17). According to the national survey I've cited earlier, the figures for at least one-time lifetime use for the population as a whole age 12 and older decline significantly during the 1980s and into the 1990s: 1991, 18 percent, and 1998, 11 percent; however, into the twenty-first century, this lifetime figure increased slightly—in 2007, to 14.5 percent (SAMHSA, 2008).

The point is this: Practically all surveys show a decline in the use of cocaine in the general population over time since the late 1970s. This sounds encouraging, and it's possible that yearly, even monthly, use may not present a serious problem to the society. What most experts are most concerned about are the problems posed by cocaine addicts—frequent, chronic, heavy, and compulsive abusers who stand a high likelihood of causing medical damage to themselves as a result of overdoses and heavy use, and of victimizing others in the form of violence and property crime. The problem is that such users are difficult to locate. What indicators we do have, however, indicate a trend line that is not nearly as encouraging as for casual use. While the casual, recreational use of cocaine in the general population has declined in the past decade or two, it is possible that the heavy, chronic abuse of the drug has actually increased. What we see is something of a polarization in cocaine use, with the least involved (and least criminal and least deviant) user most likely to give up the drug, and the most involved (and mot criminal and deviant) abuser least likely to abstain. Abusers who are most likely to harm themselves and victimize others are also most likely to stick with cocaine over an extended period of time.

One indicator of this increase comes from the Drug Abuse Warning Network. As we saw, DAWN plots two drug-related events over time: nonfatal drug-related emergency department (ED) admissions, and medical examiner and coroner's reports on lethal drug-related deaths or mortality. While there are many reasons why these figures would change over time (including changes in drug potency, trends with respect to taking different drugs simultaneously, taking drugs via different routes of administration, and an aging addict population), one reason is the change in the number of very heavy abusers, resulting in changes in the medical problems they exhibit. Out of 1.7 million ED hospital visits associated with drug use or abuse taking place in 2006 (the latest date at this writing for which data are available), over half of which (55%) were for illicit drugs, cocaine ranked at the top of the list (DAWN, 2008a), with a rate of 182 ED visits per 100,000 in the population—*three times* that of heroin, which had a rate of 62.8. Just as scary are DAWN's mortality statistics: In 2004 (again, the latest available figures), cocaine was mentioned in 46 percent of all drug-related deaths (DAWN, 2008b), placing it at number two on this list. (Heroin placed first, with 70% of all drug-related mortality mentions.) These figures represent enormous increases since DAWN revamped its data-collection procedures in 2003.

In its powdered form, cocaine is usually sniffed or snorted, that is, inhaled sharply through the nostril. The user usually chops the drug on a smooth surface and arranges it in the form of a fine, thin line. The user snorts each line up either directly off the surface into a nostril, or through a tiny tube, such as a short, cut-off soda straw or a rolled-up bill. Some users prefer to scoop up the powder with a tiny spoon, place it just inside the nostril, and then snort it. Snorting cocaine is slower, less efficient, less reinforcing, and less intensely pleasurable than smoking it. Perhaps nine users out of ten will snort cocaine most of the time they use it. Until 1985 or 1986, users smoked pure cocaine in the form of "freebase." After 1986, smoking users moved to crack, making it the most popular smoked cocaine substance. Crack is an impure crystalline precipitate that results from heating cocaine with baking soda; it contains only 30 percent or so cocaine.

The difference between powdered cocaine and crack is mainly in route of administration, or the way users take these substances. Taking powdered cocaine intranasally produces a high that takes roughly 3 minutes to take effect and lasts perhaps 30 minutes. There is no real "rush" or intense orgasmlike explosion of pleasure. Injected, the rush takes only 12–15 seconds to appear, and it is described as a vastly more voluptuous feeling than the high that occurs when cocaine is snorted. Users do not as often smoke powdered cocaine since the combustion temperature is extremely high. When cocaine is smoked in the form of freebase or crack, the onset of the drug's impact is even faster than injection, a matter of six to eight seconds, and the intense, orgasmlike high or rush lasts for perhaps two minutes, followed by an afterglow that lasts 10–20 minutes. The euphoria achieved in this experience is extreme—in the terms of the behaviorist psychologist, it is highly reinforcing—and, often, this impels users to want to take the drug over and over again.

However, to say that smoked crack cocaine is highly reinforcing—more so, in fact, than almost any other drug—is not to say that most users become chronic abusers. As with nearly every newly introduced drug, sensationalist exaggeration in the media accompanies its widespread use. *Feeling the urge* to take a drug over and over again does not always, necessarily, or even mostly, result in actually doing so. In the mid-1980s, newspaper headlines and television reports implied that all teenagers in the country had used, or were in imminent danger of using, crack—that every community nationwide had been "saturated" by the drug. The reality is not nearly so terrifying. The first year that the Monitoring the Future study asked about crack (1987), only 5 percent of high school seniors questioned said that they had used crack even once in their lives; in 1998, the figure was 4 percent; and in 2008, it was 3 percent (Johnston et al., 2009). The figures for annual and 30-day prevalence are, of course, much lower. (Unfortunately, high school dropouts, whose crack use is likely to be considerably higher, could not be included in this survey.) For college students, in 2007, the lifetime figure was only 1.3 percent (Johnston et al., 2008).

Just as the incidence or frequency of crack use was exaggerated by the media, the drug's demonic addictive power was sensationalized as well. A June 16, 1986, story in *Newsweek* claimed that using crack immediately impelled the user into "an inferno of craving and despair." "Try it once and you're hooked!" "Once you start, you can't stop!" These and other slogans were repeated so often that they seemed to take on a life of their own. In fact, they are a serious distortion of reality. Crack may be among the most reinforcing drugs known, and it is possible that a compulsive pattern of abuse builds more rapidly than for any other well-known, widely used drug. Still, only a fairly small minority of users take the drug compulsively and destructively.

In one Miami study of over 300 heavily involved drug users age 12–17, 96 percent of whom had taken crack at least once and 87 percent of whom used it regularly, only a minority, 30 percent, used it daily, and half used it weekly or more, but not daily. A majority of even the daily users limited their use to one or two "hits"—"hardly an indication of compulsive and uncontrollable use. Although there were compulsive users of crack in the Miami sample, they represented an extremely small minority" (Inciardi, 1987, p. 484). While there is unquestionably a certain risk of dependence in smoking crack, the hellish experiences that were described in the media in the 1980s did not typify what most users went through when they took the drug. Once again, drug users are often characterized as extreme deviants by the media, a characterization that assumes a reality in the way they are pictured by much of the public.

A good example of the way that cocaine and crack use was demonized in the media is provided by the "crack babies" phenomenon of the late 1980s and early 1990s. In his *Folk Devils and Moral Panics,* Stanley Cohen (1972, pp. 77–85, 2002) refers to the process of sensitization in the early stages of a moral panic—that is, "the reinterpretation of neutral or ambiguous stimuli as potentially or actually deviant" (1972, p. 77). Thus, a familiar, nondeviant source that causes a certain measure of harm does not generate much concern, while an unfamiliar, deviant source that cases the same level of harm will touch off a firestorm of concern, fear, and hostility. We already saw the sensitization process at work in the 1960s with LSD: Panic reactions were interpreted as an epidemic of psychotic episodes, and peculiar-looking chromosomes drawn from one mental patient who was administered LSD were interpreted as a future tidal wave of malformed, abnormal children.

The findings of the initial studies on children born to cocaine-dependent mothers were extremely pessimistic. Babies whose mothers were exposed to crack and powdered cocaine during pregnancy, compared with those whose mothers were not exposed to the drug, are more likely to be born prematurely, have a lower birth weight, have smaller heads, suffer seizures, have genital and urinary-tract abnormalities, suffer poor motor ability, have brain lesions, and exhibit behavioral aberrations such as impulsivity, moodiness, and lower responsiveness (Chasnoff et al., 1989). Findings such as these were picked up by the mass media with great speed and transmitted to the general public; within a short period of time, it became an established fact that crack babies made up a major medical and psychiatric problem for the country. It is possible, some argued, that they could never be cured. Crack babies could very well become a catastrophe of monumental proportions. William Bennett, then federal drug "czar," claimed that 375,000 crack babies annually were being born in the United States in the late 1980s—one out of ten births!—a figure that was echoed by *Washington Post* columnist Jack Anderson and *New York Times* editor A. M. Rosenthal (Gieringer, 1990, p. 4). One reporter, in a major and widely quoted article published in *Time* magazine, claimed that the medical care of crack babies would cost society 13 times as much as normal babies. There is fear, she said, that these children will become "an unmanageable multitude of disturbed and disruptive youth, fear that they will be a lost generation" (Toufexis, 1991, p. 56). A Pulitzer Prize–winning columnist describes the crack baby crisis in the following dramatic, heart-wrenching words:

> The bright room is filled with baby misery; babies born months too soon; babies weighing little more than a hardcover book; babies that look like wizened old men in the last stage of a terminal illness, wrinkled skin clinging to chicken bones; babies who do not cry because their mouths are full of tubes. . . . The reason is crack. (Quindlen, 1990)

It was not until the early 1990s that enough medical evidence was assembled to indicate that the crack baby syndrome was, in all probability, mythical in nature (Neuspiel et al., 1991; Coles, 1992; Richardson and Day, 1994). The problem with the early research on the babies of mothers who had used cocaine and crack was that there were no controls. Most of these women also drank alcohol, some heavily—and medical science has documented at least one damaging outcome of heavy drinking by the expectant mother: fetal alcohol syndrome. Likewise, no controls were applied for smoking, which is associated with low birth weight in infants, nutritional condition, medical condition of the mother, medical attention (receiving checkups, following the advice of one's physician—indeed, even seeing a physician at all during one's pregnancy), and so on. In other words, factors that vary with cocaine use are known to determine poorer infant outcomes; mothers who smoke crack and use powdered cocaine are more likely to engage in other behaviors that correlate with poorer infant health. Is it the cocaine or these other factors that cause these poorer outcomes? Expectant mothers who use cocaine are more likely to get sexually transmitted diseases; such mothers are less likely to eat a nutritious, balanced diet; get regular checkups; and so on. Were these factors at work in their children's poorer health? Or was it the independent effect of the cocaine itself that produced these medical problems?

When the influence of these other factors was held constant, it became clear that the poorer health that was observed in very young babies was not caused by the effects of cocaine use itself. Instead, it seemed to be a function of the impact of the other drugs these pregnant mothers were using, including alcohol and cigarettes, and a lifestyle that included an inadequate diet and insufficient medical care. In short, it is likely that the crack babies issue was a hysteria-driven rather than a fact-driven syndrome. In the late 1980s and early 1990s, the public, the media, and even the medical profession were sensitized to believing in the harmful effects of cocaine on newborns with scanty, skimpy evidence; at the same time, influence of the more conventional factors was normalized and ignored. Such processes are characteristic of the moral panic; in the moral panic, hostility to and condemnation of deviant behavior and deviant actors are invigorated, intensified, and reaffirmed.

For the general population, at-least-one-time cocaine use declined during the 1990s: In 1991, 18 percent had taken the drug only once during their lifetime; in 2007, this figure had decreased slightly to 14 percent. For college students, the latter statistic was 8.5 percent (Johnston et al., 2009). But the story is not quite the same for all categories or groups in the population. Among schoolchildren, cocaine use increased during most of the 1990s, then leveled off and even declined after that. Between 1991 and 1998, the lifetime prevalence of cocaine use among eighth graders doubled—from 2.3 to 4.6 percent; the percent using it in the prior 30 days nearly tripled, from 0.5 to 1.4 percent. But between 1998 and 2007, the figure for lifetime prevalence dipped slightly, to 3.1 percent. The changes for high school seniors were practically nonexistent—7.8 in 1991 and 7.8 percent for lifetime use in 2008; and from 1.4 to 2.4 percent for use in the past 30 days (1991–1998), to 2 percent in 2007 (Johnston et al., 2009). These numbers are small, and they do indicate a plateau during the past few years, but that these increases run counter to the declines that have been taking place in the adult population should give us cause for concern.

HEROIN AND THE NARCOTICS

Of all well-known drugs or drug types, heroin ranks lowest in popularity. Assuming the polls are reasonably accurate, only 1.5 percent of the American population has even tried heroin, and a fraction of that figure (two-tenths of 1%) has used it, even once, in the past month (SAMHSA, 2008). The percentages for high school seniors are about the same as for the general population—1.4 percent has at least tried it, and less that one-half of 1 percent (0.4%) has done so in the past month (Johnston et al., 2009). Less than 1 percent of college students are at-least-one-time heroin users (0.5%, to be exact) and only one-tenth of 1 percent did so in the past 30 days (Johnston et al., 2008).

Remember, however, that school surveys do not interview dropouts; in addition, infrequent school attenders and truants are less likely to show up in a survey's sample. And it is almost certain that dropouts and truants are significantly more likely to use heroin. In addition, studies of the general population are based on households. Homeless people, the incarcerated, and people who crash on the couches of acquaintances do not live in stable households, and the chances are they are more likely to use heroin than members of stable households. Nonetheless, heroin ranks extremely low on America's list of well-known illicit drugs.

The questions that arise, then, are these: Why study heroin use at all? If, compared with marijuana, cocaine, and the hallucinogens, it is used with such rarity, why study it? Why discuss heroin in a general overview of drug use and abuse as a form of deviance? One answer is that, until the advent of crack in the mid-1980s (and, more recently, the abuse of methamphetamine in the late eighties to early nineties), heroin use, and especially addiction, has been the most deviant form of drug use in the public mind. It is usually regarded as the ultimate or most serious form of drug use known. In addition, although many users take heroin once, twice, a dozen times, and abstain from it from then on, and many use it occasionally, or, if regularly, confine their use to weekends or special occasions, still, a very substantial proportion of heroin users become addicts. Most estimates of the number of narcotic addicts in the United States hover in the half million range, though it is possible that, according to a more generous definition, there may be as many as a million American heroin addicts or abusers. (It must be stressed that defining just who is an addict or abuser is not as obvious or straightforward as might be supposed.)

One reason why heroin is such an important drug for the sociologist of deviance (aside from its strongly negative image in the public's mind) is that its use seems to generate social problems of enormous seriousness and magnitude. This is not merely a matter of the society subjectively constructing a problem in a certain way; objectively speaking, heroin causes a great deal of damage to users and nonusers alike. As we've seen, it is clear that alcohol and tobacco kill more Americans than the illegal drugs. Still, among the *illicit* drugs, heroin ranks at or near the top in objective seriousness. Heroin causes a great deal of medical damage. As I pointed out, in 2004, heroin ranked first in DAWN's medical examiners' reports, being mentioned in seven of ten (70%) of all drug-related mortalities, or drug overdoses. During 2006, heroin figured in 190,000 ED episodes nationwide, ranking third for illicit drugs.

Considering that heroin is used about one-tenth as often as cocaine, its contribution to these overdose figures is truly remarkable—in fact, astounding. It is possible that, *on an episode-by-episode basis,* heroin is the most dangerous of the well-known drugs. It remains an interesting and vexing question as to whether it is the direct action of the drug or the way the legal system deals with heroin users that causes such extensive medical havoc. But clearly, given the way that heroin is currently used, its contribution to medical harm justifies attention to its use as sociologically important. Certainly the increase in DAWN's figures on lethal and nonlethal overdoses suggests increases in heavy use and abuse. (Another possible explanation: an aging addict population, leading to more deaths and medical complications. A third explanation: the increase in the potency of heroin has led to more overdoses.) Of all drugs currently in use in the United States, on a dose-by-dose basis, heroin ranks at the top with respect to its potential for damage—an excellent reason for a sociologist of deviance to pay close attention to its use.

METHAMPHETAMINE

The stories were terrifying. The abuse of methamphetamine, a more potent sister of the amphetamines, was sweeping the country like wildfire. Within just a few years, the United States would be awash in "ice"—recrystalized methamphetamine sulfate. Methamphetamine, according to the media in the late 1980s, was the drug of choice for a new generation. It would replace heroin, cocaine, and even marijuana as the nation's premier problematic drug. Law enforcement was put on notice; "crystal meth" or "crank" (other terms for illicit methamphetamine sulfate) was the drug to watch. Or so the media announced in the late 1990s (Lerner, 1989; Young, 1989).

Every decade or two, a particular drug or drug type is designated by the media as, in the words of criminologist Ronald Akers, the "scary drug of the year." A panic or scare is generated about its use, and headlines scream out the danger its use poses. A tidal wave of abuse has hit or is about to hit our shores, these stories assert, and we should be prepared. In the 1930s, that drug was marijuana; in the 1960s, it was LSD; in the late 1970s, it was PCP; in the 1985–1990 era, it was crack cocaine. Just as the crack scare had begun to die down, a smaller but no less terrifying scare emerged about the use of methamphetamine. In every case, the headlines were exaggerated. Experts do not doubt the dangers attendant upon compulsive drug abuse, but they do argue that the headlined drugs are not nearly as harmful, nor are they likely to be used as compulsively, or as widely, as most of these headlines claimed. Sober, systematic evidence eventually revealed that the vast majority of episodes of PCP use did not result in self-destructive or violent behavior, that neither LSD nor crack use by expectant mothers produced birth defects in their babies, and that very few crack users were caught up in the "inferno of addiction" described by the press.

What of methamphetamine? Is the country "awash" in "ice"? Has crystal meth become the drug of choice for our younger generation? Is it as dependency producing as the headlines proclaimed? What evidence do criminologists, epidemiologists, and sociologists have of the use of this powerfully reinforcing drug?

Compared with the amphetamines, methamphetamine use more often escalates to high-dose, compulsive abuse. Methamphetamine is more potent than any of the amphetamines; it can cross the blood-brain barrier more rapidly, and is metabolized more efficiently. A dose of methamphetamine generates more dopamine, a chemical neurotransmitter that regulates pleasure, than amphetamine or even cocaine. But a drug's effect is also influenced by route of administration, that is, how it is taken. Amphetamine has traditionally been taken orally via capsule or sniffed in powder form, while methamphetamine, in addition to being snorted, is injected and smoked; less commonly, although occasionally, it is ingested in pill or other form. John Kramer, a pharmacologist who studied amphetamine addiction in the 1960s, said at the time that the drug, administered IV, "is an ecstatic experience." The user's first thought is, "Where has this been all my life?"

At one time, methamphetamine was prescribed under the brand name Methedrine; it is no longer legally manufactured in the United States. (Another methamphetamine is currently marketed in pill form under the brand name Desoxyn; it is a Schedule II drug.) In the 1960s, Methedrine was injected intravenously in high doses; a sizable "speed scene" developed, which involved tens of thousands of youths taking huge doses day in and day out. Use peaked around 1967 and declined sharply after that. Many "speed freaks" (as compulsive, high-dose users of Methedrine were called) at the time eventually became heroin addicts, because they alternated the use of methamphetamine, a stimulant, with heroin, a depressant, so that they could come down from their Methedrine high. They began to use more and more heroin and less and less methamphetamine, and eventually the heroin took over. Considering the way that Methedrine was used by speed freaks, heroin turned out to be a safer, easier drug to take, and it had less of a deleterious impact on their lives.

Although the street speed scene did not last a very long time, it had a tremendous impact on its participants' lives. What was it like? The speed freak of the late 1960s took Methedrine to get high. More specifically, the drug was injected IV to achieve a "flash" or "rush," whose sensation was likened to an orgasm—a "full body orgasm"—or a jolt of electricity. Extremely large quantities of the drug were taken. While 5–10 milligrams of Dexedrine or Dexamyl taken orally via tablet or capsule would represent a typical therapeutic or instrumental dose of an amphetamine, the speed freak would inject as much as half a gram or a full gram (500 or 1,000 milligrams!) of Methedrine in one IV dose. Such massive doses of speed would cause unconsciousness or even death in a nonhabituated person but a pleasurable rush in the experienced user. Since amphetamine inhibits sleep, IV administration every four hours or so causes extended periods of wakefulness, often two to five days at a stretch (called a "run"). This would be followed by long periods of sleep ("crashing"), often lasting up to 24 hours (Carey and Mandel, 1968).

In the late 1980s, the heavy use of methamphetamine made a comeback; it began in Hawaii and spread to California. The current form of methamphetamine is considerably more potent than its older version, Methedrine. (Its current manufacture involves a somewhat different chemical process, in which ephedrine or pseudoephedrine, a heart and CNS stimulant, is used as its precursor drug.) The effects of methamphetamine last a long time, 12 hours, its half-life is at least as long, and it takes two days to be totally eliminated from the body. Its relatively slow breakdown rate means that if taken daily, accumulation can occur. This both boosts the effect of each subsequent dose and potentiates serious organic harm.

The chemical process to produce methamphetamine is extremely simple and its precursor chemicals are readily available. As a consequence, until the mid-1990s, most of the meth used in this country was manufactured either by biker gangs or very small "mom and pop" operations, mainly in the Southwestern United States, usually California. According to the Drug Enforcement Administration (DEA), however, beginning about 10 years ago, Mexican gangs began muscling into the bikers' turf and managed to wrest a majority of the business away from them. In 1994, a total of 263 methamphetamine labs were seized by American authorities. In 2000, 1,800 labs were seized by the DEA alone, and 4,600 by state and local police. In the last two or three years, methamphetamine originating from Canada began to be seized. In addition, methamphetamine tablets that had their origin in Southeast Asia began to show up on the streets of America's cities.

Recent media accounts on methamphetamine abuse have warned the public and put law enforcement on alert: Methamphetamine is the drug to watch. Does systematic evidence bear out these journalistic claims?

As we saw in Chapter 4 on research methods, ADAM drug tests and interviews arrestees who have agreed to volunteer information about their use; 85 percent agree to be interviewed, and of these, about 90 percent agree to be urine tested for the presence of drugs. The program looks at arrestees from the counties in and around which the nation's largest cities are located. In the past decade, cocaine has declined as the drug of choice among arrestees, and marijuana has remained more or less stable. Nonetheless, nationwide, only *one-tenth* as many arrestees test positive for methamphetamine as for cocaine. The most remarkable of ADAM's findings, however, is that the use of methamphetamine remains *extremely* regionalized. In some cities (for instance, Sacramento and Portland), meth is a, or *the,* major drug, in 2008, with between 15 and 35 percent testing positive for methamphetamine. In others (Chicago, New York, and Washington, D.C.), the presence of meth among arrestees is under 5 percent. This may change in the near future, since some cities, which, a half-dozen years ago, tested zero percent for methamphetamine among arrestees, now find that a tiny percentage test positive.

Monitoring the Future is a yearly survey of eighth, tenth, and twelfth graders, as well as college students and adults not in college. Questions about methamphetamine began the late 1990s and declined since then; for seniors, lifetime use is in the 2–3 percent range, and 30-day prevalence is under 1 percent. The data from the National Household Survey on Drug Abuse indicate that recent increases in methamphetamine use have been fairly modest, and that the drug's use nationwide is far below that of marijuana and even cocaine. In 2007, the national survey revealed that about 5 percent of the respondents said that they had ever tried meth, and two-tenths of 1 percent said that they had used it in the past 30 days. Methamphetamine does not show up at all on DAWN's "top five" drugs with respect to mortality, and the number of drug-related ED visits for meth is less than a tenth as for cocaine (80,000 vs. 958,000).

These nationwide figures mask not only regional differences but rural–urban differences as well. In some rural communities, methamphetamine has become *the* drug of abuse. In some areas, in the past few years, narcotics law enforcement spends most of its person-hours on methamphetamine, and, in these same areas, admissions to treatment programs for meth abuse have shot up several-fold and have overwhelmed regional and local facilities. Clearly, the national picture is not the same everywhere; it is clear that to get the big picture, piecing together many smaller pictures is necessary.

At the same time, the nationwide picture does not warrant alarm—yet. Methamphetamine has been dubbed "redneck cocaine," and it is principally in the poorest, more rural areas of the country that meth has taken root. Even today, almost everywhere, methamphetamine abuse is dwarfed by the use of cocaine and, as measured by harm if not by its volume of use, even heroin. That may change in the years to come, but the current picture does not justify a recent *USA Today* headline: " 'Meth' Moves East" (www.usatoday.com/news/nation/2003-07-29-meth-cover_x.htm), whose story quotes a DEA agent who says "It looks almost like a wildfire moving east." But although the potential for growth, and harm, is there, hysteria, as I indicate, is not warranted. Nationwide, meth is used *vastly* less than the media indicate, and the harm it has caused is likewise substantially lower.

Our fear of methamphetamine should be partially tempered by an examination of loyalty or continuance rates. Most at-least one-time users of meth do not go on to continued use; most give it up after a few trial experiments. But meth is second among illicit drugs only to marijuana in the degree to which persons who took the drug during the *last year* also took it within the past 30 days. In other words, a minority—albeit a substantial minority—who graduate from the experimental use of methamphetamine begins taking it more or less regularly. And if we had more precise data, we'd see that a minority *within* that minority—but again, a fairly substantial minority—begin taking the drug compulsively and abusively. It is this minority within a minority that law enforcement has to worry about. No, tasting crank does not even remotely inevitably lead to a "maelstrom of addiction." But yes, if a user escalates from tasting to occasional use, that risk is very likely as high as it is for any drug currently available on the drug menu, with the exception of marijuana. The last-year-to-last-month loyalty figures should give us cause for concern about the use of methamphetamine.

SUMMARY

Drug use has both an objective (positivistic) and a subjective (constructionist) side. On the one hand, it is an identifiable form of behavior; it has certain concrete, measurable consequences; and it is caused by and has consequences that are a product of scientific, discoverable factors. On the other hand, drug use is also categorized in a certain way by the general public, by the law, and in the media; and users, likewise, are thought about and dealt with in certain level of public concern which is not always an accurate reflection of the degree of objective danger or damage represented by drug use.

Often, there is great concern at a time when the harmful effects of drug use abuse are declining and, contrarily, concern is often relatively low when these drug effects are on the rise. In addition, the specific drug that attracts public concern has shifted over time—from marijuana in the 1930s, to LSD in the 1960s, to heroin in the early 1970s, and to crack cocaine in the later 1980s. Sociologists refer to a period in which concern over a given condition, such as drug abuse, is intense and disproportionate to its concrete danger as a moral panic. Usually, in a moral panic, a specific agent is held responsible for the condition or threat—a folk devil.

Humans have ingested psychoactive or mind-altering substances for thousands of years. Drug use is very close to being a human universal in that nearly all cultures use psychoactive drug substances. Sometimes the wrong substance is ingested, or it is taken too often, or under the wrong circumstances, or with undesirable consequences. In such cases, we have instances of deviant behavior.

Marijuana use has gone through several drastic changes as an illegal and deviant activity. In earlier centuries, marijuana was used as a medicine. Early in the twentieth century, the recreational use of marijuana was not well known; users were rarely condemned as a separate category of deviants. During the 1930s, numerous articles in popular magazines and newspapers created something of a marijuana scare or panic; in that decade, possession and sale of the drug became a crime in all states of the United States and at the federal level as well. Harmful medical effects of marijuana have been asserted but never fully documented; the jury is still out on this question. In the United States, during the 1960s and 1970s, marijuana use became much more common, more accepted, and less deviant, and the drug was decriminalized in a dozen states. In addition, it is legal as medicine in a dozen states. Since 1990, marijuana use has become somewhat more common and a bit less deviant among the young. Nonetheless, in some jurisdictions, with respect to arrests, the war on drugs has become a war on marijuana.

Hallucinogens or psychedelics include LSD as their best-known representative. During the 1960s, an LSD scare or panic erupted. Users were said to suffer temporary insanity and irreparable chromosome damage. The first effect is now regarded with suspicion by experts, while the second has been entirely discounted. LSD use has not disappeared. If anything, it has stabilized over the past decade or two. LSD is taken sporadically, with episodic infrequency. It rarely becomes a drug of serious, heavy, or chronic abuse.

Although once an ingredient in some medicines and beverages, for recreational purposes, cocaine was never a drug of widespread popularity in the United States until the 1970s. Cocaine was criminalized, along with narcotics, in the aftermath of the Harrison Act. In the 1980s, a new form of cocaine, "crack," became popular. Crack is smoked and thus produces an intense and extremely rapid high. Never widespread in the country as a whole, crack quickly became popular among a minority of poor, inner-city youth. Its use declined during the course of the 1990s. Crack use, while far from safe, was demonized by the media; its harmful effects were hugely exaggerated. Babies born to cocaine-dependent mothers were said to be permanently disabled mentally and physically. In fact, it is now clear that their medical problems were due more to the lifestyle of their mothers than to the effects of cocaine per se. In other words, the fear that crack will severely harm the fetuses of the dependent mothers was a fear-driven rater than a fact-driven syndrome. Crack abuse became another in a long line of drug panics. During the 1990s, cocaine use declined in the general population but increased slightly among the young.

Heroin is perhaps the least popular of all widely known drugs in America. As it is used, on an episode-by-episode basis with respect to lethal overdoses, it is also one of the most dangerous. (Although, interestingly, if used in a medically controlled fashion, heroin does not damage organs or bodily tissue.) Considering the small number of heroin users in the United States, an astonishingly high number of addicts die of heroin overdoses and other related ailments. Perhaps that this has much to do with the legal situation as to the effects of the drug itself. Since the early 1980s, heroin has become increasingly pure and abundant. It is now imported from a much wider range of sources than was true in the past.

Since 1989, methamphetamine, a powerful chemical analogue of amphetamine, has created a media stir. Pundits and journalists predicted that the drug would sweep the nation like wildfire. Today, while deeply entrenched in many Western and Midwestern communities, it has not yet crossed the Mississippi to become a scourge in Eastern regions. Methamphetamine has caused major disruption and devastation in Western and Midwestern cities such as Honolulu, Portland, San Jose, and Omaha, as well as in many rural areas of the West and Midwest; its abuse has failed to register at all in New York, Washington, D.C., and Chicago. Perhaps with a matter of a few years, that will change, and possibly drastically.

Account: Smoking Marijuana

One interesting aspect of illicit drug use is that there is a gulf between what the law says on the one hand, and public opinion and law enforcement on the other. Illegal is illegal. Though penalties vary from drug to drug, the fact is that both in a number of states and by federal law, one can receive a lengthy sentence for the possession of a usable quantity of marijuana—a crime most of the American public thinks should not draw a jail or prison sentence at all. In Arkansas, possession of an ounce or more draws a sentence of 4–10 years in prison; in Connecticut, a second conviction of simple possession of any amount draws a sentence of five years; and in Florida, possession of 20 grams (less than an ounce) calls for imprisonment for five years. Moreover, while the federal government seems adamant about retaining marijuana's criminal status, possession of small quantities of the drug is extremely low on law enforcement's radar screen. As we saw in this chapter, 80 percent of the population favors medical marijuana and 72 percent is opposed to incarcerating recreational pot smokers. Hence, we observe a disconnect between the law on the one hand and how the public feels and what the police and prosecutors are willing to do to enforce the law, on the other.

Brad is in his forties and is a recreational pot-smoking parent. His daughter, Tiffany, is a college student. In the eighth grade, she took a drug education course under the auspices of D.A.R.E., and was shocked, angered, and appalled when she discovered that her dad smoked marijuana.

"I had been force-fed the notion that people who use drugs are all criminals," she explains,

(Continued)

Account: Smoking Marijuana Continued

"and addicts. It angered me that he would want to do that to his body. To me, smoking pot was the equivalent of shooting heroin. A drug was a drug, and I was ashamed to have such an out-of-control father who was stuck in his little seventies world. Somehow, the fact that he took me skating every day, went to work, helped my mom, made dinner, and cleaned the house, did not matter. . . . Granted, he never smoked in front us [Tiffany and her brother]. It was just always there in the background somewhere in a smoked-filled bathroom. . . . In my family, as well as our family's friends, my dad is not considered deviant. Some of his musician friends do much harder drugs than he does. . . . In our neighborhood, though, as well as in America as a whole, his marijuana use would definitely be seen as deviant. I think this is because of the belief that fathers and mothers should set a good example for their children and that parents who use drugs are not good parents. A lot of conservative people would argue that Brad's drug use is irresponsible and immature." Tiffany adds: "Brad is an example of a person who shatters the stereotype of a parent who uses marijuana. He is hard-working, family-oriented, and responsible. That is not my own personal opinion, it is a fact. The proof is the roof still over my house, the wedding ring on my mom's finger, and the diploma I will receive in a year."

In this interview, Tiffany is asking her dad questions.

TIFFANY: How regularly do you smoke?

BRAD: Daily. I stop drinking alcohol when I'm stoned. I get my stuff from one of my fraternity brothers from college. He gets me a whole bunch so I don't have to go through some dealer I don't know. I don't think I'd do it half as much if it was hard to get. But it's cheap and easy for me. I don't smoke a lot at a time. I just pack a bowl with about half a gram, about the size of a dime [there are 28 grams in an ounce], watch TV, and don't remember what I saw, I kind of zoom out. Anyway, pot's so strong nowadays, I get much higher with less than I used to. I don't have to smoke as much pot to get the same effect that I got years ago. Strong stuff.

TIFFANY: What kind of jobs have you had?

BRAD: I've worked in the telecommunications field for a long time for a lot of different companies. I also helped my wife when we ran a daycare business out of our house. It was a great little thing we had. Just a handful of infants and toddlers—we were great at it.

TIFFANY: Were you ever high at work?

BRAD: Usually I don't smoke until I get home. I have to get up too damn early for that.

TIFFANY: How is smoking [marijuana] seen in those circles [that is, among the people Brad works with]?

BRAD: I only talk about it with people I know smoke too. Like, you could tell who did it and who didn't. The people who didn't, yeah, they probably have a big stick up their ass about it, but I really don't care. I don't advertise that I smoke or anything.

TIFFANY: So if everybody knew you smoke, how do you think they'd react? Do you think they would consider you somehow deviant?

BRAD: By a small percentage, I'd be seen as a deviant.

TIFFANY: Do you think you'd be fired?

BRAD: I don't know. I guess it depends on the boss. I don't really think about getting fired or not. That's not why I keep it hidden. It's more the fact that I don't want people judging me on their limited knowledge. . . . They lump pot in with heroin. I think pot's not even in the same galaxy as the hard drugs. It's like alcohol or cigarettes. But a lot of people think that way because they haven't had the same experiences as I have. Ignorance is bliss and there's a lot of blissful people in the world.

TIFFANY: How do you think you have been as a parent?

BRAD: Above average. I've come home every night, done laundry, washed dishes, haven't fooled around, haven't beaten my kids, sexually abused them, I've encouraged them to excel in whatever they were interested in. I've been open, honest, and supportive. We've lived within our means, sometimes above our means. We always ate well, and my kids' friends were always welcome and fed. I have the greatest relationship with my kids. They're awesome. Much better than I could have hoped. They know self-reliance, they know they can trust me with a secret, and I've continued to earn that trust by not revealing any of those secrets. They know that they can come to me with anything, day or night as a dad, friend, nurse, sounding board for ideas, devil's advocate, accountant, or a resource for information. I think I'm just a nice guy.

TIFFANY: Has being high ever affected your parenting?

BRAD: No, I don't think so. I've always been there for my family. They're the most important thing in my life. Career's a distant fifth, and pot's a little after that.

TIFFANY: If your drug use were public and obvious, how do you think people in the community would see you?

BRAD: In our community, about 10 percent would think I'm extremely deviant and the rest would think I'm normal. I know there's a ton of people out there who do a whole lot worse shit than I do. I think I'm somewhere in the middle there.

TIFFANY: How about how you're seen in your social circle?

BRAD: In my private social circle there's marijuana use and some limited cocaine use. You know, wussy stuff. And [with the cocaine], it's just snorting. I'd say a lot of my friends go further than I do. We're a diverse mix of guys, and I'd say that in that mix, I'm one of the more conventional ones.

TIFFANY: If it's no big deal to you and you don't think that most people would care, why do you keep it a secret? Do you have any fear of stigmatization?

BRAD: Not fear of stigma really. I just don't need the hassle with cops or anything. I don't want rehab, parole, or community service. Cops are the biggest hassle [with using an illegal substance]. There's just no reason for me to flaunt anything in front of them or anybody else. I don't want to be the poster boy for middle-aged marijuana use.

TIFFANY: Would you consider yourself an addict?

BRAD: Hell, yes. Just like I'm addicted to cigarettes. I quit for nine years, but when I wanted to smoke again, I did. I don't need pot to live, but it doesn't hinder my life or change how I act, so there's no need for me to quit.

TIFFANY: If your life were put into a newspaper, how do you think a lot of people would react to your drug use?

BRAD: If my life were put into a newspaper I guess I'd be considered deviant. But I don't believe in organized religion, and that's deviant too. Let me put it this way. On Dr. Phil or Oprah, yeah, I'd be considered deviant. On The Man Show, I'd be a minor hero.

TIFFANY: Do you think you're a part of a small group of people who do this? Do you feel connected to adults like you who smoke pot—maybe feel like you belong to a subculture?

BRAD: No, I'm just a guy who likes to drink beer and get high in my basement. Life is short and some things are fun.

QUESTIONS

Brad is a regular pot smoker and unconventional though not entirely a deviant parent. Is there or is there not something about the specific drug used that makes a certain lifestyle possible, and precludes other lifestyles? Is the regular use of certain drugs more demanding and forceful in intruding into the life of the user, making certain ways of life necessary, and others impossible? In other words, can you imagine Brad living the life he does and using methamphetamine or heroin? What other illicit drug could he have used and still maintained his role as a parent and reliable worker? Do you buy Brad's claim that he could quit any time he wanted? Do you feel he is irresponsible for smoking marijuana while parenting his children? Do you accept Tiffany's defense of her dad's use of pot? If you were to guess, would you agree with her that the fact that he has performed in a number of conventional roles while continuing to smoke pot indicates that the stereotype of a marijuana smoker is inaccurate?

CHAPTER 9

Sexual Deviance

As we've repeatedly seen, more than a generation ago, a critic (Liazos, 1972) attacked—indeed, mocked and poked fun of—sociologists of deviance who studied "nuts, sluts, and deviated preverts," which, in his mind, included the mentally disordered, prostitutes, and homosexuals. He regarded the emphasis by the sociologist of deviance on actors who engage in the violation of society's sexual norms as a bias, which ignored the truly important and influential forms of deviance—such as the evil and destructive deeds of powerful corporate and government actors. His message seems to be: No more sex in deviance courses and textbooks!—at least, less than in the past.

But the fact is, it is more interpersonally discrediting—and therefore more deviant—to engage in the "nuts, sluts, and preverts" forms of behavior than corporate crime and high-level political malfeasance. In spite of this supposedly misguided and biased emphasis, sociologists of deviance still focus on the study of, and continue to discuss, sexual deviance more than the "big bang" deviant behaviors. Sexually unconventional behavior remains a central topic of discussion in most courses in deviance, and with good reason: It is a prime example of deviance. Sociologists discuss sexual violations as deviance because such behavior tends to be more discrediting and stigmatizing than most other forms of deviance. Indeed, it seems perverse and wrongheaded not to emphasize social deviance in a deviance course. It is Liazos who holds the bias, not the sociologists of deviance.

Critics who claim that sociologists focus too much on sex in their courses on deviance are asking the wrong question. The right questions are these: Why do societies devise and enforce so many norms about sexual behavior? Why are the punishments for violating sexual norms so severe? The ways we violate mainstream society's norms by engaging in variant sexual acts are almost infinite. And the severity of society's punishment for many sexual transgressions is substantial. How many husbands or wives divorce their spouses for committing corporate crime? Very few. How many people become the town gossip as a result of cheating on their income tax? A few; not many. In contrast, many sexual acts are off limits or unacceptable to most of the members of this—indeed, almost any—society. The fact is societies pretty much everywhere have set forth and enforced an immense number of norms dictating acceptable and unacceptable sexual behavior. The do's and don'ts of sex are staggering in their number, variety, and complexity. And these do's and don'ts usually carry with them interpersonal penalties.

We construct almost uncountable social identities on the basis of what we do, or have done, sexually. We have—and we construct for ourselves—categories for people as a result of the fact that they, or we, engage in, have engaged in, prefer, or want to engage or try to engage or can't engage, in certain types of sexual acts. Think of these categories: homosexual, heterosexual, bisexual, adulterer, cuckold, faithful husband, faithful wife, impotent man, frigid woman, necrophiliac, pedophile, child molester, rapist, rape victim, Liazos' "prevert" (his way of mocking the sociologist's interest in sexual perversion), cougar, gigolo, escort, call girl, "dirty old man," sexual harasser, "slut," "tramp," whore, prostitute, pimp, sex fiend, sex addict, pornographer, sadist, masochist, exhibitionist, peeper, lap dancer, stripper, nude dancer, exotic dancer, "tease," a "lousy lay," gay, queer, faggot, pansy, Mary Jane, dyke, "butch," "femme"—the list goes on and on. Obviously, sex plays a very central role in defining who we are in this society. And its importance, so intricately and intimately tied in to social relations, is indicated by the number and strength of the norms attempting to govern it. Clearly, sexual deviance is an important type of deviant behavior. It would represent a bias to ignore or underplay it. Corporate crime is an extremely minor form of deviance since only a small number of people can engage in it, the interpersonal sanctions for transgressions are usually minor, and it is rarely relevant to actors' identities. Precisely the opposite is true of sexual deviance.

Consider the Bible's sexual prohibitions. It is true that, for most people, *The Holy Bible* is not the primary source of sexual norms. In fact, many people ignore most of the injunctions in the Bible as more or less irrelevant for their lives. Still, when we want to understand how sexual norms work, a good place to start is the Old and New Testaments; these texts give us a clue to what's considered wrong. A perusal of the Bible tells us a great deal about sexual norms. The number of injunctions and prohibitions against sexual acts considered wrong by the ancients, and the severity of the punishments for violating them, is impressive. Consider the fact that the Bible contains 69 different passages that refer to adulterer, adulterers, adulteress, adulteresses, adulteries, adulterous, and adultery, and 44 refer to fornication, fornications, fornicator, and fornicators. In addition, the Holy Book prohibits sex with one's father's wife, daughter-in-law, mother-in-law, sister, father's daughter, mother's daughter, mother's sister, father's sister, uncle's wife, and brother's wife—not to mention animals, another man, and one's own wife during menstruation. (It is interesting that these prohibitions are spelled out mainly for men, less often for women; the compliance of women to the norms is more likely to have been taken for granted.) Several of these injunctions carry a penalty of death, in some cases, by stoning. Clearly, the control of sexuality and the punishment of deviant sexuality were major tasks of the prophets. And the fact is the importance of sexual prohibitions remains true to this day.

WHAT'S DEVIANT ABOUT SEXUAL BEHAVIOR?

In contemporary society, what are the ways in which sex may be considered deviant? With sex norms, as with laws governing sexual acts, there are the *who, what, how, where,* and *when* questions. Who one's partner is, is clearly an important source of prohibition; "what" one's partner is, likewise, determines right and wrong in the sexual arena; how the sex act takes place also can determine its inappropriateness; and where and when sex is performed, too, can be a source of right and wrong. What makes a sexual act illegal—and deviant—is an inappropriateness along one or another of the following dimensions: (1) the degree of consent, one aspect of the *how* question; (2) the nature of the sexual object, the *who* and *what* question; (3) the nature of the sex act, another aspect of the "how" question; and (4) the setting in which the sex act occurs, the *where* question (Wheeler, 1960).

Rape, which is regarded by most observers as more an act of violence than a type of sexual behavior, and which is discussed in Chapter 6, is deviant along dimension (1)—consent on the part of the woman is lacking; force, violence, or the threat of violence is used to obtain sexual intercourse.

All societies on earth proscribe certain sex partners as unacceptable, and sex with them as deviant—dimension (2), or nature of the sex partner. The number of sex partners who are regarded as inappropriate for all members of societies around the world is enormous. In addition, all societies deem certain partners for designated persons off-limits, while those partners may be acceptable for other persons. In our society, close relatives may not have sex with one another (again, the "who" question); if they do, it is automatically an instance of deviance. The same applies to members of the same sex, strangers, anyone except our spouse if we are married, and so on. Adults may not have sex with underage minors; Catholic priests may not have sex with anyone; psychiatrists may not have sex with their patients; on most university campuses, professors should not have sex with students; and so on. Many of these restrictions pertain to the relationship we have (or don't have) with certain persons—brothers and sisters, strangers, and so on. Dimension (2), the nature of the sexual partner, also includes nonhuman sex objects, such as animals or sex dolls. (This is a "what" rather than a "who" question.)

"Kinky" sex, encompassing dimension (3)—the nature of the sex act, or the "how" question—is made up of sexual behavior that is bizarre to many people, constituting what used to be referred to as perversions. Some people receive a sexual charge out of receiving an enema; this is regarded as kinky. Others like to be tied up when they have sex, or to tie their partner up; this too may be referred to as kinky. Sadomasochistic practices (giving or receiving pain during the sex act) likewise fall under the "how" umbrella of dimension (3). Some acts that were once considered perverted are more likely to be accepted and considered normal today—for instance, oral and anal sex. Kinky sex is considered deviant specifically because what is done—the nature of the act—is considered weird, unwholesome, and worthy of condemnation. Sex with a partner of the same gender is condemned and therefore deviant in most social circles of Western society. Another widely controlled sex act in this society—by custom, if not by law—is masturbation. Adolescent boys and girls are admonished not to touch themselves, and adults are rarely willing to discuss their participation in it, even to their close friends.

And lastly, some people find sex in public and semipublic places exciting and practice it because they have a certain chance of being discovered by others. Pushed to its extreme form, this is referred to as exhibitionism, and it is regarded as deviance because of dimension (4), the "where" question—sex in an inappropriate setting. Sexual fantasies (of many men, at least) indicate that sex in an inappropriate setting excites the imagination of many people.

There are other dimensions that are not covered by the law or are less strongly governed by law than by custom that, nonetheless, dictate the inappropriateness of certain sexual behaviors. There is, to begin with, the *how often* question: The desire for sex that is widely deemed too often may court the charge of being a "sex addict" (Carnes, 1983) or being "sexually compulsive" (Levine and Troiden, 1988). On the other hand, desiring or having sex not often enough may result in being labeled "impotent" or "frigid." Generally, sex at too young an age, even if the partners are of the same age, generates condemnation and punishment among conventional others, parents especially. Not uncommonly, persons who are deemed too old will experience some negative, often condescending, reactions from others—often their own children! Sex with too many partners (a pattern that is conventionally referred to as "promiscuity," a loaded and sexist term) will attract chastisement, although more often for women than men, and more often homosexual men than heterosexuals. Exposing one's sex organs to an unwilling, coerced audience (exhibitionism), too, qualifies as an unconventional sex act, and is illegal as well. Selling, acting in or posing for, making, or, in some quarters, purchasing and consuming material that is widely regarded as pornographic is widely regarded as deviant. Selling and buying sexual favors is a clear-cut instance of sexual deviance in most people's eyes; prostitution is one of the more widely known and condemned forms of sexual deviance.

ESSENTIALISM VERSUS CONSTRUCTIONISM

As I've said, positivism—or the application of the strict scientific method to the social world—is related to a perspective that, in philosophy, is referred to as "essentialism." There is perhaps no arena of human life in which a contrast between essentialism and constructionism is sharper than with sexual behavior. The essentialist position sees sexuality as "real," as something that exists, in more or less standard form, everywhere and for all time. Sex is a "thing," a pregiven entity, a concretely real phenomenon, much like an oxygen molecule, an apple or an orange, or gravitation. To the essentialistic perspective, sex is an immanent, indwelling inherent force, it is there; it exists prior to the human consciousness. "Everyone knows" what sex is; sex is sex is sex. Essentialists recognize that sex norms and sexual custom, and behavior, vary the world over and throughout recorded time. But the sexual conservative would say that certain variations are a perversion of our "true" or legitimate sexual expression, while the libertine would say that sexual repression is a perversion of our true or legitimate sexual expression. Both agree, however, that the essence of sexuality is a thing that can be characterized in a more or less standard fashion. In other words, both are essentialists.

A completely different view of sex is offered by constructionism. This perspective asks questions about the construction and imputation of meaning (Gagnon and Simon, 1973, 2005; Plummer, 1975, 1982). Instead of assuming beforehand that a phenomenon bears an automatic sexual meaning, the constructionist asks the following: How is sexuality itself constructed? What is sexuality? How is the category put together? What is included in it, what's excluded? What are the meanings that are attached to it? How is sex thought about? Talked about? What rules do societies construct for appropriate and inappropriate sexual behavior? Constructionists argue that sexual meanings vary from person to person, setting to setting, social circle to social circle, and society to society.

Constructionists insist that behaviors or phenomena that are superficially, mechanically, and outwardly the same—that might seem formally the same to an external observer—can have radically different meanings to the participants. And the opposite is true as well: Social phenomena that, if examined from the outside, are objectively radically different can actually bear very similar meanings to observers or participants. What is sexual to one person may be totally lacking in sexual content or meaning to another.

For instance, is being strangled with a nylon cord sexually exciting? Very few of us would feel that way, but sexual asphyxia—strangling oneself to achieve sexual excitation—is common enough to be well known to every coroner and medical examiner in the country. Does wearing rubber and leather arouse our passion? What about engaging in dominance and submission games with your partner? Are children your sexual cup of tea? Do strippers become sexually aroused when they perform? Many members of their audiences certainly do; in contrast, these performers are usually going through the motions, utterly unmoved by their act. Receiving an enema or watching an entire family playing volleyball at a nudist colony may be sexual to one observer or participant and totally asexual to another. Is a vaginal examination by a gynecologist sexual in meaning? An act that sickens one person leaves another cold and causes a third to become aroused to orgasm.

Consider same-gender sexual behavior in ancient Greece. In this case, same-gender sexual behavior was accepted, even expected, if one male is older and the other is an adolescent and the older male continues to have sex with women as well. Now consider same-gender sexual behavior in the contemporary United States where homosexual contact is more likely to be stigmatized, the partners tend to be age peers, and it is not typically accompanied by heterosexual activity. Can we equate the two? Are they the same sort of behavior? Can we refer to both as "homosexuality"? To do so would make many constructionists extremely uncomfortable. In Inuit society, a custom exists of husbands offering their wives sexually to male guests; in the contemporary United States, in some social circles, married couples "swap" or "swing" or engage in comarital sex. Are these two practices similar to, or very different from, one another? They are likely to serve entirely different functions and be experienced by the relevant parties in radically different ways. Hence, to the constructionist, they are different acts; their similarities are likely to be more superficial than meaningful.

Constructionists argue that sexuality is in the service of the social world. Sexuality does not shape our social conduct so much as social meanings give shape to our sexuality (Plummer, 1982, p. 232). We are sexual because we are social. It is social life that creates, motivates, and shapes our sexuality. The social constructionists argue that sex is not a given, a hard-and-fast reality, or a bedrock biological constant—something that simply *is*—but something that is created or fashioned out of our biological "raw material," partly by our culture, partly by our partners and our interaction with them, and partly by the richness of our imagination. It is not sex that makes us who we are but we who make sex what it is.

The constructionist position goes considerably beyond the insight that understanding symbolic meaning is necessary to understand sexual behavior. It argues further that not only is the very category of sexuality constructed, in addition, but a specific evaluative meaning is read into it as well. By "evaluative," I mean, sexual categories are rendered "good" or "bad"—that is, conventional and norm abiding, or deviant, in violation of the norms—through the construction process. For instance, not only are the categories "homosexual" and "heterosexual" constructed, but they are infused with positive or negative meanings. Different forms of sexual expression do not bring with them an automatic response; they do not drop down from the skies as a reaction to their essence or basic reality. What creates the phenomenon of deviance is condemning reactions, and these reactions are variable in societies the world over, from one historical period to another, and from one social circle or context to another in the same society. What's good in one place and time is bad in another. This variability reflects the construction process that makes up the very stuff of deviance.

Traditionally, the imputation of pathology has been an aspect of the way that deviance was constructed by psychologists and psychiatrists. This has been especially true of deviant sexuality. Until the 1970s, the vast majority of research and writing on nonnormative sex cast it beyond the pale of normality. Sexual deviants, these early researchers were saying, are distinctly not like the rest of us. When the term "sexual deviant" was used to describe someone, the image that came to mind was someone who is impelled to act as a result of uncontrollable and distinctly abnormal motives—someone whose behavior is freakish and fetishistic.

Today when discussing deviant sexual behavior and proclivities, we are not referring to that which is sick or pathological but what's socially disapproved. Such a discussion includes no taint of disorder whatsoever, no implication of harm, and no sickness or illness. Sociologists of deviance do not mean "abnormal" or "sick" when they refer to deviance. To repeat the theme of this book: Sociologically deviance is made up of actions (and beliefs, and conditions) that violate one or more norms in a given place and at a given time, and are likely to touch off negative reactions.

Let's put the matter another way: *Psychological* and *social* (or sociological) deviance are not the same thing. They delineate two separate and independent dimensions. They overlap, of course; the chances are nearly all cases of psychological deviance would qualify as sociological deviance. But the reverse is not the case. Psychologically, sexual deviance implies a disorder, a dysfunction; socially and sociologically, sexual deviance refers to a violation of norms and a subsequently high likelihood of condemnation and stigma. What violates the norms in a given society may in fact be regarded by psychiatrists and clinical psychologists as quite normal (although it may not). What is accepted, practiced, and even encouraged in one society may be savagely condemned and harshly punished in another. What is a normative violation at one time may be the norm at another. Again, because the link between sexual deviance and psychological abnormality is so strong in many observers' minds, we have to be reminded of their conceptual independence.

HOMOSEXUALITY

Of the many ways that humankind is divided into categories, it is possible that sexual behavior and orientation are among the most basic and important of those categories. Why is the sex of one's partners such a crucial part of our identity? Why do we divide humanity into "straight" and "gay"? Why is such a division so much more important for us than one that, let's say, divides us into "egg eaters" and "people who don't eat eggs"? And why does this division include an evaluative component? Not all societies condemn sex with members of the same gender. In the United States, a sizeable—although slowly and unevenly shrinking—percentage of the population believe homosexual acts to be an abomination and support the laws banning them. Is homosexuality deviant in the United States? It depends on whom you ask. It is most decidedly deviant in some social circles; to the majority, it is decreasingly deviant.

Fundamentalist Christians and political conservatives point to the Bible to justify their opposition to homosexuality. As we saw, Leviticus clearly states that homosexual behavior is an abomination. "It's God's judgment, not just mine!" these opponents of homosexuality will state. But this conveniently omits the fact that the Bible also condoned slavery, patriarchy, and polygamy. Moreover, the Bible calls for the death penalty for a number of taboos besides engaging in homosexual relations—adultery, having sex with an animal, cursing and hitting one's father and mother, and working on the Sabbath. The Scriptures commanded the ancient Israelites to "annihilate" the nonmonotheistic peoples—the Hittites, the Ammonites, the Canaanites, and the Jebusites—who lived in their region. Today, hardly any fundamentalist Christian supports capital punishment for such practices. In other words, homosexuals must feel that strict Bible Christians pick and choose certain injunctions but pretend that others don't exist. They wonder, why is homosexuality considered an abomination while so many other actions that are also condemned in the Bible not nearly so condemned by contemporary Bible Christians?

And yet, for the society as a whole, things are changing. Is the United States, as some have claimed, "departing from deviance" (Minton, 2002)? A substantial proportion of Americans still regards homosexuals as deviants and feels that homosexual behavior is abnormal, unnatural, and unacceptable. But that proportion is dwindling. The segment that is consistent in its strong condemnation of homosexuality is increasingly confined to political conservatives and fundamentalist Christians. This remains a huge segment of the public, but before long, that sector may become practically the only one that feels and acts this way.

Public Opinion

For starters, public opinion has become much more accepting of homosexuality than was true a generation ago. Today, as compared with 20 or 30 years ago, the public is significantly, and in some cases, strikingly, more likely to believe that homosexual relations should be legal (43% in 1977 vs. 55% in 2008); that homosexuals should be allowed to teach in elementary schools (27% in 1977 vs. 54% in 2005); and that homosexual relations are "an acceptable lifestyle" (34% in 1982 vs. 54% in 2008). It is true that most Americans would withhold from homosexuals the right to get married on an equal par with heterosexuals (57%). Also true is the fact that the public is evenly split over whether or not homosexual relations are "morally acceptable" (48% vs. 48%). In many respects, a majority of Americans no longer regards homosexuality as a form of deviance, or homosexuals as deviants. These public opinion polls suggest that homosexuality is a transition phase with regard to its deviant status; it is exiting or transitioning away from a deviant status through a halfway house between deviance and almost-conventionality (see Table 9.1).

One indication that condemnation is slowly declining as a form of deviance is that older sectors of the population condemn homosexuality more than younger sectors do. For instance,

TABLE 9.1 ATTITUDES ON HOMOSEXUALITY, 1972–2008/2009

"Do you think that marriages between same-sex couples should or should not be recognized by the law as valid, with the same rights as traditional marriages?"

	YES	*NO*
1996	27	68
1999	35	62
2004	42	55
2007	46	53
2009	40	57

Source: Gallup Polls.

Do you believe that homosexual relations are:

	MORALLY ACCEPTABLE	*MORALLY UNACCEPTABLE*
2000	40	53
2002	38	55
2003	44	52
2004	42	54
2005	44	52
2006	44	51
2007	49	47
2008	48	48

Source: Gallup Polls.

Table 9.1 Continued

"In general, do you think homosexuals should or should not be hired for the following occupations?"

	Elementary School Teachers		*High School Teachers*	
	Should	**Should Not**	**Should**	**Should Not**
1977	27%	65%	*	*
1989	42	48	47%	43%
1994	47	46	53	40
2005	54	43	62	36

Source: Gallup Polls.

"Do you feel that homosexuality should be Considered an acceptable lifestyle or not?"

	Acceptable	*Unacceptable*
1977	43	43
1982	34	51
1992	38	57
1996	44	50
2001	52	43
2005	52	40
2008	54	43

Source: Gallup Polls.

"Do you think gay or lesbian relations between consenting adults should or should not be legal?"

	Legal	*Not Be Legal*
1986	32	57
1989	47	36
1998	50	43
2003	60	35
2005	51	45
2007	55	40
2008	56	40

Source: Gallup Polls.

"Federal law currently prohibits openly gay men and women from serving in the military. Do you think this law should be repealed or not?"

Yes, repealed	56
No, not repealed	37

(*continued*)

Table 9.1 Continued

"Some people say that allowing openly gay men and women to serve in the military is discrimination. Do you agree or disagree?"

Agree	60
Disagree	36

"Some people say that allowing openly gay men and women to serve in the military would be divisive for the troops and hurt their ability to fight effectively. Do you agree or disagree?"

Agree	35
Disagree	58

Source: Quinnipiac University Poll, April 30, 2009.

consider the question, "Sexual relations between two adults of the same sex are always wrong/ sometimes wrong/or not wrong." Nearly three-quarters of the respondents in 1973 (or 73%) said homosexual relations between were always wrong, while this figure had shrunk to a slight majority (55%). But the age differences are as important as the time change. In 1973, 56 percent of the 18- to 29-year-olds said that homosexual relations were always wrong (as opposed to 89% of the 60-and-older respondents). In 2002, these respondents would have been 47–58 years old, and in 2002, 55 percent of the 45- to 59-year-olds said that homosexual relations were always wrong, almost the identical percentage. In other words, as younger segments of the population grow older, they tend to retain the attitudes they held when they were younger, and the younger age groups at one point in time remain less condemnatory than their older contemporaries when they age. Meanwhile, the older segments of the population, the ones with the most conservative, condemnatory attitudes, increasingly die out. In other words, the more accepting attitudes of younger Americans indicate that the view that homosexuality is deviant is in fact dying out; homosexuality, it seems, as I said, is departing from deviance. Moreover, attitudes toward homosexuality are strongly related to education. The National Opinion Research Center poll I cited earlier showed that roughly seven out of ten respondents who did not graduate from high school said that homosexual relations are always wrong, but the more education someone had, this figure decreased: Forty-three percent of the sample who were college grads said this, and only 33 percent of the respondents with a postgraduate education did so. Clearly, as American society becomes increasingly educated, its condemnation of homosexuality will decrease.

One indicator of the deviant status of an activity is that it was once regarded by clinical psychologists and psychiatrists as a mental disorder. And the decline of the deviant status of homosexuality is indicated by the slow death of this pathology paradigm. At one time, many psychologists and, especially, psychiatrists believed that homosexuality was a pathology, an illness or neurosis, much like schizophrenia, clinical depression, obsessive-compulsive personality disorder, or a fear of open spaces. It was caused, many of these observers believed, by an overbearing, too-intimate mother and an absent, weak, or punishing father. And it could be cured, they claimed, through clinical therapy, whether psychoanalysis, behavioral or aversion therapy, or some other modality. This view, once dominant, has declined to the point where it is accepted by very few practicing clinicians today; the few who do accept it are older, and they are dying out. In 1973, the American Psychiatric

Association removed homosexuality from the *Diagnostic and Statistical Manual of Mental Disorders.* In 2005, when Charles Socarides, a psychiatrist and author of a half-dozen books on homosexuality (1978), and proponent of the pathology perspective, died, Gilbert Herdt, a sex researcher, stated: "His theory went from being the reigning paradigm to being considered eccentric" (January 2, 2006, *Washington Post*).

Correlates of Homophobia

"Homophobia" is the hatred of homosexuals. The homophobe is a person who says that homosexuals should be regarded as deviant and treats them as such. Which segments of the population are more likely to be homophobic? Which ones are less so? As we just saw, age and education are major factors: The older and the less educated the person, the greater the likelihood that he or she says that homosexuality is wrong and that homosexuals should not have the same rights as heterosexuals. Gregory Herek pored through the polling data and found that men, Southerners and Midwesterners, rural dwellers, Republicans, frequent churchgoers, the religiously fundamentalist, and political conservatives are more prejudiced against gays than women; people living in the Northeast and on the West Coast, urban residents, Democrats and independents, people who attend religious services infrequently or not at all or who have a more secular view of religious beliefs, and political liberals and moderates are less prejudiced against gays (http://psychology.ucdavis.edu/rainbow/html/prej_corr.html).

Two psychologists used polling data from the General Social Survey, conducted by NORC (National Opinion Research Corporation, at the University of Chicago), and determined that the most important variable determining whether and to what extent the public condemns homosexuality is the degree to which the respondent held a general traditional belief system (Shackleford and Besser, 2007). Someone who is "open to novel experience" ranks low in traditionalism; being open to experience involves being curious, imaginative, and willing to entertain novel ideas and unconventional values. People who are closed to novel experience tend to be conventional in beliefs and attitudes; conservative in tastes; and more dogmatic, rigid in their thinking and beliefs (2007, p. 108). The open/closed dimension is related to age, education, political conservativism versus liberalism, and religious fundamentalism. Persons who are more "closed" tend to be older, more politically conservative, and religiously fundamental, and have a low level of education; those who are more "open" tend to be younger, politically liberal, secular or religiously moderate and ecumenical, and have a higher level of education (pp. 108–109). To the extent that the tendency to be open to novel experience is on the increase, acceptance of homosexuality will grow; to the extent that it declines over time, intolerance or homophobia will increase.

Homosexual Behavior as a Crime?

Until June 2003, 11 states of the United States had laws on the books criminalizing what it referred to as "sodomy," which applied equally to homosexual and heterosexual acts; 4 states had sodomy laws that applied only to homosexual acts; and 35 states had by then repealed their sodomy laws. In that month, the Supreme Court of the United States ruled that the Texas sodomy laws were unconstitutional, a decision that repealed the sodomy laws everywhere. This decision, referred to as *Lawrence v. Texas,* overturns a 1986 ruling, *Bowers v. Hardwick,* that affirmed the right of states to criminalize homosexual sodomy. The 2003 Supreme Court decision, say legal scholars and movement spokespersons, represented a "landmark victory for gay rights" (Lane, 2003).

Homosexual Marriage and Civil Unions

In September 2003, Canada's Parliament endorsed homosexual marriage. The vote was close (137 to 132) but binding; the ruling went into effect the moment it was rendered (Brown, 2003). American public opinion is largely opposed to homosexual marriages; in 2000, according to a Gallup poll, respondents were opposed to making gay marriage legal by a margin of almost two-to-one (62% opposed, 34% in favor). In the United States, Vermont's "civil union" law went into effect, authorizing a marriagelike bond between partners of the same sex. Couples joined in civil union shall have all the same benefits, protections, and responsibilities that are granted to spouses in a marriage. In November, the Massachusetts Supreme Court ruled that homosexual marriage is a constitutional right (Von Drehle, 2003). As we see in Table 9.1, a Gallup Poll conducted in 2009 showed that, in spite of a mellowing of mainstream public opinion toward gays over time, 57 percent of the American population opposed gay marriage.

The Media

In the September–October 2003 issue, *Bride's* magazine published an article about homosexual weddings. The appearance of this article was such a radical departure from tradition that *The New York Times* devoted an article to reporting the event. It was the first time that any of the five top-selling bridal magazines devoted a feature to the subject (Carlson, 2003, p. C2). On October 1, 2003, on its "Weddings, Engagements, and Anniversaries" page, *The Washington Post* announced the marriage of James Gasser and Gregory Ramsey in Toronto, Canada. A month later, the announcement said, the couple also celebrated their twenty-fifth anniversary together. Both Gasser and Ramsay are "active parishioners" of All Souls Memorial Episcopal Church. Two months later, on November 30, 2003, *The New York Times* announced the wedding, in Canada, of two men in their fifties, Richard Mohr and Robert Switzer. Whether this portends a developing trend can only be speculated upon at this point. Still, these announcements certainly indicate a radical change of media representations that have taken place over the past two or three years.

The early years of the twenty-first century witnessed the release of a remarkable array of gay-oriented television programs. To appreciate how truly remarkable this development is, consider the fact that 30 years ago, prime-time television tended to depict homosexuals as mentally disordered. The hero of *Marcus Welby, M.D.* urged a "tormented patient" of his to "win that fight" against his homosexual impulses. An episode of *Police Women* portrayed three lesbians murdering the residents of a retirement home. As late as 1995, *Serving in Silence,* the first sympathetic depiction of a homosexual character, Col. Margarethe Cammermeier, who was dismissed from the Washington State National Guard for her lesbianism, elicited a refusal of many sponsors to advertise, and a kiss between the two main characters brought forth protests against the stations that aired the show. All that has changed. In January, 2001, Showtime launched *Queer As Folk,* a remarkably sexually explicit program depicting gay men and women living in Pittsburgh—with a great deal of kissing, caressing, nearly total nudity, and homosexual bedroom scenes. Buoyed by its success, in January 2004, Showtime released *The L Word,* which is centered around a social circle of lesbians living in Los Angeles. In 2003, Bravo aired *Queer Eye for the Straight Guy,* a program depicting five gay men who each week give style and fashion advice to a different (and usually clueless) heterosexual man. The audience watching the first two broadcasts of this show was the largest in Bravo history. So successful has the program been that NBC, Bravo's parent station, broadcast the program; it was the network's second most-watched program in that time slot in more than two weeks. Advertisers—including Bausch & Lomb (an optical company), Levis, Volkswagen, and the movie *Seabiscuit*—lined up to sponsor the show; none objected to its content. This development is not without its critics, including representatives of the Parents Television Council, a conservative lobby group. Interestingly, some homosexual spokespersons also object to such programs, contending that they feed into gay stereotypes. "You're not seeing diverse images on these shows," said Martin Duberman, a historian of the homosexual rights movement. But Randy Barbato, cocreator of *Gay Hollywood,* disagrees. "There are a few visible stereotypes right now. That'll open the door for different kinds of characters" (Weintraub and Rutenberg, 2003, pp. A1, C5).

Homosexual Clergy

In 2003, an openly gay New Hampshire priest, Gene Robinson, was elected bishop of the Episcopal Church. The Episcopal Diocese is affiliated with the Anglican Union, a denomination with 80 million members worldwide. As we saw earlier, Leviticus declares homosexual acts to be an abomination. In Romans, St. Paul refers to same-sex act as "unseemly," "unrighteous," and "unnatural," depending on the translation. These and other passages—for instance, in Timothy, Corinthians, and Genesis—are what gay rights activists refer to as "clobber passages," that is, they have been used to denounce homosexuality. An increasing number of Christian theologians, however, are redefining homosexuality in ways that challenge traditional views of scripture. Robert Goss, a former Jesuit priest and an advocate of what's called "queer theology," argues that God created humans in His image; hence, homosexual behavior, an expression of that humanity, is a blessing, not a sin. Several theologians have even gone so far as to argue that Jesus' relationship with his disciples was "homoerotic." Christians "have so much baggage around sexuality, so much shame that short-circuits pleasure," explains Professor Goss; it's time, he says, for Christians to "reconnect with their lovers, their community, and their God" (Broadway, 2003, p. B8).

Holdouts Such pro-gay interpretations of Christian theology are controversial, however. If we are to compile the "score card" I mentioned earlier, detailing the many ways that homosexuality is departing from deviance, to be balanced, such changes would have to be compared with those ways in which the deviant status of homosexuality is not changing. Who are the holdouts, those segments of American society who continue to regard homosexuality as deviant?

Conservative Clergy One such segment is, as we might expect, conservative Christianity, both among the clergy and the laity. Contemplating the election of Bishop Robinson, Richard Land, head of the Southern Baptist Convention's Ethics and Religious Liberty Commission, stated: "Homosexual behavior is deviant behavior according to the clear and consistent teaching of Scripture, from the Book of Genesis to the end of the New Testament." Bishop Robinson's election is, he said, "the antithesis of Scripture" (Broadway, 2003, p. B8). The election of Bishop Robinson threatens to split the Episcopal Church right down the middle. Regardless of which interpretation prevails—or whether the impending split actually takes place—it is clear that these issues were not seriously discussed a decade ago, nor was the traditional perspective so seriously challenged. Christianity has moved from monolithic opposition to homosexuality to a consideration of overturning at least a millennium of that opposition. If such a change were to be institutionalized, it would be as momentous and far-reaching in its impact as the Protestant Reformation of the sixteenth century.

The Laity The laity also has its views on the deviance of homosexuality. A nationwide poll conducted by *The Washington Post* in August 2003 revealed that a clear majority (63%) felt that their own denomination should not bless "committed relationships of gay or lesbian couples." Only a third (31%) approved. Evangelical Protestants, most of whom have a literal interpretation of the Bible, were more likely to disapprove (81%) than the majority. Respondents who were members of a congregation were evenly split on the question of whether, if their local church did bless homosexual unions, they would continue to attend (48%) or look for another church (47%). Not quite six in ten (58%) opposed a law "that would allow couples to legally form civil unions, giving them some of the legal rights of married couples"; roughly a third (37%) favored such a law. Interestingly, public support favoring civil unions or marriagelike arrangements for homosexual couples declined in the aftermath of the Supreme Court's decision repealing the sodomy laws nationwide. Earlier polls showed roughly half the population in favor of such unions (Morin and Cooperman, 2003). Clearly, both the church's and the general public's views on homosexuality are in transition.

The Military The United States military is another institution in which homosexuality is regarded as unacceptable—by its very rejection of gays, dealt with as deviant. In 2001, more men and women were discharged for declaring themselves as homosexuals or for being caught at engaging in homosexual acts (a total of 1,200 personnel), the highest figure in 14 years. In addition, the number of incidents of antigay harassment in the four services increased by 23 percent since 2000. In one base, roughly a third of all military discharges are for reasons relating to homosexuality (Marquis, 2002). But the prevailing military policy ("Don't ask, don't tell") has come under fire. *Lawrence,* the Supreme Court's 2003 decision overturning the sodomy laws, will very likely be applied to military personnel. If, as *Lawrence* ruled, criminalizing sodomy is unconstitutional because of the fact that it restricts individual liberties and serves "no legitimate state interest," then the same applies to military personnel. Article 125 of the Uniform Code of Military Justice prohibits "unnatural carnal copulation with another person of the same or opposite sex or with an animal." While Article 125 is rarely directly invoked, its application is implied in the discharge of gay military personnel. Such discharges raise the obvious question, "What interest do you have in regulating private consensual activity?" Clearly, a court challenge to the military's definition of homosexuality as deviant is likely to be brought at some point. Over seven Americans out of ten (72%) believe that homosexuals should be allowed to serve in the military.

The exclusion of gays in the military is also under fire from another source: the empirical evidence. A think tank located at the University of California at Santa Barbara, The Center for the Study of Sexual Minorities in the Military, has investigated the impact of including homosexuals in the armed services in Canada, Israel, Great Britain, Australia—and the United States. (A total of 24 nations allow gays to serve openly in their military forces.) The conclusion of all these studies is that allowing gays to serve in the military does not decrease military performance or undermine combat effectiveness (Frank, 2002; Belkin, 2003; http://www.gaymilitary.ucsb.edu/Publications/PublicationsHome.htm). One military sociologist, Charles Moskos, claims that the "empirical data" demonstrate the opposite, but the evidence he cites consists of a Roper poll conducted almost two decades ago which shows that 45 percent of military personnel who served in mixed-sex units said that "there was enough sexual activity to degrade military performance" (Frank, 2002). Notice that this was an opinion, not a fact, and that this applied specifically to male–female sexual relations—and yet hardly anyone now questions the presence of women in the military. Notice, too, that similar claims of lowered troop performance were made about the integration of African Americans into the military before they achieved equal footing with whites (Evans, 2003), a claim long since regarded as not only false but ludicrous. Before Canada permitted gays to serve in the military, 62 percent of the personnel questioned said that they would refuse to share showers, undress, or sleep in the same room as a gay soldier. In Britain, two-thirds of male personnel said they would not serve if gays did. In neither country did any service member resign in protest when the ban was lifted (Belkin, 2003). Increasingly, the American military brass will have to deal with the fact that the evidence does not support the exclusion of openly gay personnel in the military, and that their closest allies have accepted homosexuals in the ranks without serious negative impact. As far as the armed forces of the countries that have lifted the gay ban are concerned, inclusion has been a nonevent (2003, p. 110).

Is Homosexuality Departing from Deviance? A Summary

In many respects, homosexuality is "departing from deviance" (Minton, 2002). Gay couples are, increasingly, permitted to adopt children (Brody, 2003); the media are depicting homosexuals in a more realistic, less negative light; three-quarters of gays and bisexuals feel more accepted by society today than a few years ago; an increasing percentage of Christians, both clergy and laity, believe that homosexuals should be accepted on an equal basis; sodomy laws outlawing homosexual acts have been struck down as unconstitutional; the majority of psychiatrists and psychologists no longer believe that, in and of itself, homosexuality is the manifestation of a mental disorder; gay marriage is legal in Canada, and marriagelike civil unions between two persons of the same sex are legal in several states of the United States; today, heterosexuals are vastly more accepting of homosexuality than was true even a decade ago; and in society's more traditional sectors and institutions, monolithic opposition to homosexuality has given way to conflict, dissension, and schisms. In short, the deviant status of homosexuality is eroding. "The war for acceptance" of gays, says a *New York* magazine writer, "is practically won" (Green, 2001, p. 27). Consider the fact that a deviance textbook published 1976 included a chapter on premarital sex (Bell, 1976, pp. 37–59). Today, no one would think of writing such a chapter because premarital sex is no longer regarded as a form of deviance. Although, as we saw, in some sectors of the society, homosexuality is still seen as an abomination, those sectors are shrinking, and this position is becoming, increasingly, a minority view, much like belief in creationism, masculine dominance, and uncompromising opposition to abortion. In other words, if we look at deviance in horizontal terms, we will still be able to find categories in the population—political conservatives and strict Bible Christians—who retain the view that homosexuality is immoral, a sin, and hence, deviant. However, within a generation, for the society as a whole, homosexuality's deviant status will shrink to the point where it will no longer be a form of societal deviance. Then, in all probability, homosexuality will no longer be discussed by sociologists as a form of deviance.

SEX WORK

Sex workers sell sexual services. For them, sex is a job, a source of income. For the most part, their motive is financial, not sexual. Prostitution is a major form of sex work, but it is far from the only variety. In fact, the street (or outdoor) prostitute has been studied extensively and in great detail while a variety of indoor sex workers, such as call girls, women who work in a house of prostitution, masseuses, telephone sex worker, actors and actors in pornographic videos and films, and topless dancers have received much less attention (Weitzer, 2000, p. 5). It is entirely possible that 5–10 times as many sex workers are employed in indoor enterprises than is true for outdoor or street prostitution. This exclusive emphasis on a single variety of sex worker is very likely to yield a biased and distorted picture of the job situation of women who sell sexual services. To put together a more accurate picture, therefore, it is necessary to examine a full range of sex work.

Sex work—mainly prostitution—has been approached or analyzed from a variety of perspectives. Throughout history, perhaps the most common of these perspectives has been the moralistic perspective: Sex work and its workers are evil, immoral, and vile corrupters who deserve the contempt and condemnation they receive. A variety of this perspective might be called the "social worker" approach: Sex work is evil, but sex workers have been corrupted and need to be saved or salvaged, shown the straight and narrow path, shown the error of their ways, and offered a decent job at a decent wage so that they don't have to demean or debase themselves by selling their bodies. In contrast, *functionalism* argues that prostitution offers hidden benefits to the society that no other institution can supply (Davis, 1937). *Marxism* has argued that prostitution is a manifestation of class exploitation; since capitalist society offers working-class women few opportunities to earn a living, many are forced to sell themselves to survive. Van der Veen (2001) quotes Karl Marx's *Economic and Philosophical Manuscripts* on the subject: "Prostitution is only a specific expression of the general prostitution of the laborer." Such a position denies the central role played by gender that feminists would stress.

Feminism versus Ethnography: Tourism in Southeast Asia

Two social scientists, Jody Miller (2001) and Marjorie Muecke (1992), studied the same phenomenon, sex tourism in Southeast Asia, and reached almost exactly the opposite conclusions. Each analysis operates on the basis of a very different theoretical perspective: Miller is a feminist and Muecke is an ethnographer who attempted to understand her subject from the inside, as a participant or member of the society understands it.

In the field of anthropology, the term "etic" refers to an approach that looks at behavior or a society from the outside, from a perspective that, in a sense, is imposed on the phenomenon. It is an objective or outsider's perspective, an approach not necessarily shared by the member of that society or group. An "emic" approach is one from the inside, a "subjective" perspective. It is an interpretation of the world held and acted upon by the member or the society or group under study. Saying that some members of Renaissance society were witches who deserved to be burned at the stake is an "emic" or insider's approach; saying that there were and are no such thing as witches and that no one "deserves" to be burned at the stake is an "etic" or outsider's approach. Clearly, Miller's feminist approach is "etic": It argues that certain features of Southeast

Asian society (and ours as well) are exploitative and should be ended—even if members of that society do not agree with that interpretation. Muecke's approach is "emic"; it attempts to understand how members of Southeast Asian society think about and understand the sex tourism taking place in their midst and how they feel about what part it plays in the functioning of their society.

There is no doubt about Jody Miller's position on sex tourism: She most emphatically denounces it. Using women as prostitutes to service the many tourists who come to Southeast Asia—many of them for the very purpose of have sex with Asia prostitutes—is an abomination. In fact, she says, the sex trade "is at the heart" of the tourist industry in the region. It is a "new form of exploitation" which "calls for using women as sex slaves," she argues. Miller's points are discussed in the following sections.

Who Is Responsible? The parties responsible for the tourist sex trade are the higher-ups, the fat cats and top dogs, usually foreigners: the World Bank and the International Monetary Fund (IMF), which lend money specifically for the purpose of investing in tourism, knowing that the majority of that loan will be invested specifically in the sex trade; the U.S. military, which sends its troops for rest and recreation jaunts to locales where sex tourism is rampant; multinational corporations, such as airlines, the hotel industry, the travel industry, all of which collude in the sex trade through blatantly sexual advertising and encouraging tourists to travel Southeast Asia; and the government of Thailand, whose representatives are aware of the exploitation of their women, yet do not invest in the country's poorest regions so that those regions will remain poverty stricken, thereby ensuring a plentiful supply of women willing to migrate to Bangkok and work in the sex trade for extremely low wages.

Who Profits from the Tourist Sex Trade? The sex business is extremely profitable for multinational corporations, a small local elite, and the Thai government, says Miller, but it "does little to improve the standard of living or availability of services for the majority of the people" living in the regions in which it operates (2001, p. 147).

Can the Prostitute Earn a Decent Wage? Miller says no. She argues that prostitutes "receive only a small percentage of the money they earn" (2001, p. 148). In fact, attempts to unionize to improve working conditions and raise their standard of living, Miller says, "have been unsuccessful" (2001, p. 148).

Do Women Choose to Work in the Sex Trade? Miller approvingly cites a publication that quotes a prostitute, who says: "Believe me, if it was not necessary, no one would ever want to live like this. . . . But we have no choice" (2001, p. 148).

Are Women Stigmatized by Being Prostitutes? Although prostitution flourishes, it is illegal. Hence, prostitutes "are stigmatized"; they "must continually interact with men" who "consider it their right . . . to buy themselves exotic women" (2001, p. 148).

Is Prostitution a Traditional or Recent Institution? Miller admits that prostitution "has a long history in Thailand and other Asian countries." However, it was not until the War in Vietnam during the 1960s and early 1970s that Southeast Asian women "were turned into prostitutes on a mass scale" (2001, p. 147). In other words, sex tourism is a new form of exploitation (2001, p. 148).

Is Prostitution a Local Product or a Consequence of Imposing a Practice from the Outside? Miller argues that sex tourism is a recent form of exploitation in a long history of Western imperialism, in which poor, Third World countries, because of their poverty, are forced by the industrialized countries, to engage in practices that are repugnant, humiliating, and abusive. The Thai government's collaboration with the U.S. military and multinational corporations can't disguise the fact that sex tourism in Thailand is imposed from outside the country on a small, poor country. It is in fact yet another example of exploitation by the imperialist West (2001, p. 147).

Marjorie Muecke's analysis of sex tourism in Southeast Asia contradicts Miller's in nearly every particular. In fact, the very question that guides her investigation—"Why is the rapid growth of female prostitution not culturally problematic for the Thai?"—argues against Miller's thesis. While Muecke does not argue that the institution is completely benign or beneficial, she does emphasize a very different side of the sex trade. Muecke's conclusions are drawn from years of fieldwork or ethnographic research, entailing a close look at the practices she studied from the point of view of the insider (while Miller's conclusions are drawn mostly from already-published work). Muecke's points are discussed in the following sections.

Who Is Responsible? While Muecke does stress the role of the military as influential in the recent explosion of prostitution in Thailand, nowhere does she mention the IMF or the World Bank, multinational corporations, or the Thai government. The institutions she stresses are national and local—the Buddhist temple; the prostitute's family; and Thai norms, traditions, customs, and culture.

Who Profits from the Sex Tourist Trade? Muecke emphasizes that the women themselves, and the regions in which they work—mainly Bangkok—profit hugely from the sex trade. As we'll see momentarily, prostitutes earn enough to enable their families to purchase what most Thais are unable to buy—financial security, a house, expensive household appliances. Though Muecke would not deny that big business, local elites, and the Thai government profit from sex tourism, unlike Miller, they are not depicted as the sole beneficiaries of the sex business. In fact, Muecke's roster of characters who earn money from prostitution is quite lengthy: "pimps; procurers; owners (at least some of whom may be highly placed officials or their agents) of massage parlors, escort agencies, bars, and brothels; police and government officials," as well as taxi drivers. In addition, "minor wives," who are much like prostitutes, earn money in the service of sex.

Can the Prostitute Earn a Decent Wage? Prostitution enables women to extricate themselves from poverty. Sex workers can earn enough "to help the family of origin out of poverty or to build a foundation for their own futures." Entering the sex trade satisfies "the young woman's craving for security, both economic and domestic" (Muecke, 1992, p. 155). Sex workers can send money to their families so they can buy, as Muecke explains, both necessities and luxuries. In addition, they can pay for their younger siblings' education.

Do Women Choose to Work in the Sex Trade? The lot of the prostitute is not easy, Muecke emphasizes; typically it involves suffering in the form of physical and verbal abuse, illness, exhaustion, the possibility—and all too often, the reality—of sexually transmitted diseases, including AIDS, unsafe abortions, and of course, stigma. But she also emphasizes that, typically, the young woman's choice—Muecke specifically uses that word—is between poverty and/or abusive parents and comparative affluence and abusive clients, agents, and bar owners. For many women, the choice is made by the woman herself. Both Miller and Muecke point out that roughly one out of five Thai prostitutes are under the age of 16, and clearly, the younger the girl, the less that her personal choice comes into the picture and the more that force of one kind or another determines her behavior. Nonetheless, says Muecke, far from being a puppet on a string, she makes her decision on the basis of traditional—mainly familial and religious—values, factors that do not enter into Miller's analysis.

Are Women Stigmatized by Being Prostitutes? Prostitution is stigmatized pretty much everywhere. However, in Thailand, there are ways of washing away the stigma of prostitution. One is accomplished through making merit, that is, doing good and, hence, compensating for her stigmatizing career. There are two forms of making merit. The first is accomplished by contributing money to the local Buddhist temple, thereby providing food for its monks. Bad actions earn demerit, good actions earn merit, says Muecke. What counts is that the merit of helping the temple outweighs the demerit of prostitution. "When making merit, [the prostitute] avoids presenting herself as a prostitute." Instead, she is seen as a good Buddhist. The second way is, of course, helping her family, as we saw. Contributions to her family not only improve their material lot in life, they also give her family prestige. In short, working in the sex business removes the stigma from village daughters.

Is Prostitution a Recent or Traditional Institution? Muecke agrees that prostitution in Southeast Asia mushroomed recently, initially as a consequence of the U.S. military presence in Asia. But in discussing the historical background of Thai prostitution, Muecke goes back hundreds of years to an era when Thai women served as prostitutes to Cambodian and Chinese men, and parents and husbands could legally sell their daughters and wives into prostitution. Sex for monetary gain, she explains, has ancient roots in the region.

Is Prostitution a Local Product or a Consequence of Imposing a Practice from the Outside? According to Muecke, prostitutes uphold the same family values that their mothers—who sold food—did, but in a "grander, almost grandiose, scale." In other words, far from undermining traditional Thai norms and culture, the financial support that earning money as a prostitute yields to the prostitute's family upholds tradition—in much in the same way that their mothers in an earlier generation helped the family by selling food. Likewise, contributing money to the local Buddhist temple, again, supports traditional Thai values and norms. "Prostitutes who fulfill the cultural mandate for proper daughters are considered justified [in their actions]. They take care of parents and younger siblings financially, they return home at traditional new years . . . with gifts to receive the blessings of their elders, and they fulfill the Buddhist expectation that women support [the Buddhist monks] by donating to temples."

Jody Miller and Marjorie Muecke portray the sex business in Southeast Asia in a sharply contrasting fashion. Which of these two analyses makes the most sense to you? Are their two portraits as much a matter of empirical contradiction or are they emphasizing different aspects of this complex, many-sided deviant institution?

Feminism versus Sociology: New Directions on Prostitution?

A manifesto distributed in 2005, "Trafficking and Sexual Exploitation: Who Represents Women in Prostitution?" argues for what it refers to as the feminist position on prostitution. It claims to be the voice of women "survivors" of prostitution and includes some of the following points. (1) Women do not "choose" to become prostitutes; it is "chosen for us by poverty, past sexual abuse, the pimps who take advantage of our vulnerabilities, and the men who buy us for the sex of prostitution." (2) Prostitution is, by its very nature, a form of sexual exploitation, "one of the worst forms of women's inequality, and a violation of any person's human rights." (3) Prostitution is by its very nature violence against women. (4) Making prostitution illegal but ignoring the crimes of pimps and johns exploits and degrades prostitutes; making prostitution legal also exploits and degrades prostitutes. (5) Prostitution begins at an early age; the average worldwide is 13. (6) Prostitution should be eliminated. (7) Prostitutes need financial resources and services to leave the life of prostitution. (8) Prostitutes should not be arrested; traffickers and customers of prostitutes should be arrested. (9) Prostitution is not "sex work."

In contrast, Ronald Weitzer (2005) summarizes the sociological literature on prostitution and comes up with some very different conclusions. The radical feminist claims that prostitution is by definition exploitation and violence and that all male customers of prostitutes are woman haters, says Weitzer, "are not supported by the evidence" (p. 212). Customers vary in a variety of respects, and the vast majority of prostitute–customer relations are distinctly nonviolent. Radical feminism, Weitzer argues, uses loaded, emotive rather than scientifically neutral language. For instance, referring to prostitutes as survivors implies that they have "escaped a harrowing ordeal," does not describe the experiences of most women who engage in sex for pay. Most importantly, the radical feminist position denies workers' agency, that is, that women make a choice to enter into sex-for-pay relationships. Prostitution is not "paid rape"; in the United States, very few prostitutes are forced into sex for pay, many prostitutes are not poor, and this is especially true of most women who engage in indoor sex for pay relations. Moreover, the vast majority of women who are poor do not become prostitutes. And lastly, prostitutes themselves do not adopt a radical feminist position, contrary to the radical feminist manifesto. Almost all of the nearly 300 Miami prostitutes in one study (Kurtz et al., 2004, p. 359) refer to themselves as *sex workers* and *working women.* While the radical feminist position argues that prostitution is an essentialistic condition, true and valid for all times and places, the sociological perspective sees prostitution as a negotiable, socially constructed category whose meaning varies according to time and place, the experience of which is likewise variable in different social contexts.

EXTRAMARITAL SEX

According to Jewish and Christian tradition, Moses received the Ten Commandments directly from God. Among them, the seventh is this: "Thou shalt not commit adultery." Like the other proscriptions, it forbids an action that is tempting to many and hence frequently engaged in, and deviant as well. In fact, because it is so tempting—and because of its potentially harmful consequences—it had to be prohibited. In the absence of the prohibition, adultery would be far more commonplace than it is.

"It used to be, I'd get in the shower and my wife would come in there, too, impulsive and sexy and all," says Anthony. Not long ago, he snuck up on her in the shower. "What are you doing?" she asked. "Grow up. The kids will hear us." Anthony and his wife no longer have sex. He has had three extramarital liaisons; they only take place on business trips, far from home. "I've cheated because I just wanted to have sex and that was something my wife and I weren't doing. . . . And if what I did was away from home it doesn't count" (Konigsberg, 1998).

We already know a thing or two about the deviance of adultery.

One: Most Americans disapprove of it. In the "Sex in America" survey, as we saw, three-quarters of the sample (77%) agreed with the statement "Extramarital sex is always wrong." This condemnation is even more widespread than that for teenage sex and same-gender sex. The same finding turned up in a comparable survey conducted in Great Britain (Johnson et al., 1994, pp. 238–240, 471). Interestingly enough however, given how widespread the condemnation of adultery is, the strength of this condemnation is rather muted and qualified. In a recent national poll, only a third of the population (35%) said that adultery should be a crime (Goldberg, 1997), and a majority of the American population opposed the impeachment of President Bill Clinton, an event that was launched by his lies, under oath, about an extramarital liaison with a White House intern. In a *Newsweek* poll, only a third of the sample (35%) considered the adultery of a political candidate a sufficient reason to vote for someone else (Adler, 1996).

Two: In every Western society in which a nationally representative survey has been conducted—France, the United Kingdom, Finland, and the United States—the majority of married respondents said that they were faithful to their spouses for the entire length of their marriages. In the United States, only a quarter of the men (25%) and a bit more than one-seventh of the women (15%) in intact marriages said that they had ever had even one extramarital affair (Laumann et al., 1994, p. 216). If this survey is valid, it is clear that adultery is far less common than most of us imagine.

Three (and related to point two): As we just saw, men are significantly more likely to engage in extramarital sex than women. However, the gap may be closing: Among the oldest respondents (age 54–63) in the "Sex in America" survey, the male-to-female infidelity gap was three to one (37 vs. 12 percent), whereas among the youngest, the gap was much smaller—12 percent versus 7 percent (Adler, 1996, p. 60).

And *four:* In most of the societies of the world, a double standard exists; women are more likely to be condemned for adulterous sex than men are. As we saw, it is extremely common for societies around the world to completely tolerate (43% of all societies studied did so) or at least condone (22%) extramarital sex for the man but condemn the same behavior for the woman (Broude and Greene, 1976, pp. 415–416). Recently, however, some observers have argued that the reverse has become true: "When men cheat, they're pigs. When women do it, they're striking a blow for sexual freedom" (Roiphe, 1997, p. 54).

The motives for extramarital sex are many and varied (Hunt, 1971; Wolfe, 1976; Atwater, 1982; Lawson, 1988). The simplest reason for men and women straying from the marital bed is a response to a failing marriage. This is indicated by the fact that couples in marriages that end in divorce are vastly more likely to have adulterous sex than those in intact marriages. In this case, extramarital sex may be both cause and consequence of marital instability. At the same time, it is clear that a substantial number of stably married men and women (though not, as we saw, a majority) have intercourse with partners other than their spouses. Why? Why risk getting into trouble, being defined as a deviant, disrupting a marriage that is more or less satisfying?

Evolutionary psychologists think they have found the answer. The key, they say, can be located in the tendency of organisms, humans included, to act in such a way that they maximize the transmission of their genes to later generations. And one way of understanding this process, they claim, is the differences between males and females in responses to questions about what would be most upsetting about the infidelity of their spouse or partner. "What would distress you more," these researchers ask respondents, "discovering that he or she has formed a deep emotional attachment" to another person, or discovering that your spouse or partner "is enjoying daily passionate sex with the other person"? As it turns out, women are much more likely to be distressed by the emotional involvement of their partner, while men become more upset at their partner's sexual infidelity. Evolutionary psychologist David Buss has asked this question of samples of respondents in Germany, the Netherlands, and the United States; the differences are, says Buss, "quite solid."

The reason for the findings? This "jealousy gender gap" is encoded in our genes, says Buss and his colleagues (Buss, 1994, pp. 125–131; Buss et al. 1992). Think back to the early ancestors of humans, these researchers argue. Since men could never be certain of the paternity of their children, they are most threatened by their partner having sex with another man; if their partner becomes pregnant by him, they will thereby end up being tricked into supporting offspring who are not biologically their own. Moreover, when the male's partner is pregnant with another man's child, he is thereby prevented from impregnating her himself. What heightens a man's chances of ensuring the survival of his genes is a faithful wife. It is the winners in this competition to keep their female partners faithful who are our ancestors, evolutionary psychologists claim.

The female has a different task, they argue. If a woman's partner strays, the sexual aspect of the encounter could be over in minutes, or even seconds, and that may very well be the end of it. No threat to the long-term relationship is implied by such a liaison. But if he were to become emotionally involved with another female, he might abandon his long-term mate and thus threaten her likelihood of survival and that of her children as well—and therefore, the survival of her genetic material. In short, women are "evolutionarily programmed to become more distressed at emotional infidelity than sexual infidelity" (Begley, 1996/1997, p. 58).

Not all observers agree that jealousy is genetically encoded. Enormous variation exists from one society to another with respect to how jealous its members are at the infidelity of their partners. The male–female gap predicted by the evolutionary biologists is found everywhere, it is true, but the size of the difference varies considerably. In the United States, three times as many men as women are upset at their partner's sexual faithlessness versus their emotional infidelity; in Germany, the gap is only 50 percent. Moreover, while the relative differences between men and woman support the theory, the absolute size of the percentages runs counter to it. Evolutionary biologists predict that more men would care about sexual than emotional fidelity, in fact, most men are not disturbed more by sexual than emotional infidelity, which is totally contrary to the theory (1996/1997, p. 58).

What triggers sexual jealousy, many observers argue, is how members of each sexual category picture the connection their partner has in his or her mind between sex and love. Men's conception of female sex has it that her sexual infidelity implies emotional infidelity as well. In other words, if she has sex with another man, he assumes, that pretty much means that she loves him, too. In addition, some women can be in love with another man but not have sex with him. Hence, the man loses twice when his partner is sexually unfaithful, a more threatening situation than simple emotional infidelity, which may imply nothing beyond that. In contrast, women are aware of the fact that their male partner can have sex with another woman without loving her. But when a man forms a romantic or loving attachment to another woman, it is much more likely to be a serious threat to his relationship with the first woman.

Our awareness of what sex and sex roles mean to our partners determines the differences researchers observe. The jealousy gender gap, critics of evolutionary psychology argue, is the result of a cultural, intellectual, and to some degree "rational" process, not the nagging and largely unconscious demands of our genes. Regardless of which explanation is correct, marital infidelity is not likely to be accepted any time soon. It remains a major form of sexual deviance.

GENDER: THE CRUCIAL INGREDIENT

Understanding sexual behavior demands that the observer and analyst have a firm grasp on gender. "Heterosexuality," writes Diane Richardson, "is a category divided by gender" (1996, p. 2). The same applies to homosexuality; gay males and lesbians are not merely homosexuals but also—it seems almost obvious to say this—men and women. With regard to sexual behavior, a gender disparity looms between men and women. Male sexual behavior "is less subject to social strictures than female sexual activity" (Weitzer, 2000, p. 7). For instance, evaluations of sexual behavior vary according to the sex or gender of the actor. Thus, a sexually active teenage girl is condemned more strongly than a teenage boy; an adulterous wife is condemned more harshly than an adulterous husband. Hence, the very foundation of deviance—that is, stigma or condemnation—is dependent on who is being stigmatized or condemned, which, in turn, is based on the sex or gender of the enactor. The problem of teenage sex, pregnancy, and subsequent out-of-wedlock births is widely regarded as a problem almost exclusively of the behavior of girls. The sexual behavior of boys is considered natural, understandable, inevitable, and beyond society's control. When the authorities attempt to control teenage sex, it is specifically the sexual behavior of teenage girls that is the target of such control. Even more specifically, "female sex workers are [regarded as] quintessential *deviant women,* whereas [their] customers are seen as essentially *normal men*" (Weitzer, 2000, p. 7). Condemnation for participating in sexual deviance is much stronger for women than for men. (Of course most of the time, for women, the behavior is more central: It is a full-time paying job; whereas for men, it is little more than a part-time recreation.) The stigma of having to pay for sex is vastly less than the stigma of being paid. "The very terminology used [for women]—whore, hooker, harlot, slut—is heavily laden with opprobrium." By contrast, the terms used for male customers are "fairly tame labels." In short: "You may be a bit surprised to learn that a male friend has visited a prostitute, but shocked to learn that a female friend *is* a prostitute" (2000, p. 7). The same applies to a one-time experience.

An experiment conducted by Russell Clark and Elaine Hatfield, two social psychologists, indicates that men are much more likely to take up sexual offers from female strangers than women are to do so with male strangers; in fact, the authors suggest, women hardly ever take men up on such offers, whereas men often, even usually, do (Clark and Hatfield, 1989; Clark, 1990). Sexual behavior generally and sexual deviance more specifically are expressions or manifestations of the roles of men and women. Sex as behavior cannot be understood independent of sex as a role. In short, sex is gendered, and our understanding of sex, sexual deviance included, must incorporate gender as its foundation. It is naive to assume that a given sexual encounter between a man and a woman means the same thing to the two participants, has the same consequences, or is interpreted by members of the society in the same fashion. While men and women act and interact together, in a way they inhabit social worlds that are in large measure separate and distinct. Gendering must always inform our view of sexual deviance. Sexual nonnormativeness is usually more deviant when engaged in by women than by men; women are expected to conform more closely to sex and gender roles than men, and their transgressions are typically noticed and condemned by men (Schur, 1984).

When the paper reporting a study concluding that men are more likely to accept invitations to engage in adventurous, risky sex than women—documenting what may be the most important and significant difference between men and women—was first circulated for consideration for publication to academic journals, it attracted a great deal of hostility among researchers. One reviewer's evaluation branded the "nature and situations" of the study as "comical" and "hilarious," its propositions "incredibly naïve," and its conclusions likewise "naïve." It should, said one reviewer, "be rejected without possibility of being submitted to any scholarly journal." The study itself "lacks redeeming social value," said another reviewer. It "is too weird, trivial and frivolous to be interesting. Who cares what the result is to such a silly question"? (Clark and Hatfield, 2003, pp. 229–230). The paper, rejected by numerous journals, sat on the shelf for four years before it was sent to *Journal of Psychology and Human Sexuality.* "Times have changed," say the authors. "Today, most scientists recognize the importance of scientific knowledge about topics that were once considered taboo—love, emotions, sexual desire, sexual behavior" (2003, p. 230). Clark and Hatfield experienced a transition that Kinsey never went through: Research on sexual behavior, once itself a deviant activity, had become important and scientifically respectable.

SUMMARY

Throughout this book, I have emphasized the difference between how constructionists and essentialists view deviant phenomena. The essentialist sees sex as a drive that exists to some degree independent of and prior to social context or definition. In contrast, the constructionist position, argues two points. One, sex is constructed by the society and social contact through the imputation of meaning. And two, the sex drive itself is, in large part, a product of human contact. Constructionists argue that social dynamics are lurking behind all things sexual; sexuality is in the service of the social world. Sexuality does not shape our social conduct so much as social meanings give shape to our sexuality. We are sexual because we are social; it is social life that creates, motivates, and shapes our sexuality.

The construction process applies not only to infusing phenomena and behavior specifically with sexual meaning, but also to filling the content of sexual definitions with a certain type of evaluation—positive, negative, or neutral, "normal" or "abnormal," conventional or deviant. How deviance is socially constructed is central to any understanding of sexual behavior. It is likely that sexual deviance is more likely to be regarded as "sick," abnormal, and pathological than any other type of deviance. A central feature in the psychiatrist's and the psychologist's conception of sexual deviance is dysfunction or disorder—an undesirable condition in need of treating or curing. However, the notions of dysfunction and disorder are alien to the sociologist's, particularly the constructionist's, notion of sexual deviance. Sociologically, what defines sexual deviance, as with all other varieties of deviance, is that it is nonnormative and likely to result in the condemnation of the actor. No implication of dysfunction or disorder whatsoever is implied. Hence, the sociological conception of sexual deviance overlaps extremely imperfectly with the psychological conceptions.

A variety of dimensions determine judgments of deviance with respect to behavior in the sexual arena. Several include degree of consent, who (or what) the sexual object or partner is, specifically what behavior is engaged in, where it takes place, who engages in the sex act, how often, when, with how many partners, and so on. These dimensions proscribe or render deviant a substantial number of sexual acts. How does the sociologist of deviance decide which ones should be studied? How strongly a given behavior is condemned (some acts are not deviant enough), how frequently it is enacted (some acts are not common enough), whether it makes up a category that is well-known enough to be a form of deviance in the public's mind (some acts are not conceptualized as a deviant category, and some are too obscure to be thought about or condemned), and whether it generates a social structure (some acts are enacted by scattered, isolated individuals), will all influence the sociologist of deviance's decision.

In Western society, homosexuality is decreasingly regarded as a form of sexual deviance. Over time, a decreasing proportion of the American population believes that homosexual relations should be against the law; the media are increasingly depicting gays in a nondemeaning, nonstereotypical fashion; a growing number of Christian denominations are accepting gays as both members and clergy; the sodomy laws have been struck down as unconstitutional; Canada has legalized gay marriage; and in a growing number of jurisdictions, "civil unions," which grant partners the same rights as married couples, have been legalized. Albeit with important exceptions, increasingly, homosexuality is "departing from deviance."

Sex work encompasses a wide range of sex, both simulated and real, for pay: prostitution, massage, pornography, telephone sex, nude dancing, and being an escort. In the past, vast majority of research has been conducted on street prostitution or outdoor sex work. In contrast, indoor sex work has rarely been studied; this deficiency is currently being corrected. Sex work has been approached from a variety of perspectives, including conventional morality, functionalism, Marxism, and radical feminism, which draw very different conclusions about it. For our purposes, the ethnographic perspective, which examines prostitution from the inside, and the sociological approach, which attempts to understand how the institution works, yield the maximum intellectual payoff.

Extramarital sex is widely condemned and far more rarely practiced than most of us believe. Men and women differ in their response to their partner's infidelity. Women are more likely to be distressed by their partner's emotional faithlessness, while men are more likely to become upset about their partner's sexual infidelity. Evolutionary psychologists believe that these responses are dictated by messages encoded in the genes; social psychologists argue that it is a result of reasonable inferences about the meaning of sex roles in our society.

Sexuality is gendered. By that, sociologists mean that it is impossible to understand sexuality of any kind apart from men's and women's gender roles. Everything that we do sexually is informed or saturated by our maleness or femaleness. What are seemingly the same acts mean very different things if performed by men versus by women—both to the participants and to the society at large. We cannot understand sexual behavior without simultaneously considering who we are as males and females.

Account: Bondage and Discipline Sex

The following account was written by Jackie, a college student at the University of Maryland. She describes her participation in "bondage and discipline" sex.

I am a 21-year-old bisexual female, who, in the BDSM [bondage-discipline-sadism-masochism] community, is known as a "switch." I was raised Catholic in an interesting sort of family life. My mother is a diagnosed antisocial psychopath. My father raised his siblings because his mother was the town drunk while his dad abused both him and his siblings; he then in turn grew up to be a rage-aholic, a verbal and physical child abuser. I lived off and on with my "grandmother"—one of my half sister's grandparents—who has been more of a parent than anyone else. I began studying psychology in an attempt to work with children so I would be able to remove them from the sorts of abusive situations I had to endure as a child. . . .

I have always thought women were attractive. I remember watching beautiful women when I was younger. My mother was a beautiful woman. . . . My mother was a very sexual woman, and there was a constant stream of men in the house. She used them to get things, not for sex—that was part of her disorder. Because of this I grew up seeing men and women in much the same light. I don't think I fully admitted this to myself until I was in college. I have always done a lot of nudes in my paintings, females preferably because I like their lines better. When I visited my high school art teacher—also a close friend—because I was having a crisis over the stress of admitting I was gay, she informed me she had known that since she met me. Even my guy friends in high school knew. Recently, I asked John how he knew about me. He said the

(*Continued*)

Account: Bondage and Discipline Sex Continued

whole time he had known me I had looked at men and women with the same interest and desire, whereas usually, people choose one or the other. Specifically, he said, most men look at women and drool, whereas he looked at other attractive men and wished he looked more like them. John said I looked at attractive women *and* men with a drooling look. . . .

At one point, I tried telling my grandmother. I could never tell my mother—she was a gay-basher—or my father, whom I don't feel close to. My grandmother said it was a phase. At some point or another, every woman had fantasies about other women. She "knew me," she said. I'd meet some knight in shining armor and get married; I'd live in a nice house surrounded by a picket fence. Besides, she'd say, even if I were a lesbian—it wasn't possible to like both sexes, she believed—I could never marry another woman. And I couldn't live in sin—I was a Catholic, after all. And so I'd have to live my life alone.

I've had relationships primarily with men, but a few with women. Men are easier to come by. There is more of a selection of males to choose from, and I am picky with the people I date. It's harder finding same-sex partners, although it's easier living so close to a big city than in a less urban area. I'm not openly gay. My first gay relationship was with Emily, my best friend in high school. I was at her house, fooling around with a guy friend. I was young and most definitely stupid. I remember feeling uncomfortable with this guy. . . . I really wasn't into fooling around with this guy, but he was and he kept going. Finally I called Emily over and she began kissing me on the neck and breasts and I felt exhilarated. We drove our friend home and she and I talked. Apparently, we have been attracted to each other since we had met but we were just afraid to act on your desires. Within the week, we were dating and were constantly with one another. My family knew that she was my best friend, so they didn't suspect anything. Her mom knew about us but she also knew how much we cared for each other as friends, so she never minded me staying over, although we never had sex when we stayed over. There are some things I just considered too uncomfortable.

I've always believed in monogamy no matter who my partner was. I always hated the stigma that bisexuals are "easy," into having sex with as many people as possible simply because they like both sexes. . . . Even now most of my friends don't know I am bisexual. Definitely not my roommates or my mother. My roommates are a little more tolerant than my mother, but when you're living in a house full of girls, they start getting uncomfortable. One of my housemates in particular, Jennifer . . . had a run-in because one of her past roommates was bi and told her not to worry because she wasn't attracted to her. Instead of feeling less anxious, she got insulted. It's like me saying, I am not going to grope you in your sleep so you can rest easy and not live in terror.

During my freshman year . . . , I worked in an office in a work-study program. I didn't think anything of being bisexual until one day my supervisor began talking about a guy in the department she thought was gay. I couldn't believe it when I heard her refer to this kind, intelligent man as a "fag," then she began making jokes about the fact that he was a homosexual. I wanted to crawl into my skin . . . and never come out. I knew if anyone at my job found out I would be harassed or, even worse, I'd lose my job. . . . Sometimes the nicest people make a complete change of face when they find out someone is gay. There is a lot of stigma associated with being bisexual. Most people think we are lascivious, can't make up our minds, sick, perverse—you name it, we are pretty much labeled. . . .

I think about who will be reading this account. I hardly share any of this with outsiders. If anyone were to find out how I lead my sexual life, I could lose all credibility as a therapist simply because of the stigma of how perverse I am. . . . The things I do would shock anyone I guess. For as long as I can remember seeing men and women tied up, spanked, smacked, or interacting in violent or sexually aggressive ways has always been a turn-on [for me]. No one else I knew seemed to have these feelings. Having had the background I did, I couldn't tell if it was my own form of self-abuse, mental illness, or seeking the familiar. My childhood was very abusive. . . . I thought it may be possible that I seek humiliation, abuse, and power in relationships because I was trying to act out familiar patterns. That didn't really make sense, though, since in sex, I played the dominant or dominatrix role. I have always had some form of a power dynamic in my relationships, even with partners who weren't into being kinky. The first woman I dated I told her that I had a surprise. I came home blindfolded and I tied her up and tickled and tease her as I watched her writhe until I was satisfied that her release and satisfaction were completely dependent on my will. In the beginning, I didn't really consider it kinky, I saw it mainly as experimentation.

Most of the time my actions got really negative responses. I can remember one guy I dated in high school. When I pulled his hair and tried to bite his neck, he kinda freaked out. From then on in that relationship, I never tried anything out of order again. I did remain the "top" partner, though, the person who causes the sensation. That was doing what I wanted—getting my way, staying in control, and enjoying every minute of it. I wanted to take the dominant role in pleasing a partner. At the time, I didn't realize there was a community and a literature about all this that explained that what I was doing could please both me and my partner. Women were a lot more welcoming with my tendencies than men. Men never seemed to understand what I was up to, or they would see my dominance as challenging their masculinity. The women I dated liked being tied up, blindfolded, bitten, degraded, smacked, and used sexually. I guess this is one reason why I always like to dominate women. I don't think another woman could ever dominate me. I just don't have that mind-frame. I enjoy watching them too much.

You could look at this and say that I am trying to assume a power role because I was badly abused in childhood. Being dominant in my sexual relationships is safer because I call the shots. But the fact is, I never really saw myself as a victim. In school, when I was living with my parents, I thought these behaviors—shaking, hitting, punching, being thrown across the room, leaving bruises—happened to everyone. When I was living with my mom, I hadn't known anything different. My sense of what should happen in a family was kind of skewed. I've thought a lot about it, though. Maybe my whole reason for seeing this as interesting and arousing is that it uses sex as manipulation as my mom did. It's a possibility; she was my earliest role model. No one can be born liking this, right? When I was younger, I still viewed this as sick and twisted.

Every time I was abused at home, I swore I would never hurt anyone like that. So I went through extreme bouts of cognitive dissonance. I was thinking along one track while trying to do the exact opposite. For me, sexual activity was fun, but without certain elements, I never really got fulfilled. There came a time when I knew I wanted to try something different. I wanted to be in the other role. I wanted to be subservient. I craved it. I tried prompting boyfriends at the time by bringing up non-scary items, such as scarves. I could tell there was something wrong with me. I still wasn't fulfilled because those boyfriends were terrible at doing what I wanted them to do, but I was also terrible at trying to explain how to do it in a way that wouldn't send them running. So I continued to remain dominant.

Don't get me wrong: Bad things can happen during both during sex and during a relationship. There is a population of people who believe that bondage and discipline is all about force—real abuse, real rape. I had a relationship with a guy. For a while, things were pretty good. I was usually dominant, but occasionally, things switched the other way. He became verbally and emotionally abusive, taking out his anger at his exes on me. He eerily reminded me of my father. We were very volatile, providing catalysts for one another. We went through phases when we

(*Continued*)

Account: Bondage and Discipline Sex Continued

would cut things off and end up sleeping with one another, over and over again. I thought maybe we could be just friends, but I realized I was being naïve and foolish. One night, I went to his place thinking that he was going to help me find parts for my car. When he wanted to have sex, I told him no. I tried to pull away from him but couldn't because he was stronger. He tied me up from hand to foot. Before, we had played with handcuffs and ropes, but I just never thought he would use them without my consent. I felt very violated that night. I walked home, shaking. I couldn't sleep. I sat on the fire escape outside my bedroom, smoked two packs of cigarettes, and watched the sun rise. . . . I thought that if I kept doing these bad things I would end up with more people who would take advantage of me. My next relationship was with a very conventional guy. I guess there's a Catch-22 situation here: When I engaged in bondage and discipline, bad things happened; when I didn't, bad things happened.

The conventional guy, we talked about marriage and kids, but he hated anything even remotely kinky, even the non-scary things. He saw bondage and discipline as abusive to women. He accused me of being a nymphomaniac—apparently all I wanted was sex. I became extremely depressed and began taking antidepressants. I realize now that I wasn't satisfied with the sex I engaged in, so I tried to make up with it in quantity. He ended the relationship, and I got upset because he was perfect for leading the life my family wanted me to lead: the husband, the family, a two-car garage, a good income—and most definitely no collars or handcuffs. I felt guilty about the failure of the relationship. I had screwed up what would have been perfect if I could just be normal. This was everything I was supposed to want by conventional standards. I won't ever have a normal life, I thought. . . .

I started visiting specialty adult stores. I accumulated a little collection of the toys I enjoyed. This is part of me, I realized. When I fight who I am, I end up miserable. It didn't take me long to get over this guy.

Through a friend, I met Jason, the guy I've had my most recent relationship with. I completely brushed him off, and he thought I was a total bitch. We met again three months later. We decided to change our stances toward one another. At first, we talked as friends online. He told me things about myself no one had ever bothered to notice. He was supportive when we were talking about sex. He felt the same things. He had problems with sex earlier because he didn't want to see himself as abusive. He took the teacher role, showing me books and answering my questions. He wasn't sickened by me and he gave me an opportunity to fulfill my need for being submissive. He became my friend, lover, and above all, master. He explained what being submissive entails. The dominant partner has to earn the trust and respect from the submissive to play the role. He told me that whatever may go on in the bedroom—degradation, humiliation—they happen because the submissive partner wishes to fulfill the role that involves those activities. He would treat me in this way because he respects the dynamic between us. In turn, I would allow him to treat me like that because I would have the control to say who treats me as such and when. He also set up what's called a "safe word" for me. Sometimes things can become so intense that the words you might speak in a typical dialogue during a scene won't stop the action. You need a safe word that you would never say during a scene that would be a signal to stop the action so that the participants can try to fix anything that may be going wrong. S&M is all about communication. My safe word is "blue." I think I picked it because I think primarily in colors and it reminds me of feeling scared. It seemed right.

We have a library of books that explain techniques of the bondage and dominance "lifestyle." Occasionally, when I'm reading one of them, one of my roommates will walk in and see my book, and so I explain it away as a book for research on deviance or aesthetics or some other such thing. As for my toys, they are usually kept in a duffle bag or in drawers in my closet. . . . One aspect of the bondage and discipline lifestyle is covering up evidence of how we live, including bruises and bite marks, or simply putting away the toys so that no one will ever find out about it and accuse us of abuse. We have many friends in the bondage and discipline community because it tends to be very tight-knit. We choose to keep it private among ourselves. . . .

Some people in this community find romance in pieces of glass—that is, bloodletting, cutting the skin to achieve sexual arousal. I enjoy many different things. Sometimes the simple act of being tied or having something placed around my neck will send me into a frenzy of arousal, wanting to do anything to please to earn pleasure. Sometimes I surprise Jason by setting up a scene for him when he comes home from work. One such scene involved 12 lit candles lining each side of the corridor to the bedroom door and red rose petals scattered on the floor. Inside the bedroom, I trailed petals up to the bed with candles lighting the windowsill. A rope trailed zig-zag through the petals under the door and onto the bed, there, connected to the collar I was wearing. It was then my turn to wait, having mentally prepared myself for him to come home, when he would decide what happened next. One night, paddling or flogging; the next night, maybe hot wax, anal intercourse, or bondage and teasing.

There is a sensation called "floating" a lot of submissives describe. It's when you get so far into your personal head-space that sensation floods you and everything feels like soft pillows. After we have a vigorous scene, my master usually gathers me into his arms or holds me and we talk about everything we felt and went through in our minds, things that happened—and maybe didn't happen—during the session. This is the most fulfilling and loving relationship I have been in. . . . In the morning, we're like every other couple. We get up and shower, brush our teeth, dress and the like, and go about our normal lives, for him it is his work, for me to school and therapy sessions—where we await the next time we see each other. When we get together, we're distinctly not like other couples. . . .

It excites me to think I will be able to spend the rest of my life with someone who fills me with such joy—emotionally, intellectually, and physically. Someone who pushes me to be the best I can, someone who makes me dinner when I am stressed or gives me a backrub or surprises me by putting up Christmas lights, or bringing my favorite candies for a devious blindfolded study break. Someone who won't judge me. To me that doesn't seem deviant. It's really all in the way you look at it.

I have a job I enjoy tremendously, trying to make the lives of children better. I am in my last year of college. I won't talk about private members clubs for bondage and discipline participants in my deviance course because all eyes would turn to me in accusation. If people in my everyday life knew about my sex life, they would accuse me of bring sick, being just like a child molester, accuse me of doing things with my clients with the same ignorant thought processes that lead people to think you can "catch" homosexuality. I won't discuss anything that happened the night before, when I subjected myself to any number of abuses and perversities. I will put on the mask of a confident, conventional, heterosexual woman. I will hope that I remembered to put all my toys away, that I haven't left a trail that may lead to being scrutinized, judged, evaluated, stigmatized. And I will love being comfortable, finally, with who I am.

Everyone wants to feel accepted. I spent most of my life either not admitting things to myself or thinking I was a bad person because I felt a certain way. Now that I feel accepted in one area of my life, I have a much easier time separating the two halves of my life and not worrying about one affecting the other as much. Now that I have confidence in my sexual self, I am much more confident in my social self. Jason says it is funny that my family never liked any of the guys I dated in the past who were supposed to be so acceptable. Now that my family knows Jason—the one person who shouldn't be acceptable—they've fallen in love with him. Jason says, "Being comfortable allows other people to be comfortable with you."

(*Continued*)

Account: Bondage and Discipline Sex Continued

I don't consider myself "normal" in the way that the "American dream" is normal, but I am the way I want to be.

Questions

What's your reaction to Jackie's behavior? Do you accept her notion that it should be regarded as normal? Does it challenge the meaning of the concept "normality"? Sociologists do not use the term "normal"; instead, they prefer to refer to such behavior as "nonnormative" or deviant. Jackie's behavior would certainly be regarded as nonnormative or deviant by the majority of the American public. She is aware of that fact by keeping her sexual activities a secret from others. How would a psychologist or psychiatrist regard this behavior? Is it likely to disrupt conventional social arrangements? Or, if it is kept secret, is it more likely to have no impact on them at all? Do sociologists of deviance pay too much attention to what Alexander Liazos (1972) contemptuously referred to as "nuts, sluts, and deviated preverts"? Or is that attention appropriate, given its subject matter? Why have radical sociologists such as Liazos argued that the attention sociologists of deviance pay to behavior such as Jackie's is a kind of bias? Do you agree? Which is more interpersonally stigmatizing: corporate crime or Jackie's sexual activities? Which shocks the public conscience more? What theories might positivist sociologists and psychologists have about devotees of S&M sex such as Jackie?

CHAPTER

10

Deviant Organizational Behavior

During the course of at least two decades, Bernard Madoff, an investment broker, committed the largest financial fraud ever carried out by a single individual. He swindled his 4,800 clients out of between $50 and $65 *billion.* Chances are investors will retrieve only pennies on the dollar for their losses. His victims included charities and foundations, banks, schools and universities, corporations, a senator, a motion picture producer, a motion picture director, a famous motion picture actor, a Hall of Fame baseball pitcher, the owner of the Philadelphia Eagles, the owner of the New York *Daily News,* lawyers, accountants, and investors—the list is long, impressive, and hugely monied. Many of his clients invested everything they had with Madoff, and lost their entire investments to his flimflam.

Madoff ran what is called a "Ponzi scheme," named after a 1930s swindler who looted funds from later investors so that he could pay off earlier ones. And meanwhile, he and his wife enjoyed a lavish lifestyle beyond the imagination of most of us. In the courtroom, victims expressed their outrage at Madoff and his crimes, calling him a "monster," a "beast," and "an evil lowlife." Judge Denny Chin, who presided over the case, noted that of the more than 100 letters he had received about the case, not one expressed support for the defendant or described a single good deed he had performed. "The absence of such support," said Judge Chin, "is telling." He sentenced Madoff to a 150-year sentence; the swindler's release date is listed as November 23, 2754. Barring a fatal illness and early release, Madoff will spend the rest of his life in a federal penitentiary in North Carolina. In addition, the court stripped Madoff and his wife of their financial assets, including a $7 million Manhattan apartment, an $11 million estate in Palm Beach, a $4 million property at the tip of Long Island, and a $2.2 million yacht. Madoff represents a classic case of a white-collar crime; he could not have committed his theft if he had not been in a position to convince his victims to hand over their billions to him, willingly, in the expectation that they would earn more by investing with him.

For our purposes, two features of the Bernard Madoff case are interesting: One, the perpetrator could not have committed his crimes without occupying a position as investor; and two, he did not commit his crimes by means of violence or the threat of violence. Almost as interesting: Unlike the past, when white-collar criminal received a "slap on the wrist" penalty for crimes that entailed frauds totaling huge sums of money, Madoff received a sentence characteristic of violent offenders, such as murderers. Perhaps this is a tendency that will carry over into the future.

The agency of most deviant acts we've looked at in this book can traced to a single individual—as influenced by the usual cultural, social, and collective forces, but individual (or group) actions nonetheless: murder, rape, robbery, drug use, alcoholism, and so on. And it is these individuals who are socially designated as "deviants." This is a form of deviance in which *any* member of the society could engage or be designated as "having." (Or, in the case of rape, any member with the anatomically correct characteristics could enact.) It is the individual who is the focus of the origin of judgments of deviance; *all* individuals in the society are designated with respect to the deviance or conventionality of their beliefs or mental or physical condition. Individual deviance corresponds to two of Goffman's famous trilogy—that is, first, behavior or conditions that indicate blemishes of individual character, and second, physical traits that are considered abominations of the body. And Goffman's "stigma of tribe, religion, and nation" likewise locates *each and every person* along an axis of degrees of acceptability versus unacceptability. They are relevant for *everyone* (or almost everyone) in *every* society on earth.

A different type of deviance entails individuals who act as embodiments of a particular organization and *within an organization setting.* The act *could not* have been performed without the actor's location *within* that setting. In this category, we find embezzlement by bank tellers, the sexual molestation of children by priests, sexual harassment by professors against students, and the police use of excessive force against citizens. This is a form of deviance that results in condemnation and judgments of deviance against the perpetrator, if caught, but it is a form of deviance that *cannot* be enacted by just anyone; it is the individual's position within a given organization setting that facilitates, permits, or *enables* the perpetration of the act. In other words, only *some* members of the society, those who are embedded within a given organizational structure, can be designated as falling along a continuum of deviance or conventionality. Most of the members of the society never fall within the scope of this evaluation process because they never hold a position that gives them the opportunity to engage in the relevant deviant behavior.

Even less individual are the forms of deviance that entail actions whose *setting* is organizational and whose *agency* is organizational, where, in a sense, individual initiative is of no consequence, where, strictly speaking, it is the organizational setting that generated the act. Here, we find most corporate crimes. In most such schemes, the actions are collective products of many minds that rarely if ever have a single author or originator; take one or another actor out of the picture and the outcome is the same.

In this sense, organizational deviance stands outside Goffman's trilogy. They can *only* be enacted by persons who have a particular position in a particular organization. Only a corporate executive can engage in corporate crime. Only a police officer can engage in police corruption or police brutality. Anyone can steal, but only an employee can pilfer *as an* employee; only an employee of a firm can embezzle, for instance. Only a professor (or a teaching assistant) can demand sex for a grade from a student. And so on. In other words, with respect to *being judged as a deviant,* a given form of organizational deviance is completely *irrelevant* for most of the members of the society. Unlike individual and even collective deviance, with organizational deviance, most of us stand *outside* the process that evaluates the behavior, beliefs, and traits of the members of the society as potential forms of deviance. As *actors,* many forms of organizational deviance do not touch our lives at all. Of course, as *victims,* many forms of organizational deviance touch all our lives.

One of the most interesting aspects of behavior that takes place within an organization is that judgments of deviance vary considerably according to where someone stands. By that I mean acts that are *not* regarded as reprehensible *within* the organization, or in different segments of the organization, *are* regarded as wrong in the society at large, by people who hold certain political views, or by the law. In other words, judgments of deviance *by* different audiences are to some degree separate and independent of one another. For instance, the police have their own interpretation of what constitutes "normal" force required to subdue a suspect. This interpretation differs from what they learned in the academy, different from what the law says, and different from what members of the community regard as acceptable (Hunt, 1985). Likewise, business executives recognize that no product can be risk free, that all products carry a certain measure of potential harm to consumers—a position many consumers are unwilling to accept. Employees often convince themselves that a little pilfering from the company they work for is just compensation for low pay; executives in that company are likely to disagree. In other words, condemnation of the behavior—the designation or social construction that the behavior is deviant to begin with—depends on where one stands, either inside or outside the organization, as well as within the organization itself.

In addition, a great deal of organizational malfeasance is kept secret by the higher-ups in organizations. Trusted employees who are discovered to have abused financial trust by embezzling funds are rarely turned over to the police. (Unless the sums are very large.) Instead, they are simply fired. For many years, when the criminal abuse of children by priests was reported to authorities in the Catholic Church, it was nearly always covered up; offending priests were simply transferred to another parish, and the police were almost never notified. (Now that the media have uncovered and reported this scandal, this age-old practice is no longer as possible.) The "blue wall of silence" in police departments around the country is legendary (although we'll see in this chapter that the matter isn't quite as simple as this phrase suggests). In short, typically, organizations protect their own. This doesn't always occur, but it is the modal or most common response. Cover-ups are an interesting and important aspect of the deviance process.

Organizational deviance is important not only with respect to judgments made against its enactors but also with respect to its causes. The opportunity to engage in certain forms of deviance is *structured* according to occupational position. The most basic reason why the occupants of certain organizational statuses engage in specific forms of deviance is that they are in a position to do so. On the most fundamental level, as I just pointed out, some forms of behavior *cannot be committed at all,* except by occupants of particular positions. Corporate crime is the obvious example. With others, a given position gives the occupants almost unparalleled *opportunities* for committing deviance. Bank tellers handle thousands upon thousands of dollars in cash every day; they have the opportunity, and the skills, to embezzle money that the occupants of almost no other position enjoy. Since employees are exposed to volumes of merchandise and office supplies, they too have access to the crime of employee theft and pilferage. Professors who have a monopoly on the distribution of what is a valued commodity to large numbers of young, attractive students—good grades—are in a *structural* position to engage in an illicit, unethical exchange of grades for sex. What I'm saying is that anyone with the inclination to engage in certain forms of behavior will be tempted by the prospect—*which is generated by structural position alone.* Many, probably most, occupants of these positions will *not* be tempted by the prospect of violating organizational norms. Unethical professorial threats of low grades unless a student engaged in sex were much more common in the past; because of extremely strong sanctions against such threats, they are less common today. Only a very tiny percentage of priests are interested in, let alone have sex with, children in their pastoral care—but the position they occupy will provide opportunities for those who are so inclined. In some organizations, the norms and the sanctions against deviant actions are so strong as to minimize them.

Organizational deviance helps in our quest to explain deviance in a second way as well. In addition to the structural difference between occupants of certain organizations and the persons who do not occupy an organizational position, causality also comes into the picture when we compare organizations with one another. Some organizations have extremely high rates of deviance within their ranks, while others have low rates. Why? While there are many reasons, it is clear that *institutional climate* influences the enactment of deviant acts within a given organizational setting. Corporations whose executives strongly and openly oppose, monitor, and sanction the illegal behavior of their underlings are likely to have less of it than the corporations whose executives seem indifferent or even encourage such behavior. The same principle applies to police malfeasance in different precincts. Hence, if we are explaining organizational deviance, clearly, we have to look to institutional climate, which is itself largely a product of social control issuing from the top of the organization. Institutional climate also applies to changes in time. The police are vastly less likely to use the same level of force that was routine a generation or more ago. Today, Catholic priests cannot molest children and get away with it as they did a few years ago, because the institutional climate of the Church has changed.

The members of organizations, taken as a whole, seek to perpetuate the organization in which they are located—in a phrase, to ensure that it will survive and succeed. Certain actions that are regarded as deviant *outside* the organization are actually endorsed, encouraged, and rewarded *by* and *within* the organization. They are endorsed because they are thought to further the organization's interests. Other actions are discouraged, punished, and regarded as deviant by the organization. They are believed to be (and, objectively speaking, they actually are) harmful to the organization. In the former category we find much (although not all) corporate crime, where the perpetrator is the organization. To be more precise, the perpetrator *is* made up of the top echelon of the corporation. Corporate crime is by definition illegal behavior that is enacted *on behalf of* the corporation. In the latter category we find most (although not all) embezzlement, when an employee steals *from* a corporation. Unlike corporate crime, embezzlement is a crime *against* a corporation. The police are enjoined to enforce the law, but certain law enforcement circumstances lead individual officers to engage in actions, originally thought to be a product of police mandate, that turn out to have been a mistake: firing at a suspect who *might be* reaching for a gun but isn't, stopping and frisking suspects who are completely innocent but fit a certain profile, and searching a dwelling that turns out to have been a wrong address.

WHITE-COLLAR AND CORPORATE CRIME

Here, I'd like to focus on corporate crime, but to do so, I have to introduce the parent concept that gave birth to it—white-collar crime. Corporate crime is a subset of white-collar crime. That is, all corporate crime is white-collar crime, but not all white-collar crime is corporate crime. What is white-collar crime? As it was originally defined by Edwin Sutherland in a speech to the American Sociological Association in 1939 (and later formulated in print), white-collar crime is *an illegal action that is committed by the occupant of high occupational status in the course of his or her professional activity* (1940, 1949).

Exactly how "high" the occupational status in question must be to qualify need not concern us; clearly, we are not referring to manual laborers, but it does include bank clerks. Even embezzlement, a relatively lowly white-collar crime, is committed by persons who work in occupations that rank in the top half of the class structure. This definition *excludes* "common" or conventional crimes. An executive who murders his wife (or her husband) has committed a crime of violence, not a white-collar crime. It also excludes theft and pilferage from the job; this is larceny-theft, an Index Crime category in the Uniform Crime Reports. And it excludes acts that someone may see as unethical and/or harmful but are not against the law, such as manufacturing and selling cigarettes, selling legal but dangerous products, and taking "three martini lunches." If an act is not a violation of a legal code and does not call for a punitive sanction, that is, a jail or prison sentence—or at least a punitive fine—then it is not a white-collar *crime.*

The stereotype of white-collar criminals is that they are all rich and powerful. In fact, this is far from true. In fact, Weisburd et al. (1991), who examined a cross-section of offenders convicted in federal court of a variety of white-collar crimes, including securities fraud; antitrust violations; bank embezzlement; and postal, tax, and credit fraud, found that these offenders did not fit the usual portrait of white-collar criminals as occupying high-status positions. True, given the fact that they are *white-collar* offenders, by definition, they were not manual laborers. But a remarkably high proportion occupied the very lowest rungs of the white-collar status hierarchy. Many were unemployed at the time of their arrest or held fairly humble jobs, did not have a college education, and did not own their own house. At the time of the arrest that led to their conviction, offenders were twice as likely to have had a past criminal record than the national average. The authors (p. 190) conclude that most white-collar offenders are ordinary people who got into financial difficulty and who saw their way out of it through illegal and fraudulent measures. They were "struck by the banal, mundane quality of the vast majority of criminals" in their sample (pp. 45–46); the majority of their crimes "have an undramatic, local or regional quality," a "common, familiar ring." Say the authors, business fraud is "as familiar in their business context as are street crimes in poor communities" (p. 46).

I would not refer to most of the white-collar criminals who are caught and convicted as organizational deviants. Most are individual deviants—petty thieves who act on their own, outside an organizational setting, criminals who engage in acts that are not classified as street crimes. What they do, anyone can do; their actions are not specific and unique to any particular organization setting. Hence, their actions fall outside the scope of this chapter.

The fact is, what most people mean by white-collar crime is *corporate crime.* While all corporate crime is white-collar crime, corporate crime is a specific *form* or *subtype* of white-collar crime. To be precise about it, corporate crime entails executives and executive officers engaging in illegal actions that are intended to further the interests of that corporation; they are actions taken *on behalf of* the corporation. (In so doing, they may *also* benefit the careers of the individual corporate actors, but that is a different matter.) This type of crime clearly contrasts with individual embezzlement, which is undertaken *against* the corporation *on behalf of* a given employee or several employees. In embezzlement, the victim is the corporation. In corporate crime, the victim, or potential victim, is the *general public* (in the case of illegal pollution), the *consumer* (in the case of price-fixing or the sale of illegally unsafe products), the *employee* (such as illegally unsafe working conditions), the *government* (for instance, illegal tax avoidance), or a *competitor* (two firms forming a price-fixing conspiracy against a third). And the criminal act was performed not only *in the context* of the corporation but also *on behalf of* the corporation. While, as we saw, the majority of white-collar criminals are low level, unsuccessful bottom-feeders who are trying to scrape by with petty, illegal scams to cheat and defraud their victims, the same is not true of corporate criminals.

Corporate crime is not a classic, clear-cut case of deviance. *In some respects,* it is a form of deviant behavior; in some respects, it is *not.* In the sense that audiences designate corporate actions that harm people physically and take money out of their pockets as serious crimes (Friedrichs, 2004), they are a form of deviance. To the extent that illegal corporate actions are likely to result in prosecution and a jail or prison sentence, they are deviant. To the extent that a conviction and a jail or prison sentence for a corporate crime is stigmatizing, *personally discrediting,* that it *taints* the character of the offender (for instance, if friends and loved ones regard mention of it in an obituary inappropriate, a "smear"), then clearly, it is a form of deviance. To the extent that there are social circles in this society made up of persons who define executive misdeeds as serious wrongdoing, and attempt to legitimate that view in the society as a whole, then they are indeed a form of deviance *in those circles.*

On the other hand, to the extent that seeing harmful corporate crime, however serious, does *not* result in jury conviction for offenders or stiff prison sentences (Friedrichs, 2004), then it is *not* deviant. To the extent that social circles define the actions that corporate offenders engage in as acceptable and characterize their prosecution a "witchhunt," then, clearly, in those circles, such actions are *not* deviant. Just because corporate actions are unethical, harm people, and are formally against the law, it does not automatically make them deviant *to relevant audiences.* Just because we, or persons very much like us, don't like what executives do, it can't magically make their behavior deviant. *Are corporate misdeeds condemned by the public?* Are they commonly *prosecuted* by the criminal justice system? Can corporate wrongdoers get into *trouble* as a result of their actions? Are such corporate actors socially *stigmatized* by their actions? If the answer is yes, then absolutely—corporate crime is deviant. If the answer is no, then corporate crime is *not* a deviant act. What we see, instead, is something of an in-between case. Clearly, corporate crime has one foot in conventionality and one in deviance. This is one of the reasons why it is so interesting.

Corporate crime is wrongdoing in high places. We do not expect the executive or lawyer to engage in crime, or to be prosecuted, convicted, and be sent to prison. Most of us have a conception of crime that *precludes* the respectability of the offender. Crime is what street people—or at least, poor people—do. There is, as many observers have pointed out, a certain *incongruity* in seeing an affluent, 60-year-old banker in handcuffs and a prison uniform, being marched off to a prison cell, to serve time with murderers, rapists, and burglars. Many of us can understand the motives of poor, powerless criminals, who steal out of desperation or commit violence as a result of anger and frustration. The crimes of the rich and the powerful are puzzling to us, however; if someone can earn a sizable income legally, why try to earn even more in an illegal fashion? Why risk one's current material comfort and freedom simply to gain an edge over one's competitors? Is it greed? To many casual observers, corporate crime doesn't make a great deal of sense.

The fact is corporate crime is similar to all *instrumental* actions, that is, those that are designed to achieve a certain goal; under certain circumstances, achievement of the goal assumes far greater importance than the means by which the goal was attained (Merton, 1938). One major *subtype* of—but by no means all—deviant behavior takes place when the actor resorts to *illegitimate* means to achieve a *legitimate* goal. If the likelihood of detection is extremely low, resorting to *legal* or *legitimate* means to attain that goal is actually quite *irrational,* since, typically, they are less efficient and less effective. Following legal procedures usually ties the corporate actor down to rules, regulations, and restrictions that may actually prevent or frustrate the achievement of desired goals. In the corporate world, we are forced to ask this: "Given the great rewards and low risks of detection, why do so many business people adopt the 'economically irrational' course of obeying the law" (Braithwaite, 1985, p. 6)?

The same logic is not unique to the business world—nor even to capitalist society. Students often cheat on exams because it gets them what they want—a higher grade; shoppers may shoplift clothes, again, because it permits them to have what they cannot otherwise afford; many of us lie because, once again, in so doing, we attain what we desire—respect, admiration, or getting out of a sticky situation. When legitimate or conventional avenues make the attainment of a goal difficult or impossible, many of us, whether as individual or as corporate actors, will resort to illegitimate or deviant avenues. But the conditions that create the impulse to deviate are widespread, not confined to business dealings. "Some organizations seek profits, others seek survival, still others seek to fulfill government-imposed quotas, others seek to service a body of professionals who run them, some seek to win wars, and some seek to serve a clientele. Whatever the goals might be, it is the emphasis on them that creates trouble" (Gross, 1978, p. 72). The problem here is not the worm in the apple—it is the apple itself.

CORPORATE CRIME: CORRELATIVE FEATURES

There are also *correlative* features of corporate crime, aspects of what it is like that are a *product* of its defining criteria. What are they? Imagine describing corporate crime to someone who knows nothing about the phenomenon; what would our description look like? Let's look at eight of the most essential features of corporate crime.

First, as to the nature of the behavior itself: Corporate crime tends to be made up of *complex, sophisticated,* and relatively *technical* actions. Imagine witnessing or watching a videotape of a robbery or a murder; most of the time, we'd be able to unambiguously identify the act *as* a crime. In contrast, corporate crime would not be so readily identified. How do we know a corporate crime when we see one? When we watch a videotape of an armed robbery, we know an armed robbery is in process. In contrast, a videotape of a corporate crime would result in a more ambiguous judgment from an audience. It might even take an expert—an accountant, for example, an industrial chemist, a physician, or a government official—to determine its illegal status. The way that a corporate crime is committed is complex and interactional. At a board meeting of executives, a proposal is made and discussed. Memos are exchanged; decisions are made, policies are put into practice. Much of the time, it is not clear whether a crime in fact took place. Even experts may have trouble deciding. Even *victims* may not know that they have been victimized. Of course, the criminal status of some actions is more clear-cut than others, but for most, it is far less clear-cut than for most street crimes. This is because these actions tend to be complex, sophisticated, and technical. In contrast, the meaning of street crime is more direct and unambiguous.

Second, corporate crime tends to be *intermingled with legitimate behavior.* Illegal advertising claims are made in the context of a legal, legitimate advertising industry; some exaggeration is considered acceptable and is legal. But how much is too much? Monopolistic restraints of trade are carried out in a capitalistic business environment in which all corporations attempt to capture a larger share of the market; most of such attempts are legal and are considered good business practice, while some are illegal and go too far. Even embezzlement is enacted within the context of ordinary, routine workaday activities, such as entering numbers into an accountant's ledger. While *some* traditional street crimes are also "intermingled with legitimate behavior" (date rape, e.g., is a product of extremely aggressive courtship practices), most is not. It is difficult to imagine, let's say, what legitimate behavior a robbery or a burglary is intermingled with. With street crime, the crime act is illegal *in its totality.*

A third characteristic of corporate crime is that *victimization tends to be diffuse.* Harm is not always conceptualized or identifiable as such because it is usually spread out over a substantial number of victims. Again, this represents a sharp contrast with street crime. A rape harms a specific woman; a robbery, a specific store; a murder, obviously, the deceased victim as well as his or her survivors. But with corporate crimes, harm is usually spread out, usually thinly to many victims. Monopolistic practices may result in us being charged, let's say, $1,000 more for the purchase of a new car, a quarter more for a half-gallon of milk, and $2 more for a pair of jeans. Even where there is physical harm, victimization can usually be measured in terms of *statistical odds* and *chances* rather than in a direct, one-to-one fashion. Pollution hardly ever kills or harms everyone exposed to it. Instead, it increases our *likelihood* of getting sick and dying prematurely. For instance, if a factory pollutes the air in a given area at a given level for a given period of time, the 10,000 people living nearby have a 1 in 100 lifetime chance of contracting a certain form of cancer as opposed to a 1 in 200 chance. The harm that embezzlement inflicts is usually more direct, but even there, the loss is pretty much always insured and hence is spread out over many policyholders.

A fourth characteristic of corporate crime is that the monetary sums that are involved tend to be quite large. The total amount of money that is stolen by a single extremely successful corporate criminal in a single year is usually considerably greater than, for example, the take of *all* of the robberies in the country in that same year. As we saw in the chapter on property crime, the FBI estimates that roughly $525 million were stolen in all robberies in the United States during 2004; this is roughly the same sum of the *fines* the government levied against convicted stock swindler Michael Milken. The savings and loan scandal resulted in the disappearance of well in excess of $300 *billion,* perhaps 70–80 percent of which were a product of illegal acts. Since the money was insured, it will be the government—and ultimately the American taxpayer—who will foot the bill. The per capita cost? Roughly $1,500 for every man, woman, and child in the United States. Sums such as these simply *cannot* be stolen by ordinary thieves. Illegal price-fixing may add as much as $250 *billion* a year to the cost of the products we purchase. It is *only* for "respectable" crime that thefts entailing sums in the hundreds of millions and the billions of dollars are possible.

There are two reasons why corporate crime is so much more lucrative than ordinary burglaries, robberies, and larcenies. The first is that street criminals have to steal money in the form of a *physical object,* and hundreds of millions of dollars are rarely found in the same place at the same time; even when it is, it is usually inaccessible except to trusted employees. In contrast, corporate criminals steal by *manipulating symbols,* which means that they can steal money they don't even have to pick up and carry away; indeed, that doesn't even have to *exist* in the form of a physical object. A second reason why so much more can be stolen by the executive thief than the street criminal: Street crime tends to be a "one shot deal," a single theft involving a specific sum of money. In contrast, white-collar crime is usually made up of a *number* of *interrelated* actions that extend over a period of time—months, years, and even decades.

A fifth characteristic of corporate crime is that it is *rarely* prosecuted; when prosecuted, and if a conviction is obtained, penalties tend to be *extremely* light. With respect to prosecution, evidence indicating that a crime has taken place is not as clear-cut as with street crime. Police officers do not patrol business suites looking out for corporate crimes being committed. Indeed, following up on the point on the complexity of corporate crime, how would the police even *know* when one is being committed? (In addition, business suites are private property, and hence, the police cannot enter them until crimes are reported.) Relative to their incidence, arrests are very, very rarely made; the ratio of violations (were this known) to arrests almost certainly approaches and may even surpass that for crimes that entail no complainant, such as drug possession and sale. In addition, even if evidence does indicate criminal behavior, arrest is rare and business executives are rarely convicted for their crimes; conviction, when it does occur, is *extremely* unlikely to lead to a lengthy prison sentence. This is especially striking in view of the amount of money that is stolen. Jail or prison time tends to be almost nonexistent. But this is changing.

Sixth, for the most part, corporate crime does not fit our stereotype of real crime; it is rarely condemned to the same degree that street crime is, and there is very little public stigma attached to white-collar crime. When harmful corporate actions are listed on rosters of actions the public is asked to evaluate the seriousness of, for corporate crimes, condemnation tends to be commensurate with harm. The public regards corporate crime in which injury occurs as *serious* crime. However, when members of the public are asked to act in the capacity of jurors and pass judgment on and sentence corporate suspects, they tend to be extremely lenient toward them. In other words, as Friedrichs says, although the public is perfectly willing to see corporate crime as having serious consequences, this does not always translate into being willing to impose harsh sentences on offenders or support legislation calling for such sentences (Friedrichs, 2004). To put the matter another way, as we've seen, in some ways, there is some question about whether corporate crime even *qualifies* as a form of deviance.

Seventh, the media tend not to cover corporate crime in as complete or detailed a fashion as is the case with street crime. True, there have been a few notable exceptions in recent years: It's hard to ignore the theft of billions of dollars. The fact is, as we've seen, corporate crimes tend to be complex and technical; they are difficult to explain and understand, they are intrinsically unexciting, and there is virtually no way to present them on television in an even remotely dramatic fashion. They do not make "good copy," as members of the media say, they do not provide dramatic "sound bites." They do not make for juicy, sensationalistic stories that get page one coverage and a prominent place on the six o'clock news. When they do get space in newspapers, they tend to be buried in back pages, usually in the financial rather than the hard news section. In order for a story of a corporate crime to appear on television news, one of three conditions has to prevail: One, as I said, the sums stolen have to be huge; two, a scandal must be connected with the theft; or three, the accused must be prominent. For the most part, the public finds news stories of corporate misdeeds boring. It is rare that we have the financial training even to understand the nature of corporate offenses; for most of us, there is little intrinsic *drama* in these stories. The shotgun robbery of a downtown bank, complete with hostages and a standoff with the police—now, that's a story! The gangland execution of a mob figure while he's eating a plate of linguine—that grabs our attention! A daring jewel heist from a famous store, again, captures our fancy and interest. We need not invoke conspiracies among the rich and powerful to account for this; the fact is, for most of us, corporate crimes just don't make it as news. Most of us would turn the channel or the page if confronted with such a story. With rare exceptions, we are just not as interested in such stories as we are in reports of meat-and-potatoes, nuts-and-bolts street crime, which most of us find exciting and entertaining. Of course, fanciful fictional depictions of supposed corporate misdeeds, complete with the murder of rivals or crusading journalists, always sell, but I'm talking about real-life corporate crime.

And eighth, as a result of its lack of correspondence to a crime stereotype and its lack of stigma, corporate criminals, even after being convicted, rarely think of themselves as real criminals. They use a "vocabulary of motives" that permits them to see themselves in a respectable, law-abiding light; they tend to "deny the guilty mind" and insist that, though their actions may have been technically illegal, they did not *intend* to commit a crime. While corporate criminals use a somewhat different vocabulary, depending on the crime in question, to explain the crime, they are "nearly unanimous in denying [the] basic criminality" of their illegal actions (Benson, 1985, p. 591). While some persons convicted of street crimes and their defenders will insist that they "didn't do it," corporate criminals and their defenders take a different tack: They insist that, even though they engaged in the action of which they were accused, what they did *wasn't a crime*.

Another feature of corporate crime: For the majority of corporate crimes, this *intention* to do harm to a victim is absent. Instead, corporate executives expose parties to a certain measure of *risk*. Whether this risk is acceptable or unacceptable, legal or illegal, is a matter of interpretation. Some corporate actors *knowingly* expose other parties to risks that those parties, and the law, would regard as unacceptable, while other corporate actors do so in the *absence* of such awareness. But nearly all take risk into account and weigh their actions accordingly (Short, 1990). All executives would prefer that the actions they take on behalf of their corporation cause no one any harm. But in the real world, this is not possible. On the one hand, no work site, product, or industrial waste can be made completely safe; some level of risk is an inevitable feature of modern existence (Friedrichs, 2004); if corporate risk were to be eliminated altogether, all business activity would cease to exist (Perrow, 1984, p. 311). For instance, no automobile can ever be manufactured in which the likelihood of injury or death is zero. On the other hand, some work sites, products, or waste products are so *blatantly* unsafe, the risk so *immense,* that harm is nearly certain; some corporate actors can be said to *deliberately* expose potential victims to unnecessary and substantial risk.

How does the observer make a judgment that the risk was unacceptable and the action that brought it on is a crime? How do we assess risk? According to what criteria? And *who* assesses it?

Do persons who are themselves exposed to the risk of harm assess its magnitude and the acceptability of that exposure? (In effect, they often do, in civil cases, but only *after* the damage has been done, not at the decision-making stage.) One problem is that people assess risk in an extremely inaccurate fashion, exaggerating the likelihood of certain types of harm and minimizing others (Slovic, Fischoff, and Lichtenstein, 1980; Erikson, 1990; Slovic, Layman, and Flynn, 1991; Friedrichs, 2004). On the other hand, in determining the culpability of corporate actions, do we rely on corporate actors to assess what constitutes "acceptable risk"? Clearly, we do not, for it is members of the general public who sit on juries in civil trials, not hand-picked panels of corporation executives, who are likely to decide on the basis of what's good for the corporation, not what's good for the customer, the public, or the worker.

There is a second risk the corporate actor calculates in addition to risk of harm to customers, the public, and employees. This is the likelihood of *accountability*—in the case of the criminal law, the risk of arrest and prosecution, in the case of civil and administrative law, and the risk of lawsuits and punitive fines. Corporate offenses very rarely result in criminal prosecution, and administrative agencies rarely slap corporations with huge fines. But torts do result in a *great many* civil trials and, occasionally, extremely large settlements. In fact, today, product liability is the largest field of civil law (Priest, 1990). Here we see the inhibitory impact of civil law: It forces executive actors to consider in their cost-benefit analysis the cost of harmful consequences of their operations or products in the form of substantial settlements.

Let's be clear about this: We live in a capitalist society. Corporations are not philanthropic organizations; they are designed and run to earn a profit. So far, all government experiments based on a socialist economy, or any markedly noncapitalist alternative, have either collapsed or been seriously compromised. To a corporation, what counts is the "bottom line." This means that their executives make decisions based almost exclusively on *cost-benefit analysis*: They weigh potential costs against earnings to determine possible or likely profit. To earn a profit, they make decisions to engage, or not to engage, in certain business ventures that may or may not pay off. Business ventures may be costly in various ways. Some may entail huge expenditures and offer little potential reward. Still others are likely to result in extremely unfavorable and irreparable public relations, and hence, be costly in indirect ways. Others are highly certain to result in criminal prosecution, while still others are so likely to cause damage to customers that extremely expensive lawsuits, along with the possibility of bankruptcy, loom on the horizon. Corporations do not avoid certain actions for the public good or as a service to humanity; they do so because they would be unprofitable.

At this point, a crucial issue needs to be addressed: *Who is the corporate actor?* It is often stated that corporate crimes are distinct, different from practically all others in that they are, *by their very nature,* enacted by a collectivity rather than individual persons. Decisions are arrived at in consultation with higher-ups and approved—or initiated—at the top. It is the *corporation* that acts, as a whole, not scattered, isolated actors, one at a time. Often, after conviction, it is the corporation that is fined, not specific persons working for that corporation. On the other hand, individual corporate actors may be fined and, occasionally, sentenced to a term of incarceration. (Clearly, a corporate entity cannot serve a prison sentence!) When the Pennwalt Corporation was convicted and fined more than $1 million for illegally dumping a toxic substance into Puget Sound, a federal district judge insisted on seeing the company's top executive in court before he would accept a guilty plea; "Who is the corporation?" the judge asked; "I think the public is entitled to know who's responsible" (Egan, 1989). Suffice it to say that, though individual persons act, they always do so within certain social structures. In the case of corporate crime, these social structures are formal organizations or bureaucracies. As to whether persons or organizations are responsible for a given corporate crime depends on the specific crime in question. But clearly, structural entities play a larger role in acting for corporate crime than, perhaps, for any other type of crime. (For a contrary argument, see Cressey, 1988, who argues that a corporate actor is a fiction—only individual executives act.)

The question of who the corporate actor is plays a central role when we attempt to determine the *incidence* or *rate* of corporate crime. If the corporation is considered as the actor (and if the entire period of its existence is considered as well), then clearly, *most* (and in Sutherland's pioneering study, *all*) corporations are guilty of committing corporate crimes at least once, since at least some executives made decisions that turned out to be illegal. Hence, their *rate* of corporate crime would be enormous. However, if all the executives are included in the total number of actors (and if a year-by-year tally is made), it is possible that rates of corporate crime would be quite low. Most observers who argue that corporate crime is rampant have not devoted much thought to determine its rate relative to the number of persons who are in a position to commit it. Sutherland's study was based on *corporations* as the unit of analysis, but his explanation for white-collar crimes took place within them—differential association theory—was fundamentally *individualistic,* an obvious *contradiction* (Gottfredson and Hirschi, 1990, pp. 188, 191).

Four Recent Examples of Corporate Deviance

According to the Securities Fraud InfoCenter, securities fraud occurs "when one party deliberately misinforms another party during the trading of stocks, bonds, and other securities." Corporations "are required to submit particular information to the Securities and Exchange Commission [SEC]; if this information is incorrect or incomplete, the company may be liable" (www.securitiesfraudinfocenter.com/information.php).

For years, WorldCom, once the nation's number two Internet services provider, hugely overstated its profits and assets to the SEC. By late 2002, the corporation admitted that it had juggled its books by concealing $9 billion in expenses by claiming them as assets, falsely inflating their company's net worth. The corporation is now in Chapter 11 bankruptcy and half a dozen of the corporation's top executives, including its former chief executive office and its former chief financial office, have been indicted for conspiracy to commit fraud; they face possible substantial prison sentences. In addition, WorldCom is in the process of settling its civil lawsuit with the SEC (http://news.bbc.co.uk/1hi/business/2407991.stm; www.securitiesfraud.fyi.com/worldcom_fraud.html).

In 2002, the SEC filed civil fraud charges against Dennis Kozlowski, then chief executive officer of Tyco—a conglomerate selling a variety of products including health care products, electronic equipment, valves, and fire alarms—and two other Tyco executives. (All three have since been fired from the company.) The trio, said the SEC's Director of Enforcement, "treated Tyco as their private bank, taking out hundreds of millions of dollars of loans and compensation without ever telling investors." The complaint seeks monetary penalties, a recovery of the ill-gotten gains, and barring the three from ever serving as officers or directors of a publicly traded company. In tandem with the SEC's suit, Kozlowski and one of the other executives faced criminal charges for stealing $170 million in company loans and obtaining more than $430 million through fraudulent sales of securities, as well as avoiding the payment of sales taxes totaling more than $1 million. As of 2002, Kozlowski owned a $30 million mansion in Florida and a $5 million house in Massachusetts; he gave a $17 million apartment to his ex-wife. He also used company funds to pay for a $1 million party for his second wife (which featured an ice sculpture of Michelangelo's David that spouted vodka from its penis), expensive trinkets for himself, including a $15,000 umbrella stand, a $2,000 wastebasket, and two sets of sheets for $5,900. Revelations caused Tyco's stock to plummet from $15.86 to six cents a share, snatching millions away from the portfolios of shareholders (www.sec.gov/news/press/2002-135.htm; http://money.cnn.com/2002/09/19/news/companies/kozlowski_jail/; http://www.nydailynews.com/news/story/1866p-17595c.html).

In 1997, Gary Winnick took on AT&T's request to lay an undersea cable linking Europe with the United States; the job raised billions of dollars in revenue, and Global Crossing was born. Eventually, the company laid 100,000 miles of fiber-optic cable connecting four continents and

(*Continued*)

27 countries. At one time, Winnick was the richest man in Los Angeles, with $6 billion in wealth. In 1998, he bought the most expensive single-family house ever purchased in the United States, at a cost of $60 million; renovations cost another $30 million. At its height, Global Crossing traded on Wall Street for $64 a share. In 2001, saddled with a debt of $12.4 billion and the company's stock down to 30 cents a share, Global Crossing filed for bankruptcy. During the quarter ending in September 2003, Global Crossing lost $3.3 billion as against a total revenue of only $286 million; demand for high bandwidth cable, it seems, has been plummeting. The company simply never generated enough revenue to sustain its massive debt. Several months before the company filed for bankruptcy, Winnick cashed in $120 million in stock. In 2002, amid allegations of insider trading, he resigned from the company he had started up. Several lawsuits have been filed against the company (www.wired.com/news/business/0,1367,50114,00.html; www.texassecuritiesfraud.com/securities_pages/ suspect-stocks.html).

Between 1998 and 2001, executives at Enron, a company that shipped natural gas through pipelines, made false and misleading statements about the financial performance of the corporation. A growing debt problem was concealed by illegal, undisclosed transactions and partnerships; income was inflated and debts were incomplete and underestimated. The corporation's cooked books sent Enron stock to a high of $90.75 a share. But in 2001, news began leaking out that the corporation was worth considerably less than its stated value. Eventually the SEC stepped in and investigated Enron and Arthur Andersen, the accounting firm that audited the cooked books. A total of 29 Enron executives have been charged with securities, wire, and mail fraud and accused of money laundering and conspiracy; Arthur Andersen was convicted of obstructing justice, paid a fine of a half million dollars, and was placed on probation for five years. The case is so complicated that it will take years for these many cases to be decided (www.enronfraudinfocenter.com/information.php).

WAS THE 2008 FINANCIAL CRISIS A FORM OF DEVIANCE AT ALL?

Late in 2008, the financial world—at first, in the United States and eventually, in every corner of the globe—suffered a catastrophic "meltdown." Banks, bonds, the stock market, property, and businesses of every conceivable description declined 30–80 percent in value. Investors lost fortunes practically overnight. Huge corporations that had stood for a century or more as beacons of stability and profitability filed for bankruptcy; unemployment rose to 10 percent of the labor force; everyone began spending less money and so companies that relied on retail sales struggled to stay afloat; and entire residential neighborhoods became festooned with "For Sale" signs. Between September and November, the stock market lost nearly half of its value. In October, the Federal Reserve lent the money market half a trillion dollars to stay in business; in November, it agreed to buy $800 billion in mortgage-backed investments. No one was immune; everyone was affected. Home mortgages, pension funds, insurance companies, and mutual funds—financial instruments that affect all our lives—found themselves burdened with debt, undercapitalized, and on the verge of collapse.

The government took over Fannie Mae and Freddie Mac, the two largest and most venerable home mortgage corporations. Who owns General Motors and Chrysler? You do—the taxpayer owns most of these long-established auto giants, because they were unable to stay in business without huge government bailouts. The government converted Goldman Sachs and Morgan Stanley, previously unregulated investment banks each one of which owned more than a trillion dollars in assets, to ordinary banks, now subject to strict regulations. Lehman Brothers and Bear Stearns, together once worth a billion dollars in assets, are now bankrupt. Merrill Lynch is taken over by Bank of America. And meanwhile, because of the "ripple effect," millions of ordinary workers find themselves on the unemployment line, unable to find a job.

What caused this global financial crisis? What crimes were committed? Who did what to make this happen?

Most financial experts point to two sources of the crisis: overvaluation of property and underregulation of the finance industry. In the early 2000s, because of the low rate of interest from the Federal Reserve (1%), investors began borrowing huge sums of money to leverage financial deals. They began packaging bundles of mortgages, some safe, some risky, into investment instruments they bought and sold. The safe or *prime* slices of these mortgage investment instruments proved to be very profitable, so investors sought more mortgage investments, and soon, they began dipping into the risky slices of these packages. The risky or *subprime* slice of the investment packages were made up of mortgages where the buyer needed no down payment, paid high mortgage rates, and was asked for no proof of income. Inevitably, a high proportion of such homeowners defaulted on their mortgages, and the lender got their houses; eventually the market was flooded with houses for sale, and all the houses in their neighborhoods lost value. As a result the homeowners who were able to make their mortgage payments found themselves paying mortgages on houses worth a third or a quarter of what they originally paid for them; increasingly, mortgage holders walked away from their payments, further swamping neighborhoods with unsold houses and further reducing the value of the occupied houses. Insurance companies that had insured the payment of mortgages lost billions on their investments, and, as I said, the ripple effect spread from there to nonfinancial companies and hence, to the jobs of ordinary worker. The world found itself in an economic crisis not experienced since the Great Depression of the 1930s, when one out of three workers were unemployed (www.mikesdailylockup.com/2009/02/the-financial-meltdown-explained.html). Most experts trace the worldwide financial meltdown to the *subprime mortgage collateralized debt obligation.*

Sounds technical, doesn't it? It is, and there's no single villain in this drama. Many thousands of investors, homeowners, bankers, stock and bond traders, government employees, money managers, executives, and ordinary workers—they're all tangled up in this fiasco, the toxic effects of which may last as much as a decade. This crisis has snatched trillions from the pockets of people worldwide, turned houses worth half a million dollars into eyesores and liabilities, princes into paupers, and retirement funds into scraps of paper, and yet, though experts have some understanding of what caused it, it's not clear that such actions are criminal or deviant. The financial crisis that began in the fall of 2008 is a prime example of an interlocking set of actions that take place within an organization setting whose agency is likewise organizational. It's almost as if individual initiative played no role at all in the cascading meltdown.

POLICE USE OF EXCESSIVE FORCE

Some actions grow out of organizational mandates but turn out, in retrospect, to have been a mistake. Others depart so wildly from organizational expectations that hardly anyone in the organization supports them or their perpetrators. Still others are disputed; disagreement exists within the organization as to their acceptability. In this section, we'll look at three cases of the use of excessive force by the police—indeed, all are violent actions, two of which resulted in serious injury to their victims and one resulted in death. From the perspective of the organization—that is, the police—they are significantly different from one another, although much of the public saw them in a similar light.

At 12:45 in the morning of March 3, 1991, George Holliday, 33, manager of the local office of a national plumbing firm, was awakened by the sound of police sirens. Looking out of his window, he saw a helicopter spotlight trained on a white Hyundai sedan surrounded by six police cars. Holliday grabbed his videocamera and began shooting. What he captured on tape was astounding: Two police officers were beating a large black man with metal truncheons, while a third stomped him and 10 others watched. (A fourth was later discovered to have been directly involved in the beating.) A total of 23 officers of the Los Angeles Police Department, as well as four from other departments, had been present at the scene. The man being beaten, Rodney King, had received a total of 56 blows, to his head, neck, back, ankles, legs, and feet (Skolnick and Fyfe, 1993, p. 3).

On Monday, Paul King, Rodney's brother, reported the incident to the police but received a bureaucratic runaround. When King mentioned the existence of a videotape, the officer he spoke to told King he was in "big trouble" because he was riding in the car with his brother. No complaint was taken by the desk. Independently, George Holliday, incensed at the beating, contacted his local police station to report the incident, but the desk officer he talked to was clearly uninterested. Again, the police refused to take an official complaint. Frustrated, Holliday called television station KTLA in Los Angeles. A 19-second segment of the 81-second videotape was aired that evening. Not shown in the broadcast footage was the fact that King was zapped with several jolts from an electronic Taser gun, yet got up and "advanced" on several officers. In addition, the police said that King was obviously drunk or high; King's passenger admitted that they had been drinking. None of this exonerates the behavior of the officers, but these are factors that do influence police behavior.

The story attracted national, even international media attention. The tape was played repeatedly "until it was seen everywhere in the world, from Tokyo to London to Zaïre. The beating of Rodney King . . . [was] the most explicit and shocking news footage of police brutality every to be seen on television" (Skolnick and Fyfe, 1993, p. 3). Just about everyone who saw the tape was sickened and horrified. Police Chief Darryl Gates condemned the King beating, calling it an "aberration." But it turns out, in the three full years before the incident, over 4,000 citizen complaints were filed against the Los Angeles Police Department. In 1990, the year before the incident took place, the city of Los Angeles paid out over $11 million for police misconduct, including civil rights violations, excessive force, and wrongful death. "What made the King beating different from those earlier events was not the conduct of the police, but the presence of George Holliday's video camera" (p. 3).

King's offense? Speeding, not pulling over when told to do so, and resisting arrest. Four days after the incident, Chief Gates announced that the four officers who beat King would face criminal charges. Against the nonparticipants, whom Gates said should have restrained their fellow officers, no criminal charges could have been filed since their inaction was not illegal. On March 15, the four officers, Stacey Koon, Laurence Powell, Theodore Briseno, and Timothy Wind, were officially charged with the use of deadly force and assault with a deadly weapon. The venue of the trial was transferred from Los Angeles to Simi Valley, a suburb. All four officers were white. The jury was entirely white. The trial began a year later, in March 1992, and on April 19, the jury rendered its verdict—an acquittal on all charges.

The decision was almost universally regarded as unjust. In a *USA Today* poll taken soon after the trial, 86 percent of the whites and 100 percent of the blacks interviewed said that the verdict was "wrong." The outrage was felt especially acutely in the inner city community, which exploded with six days of rioting, violence, arson, and looting. By the time the flames had died down, 54 people had been killed, over 2,000 were injured, 13,000 arrested, and rioters wreaked $700 million in property damage.

In August 1992, the four officers were indicted by a federal grand jury for violating Rodney King's civil rights. (This was not a case of double jeopardy, since both the charge and the court system were different.) The trial began in February 1993, and in April, the jury rendered its verdict: Koon and Powell were found guilty, and Briseno and Wind were acquitted. This time, riots did not break out. The two convicted officers received a sentence of 30 months imprisonment. The vote was split on King's beating; 55 percent of blacks but only 21 percent of whites felt that the officers were not punished enough by the conviction of only two officers. Some public commentary was generated by the venue of their incarceration. The prison in which they served their time is nicknamed "Club Fed" for its loose control of inmates and well-appointed facilities (www.crimsonbird.com/history/rodneyking.htm).

At four in the morning of August 9, 1998, a report of a disturbance outside a Haitian social club in Brooklyn, the Rendez-Vous, was called in to the local police precinct. While attempting to disperse the crowd, several officers began pushing people around, including, some eyewitnesses reported, a pregnant woman. A verbal altercation ensued, and a fistfight broke out between an unidentified man and one officer, Justin Volpe. Volpe was knocked to the ground, and the man who hit him ran away. The police, enraged, began insulting the crowd, hurling, some bystanders said, racial insults at them. Several scuffles broke out between officers and members of the crowd.

Abner Louima, 30, was watching the melee when an officer told him to shut up. Louima was shoved to the ground, handcuffed, put into a patrol car with two officers, and driven two blocks, where he was put into another car, then kicked and beaten with police radios. Clearly, Louima had been mistaken for the man who punched Volpe. The cops proceeded to drive him to an unlighted, more deserted area, where they were joined by two more officers, at which point, the beating resumed. Louima was then taken to the 70th Precinct's station house, where, at the booking desk, he was stripped—supposedly for guns and drugs—his pants around his ankles, "in full view of the cops." Two officers then walked Louima to the bathroom and closed the door. Shouting racial slurs, one officer, reported Louima, said, "If you yell or make any noise, I will kill you." While one officer held Louima down, the other shoved a stick (some said a toilet plunger, others, a broom handle) up his rectum, pulled it out, shoved it into his mouth, breaking several teeth, and said, "That's your shit," ending with a racial insult (www.nubeing.com/archives/torture.htm). The police then put Louima in a jail cell.

There, Louima began hemorrhaging; his condition looked serious. A fellow prisoner managed to convince an officer that Louima needed immediate medical attention. Several hours later, an ambulance was dispatched to a Coney Island emergency room. No officers accompanied him to the hospital. Louima had a punctured bladder and a severed colon, and required extensive surgery. He was handcuffed to his bed. He remained in critical condition for four days following his operation, and had to undergo several additional surgical procedures. He was not released from the hospital until mid-October, over two months after he was assaulted (www.radcliffe.edu/quarterly/199703/page25a.html).

The torture of Abner Louima touched off an international firestorm of outrage. Almost universally, without regard to race, the public deemed the station house abuse as a deviant act. Outside the Brooklyn Supreme Court building, demonstrators waved toilet plungers and Haitians held posters that read "Yes, Massa," "Close Down the 70th," and "NYPD: KKK!" Hundreds of editorials were published expressing horror at the atrocity and demanding justice. Members of the 70th Precinct were dubbed "Rapist Pigs." Johnny Cochran, famed courtroom lawyer, offered his services on behalf of Abner Louima. Don King, flamboyant boxing promoter, handed Louima a check for $5,000 (www.mariebrenner.com/articles/incident/70.html). Eventually, Louima won a $8.7 million civil settlement, $7.1 from the City of New York and $1.6 from the NYPD's Police Benevolence Association. It was the largest settlement involving the police in the history of the city.

Five officers in the 70th Precinct were indicted for a variety of crimes, including assault, conspiracy, and obstruction of justice. In May 1999, they went on trial. Within three weeks, Justin Volpe, the man who assaulted Louima with the stick, tearfully pled guilty to the charges; he received a sentence of 30 years in prison. In June, Charles Swartz, the man who was accused of holding Louima down, was found guilty; after appeal, he was convicted again and received a sentence of five years. (Swartz's guilt was based on conflicting testimony; it remains controversial to this day.) After several trials, the other three defendants were acquitted of all charges.

During the evening of February 3, 1999, Edward McMellon, Sean Carroll, Kenneth Boss, and Richard Murphy, officers working for the Special Crime Unit of the New York Police Department (NYPD), were patrolling a neighborhood in the South Bronx, looking for a reported serial rapist who was said to be in the area. All four were in plainclothes and wore bulletproof vests. At 12:45 in the morning of February 4, they came upon Amadou Diallo, a 22-year-old street peddler and West African immigrant, near the doorway of an apartment building. McMellon and Carroll had mounted the steps in front of the building, Murphy was on the sidewalk, and Boss was crouched behind a parked car on the street. The officers identified themselves, flashed their police shields, and demanded that Diallo freeze and raise his hands. The young man darted toward the vestibule of the building, then stopped and seemed to reach for something in his pocket. The officers opened fire with a barrage of bullets. McMellon and Carroll fell backwards off the stairs, then they unleashed another barrage of bullets. In all, 41 rounds were fired; 19 of them struck Diallo. Murphy fired four times, Boss five; both McMellon and Carroll emptied their 16-round clips.

The young man lay dead by the doorway of his apartment building.

The police officers approached the body and quickly realized that Diallo was unarmed and probably reaching for his wallet, presumably to provide documentation of his identity. According to an officer called to the scene of the shooting, Carroll was hunched over Diallo's body, "crying profusely." According to the police, the killing had been "a tragic mistake." Militant African American spokespersons claimed it was the "execution" of an innocent, unarmed black man. Even many moderates argued that had Diallo been white, the police would not been so quick on the trigger; chances are, they say, he would still be alive today. It was agreed in nearly all quarters that the 41 bullets, and the 19 that struck Diallo, were compelling evidence of police recklessness. As with the Louima case, the killing of Amadou Diallo ignited a torrent of invective against the police and cries for justice. Clearly, much of the public regarded the shooting as *deviant*.

At the end of March 1999, the four officers were suspended from the NYPD. In April, the suspected serial rapist they had been looking for was arrested. In December, the trial was moved from New York City to Albany, where, supposedly, the emotions of the local public would be less heated. The officers were charged with intentional murder and second-degree murder with depraved indifference to human life and reckless endangerment. They faced the possibility of spending the rest of their lives in prison. On February 1, 2000, the jury was selected for the trial; it consisted of eight whites and four African Americans. The next day, the trial began. Not admitted at trial was the officers' history of gunplay, civilian complaints, and brutality. Three of the four officers had fired their weapons on the job; three had civilian complaints lodged against them. McMellon, who wounded one suspect, had five such complaints, and Boss, who had three, had killed a man threatening people with a shotgun.

On February 25, 2000, the jury returned its verdict. All four officers were acquitted on all counts. Critics of police brutality were horrified and outraged. How could such a thing have happened? Wasn't it a clear-cut case of the murder of an innocent, unarmed black suspect? At the very least, wasn't it a display of a reckless and depraved indifference for human life? Surely racism was involved. How could such a brutal act go unpunished? Two days after the trial was over, 1,400 people held a prayer vigil outside the United Nations in New York City to protest the decision. The same day, the foreperson of the jury, an African American woman who used to live in the Bronx, was quoted by a reporter as saying that the verdict "has nothing to do with race" (http://crime.about.com/library/blfiles/bldiallo.htm; www.courttv.com/archive/national/diallo/02800_background_ctv.html).

The police are charged with protecting the public, keeping the peace, and enforcing the law. With the exception of a military situation, the police, and only the police, have a monopoly on *general, legitimate, and coercive force.* The police are authorized to issue a lawful command to any and all citizens, and they can back up that command with the force of the state. And violence is, of course, the most *extreme* form of coercive force. Representatives of no other entity or institution in society has that power (Bittner, 1970, pp. 36–47). Clearly, if more than one entity had that power, chaos would be the inevitable result, since all institutions have *some* conflicting goals or practices with all others. But just as clearly, the police sometimes abuse this power; hence, we encounter cases such as those I just described. These three cases attracted a huge volume of public and media attention. Consider the sheer number of Web sites, contemporaneous with each event, that Google devoted to each: Rodney King (70,000), Abner Louima (10,000), and Amadou Diallo (20,000). Many of these sites express outrage against police abuse; they argue that these three black men were the victims of police brutality.

When one sector of the society is authorized to use force under certain circumstances, this inevitably raises the question of *at what point* police force is acceptable, and when does it become too much force—unacceptable, inappropriate, or deviant. However, this begs an even thornier issue: *Who* decides what's too much force? To put the matter another way: What are the "understandings and standards" of the police about the use of force (Hunt, 1985, p. 316)? And what are *the public's* understanding of what constitutes excessive force? And *which sectors* of the public hold what understandings on this issue? Does this vary by race? Political orientation? How does the court system render its judgments? Clearly, these questions are directly relevant to the constructionist approach to deviance. They address the matter of how different observers, located in what sector or institution in the society considers the illegitimate or deviant use of force.

According to Jennifer Hunt (1985), the police themselves "classify and evaluate" acts of force into three categories—legal, normal, and excessive. Legal force is "going by the book." It is that degree of force that is necessary to subdue a modal suspect and take him or her into custody. *Normal* force is made up of those coercive acts that the police consider "necessary, appropriate, reasonable, or understandable" (p. 317). The important thing to note about normal force is that it may or may not be legal, but it is considered a "natural response to normal police to particular situational exigencies" (p. 317). This means that under certain extraordinary circumstances, the police may have to bend or break the law to do their job. In contrast, the third type of force, *excessive* force—popularly known as "police brutality"—is not deemed by the police as normal, necessary, or justified. This type of force is considered *by the police* illegitimate, unacceptable—and deviant. The police learn to make these distinctions not in the academy, but on the street, as rookies, in their working interaction with more experienced officers. The police phrase, "It's not done on the street the way it's taught in the academy," expresses "the perceived contradiction between the formal world of the police academy and the informal world of the street" (p. 318).

The three cases of police violence I discussed earlier illustrate the distinction the police make between "normal" and "excessive" force, and the fact that *their* understanding of what constitutes normal force varies substantially from what the public's understanding is. Let's look at two of these cases, the beating and torture of Abner Louima and the shooting of Amadou Diallo.

No police officers or representatives of the police force or defenders of the police defended the treatment of Louima. (Some observers felt that Swartz was wrongfully convicted, not because what he did was acceptable but because, they say, he wasn't the second man in the men's room. And some felt that the original—life—sentences were excessive for aggravated assault, since murder often draws a lesser penalty.) If one were to look through the 10,000 Web sites called up by a Google search for the entry "Abner Louima," one would search in vain for a single one defending the actions of the police in the Louima case. In other words, the beating and torture of Abner Louima was regarded by the police, public, and courts as a case of police brutality, that is, excessive, over-the-top coercive force—illegitimate, illegal, and deviant. The police and the public agree completely on this case; it was completely noncontroversial. The fact that the principal actor was convicted and sentenced to a 30-year term indicates that the court agreed with this view.

While the beating and torture of Louima found no supporters on the part of either the police or the public, on the matter of the shooting of Amadou Diallo there was a much more complicated reaction. African Americans overwhelmingly opposed the action of the police; most in fact regarded it as a crime. The fact that the young man was shot 19 times, and officers on the scene fired a total of 41 rounds, displayed for many observers the fact that the police displayed a "reckless and depraved indifference for human life." And the fact that Diallo was black underscored the fact, many argued, that the police resort to violence more readily, and more brutally, when suspects are members of a racial minority.

Still, a division did exist. A *New York Times*/CBS poll taken of New York State residents just after the decision found that half of respondents (50%) felt that the jury decision to acquit the officers was wrong, 30 percent said that it was right, and 20 percent said they weren't sure. The fact that Diallo refused to obey orders, did not raise his hands, seemed to be reaching for something in his wallet, and was standing in a dimly-lit doorway led some members of the public to believe that his killing was a tragic mistake, not a brutal crime, and hence, that the officers who killed him should have been acquitted of murder. However, this opinion was sharply divided by race. Only 8 percent of blacks said that the acquittal was the "right" verdict, 77 percent said it was "wrong," and the remainder weren't sure. Whites were more nearly evenly split: 37 percent right, while 40 percent said it was wrong. Residents of New York City were more likely to think the decision was wrong than those living elsewhere, and women were more likely to think it was wrong than men.

While the public was divided but more opposed to the action of the officers than accepting, among the police, the view that the officers who shot Diallo made a mistake but did not commit a crime was practically universal. In fact, it was as a result of the testimony of the police that an acquittal was rendered. Probably the most compelling testimony at the trial was given by James Fyfe, a former police officer, criminologist, and coauthor of a book on police brutality (Skolnick and Fyfe, 1993). In point of fact, Fyfe usually testifies *against* police officers in cases of police brutality. He is keenly aware of the distinction between justified and unjustified police force. In all likelihood, his views on the shooting reflect those of urban police generally. Fyfe told jurors that Diallo had refused to stop when he was commanded to do so. "It is the job of the officers to protect life," Fyfe said. Diallo, he continued, "ran from the officers into a building with innocent citizens. It is the job of the officers to prevent him from entering the building and putting its occupants in danger. . . . Things can only get worse if he gets out of sight" (www.courttv.com/archive/national/diallo/021600_ctv.html).

Patrick Lynch, president of the NYPD's Police Benevolence Association—which paid a portion of the officer's legal bill—was quoted as saying:

> The fear for your life you have . . ., your adrenaline is pumping. You have an obligation to save yourself, save the other officers, the citizens that might be behind you. [All] this comes into play. When we're in the quiet of the courtroom where you can hear a pin drop, it's easy to second-guess. But when you're standing on that stoop and everything is breaking loose, that's what the police officer is dealing with.

When asked whether if Diallo had been a white man, he'd be alive today, Lynch emphatically disagreed. "If it was a white person who ran into a dark alley and turned like they had a weapon, I'm going to save my life, I'm going to save my partner's life—regardless of who's trying to kill me" (www.pbs.org/newshour/bb/law/jan-june00/diallo_3-3.html).

At the end of January 2001, the Justice Department issued a statement to the effect that after an investigation, its Civil Rights Division and U.S. Attorney Mary Jo White concluded that federal charges against the officers "were not warranted." Federal officials determined that they "could not prove beyond a reasonable doubt that the officers willfully deprived Mr. Diallo of his constitutional right to be free from the use of unreasonable force." The Acting U.S. Attorney General Eric Holder agreed. This decision indicates the courts agreed with the police that a tragedy mistake took place—not a crime (www.cbsnews.com/stories/2000/03/02/national/main167178.shtml). And in this respect, they drew a sharp distinction between the cases involving the beatings of Rodney King (which resulted in no conviction in state court but two in federal court) and Abner Louima (two convictions at the state level). And clearly, in this respect, the judgments of the police and the courts are the same (the killing of Diallo was not a crime, and was not a deviant act), while both differ sharply with the judgments of the vast majority of the African American community and roughly half of the white community (who believed the killing of Diallo *was* a crime, and deviant act as well). Once again, judgments of deviance depend on where one stands.

Let's return to the distinctions I made at the beginning of this section. The beating and torture of Abner Louima was considered totally contrary to the mandates of the police, and had no supporters within the force. In contrast, the shooting of Amadou Diallo was regarded as a tragic accident that grew out of acceptable police mandates, namely, to enforce the law and protect the public. *To the police,* it was considered a mistake only in retrospect, that is, the policy that caused it was considered good, but in this case, the outcome was bad. The beating of Rodney King was even more complicated. Here, the police were split on the issue. When the unabridged version of the tape was shown to them, many police officers agreed that King was probably intoxicated, that he had "advanced" several times on the officers, that he refused to obey a command to lie on the ground, and that the two charges from the Taser gun and successive blows from police truncheons had failed to subdue him. Not all officers agreed and believed that King should have been subdued by some other means. Again, what we are addressing here is not the *reality* of these cases but the *perceived* or *constructed* reality. And in this respect, the officers who attacked Abner Louima committed a deviant act, the ones who shot Amadou Diallo did not, while those who beat Rodney King engaged in an action that was not clear-cut either way.

THE SEXUAL ABUSE OF CHILDREN BY ROMAN CATHOLIC PRIESTS

Sexual contact between an adult and a child is both deviant and criminal. The child molester is considered "the lowest of the low," beyond the pale—the deviant *par excellence.* Even in prison, he is despised and persecuted by other prisoners. And since, below a certain age—and the age depends on the jurisdiction—a person is not legally capable of granting sexual consent, any adult who has sexual contact with a child has committed a crime, even if the child initiated the contact.

The sexual abuse of children by priests is both deviant and criminal, but it poses special issues that make it worth exploring in a discussion on the sociology of deviance. Reports of priestly molestation indicate that the abuse of boys outnumbers that of girls by a factor of 10 to one. This makes it a form of homosexuality, and hence, doubly deviant. And sexual abuse by a Roman Catholic priest is regarded as an especially heinous act because of the priest's prestige and aura of holiness, as well as the trust parishioners place in their clerics. Catholics consider the priest God's representative on earth, in a sense, a reflection of divinity. As a result, when a Catholic cleric molests a child in his pastoral care, he is corrupting the Church, soiling the cloth of the priesthood, defiling God, and betraying the trust believers have in him. And while the abusive priest tends to act alone, he holds a position in a very large organization. More important for our purposes, the *reactions* of the Catholic hierarchy to charges of sexual abuse of children by priests reveals that *enacting* deviance is not the same thing as *being sanctioned* for deviant acts. In many social circles, tolerating and covering up priestly abuse is regarded as even more deviant than the abuse itself. In this respect, we have a perfect example of organizational deviance on our hands.

Imagine a spectrum of organizational deviance that stretches from those that are *completely acceptable* within the organization to *completely unacceptable.* "Completely acceptable" organizational deviance would be those acts *members of the organization* deem acceptable, but which are judged *un*acceptable outside the organization—say, to the general public, or sectors of the public, to law enforcement, or to the media. Many forms of corporate crime fit this characterization. At the other end of this spectrum we find acts committed by individuals in an organizational structure that are *discouraged* by the norms of the organization, *contrary* to the mandates of the organization, negatively *sanctioned* by the organization (although they may be concealed from the general public), and that may in fact *undermine* the interests and goals of the organization. In between, we find acts supported by organizational mandates but whose specific execution may hurt the organization. Clearly, some instances of police violence—the Amadou Diallo case included—qualify for the last of these types.

The sexual abuse of children by the priests is one of the most extreme cases we could find of a deviant act that is committed *within* an organizational context, *by* individuals, who are representatives of the organization, that *corrupts* organizational mandates. The sexually abusive priest, like the police officer who engages in excessive force, acts *under the cloak of the organization.* Priestly abuse is similar to the case of the police torture of Abner Louima—but very different from the shooting of Amadou Diallo—in that the former was totally contrary to organizational norms, guidelines, and mandates, while the latter was not. As we saw, members of the organization regarded the Diallo shooting as a tragic mistake rather than deviant and criminal behavior *in its totality.* As with the Louima case, there are virtually *no* justifications that are likely to work in the case of abusive priests. Claiming mental disorder is likely to be regarded as a self-serving rationalization, at least to the general public. However, while at all stages in Louima's beating, at least one other officer acted in concert with Volpe's actions, abusive priests nearly always act alone. In fact, so extreme is the case of abusive priests, the act itself is only marginally an instance of organizational deviance. What makes it most interesting as a case of organizational deviance is how Catholic authorities have tolerated it over the years.

To truly launch our discussion, we need to clear away the conceptual and empirical underbrush. The issue has become so tangled and confused that we need to clarify what's being said and what is implied. For starters, as Philip Jenkins points out (1996), the Catholic clergy does not have a monopoly on sexually abusing their youthful parishioners. Sexual scandals have rocked Orthodox Judaism (Cooperman, 2002), Jehovah's Witnesses (Goodstein, 2002), and, indeed, all religious faiths. Jenkins calculates that for Catholic priests, the figure for sexual abuse is no higher than 2 percent. Until the hierarchy of other faiths publish complete records, he says, it is fair to say that there is no evidence that priests are any more likely to molest children in their care than are non-Catholic clergy. Second, a corollary of this point is that the vast majority of Catholic priests do *not* molest the children in their flocks. As a result of the recent revelations of abuse, the sins of the few have tainted all Catholic clergy. Third, Jenkins continues, the *stereotype* of sexual molestation by priests is that, typically, very young prepubescent children—six or seven years of age—are being molested. In fact, Jenkins asserts, the *reality* is that priests are most likely to sexually approach minors in their adolescent years—15, 16, and 17 years old—rather than small children. On top of this, we have to add the fact that not every accusation is valid. False accusations have been, and continue to be, made, harming the accused and tainting the Church.

There are many interesting and distinctive features of organizational deviance. Among them, none is so crucially tied in to the importance of social reactions as *how the authorities within the organization react to and deal with the wrongdoing*. In other words, we should not be surprised by the fact that *some* cops use excessive violence on citizens, or that *some* priests sexually molest children in their pastoral care. Deviant behavior has been, is, and will continue to be a fixture in all societies, everywhere, and at all times. *Some* members of *every* society and social collectivity on earth will violate *some* of that society's, and that collectivity's, rules. *No* social grouping on earth is immune from deviance. Incidents of police use of excessive force against citizens and priestly molestation of children can be substantially reduced, but they will never be totally eliminated. In contrast, organizational tolerance by the hierarchy of wrongdoing by the rank-and-file is far more amenable to change.

Organizational tolerance of wrongdoing gets to the heart of the subject matter of the study of deviance. And it is directly relevant to the molestation of children by Roman Catholic priests. Are priests punished for this act? Have they been punished in the past?

Reactions by the Catholic Church in the United States to allegations of child molestations by priests can be divided very roughly into three eras—pre-1985, 1985–2002, and post-2002.

The pre-1985 era can be summed up quite simply. The Catholic Church did very little to punish priests who sexually abused the children in their care. Complaining families were told to keep the matter quiet, authorities in the Church did not contact law enforcement, and priests were typically sent to a program of psychological or spiritual counseling, then transferred to another parish. This radically changed in 1985.

In 1983, six Henry, Louisiana, families sued their local diocese and Gilbert Gauthe, the priest of their church, claiming their boys had been sodomized by the priest. The diocese transferred Gauthe to a treatment center in Massachussetts and made a monetary settlement with the families. The judge who officiated in the case sealed the papers that dealt with the case. But in 1984, another boy stepped forward, and his lawyer filed a suit with the same Lafayette court. The boy, Scott Gaskell, refused to accept the "hush money" settlement. His lawyer, Minos Simon, said, "the whole damn thing was wrapped in a cocoon of secrecy. The church knew damn well this dude had gone ape-wild down in Henry" (Powell, 2002, p. F4).

The civil lawsuit that followed caused the Lafayette district attorney to initiate a criminal investigation. During the investigation, it became clear to Ray Mouton, Gauthe's attorney, that Gauthe was not the only Louisiana priest who had molested children. Mouton, Michael Peterson, a psychologist specializing in treating priests, and the Reverend Tom Doyle, a representative of the Church, prepared a report on the problem of priestly abuse. In it, they warned of the problem and the impending blizzard of lawsuits the Church would have to deal with, and they suggested some solutions. In 1985, the Church announced that it would form a committee and launch its own probe, and recommended that Mouton, Peterson, and Doyle shut down their investigation. But the Church did not appoint a committee, and did not conduct an inquiry. Meanwhile, in 1985, Gauthe pled guilty to molesting children and was sentenced to a 20-year sentence and psychiatric treatment. He was released after serving nine years, was arrested in Texas after fondling a 3-year-old boy, and was sentenced to a seven-year term of probation. For a time, he counseled sex offenders in a Texas prison. Then, in 1998, a woman accused Gauthe of raping her 17 years previously; he got off on a legal technicality. Most recently, he worked as a groundskeeper in Houston (Powell, 2002).

The 1985 Gauthe case touched off a firestorm of anger toward the Catholic Church and encouraged dozens of boys, and men who had been molested much earlier, to step forward and lodge accusations against their abusers. Charges were made, investigations—civil, criminal, and ecclesiastical—were launched, offenders were formally charged, and sanctioned. Suddenly, the media were ablaze with stories about the sexual abuse of children by priests. Hundreds, indeed, thousands, of stories were broadcast about the subject. For the first time, the Roman Catholic Church was forced to acknowledge that this was a major problem and that steps had to be taken to deal with it. Lawsuits mounted. Unlike the stereotype many non-Catholics hold, the Vatican cannot simply write a check every time a local diocese needs cash. Officials had to scramble to compensate the litigants. They sold property, held fundraisers. Many believers began questioning the integrity of their church—even their faith.

If that had not been enough, in February 2002, John Geoghan, a defrocked priest, was sentenced to a 10-year prison term for fondling a 10-year-old boy. Between 1995 and 2002, more than 130 boys and men charged that Geoghan fondled or raped them. He has been named by more than 80 persons who have brought civil suits against the Boston diocese. Geoghan's career of molesting boys stretched back for 40 years. Each time an incident was reported to authorities in the Church, the Church hushed it up, sent Geoghan for counseling, and transferred him to another parish. Nearly all of Geoghan's sexual abuse took place under the auspices of dioceses in Massachusetts.

Here are a few highlights of Geoghan's career as a priestly pedophile:

- In 1966, Geoghan's superior in Blessed Sacrament, the parish church at Saugus, reports that the priest had brought boys into his bedroom—a report his superior later denied having made. Geoghan spends an extended stay in a rectory at Concord. No explanation is given by the Church as to the nature of that stay.
- In 1967, Geoghan is transferred to St. Paul's Church in Hingham. In 1968, a father complains to Church authorities that his son was molested by Geoghan; several members of the same church lodge the same accusation. Geoghan is sent to a therapeutic institute in Baltimore.
- Geoghan is sent to St. Mary's Church Melrose. There, in the early 1970s, a mother complains to authorities that her four boys had been molested by Geoghan. She is told to keep quiet; a financial settlement is reached.
- In 1974, Geoghan is sent to St. Andrew's in Jamaica Plain. There, Geoghan is accused of molesting seven boys in the same family; the lawsuit is later settled. Geoghan admits the abuse but says he "does not feel it a serious or a pastoral matter." In 1980, Geoghan is placed on sick leave and undergoes psychotherapy.
- In 1981, he is sent to St. Brendan's in Dorchester. There, parents lodge numerous complaints of molestation against Geoghan to authorities. In March 1984, Cardinal Law is installed as archbishop of Boston. He is elevated to cardinal in 1985.
- In September, 1984, Law removes Geoghan from St. Brendan's, transferring him to St. Julia's parish in Weston. There, he is put in charge of three youth groups, including altar

boys. An auxiliary bishop complains to Law about Geoghan's "history of homosexual involvement with young boys." In December, the therapist who had been working with Geoghan declares the priest "fully recovered."

- Between 1986 and 1989, several fresh allegations of molestations involving Geoghan are lodged with the Church. In 1989, Geoghan is placed on sick leave and undergoes therapy in institutes in Maryland and Connecticut. In November, he is released; his evaluation states that he is "moderately improved" and that the likelihood that he will "act out again" is "quite low," though there was no guarantee he wouldn't offend again. However, one psychiatrist who treated Geoghan tells the priest's bishop: "You'd better clip his wings before there is an explosion. . . . You can't afford to have him in a parish." Cardinal Law tells Geoghan: "I am confident that you will again render fine priestly service to the people of God in Saint Julia's Parish."
- In 1990, Geoghan is OK'd for return to priestly duties at St. Julia's. During the early 1990s, more than a half-dozen parents make complaints about Geoghan molesting their boys. In 1995, the Church receives a psychiatric evaluation of the priest that recommends that "Father Geoghan should have no interpersonal contact with male minors that is unsupervised." In the same year, Geoghan is accused of molesting a boy during the boy's sister's confirmation ceremony. In 1996, he spends six months in therapy at a psychiatric institute in Ontario.
- In 1996, after approving his retirement status, Cardinal Law says to Geoghan: "Yours has been an effective life of ministry, sadly impaired by illness. . . . God bless you, Jack." He is recommended for retirement.
- In 1997, Church officials review Geoghan's history of sexual abuse.
- In 1998, after suing the Boston diocese, a small portion of Geoghan's accusers are awarded $30 million (later reduced to $10 million). The accusations and lawsuits against Geoghan—and the Boston diocese—mount. Cardinal Law flies to Rome and requests the Vatican to relieve Geoghan of his collar. Geoghan is defrocked (www.kenanderson.net/bible/john_geoghan.html; Miller et al., 2002).

Geoghan's 2002 criminal conviction ignited a firestorm of commentary from the media, and soul-searching by the Catholic Church. In August 2003, Geoghan, then 68, an inmate in a maximum security penitentiary, was murdered by Joseph Druse, a fellow convict, and a neo-Nazi, racist, and homophobe. Some observers, including Geoghan's victims, said it was a fitting end for a man who caused a great deal of harm to a great many people who trusted him. However, the case of the infamous Father Geoghan produced two seismic changes in how the Roman Catholic Church and its parishioners handled instances of child abuse by priests. The first was the decision by the Catholic hierarchy in 2002 to dismiss abusive clerics from priesthood. And the second was that lay Catholics were no longer willing to keep silent when a priest abused their children. Geoghan's case unleashed a torrent of revelations of abuse stretching back decades.

The New York Times undertook its own investigation and found that the sexual abuse crisis that engulfed the Roman Catholic Church in the year after the conviction of John Geoghan "has spread to nearly every American diocese" (Goodstein, 2003, p. 1). As of the last day of 2002, the *Times* documented more than 1,200 cases of abusive priests nationwide involving over 4,200 people "who have claimed publicly or in lawsuits to have been abused by priests," although experts believe the number who have remained silent is certainly much larger (p. 1). The fact is, after 2002, the Roman Catholic Church would never be the same again.

Interestingly, in 1993, before the Geoghan case broke open, Cardinal Law had to deal with another abusive priest, Father James Porter of Fall River, who was criminally convicted of abusing 28 children and was sentenced to 20 years in prison. In response, Law formed a panel of experts to lay down policy for such cases; a copy of the panel's report was given to every priest in Law's diocese. But the report did *not* recommend that cases be turned over to the police; they were expected to be handled within the Church. Moreover, media attention to the Porter case, as well as to Geoghan, "sent the cardinal around the bend." He especially attacked *The Boston Globe,* whose writers later produced a series of articles, which was eventually collected into volume entitled *Betrayal: The Crisis in the Catholic Church.* Law's response to the attention the media devoted to priestly abuse was this: "By all means," he intoned, "we call down God's power on the media, particularly *The Globe*" (Miller et al., 2002, p. 49).

Geoghan is atypical, perhaps the very worst offender of a type of offense that is itself statistically atypical. The two sides of the Geoghan case are laid out by the two "missions" I spelled out in Chapter 2—the positivist's and the constructionist's mission. The positivist asks the "Why do they do it?" question. What causes child molestation by priests? Are the priests who molest different from those who don't? Is there something in their personalities or background that leads them to abuse the minors in their care? Or is it perhaps the distinctive qualities of the Roman Catholic Church that leads to molestation by the clergy, as some have argued (Wills, 2002)? The constructionist asks a very different question: How do different audiences *define* child abuse by clerics, and *react to* and *deal with* accused offenders? And here, the relevant audiences include the Catholic hierarchy, the offending priests, the Catholic laity, the families of molested boys, the public at large, the media, and law enforcement.

As I said earlier, by itself, priestly sexual abuse is an imperfect case of organizational deviance, since it is committed by individuals (albeit those who occupy an institutional position), and their actions subvert the intentions of the organization. In contrast, the cover-ups by Church authorities is a *perfect* case of organizational deviance, since it is usually done by a collectivity—one or more authorities who consult with one another and reach a decision together—and it is done with the (misguided) intention of protecting the organization. And here, it is the cover-up that has been the primary focus of criticism by the media and the public. The cover-up has two aspects. The first aspect relates to civil sanction, and the second, ecclesiastical.

First, unless a case independently came to the attention of secular authorities, prior to 2002, the Church *rarely,* and prior to 1985, the Church *practically never,* reported a case of priestly abuse to the police. The sexual molestation of a child is a crime. Says media pundit Charles Krauthammer: "Why didn't the Church call the cops?" Priests, and the bishops who preside over their conduct, are citizens of nations with laws that apply to everyone living within a jurisdiction. The surprise, says Krauthammer, is not that a tiny minority of priests abused the cloth and their charges. "The surprise is that when it happened—when the first child was abused by a priest—his superiors could see only the need for therapy and ministry." How the Church treats sin, he continues, is not a concern for non-Catholics. How the Church treats crime, "whether it reports criminality occurring within its gates for adjudication and punishment by secular authorities," is of absolute concern. The fact that such cries of outrage have sounded throughout the country by Catholic and non-Catholic alike are a sure-fire indication that the cover-ups of these crimes by Church authorities are regarded as a serious form of deviance by a substantial portion of the American public (Krauthammer, 2002).

The ecclesiastical side of the cover-up is this: In the past, when Church authorities received reports of priestly abuse, they almost never "defrocked" the priest, that is, removed him from the priesthood. In 2002, *The Washington Post* requested from the nation's 178 Roman Catholic dioceses complete records of cases of accusations of sexual abuse by priests going back to the 1960s. Ninety-six dioceses supplied the records, 82 refused to do so. In these records, there were a total of 855 priests against whom accusations were made, 218 of which were lodged specifically between January and June, 2002. Of the 355 priests who were removed from office prior to 2002, only 20 were defrocked. The remainder were asked to retire or were kept on as priests but not allowed to say Mass or engage in the ministry. Indeed, anecdotally, prior to 1985, *nearly every* priest against whom parishioners lodged sexual abuse charges was ordered to undergo psychological counseling or therapy and then simply transferred to another parish. Considering the seriousness of the charges, most observers, whether Catholic or non-Catholic, would regard the penalty so minor as to be "a slap on the wrist."

The question many observers have about such lenient punishments is why? Why the silence, the cover-ups, the shuffling of abusive priests from parish to parish, and the inability to punish offenders with a sanction as serious as the offense deserves? Why have abusive priests been protected by the Church for so long? Why did it take a series of scandals and criminal convictions for the Church to face and deal with the problem?

All organizations are self-protective; all act, in varying degrees, to cover up revelations that would be harmful to their interests. In this respect, as a religious organization, the Roman Catholic Church is different from other religious organizations only in the *degree* to which it is secretive of its sins. And it is clear that the difference lies in the fact that other denominations are far more decentralized. An accusation against an individual rabbi or Protestant minister is not typically considered an accusation against God (two possible exceptions: charismatic Protestant sects and the Jewish *haredim,* or the ultra-Orthodox). In contrast, the belief that priests are the embodiment of God's holiness is far more ingrained in Catholics, from the humblest layperson on up to the Pope himself. An attack on any aspect of the Church is regarded as an attack against God. Just as God must be defended, if anyone in the Church is venal, corrupt, or sinful, the Church must be protected from being undermined, even if it means covering up the venality, corruption, and sins of the wrongdoers. One of the boys in Boston "was struck in the face by his mother when he told her a priest had molested him" (Wills, 2002, p. 9). "By Vatican lights," says Jason Berry, author of *Lead Us Not Into Temptation,* a book about priestly abuse, "the worst thing a bishop can do is become publicly associated with a scandal" (Miller et al., 2002, p. 48).

Priests—and that most emphatically includes bishops and cardinals—feel that "the source of their wisdom must be their supernatural powers" (Wills, 2002, p. 8). Says Father Donald Cozzens, who has investigated and counseled pedophile clerics, the priest believes "he is not like other men." When he asked the priests he worked with whether they were sorry for causing harm to their victims, their response lacked conviction or remorse. "I don't remember one priest acknowledging any kind of moral torment for the behavior that got them in trouble" (p. 9). Moreover, "the conviction that they are above the law has much to do with the compliance of their victims" (p. 9). A file kept by the Boston diocese on pedophile priest Paul Shanley and released to the public by Shanley's lawyers for his victims' use in court reminds us of that fact. According to Wills: "The man expresses no feelings of guilt, *and his superiors never suggest that he should*" (my emphasis, p. 9). Throughout his dealings with authorities, Shanley "continues to feel that he is the wronged person." And Cardinal Law aided and abetted in this view by regarding one of his victims as something of a stalker. Said Law to Shanley: "It must be very discouraging to have someone following you" (p. 9). Law and his bishops "express unfailing support and sympathy for Shanley, and no sympathy—indeed little curiosity—about the minors he had sex with" (p. 9). In a letter to an archdiocesan administrator, Shanley admits to having been abused as a teenager and later, in the seminary by several priests. "His superiors worried little about what he did. Was that because they were more concerned with what he knew?" (p. 9).

SUMMARY

Organizational deviance is behavior that is (a) enabled or made possible by one or more actor's position(s) within an organization and is (b) regarded as nonnormative either within or outside a given organization. As a general rule, actions that are seen as an expression of the mandate of the organization are punished mildly or not at all by the organization, whereas those that are seen as corrupting or subverting the organization are handled more severely. However, organizations tend to be self-protective, and hence, the wrongdoing is often covered up to prevent outsiders from tainting and undermining the goals and integrity of the organization.

What makes organizational deviance interesting sociologically is that, for all other types of deviance, *every single person in the society can be evaluated as acceptable or unacceptable along a given axis.* All of us are fat, less fat, or not at all fat; honest or dishonest, or everything in between; atheists, agnostics, or believers; alcoholics, moderate drinkers, or abstainers; and so on. Only for organizational deviance is the relevant dimension *irrelevant* for most of us. Most of us cannot be placed along the relevant dimension because we are not members of the organization in question. Most of us do not have an executive position, and hence, cannot be evaluated with respect to whether we have committed corporate crime or not. Only a small percentage of us are police officers; thus, we cannot be evaluated as to whether we have engaged in excessive force with a suspect. Very few of us are Catholic priests; therefore, the overwhelming majority of us cannot be evaluated as to whether or not we committed the sexual abuse of children *as* a Catholic priest. (In principle, all adults could engage in child molestation—but not as a Catholic priest.) In other words, the position makes the deviant act possible. Since most of us do not occupy the relevant position, we stand outside the dimension of evaluation.

However, even though most of us cannot *be* evaluated as having committed, or not committed, a given form of organization deviance, all of us evaluate *others* for having done so. And, since organizations are not always successful in shielding wrongdoing in their ranks from the prying eyes of others, the general public often becomes a crucial audience that evaluates organizational behavior. Often, the general public's evaluation of wrongdoing within a given organization is radically at odds with evaluations made by members of the organization. Some acts are judged more harshly by the general public than by organizational members; occasionally, it is the reverse. Law enforcement, the courts, and the media are additional relevant audiences who render judgments about organizational behavior.

White-collar and corporate crime constitute an important form of organizational deviance. Most of the time, when the term "white-collar crime" is used, it refers to corporate crime. Not all white-collar criminals are rich and powerful. In fact, in the world of white-collar crime, there are a lot more "small fry" than "big fish." Perhaps the best way of dividing up white-collar crimes is those that are on behalf of an individual against the corporation (embezzlement); those that are *on behalf* of the corporation *against* the general public, consumers, or employees (corporate crime). Other types include governmental crime (receiving bribes, violating international treaties) and professional crime (performing unnecessary surgery, overcharging a client).

As deviance, the public's reaction to corporate crime is ambiguous. On the other hand, public opinion polls reveal that most people regard corporate crimes that harm people as serious offenses. On the other hand, when corporate criminals are judged by a jury, they tend to receive penalties that do not match the seriousness of the offense. Whether corporate crime is a legitimate form of deviance isn't a cut-and-dried matter. Corporate crime tends to be made up of acts that are complex and not easily determined by nonexperts; intermingled with legitimate business; cause diffuse victimization; entail sums of money that are substantially greater than those of street crimes; be prosecuted only rarely; not fit the public's stereotype of what a crime is; be underplayed by the media (unless the sums are vast); be relatively unstigmatizing for the perpetrators; and be lacking in the intention to harm victims.

We can distinguish two types of police use of force: first, cases that are seen by the police to *undermine* their law enforcement mandate, and second, those that are regarded as being *in the service of* law enforcement. In the case of the second, the action is judged only in retrospect to have been wrong—a mistake. Most officers regarded the case of the torture of Abner Louima as a clear-cut case of excessive force, both deviant and illegal. In contrast, the shooting of Amadou Diallo was seen by most officers as a case of normal force, that is, normative and lawful—although, again, a tragic mistake. The case of Rodney King's beating drew more mixed reactions from the police, though it was more similar to Louima's torture than Diallo's shooting.

Catholic priests engaging in child molestation is only marginally a case of organizational deviance. But its cover-up by the Church powers that be is a form of organizational deviance *par excellence.* For years—indeed, probably for centuries—the Catholic Church implicitly condoned sexual abuse of children by priests. The usual punishment was a slap on the wrist—counseling and transfer to another parish. A series of cases of priestly abuse that came to the attention of civil authorities, resulted in criminal prosecution and attracted media glare, awakened lay Catholics, the general public, and the Catholic hierarchy to the Church's widespread tolerance of the practice. After 2002, such practices were no longer possible on the same scale. It is possible that, as a result of the scandal, the way the Catholic Church handles cases of priestly abuse was changed forever.

Account: Employee Pilferage

At the time she wrote this account Nancy was a 22-year-old college student. She describes her involvement with employee pilferage in the following words.

During the summer, I began working in a clothing store in a mall. I became friendly with another girl, Sandra, because we had a lot in common. Both of us were pissed off that we had to work hard for a lousy paycheck—money we were saving up for college. We were more pissed because we had to spend part of that money on clothes we had to buy in the store. It was policy that all employees had to wear the store name brand to work. The clothes were pretty expensive, plus a 30 percent employee discount didn't amount to much when we only got paid eight bucks an hour.

Without specifically stating her desire to steal, Sandra often tested me to see if I would steal from the store. She'd say, "We could get this stuff for free," or "I bet they wouldn't notice this if it was missing," or "It would be so easy to take stuff from this store." Since my parents raised me in a family that didn't allow stealing, I believed it was wrong. I didn't give the implications of what Sandra was saying to me much thought. But as the customers got ruder, management got stricter about the dress code, and the realization sank in that the pay I got was going to stay low, I began agreeing with what she said. I became so fed up with the job that I thought stealing a little here and there was all right, because it made me happy to get things for free and because it helped make up for the low pay. I began believing I deserved to get all the merchandise I wanted because I had to deal with that lousy job.

One night, Sandra mentioned that all the employees except management used to steal. She said they'd take everything from wallets to sweaters to jeans. She told me no one dares to do it any more because one of their employees got busted. She said management had even started checking the employees' belongings, but had since stopped. Sandra told me it had been easy to get stuff when the store was closed when everyone was in on it because one person could distract the manager and the rest could have a field day before they quit work. The guy who got busted just took it too far; he even let his friends in on it. He had filled up three shopping bags full of uncensored jeans, belts, and sweatshirts and placed it in a bin so his friend could walk into the store, pick up the bags, and walk out without anyone suspecting a thing. His friend showed up at closing time, and the manager noticed he did not come into the store with a bag and he hadn't purchase anything. The manager had even noticed this boy before and was aware that he was a friend of one of her employees. So she approached him as he was nearing the exit and asked how he got those bags. He concocted a story about how he bought the merchandise earlier in the day. She asked him if she could see the receipt, but he said he had thrown it out. When she asked him how much it all cost, the boy was stumped. She also asked him which employee sold the merchandise. So he finally told her the whole story, and she called the police. Both boys were taken into police custody and the employee was fired. At that point, all the employees made an informal agreement that they would stop taking stuff. No one wanted to get arrested.

But Sandra and I had two advantages over the other employees in the store: We were friendly with management. We were close to them in age, we hung out at the same clubs, and we knew their friends. The other employees were high school kids. Plus, Sandra was very good friends with Rebecca, an employee who was recently promoted and trusted with the store key. This meant that Rebecca could open and close the store on her own without supervision from the manager or assistant manager. This meant that Sandra and I could now take anything we wanted, plus it decreased our chance of getting caught. Rebecca had been in on all the previous stealing jobs, before that employee got busted, so she didn't care about us stealing. Before long, Rebecca began stealing right along with us.

Usually, we took stuff the nights Rebecca closed the store. Since at that hour, she was the person in charge, she told the employees they could leave by 8:30 if they got the store cleaned up in time. Then she'd say "I'll need one person to stay and help me count down the drawers and make the evening deposit." Then she'd turn to me and say, "Would you mind staying for a bit?" Then I'd say, "Sure, I don't mind, but Sandra is going to have to stay as well because I have to drive her home." So Rebecca would say that's fine. At 8:30, Rebecca said to the employees that the store looks great, they had done a good job, and she'd see us tomorrow. Locking the door was the green light for Sandra, Rebecca, and me to take anything we wanted. Actually, we did help Rebecca count down the drawers, but while we were doing it, we talked about what we'd be taking home with us.

Some nights we took a couple of things and shoved them into our backpacks. But other nights we got really greedy. Those nights we'd take merchandise off the floor, uncensor it in the stockroom with the handgun we used, and load up bags of stuff. Then we left, locked up the store, got in our cars, and went home as if nothing had ever happened. Some nights we'd have "theme" nights—"footwear night," or "denim night"—where we'd take all of one type of item. Other nights we'd fix up our hair and makeup, pick out new outfits, get dressed in the dressing room, and go out to a party or a club.

Once in a while, we took stuff for our friends or boyfriends. Sandra used to tell a couple of her friends that she'd pick up merchandise for them using her employee discount. Then she'd take what they had requested and pocket the difference. One night Rebecca told a guy she had a crush on to come into the store at eight and go shopping for free. This guy brought three of his friends along. They picked stuff out, tried it on to see if it fit, brought it to the counter, we uncensored everything, and they walked out. Although the guy never showed any romantic interest in Rebecca, after that night they became good friends.

Sandra and I took our idea a step further. We began going to [Nancy mentions two specific stores] to find out what they were carrying from our store. Then the night Rebecca was supposed to close, we took stuff that could be returned to another store and told the sales clerk we had received the merchandise as a gift and we'd like to exchange it. This was never a problem; the clerks were always cooperative. It would have been better if these two stores gave us cash for the return, but they only gave us store credit because we didn't have receipts for the merchandise. Sandra was able to purchase a beautiful and very expensive pocket book, a television, and a pair of designer boots; I bought a pair of gold hoop earrings and a fashionable shirt.

One day, Rebecca told us management believed that one of the employees was a thief. When I heard that, I got scared. It finally dawned on me that I could get into serious trouble if management found out what we were up to. They never told her whom they were suspicious of, but we decided it would be the smart thing to quit for a while. We found out that the managers suspected one of the stock boys, and he was terminated immediately after a surprise check of all employees' belongings and lockers. At the next monthly store meeting, the managers tried to scare all the employees by saying, about the stock boy who had just been fired, "Let this be an example." After that meeting, Sandra, Rebecca, and I were laughing hysterically because each one of us was wearing something we had taken from the store. After that meeting, I realized the managers didn't suspect any of the three of us at all. I felt relieved and decided to go ahead with our plan one last time. We planned a final night to steal merchandise so that we could go back to college in style. Time to stock up before we became penniless college students again. We figured we could save the money we had earned.

Actually, that night almost never happened. When I arrived at work, I was disappointed because I saw my district manager, the store buyer, and the company president in the store. When I saw them, I figured the store managers were on to what we were doing. But as it turned

(*Continued*)

Account: Employee Pilferage Continued

out, they didn't suspect a thing. In fact, they complimented me on a window display I had decorated the night before. The district manager told me I'd be missed when I left for school; if I wanted to work during holidays, I was welcome to do so. When eight o'clock rolled around, we rushed to clean up the store and waited for Rebecca to tell us to lock the door behind the last employee. We filled up five shopping bags, each of our backpacks, and wore new jackets out of the store. I carried a brand-new brown leather coat over my arm. As walked to our cars, we casually walked past a mall security guard, who commented, "You ladies have certainly been busy shopping today, haven't you?" We laughed and told him, "We're going back to school, so we gotta look good!" He laughed and said, "Have a good night, ladies!"

Questions

According to your personal attitudes, is Nancy's behavior deviant? Would it be regarded as deviant to the American public? If management had apprehended Nancy, Sandra, and Rebecca stealing, do you feel they should have been arrested? Where would you rank their crime with respect to its severity or seriousness? In at least one respect, what they did is most decidedly deviant; what is that one respect? Do you think Nancy would have committed her crimes without group support? What is the significance of the fact that, at one time, all the employees below management stole from the store? Do you think, as some sociologists do, that management looks the other way when employees steal, enabling the store to exploit workers because stealing boosts employee morale, making them satisfied with their low wages? If employee pilferage is the largest source of the direct theft of goods and cash in the United States, why isn't more done by stores to stop it? Why was it so easy for Nancy and her friends to get away with it? What's the lesson of Nancy's account for the student of deviance?

CHAPTER

11

Cognitive Deviance: Unconventional Beliefs

Is atheism deviant? Indeed it is! In the United States, year after year, polls indicate that over 80 percent of the population believes in God. A substantial proportion of theists feel that someone who doesn't believe in God is not a moral person and "might not be fully trustworthy." In 2007, a Gallup Poll asked whether they would consider voting for a Catholic presidential candidate, 95 percent of Americans said yes; for an African American, 94 percent (in fact, in 2008, an African American *was* elected president); for a Jew, 92 percent; for a woman, 88 percent; for a Mormon, 72 percent; for someone married three times, 67 percent; and for a homosexual, 55 percent. But in this poll, only 45 percent said that they would consider voting for an atheist. In other words, more than half of the American public feels that atheism is so deviant that it disqualifies a candidate to be president of the United States. Not believing in God, it seems, is unpatriotic, and, one would conclude, deviant as well.

Not so fast, says the critic. In the past 20 years, according to the American Religious Identification Survey, the number of atheists has more than tripled—from 1 million in 1990 to 3.6 million in 2009—today, twice the number of Episcopalians in the population. The percent of religiously unaffiliated American voters has more than doubled, from 5 to 12 percent, almost the percentage of African Americans; and the percent self-identifying as Christian declined from 86 percent in 1990 to 76 percent in 2009 (Meacham, 2009). So while to the mainstream of the society, atheism remains a form of deviance, that disapproval is softening. Say some observers, atheists are "growing in number and visibility," and becoming *less* deviant over time (Goodstein, 2009). Less deviant, perhaps, but not completely conventional.

Cognitive deviance often reveals cultural differences so vast that, when revealed, and reactions play themselves out, people are killed, relations between and among nations are stretched to the breaking point, international trade is terminated and millions of dollars of revenue lost to one or the other side of the dispute, and major institutions are undermined. These unbridgeable differences between contending parties speak eloquently of the relativity of deviance, cultural and subcultural *definitions* of deviance, clashing norms about what views can and cannot be expressed, and what the appropriate reaction is when norms are violated. Cognitive or "intellectual" deviance often generates enormous hostility and punitive official reaction, and the exercise of power, or the manifestation of powerless, on one side or the other.

In Iran, China, Pakistan, and Saudi Arabia, the government censors blocks access to certain Web sites; in China alone, the government employs 40,000 censors. In 2008, sites offered a new software that allowed users to evade government censors; within a few months, "more than 400,000 Iranians were surfing the uncensored Web" (Markoff, 2009, p. A1).

In 2005, *Jyllans-Posten,* a Danish newspaper, published cartoons critical of Muslims, one of them depicting Muhammad wearing a turban in the form of a bomb. It touched off protests, demonstrations, death threats, the firebombing of dozens of buildings housing Western businesses, boycotts, screaming, rampaging mobs, the killing by the police of more than a dozen protesters storming an American compound in Afghanistan, and the torching of at least two Danish embassies in two Middle Eastern countries.

In Rome, Richard Williamson, an excommunicated Catholic Bishop who had earlier made a speech denying the existence of Nazi gas chambers and the extent, even the very fact, of the Holocaust, under pressure from the Vatican, apologized for having made such schismatic statements. His statements did not, however, address the issue of whether he still thought his statements were truthful (Donadio, 2009). Observers wondered whether such a tepid recantation was enough to stop the erosion of the Church's moral authority caused by his original statement.

Did NASA, the United States space administration, land astronauts on the moon, six times? Or was the moon mission a hoax, a conspiracy perpetrated by nefarious politicians and their agents to bolster the sagging morale of an increasingly pessimistic public during dark times? Polls indicate that about 6 percent of the American population believes that the moon landings never happened, and that they were staged on a secret movie set somewhere in the desert for political purposes. Bart Sibrel, a filmmaker and director of *A Funny Thing Happened on the Way to the Moon,* has made a career of moon-landing denial. He even pestered astronaut Buzz Aldrin by waving a

Bible in his face and calling him "a coward, and a liar, and a thief." Mr. Aldrin became exasperated to the point where he punched Sibrel in the face; law enforcement refused to charge the astronaut with a crime. "I have suffered only persecution and financial loss," Sibrel told a reporter. "I've lost visitation with my son. I've been expelled from churches. All because I believe the Moon landings are fraudulent" (Schwartz, 2009).

Cognitive or intellectual deviance is the expression of beliefs that are contrary to the views of specific audiences. Of course, such expressions are deviant *in context,* so that criticisms of Mormon theology—which are themselves deviant to the majority of Americans—would be deviant *among Mormons.* The expression of some beliefs are hostile to established interests, the ruling elite, and the regime in power; some are hostile to the views of the majority of the public; and some, to those of particular sectors or social circles within the society.

It might seem controversial to argue that beliefs and their expression make up a form of deviance. After all, isn't it true that though you can get arrested for enacting certain *behavior,* you can't get arrested for holding, or even expressing, a certain *belief*? How can holding unconventional beliefs be a form of deviance? Doesn't everyone have a right to believe whatever they please? Isn't what you believe "nobody's business but your own"?

Well, ideally, but not in practice. First of all, you *can* be arrested for expressing a belief. Not in Western society at this time, but in past centuries, yes, one could be arrested for expressing many beliefs. In Europe a few hundred years ago, the air was rank from the burning flesh of heretics and blasphemers, or supposed heretics and blasphemers. And over the centuries, even in the West, religious wars have led to the slaughter of millions of Catholics, Protestants, unbelievers, Muslims, and Jews. And people are still arrested elsewhere for expressing certain assertions; even more important for our purposes, *informal* reactions to definitions of right and wrong define what's deviant, and, by this definition, there's no doubt that expressing certain ideas is deviant in some social circles. Cognitive deviance may not be an appropriate subject for a *criminology* course, but it is for a *deviance* course.

Many audiences *do* react negatively to the expression of certain beliefs. Certain audiences do *not* feel that beliefs and their expression are "nobody's business but your own." In the West, even if people aren't arrested for expressing unconventional views today, they can be criticized, denounced, and can lose their job. The fact is, almost as many—and in some eras of history, even more—people have been punished, stigmatized, and condemned for expressing their beliefs as for their behavior. One of Erving Goffman's types of stigma is "blemishes of individual character," one portion of which includes "treacherous and rigid beliefs" (1963, p. 4). And a belief that one person regards as "treacherous and rigid," another sees as just and righteous, and vice versa. So, *of course,* holding beliefs that wander off the beaten path is a form of deviance. William Newman identified three minority groups: behavioral, cognitive, and physical. "Behavioral" minorities varied from the norm in conduct; an example: homosexuals. "Cognitive" minorities varied from the norm with respect to their beliefs. An example: members of religious sects and cults. And "physical" minorities varied from the norm in appearance; for example: the handicapped (Newman, 1973, p. 35). Holding unconventional beliefs is an *important* form of deviance.

Cognition refers to knowing—that is, what one believes to be true. It encompasses "beliefs, disbeliefs, guesses, suspicions, judgments, and so forth" (Douglas and Waksler, 1982, p. 364). When sociologists refer to "knowing," we do not imply that these views are empirically correct (or that they are wrong). What we mean is that people *think* that they are true. Cognition refers to the belief that a given assertion or claim is valid. Cognitive deviance refers to holding beliefs that are unconventional and nonnormative, which, in some social circles, causes their believers to be shunned, isolated, marginalized, rendered powerless, criticized, condemned, or punished. And it is the *expression* of beliefs that gets the believer in trouble. After all, the belief has to be *known* to disapproving audiences.

With respect to the central analytic features of deviance—what makes something *deviant*—in principle, deviant beliefs are identical in all basic respects to deviant acts. The same basic principles apply: Someone, or a category of persons, is regarded by the members of one or more audiences as violating a rule or norm, and the members of those audiences are likely to condemn or punish them. The content of the belief is less important than the fact that that belief is deemed normatively unacceptable. Thus, being an atheist violates a rule that says one must believe in God; belief in creationism violates the principles of scientific reasoning; belief in evolution violates a literal reading of the Bible; belief in alien spaceships violates a law that says that objects cannot travel faster than the speed of light; and so on. Because specific audiences hold certain beliefs to be nonnormative, unconventional, unacceptable, scandalous, heretical, vulgar, unseemly, improper, and/or just plain wrong, they isolate, stigmatize, condemn, and/or punish the persons who hold them. Of course, precisely the beliefs that *one* audience finds unconventional, *another* accepts as normatively correct. In these respects, holding unconventional beliefs is no different from engaging in unconventional behavior. Both result in stigma and condemnation. In other words, social rules apply "not only to how one behaves but also *how and what one thinks*" (Douglas and Waksler, 1982, p. 366). And to the extent that audiences treat others negatively—for instance, that they consider them immoral, unpatriotic, and, let's say, refuse to vote for them if they are a political candidate—how one thinks is a form of deviance.

It is not always a simple matter to separate beliefs from behavior. Often, unacceptable beliefs *translate into* or *become a basis for* unacceptable behavior. Someone who holds a certain belief announces to the world that he or she has the potential to act in a certain way. In other words, the *believer* can become an *actor*.

The belief that Jews are parasites who are organized into an international conspiracy to enslave the Christian world (Abanes, 1996, pp. 175–178; Lamy, 1996, pp. 118–134) is far more than a mere belief: Some members of organized groups who hold such beliefs have committed overt violence against Jews. In the 1950s and 1960s, many politically mainstream Americans feared and stigmatized communists not merely because of their unconventional political ideology but also because they sincerely believed that communism was actively dedicated to the destruction of everything they valued: religion, spiritual values, the conventional family, democratic elections, the work ethic, a free market economy, a free press—in other words, that which defined the "American way of life." Hence, audiences may label or condemn people who hold unconventional beliefs because they fear that these believers pose a clear and present danger to the way of life—indeed, the very physical existence—of right-thinking people everywhere. Hence, many cognitive belief systems are not deviant *merely* because they violate mainstream notions of what's true. Their proponents are *also* regarded as deviants because of the behavior those beliefs could potentially call forth. The deviant nature of terrorists is not that they criticize the U.S. government; it is that they are likely to commit violence against innocent victims.

Cognitive deviance overlaps with mental disorder. Psychiatrists and clinical psychologists regard the expression of certain beliefs as a manifestation or an indicator of a pathological psychic condition. For instance, schizophrenics are said to suffer from *delusions* and *hallucinations*. One man describes a transmitter that has been implanted in his teeth that receives signals from a distant galaxy commanding him to deliver a message to everyone on earth about a coming catastrophe. A woman believes that her thoughts have been sucked out of her mind by a "phrenological vacuum extractor" (Kring et al., 2010). A man believes that X-rays have entered his body through his neck, passed down to his waist, and settled in his genitals, preventing him from getting an erection. A woman claims that she is "just a puppet who is manipulated by cosmic strings. When the strings are pulled my body moves and I cannot prevent it." Clearly, then, people who are diagnosed as having a mental disorder often hold deviant beliefs.

Just as there are parallels between mental disorder and cognitive deviance, however, there are differences as well. Schizophrenia is nearly always accompanied by a number of other disturbances in addition to cognitive delusions and hallucinations. Some of these include flat or inappropriate emotions, bizarre motor activity, and the use of jumbled words ("word salad") and thoughts. Clinical depression, too, is marked by inappropriate beliefs, but in addition, it is a *mood* disorder characterized by feelings of sadness, dread, apprehension, worthlessness, guilt, and anhedonia, or an inability to take pleasure in life.

In contrast, *by itself,* cognitive deviance, or holding unconventional beliefs, is not necessarily linked with any psychiatric disorder. Mental disorder and cognitive deviance are *empirically* related but *definitionally* separate and distinct. In other words, while mental health professionals would classify many cognitive deviants as mentally disordered, and many of the persons they classify as mentally disordered would also be regarded as cognitive deviants, neither category demands or necessitates the other.

Beliefs are not deviant simply because of their content. No belief, however bizarre it might seem to us, is *inherently* or *objectively* deviant. A belief is deviant in two ways—one, normatively, and two, reactively. In other words, one, because it violates the tenets of the dominant belief system, or simply a different belief system, and two, because its adherents are likely to be condemned or punished by the members of the society at large or specific subgroups within that society, that is, a given audience. A belief is deviant both because it is *considered* wrong and its believers are *treated* as socially unacceptable—*in* a given society or collectivity.

Many ideas have been regarded as heretical—and therefore *deviant*—at one point in time, yet later *came to be* accepted as true or valid. In 1633, the Catholic Inquisition imposed the penalty of house arrest in Galileo because he argued that the earth revolved around the sun, an assertion that was contrary to Catholic dogma, which held that the earth is the center of the universe. In 1854, Viennese physicians ridiculed Ignaz Semmelweis for asserting that physicians could transmit disease to patients after they dissected rotting cadavers; *in* the 1850s, the medical establishment regarded Semmelweis as a deviant. Today, any physician asserting that physicians should *not* wash their hands before thrusting them into patients' bodies would be regarded as the deviant. Beginning in 1915, and, in revisions throughout the 1920s, a German astrophysicist Alfred Wenger proposed the theory that 300 million years ago, the earth's crust formed one giant continent, Pangaea, that broke apart over time into the continents we know today. They are still drifting, and will continue to do so for as long as the earth exists. For nearly a half-century, Wenger's theory met with scathing derision almost uniform hostility; it was not until the 1960s that virtually all earth scientists accepted continental drift and plate tectonics as a valid description of geological processes.

Because of his astronomical statements, *to* the hierarchy of the Catholic Church, *in* the 1600s, Galileo was a cognitive deviant; *because* of his medical claim, *to* physicians *in* the 1800s, Ignaz Semmelweis was a cognitive deviant; *because* of the publication of his books espousing the theory of continental drift, *to* geologists between 1915 and the 1950s, Alfred Wenger was a cognitive deviant (Ben-Yehuda, 1985). The fact that these theories have proven to be valid is *irrelevant* to the fact that *at* one time, *to* a certain audience, these theories *were* heretical, and hence, their creator *was* condemned and punished—and hence, deviant.

To repeat a point I've made throughout this book: Deviance makes sense *only* with reference to the beliefs and reactions of certain audiences. Beliefs that are regarded as wrong, unacceptable, and deviant in one social circle may be considered right, good, proper, and true in another. Among political radicals, conservativism is anathema—unacceptable and deviant. Contrarily, among conservatives, radicals are on the hot seat. To the fundamentalist Christian, the atheist is the spawn of Satan, most decidedly a deviant. Turn the picture around: To the atheist, fundamentalist Christians are ignorant, narrow-minded fools. Here, we encounter the process of "mutual deviantization" (Aho, 1994, p. 62).

But let's be clear about this: Deviance is never *solely* a matter of the word of the members of one social category against that of another. Yes, we live in a society that is an assemblage of different and mutually antagonistic belief systems. But society is as much a ladder as a mosaic. This means that some beliefs are more *dominant* than others; their adherents have more power and credibility, and hence, can legitimate their beliefs and discredit those of their opponents. To the extent that a particular belief is taught as true in the educational system, it is dominant, legitimate, and credible; to the extent that, when a belief is expressed in schools, its proponents tend to be *disparaged,* that belief is deviant. To the extent that holding a certain belief is a criterion among a majority of the electorate to vote for a given political candidate, it is a dominant belief. To the extent that a substantial segment of the electorate *refuses* to vote for a political candidate because he or she is known to hold a certain view, that view is deviant. To the extent that a given belief is taken for granted as true in the mainstream media, it is dominant; to the extent that holders of a given belief are scorned, rebuked, and ridiculed—that belief is deviant. In each of society's major institutions, we can locate beliefs that are mainstream, "inside the lines," and conventional, dominant, or hegemonic; *and* we can locate those beliefs that are nonmainstream, outside the lines, beyond the pale, and unconventional—in a word, from the societal point of view, *deviant*.

THE SOCIAL FUNCTIONS OF BELIEF SYSTEMS

Are beliefs just beliefs? To put the matter even more emphatically, are beliefs *ever* just beliefs? How does the sociologist approach deviant beliefs? More generally, how do *we,* as students of the sociology of deviance, approach beliefs? As Berger and Luckmann say, the task of sociologists who study beliefs is not to look at beliefs for their own sake, to take them as just beliefs, and attempt to prove them right—or, on the other hand, debunk or prove them wrong. Instead, sociologists attempt to understand the social conditions that *generate* or *encourage* them (Berger and Luckmann, 1966, p. 12). The basic insight of sociology is that beliefs serve social functions that *transcend* their uniqueness *and* their empirical validity or truth value. We argue that the way humans think is rooted in the material and social world. Beliefs usually grow out of real-world conditions and tend to have real-world consequences.

For thousands of years, theorists, philosophers, intellectuals, academics, social scientists, and other observers of social reality have commented on the relationship between the *ideational* world—the world of thoughts, beliefs, and ideas—and the *material* world, such as what people do for a living, where they live, and what social categories they belong to and participate in. Theories have been proposed to account for that relationship. The central thrust of these writings is that beliefs spring from social conditions, they serve social functions, and they have social consequences.

Most of us think that what we believe comes from our own special, unique individuality. We convince ourselves that our beliefs would be the same, even if we had been subject to very different social influences. Sociologist Joel Charon asks the question "Why do we believe what we believe?" To answer it, he invites the reader to ask the following questions: "If my life had been different, if I had been born at a different time or place, would I still believe in God? Would my beliefs about God be the same as they are now?" (Charon, 1995, p. 99). Do you really think your beliefs would be the same if you had grown up in a different time and place? If you had grown up two centuries ago the child of a white slave owner, would you have believed that slavery is evil? If you had been a gentile child in Nazi Germany, would you have believed that Jews are good, decent people who deserve the same rights as everyone else? If you had been born a thousand years ago in the New Guinea highlands, would you have had the same religious beliefs you have now? Or had you been born on a Polynesian island half a millennium ago, would you have thought that public nudity was immoral? Do you really believe that, in a different society in a different time period, you would have had exactly the same notions of right and wrong and true and false that you have now? "Can you think of *any* idea you believe that does not have primarily a *social* foundation? Is there anything we believe that has not arisen primarily though *interaction* with others" (p. 99)? The first and more or less universally accepted sociological principle of beliefs is that they arise through social interaction with others. In short, *human consciousness is determined by social existence* (Berger and Luckmann, 1966, pp. 5–6).

Karl Marx, a nineteenth-century German intellectual who, for more than a century and a half, had a profound impact on sociology, philosophy, history, and economics, argued that the way we think at a particular time and place is a *reflection* of the economic arrangements of the society in which we live. "Morality, religion, metaphysics, all the rest of ideology and their corresponding forms of consciousness," Marx wrote, "thus no longer retain the semblance of independence. . . . Life is not determined by consciousness, but consciousness by life" (1846/1947, pp. 14–15). And by life, Marx meant *economic* life. It is the nature of the economy that determines the nature of a society's art, politics, religion, science, and system of justice—in short, the ideational world, the world of beliefs and ideas. Moreover, in any society, it is the dominant social class whose ideas tend to be most influential.

> The class which has the means of material production at its disposal, has control at the same time over the means of mental production. . . . The individuals composing the ruling class . . . rule also as thinkers, as producers of ideas, and regulate the production and distribution of the ideas of their age: thus their ideas are the ruling ideas of the epoch. (p. 39)

The influence of Marx's theories has declined considerably during the past generation or so. Most social scientists and intellectuals see a much more complex and less deterministic relationship between the economy and beliefs. They argue that ideas can influence the economy as much as the economy can influence ideas and see the many institutions, including art, religion, and politics, as "codeterminate," or equally capable of influencing one another. For instance, Max Weber, an early twentieth-century sociologist, argued that religious beliefs influence the economic life of a society as much as the other way around. It was ascetic, rationalistic seventeenth-century Protestantism, he said, that stimulated industrial capitalism—a case of ideas generating material conditions rather than the reverse. The Industrial Revolution could not have emerged in a society dominated by religions such as Hinduism and Buddhism because they denied rationality and the central importance of the material world.

Max Weber wrote of the *elective affinity* people have for certain ideas and beliefs (1946, pp. 62–63, 284–285), that is, the social and material conditions in which they live influence the likelihood that they would be receptive to certain ideas. They do not choose (or "elect") their beliefs—their social and material conditions do. The privileged classes tend to be attracted to religions that assure them that their status is justified and legitimate. For the poorer strata, religious beliefs (or, alternatively, political beliefs) will be appealing to the extent that these beliefs offer a salvation of compensation, that is, righting the wrongs they feel have been inflicted upon them, whether in this world or the next. The prophecy of seventh-century Islam was especially appealing to warriors. The religious expression that middle-class urban dwellers during early Protestantism found compatible with their way of life was practical, rational, based on a mastery of nature and relations with others. Members of the bureaucratic class—whether in ancient Rome or in the contemporary West—have found irrational, ecstatic, or completely otherworldly religious expression unappealing, but were comfortable with a religion that offered ways of controlling the masses (Weber, 1922/1963, pp. 89, 107, 108, 265). Weber sees much more diversity in the ideas of the many social classes in the society than did Marx—who pictured only two social classes. Weber neither sees the ruling class so overwhelmingly dominant that their ideas are the ruling ideas of the era, nor does he see liberation as the only function of the ideas of oppressed peoples. Ideas and beliefs may serve many functions aside from their economic interests.

In other words, unlike Marx, Max Weber saw a *two-way street* between the ideational world—the world of beliefs and ideas—and the material conditions of people's lives. People are attracted to beliefs because they are compatible with the way they live. But the way they live is much more than economic circumstances alone. It includes the many and myriad facets of our existence. And ideas and beliefs, in turn, can act back on material conditions. For instance, a religion can generate ideas that either stimulate or inhibit a certain kind of economic system. Buddhism, practiced in Tibet and Bhutan, rejects materialism—and therefore the very basis of industrial capitalism. In contrast, as we saw, according to Weber the beliefs of seventeenth-century Protestantism actively encouraged the Industrial Revolution. So, to Weber, there is reciprocity here. In contrast, to

Marx, it was more of a one-way relationship—economic circumstances cause beliefs. On this issue, most contemporary theorists prefer Weber's way of thinking to that of Marx.

The functions that deviant belief systems serve can be looked at from two different approaches—one, the functions they serve for the believer, and two, the functions that *opposing* unconventional beliefs and *condemning* their believers serve for the society at large or, more specifically, for their condemners.

Each of the belief systems discussed in this chapter functions in one way or another for certain strata or social circles or segments of the society. Each affirms the believer's way of life or upholds a certain vision of the way things are. Each is supported by a specific epistemology or way of knowing, and each points to a way of looking at things, a belief system that it rejects or which rejects theirs. Some are backed up by a *demonology*—the designation of an immoral, fiendish wrongdoer who represents evil in the flesh—while others merely point out the errors perpetrated by persons who fail to see things the way they see them. Beliefs respond or correspond to issues that are a vital part of the way their believers live their lives; all answer questions and provide solutions to problems that make them believable or credible to some of the members of a society rather than others.

Thus, in cognitive deviance there are usually two sets of deviants—to each side of the controversy, the *other* side. To Martin Luther, Catholicism was deviant—indeed, evil. To the pope, Martin Luther and his Protestant followers were deviant, a representative of the devil. To the person who believes that UFOs are spaceships from another planet, anyone who denies that belief is wrong, cognitively in error—or part of the cover-up to hide the fact that aliens are all around us. Looked at from the other end of the controversy, the parties who are wedded to the mainstream institutions, UFO believers are wrong, silly, irrational, and most decidedly deviant. To the fundamentalist Christian, proponents of evolution are secular humanists and hence the spawn of Satan; to the traditional scientist, creationists are ignorant, closed-minded enemies of reason and enlightenment. The list could be multiplied endlessly. In this sense, we are talking about looking at definitions of deviance in horizontal terms—from one group, category, or social circle to another.

But there's another dimension, the vertical dimension: What is central in any controversy is which side has the influence to legitimate and validate its own special view of right or wrong and true or false. *Whose* notion of right and wrong are we talking about here?

It is true that *in* creationist circles and *to* creationist audiences, evolutionists are considered deviant. But it's also true that with respect to power, influence, legitimacy, and credibility, creationists are *marginalized;* their views are *not* mainstream in the society at large. This is what makes creationism a deviant belief system—not because they are empirically wrong. (That is a separate issue.) Evolution, not creationism, is taught in the dominant institutions, promulgated in the dominant media, believed among the most well-educated strata. In the event that the mainstream institutions were to legitimate creationism and stigmatize and marginalize evolutionist thinking, then it would be the evolutionist whom the sociologist would designate as the cognitive deviant.

The same applies to the belief that UFOs are real. The belief that unidentified flying objects (UFOs) are alien spaceships is held by just under half of all Americans; the belief that they are not is held by the same proportion. So what then makes the belief, "UFOs are real," deviant? It is deviant *societally* because it does not have hierarchical legitimacy. The most influential media (the news divisions of the television networks, *The New York Times, The Washington Post, Time, Newsweek,* etc.), the relevant departments in major universities, and the major, mainstream churches do not accept the belief as true. If a political candidate were to announce the belief in a speech—or to urge that its truth be adopted by educational curricula—he or she would be ridiculed by the media. When John Mack, a Harvard professor, published a book asserting his belief that people had been kidnapped by aliens (1995), a shockwave of horror rumbled through the university community. When Minister Farrakhan announced that he had visited an extraterrestrial spaceship, observers denounced him as a crackpot (Brackman, 1996). Again, charges of deviance can more easily be legitimated by influential representatives of social institutions than by those who are weaker and more marginal. But once again, *within* those weaker, more marginal sectors of the society, the dominant definitions of right and wrong may nonetheless be regarded as deviant. To repeat, as students of deviance, we need to think in terms of *both* the vertical *and* the horizontal dimensions of deviance.

RELIGIOUS SECTS AND CULTS

An "ecumenical" denomination or church is one that promotes cooperation and mutual tolerance among all churches and denominations. The Episcopal, Congregational, Presbyterian, Methodist, Lutheran, and, today, Catholic churches tend to be ecumenical. Most mainstream, old-line American religious denominations tend to be moderate, ecumenical, and comfortable with secular society. But the cost of adapting to secular society is promoting a lukewarm, unemotional, unenthusiastic, and unzealous form of religious expression. In other words, the more tolerant a religious body is toward the faith of other religious bodies, the more cooperative it is toward those other faiths, and the more accepting it is with the compromises the material world has wrought on the faith of its members, the more reserved, the more tepid, and the less muscular its members' faith is likely to be. The 2001 Barna Poll revealed an extremely strong correlation between evangelism and church attendance, and evangelism and orthodoxy of religious belief. ("Evangelism" is a fervent, zealous belief in heavenly salvation through Christian faith, especially in the Gospel, that is, the first four books of the New Testament, and the impulse to spread the good news of the Gospel to others.) All religious bodies, including the mainline ecumenical churches, harbor members with evangelical tendencies, but the largest religious bodies that are evangelical as a rule include the Southern Baptist, Pentecostalist, and Assemblies of God churches.

Members of the old-line, ecumenical denominations attend church services less frequently than members of the strong evangelical faiths. In the 2001 Barna Poll, only 30 percent of the members of Episcopal churches attended weekly, but 50 percent of Baptists, 66 percent of Pentecostalists, and 69 percent of the members of the Assemblies of God did so. Only 12 percent of Episcopalians said they must tell their faith to others, whereas 51 percent of Baptists, 61 percent of Assemblies of God, and 73 percent of Pentecostalists felt this way. Satan is real? Only 20 percent of Episcopalians agreed, but 34 percent of Baptists, 47 percent of Pentecostalists, and 86 percent of Assemblies of God did so. In short, mainline denominations offer a *weaker, milder* version of Christianity, while the evangelical sects offer a *stronger and more intense,* more *zealous* version. In contrast with the mainline denominations, members of the more fervent and muscular evangelical faiths are much more likely to accept articles of orthodox Christian dogma and to believe that they must vigorously proselytize their faith in the Gospel to others (www.adherents.com/misc/BarnaPoll.html and www.adherents.com/rel_USA.html).

In addition, *social* and *political* ideology is strongly related to *religious* beliefs and practices. Another Barna Poll, conducted in 2009, indicates that conservatives are significantly more likely to hold more intense religious views; engage in regular religious practices, such as church attendance, prayer, and reading the Bible; believe that the Bible is the literally accurate word of God; live a spirituality centered life; and believe that they have a "personal responsibility to share their religious beliefs with others," than is true of liberals. Liberals, in turn, are more likely to live a secular life, believe that religious faith is not a basic moral guide to their lives, and reject the notion that they have a responsibility to share their religious beliefs with others. Liberals are also more likely to have discovered their own religious beliefs instead of embracing those promulgated by an organized church or religion and are more open to "accepting different moral views" than the ones they currently hold (www.barna.org/barna-update/article/13-culture/258-survey-shows-how-liberals-and-conservatives-differ-on-matters-of-faith). Conservatives tend to hold and express a "stronger" version of religiosity, while that of liberals is typically "weaker."

Weak denominations do not answer the need of the more fervent parishioners who long for a strong expression of their faith. Hence, they tend to stimulate "new, more vigorous religions to replace them" (Stark and Bainbridge, 1996, p. 103). Two types of religious bodies contrast with established, mainstream bodies. The first is the *sect,* a religious group that breaks off from the mainstream religion and is "within the conventional religious tradition(s) of a society, but one that imposes stricter demands on its adherents than do mainstream groups" (pp. 103–104). Such groups are only "moderately deviant." And what *makes* them deviant is that they are "*too* religious" (p. 104).

Even more deviant is the *cult.* As with "deviant," the term "cult" has become such a pejorative word that it seems to connote a religion that is kooky, bizarre, pathological, creepy, and strange; in other words, it is an "insult to stir up fear and oppression" (p. 104). In a straightforward definitional sense, however, cults are simply religious groups that are "outside the conventional religious tradition(s) in a society" (p. 104). They differ less with respect to the intensity of their members' religiosity as to their *difference from* the mainstream religious body. They are not a *variation on* the usual theme, they are *outside* the usual theme altogether. Some cults are imported from a cultural tradition foreign to a specific country's religions, while most arise "because someone creates or discovers [a] new religious culture and successfully attracts a group of followers" (p. 104). In the United States, examples of domestic cults include The Church of the Latter Day Saints (the Mormons) in the nineteenth century, Christian Science in the 1920s and, today or in the recent past, and the Church of Scientology; imported cults include Hare Krishna, the Divine Light Mission, and the Unification Church (or "Moonies"). Cults "engender far more concern, antagonism, and repressive efforts than do sects" (p. 104). While sects are *moderately* deviant to the mainstream, cults tend to be *very* deviant.

Many conventional religionists adopt the "absolutist" perspective I spelled out earlier; they argue that cults are *not like* traditional or conventional religious bodies, believing them to be evil, sinister, or at the very least, strange. Their leaders are said to engage in "manipulative mind control" to seduce, capture, and "brainwash" their young acolytes. These leaders are up to no good, and they must be stopped from engaging in their nefarious practices. "Cults are groups that often exploit members psychologically and/or financially, typically by making members comply with leadership's demands through certain types of psychological manipulation and through the inculcation of deep-seated anxious dependency on the group and its leaders" (Chambers et al., 1994, p. 90).

To the absolutist, the evil nature of cults must have a sinister origin, cause, or dynamic. "No rational or sane person would choose to join a cult. Given such assumptions, how does one explain cult involvement?" (Perrin, 2005, p. 6). The absolutist responds by invoking such mechanisms as brainwashing, by arguing that clever but malicious leaders trap, seduce, manipulate, and hypnotize innocent parties into their spider's web of deceit (Singer and Lalich, 1995). Note that the absolutist perspective demands that a truly anomalous, aberrant phenomenon such as cult membership demands an explanation that invokes anomalous, aberrant causes. The proposition that cult members are recruited in much the same ways that members of mainstream churches are is unacceptable. This is what experts who study the logical structure of arguments call the "evil causes evil" fallacy: that something the observer doesn't like must have an origin that the observer also doesn't like. As some researchers have pointed out (Perrin, 2005), the brainwashing explanation for cult membership goes back to the 1950s, when the Chinese communists were said to brainwash American prisoners of the Korean War into betraying their country.

Perrin (2005) locates four interest groups whose members compete to define the nature of cults: the anticult movement, the media, the cults (or new religious movements) themselves, and academics, including sociologists of religion, who study them from a social science perspective.

The anticult movement attempts to define cults as deviant and, in so doing, to drive them out of business. Most anticult organizations were started by parents who lost their children to cults, whose theology and religious practices these parents found puzzling, incomprehensible, troubling, very different from the conventional Christianity or Judaism these young people grew up with. Many parents, says Perrin, "were confused by their child's conversion and fanatical commitment, and were anxious to 'expose' the sinister cults and get their children back" (p. 15). "Deprogrammers" and "exit counselors," some health professionals, others Christian ministers or committed Christian laypeople, attempt to "unbrainwash" converts and to indoctrinate potential converts into the evil nature of cults. Some parents of cult members have even hired deprogrammers to kidnap their children from a cult setting and force deprogramming on them. Many anticult activists have been defectors, former cult members who became disillusioned and now "want the evil practices of the cult exposed" (p. 16). Many Christian clergy and laypeople oppose cults because they "want to win the world for Jesus."

The media don't necessarily attempt to define cults as evil or deviant. "However, faced with time and space restrictions, and obviously drawn to sensationalistic and controversial topics, media accounts sometimes ignore the mundane and non-newsworthy elements of NRM [new religious movements, or cults], and thus contribute to a distorted perception of NRMs" (p. 16). Hence, by making sensationalistic and distorted claims, the media unwittingly serve the interests of the anticult movement in defining cults as deviant.

Jostling on this stage where interest groups attempt to define cults as deviant—or as legitimate religions—are the cults themselves. Clearly it is in the interests of cult participants to themselves, and to convince others, to define cults as not only legitimate but also as altruistic, as dedicated to saving a corrupt world. Cult leaders also have a material interest as well: As a given cult organization grows, its leadership prospers.

Sociologists and other academics usually provide a more sober and balanced, if not necessarily objective, view of cults. In their effort to produce original, nontrite, and counterintuitive findings and conclusions, academics often find themselves defending cults. Moreover, since sociologists often attempt to understand social phenomena as their participants understand them, they may present cult members' views of reality as one version of acceptable and believable truth. Outsiders, especially those with an anticult agenda, often see such efforts as a defense of cults. However, psychologists, who are more interested in the special means by which cults convince their members of the truth of their vision, are more likely to see the dark side of these new religious movements. For instance, *Cultic Studies Review,* "an internet journal of research, news and opinion," is dedicated to disseminating "information on cults, psychological manipulation, psychological abuse, spiritual abuse, brainwashing, mind control, thought reform, abusive churches, extremism, totalistic groups, authoritarian groups, new religious movements, exit counseling, recovery, and practical suggestions." Clearly, this journal focuses mainly on the negative, deviant side of cults.

Conflicts between cults and mainstream society were depicted prominently in the news in the 1970s and early 1980s. But into the 1980s and the 1990s, cult membership declined and defections increased (Perrin, 2005, p. 18). About 20 or 30 years ago, Hare Krishna members danced in the street and begged in airports. Since that time, events, media reports, and defectors have exposed many cults as anything but normal, legitimate, or altruistic. In 1978, Jim Jones, a charismatic but mentally unstable leader of his self-created new religious movement, exhorted his flock to commit mass suicide. By the end of the day, nearly a thousand of his followers lay dead in the jungle compound. A book entitled *Monkey on a Stick* revealed that a Hare Krishna organization was deeply involved in stealing, the rape and beating of members, murder, drug smuggling, and building an arsenal of weapons that would equip a small army (Hubner and Gruson, 1989). These and countless other revelations hurt the cause of the new religious movements, convinced nonmembers that they were right to denounce and attack these movements, and contributed to the movements' demise.

CREATIONISM, INTELLIGENT DESIGN, AND EVOLUTION

In December 2005, a federal district court judge rejected the suit brought by the school board of the Dover, PA school district (by the time of the ruling, already voted out of office) to introduce intelligent design into the science curriculum. Intelligent design does not belong in the science classroom, the judge ruled, because it is a religiously motivated belief that violates the constitutional mandate of separation of church and state. The judge, John Jones III, a conservative and a Republican appointed by President George W. Bush, went further; he lashed out at school board members for lying under oath and for being guilty of "breathtaking inanity" in their attempt to infuse religion into science courses. Intelligent design, declared Judge Jones, "relies on the unprovable existence of a Christian God and therefore is not science" (Powell, 2005, p. A1).

From our point of view, the decision raised the issue of whether and to what extent the struggle between supporters of intelligent design and advocates of evolution to define reality illuminates an aspect of cognitive deviance. Clearly, the position of most scientists is that both creationism and intelligent design are *deviant* explanations for the origin of the universe and the origin of the species. It is their intention to rule these theories invalid and inappropriate for inclusion in the science curriculum. They are not scientific, most scientists argue, and have no more place in the teaching of science than Zulu, Navajo, or Australian aborigine explanations of the origin of the universe and the species. On their behalf, fundamentalist Christians wish to relegate evolution to the nether world of error, untruth, falseness, and Godlessness. In short, the creationism–evolution controversy is a classic case of *mutual deviantization* (Aho, 1994, p. 62).

This controversy is fraught with conceptual and theoretical confusion and misunderstanding which I'd like to dispel. To begin with, Charles Darwin was not the first to advocate the evolution of the species. Dozens of scientists before him thought of the same thing; Darwin was the first to have thought of the *mechanism* that drove or caused evolution. (More on this momentarily.) Actually, to be more precise, Darwin and Alfred Russel Wallace published a summary of their ideas simultaneously. Moreover, one or another form of evolutionary thinking had been accepted as valid by many scientists and intellectuals for more than a half-century before Darwin published *On the Origin of Species* in 1859. In addition, it's not clear why creationists focus specifically on evolutionary theory in biology as subverting Biblical literalism since the findings of astrophysics, paleontology, genetics, and geology also contradict a literal interpretation of the Bible. Biology is just one of a number of fields whose findings contradict Genesis as a scientific tract.

In addition, in spite of their equation in the media, creationism is not the same thing as intelligent design. In fact, these two perspectives disagree on most of their claims and agree on only one point. There are many versions of creationism, but classic, "new Earth" or Biblical creationism holds that the universe, Earth, and all species on Earth were created by God in six 24-hour days less than 10,000 years ago. In sharp contrast, intelligent design accepts the fact that the universe and the Earth are billions of years old and that the process of evolution produced all the species on Earth. Where intelligent design parts company with the scientific view of evolution is that it argues that the hand of God *guided* the process of evolution and designed and created all species on Earth, including humans. Hence, intelligent design and evolution have a great deal in common, in fact, in many ways, more in common than creationism and intelligent design do.

Much of this confusion is caused by the designation of evolution as a "theory." Most laypeople think that theory means speculation or an unproven hypothesis. This is wrong. The scientific definition of theory is an *explanation,* a cause-and-effect account for a general class of phenomena or observations. When people say "evolution is just a theory," what they mean is it hasn't yet been shown to be true. But scientifically, what the phrase really means is that evolution is an *explanation* for something. But what?

People who refer to evolution as a theory confuse *the fact* of evolution—that is, whether the species evolved over millions, even billions, of years—with *the mechanism* of evolution. Intelligent design theorists accept the *fact* of evolution but reject a materialist mechanism or *explanation* of the process. Their theory is that "God did it," the "it" being the actual causal mechanism of evolution itself. In contrast, the scientific explanation of evolution holds that the explanation, cause, or mechanism for the process is *natural selection,* that is, genetic variation, the adaptation of organisms to a particular environment, and differential survival, and hence, differential productive success. Hence, the "theory" that is referred to in the phrase "the theory of evolution" is not a theory of evolution at all, but the theory of natural selection—that is, an explanation for *why* evolution occurred. Scientists take evolution as the observation or *fact,* and natural selection as the theory or explanation *for* the fact of evolution. Intelligent design advocates accept the fact of evolution but reject the mechanism of natural selection. And most scientists believe that the concept, "guided by the hand of God," is an unprovable, supernatural explanation. It cannot be tested with the tools of natural science, they say.

In spite of the fact that intelligent design and creationism are almost totally contradictory theories on the fact of evolution, the point they agree on is that God plays a causal role in observable material reality. In contrast, the scientific version of evolution, and all natural phenomena, is that material reality has material causes; the observer need not invoke the hand of God in these processes. So important is the role of God here that most observers believe that intelligent design is a "foot in the door" or a "wedge" for creationism to enter into the biology curriculum. Grant intelligent design in the public schools, say its opponents, and creationism will follow. Hence, their strong opposition.

Information on the beliefs of different segments of the population will make this controversy clearer and will situate it more firmly within the topic of cognitive deviance. Polls have been conducted yearly on the public's attitude on creationism, some form of intelligent design, and evolution, and the results are fairly consistent. In 1987, *Newsweek* magazine estimated that of the nearly half a million life and earth scientists (mainly biologists and geologists) in the world, less than 1 percent believe in some form of creationism. Another estimate has it that 99 percent of scientists take the strictly naturalistic view of evolution (Shermer, 1997, p. 156). In the United States, in poll after poll, in the general public, roughly 45 percent of respondents believe in creationism, that is, the universe and all species on Earth were created by God less than 10,000 years ago. About 40 percent believe in some form of intelligent design, that is, that evolution occurred, but the process was guided by the hand of God. Less than 10 percent of the American population believes in evolution and a materialist cause-and-effect mechanism, that is, "Man has developed over millions of years from less advanced forms of life. God had no part in the process." The level of support for creationism and intelligent design in the United States is unique in the Western world. A British survey of over 100 Catholic priests, Anglican bishops, and Protestant ministers and pastors found that 97 percent did not believe the universe was created in six days, and 80 percent did not believe in the existence of Adam and Eve.

Here we have a belief that 99 percent of scientists hold (depending on the year the question is asked and the wording of the question), but only 9 percent of the general public accepts. Says one observer: "It would be hard to imagine any other belief for which there is such a wide disparity between the person on the street and the expert in the ivory tower" (Shermer, 1997, p. 156). Moreover, nearly all the dominant social institutions affirm that evolution took place: the educational system, especially higher education, and most especially, the most prestigious institutions of higher learning; the most influential media, such as network news, *The New York Times, The Washington Post;* all the science magazines, such as *Smithsonian, The National Geographic, Scientific American,* and *Science;* every major science museum in the country, all its zoos and aquariums; and the mainstream, old-line, ecumenical churches, such as the Catholic, Episcopalian, Presbyterian, Methodist, Congregationalist, and Lutheran churches. For us, as students of deviance, the interesting questions become, first, why do we find such a discrepancy, second, what functions does such a belief serve for the social circles holding them, and third, what does this discrepancy say about definitions of deviance in different audiences?

It might seem strange to refer to beliefs, such as creationism and intelligent design, held by nearly half of the population, as deviant. How could such common beliefs be deviant? The answer is that deviant cannot be equated with different; conventional cannot be equated with common or usual. Many common actions, beliefs, and physical traits are deviant. Most of us—in fact, very possibly, nearly all of us—lie once or more in our lives, but lying is a deviant act; the people we lie to don't like it, resent us for doing it, and would punish us in one way or another if they knew we did it to them. A very high proportion of the population has taken something that's not theirs at least once, but that doesn't mean that stealing isn't deviant. Most American women are not happy with some feature of their bodies, consider their bodies, in one way or another, deviant. Contrapositively, owning a house with five bathrooms, receiving 100 items of mail a day, and taking three showers a day is unusual—but not deviant. As I said in Chapter 1, sociologists do not define extremely common acts, beliefs, or traits as conventional statistical, nor those that are different as deviant.

What makes creationism and intelligent design deviant? What makes evolution deviant? Deviance is something that's "out of place." It is that which is judged invalid or bad or silly or evil or reprehensible *by* a particular audience *in* a particular context. Deviance is defined or *constituted by* the negative reactions it generates in certain audiences, in certain contexts. Evolutionists are emphatic in insisting that creationism, creation science, and intelligent design are *out of place,* and therefore deviant, in any science context. Anyone who believes in them is, by definition, not a scientist, and has no place in that context. Any attempt to teach science to students, whether at the elementary or the graduate school level, *cannot* include Biblical teachings on the subject. In contrast, among creationists, believing in evolution is evil, contrary to God's teachings, certain to bring forth divine retribution; their attacks on proponents of evolution are powerful, denunciatory, and savage.

Make no mistake about it: The struggle between creationists and intelligent design advocates on one side and materialist evolutionists on the other is a battle to define a particular body of knowledge as valid and another as *deviant.*

Michael Dini, associate professor of biology at Texas Tech University, has a strict policy of never giving a recommendation to a student who does not accept what he refers to as "the most important theory in biology," that is, evolution. Michael Spradling, a senior at Texas Tech who needed a recommendation to medical school, enrolled in, then dropped, Dini's course when he found out about the professor's policy. Spradling transferred to Lubbock Christian University and enrolled in that same course so that he could obtain a recommendation from its instructor. Dini feels that believing in creationism is a simple case of looking at rock-solid evidence and being incapable of reaching conclusions, in a phrase, being incapable of reasoning scientifically. Denying evolution is no different from denying that gravity exists, he says. Most, although not all, of Dini's colleagues agree. Spradling appealed to the Department of Justice, arguing that Dini's policy is a case of discriminating against a student's religious beliefs (Brulliard, 2003; Madigan, 2003).

Commenting on one creationist's claim that evolutionary theory can be traced back to the early Greek atomists and before, to Babylonian philosophy—and was, perhaps, revealed by Satan himself—an evolutionist comments that he finds it "hard to believe that anybody . . . accepts this shaggy-dog story" (Kitcher, 1982, p. 193). After a scientific meeting, commenting on the efforts of creationists, one scientist declared "*we've got to stop the bastards*" (my italics). This, comments a historian of creationism, is the prevailing attitude among scientists (Numbers, 1992, p. xvii). Says the guidebook of the Museum of the Earth in Ithaca, NY: "Essentially all available data and observations from the natural world support the hypothesis of evolution. No serious biologist or geologist today doubts whether evolution occurred" (Kates, 2005, p. A22). Clearly scientists wish to define creationism as intellectually and cognitively unacceptable—in a word, deviant.

After the citizens of Dover, PA, voted for a school board whose members opposed intelligent design (and voted out of office a board whose members supported it), Pat Robertson, a religious broadcaster, announced that the "good citizens of Dover . . . voted God out of your city. . . . If there is a disaster in your area, don't turn to God. You just rejected Him from your city. . . . If they have future problems in Dover, I recommend they call Charles Darwin. Maybe he can help them." Robertson also called for the assassination of President Hugo Chavez, a radical; recommended that the State Department be blown up with a nuclear device; and asserted that feminists encourage women to "kill their children, practice witchcraft, destroy capitalism, and become lesbians" (Associated Press release, November 11, 2005).

In his well-known antievolutionist tract, *The Icons of Evolution,* Jonathan Wells writes that his prayers convinced him that he should devote his life to "destroying Darwinism." When the Rev. Sun Myung Moon chose him to enter a PhD program, he said, he "welcomed the opportunity to prepare" himself for battle (Wells, 2000). Indeed, "battle" is an excellent metaphor for the debate between creationists and evolutionists since many of its participants believe that it is a struggle between good and evil, right and wrong, and light and darkness.

One Louisiana case, *Edwards versus Alluigard,* intended to bring "creation science" into the educational curriculum; creationists sent letters to the scientists testifying on behalf of evolution. One letter sent to Murray Gell-Mann, a Nobel Prize winner, read:

> The blood of Jesus Christ cleanses us from all sin. Whosoever is not found written in the book of life will be cast into the lake of fire. The wages of sin is death, but the gift of God is eternal life through Jesus Christ our Lord. Ask Jesus Christ to save you now! The second law of thermodynamics proves evolution is impossible. [Actually, the Second Law of Thermodynamics states that energy cannot be increased in a closed energy system. Since the Earth receives energy from the sun, it does not constitute a closed energy system.] Why are you so afraid of the truth of creation-science? (Shermer, 1997, pp. 169–170)

Says Henry M. Morris, a prolific creationist: "Evolution is the root of atheism, of communism, nazism, behaviorism, racism, economic imperialism, militarism, libertinism, anarchism, and all manner of anti-Christian systems of belief and practice" (1972, p. 75).

The elementary school superintendent of Marshall County KY, Kenneth Shadowen, glued together two pages of his fifth and sixth graders' science textbooks dealing with the "big bang" 15 billion years ago—according to scientific theory, the origin of the universe—so that his students could not read them. Shadenow claimed he had done it because the text didn't present alternatives to the big bang theory (Shermer, 1997, p. 138). Governor Fob James of Alabama used the taxpayers' money to purchase and send a copy of a book supporting intelligent design and critical of evolutionary theory to all high school instructors of science courses (p. 139).

To repeat: It is the goal of creationists to depict evolutionary theory as cognitively, intellectually, theologically, and morally bankrupt, in error, and hence, deviant.

What makes the conflict between creationists and evolutionists so particularly bitter and protracted? Why are the differences between them so quickly and readily translated into denunciation and reproach? And why is this conflict such an ideal example of cognitive deviance labeling?

Belief in creationism versus evolution is very strongly correlated with several key and basic factors, including education, urban–rural residence, and blue state–red state, or "metro" versus "retro" residence. (Liberal or "blue" states are located in the northeast and mid-Atlantic, from Maryland to Maine, the upper Midwest, and the west coast; conservative or "red" states are in the South, much of the Midwest, and the Rocky Mountains.) Creationists are more likely to be uneducated, politically conservative, and reside in a less-populated area of a red or retro state. Believers in some form of evolution are more likely to be better educated, politically liberal, and live in a more metropolitan area of a blue or metro state. (We can find many exceptions, of course, as we can for every valid generalization.) Hence, this controversy expresses not merely the merits of one or the other side, but also entire worldviews, indeed, ways of life as well. Both sides have a substantial investment in their positions as well as a great deal invested in discrediting the other side. "Live and let live" is an impossibility for many adherents of both positions. While homosexuality does not necessarily discredit heterosexuality and vice versa, in contrast, creationism and evolution *automatically* contradict one another. Each, inherently and by its very nature, provides a critique of the other. If one is right, the other *must* be wrong, and vice versa. (There's another logical possibility: In theory, both could be wrong.) Hence, the special vehemence of the adherents of these two positions.

For creationists, the dominance of evolution in the educational curriculum represents the triumph of secular materialism. If we descended from animals, we must have a kinship *with* animals; if what brought humanity out of the slime is a random, Godless power, it follows that humanity itself is guided *by* a Godless power; and if apes are our ancestors, we must *be* apes. Clearly, the propositions on which evolutionary theory is based must be false, reasons the creationist, otherwise we live in a society dominated by bestiality, not Christianity. Humans stand next to angels; they are touched by the hand of God; they share no kinship with beasts of the forest. To the creationists, the implications of evolution are terrifying: They seem to undermine the very foundation of Christianity, indeed, their very notion of their intimate bond with God. Evolution implies that the forces that created humanity were accidental, indifferent, unguided, capricious, and purposeless. If certain events had turned out differently, humans would not have evolved at all. Humans were not fated or destined to appear on Earth, as Christianity decrees; we appeared at a particular time and place by a roll of the bio-geological dice. Evolution seems to deny every particular of the Christian cosmology. To the unsophisticated Christian who reasons in Manichean, black-or-white, either-or terms, evolutionary theory is anathema, a plot concocted by Satan himself, a conspiracy to undermine Christian faith and annihilate the Christian world altogether. It should come as no surprise that evolution has become a lightening rod for creationists everywhere, and that evolutionists have become labeled as deviants.

For their part, evolutionists regard the belief in creationism as a failure in the scientific program. Like Professor Dini, scientists believe it is their task to draw reasonable conclusions from the available evidence, and the task of science educators to teach their students to reason likewise. The fact that some of their students, not to mention nearly half of the American public, hold a belief that contradicts the very foundation of modern biology indicates that scientists have failed at their task. In a sense, creationist belief represents an *indictment* of science education, a failure of one of the central missions of science itself. Evolutionists rarely bother to address the creationist challenge, which they find frustrating and puzzling; rather, most ignore it. To the extent they do address that challenge, creationists are depicted as ignoramuses, country bumpkins—or charlatans who hoodwink the masses into believing bogus assertions about how nature works.

Rationalistic nineteenth-century thinkers such as Karl Marx (1818–1883), Auguste Comte (1798–1857), and Herbert Spencer (1820–1903) argued that as societies became increasingly educated, and as scientific knowledge became widely disseminated, mystical, occult, and superstitious beliefs, including Christian and other religious dogma, would disappear. These writers would have been astounded by the persistence of religion in the modern age, in particular, the belief in Biblical creation. In a conversation, a prominent evolutionist predicted that when the implications of the relevance of DNA research for evolutionary theory sinks in to the public at large, creationists will be convinced of the error of their ways; they'll pack up their road show and slink off into the night. I disagreed; I said there is no conceivable accumulation of evidence that will change minds on either side of this issue. Clearly, the belief that the account of the origin of the universe described in Genesis plays a major role in the lives of fundamentalist Christians. It is not going to go away any time soon. Clearly, the evolution–creation debate provides a major source of defining cognitive deviance—on both sides of the debate.

PARANORMAL BELIEFS AS DEVIANT

What makes paranormal beliefs—those that contradict what scientists believe to be the laws of nature—a form of cognitive deviance? As with creationism, how can beliefs held by half, or more than half, of the population be regarded as *deviant*? Gallup and Harris polls show that nearly half the American public believes in ghosts, a third in astrology, three-quarters in miracles, and six in ten in the devil. How can beliefs with such widespread support be unconventional or nonnormative? It's simple: *In* certain contexts, these beliefs are derided, scorned, and not permitted a serious hearing. These beliefs are not valorized in the dominant institutions; they are nonhegemonic, not validated by the dominant educational, media, and religious institutions. The higher we move on the ladder of prestige and power, the less and less acceptable—and the more deviant—they are.

Sociologically, we look at paranormal beliefs by focusing on how they are generated and sustained. The routes through which this takes place are many and varied. Perhaps five are most likely to be interesting to the sociologist. For each, we should ask the basic question: "Who is the paranormalist's social constituency?" And for each belief, the answer is significantly different.

First, there are paranormal beliefs that originate from the mind of a social isolate, a single person with an unusual, highly implausible vision of how nature works. The isolate's message is presumably directed mainly at scientists, although any connection with the scientific community is tenuous or nonexistent. Scientists refer to these people as cranks. Here, the social constituency of the crank usually does not extend beyond himself (most cranks are men). It is deceptive to think that cranks address their message to the scientific community, since they do not engage in sciencelike activities or associate with other scientists; their goal is to *overturn* or *annihilate* conventional science, not contribute to it. Not enough attention has been paid to the crank, but it is a sociologically revealing subject nonetheless. Donna Kossey devotes an entire book, entitled *Kooks,* to the topic (1994).

Second, there are paranormal belief systems that begin within a religious tradition that existed long before there was such a thing as a scientist. Such beliefs sustain, and continue to be sustained by, an identifiable religious organization. Creationism is a prime example. The social constituency of the creationist is the like-minded religious community.

Third, there are beliefs that depend on a client–practitioner relationship. In other words, the key fact of certain belief systems is that they are validated by professionals who possess special expertise that is sought by laypersons in need of personal assistance, guidance, an occult interpretation of reality of their lives, or a demonstration of paranormal proficiency. Astrologers and other psychics exemplify this type of paranormalism. The social constituency of the astrologer and the psychic is made up primarily of the client, and secondarily, of other astrologers and psychics.

Fourth, another form of paranormalism is kept alive by a core of researchers who practice what seems to be the *form* but not the *content* of science. Many adherents are trained as scientists, who conduct experiments, publish their findings in professional journals, and maintain something of a scientific community of believers, but most traditional scientists reject their conclusions. As we've seen, parapsychology offers the best example here. Unlike astrologers and psychics, parapsychologists do not have clients. They are researchers and theorists, not hired for a fee. While a substantial number of laypersons may share the beliefs paranormalists claim to validate in the laboratory, these paranormal scientists or "protoscientists" form the sociological core of this system of thinking. For the *professional* parapsychologist, that is, the parapsychological *researcher,* the social constituency is that tiny band of other professional parapsychologists and, ultimately, the mainstream scientific community.

Fifth, there are paranormal belief systems that can be characterized as "grassroots" in nature. They are sustained less by individual theorists, a religious tradition or organization, a client–practitioner relationship, or a core of researchers, than by a broad-based public. In spite of the fact that it is strongly influenced by media reports and the fact that there are numerous UFO organizations and journals, the belief that UFOs are "something real" has owed its existence primarily to a more-or-less spontaneous feeling among the population at large. The ufologist's social constituency is primarily other ufologists, secondarily the society as a whole.

The assertions of the scientific "crank" represent one of the more interesting of all paranormal belief systems. He is a self-styled scientist or (from most scientists' point of view) a *pseudoscientist* who persists in advancing views of how nature works that are regarded as either nonsensical or contradicted by the available evidence (Gardner, 1957, pp. 7–15). While many legitimate scientists have advanced theories that were later overturned, falsified, or refuted by evidence, most of their peers regarded their theories as plausible, even though they were ultimately proven false. Moreover, many of the legitimate scientists who propose erroneous theories are able to recognize the error of their ways once the evidence against their hypotheses begins piling up. (To the extent that a real scientist continues to advance an incorrect theory, even after it has been disproven, he or she is more likely to be called a *curmudgeon* than a crank.) In contrast, the crank usually advances theories that are completely implausible to most scientists, or irrelevant or contrary to the way the world operates, or simply impervious to empirical test.

Have proponents of novel theories that were eventually validated and accepted regarded as cranks? Why aren't Albert Einstein (whose theory of relativity subsumed Newton's laws of physics), Alfred Wegener (who proposed the theory of continental drift), Karl Jansky and Grote Reber (who discovered radio waves), and Ignaz Semmelweis (who discovered that germs could infect mothers who were delivering babies)—all of whose theories were initially either rejected or considered controversial (Ben-Yehuda, 1985, pp. 106–167)—cranks?

For instance, did any physicist in 1905 regard Albert Einstein a crank for proposing his theory of relativity? One physicist says no, that is, that Einstein's contemporaries did not and would not have branded him a crank (Bernstein, 1978). To begin with, Einstein published his ideas in a recognized journal of physics. Second, his theory of relativity passed the test of the "correspondence" principle, that is, it proposed exactly *how* it fit into or extended existing and established theory. In other words, Einstein's theory was very clear on just where Newton's principles ended and where his own theory began. In contrast, crank theories "usually start and end in midair. They do not connect in any way with things that are known" (p. 12). Third, most crank theories "aren't even wrong." Says physicist Jeremy Bernstein, "I have never yet seen a crank physics theory that offered a novel quantitative prediction that could be either verified or falsified." Instead, they are "awash in a garble of verbiage . . ., all festooned like Christmas decorations." Einstein's paper was very clear about its predictions; it virtually cried out to be empirically tested (p. 13).

Cranks tend to have at least two basic characteristics. First, they usually work in almost total isolation from orthodox scientists. They have few, if any, fruitful contacts with genuine researchers and are unaware of, or choose to ignore, the traditional canons of science, such as falsifiability and reproducibility. Cranks tend not to send their work to the recognized journals; if they do, it is rejected for what scientists regard as obvious, fundamental flaws. They tend not to be members of scientific academies, organizations, or societies. And they tend not to receive grants or fellowships or awards from scientific organizations. In short, they are not members of the scientific *community.*

Second, cranks have a tendency toward *paranoia,* usually accompanied by *delusions of grandeur* (Gardner, 1957, pp. 12–14). I am not using these terms in the clinical or psychiatric sense, but descriptively. That is, they believe they are unjustly persecuted and discriminated against because they are geniuses, because their ideas are so important and revolutionary they would threaten the scientific establishment. Cranks argue that practitioners of entire fields are ignorant blockheads; they are wrong, blinded by pigheaded stubbornness and stupidity. Only they themselves, the true visionaries, are able to see the light. Consequently, they have to continue to fight to expose the truth. If the scientific establishment ignores them, that only demonstrates their arguments are unanswerable. If scientists challenge their charges and attempt to answer their arguments, that only shows they are out to destroy them. It is all part of a plot. It never occurs to cranks that this opposition is, in all probability, generated by basic flaws to their work (Gardner, 1957, pp. 8–15). As a consequence, cranks are usually *driven,* compelled to spell out their theories and get them recognized as valid. Like many other paranormalists, they are seized with a messianic zeal (Kossey, 1994, p. 56).

The central concept in the field of sociology is the group. In fact, it can be said that sociology is the *study* of group life. Sociologists are very interested in the social "glue" that binds the members of a society—the networks of relations and associations, both formal and informal, that make interaction an ongoing enterprise. It is the shared expectations people have of who we are and what we should be doing, as well as the sanctions we apply to transgressors, that bring most disruptive and destructive behavior under control. In the absence of such communal links, mutual obligations, and shared meanings, social life as we know it would be impossible. It is the sociologist's job to understand exactly how social life operates.

Social isolates choose to live apart—or have been driven—from the bosom of the conventional group, and hence, from these social influences.

(Although, even before their isolation, all of them have already been influenced by the groups that have shaped them and will manifest that influence to their dying day.) As a result of this social isolation, sociologists have not paid much attention to cranks.

In my estimation, this is a mistake. Cranks and their theories are worth examining, even by sociologists. In fact, I'll state this even more strongly: Sociologists ought to be *especially* interested in cranks. They seem to defy the sociologist's insistence that the group is the measure of all things. In a way, the crank offers an example of the limiting or negative case: someone who pursues a line of action that is not validated by any relevant social groupings. How did the crank come to generate ideas that practically everyone else considers crackpot? Where did these ideas come from in the first place? What motivates the crank? What keeps him (again, they are usually male) at the task of churning out missive after elaborate, detailed missive, spelling out theories or interpretations of reality that only he grasps? Where does the crank fit into the sociologist's relentless pursuit of understanding group dynamics?

All crank theories take scientists to task for the error of their ways, their inability to see what is clearly and plainly in front of their noses. Nearly all deride or demean the existing scientific hierarchy of power, prestige, and influence. All argue that the crank creators and proponents are vastly wiser and more intelligent than the scientific establishment. Nearly all assert the wisdom of good common sense and challenge the warping, distorting perspective of encrusted scientific dogma. Many challenge the narrow specialization of practicing scientists and respond with their own broad, sweeping view of things. Most offer a critique of the dehumanizing tendency of science, especially its emphasis on rationality (Kossey, 1994, p. 58). It might be said that cranks possess much the same hubris, arrogance, and self-righteous audacity manifested by biblical prophets. They offer a kind of apocalyptic vision of how we ought to view reality and, hence, to re-order our lives, reform our behavior, and transform the society. Cranks are a cultural phenomenon; rather than debunking or dismissing them, we should attempt to understand them.

In a way, then, cranks want it both ways.

On the one hand, they want to *annihilate* the prevailing theories of established science. Scientists are wrong, I am right; they are ignorant, I am well informed—this seems to be the prevailing position of the crank. The hubris or arrogance of the person possessed of superior wisdom and knowledge seems to suffuse the crank's self-presentation.

But, on the other hand, cranks also lust to be *accepted* by the scientific fraternity as well. Otherwise, why do they send established scientists their writings? Cranks deeply and sincerely believe that, through the presentation of their evidence and the sheer power of their argument, they will convince the scientific powers that be that they are right.

What they want is contradictory, of course; it can be said that cranks have a *love–hate* relationship with established science. On the one hand, they do not play by the rules of conventional science. But on the other, they are sufficiently removed from social contact with those who set those rules that they are either unaware of what those rules are or are deluded into thinking that such rules are mere technicalities that can be swept away by the tidal wave of truth. And it is they alone who are possessed of that truth.

SUMMARY

The processes by which some members of the society come to hold beliefs thought in mainstream social circles to be unacceptable is interesting and significant. Sociologically, we can refer to such beliefs as *cognitive* or intellectual deviance. Yet few sociologists of deviance discuss or deal with the topic. Atheism is a prime example of cognitive deviance; many Americans, for example, believe that an atheist cannot be trusted, and less than half of the public would even consider voting for an atheist as president. As with deviant behavior, unacceptable beliefs elicit negative reactions from audiences, including stigma, social rejection and isolation, criticism, and even punishment. Different audiences deviantize different beliefs. Indeed, different audiences deviantize *one another:* Liberals deviantize conservatives and vice versa; evolutionists deviantize creationists, and vice versa; and atheists deviantize theists and vice versa. At the same time, it's not a matter of a random hodgepodge of different, separate, and independent belief systems: Some audiences have more power to define what's cognitively acceptable and what's deviant.

Some conceptual distinctions are in order here. Not all deviant beliefs lead to deviant behavior; many beliefs remain in the cognitive realm. Hence, the topic is important in and of itself; it is not a simple extension of the fear that deviant beliefs will translate into deviant behavior. Deviant beliefs should be distinguished from mental disorder. While nearly all mental disorder has a cognitive manifestation—just about all mental disorder entails deviant beliefs—most holders of deviant beliefs are psychologically normal. Beliefs are deviant not because they are wrong in some empirical sense, but because they are *regarded as* wrong by specific audiences. Galileo was *right* about the Earth revolving around the sun, but in the 1600s, that belief ran afoul of the Catholic Church hierarchy, and hence, Galileo was defined *by* the Church at that time as a deviant. The fact that Galileo made empirically correct observations has no bearing on his deviant status. Some beliefs become dominant (and therefore conventional) at a later point in time. In the 100s, Christians were persecuted for their beliefs; by the Medieval era, Christianity was the dominant religion in Europe, and it was non-Christians who were persecuted.

Belief systems are never just beliefs; beliefs are never a simple matter of what one individual believes. Human consciousness is a product of social existence. Marxism argued that our beliefs are a product of our economic life. Scholars no longer accept a simple Marxist theory of social and ideological beliefs. Max Weber, an early twentieth-century sociologist, held a more sophisticated view of the origin of belief systems, arguing that people tend to have an *affinity* for certain beliefs, based on their social circumstances and their position in the society's system of ranking. In addition, Weber argued that ideas could influence social position as much as social position influences ideas.

Religion is a major source of differing definitions of true and false; hence, religion spawns a substantial sector of cognitive deviance. People know religious truths to be valid in the same way that they know that the sun sets every night. Religion and deviance intersect in a variety of ways. Religion influences, and hence, correlates with acts the society defines as deviant; this is a case of religion *and* deviance. Mainstream religions define certain religious sects and cults as unorthodox and heterodox, that is to say, deviant; this is a case of religion *as* deviance. In addition, religious bodies define certain secular practices as deviant; this is deviance *according* to religion. Theological disputes among practitioners of a particular religion and wrongdoing by religious functionaries may be referred to as deviance *within* a religious organization. And religious bodies attempt to define other religious beliefs and bodies as deviant; this might be referred to as deviance *between and among* religious organizations.

One of the more interesting instances of religious deviance is how a mainstream body defines and reacts to sects and cults. A "sect" is a religious body that breaks off from an established, mainstream body. A "cult" is a religious body that is radically different from an established, mainstream body; some cults stem from within the same society, while others stem from outside the same society, as the established body. In the United States at this time, sects that offer a stronger, more evangelical, more zealous, and more dogmatic version of Christianity are growing faster than the old-line, established, mainstream ecumenical denominations. In a sense, sects are deviant—albeit only moderately deviant—because they are "too religious." In contrast, cults are deviant because they contrast too sharply with the established denomination. In the nineteenth century, the Church of the Latter Day Saints (the Mormons) was an example of a cult. Their difference with established denominations has declined over the years.

The struggle to define creationism as deviant and evolutionary theory as intellectually acceptable, and vice versa, is one of the more interesting examples of cognitive deviance we might examine. The controversy is fraught with conceptual confusion. In the past two decades or so, "intelligent design," the view that evolution occurred but it was guided by the hand of God, has been added to the struggle. Nearly half of the

American public believes that the Earth is less than 10,000 years old and that all species on Earth were created in six days, as spelled out in the Genesis account. Less than 10 percent accepts a materialistic version of evolution, that is, that evolution occurred but God had nothing to do with it; in contrast, roughly 99 percent of biological and geological scientists accept this belief. In addition, representatives at the pinnacle of society's major institutions accept the evolutionary account. Perhaps for no other major belief is there such a yawning gulf between what the public believes and what scientists believe. Since both creationism and evolution are tied in to a larger worldview, this controversy is unlikely to disappear any time soon.

Paranormal beliefs, those that scientists argue contradict the laws of nature, are extremely widespread. Some paranormal beliefs originate with a crank, someone disconnected from the scientific establishment who attempts to overturn conventional science by proposing a theory that challenges what scientists believe to be true. Observers argue that cranks are completely different from legitimate scientists, like Einstein, who propose a revolutionary theory that challenges conventional paradigms. The theories of cranks usually cannot be empirically tested, falsified, or verified. Other paranormal beliefs originate from a religious community; examples include creationism and the belief that angels and the devil exist as material beings that influence worldly events and behavior. Still other paranormal beliefs are sustained in a client–practitioner relationship; here, astrology is a prime example. And some paranormal beliefs are sustained through the activities of a body of researchers whose work, in the estimation of scientists, is deviant because it lacks the form but not the content of science. Here, parapsychologists offer the prime example, since, in the judgment of the vast majority of scientists, its practitioners are unable to offer a satisfactory, testable, cause-and-effect model for how the mind can influence material phenomena. Finally, many paranormal beliefs have a grassroots or popular origin; they are an aspect of the traditional culture. Examples include beliefs that UFOs, ghosts, and witches are real.

Account: The Belief That Extraterrestrials Are on Earth

Steven, 35, who works as an office manager in a physician's office, holds a belief in paranormal phenomena. He was interviewed by Gretchen Kowalick, then a student at the University of Maryland. Steven, says Gretchen, "has a family and a job and seems to live a normal life. But he has beliefs that are considered to be deviant. They stray from mainstream beliefs and the beliefs of the scientific community."

GRETCHEN: What are your beliefs about aliens and UFOs?

STEVEN: They have been here and are still here. They may just be in the skies, not actually living in the population. I think it has to do with some type of technology exchange between the government and the aliens and we want to keep the upper hand in the situation. There are multiple groups of aliens visiting the earth. Ancient texts speak of multiple beings visiting the earth.

GRETCHEN: What type of technology?

STEVEN: I believe we allow them to abduct people and do experiments on them in order to get technology from them. Some of the technology we have gotten from them has been night vision and the stealth bomber. I think we have been close to developing this type of technology but we were missing things and they gave us the missing links to add it all up. I also believe they have given us technology that can end our dependence on fossil fuels, but that's the global economy so they don't want to tell us they know. The people who are in charge want to stay in charge so they can't allow the technology to come out. In 1947, the government came out and said they had crashed a saucer, but 24 hours later they took back the statement. . . .

(*Continued*)

Account: The Belief That Extraterrestrials Are on Earth Continued

GRETCHEN: Where do you get your information?

STEVEN: I read a lot. I watch the History Channel, Discovery Channel, and the Learning Channel. With Internet access, there is a lot of information out there and I can even check some of the sources out. There are a lot of firsthand witnesses so either there is mass hysteria or people are telling the truth. There are even pictures that can't be explained, or the explanations that are given aren't feasible. For example, for one picture, they said it was swamp gas that made the image.

GRETCHEN: Are you in any [UFO] clubs?

STEVEN: No. Many of them are dangerous and take this to extremes and kill themselves [such as the "Heaven's Gate" UFO cult, 39 of whose members committed suicide in 1997]. I don't like to think of myself as an extremist. My views can be considered extreme. But I just look at things with an open mind and a lot of things get explained.

GRETCHEN: Do you ever go to conventions or [listen to] speakers?

STEVEN: Absolutely. Stephen Greer and Jim Marrs are two speakers I have been to see. Jim Marrs is a journalist who came from Texas and wants to get at the truth. They have over 400 government witnesses on videotape who are talking about their experiences and say they were told by the government not to talk about it. There are generals and colonels, not just average citizens. People with high-ranking positions talking about things they have seen and experiences they have had with UFOs. . . . Dr. Greer spoke about government secrecy, about 9/11, and our dependence on fossil fuels. . . . I also went to a conference with multiple speakers who talked about alien abductions, crop circles, and ancient Sumerian texts. There were a variety of people there, from all walks of life. Of course, there were some extremists there who would believe anything they were told. In order to understand this phenomenon, you have to understand that it's . . . been here since we've been here. Indian texts talk abut being coming and building anti-gravity vehicles. Most are dismissed as myth, but if you put this together with the stories in the Bible, it makes sense.

GRETCHEN: But are all aliens good?

STEVEN: No. Some have good intentions and some have bad intentions. I relate this to when you go to the doctor when you are a young kid. You don't know what the doctor is going to do to you, but you let him do it because you think it's going to be OK. It's the same way with aliens. If you get abducted, you don't know exactly what they are doing to you because you really don't have a choice. The aliens are crafting a new race. They have done this before, and this explains gaps we've found in the fossil records. There was a type of being already here, and the aliens manipulated what was here to help humans get to where we are today. We got our jump-start from another race of beings. This is another reason why the government doesn't want us to know. Again, a lot of ancient texts speak of this. People who have been abducted have had sperm taken from them and they are taken back afterwards to see what they have helped to create. . . . [In 1938, Orson Welles broadcast a radio drama of the novel of H.G. Wells, *War of the Worlds,* about an invasion from Mars] and people thought that it was really happening, that aliens were invading. There were people committing suicide. It was just mass hysteria. Some say this was a test to see if we were ready to know all that the government knew about the aliens here, but that proved we weren't ready. In the 1960s, there was a report that was done that said we would be likely to find alien artifacts on the Moon, on Mars, and on Saturn, and that this information should be kept from the public. Many people believe that Roswell was the first crash of an alien craft, but it wasn't. One time in California [during World War II], they thought they were being invaded by the Japanese, and they shot at the thing in the air, but this was never explained. There are some very famous paintings that have pictures of UFOs in the background.

GRETCHEN: Why do you think the government has kept everything a secret?

STEVEN: People begin to question reality when they talk about all this. The amount of evidence is overwhelming. In a court of law, the evidence would be enough. The cover-up may be grander than we can ever understand. . . . The two main reasons for the cover-up are, one, people can't handle change in their belief system, and two, the change it would cause in the economy.

GRETCHEN: Does everyone you know know about the beliefs you have?

STEVEN: No, not everyone. The ridicule factor is very high and I know that. If you are going to discuss this, you have to sneak it in through the back door. Global politics is a good subject to talk about and then sneak the discussion in about aliens and UFOs.

GRETCHEN: What about your family? How do they feel about your beliefs or do they even know about them?

STEVEN: I talk to some of them about it. I'm more comfortable with my family. We talk about religion and I can slip in the UFO topic. Some of them believe it to a certain extent but they think I go too far with it, especially when it comes to religion. My mom knows I believe in aliens and UFOs and stuff, but she doesn't believe in it at all. This is more a hobby to me and they know that. . . . I just want to know the truth.

GRETCHEN: When did this all begin for you?

STEVEN: It was like a ball of yarn unraveling. I was watching the TV show, "Sightings." It showed a face on Mars, just a quick glimpse, and it intrigued me. NASA [the National Aeronautics and Space Administration, a government agency] said it was a trick of light and shadow. So they found another picture at another time of day and the face was still there. They have done research on the picture and the eyes were in the right place, and the nose was in the right place, so I don't think it was just a coincidence. There have also been pictures of a five-sided pyramid, and as of today, there is no natural explanation for a five-sided pyramid. The aliens used pyramids as beacons. They came here to mine for gold and to help fix their atmosphere. Sumerian texts say that man got started this way, because aliens made humans mine gold for them.

GRETCHEN: What have you done to get this information out?

STEVEN: I volunteered for Stephen Basset in the last election. He was an independent who ran for Congress in the Eighth District in Maryland. He was the first person to run with UFOs as his main platform. He knew he wasn't going to get elected. His main goal was to get exposure for the subject. The other people running wouldn't even let him take part in the debates. . . . I volunteered for him and helped by handing out flyers and things like that.

GRETCHEN: Does it bother you that people think you are crazy?

STEVEN: It doesn't bother me. If they stopped to listen, they will hear that I know what I am talking about. I have made people begin to question reality. . . . This is serious and I am serious about it. Why all the secrets? That's what I want to know. What is so secretive that you have to make up stories to explain things? You have to gather all the information before making credible judgments [and I've done that]. It is part of our mental conditioning that when you believe in this [sort of thing] you are [supposed to be] crazy.

GRETCHEN: What do you think about crop circles?

STEVEN: They are real. Some paranormal entity makes them. There is no man-made reason for them. They go back three hundred years. . . . The government puts out misinformation [about them].

QUESTIONS

Do you agree that belief in UFOs should be regarded as a form of cognitive deviance? If so why? If not, why not? What is or what are your

(*Continued*)

Account: The Belief That Extraterrestrials Are on Earth Continued

criteria for determining whether and to what extent a given belief is, or is not, deviant? In your estimation, *is* the government concealing evidence that extraterrestrial spacecraft crashed on Earth? What motive would officials have for doing something like that? Is it possible for the government to keep something like that a secret? And since there are so many people who work for the government—and who hold conflicting views on almost every imaginable subject, *who,* exactly, is "the government"? And if the evidence is as "overwhelming" as Steven says it is, why are so many scientists—any one of whom could, if he or she revealed evidence of aliens on Earth, would be making perhaps the most important discovery of all time—dubious about the claim of aliens on Earth? And why, if aliens are in our backyard, are scientists spending so much time and money to communicate with intelligent beings in other solar systems? Is Steven someone you would want to talk to? Hang out with? Do you buy his beliefs about paranormal forces at work along a broad range of fronts? If nearly half of the American population believes in many of these beliefs, does it make sense that sociologists refer to them as deviant?

CHAPTER 12

Mental Disorder

We all know someone who seems odd, bizarre, and acts in a totally inappropriate fashion. A stroll down many streets in the nation's larger cities will reveal men and women who look disheveled and mutter incomprehensible phrases to no one in particular. Some people are so fearful of lurking, unmentionable forces that they are literally incapable of walking out of their front door. Others are unable to hold a conversation anyone else would regard as intelligible. Some people are convinced that their dentist has implanted an electronic receiver in a filling in their teeth that is sending bizarre messages into their brain. Some people wear a perpetual, peculiar smile, and seem to exist in "their own little world."

In everyday language, we have terms for such persons. "He's whacko," we say. "She's out of her mind," "He's a nut," "She's completely cracked," "He's a weirdo," "She's a sicko," or "He's off his rocker," we declare, pointing to the people who display what we regard as manifestations of a mind that's "not right." More formally, the condition such people suffer from is referred to as *mental illness* or, more broadly, *mental disorder.*

What is mental disorder? In what way can a mind be said to be "disordered"? What is a mental "illness"? How can a mind be said to be "ill"? Is disorder an instance of deviance? If so, in what specific ways?

WHAT IS MENTAL DISORDER?

At first glance, defining mental disorder is not as easy or as straightforward a task as might appear. Even explaining specific deviant behaviors such as murder, homosexuality, drug use, and prostitution proves to be an extremely thorny matter. Mental disorder presents a much more formidable definitional problem because it is not a type of behavior as such; instead, it is seen as a mental condition that presumably *manifests* itself in certain behaviors, thought patterns, and verbal utterances. And, as we just saw, even the behavior supposedly associated with it cannot be pinned down to any one type of action with much precision. (Of course, certain specific *categories* of mental disorder have more clear-cut symptoms than others, but mental disorder *as a whole* does not.) Rather, mental disorder is a set of conditions that exhibits itself in a *wide range* of behaviors. Hence, no general definition of the phenomenon can be completely satisfactory.

The term "mental *illness*" does not appear in the table of contents or the index of the latest edition of the *American Psychiatric Association's Diagnostic and Statistical Manual,* its fourth (text revision), or *DSM-IV-TR* (2000), nor is it in the leading textbook on abnormal psychology (Kring et al., 2010). Psychiatry and clinical psychology, the "healing professions" that deal with and attempt to treat persons who are emotionally troubled, prefer the term "mental disorder" to "mental illness." The term "mental illness" has been used until recently among some sociologists; witness the titles of two textbooks in the field—*A Sociology of Mental Illness* (Tausig, Michello, and Subedi, 2004) and *The Sociology of Mental Illness* (Gallagher, 2002), but such a practice is decreasingly common. And clearly there is a world of difference between the classic mental illnesses (for instance, schizophrenia and clinical depression) and the grab bag that is covered by mental disorder, including impotence, "transient tic disorder," "mathematics disorder," "reading disorder," and "disorder of written expression." Sociologists study *epidemiology*—the distribution of mental disorders in the population—and hence, are acutely aware of the fact that the broader the category, the lower the likelihood that any single generalization can cover all disorders. Clearly, no single factor or variable correlates consistently with all mental disorders. On the other hand, a number of social characteristics are statistically related to mental illness, which is much narrower and more specific a phenomenon. When I refer to mental disorder here, I'll be referring *mainly* to schizophrenia and clinical depression.

The American Psychiatric Association issues a standard reference work, the *Diagnostic and Statistical Manual of Mental Disorders.* Its first edition (referred to as *DSM-I*) appeared in 1952 and its fourth edition in 1994 (*DSM-IV*). Although its "text" was revised (i.e., edited) in 2000, the fifth edition is not due until after 2011. We might expect *DSM-IV* to be a good place to find a coherent framework for understanding mental disorder.

In this expectation we would be disappointed. *DSM-IV* does not so much define mental disorder as *enumerate* a range of mental disorders. In fact, this "manual" of mental disorders is descriptive, atheoretical, and lacking in any explanatory framework. It provides a long list of symptoms the clinician is likely to encounter in therapeutic practice, and leaves matters at that.

With all its shortcomings, *DSM-IV* offers a sketchy definition of mental disorder. Each of the disorders enumerated in the manual "is conceptualized as a clinically significant behavioral or psychological syndrome or pattern that occurs in an individual and that is associated with present distress (e.g., a painful symptom) or disability (i.e., impairment in one or more important areas of functioning) or with a significantly increased risk of suffering, death, pain, disability, or an important loss of freedom" (APA, 1994, p. xxi). The manual stresses that such suffering is not the manifestation of a mental disorder if it is in response to a temporary event, such as the loss of a loved one. Moreover, the manual stresses, mere *deviant behavior*—for example, political, religious, or sexual activities or beliefs that run counter to the norms—is *not* to be included as a mental disorder *unless* such behavior is a "symptom of a dysfunction in the individual" (p. xxii). *By itself,* political radicalism, religious heterodoxy (such as atheism), or homosexuality does *not* indicate a mental disorder. In addition, this manual states, different cultures, subcultures, and ethnic groups have somewhat different customs. Hence, the clinician must make sure to avoid making judgments of psychopathology that ignore the "nuances of an individual's cultural frame of reference" (p. xxiv).

The original edition of *DSM* listed 100 disorders. There are over 300 disorders listed in *DSM-IV.* There are those that are "usually first diagnosed in infancy, childhood, or adolescence," such as mental retardation, learning disorders, autism, attention deficit disorders, and Tourette's syndrome. There are "delirium, dementia, and amnesiac and other cognitive disorders," including Alzheimer's and Parkinson's syndromes. The list includes all the "substance-related disorders," that is, abuse of and intoxication and dependence on a variety of psychoactive substances (including caffeine and nicotine). Schizophrenia "and other psychotic disorders" are listed, as are mood disorders, both simple depression and bipolar disorders (manic-depression). A variety of other syndromes follow, including anxiety disorders (panic disorder, agoraphobia, obsessive-compulsion, etc.); sexual and gender identity disorders, including sexual dysfunctions (a lack of sexual desire, male impotence, and an inability to achieve orgasm); "paraphilias" (exhibitionism, fetishism, masochism, sadism, and voyeurism); eating disorders; sleeping disorders; impulse-control disorders; and personality disorders. This represents a remarkably diverse and miscellaneous grab bag of mental disorders; they have no internal logic, and it is atheoretical; it *sidesteps* the issue of causality—what generates disorders in general, or each disorder in particular.

The public recognizes that there are *degrees* of mental disorder. This dimension is commonsensically captured in the distinction between *neurosis* and *psychosis.* We tend to reserve the concept of the psychosis for those cases that are considerably more serious, and vastly less common, than the neurosis. Without medication, the psychotic's condition, unlike the neurotic's, is almost always a barrier to academic and occupational achievement and social relationships, including marriage and the family. And, although the outbreak of a psychosis is frequently grounds for institutionalization in a mental hospital, that of a neurosis almost never is. *DSM-IV* does not mention psychosis or the psychotic, and the term "neurosis" does not appear anywhere in its index. Still, the neurosis–psychosis distinction captures most laypeople's thinking about the dimensional quality of mental disorders.

There is no assumption among experts that mental disorders can be cleanly separated from the condition of mental health. Mental disorder is not a "completely discrete entity with absolute boundaries dividing it from other mental disorders or from no mental disorder" (APA, 1994, p. xxii). In reality, most experts argue, extreme or "textbook" cases can be detected by encountering the most florid or stereotypical symptoms such as those enumerated in the *DSM.* Clinicians are emphatic in insisting that the fact that mental disorder is a continuum does *not* mean that therefore most of these disorders cannot be diagnosed or do not exist. One critic (Rimland, 1969) argues that this fuzziness does *not* mean that disordered conditions cannot be diagnosed. "While I will agree that some patients in mental hospitals are saner than nonpatients, and that it is sometimes hard to distinguish between deep unhappiness and psychotic depression, I do *not* agree that the difficulty sometimes encountered in making the distinction between normal and abnormal necessarily invalidates all such distinctions" (p. 717). Clinicians feel that because some distinctions are difficult to make—for example, deciding whether sundown is day or night—does not mean that it is impossible to distinguish grosser distinctions, such as that between noon and midnight (Kring et al., 2010).

MODELS OF MENTAL DISORDER

Two questions have to be answered in order to characterize the various approaches to or models of mental disorder. The first is this: *How is the reality of mental disorder defined?* And the second is this: *What causes mental disorder?* In asking the first question, I do not refer to the sort of formal definition such as that proposed by the American Psychiatric Association. Referring to mental disorder, I mean something much more basic and more general: *Wherein does its reality lie?* We can divide psychiatric researchers into two camps on this issue, the same two that look at all the phenomena we've discussed so far: *essentialists* and *constructionists.*

Essentialism Approaches Mental Disorder

The essentialist approach defines mental disorder as an objectivistic condition that can be located in the real world, in the concrete behavior or verbalizations of persons who are disordered. Such behaviors or verbalizations are outward signs or manifestations of a disordered mind, in much the same way that the height of a column of mercury on a thermometer indicates or measures temperature. To this perspective, we can locate mental disorder much as we can locate a specific geological formation or a biological organism. True, defining and locating mental disorder is a bit more complicated, difficult, and intellectually challenging than identifying entities in the physical world, but the essential reality of mental disorder is an objective fact, identifiable by behavior and speech that persons with the conditions manifest. Of course, mental disorder appears in somewhat different ways in different societies, but there is a *common core* to mental disorder everywhere. A severe schizophrenic in Zambia would be a severe schizophrenic in Thailand, Panama, or Norway. What counts are not the social definitions or constructs of the condition but *the nature of the condition itself* (Murphy, 1976).

The "hardest" or most extreme version of the essentialistic approach is often referred to as the *medical* model. It argues that mental disorder is very much like a medical disease; a disease of the mind is very much like a disease of the body. The bizarre and inappropriate behaviors exhibited by mentally disordered persons are *symptoms* of an underlying or internal pathology of some kind. Mental patients present symptoms, those symptoms can be *categorized,* and the sane are *clearly distinguishable* from the insane (Rosenhan, 1973, p. 250). More colloquially: "Some people *are* more crazy than others; we can tell the difference; and calling lunacy a name does not *cause* it" (Nettler, 1974, p. 894). The medical mode stresses the *intrapsychic* forces in mental disorder; it is an internal *condition* within the psyche of the disordered person. Once someone has "become" mentally disordered, that condition will manifest itself in *any and all* situations and contexts, at least until psychiatric intervention treats or cures that person. Much as a physical disease is internal to the sufferer, a mental disorder is a disease that is "in" the insane.

Essentialists are interested in, and study, the *epidemiology* and the *etiology* of mental disorder. "Epidemiology" refers to how mental disorders are distributed in categories in the population; "etiology" refers to explanations of the *causes* of mental disorder. Essentialists would argue that there is a "true" rate or incidence of mental disorder in a given population and a given society. They investigate whether men or women have higher rates of mental disorders, and more specifically, *which* disorders. Are married or unmarried men and women more likely to become mentally disordered? Blacks or whites? Urban or rural dwellers? How is socioeconomic status (SES) or social class related to mental disorder—and to *which* disorders? Are lower-class people more mentally dysfunctional because lower-class life is more stressful than middle-class life? Or because, if you're disordered, it's very difficult to become successful? These and other questions are asked by epidemiologists who regard mental disorder as a concretely real phenomenon with essentialistic qualities. Essentialists hold that there exists a pregiven entity or syndrome that researchers can define, identify, locate, lay their hands on, and eventually explain or account for. Mental disorder is not merely a label or a social construction. *It does not matter* how the disorder is socially defined—the reality exists *independently* of that definition. The application of the label and the treatment of persons so labeled are not the most interesting things about it. The most interesting thing about mental disorder is what it is, its dynamics, how it works, and what causes it—and how we may cure it and restore the mentally disordered to mental health.

Epidemiology is usually seen as being in the service of etiology. The goal of studying how diseases are distributed in the population, many experts feel, is so that an explanation of illness can be devised and tested. Someone with an essentialistic orientation sees the primary task of anyone who studies mental disorder as devising a valid theory or account of etiology: *What causes it?* Again, whether this theory is sociological, psychological, or biological does not determine the essentialist's model. The sociologist of mental disorder would argue that it is caused, at least in large part, by social factors: stress, for instance, brought on by lower-class status, gender membership, or racial and ethnic prejudice. Most sociologists agree that social factors combine with genetic, neurological, hormonal, and/or psychological factors. Certain persons who are *genetically predisposed* could experience socially induced stressful conditions, which push them over the edge into mental disorder. Still, these sociological etiologists would say, social factors are *crucial* in the causal dynamics leading to mental illness. Again, simply because a theory is sociological does not mean that it is any the less essentialistic: Even sociological theories of mental disorder hold that mental disorder is an identifiable clinical entity. What counts is how the condition is caused, how it came about, what brought it on. And what does not count, what is not interesting or problematic—or at least is of secondary significance—is the creation and application of the label. The enterprise of mental health diagnosis and treatment is crucial only insofar as it relates specifically to the success of treatment outcomes. It is important to know which treatments work and which ones don't, but it isn't important to study treatment as an intellectually or theoretically problematic dynamic in its own right, as a phenomenon to be explained and understood for its own sake.

The strict medical model argues that mental disorder is largely or always a manifestation of abnormal biophysical functioning—brain damage, a chemical imbalance, pathological genes, neurological malfunction, and so on (Torrey et al., 1994). This school suggests that certain environmental factors, such as stress or early childhood experiences, have little independent etiological significance. Of course, they may act as "triggering" mechanisms that exacerbate an already established susceptibility to mental disorder. Consequently, any legitimate and effective therapy for psychic disorder must be physical in nature, such as drugs, electroshock therapy, or surgical intervention. The strict medical model has been gaining adherents in recent years. Electroshock therapy has been making a comeback in the past decade, while the use of psychoactive drugs has almost literally overtaken all other forms of therapy since their introduction in the 1950s. (In contrast, surgery, such as prefrontal lobotomies, has been almost completely abandoned as treatment for mental disorder.) At the other end of the spectrum, psychoanalysis, the "talk" therapy introduced by Sigmund Freud, has plummeted in popularity since the 1950s; in some professional circles, it has been completely discredited (Gruenbaum, 1993; Torrey, 1994; Crews, 1995).

Just as biological and genetic theories of mental disorder, which hold that sociological factors are of secondary importance, could be seen as "hard" essentialistic theories, psychological and sociological theories could be seen as "soft" essentialistic theories. Both agree that the clinical entity, mental illness, or mental disorder, is concretely real, and that diagnoses tap or measure something in the real world. Both agree that mental disorder represents a genuine malfunction or dysfunction, a true or objectively real disorder above and beyond the mere label or diagnosis itself. But these approaches—the biological on the one hand and the psychological and the sociological on the other—part company on the *cause* of mental disorders. Psychological and sociological theories emphasize that they are caused by the patient's experiences, not by an inherent or inner biological or chemical condition. That is, they stress *nurture,* or environment, rather than *nature.* A mentally disordered person may have nothing physically wrong, yet, as a result of his or her experiences, still have a dysfunctional mind. Since physical, biological, or congenital theories posit causes that are more indwelling, more inherent, the only way that mental disorders can be cured or treated is changing the very physical factors that caused them. This means surgical, chemical, hormonal, genetic, or electrical treatment. Merely changing the conditions of the patient's life, or attempting to cure by means of "talk" therapies, will not change that pathological mental patient's condition. Still, these approaches or theories agree that, because the condition is concretely real, researchers can identify and explain it and, possibly, eventually, treat and cure it. The sociological and psychological theories of mental disorder argue that certain experiences exist in some person's lives that cause or influence them to "go crazy." And being disordered can be measured by means of certain concretely real objective criteria or indicators. So the psychological and sociological essentialists don't differ on this particular point with the biological essentialists: Mental disorder is concretely real; it is not simply a label.

Before, I introduced the term, the "medical" model. The medical model sees mental disorder as a condition that is internal to, or in, the mental patient, just as cancer, say, is in a medical patient. Once a person "has" a mental disorder, it manifests itself under any and all conditions. The medical model is the most *extreme* version of essentialism. Not all essentialistic models of mental disorder conform strictly to the medical model, however. Many sociologists and some psychologists believe that mental disorder will manifest itself more under certain conditions than others. For example, some persons who are vulnerable or susceptible to mental disorder may be perfectly normal or healthy under certain conditions—for instance, those who are less stressful, or when they have a social support network. Essentialists who adhere to the nonmedical model stress that mental disorder may be a *temporary* condition, one that is not solely in the individual, one that is as much dependent on the social environment in which the individual interacts as on the individual's internal condition. Again, nonmedical essentialists retain the idea of mental disorder as a real "thing" in the material world as well as a disorder. But they see its appearance as much more heavily dependent on external factors than do proponents of the strict medical model. Biogenetic and biochemical theories of mental disorder most definitely adopt a medical model; mental disorder is a condition in the individual, again, that manifests itself pretty much everywhere. Psychoanalysis, too, adopts a medical model, although it could be seen as a softer version, since mental disorder can be treated by means of a form of therapy that does not entail physical or strictly medical intervention. Once someone has gone through certain pathological childhood experiences, again, one will remain mentally disordered until treatment intervenes.

Constructionism

A social constructionist model would argue that whether or not there is a common thread or common core to mental disorder is not the most theoretically challenging, interesting, or problematic issue. What counts is the *enterprise* of mental disorder, again, what is *said* and *done* about persons who are *defined* as mentally disordered. One major reason why this is such a crucial question is that diagnoses differ in societies around the world; hence, the reality of mental disorder varies along with them. Definitions of mental disorder are culture-bound; what is labeled dysfunctional in one society or social context may be seen as perfectly normal in another—or possessed, extraordinary, saintly, inspired by the holy spirit.

The constructionists regard mental disorder as socially defined, by both the general public and the psychiatric profession. In other words, as with deviance, constructionists do not think that mental disorder can be defined objectively by focusing on the common thread that all disorders share. Instead, they argue, what mental disorder is is how it is seen, judged, reacted to, treated, and evaluated in a given society. There exists a mental illness *enterprise* or, in the words of Michel Foucault, a mental illness *discourse:* the psychiatric, legal, and social machinery designed to deal with persons designated as mentally disordered; the writing; the research; the diagnostic manuals; the mental health industry and the drug industry built around administering medication to the mentally disordered; not to mention public attitudes focusing on mental disordered; the popular beliefs; stereotypes; prejudices; legend and folklore; media attention; and so on. Thus, what mental disorder is is what we *say* and *do* about it, what we say and do about persons designated as mentally disordered. Mental disorder has no "essential" reality beyond these social constructions, this "discourse," these reactions, and the social enterprise surrounding it.

The constructionist model of mental disorder argues the following points: (1) *It is a form of deviance,* (2) its reality is *called into being* by the labeling process, and (3) the application of the label is influenced at least in part by a variety of *extrapsychiatric* factors or variables. The mentally ill are derogated and stigmatized, excluded from full social acceptance; the process of judging persons *to be* mentally ill makes their behavior or mental states sociologically relevant (although, of course, such judgments do not *create* the condition in the first place); and these judgments are influenced by a number of factors *in addition to* the severity of their condition. In a nutshell, these are the basic assumptions of the constructionist approach to mental disorder. It is not a theory that attempts to explain *why* some people are or become mentally ill; instead, it is an approach or framework, or set of "sensitizing concepts" that help to understand one major aspect of the phenomenon.

Consider the fact that, in the first edition of the *Diagnostic and Statistical Manual of Mental Disorders* (1952), homosexuality was deemed an instance of a "sociopathic personality disturbance." In the second, it was listed as belonging under the category "sexual deviance." In 1973, under pressure from movement activists and militants, the American Psychiatric Association (APA) decided that, in and of itself, homosexuality was not a disturbance; it represented a disorder only if it created conflict and generated the wish to change one's sexual orientation. In the third edition (1980) this was further modified to apply only to persons for whom such a wish was a "persistent concern"; the APA referred to this condition as "ego-dystonic homosexuality." In the revised third edition (1987, p. 426), an explanation as to why this condition was dropped was offered ("it suggests to some that homosexuality was considered a disorder"). In the fourth edition (1994), there is no mention of homosexuality whatsoever as a disorder of any kind. It is difficult to imagine such contortions taking place, in the era we're discussing (i.e., after 1950 or so), for a physical state or condition.

The influence of extrapsychiatric factors is in large part due to the vagueness of psychiatric diagnosis. Although certainly more precise and reliable today than in the past, diagnoses of mental disorder are considerably less so than are strictly medical diagnoses, that is, those concerning strictly physical conditions. It is clear that agreement among psychiatrists as to patients' conditions is high only when they present "classic" or "archetypical" symptoms. In contrast, agreement is low for patients who present symptoms that are less clear-cut and more ambiguous. In fact, the majority of cases psychiatrists see are less classic and more ambiguous in their symptomatology (Townsend, 1980, pp. 270–272). A summary of the reliability of psychiatric diagnoses found it to be high only when the categories were extremely broad or the symptoms extreme and clear-cut; where the categories were specific or detailed or the symptoms less than clear-cut, disagreement between and among psychiatrists was high (Edgerton, 1969, pp. 68–69). Two commentators conclude that "art far outweighs science" in psychiatric judgments (Stoller and Geertsma, 1963, p. 65). An author of a textbook on psychiatric methodology states that expert judgments on mental disorder "are of a social, cultural, economic and sometimes legal nature" (Loftus, 1960, p. 13).

In one study (Kendall et al., 1971), videotapes of diagnostic interviews with patients were shown to a large number of psychiatrists in the United States and Great Britain. Those patients presenting "classic, textbook" symptoms generated almost unanimous agreement as to psychiatric condition. However, patients manifesting less than clear-cut symptoms touched off less than unanimity in diagnosis. One patient was deemed schizophrenic by 85 percent of the American psychiatrists, but only 7 percent of the British; another was judged to be schizophrenic by 69 percent of the Americans, but only 2 percent of the British. Clearly, the American concept of schizophrenia is much broader than is the British. Again, it is difficult to imagine such disparities in the diagnosis of a strictly medical disease, such as cancer or tuberculosis.

Examining *informal* mental disorder labeling around the world, even greater variation prevails. Cross-culturally, certain terms or labels are applied everywhere to persons "who are thought to be conducting themselves in a manner that is inappropriate, abnormal, or unreasonable for persons in that culture who occupy a similar social position; that is, to persons who can provide no otherwise acceptable explanation for their conduct" (Edgerton, 1969, p. 50). Every culture has a label that indicates some version of mental disorder or illness. How are these labels applied? A summary of the available anthropological literature points to two conclusions. First, the recognition and labeling of persons "who are both severely and chronically psychotic" typically occurs with a high degree of consensus "because persons such as these are typically so dramatically, and enduringly, far beyond the pale of everyday rationality" (p. 51). And second, most people who act strangely or "crazily" do not do so in an extreme or chronic fashion; consequently, being labeled for these persons is a complex matter, influenced by a wide range of contingencies. As to whether someone is or is not regarded socially and publicly as psychotic is open to *negotiation* (pp. 51, 65)—that is decided in a give-and-take interaction between two or more parties on the basis of factors unrelated to objective psychiatric condition.

Thus, the constructionist is vastly more likely to be concerned with the dynamics of mental disorder labeling than etiological issues. What factors are related to being labeled as mentally disordered? Is it psychiatric condition alone? Or do extrapsychiatric factors play a role in this process? And how prominent is this role? The medical model would hold that psychiatric diagnoses (although not popular or public labels) are an accurate reflection of the patient's "objective" condition. The constructionist and labeling approach argues that this process of mental disorder labeling is considerably less rational than the medical model holds, and that factors other than severity of psychiatric symptoms influence diagnoses and the decision to admit and discharge patients. (However, labeling theorists do *not* claim that this process is random, that persons are singled out randomly or capriciously, or that patients do not differ in any appreciable way from the population at large.) This process is guided by a number of contingencies, they argue. There is, in other words, "a clear tendency for admission and discharge of mental patients to be related more to social than to psychiatric variables" (Krohn and Akers, 1977, p. 341). Sociocultural factors, such as family desires and living arrangements, adequate patient resources outside the mental hospital, cultural conceptions, region of the country, and the danger the patient represents to others can be determinants of psychiatric case outcomes (Townsend, 1978; Krohn and Akers, 1977).

Thus, constructionism argues that, *independent of etiology,* independent of the *consequences* of labeling, and independent of the *validity* of psychiatric diagnoses, the sociologist is obliged to study *the social organization of the labeling process* that leads to a judgment or diagnosis of mental disorder. Over a half-century ago, Edwin Lemert, an important precursor of labeling theory, stated: "One of the more important sociological questions here is not what causes human beings to develop such symptoms as hallucinations and delusions, but, instead, what is done about their behavior which leads the community to reject them, segregate them, and otherwise treat them as . . . insane" (1951, p. 387). As a qualification: "Hard" or strict constructionists see *all* views of mental disorder, including those held by psychiatrists, as constructions, and sidestep the issue of whether any of them is more valid than any other. In contrast, "soft" or moderate constructionists argue that the reality of mental disorder is not *solely* a construction, and would grant that some constructions strike closer to the empirical reality of mental disorder than others.

LABELING THEORY

A theory that has always been treated as a variant of the constructionist model, but which in fact harbors a strong essentialistic component, is the labeling theory of mental disorder. It may sound confusing to stress the essentialistic strains in labeling theory, since I discussed labeling theory as a constructionist approach in Chapter 3. But, as with Lemert's theory of secondary deviation, the labeling theory of mental illness emphasizes the causal dynamics or etiological factors underlying mental illness, *not* the nature and dynamics of the social construction of mental illness. To be more specific, it argues that mental disorder *is* concretely real, a material phenomenon in the physical world. (Remember, Lemert's theory of secondary deviation emphasizes that it is *being labeled* that often strengthens one's commitment to a deviant role and further deviant behavior.) Thomas Scheff, the primary proponent of the labeling theory of mental illness takes this mechanism several steps further. Being labeled as crazy for engaging in mildly eccentric, slightly bizarre behavior results in *really, actually,* and *concretely going crazy.* The definition becomes a *self-fulfilling prophecy.* One learns to act out the symptomatology of mental illness as a result of being exposed to the definitions that are prevalent in a given society; behaving like a crazy person is how one is supposed to act if one has been defined *as* a crazy person. Hence, engaging in odd, eccentric, and unconventional behavior for which there is no ready label—"residual deviance"—results in being *labeled* crazy, which, in turn, results in acting the way a crazy person is *supposed* to act, which eventually results in actually *going* crazy. But note: The labeling theory argues that there really *is* such a thing as being crazy; although the label creates the condition, *the condition becomes concretely real* (Scheff, 1984, 1999).

It should be emphasized that, although the two approaches have often been confused, Scheff's labeling theory of mental illness and the more general interactionist theory of Becker and his associates are substantially different approaches. Although for Scheff the *initial* process of labeling *is* a social construction, the process of labeling actually *produces* an identifiable condition all can point to and identify as "true" mental illness. In other words, Scheff is not quite a true constructionist, since his primary concern is etiological. In contrast, labelists' concerns are much more heavily concentrated on constructionist matters and far less on issues of causality. Becker and the other labeling theorists never *intended* their theory to be an explanation of deviance in the sense of accounting for its origin or etiology (Kitsuse, 1972, p. 235; Becker, 1973, pp. 178–179). Nor did it insist that the process of labeling always and inevitably results in an intensification of a commitment to deviance, the deviant role, or deviant behavior; this is an empirical question and must be studied in individual cases (Becker, 1963, pp. 34–35, 1973, p. 179). For Scheff, in contrast, the whole point is to devise a theory accounting for the origin of mental illness. Note that Walter Gove, a critic of Scheff's harder version of labeling theory of mental illness, *supports* a softer version of labeling theory "that is not concerned with specific predictions [of causality] but is concerned with how social institutions function and how such functioning is related to our understanding of mental illness as a social category and as a social career" (Gove, 1989).

For Scheff, then, the *initial* process of labeling *is* a social construction; "normals" will often label eccentricity or "residual deviance" *as* mental illness. To the extent that this process is arbitrary and not based on scientific or real-world criteria, Scheff adopts a constructionist approach. Why are eccentrics being labeled as crazy? Is it because of their condition? Clearly not; a variety of extrapsychiatric social and cultural factors rule this process. However, *once the labeling process has been launched* and the person who is labeled as crazy begins to take on a crazy role, a very real condition of mental illness begins to take over. What was *defined* as real *becomes* real. Thus, Scheff has one foot in constructionism and one foot in essentialism, more specifically, in etiology.

Scheff emphatically states that he is *not* a constructionist (personal communication). His theory is *etiological;* it is an attempt to explain the origin of mental illness (1966, 1984). To Scheff, the *how* and *why* of the social construction of mental illness is secondary; what counts is its power to generate behavior and a condition the psychiatric profession knows as mental illness. Hence, he must be regarded at least as much an essentialist as a constructionist. It must be said that labeling theory, in the form stated by Thomas Scheff, has very few followers among clinicians; it is of interest almost exclusively to a very small circle of sociologists. Today, the overwhelming majority of psychiatrists adopt some version of the biomedical model. But Scheff's theory has received, and continues to receive, a great deal of attention in the sociological study of deviance.

THE MODIFIED LABELING APPROACH

Gove (1975a, 1975b, 1979a, 1980, 1982) argues that Scheff's labeling theory of mental illness is empirically wrong. Gove argues that mental patients are unable to function in the real world not because they have been stigmatized but because they are mentally ill; the mentally disordered have a debilitating disease that cripples their capacity to function normally and effectively. Moreover, Gove argues, the process by which the psychiatric profession singles out someone as mentally ill is not significantly influenced by sociological or other extrapsychiatric variables. Instead, this process is almost exclusively determined by the nature and severity of the illness. Labeling, the medical model argues, is neither capricious or arbitrary nor is it based on such hierarchical factors as race, sex, SES, or power. Persons who are sick tend to be labeled as such; in turn, those who are well are extremely unlikely to be labeled as sick.

With respect to *informal,* as opposed to professional, far from being eager to label someone as mentally ill, the general public is extremely reluctant to do so and, moreover, does not hold particularly strong, negative, or stigmatizing feelings about the mentally ill. This is especially true for intimates—spouses, children, parents, close friends—of the mentally ill, who avoid labeling until the disturbed person's behavior becomes intolerable. Lastly, hospitalization and other treatment intervention, far from making the patient's condition worse, as the labeling approach claims, most often results in an amelioration of his or her symptoms. In short, a genuine healing process does seem to take place. Gove, the most outspoken and persistent of the critics of the labeling theory of mental illness, argues that these generalizations are so empirically well founded that he flatly states: "For all practical purposes, the labeling explanation of mental illness is of historical interest only" (1979a, pp. 301–304).

Which model is correct? Which one approximates empirical reality most closely? To begin with, we need not be forced into an either-or, black-or-white position. It is possible that there is some middle ground here; labeling theory may be correct on some points, while its critics may be right with respect to some others. In my opinion, what has come to be referred to as a soft or *modified* labeling theory approach seems to fit the facts of mental illness most faithfully (Link et al., 1989). The modified labeling approach both accepts certain aspects of the medical model and stresses the importance of the labeling process.

Mentally disordered persons, while they do have difficulty in their everyday lives because of their psychiatric condition, also suffer serious debilitation and demoralization as a consequence of stigma and labeling. Everyone who grows up in this society, including the disordered, is aware of the negative image of the mentally ill. Persons who suffer from a mental disorder anticipate negative treatment from others, and these beliefs taint their interaction with normals and with mental health professionals (Thoits, 1985; Link, 1987; Link et al., 1989).

As we've seen, constructionism is concerned with how judgments of reality and imputations of deviance are made and put into practice; but labeling theory is, in addition, concerned with the *consequences* of such judgments and imputations. Constructionism also argues that there exists a certain measure of arbitrariness when applying psychiatric labels to psychiatric conditions. As we saw, American psychiatrists are far more likely to apply the label of schizophrenia to patients than

British psychiatrists are (Kendall et al., 1971); in a civil case that centered around psychic damages to plaintiffs, psychiatrists for the defense found no psychic damage, while psychiatrists for the plaintiffs found considerable psychic damage (Simon and Zussman, 1983); in fact, a wide range of extrapsychiatric factors influence psychiatric judgments (Krohn and Akers, 1977; Townsend, 1978, 1980). While this must be tempered by the qualification that, as seriousness of the condition increases, the uniformity of the psychiatric judgment increases correspondingly, *most* of the judgments that psychiatrists make are of patients with a less rather than more serious condition. It is clear that extrapsychiatric contingencies do play a major role in psychiatric labeling.

The labeling approach is clearly wrong when it comes to treatment outcomes, however. Enough valid, reliable studies have been conducted on treatment outcomes to demonstrate that psychiatric intervention is more likely to be beneficial to the patient than harmful. Far from entrenching the mental patient more deeply in the mentally ill role, treatment does appear to have some positive effects (Smith, Glass, and Miller, 1980; Landman and Dawes, 1982). Some of these effects are not profound, and many do not persist over time; nonetheless, "it would be difficult for societal reaction theorists to argue that the effects of [psychiatric] labeling are uniformly negative" (Link and Cullen, 1989). Psychiatric intervention is more likely to move the patient out of rather than more deeply into disordered behavior, and undetected, untreated mentally disordered conditions often persist over long periods of time (Fischer et al., 1979), refuting "the labeling theory notion that symptoms are transient in the absence of labeling" (Link and Cullen, 1989).

Although it is difficult to deny the impact of the objective nature of mental disorder, stigma, labeling, and societal reaction remain potent and crucial sociological factors to be taken into account in influencing the condition of the mentally disordered. Proving or disproving the strict labeling or the strict medical model *in toto* seems a futile exercise. Both have a great deal to offer; in short, a "modified" labeling theory approach seems to be the most productive model in understanding mental disorder (Link et al., 1989).

On Being Sane in Insane Places

"If sanity and insanity exist, how shall we know them?" Psychologist and law professor David Rosenhan decided to answer the question by having eight normal or "sane" persons, including himself, take part in an experiment. A "varied group" of people, they included three psychologists, a psychiatrist, a pediatrician, a painter, a full-time homemaker, and a graduate student; three were women, five were men. They "gained secret admission" to 12 different mental hospitals around the country by complaining of hearing hallucinatory voices, which said "empty," "hollow," and "thud." All but one were admitted with a diagnosis of schizophrenia. (That one was diagnosed as a manic-depressive.) Once admitted, the pseudopatients acted normally, that is, did not simulate any symptoms of mental illness or abnormality. No psychiatric staff detected that these pseudopatients were normal; they were hospitalized for an average of 19 days, and were released with a diagnosis of schizophrenia "in remission," that is, without signs of mental illness. Rosenhan's conclusion is that psychiatry "cannot distinguish the sane from the insane" (1973). His view is extremely critical of the medical and psychiatric approaches toward mental illness, and it supports some version of the constructionist or labeling theory.

Rosenhan's study has received a great deal of attention, the bulk of it favorable. A review of 31 psychology textbooks published three years after the experiment found that 15 cited the

(*Continued*)

article, 12 of them favorably (Spitzer, 1976). And most of the articles that appeared in mental health and psychology journals commenting on the experiment had positive things to say. The media, too, gave the Rosenhan study a great deal of attention and overwhelmingly favorable coverage, in large part, said one critic, because "it said something that many were delighted to hear." This single study, this critic stated, "is probably better known to the lay public than any other study in the area of psychiatry in the last decade" (Spitzer, 1976, p. 459).

Not all the attention paid to "On Being Sane in Insane Places" has been favorable, however. *The Journal of Abnormal Psychology* devoted its volume 33, April 1976, issue to comments on Rosenhan's piece; most were critical. Robert Spitzer (1975, 1976), a psychiatrist and copreparer of and consultant to several editions of the American Psychiatric Association's *Diagnostic and Statistical Manual of Mental Disorders,* is perhaps the most articulate and outspoken of Rosenhan's critics. He sees the experiment and the article, which summarized it as "pseudoscience presented as science"—prompting a diagnosis of "logic, in remission" (Spitzer, 1975, p. 442). Why?

"One hardly knows where to begin," says Spitzer (1975, p. 443). The study "immediately becomes confused" on terminology. As Rosenhan should know (he is a professor of both psychology and the law), the terms "sane" and "insane" are legal, not psychiatric concepts. The central issue for the law (inability to distinguish right from wrong) "is totally irrelevant" to the study, which is concerned with whether psychiatrists can detect a psychiatric condition. But let's assume that Rosenhan is referring to mental disorder, not "insanity." The pseudopatients *simulated mental illness* in gaining admission to a mental hospital. Said another critic, "If I were to drink a quart of blood and . . . come to the emergency room of any hospital vomiting blood," the chances are, he would be labeled and treated as having a bleeding peptic ulcer. But "I doubt that I could argue convincingly that medical science does not know how to diagnose that condition" (Kety, 1974, p. 959). These pseudopatients claimed to present symptoms of schizophrenia, and that is how they were diagnosed. What reason did the admitting psychiatrists have to doubt the genuineness of the stated symptoms?

For Rosenhan, the fact that no one detected the pseudopatients as "sane" and they were released with a diagnosis of "in remission" was significant; this means, he said, that, in the judgment of the hospital, they were neither sane, nor had they been sane at any time. Spitzer argues exactly the reverse: The fact that these patients were discharged "in remission" indicates that the psychiatric profession is able to detect mental disorder. The diagnosis in remission indicates that patients are free from any signs of mental illness, which characterizes these cases in a nutshell. It is an *extremely rare* diagnosis, appearing, in one hospital, only once in 100 discharges; in a check of 12 hospitals, 11 *never* used the diagnosis, and in the remaining hospital, in only 7 percent of its discharges. Says Spitzer, "we must marvel" at the fact that, in Rosenhan's study, the 11 psychiatrists who discharged the pseudopatients "all acted so rationally as to use at discharge . . . a category that is so rarely used with real schizophrenic patients" (1975, p. 445). *Not one* used any of the descriptions that were available to them that would have demonstrated Rosenhan's point far more effectively: "still psychotic," "probably still hallucinating but denies it now," "loose associations," or "inappropriate affect" (p. 445).

Spitzer admits that "there are serious problems with psychiatric diagnosis, as there are with other medical diagnosis" (p. 451). However, diagnosis is *not* so poor "that it cannot be an aid in the treatment of the seriously disturbed psychiatric patient" (p. 451). But, this critic of Rosenhan's experiment says, a correct interpretation of "On Being Sane in Insane Places" contradicts the author's conclusions. "In the setting of a psychiatric hospital," argues Spitzer, "psychiatrists are remarkably able to distinguish the 'sane' from the 'insane' " (p. 451).

THE EPIDEMIOLOGY OF MENTAL DISORDER

Epidemiology is the study of the distribution of diseases in the population. Psychiatry makes the assumption that the distribution of mental disorders can be determined in much the same way that the distribution of physical diseases can be determined. The field of psychiatric epidemiology is based on the idea that there is, or can be, a "true" rate or prevalence of mental disorder, just as there is a true rate of cancer or AIDS. Clearly, this is an essentialist assumption, that is, that mental disorder is a concrete entity on whose reality all reasonable and informed observers can agree. The constructionist, in contrast, seeing mental disorder as a socially determined judgment, does not make the assumption that a true rate or prevalence of mental disorder can be determined. Instead, constructionists are interested in how mental disorder is conceptualized and defined, how certain categories in the population come to be *designated* as having higher, or lower, rates of mental disorder, and what extrapsychiatric factors influence rates of institutionalization.

All epidemiologists agree that measuring mental disorder in the population, or in certain segments of the population, is problematic. The issue of how mental disorder is diagnosed and determined for the purposes of an epidemiological study has filled a substantial number of very fat tomes. The rate of admissions to mental hospitals has been used as one measure or index of mental disorder in the population and categories in the population. However, we all recognize that there are many factors that make it likelier that some persons, and persons in certain categories, will end up in a mental hospital than others, holding mental condition constant. Some conditions cause a great deal of trouble for others, while for other conditions, the mentally disordered person suffers in isolation; clearly, the first is more likely to be hospitalized than the second. Some people live among groups and categories who consider mental hospitalization a viable option only under extreme circumstances; others look to institutionalization much more quickly and readily, upon signs of relatively minor abnormality or dysfunction. The point is there is a huge noninstitutionalized segment of the population who *would be* diagnosed as mentally disordered were they to be evaluated by a psychiatrist. Because of problems such as these, another measure of mental disorder has been developed: a diagnostic interview schedule, which, presumably, can determine mental condition in a sample of respondents. Over the years, different interview schedules have been used, and somewhat different findings have been obtained. Still, many experts believe that, over time, these research instruments are becoming increasingly accurate. Currently, a huge ongoing study, the Epidemiological Catchment Area Program survey, is measuring mental health and disorder in a random sample of the noninstitutionalized population at large (Kessler et al., 1994).

A large number of studies have been conducted that have reached conclusions concerning the differential proneness of the groups and categories in the population to mental illness or disorder. Most sociologists believe that specific social processes are related to mental disorder and that these processes are more characteristic of certain groups than others. What characteristics are most important? How do members of these social categories fare with respect to mental health and disorder? Perhaps the most basic and often-studied characteristics studied by psychiatric epidemiologists have been *sex* or *gender, marital status,* and SES.

Gender: Men versus Women

It is not clear that there is a consistent relationship between sex or gender and a crude, unidimensional, and undifferentiated measure of mental disorder. Reviews of the literature (for instance, Dohrenwend and Dohrenwend, 1976) have revealed that some studies find that women have higher rates of mental disorder than men, while others show men to have higher rates. This is the case for two reasons.

When it comes to *surveys* of the general population, women have somewhat higher rates of mental disorder. One nationally representative study of households across the United States conducted jointly by the National Institutes of Health and the National Center for Health Statistics identified 1.94 million females and 1.32 million males as having a serious mental disorder; rates of mental disorder were 20.6 for females and 15.5 for males. The Epidemiological Catchment

Area Survey mentioned earlier, which was focused on five urban centers, found rates of mental disorder of 16.6 for females and 14.0 for males (Reiger et al., 1988). A later study using the same research instrument, based on a more nationally representative sample, reached the same conclusion (Kessler et al., 1994). A major textbook sums up the recent evidence and concludes that "women have greater tendencies toward mental disorder than men" (Cockerham, 2003, p. 163).

On the other hand, males are significantly more likely to be *admitted to mental hospitals* than females (p. 164). Moreover, during much of this country's history, the ratio of males to females was increasing over time. For instance, in 1900, there were 106 males admitted to state mental hospitals for every 100 females; by 1975, this had risen to 193, and in 1985, it reached a high of 199. Since then, the ratio has subsided somewhat. In 1997, there were 162 male admissions per 100,000 males in the population, and 89.0 males versus 54.9 female admissions per 100,000 females in the population (Cockerham, 2003, p. 165). It is entirely possible that both essentialists and constructionists would have something to say on the subject. In fact, experts believe that this disparity is due to the conjunction of the specific *type* of mental disorder males are more likely to suffer from (an essentialistic phenomenon) and professional stereotyping (a constructionist phenomenon). While men are strikingly more likely to fall victim to antisocial personality disorders, women are far more likely to suffer from a mood disorder, especially depression. These disorders manifest themselves in strikingly different ways. More specifically, the antisocial personality is highly likely to cause havoc in the lives of others—for instance, in the form of aggressiveness and violence—while depressive mood disorders are more likely to result in withdrawal and isolation. Someone who causes disruptive social and interpersonal trouble is more likely to be institutionalized than someone who withdraws.

The mental disorder of men, even holding severity of disorder constant, is regarded as more disabling, threatening, and dangerous to the society than is that of women (Gove, 1972; Rushing, 1979a, 1979b). Women are regarded as more cooperative and compliant and more readily influenced by the hospital staff and, therefore, are more likely to be released (Doherty, 1978). Some researchers also feel that the social roles men and women and boys and girls are forced to play impacts on their mental health—or lack of it. Males are expected to be more aggressive, independent, and adventurous; consequently, the disorders they manifest (again, antisocial tendencies, especially toward violence) reflect that role expectation. Females are socialized to be passive, dependent, and lacking in confidence; they, too, exhibit this tendency in extreme form in their characteristic disorder, depression (Gove and Herb, 1974, p. 259).

There is something of a "double standard" among clinicians in the diagnosis, hospitalization, and release of mental patients with respect to gender (Cockerham, 2003, pp. 174–176). Psychiatrists and clinical psychologists seem to have a lower standard of mental health for women than for men. They are more likely to diagnose mental disorder for men, other things being equal; a woman's condition would have to be more severe to warrant hospitalization, and a man's less severe, to warrant release. In addition to the nature of the symptoms (disruption and violence versus withdrawal and isolation), one hypothesis that has been put forth to explain this observed regularity is that in a sexist or patriarchal society, males are expected to perform in a society to more exacting standards. Being a man in a very achievement-oriented society is incompatible with being mentally disordered; the penalties for stepping out of line are swift and strong. On the other hand, where women are relegated to an inferior and dependent role, their performance in that role is met with more indulgence and leeway. Clinicians and the general public, both male and female, feel that a mildly psychically impaired woman can perform in an imperfect fashion and still "get by." Ironically, these sexist values result in a higher rate of mental disorder labeling for men, supposedly the more powerful social category, and less for women, who are generally less powerful. As sex roles become more equalitarian, one would expect these gender disparities in diagnosis, hospitalization, and release to diminish and eventually disappear.

Marital Status

Among men, a very consistent finding emerges from the many studies that have been conducted: Single, never-married men are strikingly more likely to score high on every available measure of mental disorder than are married men; separated and divorced men rank somewhere in between. Two hypotheses have been advanced to account for the observed relationship. The first is that men who are married and stay married are more stable, psychologically healthy, and conventional than men who never marry—and therefore, they are less mentally disordered. The experience of marriage itself, these observers argue, has little or nothing to do with this regularity: It is only that the kind of man who marries is also *the kind of man* who exhibits relatively few personality problems, while the man who does *not* marry is far *more likely* to exhibit those same problems. Getting married entails a certain degree of social competence to attract a spouse; men with severe mental problems are not considered desirable partners and thus, will be socially avoided by women (Rushing, 1979b). "The more symptomatic and/or ineffective an individual, the less likely [it is that] he will find a marital partner . . ., and the more likely [it is that] he will spend extended periods in the hospital" (Turner and Gartrell, 1978, p. 378). It is, some say, "the inadequate man who is left over after the pairing has taken place" (Gallagher, 2002, p. 203).

A second hypothesis is that marriage confers a kind of immunity on a man: Married men have fewer mental problems than do bachelors because the experience of being married is conducive to a man's mental health, security, and well-being. "Marriage does not prevent economic and social problems from invading life," two researchers argue, "but apparently can help fend off the psychological assaults that such problems otherwise create" (Pearlin and Johnson, 1977, p. 714). Bachelors are more socially isolated from others; they lack the social supports and resources that married men have at their disposal. Hence, they are more likely to be psychologically vulnerable and fall victim to mental disorders. Again, whether this is a question of social selection or differential experiences, the tendency for single men to exhibit strikingly more, and more serious, symptoms of mental disorder is well documented in the literature (Gallagher, 2002, pp. 203–204; Cockerham, 2003, pp. 177–179).

This generalization does not hold in the same way for women. Some studies show single women to have the same rates of mental disorder as married women (Warheit et al., 1976), while other studies show married women to have *higher* rates of disorders (Gove, 1979b). In short, the special protection that supposedly extends to men seems to offer no special protection for women. It is even possible that the opposite is the case: Some observers argue that marriage is a stressful, anxiety-provoking, oppressive, and exploitative institution, incompatible with the mental health of women (Bernard, 1982). Men have all the advantages in marriage, they feel, and thus profit from the experience; in contrast, women suffer as a result of being married because marriage is more demanding on women. It is frustrating, unsatisfying, and lacking in gratification for them (Gove, 1972). It is also possible that the social selection process that operates so strongly for men does so far less for women. That is, sexual stereotyping rejects mentally impaired men far more strongly than women (Phillips, 1964); a man who is mentally ill is seen by all women as an undesirable partner, while a woman who displays certain mental disorders may still be considered marriageable. In any case, the differences are far less strong among women than men. The evidence seems to favor few differences between married and unmarried women in mental health and disorder (Warheit et al., 1976), yet the remarkable difference in the impact of marriage between men and women should strike the observer forcefully. While it is probably a bit too rash to state that, in terms of mental health, marriage is good for men and bad for women, the evidence does at least suggest it may be good for men and of considerably less consequence for women. In a less patriarchal society, marriage will become more equalitarian and, possibly, equally good for both sexes.

Socioeconomic Status

Of all sociological variables, the relationship between social class or SES and mental disorder has probably been the most frequently studied. And the most commonly used indicators measuring socioeconomic status are income, occupational prestige, and education. The higher someone ranks on any one or all three of these dimensions, the higher is his or her socioeconomic status or social class, sociologists hold. Mental disorder is very closely related to socioeconomic status: The higher the SES, the lower the rate of mental disorder; the lower the SES, the higher the rate of mental disorder (Kessler et al., 1994; Gallagher, 2002, pp. 168–190; Cockerham, 2003, pp. 138–155). This holds regardless of the specific measure or indicator of SES that is used—occupational prestige, income, or education. People at the bottom of the class ladder are far more likely to suffer from psychiatric distress, especially schizophrenia, than those at the top. There are a few mental disorders that are more common toward the top of the class structure, such as obsessive-compulsive neuroses and some mood disorders, but the most serious illnesses, especially schizophrenia, are most common toward the bottom of the class structure. In dozens of studies, conducted in countries on three continents, the relationship between mental disorder and SES has been studied; almost without exception, these studies find schizophrenia significantly and strikingly more likely in the lower socioeconomic strata. This generalization has been verified empirically by studies stretching back two-thirds of a century (Hollingshead and Redlich, 1958; Srole et al., 1962; Leighton et al., 1963).

Why should this strong inverse relationship between psychopathology and SES exist? There are at least four possible explanations.

The first stresses *types* of disorder. The kinds of disorder exhibited by lower-status persons are more likely to come to the authorities than the kinds of disorders exhibited by middle- and upper-status persons. Lower-status persons are less likely to attribute their problems to a psychiatric condition, since they are more likely to feel that some stigma adheres to consultation with a "shrink" or being committed to a mental hospital. Hence, they are less likely to seek out psychiatric assistance voluntarily. Lower-status persons are most likely to come to the attention of psychiatric authorities as a result of referral by the police or a social worker. In contrast, upper- and middle-status persons are more likely to be referred by relatives or a private physician. A great deal of lower-status mental disorders, especially among men, manifests itself in the form of "antisocial" behavior, particularly violence, which is likely to attract the attention of agents of formal social control, the police. This explanation does not say that lower-SES persons are more mentally disordered than middle- and upper-SES persons overall so much as it focuses on how certain conditions, differentially distributed by social class, intersect with the social structure.

The second is the constructionist explanation. Some observers have argued that this strong inverse relationship between SES and mental disorder may be due to class bias and the labeling process. Middle-class psychiatrists find lower-class behavior troublesome and are more likely to label it disordered than the behavior of middle-class persons (Wilkinson, 1975). There is something of a built-in bias in psychiatric diagnosis against lower-class subculture and lower-class persons. Mental health is judged by a middle-class yardstick; lower-class values and behavior are more likely to be regarded as disordered by the psychiatric profession, composed, as it is, of persons who are toward the middle or near the top of the social class ladder. It seems almost unarguable that class bias plays a role in psychiatric diagnosis. Nonetheless, this explanation cannot be the whole story, since much of the behavior of the psychiatrically disordered is deemed undesirable by members of *all* social classes. Characteristically, the lower-class person comes to psychiatric attention as a result of being troublesome to, and being reported by, other lower-class persons.

A third hypothesis attempting to explain why mental disorder is more heavily located at the bottom reaches of the SES continuum focuses on the greater *stress* experienced by persons located there. Economic deprivation, poverty, occupational instability, and unemployment are strongly related to psychological impairment (Liem and Liem, 1978). As a result of having to deal with living in an economically deprived existence and coping with this deprivation, the lower-status person suffers a higher level of emotional stress and consequently is more vulnerable to a psychiatric breakdown (Kessler, 1979). The pressure of daily living under deprived circumstances becomes overwhelming; problems that cannot be solved mount, become unmanageable, and force the person into a break with reality (Cockerham, 2003, pp. 149–150).

A fourth hypothesis attempting to explain the strong inverse relationship between SES and mental disorder is the *social selection* or the *drift* hypothesis. This theory argues that social class is a *consequence* rather than a *cause* of mental disorder. The mentally disordered are incapable of achieving a higher position on the SES hierarchy *because* they are mentally disordered (Dunham, 1965). Members of the lower class who are mentally disordered are either stuck there or have drifted there because their mental disorder prevents them from achieving a higher position. Their disorder retards their social mobility (Harkey, Miles, and Rushing, 1976).

CHEMICAL TREATMENT OF MENTAL DISORDER

By the 1950s, it had become clear to psychiatrists who worked with mental patients that conventional therapy was not working; in the treatment of the most serious mental disorders, especially schizophrenia, psychiatrists "functioned mainly as administrators and custodians" (Berger, Hamburg, and Hamburg, 1977, p. 264). In 1952 in France, and in the United States in 1954, a drug was first used that seemed to show some promise in reducing the most blatant, florid, and troublesome symptoms of institutionalized schizophrenic mental patients. Bearing the chemical name chlorpromazine and the trade name Thorazine, it belonged to a major type of psychoactive drugs that are regarded as having an *antipsychotic* effect. Antipsychotics do not produce a high or intoxication, they are not used recreationally, and are not sold illegally on the street. Nearly all the antipsychotics have legal, licit prescription use for the purpose of controlling mental illness. Antipsychotics in addition to Thorazine include Mellaril, Compazine, Stelazine, and Haldol.

It is likely that experts would say that the two most dramatic changes that have taken place in the United States since the 1950s with respect to mental illness are the degree to which antipsychotics are administered to the mentally disordered and, correlatively, the number of patients who are in residence in mental hospitals. There is some controversy concerning the role that antipsychotics have played in depopulating the mental hospitals; some observers argue that the antipsychotics were less a cause than an opportunity (Gronfein, 1985), while others hold to a more directly pharmacological explanation (Pollack and Taube, 1975, p. 49). Regardless of the exact mechanism, the fact is, in 1955, there were nearly 560,000 patients in residence in public mental hospitals; this figure dropped almost every year until, by the 1990s, it was roughly 80,000. This decline is not due to the number of *admissions* to mental hospitals, which actually increased from 178,000 in 1955 to 385,000 in 1970, and then declined to about 255,000 in 1992. The fact is that length of stay was roughly six months in 1955; for the past decade or so, it has leveled off at two weeks. (Data are supplied by the National Institute of Mental Health.) As a result of much quicker discharges, mental hospitals are emptying out. Regardless of the precise timing and the causal mechanism of this change, it is impossible to argue that it could have come about in the absence of the administration of antipsychotics to schizophrenic mental patients. Roughly 85 percent of all patients in public mental hospitals are being administered some form of antipsychotic medication.

When the drug was initially introduced, Thorazine was described as having the following effects on agitated, manic, schizophrenic patients: The drug, an observer wrote, "produces marked quieting of the motor manifestations, patients cease to be loud and profane, the tendency to hyperbolic [that is, exaggerated] association is diminished, and the patient can sit still long enough to eat and take care of normal physiological needs" (Goldman, 1955). The emotional withdrawal, hallucinations, delusions, and other patterns of disturbed thinking, paranoia, belligerence, hostility, and "blunted affect" of patients are significantly reduced. As a result of the use of the antipsychotics, patients exhibit fewer and less dramatic symptoms of psychosis, become more manageable, and, as a result, have permitted hospitals to discontinue or reduce such ineffective or dangerous practices as hydrotherapy and lobotomies. And, as a result of the administration of these drugs, hospitals have, in the words of one observer, been transformed from "zoo-smelling, dangerous bedlams into places fit for human beings to live and, at times, recover from psychosis" (Callaway, 1958, p. 29). By inducing a more normal psychological condition in patients, it has been possible to release them into the community as outpatients, with only minimal treatment and care in aftercare facilities. This process is referred to as *deinstitutionalization;* unfortunately, what this has produced is a huge population of mentally ill homeless people who are subject to virtually no supervision or treatment whatsoever. (See the boxed insert on deinstitutionalization.)

Studies have shown that roughly three-quarters of all acute schizophrenics demonstrate significant improvement following the administration of antipsychotic drugs, and between 75 and 95 percent of patients relapse if their medication is discontinued (Ksir, Hart, and Ray, 2006, p. 182). The use of the antipsychotic drugs is regarded as not only effective for most mental patients, but it is also the least expensive of all treatment modalities. However, it should be added that although these drugs do reduce the most bizarre symptoms of schizophrenia, they are not a "cure" for mental illness. They calm the agitated, disturbed patient; the symptoms of mental illness are reduced, and patients are no longer as troublesome to others as they once were: They do not manifest their former signs of craziness. Antipsychotics permit the patient to behave in a more socially acceptable fashion; the patient's problems do not surface so painfully or disturbingly. Surely that represents progress of a sort. However, it is a stopgap measure rather than a genuine cure; no mental health specialist can be satisfied until a more substantial and more permanent treatment modality has been developed. Unfortunately, there is no prospect of this for the foreseeable future.

It is not known just why the antipsychotic drugs have this calming effect on mental patients. In any case, psychiatry has not been successful in treating seriously ill patients by means of any of its more conventional "talking" cures, such as psychoanalysis. Using the antipsychotics keeps patients out of trouble and out of the way of normals, and enables some to function in important social roles, such as education, marriage, and occupation. Some observers see the use of antipsychotics as a "revolution" in the field of psychiatry (Gove, 1975a, p. 245). Others (Townsend, 1980, p. 272) are more cautious and see the change not as a genuine treatment but merely as the suppression of troublesome, disruptive behavior.

The antipsychotics are not addictive, and very rarely result in lethal overdoses. However, there are some serious side effects that are experienced by many patients with the administration of these drugs, including abnormal, involuntary, and sometimes bizarre movements of the tongue, lips, and cheeks; facial tremors; rigidity; and a shuffling gait. These symptoms can be treated with a separate type of drug, the anti-Parkinsonian drugs. Patients also complain of feeling "doped up." At higher, often therapeutic, doses, their responses are often sluggish, they tend to be less acute mentally than usual, display less interest in external stimuli, including other people, and slower in arousal and response. Thus, the reduction of the socially and culturally bizarre and unacceptable behavior and thinking of mental patients is bought at a not inconsiderable price.

Deinstitutionalization

In 1961, the Joint Commission on Mental Illness submitted a report that criticized warehousing mental patients in huge, dehumanizing, impersonal, and ineffective publicly funded asylums. Smaller facilities should be maintained in local communities that care for the mentally ill on a more personal and humane basis. In 1963, President John F. Kennedy signed federal legislation into law mandating local community care facilities for the mentally ill (Mechanic, 1989). Any complex and large-scale change is likely to be a product of many actors and a variety of motives. Still, the desire to improve the lives of mental patients must be counted among the original reasons for deinstitutionalization—releasing the mentally ill from large hospitals into the community. In addition, some politicians reasoned, these asylums were extremely expensive to maintain (not to mention ineffective). Thus, community care facilities will save the taxpayer a great deal of money. And third, as we saw, starting in the mid-1950s, psychiatric medicine possessed an inexpensive and seemingly effective treatment modality at its disposal: psychotropic drugs. Thus, as we've seen, within a few short years, the mental hospitals were practically emptied of patients. By the mid-1970s, only the most untreatable patients remained in public mental hospitals.

Unfortunately, things did not go as these early idealists planned. The war in Vietnam (which United States troops entered in 1961 and departed from in 1975) drained an almost unimaginably huge proportion of resources from the public coffer. And President Richard Nixon (1969–1974) proved to be hostile to the idea of community mental health; in 1972 he announced plans to phase out federal support for its programs. Though partially restored, Presidents Ronald Reagan (1981–1989) and George Bush (1989–1993) continued to put the axe to federal support for local halfway houses and treatment centers.

The upshot of these cuts was that the mentally ill were often released into the community with little more than a vial of pills and a prescription for more. Some lived with relatives (many of these were eventually ejected), while others were simply on their own. A high proportion gravitated to low-income areas in the community where disorganization and violence are common. Hundreds of thousands became homeless. (Experts estimate that roughly a third of America's homeless are released former mental patients.) Half of all mental patients released into the community are reinstitutionalized within a year. While the majority of released mental patients prefer living in the community, even under adverse conditions, to life in a mental ward, the fact is most do not receive the kind of care they need—the kind of care that was envisioned in the idealistic 1960s. Meanwhile, city streets have become "open mental wards" (Goleman, 1986). We see the mentally ill on the streets of our cities—and even in smaller communities—wandering into traffic, looking wild-eyed and disheveled, screaming incomprehensible phrases to no one in particular. They have been dumped there, transferred from the asylum to the streets, the victims of massive budget cuts. The system has failed to help them; they are "a silent witness to the heartlessness and befuddlement that has created no better alternative for them" than the street (Goleman, 1986, p. C1).

MENTAL DISORDER AS DEVIANCE: AN OVERVIEW

Mental disorder has both parallels and dissimilarities with the other forms of deviant behavior we encountered in earlier chapters, such as drug use, crime, and unconventional beliefs and sexual behavior. Both deviance and mental disorder represent a departure from the normative order. Being regarded as mentally abnormal by others is usually a result of breaking the rules of the society; one behaves in a way that is considered odd, eccentric, bizarre, and/or troublesome. One says things that others regard as "crazy," one interacts with others in ways that make them feel uncomfortable. To the extent that manifestations of mental illness result in normative violations, the disruption of smooth social relations, and attracting a socially undesirable label, it represents a form or type of deviance.

In addition, deviance is nearly always located in specific actions, that is, in clearly locatable behavioral and attitudinal spheres. One is not a deviant generally; few people even use the term. One is a deviant in specific areas of life—sex, drug use, politics, harming others, and so on. The label of mental disordered is almost unique in that it is free floating, eminently generalizable. One is considered mentally disordered not because of having done anything in a delimited area of life, but because one has done many things in many areas that are supposedly manifestations of a psychiatric disorder, dysfunction, or disorganization. This is true of practically no other form of deviant behavior.

The major thrust of psychiatric writings published in past decades has been in the direction of adopting the medical model of mental disorder, that is, regarding it as perfectly analogous to, or literally and concretely, a manifestation of a physical pathology. The implication of this model is that the mental patient should be treated in much the same way as the sufferer of a physical disease, by both clinicians and the lay public. The social stigma that adhered to the mental patient in the past is regarded in some quarters as an archaic remnant of the past. Being regarded as crazy, this view holds, does not cause others to view the person as deviant but instead will "redefine the deviance in a fairly positive way." Commitment to a mental hospital "tends to shift the person's label from that of being obnoxious and intolerable to that of being mentally ill and in need of help" (Gove, 1975a, p. 245). Insofar as this is true, *mental disorder is not a form of deviance.* To the extent that the public sees mental disorder on a par with physical disorder, qualitatively no different from, and attracting no more stigma than contracting cancer and regards the mentally disordered as not responsible for their actions, it is not a form of deviance. But remember, earlier in this century the cancer patient suffered some degree of stigma, and even today certain diseases, such as AIDS and leprosy, are considered loathsome, so physical disease is not always exclusively physical. Even for some physical diseases, the sufferer is seen in some social circles as a deviant.

But consider this: Being physically disordered in our society does harbor a dimension of deviance. By that I mean that it represents a departure from being self-reliant, taking care of one's obligations; it is a failure to be healthy, productive, and normal (Parsons, 1951, pp. 428–479; Freidson, 1970, pp. 205–223). Illness, then, is a violation of a number of strongly held values. To a degree, being mentally disordered will always be regarded as a form of deviance in the *same* sense that physical illness is. Falling down on the job, being unable to cope, failing to meet one's obligations, and disrupting interpersonal relations will always be despised in a society that values performance and achievement. Being mentally ill emphasizes one's incapacity and incompetence. As such, it will always be looked down upon.

SUMMARY

Of all deviant phenomena, mental disorder comprises the most diverse and miscellaneous category. Mental disorder is a set of conditions that characteristically manifests itself in actions, mental patterns, or speech utterances that are deemed bizarre and deranged by both clinicians and the lay public. Even the behaviors associated with this condition are vastly more diverse than any other deviant behavioral category, however broad it may be, we have discussed so far.

In the fourth edition of its *Diagnostic and Statistical Manual of Mental Disorders,* the American Psychiatric Association (1994, 2000) defines mental disorder as a syndrome or condition that is associated with distress, disability, or an increased risk of "suffering, death, pain, disability, or an important loss of freedom." Over three hundred disorders are listed; however, *DSM-IV* does not provide a framework or a theoretical model for disorders, but a listing of them and a description for each of the symptoms the clinician is likely to encounter in practice. Schizophrenia (a thought disorder entailing hallucinations, delusions, and disorganized speech) and mood disorders (particularly depression) are two of the most commonly encountered and most often studied mental disorders.

Experts approach the subject of mental disorder through the lens of several different perspectives.

Essentialism, is the view that mental disorder is a real, concrete "thing" the observer can identify, locate, and explicate, much as one can pick an apple off a tree. Essentialists examine issues such as etiology (a study of the causes of mental disorder), epidemiology (a study of how mental disorder is distributed in the population), and the effectiveness of treatment. "Strict," "hard," or "radical" essentialism sees mental disorder as the manifestation of a disease, much like cancer; in its most extreme form, essentialism regards the condition as an actual, literal disease, that is, a product of biophysical pathology.

Constructionism, in contrast, focuses not on the condition but on how it is regarded, thought about, talked about, and dealt with. Here, treatment is looked at not as a means to a cure, but as a social enterprise that is itself to be explained and understood. The hard, strict, or radical constructionists deny the existence of mental disorder in the real or concrete world and focus exclusively on judgments of and reactions to a "putative" or so-called condition. Softer or more moderate constructionists either set aside the question of the reality of mental disorder, or agree that it exists and make comparisons between such judgments and reactions and the condition itself. Constructionists emphasize contingency (factors other than condition influence judgments about mental disorder), stigma (judgments of mental disorder are stigmatizing), and the creation of mental disorder through labels.

Labeling theory is a distinct perspective from constructionism. While constructionism focuses on the *conceptual* creation of mental disorder through judgments and reactions, labeling theory focuses on its *literal* creation through these processes. It is a perspective that argues that being labeled and treated *as* mentally ill is the primary *cause* of mental disorder. Labeling theory straddles essentialism and constructionism, in that the *initial* or *primary* judgments about mental condition are made to some degree independent of true mental condition; they act to *create* a true mental disorder. In the past decade or so, a "modified" labeling perspective has arisen, which adopts bits and pieces of the approach but not all of its particulars. It emphasizes the stigma of being labeled as mentally ill, the contingency involved in applying such labels, and the fact that treatment is often effective.

Some sociologists study the epidemiology of mental disorder. Three of the most often studied characteristics that correlate with mental disorder are gender, marital status, and socioeconomic status.

While women are more likely to be diagnosed as mentally disordered in surveys, men are much more likely to be institutionalized. The conditions that men are more likely to manifest (for instance, character or personality disorder, which often leads to violence) often cause more trouble for others and result in more official intervention and, hence, psychiatric labeling and commitment. In contrast, the conditions that are more prevalent among women (for instance, depression) often result in withdrawal and isolation and, hence, no official notice.

Married men are significantly less likely to be disordered than single men. This may be because marriage offers a kind of immunity or psychological protection for them; they receive support in times of trouble. It may also be because men who are mentally disordered can't get married, since they make undesirable marital partners. With women, the picture is not so clear-cut. Many studies show no differences in mental disorder between married and single women, and some studies actually show married women to have higher rates of disorder than single women. It could be that marriage is more stressful for women than for men, or it could be that disordered women are deemed not nearly as undesirable as marital partners by men as disordered men are by women.

Socioeconomic status is the single social characteristic that correlates most strongly with mental disorder. Studies conducted in the past and studies conducted today, and studies around the world as well as in the United States, agree: The lower the SES, the higher the rate of mental disorder, most specifically, schizophrenia, regarded as one of the most common, and perhaps the most serious, of all the disorders. Why? At least four explanations come to mind. Personality disorder, which is common among lower-SES men, frequently results, as we saw, in official and therapeutic intervention, whereas the disorders most characteristic of middle- and upper-middle-status persons are less troublesome and intrusive to the society. Second, labeling may play a role: Middle-class psychiatrists may be quicker to judge pathology in lower-class persons, particularly males. Third, lower-class life is more stressful than middle-class life, and hence, more likely to lead to a psychiatric breakdown. And fourth, the mental condition of the mentally disordered *precedes* achievement in the social class ladder and inhibits that achievement; hence, they "drift" into the lower class.

In 1954, psychoactive chemicals began to be used on a widespread basis to treat the mentally ill. That year, there were over half a million patients in publicly funded mental hospitals, and their average length of stay was six months. While the use of drugs was not the only cause, it was certainly instrumental in emptying out insane asylums. Today, there are roughly 80,000 patients, and their average length of stay is two weeks. Antipsychotic drugs make schizophrenic patients less agitated and more manageable, and their symptoms less bizarre. They also produce a number of undesirable side effects. The "deinstitutionalization" of these patients has resulted in relatively little medical care for many of them, and a very high proportion of those who lack family or social supports become homeless and live on the street, often neglecting to take their medication. They have been "dumped" there in large part because the society is unwilling to pay for their shelter and an adequate system of halfway houses or treatment facilities that would alleviate the problem of the huge numbers of mentally ill homeless street people.

Account: Interview with Anna-Maria, a Manic-Depressive

Anna-Maria is a retired university professor in her sixties. She has been diagnosed as a manic-depressive. "E" refers to the interviewer, Erich Goode.

E: OK, you say that the depression part of your disorder is just you feeling lousy, but the manic part of it is what gets you into trouble.

A-M: That's right.

E: And you have delusions of grandeur.

A-M: Yes.

E: OK, could you tell me about the most recent episode you had? You mentioned that something happened in a restaurant.

A-M: Yes, well, I had an episode and it was coming on gradually because I had retired the Fall before I had this episode. . . . So basically I was living a very unstructured life and I was kind of giving reign to my fantasies and all kinds of thoughts that I was having, some of which were verging on the manic but not quite getting me into a manic state as yet. As a matter of fact, around that Easter time, I started having an episode. And I was just completely removed from people. I just felt that I didn't care what they thought, I didn't care whether they knew I was manic, I just sort of went outdoors and yelled at the sky, and I yelled about the United States' involvement in the war in Iraq. I was being sort of the supreme judge of all this in my manic grandiosity. And my neighbors downstairs got frightened, I guess, and they called up the ambulance, and before I knew it, the ambulance was in my front yard manacling me into a straightjacket, not that I was violent or anything. . . . They didn't pay any attention to anything I said, they just treated me like a crazy person, they put me in the straightjacket and they took me off to the hospital. . . . And I remember in the hospital being very outspoken. You know, I'm really sort of a *shy* person, but there, I just said *everything*. Everything that I thought, I said. And I looked at the Bill of Rights of Patients, and I told the orderly what my rights were. I went around giving everybody orders and being very assertive. So that was more or less my most recent episode. It took me a while to get back to some sort of normal stance. Even when I got out of the hospital, I wrote letters to people in my past, saying nasty things about them and our relationship.

E: I see. How many of these letters did you write?

A-M: Oh, I wrote a couple of them. Mostly to ex-boyfriends.

E: I see.

A-M: I am a believer, so I ask God for help in having more patience with other people, more compassion, less judgmental feelings. And I ask Him to help me with that because I do have a problem with these negative feelings. Everybody has them, but I definitely have them and I've tried to deal with them the best way I can.

E: The people you wrote these letters to [ex-boyfriends] go back quite a ways. Not necessarily very recent.

A-M: That's right. I mean, I haven't had a relationship with a man for 20 years. The last man I had a relationship with, I called him up, also, and I said something very nasty to him, too. But that was the last one. I was in my forties. I was cycling in and out of my manic-depressive phases. I was having these episodes every few years, even when I was teaching. But I was pretty quiet about things then, I more or less had them privately at home, and when I would come out of them, I would just go back to work and nobody was that much the wiser. I *think,* I'm not sure. I think the chair of my department knew something was going on because I told him that I was coming back to work at one point. And he said, please come back, please come back, and I went back and I got back into the swing of things again, and I didn't really get very wayward the way I did when I ended up in the hospital, you know, for going outside and screaming at the sky. I'm trying to think of the question you were asking me.

E: I just said that these episodes involve trashing people that go back quite a ways.

A-M: Go back quite a ways. Yes. What I started to say was that I really didn't have any relationships after that kept me cycling. And I don't know why I didn't have any relationships. I was getting older, and older women don't normally attract the men they're interested in, and for another thing, I was just out of it. I couldn't have sustained a relationship at that point. And so there was nobody I was angry at. I was angry at these people from my youth and up to my early forties. But after that, there was nobody to be angry at.

E: Why don't you say a little bit about what led to your sudden retirement. I believe you retired in the middle of the semester.

A-M: I told my department I was retiring, and I stopped teaching, and somebody had to take over for me. My contract ran until October of that year, and so I kept getting a paycheck up until that time. But I wasn't working from the middle of the spring until early fall. And what led to my retirement was that for some time, I had been having a manic episode on the average of every two years. We call that "cycling." And at one point, I felt that the stress of my job was contributing to this, in the sense that women who get senior positions—because I was promoted to Full Professor, and I was saddled with a lot of administrative work. I had to be chairperson, I had to be director of graduate studies, I had to be director of undergraduate studies, I had to write all these *memos*, and that's not what I liked about the academic profession. What I liked about teaching was the teaching itself and doing research and writing articles and books. And I liked some of the conviviality, although you didn't always find a lot of that here, because people were pretty much into their own thing and their own work. I did have that kind of conviviality with my first job [at an Ivy League university], when I taught there. I had a group of friends that I saw almost every day, and then we would all go and do our own work, but we knew we would see each other the next day, so it was kind of comforting and friendly in that sense. But here, living alone and having this disorder and being isolated, and then getting stuck with a lot of work that I didn't want to do that was only worsening my situation, so I decided to retire. I was in my late fifties at the time, which is young to retire, basically. But I felt I had done the right thing and I still feel that way. Sometimes I feel I really wish I had more *raison d'etre* in my life. But I have gone into some other things along those lines. For one, I volunteered at the Museum of Natural History. And the rest of the time, I can make do, fill in the gaps in my education by reading things I've never read.

E: When you were cycling in and out of these episodes, what would happen *during* those episodes.

A-M: Well, I would mostly stay at home. I wouldn't go to the City and I wouldn't go to the office.

E: Would you teach?

A-M: Sometimes I taught.

E: And when you *did,* what would happen?

A-M: When I did teach, I fulfilled my obligations. Usually these episodes occurred for some reason when I was on vacation or mid-semester, or toward the end of the semester. And I wasn't obliged to keep to my schedule. And when I was, I did do what I had to do.

E: During this 12-year period of time, you would be teaching and you would have these

(*Continued*)

Account: Interview with Anna-Maria, a Manic-Depressive Continued

cycles of episodes. So what would be the nature of these episodes.

A-M: A lot of them were about the Aga Khan [the leader of a Muslim sect, whom Anna-Maria knew in college]. A lot of them involved hearing voices saying, "He's coming for you tonight, so be ready." That sort of thing.

E: Did you dress up?

A-M: I would dress up, yeah, I would get ready to go out. Then he wouldn't come. And it would be a sort of conversation that I would have with him. He would say, "You're not ready yet, so why don't you take yourself over to Café Urbino and have a nice dinner for yourself, then come back and we'll talk about this further."

E: Would you actually speak out loud?

A-M: Well, I wouldn't speak out loud, but I would have an internal dialogue going on, when we were going to get together and whether or not I spoke French well enough, different things like that. What I remembered from my slight contact with him. So basically the feelings I would have during one of these episodes was one of euphoria. I felt very high and very good, I think you—as somebody who has been interested in drugs and what people feel when they take drugs—would have some sort of notion of the *high* that one gets one gets from certain chemicals being released in the brain. I think this is what was happening with me. When I was getting manic, there was some element in my brain that was making me feel *extremely* high, very euphoric. And so it wasn't a painful feeling when I was high. In fact, it was a *good* feeling. I was indulging all my fantasies, all the things that I wanted to happen were going to happen. And when I came *off* the high and none of these things happened, then I would be very depressed, that would get me into the depressed part of the cycle.

E: Would somebody who's just walking by be able to notice that you were in any special psychic state?

A-M: I don't think so. Unless I spoke to them. For instance, I did go to Café Urbino and I created a *scene* when I was there, and they must have realized that there was something wrong with me. But I didn't do that very often.

E: Why don't you repeat the nature of that incident?

A-M: Well, I went to Café Urbino, and I think I had been a little annoyed at them because sometimes I didn't get a good meal there and sometimes I felt their prices were too high, and I told them all this, I said, my father had a restaurant and the food was much better than the food is here, and he didn't charge as much money—of course, it was many years ago, so obviously he didn't charge as much money. Anyway, there was a man smoking at the bar and I really *commanded* the waiter—you know, I was *commanding* everybody to do everything—bring the check over here, I don't want to get close to anybody who's stupid enough to smoke. And I really created quite a scene. And people just minded their own business. It's like New York; in general, New York is like that. I've been on the bus in New York City where somebody is acting strange and nobody pays any attention to them. And the bus driver, when the person gets off, the bus driver will say, "There's a full moon out tonight."

E: Let's go back a ways because I'm interested. You sort of slid over this in the autobiography. You entered college, and then, at some point, you're in a couple of classes with the Aga Khan. Then a couple of girls noticed that you're staring at him and they kind of giggled, and you tossed your hair and stuck your nose up in the air and walked away. Then after that, you mention that you have an episode, you get committed to first one mental hospital then another. Now, was that your first episode?

A-M: Yes.

E: I see. What was the nature of that episode?

A-M: Well, I got very manic. I was laughing a lot. I was finding things so amusing. Also, at one point, in one of these classes I was in with the Aga Khan because the professor started putting all these mathematical formulae on the board and math had always been my weak point. And so I got *overwhelmed* by the experience I was having. I was away from home for the first time, really on my own, and I just lost it. I got as high as a kite. And part of it took place in the classes I was attending, when I would find something the professor or that another student said very hilarious and I'd just be laughing and laughing and laughing and carrying on. And then of course all through this episode I had discovered the Aga Khan and he became one of my focal points. I used to look at him as if he could save me. [Laughs.] And one morning, I had been awake all night, I hadn't been able to get to sleep because I was so manic, my roommate was reading the school newspaper, and it had an article about people *buying* their PhDs. And I said, "I can't believe that people would be so low as to do something like that." And my roommate said, "It's right there in the paper." I felt very idealistic and holier-than-thou about everything, you know. And that afternoon, after I had come out of my class with the Aga Khan, I sort of debated with myself whether I would continue to stay at my college or whether I should go to another college. I kind of hesitated on the street for quite a long time, trying to make up my mind to go back. Finally, I walked back up to the Quad and I saw a girl sitting in the Quad, sunbathing. And I said, "Shall I take off my clothes?" You know, which I suppose had something to do with the Aga Khan, but I wasn't conscious of it at the time. And she responded in some sort of rather vague way, so I just went about my business. And then, that evening, the professor from the class I was in with the Aga Khan came to eat at our dining hall, and I sat at the table. He was teaching astronomy. And I said, "Oh, I can't eat these, don't they have something to do with outer space?" And the professor said, "Oh, she needs help." So they took me to the head resident's room and they called the ambulance. And when the head resident lit up a cigarette, I was very worried. Because in my mind, with my Catholic upbringing, that meant that the world was going to end in fire. Her lighting a cigarette was an indication that that would happen. And they took me away in the ambulance. And then in the hospital, one of the things I was most concerned abut was my hair. Because at the time, I would straighten my hair. I used to go to a hairdresser to have it done. And I *hated* having the hairdresser do my hair. I wanted to do my own hair. So I was trying to wash my hair. And they had me in an observation room, they were observing all of the things I was doing. And they wanted to know from my sister why I was so intent on washing my hair at that juncture, and so my sister explained what that was all about. The hospital was sort of the country club of mental hospitals. [Laughs.] They gave you a lot of good care. They also gave me shock treatments, which were quite frightening. I would go in and out of this state that I was in. I would have relapses and then I would come back and then I would start to get better, then I realized that all I wanted to do was to go home. They told me at college that I had to wait a whole year before I could re-enroll. And I always knew I would come back. Perhaps I should have transferred to another school. Then, seven years after I graduated from college, I started working on my PhD. I had gotten married and most of the time when I was with my husband, I was quite unstable and I think that from his point of view—and this is my objective analysis of it—it's very difficult to be married to a manic depressive. It's very difficult to be married to anybody for that matter, but to be married to a manic depressive is really hard and he did the best he could. I'm not saying he was perfect, but he gave me a lot of support and I actually, considering the men I was involved with afterwards, I have a very good opinion of my former husband now. He was quite selfless in regard to my illness. But it wouldn't have been much of a life for him and maybe it would have been different for me, too, if we had stayed married, because I would have grown into a terrible dependency on him, which I really wouldn't like to have had. I see it in some of my neighbors, where one spouse is sick and the other is all right. And it's a kind of awful thing to watch. I wouldn't want to have been dependent on him. And I wouldn't have wanted him to have sacrificed his life for me, which is basically how things would have headed or were heading. During my marriage, I was cycling then, too. . . . I was giving vent to all of my fantasies. And my husband just had to pick up the pieces. He had to kind of humor me. If anybody was at fault, it was me. What really went

(*Continued*)

Account: Interview with Anna-Maria, a Manic-Depressive Continued

wrong with the relationship was my mood disorder. I decided I didn't want to be controlled and cared for the way he was doing. I also had the feeling that maybe in another relationship, I would have done better than I was doing with him. I had all kinds of illusions about myself. The relationships I had after my husband were with men who were not as good as my husband was. Not as good to me as he was. . . .

E: Is there anything you want to ask me?

A-M: I'd sort of be interested in knowing something about your particular interest in people who have had unusual experiences in life. Why this appeals to you. Because as I recall, it seems to me that some of your earlier work is about deviance and why it is that this attracts you in a particular way.

E: First of all, it's important to know that a sociological definition of deviance is not the popular definition of deviance. To a sociologist, deviance is any activity, any belief, any characteristic that the mainstream society reacts to in a censorious way or a rejecting way or an isolating way. So that sociologically, a deviant would be, for example, a militant feminist, where a conservative politician would say, she's a "woman's libber" and reject her and her cause, you know what I'm saying? So it's not a quality of the thing itself, it's a quality of a judgment made by a conventional person of somebody who has an unconventional characteristic. Or you mentioned this fat woman who got on the bus and everybody stared at her. That would be deviant from the sociological point of view, because the mainstream regards her obesity as unacceptable. Or manic episodes. *To the extent that* they call forth certain negative reactions, for instance, neighbors calling the ambulance, then it is deviant in that sense, because somebody who has a more conventional or mainstream approach with regard to how we should act regards such behavior in a negative light and takes action against it. So that's the first thing. The term "deviant" in the popular imagination is different from the sociological definition. To most people, "deviance" means deranged, pathological, something sick and twisted. The sociological definition has no notions of pathology or anything along those lines.

The second question is, why am I interested in deviance and various forms of unconventionality? To some extent, it's because, to some extent, my life has not been on the straight and narrow, either. I feel as if I've had certain experiences that don't fit into the mainstream. And I find a lot of things that sociologists study boring. The organization structure of General Motors, for example. The composition of a local school board. The abstract laws of interaction, without regard to the nature of the group. To me, my interest gets excited most when people break the rules, when people deviate from the norms, when somebody goes off the straight and narrow path. There's something about it that attracts me. I'm interested in delinquency, I'm interested in illegal drug use, I'm interested in prostitution and homosexuality. These are some of the things I find intrinsically interesting. the introduction to the book or any part of the book, you are certainly welcome to do so.

E: By the way, why *did* you give up driving a car?

A-M: That had to do somewhat with a couple of things. One thing is that when I was manic and I was driving, quite often I would feel like driving right into those headlights coming towards me.

E: I see. Well, I guess it was a good thing that you gave up your car.

QUESTIONS

Do you think that Anna-Maria's condition is "just a matter of definition"? Do you believe she would be diagnosed as normal under a different psychiatric construction of mental disorder? Would her condition be defined differently in another country, or at another time? Can her condition be found in the DSM? Was her decision to retire and give up driving a wise one? Was her condition, as some experts argue, a simple matter of a problem of negotiating interpersonal relations? Or did her condition point to a material and "essentialistically" *real* condition? Was her condition an example of "residual deviance," as Scheff argues? Or did it emerge out of a biochemical imbalance, as most psychiatrists assert? Which model of mental disorder best accounts for Anna-Maria's condition?

CHAPTER

13

Physical Characteristics as Deviance

> Whoever he be . . . that hath any blemish, let him not approach to offer the bread of his God. For whatsoever man he be that hath a blemish, he shall not approach [the altar]: a blind man, a lame, or he that hath a flat nose, or any thing superfluous, or a man that is brokenfooted or brokenhanded, or crookbacked, or a dwarf, or that hath a blemish in his eye, or be scurvy, or scabbed. . . . No man that hath a blemish. . . . shall come nigh to offer the bread of his God. . . . [He] shall not go unto the veil, nor come nigh unto the altar, because he hath a blemish; that he profane not my sanctuaries: for I the Lord do sanctify them.
>
> (*Leviticus* 21:17–23)

> Judge not according to the appearance.
>
> (*John* 7:24)

Can we regard undesirable physical characteristics as a form of deviance? In Chapter 1, I've already answered that question in the affirmative. Here, let's discuss the matter in more detail. Permit me to lay out my rationale for this position.

Erving Goffman's *Stigma* (1963) focuses on the *grading system* of stigma based on behavior, belief, and physical characteristics. Stigma is the manifestation or outward appearance of an inner deficiency, one that either has been or may be noticed, which results or would result in *infamy* and *dishonor.* Clearly, deviance and stigma are closely related concepts; in fact, the parallels between them are so strong it is difficult to distinguish them. Someone who has been stigmatized, Goffman writes, is "a blemished person," a person who is "disqualified from full social acceptance" (p. 1). We realize, he says, that such a person is "different from others . . ., reduced in our minds from a whole and usual person to a tainted, discounted one" (p. 3). In short, "the person with a stigma is not quite human" (p. 5).

A stigmatizing trait is rarely isolated. Few people who do not possess such a characteristic (whom Goffman refers to as "normals") think of those who do as possessing only one. They regard a single sin as housing a multitude of other sins; they think of the visible sin as only the tip of the iceberg. The one stigmatizing trait that is known about is presumed to hide "a wide range of imperfections" (Goffman, 1963, p. 5). If someone is guilty of one sin, they are automatically guilty of a host of others along with it. The one negative trait is a *master trait* or a master status. Normals interpret everything about the stigmatized person in light of the single trait, status, or characteristic. "Possession of one deviant trait may have a generalized symbolic value, so that people automatically assume that its bearer possesses other undesirable traits allegedly associated with it." Thus, the question is raised when confronting someone with a stigma: "What kind of person would break such an important rule?" The answer that is offered is typically: "One who is different from the rest of us, who cannot or will not act as a moral human being and therefore might break other important rules." In short, the stigmatizing characteristic "becomes the controlling one" (Becker, 1963, pp. 33–34).

To be stigmatized is to possess a *contaminated* or *discredited* identity. Interaction with normals will be strained, tainted, awkward, and inhibited. While normals may, because of the dictates of polite sociability, attempt to hide their negative feelings toward the stigmatized trait or person, they remain, nonetheless, acutely aware of the other's blemish. Likewise, the stigmatized person remains self-conscious about his or her relations with normals, believing (often correctly) that the stigma is the exclusive focus of the interaction: "I am always worried about how Jane judges me because she is a real beauty queen and the main gang leader," explains a girl who considers herself—and would be widely considered—overweight. "When I am with her, I hold my breath hard so my tummy doesn't bulge and I pull my skirt down so my fat thighs don't show. I tuck in my rear end. I try to look as thin as possible for her. I get so preoccupied with looking good enough to get into her gang that I forget what she's talking to me about. . . . I am so worried about how my body is going over that I can hardly concentrate on what she's saying. She asks me about math and all I am thinking about is how fat I am" (Allon, 1976, p. 18).

Highly stigmatized persons walk along two possible paths.

One is to resist or reject their stigmatized status by forming subcultures or collectivities of persons who share their characteristic, and to treat their difference from the majority as a badge of honor—or at least, no cause for shame. The homosexual subculture provides an example of this path: Most homosexuals feel that mainstream society is wrong in denigrating homosexuality—that its judgment of them as tainted is invalid, illegitimate, and just plain wrong. Homosexuals typically reject the very legitimacy of the stigma—the basis or foundation for the judgment.

The second path the stigmatized may take is *internalization.* Here, the stigmatized person holds the same negative feelings toward themselves and their disvalued trait as the majority does. Such a person is dominated by feelings of self-hatred and self-derogation. In these cases, persons who put others down make them feel they deserve it; the stigmatized person comes to accept the negative treatment as just; they feel that the majority has a right to stigmatize them for what they are or do.

Goffman (1963) distinguishes stigma that manifests itself in physical characteristics from stigma that appears as violations of notions of proper behavior and belief. He refers to physical stigma as "abominations of the body—the various physical deformities" (p. 4). Goffman refers to behavior and belief as "blemishes of individual character perceived as weak will, domineering or unnatural passions, treacherous and rigid beliefs, and dishonesty, these being inferred from a known record of, for example, mental disorder, imprisonment, addiction, alcoholism, homosexuality, unemployment, suicidal attempts, and radical political behavior" (p. 4). Goffman also delineated a third type of stigma, "tribal stigma of race, nation, and religion," which is rarely discussed as a form of deviance.

In distinguishing his own perspective on deviance from that of Goffman's, Ned Polsky argues that Goffman missed the fact that he and some other sociologists excluded from their definition of deviance "people who were not *morally* stigmatized; that is, we excluded from our definition (and our courses on the sociology of deviance) various kinds of people, such as those unusually ugly according to society's current standards of physical attractiveness, who might indeed be stigmatized (e.g., by being avoided socially or joked about and discriminated against in employment) but whose condition is recognized to be 'not their fault' " (1998, pp. 202–203).

Polsky is wrong about this. Many negative definitions of statuses are entirely unearned. Is the child born out of wedlock (at one time, referred to as a "bastard") responsible for his or her status? Obviously not. In the past, was he or she stigmatized? Of course. Today, in most circles in the United States, the out-of-wedlock child is stigmatized hardly at all. But at one time, and in many societies of the world, is or was he or she regarded as a deviant? Certainly. But the moral infamy from which he or she suffers or suffered does not reside in behavior he or she enacted; we have to look to the parents, not the child, for that behavior. In this chapter, I intend to indicate my strong disagreement with Polsky's position on physical characteristics as deviance. I do not exclude physical characteristics from my definition of deviance. Clearly, people who possess traits or characteristics that are "not their fault" are stigmatized and are treated differently—in a pejorative, derogatory, or downputting fashion—by persons who are not similarly blemished, whom, as we saw, Goffman refers to as normals. In fact, the very concept, "not their fault," is not as simple as Polsky implies.

Lutz Kaelber's University of Vermont course on "Disability as Deviance" demonstrates that the Nazi regime accused the mentally and physically disabled—feebleminded, schizophrenic, epileptic, deaf, "criminally insane," and persons suffering from dementia, encephalitis, and other chronic neurological disorders—of euthanasia-worthy crimes, and exterminated them without mercy. It is possible that the Nazi extermination of the physically and mentally "unfit" paved the way for the Holocaust. To the Third Reich, the involuntary disabled were *deviants,* even though their disability was "not their fault."

Closer to home, in the first half of the twentieth century, as a result of the eugenics movement, all states of the United States passed a law that mandated that people with an unacceptable appearance, low IQ, mental disability, criminal "tendencies," and moral "degeneracy" be involuntarily sterilized so that they could not produce defective children and place an undue burden on normals. This policy was supported by "progressive" luminaries, including two American presidents, Theodore Roosevelt and Woodrow Wilson; Margaret Sanger, an early feminist, who argued that birth control and contraception would weed out the physically and mentally unfit; Ernest Hooton, a physical anthropologist and professor at Harvard, who believed blacks were closer to apes than whites; H. G. Wells, a socialist and novelist; and George Bernard Shaw, a playwright. It is possible that the Third Reich's advocacy of eugenics discredited the program. In the United States, between 1907 and 1941, 60,000 disabled people were involuntary sterilized; the laws mandating such sterilization were not repealed until the 1960s. (A eugenics program was continued in Sweden until 1975.) Again, supporters of eugenics regarded the mentally and physically defective as deviants, even though their condition was "not their fault."

Moreover, as we'll see, many condemners of possessors of unacceptable physical traits believe that these traits are "their fault." In addition to categorizing physical characteristics as deviant or undesirable, or bad, we also have to consider whether these traits are acquired voluntarily or involuntarily.

The acquisition of certain physical traits or characteristics that are widely regarded as undesirable is not always entirely involuntary. Some are chosen outright: tattoos, for example. And some are the result of engaging in risky—including deviant—behavior, for example, sexually transmitted diseases. But whether observers take note of this connection is partly a matter of interpretation, a social construction. Someone may have become paralyzed as a result of a skiing or a motorcycle accident—that is, as a result of engaging in behavior that entails a certain measure of risk—but very few of us will say the people this happens to are responsible for their condition. As I've stressed several times throughout this book, persons who do so will be charged with blaming the victim. But the fact is engaging in risky behavior is causally related to the possession of certain undesirable physical conditions. However, "cause" and "blame" are distinct and separate notions (Felson, 1991); causality is a scientific notion, while blame is a moral one. And it is blame, not cause, that is intricately intertwined with condemnation, deviance, and stigma.

For instance, most (although far from all) persons infected with AIDS received the virus as a result of unprotected, high-risk sex, often anal intercourse, or through intravenous illicit drug use. Many observers believe it is unfair to blame AIDS sufferers for their plight—and I agree with this assessment—but the fact is much of the public does hold a condemnatory attitude. Somehow, many people feel, AIDS sufferers are responsible for their plight. Early in the AIDS epidemic, fundamental Christian spokespersons claimed that the disease was God's retribution for engaging in wicked behavior. The point is this: Seeing a connection between "deliberate" behavior and possessing a physical trait is a cultural and constructed phenomenon, not a simple factual matter. Many people deem that some physical conditions are more or less entirely a product of the possessor's own behavior. Here we have the example of obesity, to be discussed in a later section. Much of the nonobese public holds negative attitudes toward the obese because they believe fat people are gluttonous and self-indulgent and "could control their weight if they really wanted to" (Katz, 1981, p. 4). Clearly on the other side of the spectrum we find persons who are heavily tattooed from one's bald, shaved skull to one's toes, and are thus totally responsible for their physical condition—which is, to many members of this society, a case of extreme deviance (Goode and Vail, 2008).

Here are a few possible routes to how a person came by certain physical traits or characteristics. First, these traits are inborn, a result of the genetic roll of the dice; here we have dwarfism and albinism. Second, they are a product of accident or disease, whether in the womb or after birth, for instance, most forms of blindness. Third, they are inflicted as a result of the actor's risky behavior, for instance, the smoker's lung cancer, the addict's or homosexual's AIDS, and the skydiver's broken neck. Fourth, they are acquired after birth as a result of culturally mandated norms, for instance, the Maori's tattoos. And fifth, they may be acquired after birth by being completely chosen by the person who possesses them, for instance, tattoos in Western culture, various forms of body piercing or alteration, and shaving or dyeing one's hair into unconventional forms, colors, or patterns.

In most non-Western societies, the view that undesirable physical traits are a punishment for wicked behavior is substantially stronger than it is in the West. In many societies around the world, certain physical traits are seen as retribution from God, or the gods, or whatever entity is responsible for such matters. Or punishment for what one did in a former life. Or perhaps punishment for what one's parents did. In any case, it is a consequence of a moral failing of some kind. For instance, among the Jewish ultra-Orthodox, the *haredim,* it is commonly believed that if a woman does not perform a monthly ritual to cleanse herself after menstruation, she may bear children with birth defects. In 1993, I spent an academic semester in Israel. At that time, a debate raged about the following issue. Some members of the *haredi* community claimed that a recent school bus crash, which killed several children, was caused by improperly inscribed biblical verses that had been placed in the mezuzah, the tiny case that holds passages from Deuteronomy, attached to the school's doorway. Such beliefs are alien to science and what we in the West like to refer to as rational thought, but they are common around the world, including some sectors of the United States.

ABOMINATIONS OF THE BODY

In earlier eras, babies born with serious deformities were referred to as "monsters." Their appearance was regarded as an evil omen, a sign of divine retribution, and a prediction of disasters and epidemics to come. In fact, the word "monster" derives from the Latin verb, *monere,* which means to warn, predict, or foretell. Throughout ancient times, many deformed children were killed or exposed to the elements and left to die. A number of Roman authors, including Cicero and Tacitus, describe the drowning or burning of deformed children, an effort to propitiate the gods. The ancient Greeks, likewise, usually put to death children with undesirable characteristics, less out of fear of the wrath of the gods than being ruled by an ethic that was strongly oriented to physical perfection. Aristotle opposed the feeding of handicapped children, believing that their appropriate end would be to starve to death. Plato wrote: "Deformed and infirm children should be hidden away in a secret place." The ancient Assyrians believed that if a woman gave birth to a disabled child, her house would be destroyed; if a woman gives birth to twins joined at the spine, "the gods will forsake the people and the king will abdicate his throne" (Monestier, 1987, p. 13).

In the European Middle Ages, for the most part, Christianity attributed all "unexplained natural phenomena" either to God or the devil. Medieval theologians reasoned that if God created man in His own image, monsters—who were clearly not in God's image—had to be created by the hand of Satan. Hence, the hunchback "bore the weight of a horrible curse on his back"; the blind baby's eyes "had surely been seared by the red-hot coals of Hell"; the "mute baby's tongue had doubtless been wrenched from his head by infernal tongs"; the deaf child "was thought to be receptive only to the murmurings of the Beast, and unable to hear the teachings of men of God" (Monestier, 1987, p. 13). In the Middle Ages, the deformed and disabled suffered most distinctly from Goffman's "abominations of the body." Today, although far less severely, and less specifically because of satanic intervention, they do so as well.

"Abominations of the body": What does Goffman mean by this term? Two distinctly different types of physical deviance come to mind: violations of aesthetic norms and physical incapacity.

Aesthetic norms represent standards that dictate how people ought to look: their height, weight, attractiveness, coloration, the possession of the requisite limbs and organs (no more, no less), the absence of disfigurement, the absence or presence of specific more or less permanent body adornment or alteration (scarification, tattoos, lip plugs, elongation of the ear lobes, etc.). For instance, the skin and hair of albinos lack pigmentation. In nearly all societies on earth, albinos are stigmatized, treated as blemished, tainted, and spoiled; they are "disqualified from full social acceptance." Likewise, dwarfs and midgets, hermaphrodites (people born with sexual characteristics of both males and females), and persons who are extremely ugly by society's standards are treated as less than fully human.

The second category of bodily "abomination," physical incapacity, is made up of bodily impairments that limit one's ability to perform certain activities considered important, such as walking, seeing, and hearing. Of course, all of us are limited in our ability to perform a number of activities. Most of us are too short, or simply can't jump high enough, to slam-dunk a basketball, or too slow to run a four-minute mile. But walking, seeing, and hearing are regarded as so crucial to everyday life that persons who lack the ability to perform them at all are treated differently, and distinctly negatively, from those who possess it.

Many explanations have been offered for why the physically different are assigned a deviant status. Many of us suspect that we could be afflicted by the same random, terrorizing forces that have afflicted the possessors of negatively evaluated physical characteristics. By interacting with them, we could, we fear, be contaminated with whatever struck them down. Hence we suspect we might very well be vulnerable to such forces and want to keep their possessors as far away from our door as possible.

In his analysis of stigma, Katz (1981, pp. 1, 5–11) introduces the notion of ambivalence. Granting that "there are important attributes that almost everywhere in our society are discrediting" (p. 2), he nonetheless argues that most of us temper our negative feelings toward the disabled and the unaesthetic with positive ones. In addition to stigmatizing them, Katz claims, most people feel sympathy for the underdog, distress over their suffering, and respect for persons who are able to triumph over adversity. So why stigmatize them in the first place?

The reasons are diverse, Katz argues, but they may be traced to a half-dozen widespread dynamics that are difficult to ignore.

The Just World Hypothesis

Interaction with persons who possess a socially undesirable trait or characteristic that is strictly involuntary (it's "not their fault") may "cast doubt" on the widely held belief that the world is a just place where the innocent do not suffer (Lerner, 1980). Many of us believe that we get pretty much what we deserve. The disabled remind us that there are many people out there for whom that is not true. Justice does not triumph, the wicked may not be punished, and extreme misfortune may befall the virtuous and the innocent. This is a painful lesson, one of which normals are reminded nearly every time they come face-to-face with someone who possesses a disability or a disfigurement.

Vulnerability

If undesirable physical traits are inflicted on people who did nothing to deserve them, the conclusion is obvious, says Katz: We are all vulnerable to sudden, catastrophic, and undeserved misfortune. The disabled and the disfigured do not merely overturn one of our ideological and moral apple-carts, they also hit home with the message that we, ourselves, could be victims of the same misfortune that befell them. This is an extremely uncomfortable message, one that most normals do not want to be reminded of. Hence, we avoid the disabled and the disfigured, we put social distance between ourselves and them, we treat them in a pitying and condescending fashion, and the cruelest of us stigmatize them. If such a misfortune befell someone else simply as a result of happenstance, it could also happen to us. Coming face-to-face with the handicapped reminds us of our own vulnerability, and many of us find that experience painful. Hence, we want to banish the possessors of these traits from our presence.

PHYSICAL DISABILITY

According to Eliot Freidson (1966), the possession of a physical disability or handicap is a form of deviance. This is so because it represents an imputation of undesirable difference from Goffman's normals. A person so designated departs or deviates from what he or she and/or others believe to be normal or appropriate. It is normal or appropriate to be able to see, walk, and hear. Not to be able to do so represents an undesirable departure from what is regarded as normal. Put another way, deviance is not merely statistical variation or difference from the average, the mode, or the statistical norm. Rather, it is that which "violates institutional expectations" (Cohen, 1959, p. 462). We are expected to be able to see, walk, and hear. When we are not able to do so, we violate the norms—the "institutional expectations" that others have of our performance. In recent years, a variety of euphemistic and politically correct terms have been applied to the physically handicapped—such as differently abled—the reasoning being that plain, straightforward, and descriptive terms stigmatize persons to whom the terms apply. Simi Linton (1998, p. 14), a disabled spokesperson, refers to such terms as "nice words," "well-meaning attempts to inflate the value of people with disabilities," which are "rarely used by disabled activists and scholars (except with palpable irony)." Many deaf militants reject the label "disabled" and claim membership in the deaf culture. But the fact is the norms in this society do call for certain kinds of performance, and persons who are unable to meet those norms are looked down upon in one way or another.

When such violations are in a significant and important sphere of life and are persistent, persons guilty of them are "assigned a special negatively deviant role" (Freidson, 1966, p. 73) and are "generally thought to require the attention of social control agencies" (Erikson, 1964, pp. 9–21). Social agencies that work with the physically disabled and handicapped distinguish between those who cooperate and work at ameliorating their condition—who, for instance, play the role of the "good" amputee—as opposed to those who are uncooperative and do not work toward rehabilitation (Freidson, 1966, p. 81). What these agencies hold out is not an exit from the disabled role—indeed, even after their intervention, those who are rehabilitated by them will still occupy the status and play the role of handicapped person—but an accommodation to that role. In other words, the "handicapped *remain* deviant, and the task of rehabilitation is to shape the form of their deviance, which is quite a different task than that of healing the sick or punishing or salvaging the delinquent" (p. 95). In the words of Erving Goffman: "The stigmatized individual is asked to act so as to imply neither that his [or her] burden is heavy nor that bearing it has made him [or her] different from us. . . . A *phantom acceptance* is thus allowed to provide the base for a *phantom normalcy*" (1963, p. 122).

Disability, like behavioral deviance, is socially constructed, "produced," or "created" (Freidson, 1966, p. 83). This does not mean that the physical conditions on which judgments of disability are based are "created" by the society. Rather, it means the definition demarcating a given condition as a disablement and judgment that a specific case or person belongs to the general category of disablement are to some degree arbitrary and based on social and cultural criteria. Agencies that deal with the disabled as well as the general public create such definitions. They "objectify" or "reify" (p. 83) disability—much the same way all social entities do with deviance in general—in that they assume every member they so classify by a given category possesses all of the characteristics the category refers to. But as it turns out, most people who are legally classified as physically "handicapped" can walk, even though the assumption is that they cannot; most people who are legally "blind" can see, even though the assumption is that they cannot. The stereotype normals hold is that the handicapped will fit the most severely impaired end of the impairment continuum, even though most are in fact at the less impaired end of that spectrum (p. 84).

One of the central tasks of the person who possesses a physical handicap and who is widely regarded as disabled is dealing with the nondisabled, that is, with normals. Rehabilitation agencies usually encourage the fiction that the population at large does not stigmatize the disabled since this fiction furthers their rehabilitative goals. But the fact is most normals do hold a stigmatizing attitude of one kind or another toward the disabled. True, as we saw, most also feel ambivalence toward the handicapped, that is, compassion is mingled with the stigma (Katz, 1981, pp. 5–11). But stigma is there nonetheless. Normals generally reject and avoid the handicapped socially. A "social distance" scale reveals this rejection with crystal clarity. When samples of respondents are asked if they would "accept" persons belonging to various disvalued categories in a range of relationships—as neighbors, as coworkers, as friends—members of none of those categories are accepted, on average, as readily as persons who are normally abled. For instance, one study asked respondents if they would accept members of 22 categories, "every one was rejected to some extent"; cerebral palsy sufferers, epileptics, and paraplegics (along with dwarfs and hunchbacks) were rejected even as next-door neighbors (p. 18). Anecdotal evidence backs up these systematic surveys. "In a host of written and oral accounts [by the handicapped], the theme of being pitied, subordinated, and ignored is expressed again and again" (p. 18). Content analyses of cultural materials, such as jokes, indicate the inferior status of the handicapped. In one study of jokes, the handicapped were made fun of 80 percent of the time, whereas jokes about farmers, dentists, and judges were vastly less likely to be insulting (p. 18). There is a measure of aversion toward the disabled, just as there is toward disfigurements, in part because they provoke anxiety in normals, reminding them that they, too, could fall victim to the same misfortune (p. 20). In other words, normals fear the handicapped as much as they pity them.

Times are changing. In 1990, the Americans with Disabilities Act, which guaranteed prohibition against job discrimination and physical access to public spaces, was passed with bipartisan support. In the late 1990s, a substantial number of books adopting the perspective of the disabled—new style activist researchers who want to change the way things are, most of whom are disabled persons themselves—have been published (Hockenberry, 1995; Thompson, 1996, 1997; Davis, 1997; Mairs, 1997; Mitchell and Snyder, 1997; Linton, 1998; Charlton, 1999; Fiffer, 1999). In 1997, Mattel introduced a "Barbie" doll friend in a wheelchair. In 1991, Dayton Hudson, an advertising firm, introduced ads using disabled models. In 1992, critics protested the muscular dystrophy telethon hosted by comedian Jerry Lewis; these protesters included some who were themselves disabled former poster children for the cause. They objected to the telethon fostering an image of the disabled as pitiable and childlike. Given these beginnings, this movement toward demanding acceptance and equality for the disabled is likely to gain momentum during the course of the twenty-first century.

CONFORMITY TO AND VIOLATIONS OF ESTHETIC STANDARDS

"I'm too ugly to get a job," declared a Miami bank robber after the police apprehended him (Morin, 2006). This felon's rationalization may have some basis in fact. One of the more remarkable pieces of evidence suggesting that ugliness is a form of deviance comes from a study indicating that, among young adults (age 18–26), ugliness is statistically associated with criminal behavior (Mocan and Tekin, 2006). The uglier the person, the greater the likelihood he or she will have difficulty in high school and, seven to eight years later, will engage in a range of criminal activities, including burglary and drug selling; this is especially true of females. One possibility: Judgments of deviance close off legitimate avenues of success and make illegitimate avenues seem more attractive. Violations of esthetic standards offer one major type of "abominations of the body." All societies hold their members to certain standards of physical attractiveness. Says Nancy Etcoff, a neuroscientist conducting research on the role of looks in human attraction and author of *Survival of the Prettiest* (1999): "Every culture is a beauty culture. . . . I defy anyone to point to a society anytime in history or any place in the world that wasn't preoccupied with beauty" (Cowley, 1996, p. 62). Moreover, in all societies on earth, there are negative consequences for not measuring up to these standards of beauty; ugly people everywhere are treated as deviants. Naturally, these consequences vary from society to society and from one period of history to another; they vary from being an object of teasing to being put to death. In one way or another, all societies reward the attractive and punish the ugly.

At one time, most anthropologists believed that aesthetic standards were completely arbitrary, that is, looks judged attractive in one society may be regarded as ugly in another. Most contemporary researchers and scholars reject this radically relativistic view. In fact, the valuation of looks is considerably less variable and relativistic than was once believed. It turns out there is a fairly substantial measure of agreement in aesthetic standards from one society to another. There is some variability, of course, and it is interesting and significant; we'll be looking at some of the sources of variability in judgments of attractiveness momentarily. The crucial point to keep in mind is that the variation is much less substantial than was believed in the past, and the consensus is probably a great deal more significant than the variation. For the most part, looks that are considered beautiful in one society are regarded as beautiful in societies all over the world; looks that are considered ugly in one society tend to be regarded as ugly in societies the world over. When researchers show photographs of faces of people from all racial categories to subjects from backgrounds as diverse as Greece, China, India, and England, they find a remarkably high level of agreement as to which ones are attractive and which ones are unattractive. The ethnic background of the subjects in these studies makes little or no difference in their judgments.

Skeptics might argue that, as a result of the influence of Western, mainly American, movies, television programs, and magazines, the aesthetic standards that rule here have spread to the inhabitants of every nation on earth. But when Judith Langlois projected images of the faces of "attractive" and "unattractive" persons—males and females, adults and babies, and whites and persons of African descent—before 3- and 6-month-old babies, the same pattern prevailed. These babies "gazed significantly longer" at the attractive than at the unattractive faces. Says Langlois: "These kids don't read *Vogue* or watch TV. . . . They haven't been touched by the media. Yet they make the same judgments as adults" (Cowley, 1996, p. 63; Langlois et al., 2000; Lemley, 2000).

What's behind these judgments? Is there something about a face or a body that dictates that we find it attractive? Does the same process take place in reverse for the unattractive face? Some psychobiologists think they have the answer: evolution. They believe that many clues point to the possibility that humans are biologically "hardwired" to make specific, distinct, and universal aesthetic judgments.

Some of the rules of aesthetic judgment are commonsensical and not especially mysterious. In nearly all persons, physical good heath is more attractive than illness. "As far as anyone knows," according to Helen Fisher, an anthropologist who studies love, mating, and physical attractiveness, "there isn't a village on earth where skin lesions [sores], head lice, and rotting teeth count as beauty aids" (Cowley, 1996, p. 63). Surprisingly, *symmetry* turns out to be a major factor in determining the physical attractiveness of human faces and bodies—a balance of each side with the other, in equal proportion. (Interestingly, the same principle holds for animals, some of them as lowly as scorpion flies. Females of many species refuse to mate with males who do not display the requisite symmetry.) Other features include, for human males, slightly above-average height, a broad forehead, prominent brow and cheekbones, a large jaw and strong chin, slightly above-average body musculature, and a waist that is 90 percent the measurement of the hips. For females, these features include youth as well as large eyes, a small nose, delicate jaw, small chin, full lips, firm, symmetrical breasts, smooth, unblemished skin, and a waist-hip ratio of 70 percent (Cowley, 1996, p. 63).

Most evolutionary psychologists believe that these judgments are genetic in origin, that, without realizing it, our bodies are telling us to seek partners who offer the maximum potential to reproduce our own genes in our children and in subsequent generations. Each of these traits, from age to smooth, unblemished skin to the flair of a woman's hips and the jut of a man's jaw, evolutionary psychologists argue are maximally related to fertility, and hence, according to their theory, maximum attractiveness. We find in a potential partner that which tells us that if we mate with him or her, our genetic material stands the highest likelihood of being propagated to later generations. Genes are "selfish"; they seek to reproduce themselves. Seeking out the most attractive available partner is a way of doing that. Our esthetic judgments are ruled by our selfish genes.

In contrast, most sociologists, anthropologists, and other social scientists argue that culture—not genes—explains judgments of attractiveness. If judgments of beauty were biologically hardwired and designed to perpetuate the judge's genes, how do we explain homosexuality? Why do same-sex partners find many of the same physical traits attractive that opposite-sex partners do? Says Micaela di Leonardo, an anthropologist who studies human attractiveness: "People make decisions about sexual and marital partners inside complex networks of friends and relatives. . . . Human beings cannot be reduced to DNA packets" (Cowley, 1996, p. 66).

Regardless of the source or cause of the consistency of aesthetic judgments about human appearance, they are a fact of life. And studies have shown that, just as conforming to a society's aesthetic standards is likely to bring forth rewards, violating those standards is likely to result in punishment. We "set narrow standards of beauty and then insult and hurt those who fall outside those standards" (Beuf, 1990, p. 1). Is the possession of an unaesthetic appearance the possessor's "fault"? Not usually. Is this punishment unfair? Most decidedly. Is such punishment a reality in the lives of many people who fail to attain the aesthetic ideal? Answering this question is precisely the point of this section.

In a classic study by social psychologist Karen Dion (1972), a sample of college women were asked to read over a teacher's notes describing the behavior of the children in her class. Attached to the notes was a photograph of the child. The notes did not describe a real child or actual behavior; in fact, they were manipulated to describe a fictional incident in which the child hurt a dog or another child in a trivial or a serious way. The photographs, likewise, were varied so that they depicted one attractive girl, one unattractive girl, one attractive boy, and one unattractive boy. The researchers asked members of the sample to evaluate the behavior and the child. Dion hypothesized that physical appearance would make a difference in these evaluations—and they did.

If the child's misbehavior was mild (stepping on a dog's tail), the women in the sample were not influenced by the children's looks. But when the misbehavior was more serious (throwing stones at a dog, causing it to yelp and limp away), for the unattractive children, members of the sample regarded this as a serious character flaw; for the attractive children, the sample of college students tended to be more lenient and indulgent, to give them the benefit of the doubt, passing off their misbehavior as trivial. One student who read the notes and saw the photograph of an attractive girl made these comments about an attractive girl who had thrown rocks at the dog: "She appears to be a perfectly charming little girl, well-mannered, basically unselfish. It seems that she can adapt well among children her age and make a good impression. . . . She plays well with everyone, but, like everyone else, a bad day can occur. Her cruelty . . . need not be taken too seriously" (Berscheid and Walster, 1972, p. 45).

In contrast, here are the remarks another student made, commenting on an unattractive girl who committed exactly the same act: "I think the child would be quite bratty and would be a problem to teachers. . . . She would probably try to pick a fight with other children. . . . She would be a brat at home. . . . All in all, she would be a real problem" (p. 45). In addition to evaluating attractive and unattractive children and their behavior differently, these respondents expressed expectations that the unattractive ones would be likelier to commit similar transgressions in the future. In short, the attribution of deviance is closely tied to looks: Other things being equal, unattractive people are more likely to be suspected of engaging in wrongdoing, more likely to be evaluated negatively, and more likely to be punished.

Standards of beauty are crucial to defining its absence—ugliness—as deviant. The fact is "uglier people are assigned all kinds of undesirable qualities. They are expected to do evil things, and their misdeeds are judged as more wicked than if the same thing was done by a better looking wrongdoer" (Jones et al., 1984, p. 53). An enormous number of studies have confirmed the impact of looks on how we are treated by others. After they have met them, people are more likely to forget about less attractive people than those who are more attractive; they evaluate work done by less attractive people more negatively than work done by more attractive people; people tend to work less hard for more unattractive people than for attractive people; and they are less likely to return something that is lost if the owner is physically unappealing (p. 53). As a result of this differential treatment, less attractive people tend to have a lower sense of self-esteem and to have less satisfactory relations with peers (p. 54). In sum, then, "ugly or physically deviant people are clearly disadvantaged both by the immediate negative effect they elicit and by the longer term cumulative consequences of coping with the avoidant and rejecting behavior of others" (p. 56).

At the age of 9, Lucy Grealy was diagnosed with cancer. To save her life, surgeons removed a third of her jaw. After the operation, when she looked in the mirror, Lucy realized she was different. She endured 30 separate operations, most of them to reconstruct her jaw so that she would look normal. The boys in her school taunted her cruelly. "Hey, girl, take off that monster mask—oops, she's not wearing a monster mask," shouted one (Grealy, 1995, p. 118). "*What* on earth is *that?*" yelled another (p. 124). "*That* is the ugliest girl I have *ever* seen" declared a third (p. 124). The taunts, which were especially frequent during lunch period, became so painful for Lucy that, in the seventh grade, she went to her guidance counselor to complain. Rather than reprimand the children who hurled them, he asked if she wanted to eat lunch in his office, an offer she decided to accept.

All societies value beauty. Hence, "the person whose appearance is impaired, who stands out because of obvious flaws and disfigurements, is perceived as a deviant." Such a person is deviant in two ways—one, by failing to live up to an ideal cultural standard of beauty, and two, by failing to live up to what is regarded as a normal or unexceptional appearance (Beuf, 1990, p. 7). Ugly or extremely unattractive persons are often stared at, teased, taunted ("How did your face *get* like that, anyhow?"), and humiliated; people with average or normal appearance often feel disgusted, repelled, even tainted to be in their presence. The cruelty of children toward the appearance-impaired "seems limitless" (p. 51). It is clear that, in spite of the fact that such people did not do anything to deserve their appearance, many audiences regard—and treat—them as deviants.

BODY MODIFICATION AS PHYSICAL DEVIANCE

Some people modify their bodies in ways that elicit suspicion, stigma, and condemnation. Erik Sprague, 27, is a "performance artist" and a Ph.D. student in philosophy at the State University of New York at Albany. Mr. Sprague "is slowly transforming himself into a reptile." Not literally, of course, but his appearance is becoming increasingly reptilian. Scalelike tattoos appear on his body from head to foot. He's having the scales filled in, one by one, with green. He convinced surgeons to implant a bony ridge on his forehead and shape his tongue into a reptile's proverbial forked tongue. His fingernails are in the form of claws, and several of his teeth are filed down to look like "crocodilelike chompers."

Sprague calls his transformation an "experiment." The idea isn't to shock, he says, but to "stimulate dialogue, to get people thinking, to make people wonder." He wants to test the limits of what it means to be human. After his metamorphosis, he wonders, can others still regard him as a full-fledged human being? He says he knows who his real friends are by their willingness to remain friends with him, even after taking on his dramatically altered appearance. "I learn a lot more about a person by their reaction to me than they could ever learn about me by just looking at my physical appearance."

Sprague works as a performer with the traveling Jim Rose Circus. He swallows swords, eats live insects, breathes fire, and sticks metal skewers through his cheeks. His ongoing bodily transformation, he says, has been great for his show business career (Anonymous, 2000).

Aside from ear piercing, which, for women, is considered conventional and normative, tattooing is probably the most widely practiced form of voluntary body alteration. No statistics are kept on the number of people who receive a permanent tattoo, but in the United States, the number certainly runs into the millions. Is tattooing a form of physical deviance?

In many societies of the world, of course, getting a tattoo is not only accepted, it is also normatively demanded. In Western society generally and in the United States specifically, people who "choose to modify their bodies" by getting a tattoo "violate appearance norms" and hence "risk being defined as socially and morally inferior. Choosing to be a physical deviant symbolically demonstrates one's disregard for the prevailing norms" (Sanders, 1989, p. 2). In many ways, persons who choose to be tattooed play on that unconventionality by demonstrating their "disaffection from the mainstream." For many people who are unconventional, tattooing is a symbolic affirmation—indeed, a public proclamation—of the tattooee's "special attachments to deviant groups" (p. 2). It is an "effective social mechanism for separating 'us' from 'them' " (p. 3). This separation may be partial, as exemplified by the Wall Street lawyer who receives a single, small, and inconspicuous tattoo to affirm his or her mild unconventionality, or it may range up to total unconventionality, as with the person who is tattooed from head to toe in wild designs and who therefore cannot move in any social circle whatsoever without being regarded as an out-and-out deviant—and wants it that way (Goode and Vail, 2008).

Tattooing is deviant for both its direct symbolic value and its symbolical connectedness with deviant groups and categories. Here we have "voluntary guilt by association." Tattooing is common among convicts, prostitutes, bikers, drunken sailors, and other disreputable types. Therefore wearing a tattoo symbolizes the "general deviance and untrustworthiness of the wearer" (Sanders, 1989, p. 126). Wearing a tattoo announces to the world, "I am a great deal like these other disreputable people who are known for wearing a tattoo." Hence, wearing "a stigmatizing mark by most members of mainstream society," one becomes aware of "the potential negative social consequences of being tattooed" from employers, relatives, one's spouse, and other representatives of "straight" society (p. 126). Many tattooed persons do belong to deviant groups for whom the tattoo is a badge of honor rather than shame.

In addition, tattooing represents a major commitment. Before the advent of lasers, tattoos could be removed only through conventional surgery, which was expensive and produced scarification. Hence, until recently, a tattoo, once on the body, remained there for life. In a phrase, the wearer was "indelibly marked" (p. 126). Although vastly more common than a decade or two ago, even today, getting a tattoo is considered a "big deal." As a result, most receivers of a tattoo "start small." Getting a small, inexpensive, and readily concealable tattoo is the usual way of limiting one's commitment (p. 126). By testing the waters in this fashion, one can determine whether, in one's group or circle, social reactions to the tattoo are sufficiently negative as to call a halt to further body alterations. If these reactions are mild among their peers, more accepting than rejecting, many recipients will escalate the process, receiving larger and more conspicuous tattoos.

In short, there is a "certain level of risk" in receiving a tattoo. One may not choose an artful or reputable tattooist, the process is somewhat painful, one risks infection, the final product may not be quite what one had hoped for, one may later have a change of heart, one may be criticized or condemned for bearing a tattoo on one's body by one's peers, one may take up with new friends or lovers who will find the connection with tattooing repugnant, one's employers may react more harshly than one had anticipated, and so on. In short, yes, tattooing is a form of physical deviance, albeit a relatively mild form. In contrast, more complete or full-body tattooing may be regarded as more "extreme" deviance. To put the matter another way, the degree of deviance of tattooing runs the gamut from mildly deviant (a small, inconspicuous tattoo) to strongly deviant (being tattooed all over one's body, including one's face). What makes it especially interesting is that, unlike many forms of physical deviance, it is voluntary. Many tattooees choose to receive tattoos on their body specifically because of its association with deviant social categories and groups (Sanders, 1989).

OBESITY

Obesity represents a prime example of an abomination of the body that violates aesthetic standards. What makes it even more interesting than most of the characteristics with which it shares this quality is that, in addition to being physical in nature, most people believe it to be the product of immoral or deviant behavior. The majority of people who are not fat feel that the obese became fat because they are gluttonous and lazy—that is, because they eat too much and don't exercise enough. Hence, obesity partakes of both of Goffman's forms of stigma: It is both an abomination of the body and a blemish of individual character.

In this society, fatness is itself looked upon with repugnance because most Americans consider it unsightly and unaesthetic, and, in addition, fatness is a sign or manifestation that the person who carries the weight got that way because of a weak, self-indulgent nature. In other words, not only does the thin majority regard obesity as unfashionable and unaesthetic, they also consider it "morally reprehensible," a "social disgrace" (Cahnman, 1968, p. 283). They set apart fat people from themselves, men and women of average size. They socially isolate the obese from normal society (Millman, 1980). Today, being obese bears something of a stigma.

In contemporary America, the obese are stigmatized. Fat people are considered less worthy human beings than thin or average-sized people are. They receive less of the good things that life has to offer and more of the bad. Men and women of average weight tend to look down on the obese, feel sorry for them, pity them, feel superior to them, reward them less, punish them, and make fun of them. The obese are often an object of derision and harassment for their weight. What is more, average-sized persons tend to feel that this treatment is just, that the obese deserve it, indeed, and that it is even something of a humanitarian gesture, since such humiliation will supposedly inspire them to lose weight. The stigma of obesity is so intense and pervasive that many, perhaps most, fat people come to see themselves as deserving of it, too.

The obese, in the words of one observer, "are a genuine minority, with all the attributes that a corrosive social atmosphere lends to such groups: poor self-image, heightened sensitivity, passivity, withdrawal, a sense of isolation and rejection." They are subject to relentless discrimination, they are the butt of denigrating jokes, they suffer from persecution; it would not be an exaggeration to say that they attract cruelty from the average-sized majority. Moreover, their friends and family rarely give the kind of understanding they need in order to deal with this cruelty. In fact, it is often friends and family who mete out the cruel treatment. The social climate has become "so completely permeated with anti-fat prejudice that the fat themselves have been infected by it. They hate other fat people, hate themselves when they are fat, and will risk anything—even their lives—in an attempt to get thin. . . . Anti-fat bigotry . . . is a psychic net in which the overweight are entangled every moment of their lives" (Louderback, 1970, pp. v–vii).

Negative feelings toward being overweight are a matter of degree, of course. If the grossly obese are persecuted mightily for their weight, the slightly overweight are persecuted proportionally less—they are not exempt. In spite of the fact that Americans are gaining weight over time (or perhaps because of it), we remain a weight-obsessed society. It is impossible to escape reminders of what our ideal weight should be. Standing at the checkout counter in our local supermarket, we are confronted by an array of magazines, each with its own special diet designed to shed those flabby pounds. Television programs and advertising display actresses and models who are considerably slimmer than average, setting up an almost impossibly thin ideal for the public. If we were to gain 10 pounds, our friends would notice it, would view the gain with negative feelings, and only the most tactful would not comment on it.

These exacting weight standards fall, not surprisingly, more severely on the shoulders of women than on men's. In a survey of the 33,000 readers of *Glamour* magazine placed in the August 1983 issue of the magazine, 75 percent said that they were "too fat," even though only one-quarter were overweight according to the Metropolitan Life Insurance Company's 1959 height-weight tables, and even fewer of them were deemed overweight by the current standards. Still more surprising, 45 percent who were underweight according to Metropolitan Life's figures felt that they were too fat. Only 6 percent of the respondents felt "very happy" about their bodies; only 15 percent described their bodies as "just right." When looking at their nude bodies in the mirror, 32 percent said that they felt "anxious," 12 percent felt "depressed," and 5 percent felt "repulsed." Commenting on the *Glamour* survey, one of the researchers who analyzed the survey, Susan Wooley, a psychiatrist, commented: "What we see is a steadily growing cultural bias—almost no woman of whatever size feels she's thin enough."

Evidence suggests that the standards for the ideal female form have gotten slimmer over the years. Women whose figures would have been comfortably embraced by the norm a generation or more ago are now deemed unacceptably overweight, even fat. In 1894, the model for the White Rock Girl, inspired by the ancient Greek goddess Psyche, was 5′4″ tall and she weighed 140; her measurements were 37″-27″-38″. Over the years, the women who have been selected to depict the White Rock Girl have gotten taller, slimmer, and have weighed less and less. Today, she's 5′8″, weighs 118, and measures 35″-24″-34″. Commenting on this trend in an advertising flyer, the executives of White Rock explain: "Over the years the Psyche image has become longer-legged, slimmer-hipped, and streamlined. Today—when purity is so important—she continues to symbolize the purity of all White Rock products." The equation of slenderness with purity is a revealing comment on today's obsession with thinness: Weighing a few pounds over a mythical ideal is to live in an "impure" condition. In the 1980s, American woman averaged 5′4″ in height and weighed 140 pounds, the same size as White Rock's model in 1894.

Advertising models represent one kind of ideal; they tend to be extremely thin. They are not, however, the only representation of the ideal female form as depicted by the media. There are, it may be said, several ideals rather than just one. Photographs appear to add between five and ten pounds to the subject; clothes add a few more in seeming bulk. (White Rock's Psyche wears very little in the way of clothes, however.) Consequently, fashion models typically border on the anorexic, and women who take them as role models to be emulated are subjecting themselves to an almost unattainable—and unhealthy—standard. It would be inaccurate to argue that all—or even most—American women aspire to look like a fashion model, and moreover, it would be inaccurate to assert that women in all media are emaciated. Still, it is entirely accurate to say that the ideal woman's figure as depicted in the media has become slimmer over the years. And that many women are influenced by that ideal, even if it only manifests itself in how they feel about themselves.

Aside from advertising, another ideal is depicted in Miss America pageants. Prior to 1970, Miss America contestants weighed 88 percent of the average for American women their age. After 1970, this declined slightly to 85 percent. Even more significant, before 1970 pageant winners weighed the same as the other contestants; after that date, however, they weighed significantly less than the contestants who didn't win—82.5 percent of the average weight for American women as a whole. Similarly, the weight of women who posed for *Playboy* centerfolds also declined between 1959 and 1979. Centerfolds for 1959 were 91 percent of the average weight for American women in their twenties; by 1978, this had declined to 84 percent. The measurements of the 1959 *Playboy* centerfold were 37″-22″-36″. In 1978, they were 35″-24″-34½″, indicating a growing preference over time for a less voluptuous, thinner, more angular, and more "tubular" ideal female figure. Interestingly, during this same period, the American woman under the age of 30 gained an average of 5 pounds (which was entirely attributable to a gain in height, not to an increase in body fat). The number of diet articles published in six popular magazines nearly doubled between 1959 and 1979 (Garner et al., 1980). This trend has continued unabated into the twenty-first century.

The increasingly slim standards of feminine beauty represent the most desirable point on a scale. The opposite end of the scale represents undesirable territory—obesity. If American women have been evaluated by standards of physical desirability that have shifted from slim to slimmer over the years, it is reasonable to assume that during that same period, it has become less and less socially acceptable to be fat. In tribal and peasant societies, corpulence was associated with affluence. An abundant body represented a corresponding material abundance. In a society in which having plenty to eat is a mark of distinction, heaviness draws a measure of respect. This tended to be true not only for oneself, but also for one's spouse (or spouses) and one's children as well. With the arrival of mature industrialization, however, nutritional adequacy becomes sufficiently widespread as to cease being a sign of distinction. Slenderness rather than corpulence comes to be adopted as the prevailing aesthetic standard among the affluent (Powdermaker, 1960; Cahnman, 1968, pp. 287–288). Over time, all social classes adopt the slim standard; while more firmly entrenched in the upper socioeconomic strata, the slim ideal permeates all levels of Western society.

Obesity is sociologically interesting, among other reasons, because the thin or average-sized majority consider it as both a physical characteristic, like blindness and paraplegia, and a form of behavioral deviance, like prostitution and alcoholism. They hold the obese, unlike the physically disabled, responsible for their condition. The nonobese majority view fatness both as a physical deformity as well as a behavioral aberration (Cahnman, 1968, p. 293; Allon, 1982, p. 130). They regard being fat as a matter of choice. The obese have gotten that way because of something they have done, many feel, as a result of a major character flaw.

Overweight persons "are stigmatized because they are held responsible for their deviant status, presumably lacking self-control and will-power. They are not merely physically deviant as are physically disabled or disfigured persons, but they [also] seem to possess characterological stigma. Fat people are viewed as 'bad' or 'immoral'; supposedly, they do not want to change the error of their ways" (Allon, 1982, p. 131). Contrary to the strictly and involuntarily disabled, "the obese are presumed to hold their fate in their own hands; if they were only a little less greedy or lazy or yielding to impulse or oblivious of advice, they would restrict excessive food intake, resort to strenuous exercise, and as a consequence of such deliberate action, they would reduce." In contrast, Cahnman argues, while blindness "is considered a misfortune, obesity is branded as a defect. . . . A blind girl will be helped by her agemates, but a heavy girl will be derided. A paraplegic boy will be supported by other boys, but a fat boy will be pushed around. The embarrassing and not infrequently harassing treatment which is meted out to obese teenagers by those around them will not elicit sympathy from onlookers but a sense of gratification; the idea is that they have got what was coming to them" (Cahnman, 1968, p. 294).

The obese are overweight, according to the popular view, because they eat immodestly and to excess. They have succumbed to temptation and hedonistic pleasure seeking, where other, more virtuous, and less self-indulgent persons have resisted. As with all forms of behavioral deviance, getting fat represents a struggle between vice and virtue. Most of us are virtuous—witness the fact that we are not fat. Some of us are consumed with vice—and the proof of the pudding, so to speak, is in the eating. Therefore, the obese must pay for their sin of overindulgence by attracting well-deserved stigma (Cahnman, 1968; Maddox, Back, and Liederman, 1968). The obese suffer from what the public sees as "self-inflicted damnation" (Allon, 1973, 1982). In one study of the public's rejection of persons with an array of behavioral and physical traits and characteristics, researchers found that the degree of the stigma of obesity was somewhere in between that of physical handicaps, such as blindness, and behavioral deviance, such as homosexuality (Hiller, 1981, 1982). In other words, the public stigmatizes the obese significantly more than they do the possessors of involuntarily acquired undesirable characteristics, but somewhat less than persons who engage in unconventional, despised behavior.

This introduces a moral dimension to obesity that is lacking in most other physical characteristics. The stigma of obesity entails three elements or aspects. (1) The obese attract public scorn. (2) They are told that this scorn is deserved. (3) They come to accept this negative treatment as just (Cahnman, 1968, p. 293). A clear-cut indication that the obese are put down because of their presumed character defects is seen in the fact that when respondents were informed that a person's obesity was caused by a hormonal disorder—in other words, it was not his or her "fault"—they stigmatized him or her far less than if their condition is left unexplained (DeJong, 1980). Unless otherwise informed, most of us assume that obesity is the fat person's fault. A trait that is seen as beyond the person's control, for which he or she is held not to be responsible, is seen as a misfortune. In contrast, character flaws are regarded in a much harsher light. Obesity tends to be seen as the outward manifestation of an undesirable character. It therefore invites retribution in much of the public's eyes.

In an editorial in *The New York Times,* one observer (Rosenthal, 1981) argues that obesity has replaced sex and death as our "contemporary pornography." We attach some measure of shame and guilt to eating well. Our society is made up of "modern puritans" who tell one another "how *repugnant* it is to be fat"; "what's really disgusting," we feel, "is not sex, but fat." We are all so humorless, "so relentless, so determined to punish the overweight. . . . Not only are the overweight the most stigmatized group in the United States, but fat people are expected to participate in their own degradation by agreeing with others who taunt them."

FREAKS

When writing his book on the physically different, literary critic Leslie Fiedler floundered around for a more appropriate and less demeaning term than *Freaks* (1978), the title he eventually chose. "I should be searching for some other term, less tarnished and offensive," he wrote, introducing his subject. All those that came to mind—anomalies, human "oddities," monsters, "very special people," "sports," mistakes of nature, and deformities—seemed inadequate and improperly descriptive, he decided. Society's hostility toward freaks, Fiedler writes, has typically been less than a "total genocidal onslaught" (p. 21). True, in the name of eugenics, the Nazis killed dwarfs and the ancient Spartans left infants with birth defects to die on a rocky mountain ledge. But most societies, Fiedler wrote, cultivated a measure of compassion and pity toward the physically different that was mixed with scorn; they manifested a kind of ambivalence that prevented an unrelieved hostility from taking root. Freaks elicited as much amusement as contempt, Fiedler argues.

For at least a hundred years, freaks were displayed in circus sideshows. But according to sociologist Robert Bogdan, author of *Freak Show* (1988), until well into the twentieth century, these human oddities were presented as awesome and amazing prodigies of nature, to be marveled at rather than ridiculed. These "prodigies" had a special niche in the society; their differences were accepted as a tolerable form of physical eccentricity rather than a source of contempt. It was not until modern medicine gained a stranglehold on definitions of normal and pathological that freaks were no longer exhibited. Medicine had developed the arrogance—the Greek term for it is *hubris*—that all such deformities could be cured rather than tolerated; any exhibition of persons who possessed such traits was exploitative and degrading, a "pornography of disability" (p. 2). Instead of correcting such anomalies, however, modern society has relegated their possessors to the "contemptible fringe," no longer marveled at but regarded as distressing, distasteful, and repulsive.

What is it about freaks that causes such a shudder of fear among normals? Fiedler asks. While eliciting some sympathy, freaks stir up "supernatural terror" in us for a variety of reasons, he argues. Most freaks are the children of normal parents. By what strange and mysterious chemistry—"forces we do not understand"—is the budding child in the womb transformed into a mythic beast, a creature no one of us wants to be, a being apart from the rest of us? The freak challenges the boundaries that separate male from female (the hermaphrodite, the bearded woman), large from small (giants and fat ladies, midgets and dwarfs), animals from humans (the hairy "wolf-man," humans with an apelike appearance), and the physical integrity of one human being as distinct from that of another (Siamese or "conjoined" twins). Consequently, Fiedler argues that freaks tear down the barrier between reality and illusion, experience and fantasy, and fact and myth. Quite literally, he says, they are a threat "to those desperately maintained boundaries on which any definition of sanity ultimately depends" (p. 24).

The "myth of monsters" originates "in the deep fears of childhood" (p. 31). The need to create and maintain firm boundaries separating these cosmic categories, Fiedler writes, stems from childhood struggles with matters of size, sexuality and gender, humanness, and togetherness/apartness.

After all, children are midgets in relation to adults, and adults are giants in relation to children. Moreover, various organs, those relating specifically to sexual functioning, change enormously in size, transforming themselves from midget-sized (those belonging to children) to giant-sized (those belonging to adults) ones; for instance, from preadolescence to adulthood, and from flaccid to aroused, the penis changes from small to large. Moreover, boys compare penis size with one another. (Are you a midget? Or a giant?) And the preadolescent girl simultaneously fears that her breasts will never grow—that is, will be midget sized—or will grow much too large (will be giant sized).

Fears and insecurities around sexuality and gender are fundamental and eternal: the little boy who is chastised for toying with his penis, the girl who is told not to kiss the little girl next door on the lips, the children who are caught playing "doctor," the tomboy, the too-effeminate boy, the boy who catches sight of his dad's vastly larger penis, and the trauma of the girl's first menstruation.

Many children are obsessed by the fear of being attacked and devoured by wild beasts, yet, at some point, they become aware that humans eat animal flesh. Hair grows in the vicinity of the genitals and in the armpits—which, in girls, is expected to be removed—and, Fiedler writes, hairiness represents our animalistic side. Perhaps the very first intellectual realization children have is the awareness of being an entity separate from the mother whose breast they suck on. As they grow older, they fear separation from their parents, yet they desperately have the need to make that separation to maintain their own personal sense of integrity. Boys, upon understanding the nature of the female anatomy, try simultaneously to imagine emerging from and at the same time entering the vagina.

In other words, says Fiedler, the freak projects our "infantile or adolescent traumas." They manifest or dramatize our "primordial fears . . . about scale, sexuality, our status as more than beasts, and our tenuous individuality" (p. 34). Fiedler's argument seems to be that both our negative and our tempered reactions to people who are different from ourselves are likely to respond to some sort of universal, transcultural appeal. Instead, they are based on who we are as human beings, where we stand in the scheme of things, and what we had to struggle with when we were growing up. They are not simply learned as a result of the accident of arbitrary cultural norms, he seems to be saying. There are limits to the capacity of social constructionism to "normalize" or routenize the extreme whimsy, caprice, and folly of nature. Our rootedness in childhood, adolescence, sex and sexuality, humanness, and our need to be a personal entity separate from all others, transcends and overwhelms any and all local customs dictating who and what should be stigmatized. They dictate our interactions with and posture and attitudes toward the persons who were once designated as *freaks.*

DISABILITY AND TERTIARY DEVIANCE

John Kitsuse (1980) introduced the concept of "tertiary" deviance—the notion of socially disvalued people standing up, fighting for their rights, demanding equality with normals. Edward Sagarin disapprovingly referred to this phenomenon as *Odd Man In* (1969)—or "societies of deviants." Over the past few years, a growing number of militant disabled spokespersons have stepped forward and confronted the abled, demanding that the blind, the deaf, and the wheelchair-bound be accorded justice and the respect and dignity they deserve. Central among their demands is that the image or public presentation of the handicapped recognize their essential humanity.

In *Nothing About Us Without Us,* James Charlton (1999) writes of "disability oppression," alienation, raising the consciousness of the disabled, and organizing "empowerment."

In *Creatures Time Forgot,* David Hevey (1992) gives us an "in your face" political argument about disability, demanding "rights, not charity."

In *Freakery,* Rosemarie Garland Thompson (1996) offers an anthology of analyses by two dozen writers who argue that, over the centuries, western society has presented "cultural spectacles of the extraordinary body."

In *Claiming Disability,* Simi Linton (1998) engages her readers, demanding that they put themselves emotionally into everyday issues and situations involving decisions about disability. "You are an architect," she says, and takes us through the decisions and emotional identifications a designer of a community center has to go through to build a facility that can accommodate the handicapped. "You are the parent of a nondisabled young woman away at college," Linton writes, and describes the experience of that parent dealing with the fact that her daughter is bringing a disabled male friend home to visit. "You are the new personnel director for a mid-sized company," she conjectures, taking us through the demands made by a disability action group to accommodate the employment of disabled personnel. "Hidden and disregarded for too long," Linton says, "we are demanding not only rights and equal opportunity but are demanding that the academy take on the nettlesome question of why we've been sequestered in the first place" (p. 185). Academics have been "complicit" in the confinement of the disabled; it's time for that confinement to end, she argues.

In many ways, the disabled represent an example of an oppressed minority group. There are many parallels between the civil rights movement and the new and most decidedly militant field of disability studies. Where this new militancy will take persons with a disability is anyone's guess. But its central message is clear: The disabled do not wish to be treated as deviants. Perhaps, one day, disability will no longer be discussed as a form of deviance.

SUMMARY

Undesirable physical characteristics represent a form of deviance. They tend to attract stigma and generate a contaminated identity for their possessors. Although some sociologists insist that involuntarily acquired traits cannot be a form of deviance because they are not the possessor's fault, the fact that their possessors do attract stigma and condemnation is specifically what defines deviance; hence, they are deviants. In fact, there is a continuum of personal causality or responsibility for possessors of deviant characteristics—yet all are stigmatized. Personal responsibility is only weakly related to the dimension of deviance. Responsibility (or "fault") for one's physical characteristics is not only a matter of degree, it is also a social construct. Many eras and cultures have claimed divine retribution for past sins as the cause for a range of disabilities and esthetic violations.

Why do we fear and avoid physical deviants? Katz argues that, though we feel ambivalence toward them, our repugnance is based on a nonconscious faith in "the just world hypothesis," that is, they believe that we all get what we deserve; if someone is disabled, maybe he or she deserves his or her faith. To deny the just world hypothesis opens up the possibility that we are vulnerable to the possibility that we, too, could end up like the disabled.

Erving Goffman referred to a form of stigma as "abominations of the body." For our purposes, two such "abominations" stand out: violations of esthetic norms and physical incapacity.

Esthetic norms refer to the way we look. Our appearance is judged by audiences and found normal or unacceptable. The latter, if extremely so, is deemed worthy of condemnation. Persons who fail to meet an acceptable standard are seen as possessing a "spoiled" identity, "disqualified from full social acceptance."

Physical incapacity is made up of the inability to perform at life's various essential tasks, such as walking, seeing, hearing, and so on.

Attractiveness is obviously the flip side of ugliness; in fact, a violation of esthetic standards is the extreme absence of beauty. Standards of attractiveness are not nearly as relative as has been assumed in the past. In fact, from society to society, from culture to culture, many of the same standards prevail. Most of the traits or characteristics that are found attractive in one place are likewise found attractive in others. In fact, beauty is not in "the eye of the beholder." Very likely, some universal causal force or dynamic influences or determines what humans (and other creatures) find attractive and desirable in a mating partner. Some researchers with an evolutionary orientation believe that it is the impulse to pass on one's genetic material to later generations that explains this panhuman tendency to judge physical attractiveness. Many culturally oriented researchers are skeptical of this explanation. Whatever the explanation, unattractive children tend to bear the brunt of the negative side of evaluations of attractiveness. That is, their actions are deemed more deviant and more worthy of punishment than the same actions engaged in by more attractive actors. In a phrase, unattractiveness is a form of deviance; it attracts stigma and condemnation.

Some forms of physical deviance are voluntary, for instance, body modification, especially extreme tattooing. Tattooing indicates identity, namely that one belongs to a category that is alienated from the mainstream. But the mainstream also "reads" a message in sporting tattoos: Such a person is an untrustworthy, reprehensible person—a deviant. In the past couple of decades, many more or less conventional people have been getting small tattoos on inconspicuous places on their bodies as a mild form of rebellion.

Obesity is a prime example of a deviant or undesirable physical characteristic. What makes obesity more interesting than most other forms of physical deviance is that it is regarded as both physical and behavioral. That is, the obese are denigrated for being fat and for behaving in such a shamelessly self-indulgent fashion—usually overeating and not being sufficiently active—that caused their obesity. Most nonobese persons feel superior to the obese, and the obese, in turn, tend to internalize stigma, that is, they usually think that they are worthy of the condemnation that average-sized persons visit upon them. The condemnation of the obese operates, in scale, on people who are only somewhat above average—that is, the hugely obese receive the harshest condemnation for their weight while the merely somewhat overweight receive condemnation in proportion to their more moderate degree of overweight. Standards of weight fall unequally on the shoulders of women: Women tend to be condemned more harshly for every degree overweight than is true of men. Over the years, the ideal standard of female beauty has gotten slimmer and slimmer; hence, the downside of being obese has correspondingly become steeper and deeper, and the stigma and condemnation, more intense and pervasive.

Freaks are both fascinating and fearful to the majority, in part because they challenge the separation between categories we regard so solid and unbridgeable: normal versus pathological, male versus female, tiny versus averaged-sized versus huge, and human versus beast. At one time, freaks were exhibited in circus sideshows. Now, such a practice is regarded as inhumane, exploitative, and politically incorrect, although some claim that, as sideshow performers, freaks had a legitimate place in the society; today, through genetic and surgical intervention, medical science attempts to correct these "mistakes of nature."

Physical deviants have challenged their demeaned status through political movements and demands for equal rights. This militancy of a previously oppressed minority may lead to the end of their categorization as deviants, although some sociologists would argue that, as with alcoholism, an inability to fully perform conventional roles will always be disvalued and regarded as a form of deviance.

Account: Jan, the Transitioning Transsexual

Being a transsexual can be looked at both as physical and sexual deviance. As physical deviance, it is voluntary: changing one's sex is something that one has chosen to do. But it is also involuntary, because transsexuals feel they have no choice in the matter: They are trapped in the body of the opposite sex, they say, and reassigning their sex is simply reclaiming what was rightfully theirs to begin with. Chromosomally and anatomically, "Jan" is a male who is convinced that she is a woman. (I will follow customary usage and refer to Jan as a "she.") The fact that she has a male body has bothered her "as long as I knew there was a difference between boys and girls." Chris Berry, a student in my deviant behavior course at the University of Maryland, wrote a paper on, and gathered the following written material from, Jan. "To the casual observer—a person passing her on the street" says Chris, "Jan looks like most any college-age male. She is tall and lanky, with a protruding Adam's apple . . ., hunched shoulders, [and] beard stubble. . . . Her manner is avoidant; she hardly ever talks to passersby, often averting her eyes as they go by. If one were to examine her closely, they might notice some characteristics a bit out of place—long, nicely filed fingernails . . ., a slightly hormonally enhanced figure, and an assortment of women's clothing worked into her regular wardrobe. Jan is 22 years old. She is poised at a very important point in her transition and in her life. . . . [She] has subjected herself to over 100 hours of facial electrolysis, and has been on estrogen for over two months. She is planning on continuing her transition while finishing up her college career at the University, and is going to start living full-time as a woman after graduation

(*Continued*)

Account: Jan, the Transitioning Transsexual Continued

and, she hopes, after facial feminization surgery. The surgery, she hopes, will enable her to pass as a woman in her day-to-day life. . . . One semester away from graduating from college, she is looking at entering the world as a woman." Here are Jan's words about the experience of her sexual reassignment.

I have a fairly typical middle-class white, male upbringing. . . . I had my little group of friends that I made in school and we kept together until we all left for college. I wasn't very popular, but I wasn't picked on. I had a girlfriend throughout high school and we broke up when we left for college. I played sports in high school. I ran track during the Spring and Winter seasons and played football in the Fall. Yes, I played football. I was reading anything I could lay my hands on from a fairly young age. I especially liked fantasy science fiction. . . . I loved pseudo-medieval stories. I can talk about books for days on end. . . . I was a smart child who didn't try very hard. I'm sure you know the type. I got mostly A's and B's through most of my early education. . . . I was always more interested in whatever little project I was working on outside of school than I was in my schoolwork. I was very quiet in school, stuck to my tried-and-true group of friends, hardly ever met new people, and coasted my way through. The truth is that anybody who really knew me would realize that I was a total dork. I personally don't think that's a terrible thing. . . . My sports were fun. I'd do them over again if I had to do the whole thing over as a guy. If I could do it over again as a girl, I'd still run, but I think I'll take a pass on football.

But my real interests were role-playing, games, and computers—Dungeons and Dragons and the like. . . . Role-playing ties into *identity.* And identity is, after all, sort of the basis for my gender issues. [However] I want to make one thing absolutely clear. *Role-playing games did not make me a transsexual.* . . . I had these feelings even before I picked up my first manual on role-playing. That being said, I do feel that role-playing games played an integral part in understanding, and beginning to accept, my gender identity. It was a creative outlet that enabled me to try on many different sets of traits, including gender, to see which ones felt right to me. I do not believe that it is a coincidence that most of the characters I made, when I wasn't the storyteller, were female. Nor do I believe it to be coincidental that I elected to be the storyteller because I felt ashamed that so many of my characters were female. Even at that young age, I realized that it was *weird* for me to want to be a girl. It was something I should be *ashamed* of. I remember making male characters many times just so my friends wouldn't question why I was always making girl characters, even though I really didn't want to play male characters.

Looking back at my life, I cannot remember a time when I did not either want to be a girl or think of myself as one. I also cannot remember a time when I didn't realize that this was not an okay thing to want or do. Those two feelings have been there for what seems like forever. New feelings did start to develop as I grew, however. When I was really little, my identity was a personal thing. I didn't need to think of myself as being part of the "real world" as I do today. My little life *was* the "real world"—to me, then. I could see myself as a girl, and bear the fact that others did not see me as one. Why? Because my whole world, back then, was nothing more than my imagination, my stories, and my small group of friends. And two out of three of them had me as a girl. As I grew up, my identity became less of my own and more of a social entity. Suddenly, all these things started to be important. Who your friends were, what your hobbies were, how popular you were, who you liked, what sports you played. These became as much a part of my identity as my imagination. Sure, I fought against them in my *personal* identity, but there was nothing I could do about my social identity. It was being formed for me, and the fact that I was male played a big role.

My body was of particular concern once I realized that my imagination wasn't going to cut it. In my mind, I had a female body. In the mirror, I didn't. I don't blame God, I don't blame fate, I don't really blame anything. . . . It's just the way it was. However, for the life of me, I couldn't figure out what to *do* about it. Puberty was hell. Any hope I might have had—however slim—that my body would feminize was quickly lost. Since everything around me told me that little people with male bodies became men and little people with female bodies became women, I was resigned to living as a guy. There didn't even seem to be any reason to talk about it. One, I knew people would think I was a freak if I said I was a girl, and two, even if I could tell people, what difference would it make? It had been decided that I was going to grow up into a bigger version of my male body and that socially, I would be a man. . . . [Still,] I never believed I was a boy despite what I was told, shown, and assumed to be. I didn't try to convince myself of it. . . . Instead, I just tried as hard as I possibly could not to think about it. And while it was always there, hurting from the inside—sometimes very little, sometimes excruciating—I managed to get through life. . . .

[In college,] I wasn't happy, and college just made things worse. I don't mean to make college sound like a terrible place. . . . There was freedom, lots of people I didn't know, and many interesting things to do. When people say college is the best four years of your life, I see where they're coming from. My experience was a bit different, however. . . . I spent the first few months learning my way around the school and meeting the people on my floor. It turns out that the people on my floor were some of the coolest people. . . . It was more of a community than you would expect from a random bunch of college students. . . . After three semesters at college, I fell apart. . . . I was a real train wreck. . . . I had tried to form a romantic relationship with a girl I met during my freshman year, and it had crumbled rather painfully. . . . I was really frustrated and starting to feel hopeless about the conflict between my gender identity and my physical body. I was [also] at odds with a lot of my peers, and had lost touch with most of the people I knew in high school. I was homesick, I was not doing well academically. . . . I contemplated suicide, and there really isn't any point in dredging up that memory for you, here. If you are contemplating suicide, *please talk to somebody.* Even—maybe preferably—a complete stranger. [And I began] skipping classes and basically doing nothing but lie in bed with a headache and the lights out for three straight days.

I would like to think that lying in bed for this long was more than just a cry for help. . . . I remember thinking that I simply did not feel like I could deal with people any more. I felt that if I had to talk to people, or go to class, or listen to anybody, or have one more assumption made about me—if I was called "Jason" one more time, or referred to as "he," or seen as just another college guy—that I would completely snap and shout at them or start crying openly or try to hurt them or myself. . . . It's kind of strange and kind of scary pulling these memories out again. I haven't felt even remotely like that in a long time. These days, I go through phases of depression, frustration, and anxiety on a more or less regular basis, but it hasn't touched near any of the extreme feelings I've had in the past.

I finally decided that I needed to escape. I called my parents and said that I absolutely needed to get out of college for a bit. . . . I want to give kudos to my parents for being understanding. I've heard so many horror stories about people going through a lot of the same things that I am [going through] only without the parental support. When she got there, we started talking. I found myself totally stuttering over my words, locking up, and crying a whole lot. Once the flood gates were open, everything began to come out. I talked about almost everything—my feelings of not having a direction, of stress, depression, anxiety, frustration, loneliness, not being understood, assumptions, and so forth. Just about the only thing I couldn't tell my mom at that point was that I felt I was a

(*Continued*)

Account: Jan, the Transitioning Transsexual Continued

girl. I don't know why. Maybe I was afraid of her reaction. Maybe she wouldn't like me or wouldn't understand me. Maybe—and this seemed worst of all—she wouldn't believe me. One thing was certain—I couldn't handle school the way I was. . . . I packed up some stuff and we headed home.

[When we got home,] my parents had a really tough time with me sitting there telling them that I—their only son—was a girl, not a boy. Or at least I did a really bad job at the time of describing what I'd been going through. . . . It was the hardest thing I've ever done. I think they left the conversation more confused than anything. It became . . . a silent issue. Never talked about. . . . Not one more word was spoken about sex or gender.

Over the next few months I saw several therapists—four, to be exact. They started out really general. The first few were all-purpose psychotherapists who I went to because of my depression. A running theme throughout my life has been people trying to put me on antidepressants. I have only been on them for two weeks of my entire life. It bothers me to treat the symptoms of something until you've dealt with the root of the depression itself. But when my therapists learned about my issues with my own gender identity, they couldn't do much since they didn't have much in the way of experience dealing with people like that. The second one referred me to another therapist in the area who had some background working with transsexual patients. Her name was Dr. Horvath and she was a godsend. We really started to talk about what I was feeling and we got it out in the open. Then we could discuss what to do about it. By this time I knew, somewhere deep inside, that my life needed to be changed drastically. It was becoming more and more obvious to me that I'd never be happy unless I was a woman to everybody else, too. I mean, I had been one to myself, inside, for as long as I could remember. But I was in severe need of validation from others. Up to this point in my life, it's just been one invalidation after another. You know, every single "Yes, sir!" really adds up over all those years.

[I attended some TS—transsexual—support groups.] In my opinion, they're not for me. I don't want to be a guy, and I don't want to be a guy "pretending" to be a girl. I want to be a girl. Therefore, I don't want any labels attached to me, like "transsexual" or "transgender." And finding groups of people based on those categories associates me with them. . . . My experiences with groups involving the words "transsexual" or "transgender" have been, for the most part, negative ones. I've attended three support groups and felt uncomfortable at all of them. In all three, I was the youngest person. I felt like the only person planning a transition in hopes of "passing" (I hate that word!). Therefore, I felt like everybody was too interested in me, which led to feeling pressured into attending regularly as well as [feeling that I was on a] "sinking ship." Basically, the groups I went to consisted mostly of people stuck living in male roles. Some of them were okay with this and just liked cross-dressing. These people were nice but I had trouble identifying with them. Some of them were resigned to using the support group as an outlet for their needs while living unhappy lives. . . . I felt like they were resigned to being miserable and were trying to live vicariously through me. . . . So I haven't really felt like attending support groups. I get the same vibes from some online forums, too. It makes me realize where people get the notions of what "transsexual" means. Most people I know think of Jerry Springer. . . . I got the same kind of feeling in some of these forums. . . .

Because I haven't been in contact with other people going through transitions at support groups, I didn't really have anyone to talk to about the whole process. Sure, I have my therapist, but I see her once a week for an hour, and she's a professional who I'm paying to visit. It's not the same thing as having a friend. Friends. I've always had a group of friends. I can honestly say I've never truly been alone in this world. Sure, they all see me as a guy, which is a real nuisance. I've talked to almost all of my friends at one point or another about my gender identity and future transition. I've gotten more or less the same response from every single one. Basically, they say, "Oh. Okay." And that's it. Then the subject gets changed to something else. This is good. I mean, they don't hate me. They don't find me disgusting. They're still my friends. We still hang out.

This is also bad because it becomes harder to bring up the subject because it's not acknowledged. I'm still treated just as much like a guy as before. I find it increasingly difficult to discuss how my transition may affect *them* in any way. Because it will. I feel that ignoring it and pretending like I said nothing is only going to make the transition more difficult to handle. But I suppose I'll cross that bridge when I come to it. Okay, so talking to my friends about my transition is like talking to a brick wall. And believe me, it's something I have to talk about! If I said nothing, I'd go crazy. I did that for 18 years. Once I started opening up to people, it felt like a great weight lifted from me. I'm not about to lock it back up and pretend like it never happened. But I can't really talk to my friends about it, so there we go. Now I have at least one reason why I'm reaching out to talk to other people who are going through this transition.

On the one hand, it's nice to find people to talk to who talk to me as the girl they consider me to be. It feels good to be validated by them since I don't get that from many people. On the other hand, it seems a shame to find people who accept me as a girl, and then talk about the transition, which admits my past (and present) guy role! I mean, I'm not the kind of person who is going to lie and make up a whole past in which I lived a girl's role my whole life. No, I've been very much a guy and am still quite a bit a guy. After all, it's my safety net which I am building up courage to let go of. I look forward to the day when I've been living as a girl long enough to be able to talk to people about my "past" experiences as a girl. That will be nice!

The guidelines [for the transition from being a guy to being a girl] say that you need three months of hormone replacement therapy and you need to be living in the desired gender role for a year before qualifying for sex reassignment—or genital—surgery. I like to think of it as a three-pronged transition. Along one prong, there's the physical stuff. Dressing the way a person of the desired sex typically dresses; hours and hours (I've logged over a hundred hours on the table, so far, and am planning quite a few more) of electrolysis to remove unwanted facial and body hair; and taking hormones—estrogens, progestins, and androgen blockers—to feminize the body. And of course, there are the surgeries. It's not just all about the sex-change operation. I consider FFS (facial refeminization surgery) a more important part of a successful transition. Having facial surgery does a lot more for passability [that is, the successful social passing as a female] than does genital surgery, which most people don't even see. One of my friends says that FFS is part of the "holy trinity" of passing. These are facial surgery, electrolysis, and voice feminization. Oh yeah, the voice. That's another part of the transition, and a really difficult one. Do *not* get any kind of surgery for the voice. It's got to be trained, which takes months, even years. So that's the first prong—the physical stuff.

The other two prongs are the emotional and the social. Emotionally, adjustment is the hardest part of the whole process. Not only are you dealing with the roller-coaster of adding hormones to your body, but then usually with a loss of friends and family members, and often employment, as well. There's a lot of emotional stuff I haven't experienced yet, but I'm sure it'll come over the next few years, probably for the rest of my life. Socially, there's a whole new role to learn. I mean, I've spent roughly 20 years of my life being a guy, and I hated it. But it isn't as if I've gotten any kind of training, formal or otherwise, in being a girl. I wasn't raised as one, so that's something I need to learn. And starting to learn ho to be a girl at 22 is a really awkward thing, you know? It's going to be really embarrassing! One of my transsexual friends says "transitioning isn't about getting rid of fear. It's

(*Continued*)

Account: Jan, the Transitioning Transsexual Continued

about getting rid of *doubt*. The fear is always there." Well, I'm scared, but I have doubt in my mind that this is the right road for me.

QUESTIONS

Do you believe that there are thousands of genetic males who believe they are really females? And genetic females who believe they are males? Does this point to a more complicated view of sex and gender than the usual dichotomy of males versus females? Or does it uphold this dichotomy? If you were a friend of Jan's, would you advise her/him to complete the sexual reassignment? Do you feel that Jan could ever be a "true" female? Do you feel that sexual reassignment is a legitimate thing to do? What do cases such as Jan's tell us about physical characteristics as deviance? Picture a typical heterosexual male being attracted to Jan—as a woman—then finding out she/he is a biological male. How would he react? Does the acceptance of Jan's status as a "wannabe" female among her/his friends surprise you? How would you react? Picture Jan growing up, say, 50 years ago? Would her/his experiences have been very different?

Summary and Conclusions

As a result of recently enacted residency restrictions promulgated by communities around the United States, thousands of sex offenders live in tent encampments, under causeways and bridges, and in parks and fields.

In Jerusalem, dozens of women, wrapped in prayer shawls, gather at the Western Wall, Judaism's holiest site, to pray—an act forbidden by the orthodox wing of the faith; the police arrest a 28-year-old medical student for "acting provocatively and in a way that upsets public order."

In New York, Muslim delicatessen owners struggle with the dilemma posed by selling pork and alcohol, forbidden by their religion, versus disappointing customers, losing sales revenues and, possibly, being forced out of business.

After the arrest of a countryman following his abortive effort to blow up an airliner, Nigerians living in the United States voice concern that they will suffer "guilt by association" because of his crime.

In Mexico City, the mother of a sailor attends a public tribute to her son, killed in a raid on a drug lord; hours later, gunmen burst into her house, spray the rooms with gunfire, and kill the mother and three relatives.

In California, an organization dedicated to the "investigation and promotion of science and rational skepticism" issues a pamphlet supporting the validity of the evolutionist's argument and refuting 25 arguments for creationism, in effect, arguing that the belief that God created heaven and earth in six days is cognitively deviant.

In New York, the garment industry holds a fashion show for women who are considered too fat to look attractive in conventionally styled clothing. In Chicago, a pediatrician administers growth hormones to a nine-year-old patient who, his parents fear, will grow up to be excessively short. Throughout Latin America, public health workers charge, the mentally and physically disabled are abandoned in institutions—filled to overflowing—that are hidden away from the general public.

These episodes express or embody the principle that certain beliefs, practices, or conditions considered socially unacceptable tend to engender negative reactions in the community, or sectors of the community. Sociologists refer to the beliefs, practices, and conditions that are regarded as socially unacceptable and that engender negative reactions as *deviance*. "Negative reactions" include disapproval, punishment, hostility, and/or condemnation. The sociology of deviance examines the *making* of rules, the *breaking* of rules, and reactions *to* the breaking of rules.

Each of these episodes can be interpreted as embodying deviance in different ways. Some observers might argue that the law should not dictate that sex offenders be forced from their communities; that women should be allowed to pray at Judaism's holiest site; that Muslims should not sell pork or alcohol; that the guilt of one Nigerian should not indicate that others are likewise guilty; that the possession, sale, and distribution of illicit substances should not be against the law; that it is evolution that is the deviant belief, not creationism; that the obese should be regarded as being as attractive as persons who are slimmer, and it's the obsessive adherence to a thin ideal for women that should be regarded as deviant; that no one should be regarded as "too short"; and that the physically and mentally disabled should be treated with dignity and respect. All of this may be true—and that's precisely the point. What is regarded as deviant is not a hard, definite, and concrete "thing," but rather is subject to debate, argument, and struggle, the outcome of exercises of power. What's deviant is what the definition *says* it is, and nothing more. As sociologists, it's our job to take note of this definition and see what its consequences are; it's *not* our job to justify the rightness or wrongness of one definition over the other. There *is* no right or wrong in the abstract; all definitions of right and wrong are social constructions of reality that sectors of the society *assert* are right or wrong in the abstract.

These examples also show us that deviance is "all over the map" in certain ways. Deviance entails wrongdoing *from* some people's point of view. It's not necessarily harmful, though it may be. The prohibitions that ban it are not always religious in origin, though they may be. Actions regarded as deviant are not, by definition, against the law, though they may be. What's judged as deviant is not usually a manifestation of mental disorder, but, again, it may be. The efforts of certain parties to define acts, beliefs, or characteristics as deviant may or may not be widely adopted or practiced, but the greater the number of people and institutions that adopt and practice a given definition, the more those acts, beliefs, and characteristics exemplify deviance. The sentiment that supports condemnation need not be widespread—there's no exact line that the sociological observer can draw and declare, *here* we have a case of deviance on our hands, *there* we don't—but, once again, the more widespread a judgment is, the more certain sociologists feel that they have a case of deviance on their hands.

And sociologists need not agree—or disagree—with the sentiment condemning deviance; all that's necessary to define deviance is that somewhere, at some time, we can observe that sentiment expressed in real-world condemnation and punishment. No value judgment whatsoever is expressed by the concept of deviance. No one is condemned when *the sociologist* uses the terms "deviant" or "deviance." But when the members of the society condemn certain actions, beliefs, and conditions, they regard them as deviant; it is the condemnation that expresses or *manifests* the sentiment. The sociologist is not the conveyor of that sentiment; it is the members of the society whose reactions the sociologist describes and analyzes who convey that sentiment.

Deviance, like pretty much every other social phenomenon we know about, is a matter of degree, not an either-or proposition. Some normative violations are so heinous, so seriously deviant, that members of the society in which such violations occur put the offender to death; other violations shame and stigmatize the offender for life; still others result in "slap on the wrist" punishments that are shrugged off, their consequences, neither long lasting nor very serious. Though all of us commit normative violations, not all of us commit violations that corrupt and taint our identities in significant ways.

Moreover, deviance is *relative* to time and place; it is an *elastic* concept: What's considered, and is reacted to, as *wrong* or *bad* changes over time and varies from one place to another. Acts for which people were once burned at the stake—religious heresy, apostasy, nonconformity, and dissent—now produce no outcry, serious condemnation, or punishment. On the other hand, what's considered "politically incorrect" behavior and utterances—now regarded as insulting to women, blacks, Jews, and the physically disabled—once went unpunished, even uncommented upon. A century ago, married politicians often engaged in extramarital affairs; such behavior was regarded as a privilege of the members of a certain class and power stratum. Now, the careers of politicians who engage in such behavior, once they are discovered and publicized, more often crash and burn in public scandal and spectacle. Times change, the norms change, and reactions to the norms likewise change.

In the past decade or two, some critics have put forth the assertion that "deviance is dead," and that the study of deviant behavior is passé, outmoded, and no longer applicable to contemporary society. This may be one of the silliest claims ever made by more than one sociologist. Deviance is an analytic concept; it is relevant to social life everywhere, and it will be relevant for all time. No earthly society has ever existed without undergoing violations of social norms, and no society could ever exist in the absence of *reactions* to violations of social norms. Utopias exist only in the human imagination; some of us will always be unable or unwilling to abide by all the rules society sets, and knowing that we can't achieve all we desire, some of us will resort to cutting corners, lying, cheating, stealing, scheming, philandering, and even engaging in violence to get what we want. It is in the nature of being human that we engage in deviance. Moreover, since deviance is also about condemnation *per se*, the reactions that deviance touches off—even unjust accusations—will always be with us. Without social control, or the effort to bring violators into line, the society will collapse into chaos and disintegration. And in every society on earth, some injustice prevails; sometimes, false accusations will be lodged, and occasional unjust legal convictions cannot be avoided. To the critic of these assertions, I say: Study the public record, examine all the societies that have ever existed, find exceptions to these rules, and determine if any such exist. To the utopian who believes that such a society can, and will, exist, I say: Pie in the sky is not empirical demonstration; I'll believe it when I see it.

Some sociologists of deviance define their mission in an *essentialistic* fashion: They define deviance as an objectivistic or concrete phenomenon, a reality in the material world whose enactment demands a deterministic or cause-and-effect explanation. To these sociologists, the study of deviance is a scientific or *positivistic* mission: How do we account for deviant behavior? Why do some people engage in deviance? In what types of societies is deviance more common; in which ones is it rare? Such a mission rarely encompasses deviant beliefs, and never attempts to explain deviant traits. Even though all explanatory sociologists agree that deviance is relative to time and place, they argue that we can devise theories that account for its enactment. Contemporary versions of causal theories of deviance have argued that untoward behavior is caused by one of an array of factors, including psychological disorder, a rationalistic calculation of pleasure and pain, social disorganization, anomie or social strain, differentially associating with peers who define wrongdoing in positive terms, a lack of social control, and a lack of self-control.

In contrast, other sociologists define their mission in *constructionist* terms: What needs to be explained, they say, is why certain rules are made and enforced, and what happens to the offenders who violate them. How are acts, beliefs, and traits *organized* into a coherent framework or set of rules, the violation of which results in scorn, stigma, pity, condescension, and/or hostility toward the violator? Is condemnation a simple product of a real and present threat or danger to the society, or is the threat or danger more symbolic, abstract, spiritual, and emblematic of a realm of meaning that exists separate and independent of threats to material survival? Constructionist theories include labeling theory, conflict theory, feminist theory, and "controlology," the attempt to explain the sociology of social control. In addition, constructionism pays close attention to the "inner world of the deviant": How do persons defined and labeled as deviant *experience* stigma and social condemnation?

Any sociologist contemplating a description of the extent and scope of deviance must consider the *realms* in which normative violations occur. Such a consideration inevitably runs into the issue of numbers, as well as seriousness: *How many* people are judged to be on the wrong side of the norms, and *how serious* are these violations? In other words, as a criterion that enables us to select topics on specific *forms* of deviance, we have to consider how many people we are talking about. Textbooks that discuss deviance in general are likely to include chapters on alcohol and drug abuse, sexual deviance, criminal behavior, economic malfeasance, including white-collar crime, deviant beliefs, deviant physical characteristics, and mental disorder. The inclusion of these topics for discussion, again, makes sense by virtue of the fact that they are relatively common, and regarded as relatively serious, normative violations. Critics who call for a discussion of very different topics usually fail to consider one or another or both of these factors.

The subject of deviance is foundational for sociology; it spells out processes, issues, and subjects that are essential for any consideration of how society works. Deviance is neither marginal to nor trivial for an understanding of the social order. It is central to everything we see and experience in the social world, from the economic to the religious realm, from birth to death, and from the intimacy of a love affair to the public proclamations made on the soap box and the drama of the television and movie screen. Without an understanding of deviance, we cannot comprehend social relations, social interaction, the workings of the community, or, indeed, what we call the human spark. To simplify the matter, "Deviance is us," and it will remain "us" forever. Every thinking person has an obligation to understand it—hence, this book, and hence, the field of the sociology of deviance.

Photo Credits

Scott Houston/CORBIS-NY: **1**

Robert van der Hilst/CORBIS- NY: **23**

Chip Somodevilla/Getty Images, Inc – Liaison: **47**

Charles Gatewood/Pearson Education/PH College: **71**

CORBIS-NY: **95**

Spencer Grant/PhotoEdit Inc: **117**

Carol and Mike Werner/Phototake NYC: **138**

Charles Gatewood/Stock Boston: **171**

AP Wide World Photos: **196**

Damian Dovarganes/AP Wide World Photos: **223**

Photolibrary.Com: **251**

Douglas Kirkland/CORBIS- NY: **275**

Jared Leeds: **301**

References

Abanes, Richard. 1996. *Rebellion, Racism, and Religion: American Militias.* Downers Grove, IL: InterVarsity Press.

ADAM (Arrestee Drug Abuse Monitoring System). 2009. *2008 Annual Report.* Washington, DC: Office of National Drug Control Policy, Executive Office of the President.

Adler, Freda, and William S. Laufer (eds.). 1995. *The Legacy of Anomie Theory.* New Brunswick, NJ: Transaction.

Adler, Freda, William S. Laufer, and Gerhard O. W. Mueller. 2006. *Criminology* (6th ed.). New York: McGraw-Hill.

Adler, Jerry. 1996. "Adultery: A New Furor Over an Old Sin." *Newsweek,* September 30, pp. 54–60.

Adler, Patricia A. 1985, 1994. *Wheeling and Dealing: An Ethnography of an Upper-Level Drug Dealing and Smuggling Community* (1st & 2nd ed.). New York: Columbia University Press.

Adler, Patricia, and Peter Adler. 1994. "Observational Techniques." In Norman K. Denzin and Yvonna S. Lincoln (eds.), *Handbook of Qualitative Research.* Thousand Oaks, CA: Sage, pp. 377–392.

Adler, Patricia A., and Peter Adler (eds.). 2009. *Constructions of Deviance: Social Power, Context, and Interaction.* Belmont, CA: Thompson Wadsworth.

Adler, Patricia A., Peter Adler, and E. B. Rochford, Jr. 1986. "The Politics of Participation in Field Research." *Urban Life,* 14: 363–376.

Agnew, Robert. 1995. "The Contribution of Social-Psychological Strain Theory to the Explanation of Crime and Delinquency." In Freda Adler and William S. Laufer (eds.), *The Legacy of Anomie Theory.* New Brunswick, NJ: Transaction, pp.113–137.

Aho, James A. 1994. *This Thing of Darkness: A Sociology of the Enemy.* Seattle: University of Washington Press.

Akers, Ronald L. 1991. "Self-Control as a General Theory of Crime." *Journal of Quantitative Criminology,* 7 (2): 201–211.

Akers, Ronald L. 1998. *Social Learning and Social Structure: A General Theory of Crime and Deviance.* Boston: Northwestern University Press.

Allon, Natalie. 1973. "The Stigma of Overweight in Everyday Life." In G. A. Bray (ed.), *Obesity in Perspective.* Washington, DC: U.S. Government Printing Office, pp. 83–102.

Allon, Natalie. 1976. *Urban Life Styles.* Dubuque, IA: W. C. Brown.

Allon, Natalie. 1982. "The Stigma of Overweight in Everyday Life." In Benjamin B. Wolman (ed.), *Psychological Aspects of Obesity: A Handbook.* New York: Van Nostrand Reinhold, pp. 130–174.

American Psychiatric Association (APA). 1994. *Diagnostic and Statistical Manual of Mental Disorders* (4th ed.). Washington, DC: APA.

American Psychiatric Association (APA). 2000. *Diagnostic and Statistical Manual of Mental Disorders* (4th ed., text revision). Washington, DC: APA.

Andrews, George, and David Solomon (eds.). 1975. *The Cocoa Leaf and Cocaine Papers.* New York: Harcourt Brace Jovanovich.

Anonymous. 2000. "He's Shedding His Human Skin." *The Chronicle of Higher Education,* January 28, p. A12.

Arrestee Drug Abuse Monitoring Program (ADAM). 2009. *ADAM II: 2008 Annual Report.* Washington: Office of National Drug Control Policy, Executive Office of the President.

Ashley, Richard. 1975. *Cocaine: Its History, Uses, and Effects.* New York: St. Martin's Press.

Atwater, Lynn. 1982. *The Extramarital Connection: Sex, Intimacy, and Identity.* New York: Irvington.

Bader, Chris, Paul J. Becker, and Scott Desmond. 1996. "Reclaiming Deviance as a Unique Course from Criminology." *Teaching Sociology,* 24 (July): 316–320.

Becker, Howard S. 1963. *Outsiders: Studies in the Sociology of Deviance.* New York: Free Press.

Becker, Howard S. 1967. "Whose Side Are We On?" *Social Problems,* 14 (Winter): 239–247.

Becker, Howard S. 1973. "Labelling Theory Reconsidered." In Howard S. Becker (ed.), *Outsiders: Studies in the Sociology of Deviance* (expanded ed.). New York: Free Press, pp. 177–212.

Beeghley, Leonard. 2003. *Homicide: A Sociological Explanation.* Lanham, MD: Rowman & Littlefield.

Begley, Sharon. 1996/1997. "Infidelity and the Science of Cheating." *Newsweek,* December 30, 1996/January 6, 1997, pp. 57–59.

Belkin, Aaron. 2003. "Don't Ask, Don't Tell: Is the Gay Ban Based on Military Necessity?" *Parameters,* Summer, pp. 108–119.

Bell, Robert R. 1976. *Social Deviance: A Substantive Analysis* (rev. ed.). Homewood, IL: Dorsey Press.

Benson, Michael L. 1985. "Denying the Guilty Mind: Accounting for an Involvement in a White Collar-Crime." *Criminology,* 23 (November): 589–599.

Ben-Yehuda, Nachman. 1980. "The European Witch Craze of the 14th to 17th Centuries: A Sociologist's Perspective." *American Journal of Sociology,* 86 (July): 1–31.

Ben-Yehuda, Nachman. 1985. *Deviance and Moral Boundaries.* Chicago: University of Chicago Press.

Ben-Yehuda, Nachman. 1986. "The Sociology of Moral Panics: Toward a New Synthesis." *The Sociological Quarterly,* 27 (4): 395–413.

Berger, Philip B., Beatrix Hamburg, and David Hamburg. 1977. "Mental Health: Progress and Problems." In John H. Knowles (ed.), *Doing Better and Feeling Worse: Health in the United States.* New York: W.W. Norton, pp. 261–276.

Berger, Peter L., and Thomas Luckmann. 1966. *The Social Construction of Reality: A Treatise on the Sociology of Knowledge.* Garden City, NY: Doubleday.

Bernard, Jesse. 1982. *The Future of Marriage* (2nd ed.). New Haven, CT: Yale University Press.

Bernstein, Jeremy. 1978. "Scientific Cranks: How to Recognize One and What to Do Until the Doctor Arrives." *The American Scholar,* 47 (March): 8–14.

Berscheid, Ellen, and Elaine Walster. 1972. "Beauty and the Best." *Psychology Today* (March), pp. 43–46, 74.

Beuf, Ann Hill. 1990. *Beauty Is the Beast.* Philadelphia: University of Pennsylvania Press.

Bittner, E. 1970. *The Functions of the Police in Modern Society.* Rockville, MD: Center for Studies of Crime and Delinquency, National Institute of Mental Health.

Black, Donald J. (ed.). 1984. *Toward a General Theory of Social Control.* Orlando, FL: Academic Press.

Black, Donald W. 1999. *Bad Boys, Bad Men: Confronting Antisocial Personality Disorder.* New York: Oxford University Press.

Blumer, Herbert. 1969. *Symbolic Interactionism.* Englewood Cliffs, NJ: Prentice-Hall.

Blumstein, Alfred, and Joel Wallman (eds.). 2000. *The Crime Drop in America.* Cambridge, UK: Cambridge University Press.

Bogdan, Robert. 1988. *Freak Show: Presenting Human Oddities for Amusement and Profit.* Chicago: University of Chicago Press.

Bolton, Ralph. 1995. "Tricks, Friends, and Lovers: Erotic Encounters in the Field." In Don Kulick and Margaret Willson (eds.), *Taboo: Sex, Identity and Erotic Subjectivity in Anthropological Fieldwork.* London & New York: Routledge, pp. 140–167.

Bolton, Ralph. 1996. "Coming Home: The Journey of a Gay Ethnographer in the Years of the Plague." In Ellen Lewin and William L. Leap (eds.), *Out in the Field: Reflections of Lesbian and Gay Anthropologists.* Urbana: University of Illinois Press, pp. 147–168.

Bourgeois, Philippe. 1995, 2003. *In Search of Respect: Selling Crack in the Barrio* (1st & 2nd ed.). Cambridge, UK & New York: Cambridge University Press.

Bourque, Linda Brookover. 1989. *Defining Rape.* Durham, NC: Duke University Press.

Brackman, Harold. 1996. "Farrakhanconspiracy: Louis Farrakhan and the Paranoid Style in African-American Politics." *Skeptic,* 4 (3): 36–43.

Braithwaite, John. 1985. "White Collar Crime." *Annual Review of Sociology,* 11: 1–21.

Brecher, Edward M., et al. 1972. *Licit and Illicit Drugs.* Boston: Little, Brown.

Broadway, Bill. 2003. "Homosexuality in the Biblical Sense." *The Washington Post,* August 9, pp. B9, B8.

Brody, Jane E. 2003. "Gay Families Flourish as Acceptance Grows." *The New York Times,* July 1, p. D7.

Broude, Gwen J., and Sarah J. Greene. 1976. "Cross-Cultural Codes on Twenty Sexual Attitudes and Practices." *Ethnology,* 15 (October): 409–429.

Brown, DeNeen L. 2003. "Canada's Parliament Endorses Gay Marriage." *The Washington Post,* September 17, p. A23.

Brownmiller, Susan. 1975. *Against Our Will: Women, Men, and Rape.* New York: Simon & Schuster.

Brulliard, Karin. 2003. "In Texas, a Darwinian Debate." *The Washington Post,* February 16, p. A7.

Bruner, Jerome. 1993. "The Autobiographical Process." In Robert Folkenflik (ed.), *The Culture of Autobiography: Constructions of Self-Representation.* Stanford, CA: Stanford University Press, pp. 38–56, 242–245.

Buettner, Russ. 2009. "Queens Teacher Accused of Sex with Boy, 14." *The New York Times,* May 29, p. A22.

Burgess, Robert L., and Ronald L. Akers. 1966. "A Differential Reinforcement Theory of Criminal Behavior." *Social Problems,* 14 (Fall): 128–147.

Burns, John F. 2009. "Poetic Justice: Briton Says She Helped Taint Rival." *The New York Times,* May 25.

Bursik, Robert J., and Harold G. Grasmick. 1993. *Neighborhoods and Crime: The Dimensions of Effective Community Control.* New York: Lexington Books.

Byck, Robert (ed.). 1974. *Cocaine Papers by Sigmund Freud.* New York: Stonehill.

Cacicio, Jennifer. 2007. "A Painful Reminder of My Ex." *The New York Times,* September 23, p. ST6.

Cahnman, Werner J. 1968. "The Stigma of Obesity." *Sociological Quarterly,* 9 (Summer): 283–299.

Callaway, Enoch, III. 1958. "Institutional Use of Antaractic Drugs." *Modern Medicine, 1958 Annual,* Part I (January 1–June 15): 26–29.

Cameron, Mary Owen. 1964. *The Booster and the Snitch.* New York: Free Press.

Carlson, Peter. 2003. "*Bride* Discovers Gay Weddings, but Plays It a Little Too Straight." *The Washington Post,* August 26, p. C2.

Carey, James T., and Jerry Mandel. 1968. "A San Francisco Bay Area Speed Scene." *Journal of Health and Social Behavior,* 9 (June): 164–174.

Carnes, Patrick. 1983. *Out of the Shadows: Understanding Sexual Addiction.* Minneapolis, MN: CompCare.

Cassidy, John. 1995. "Who Killed the Middle Class?" *New Yorker,* October 16, pp. 113–124.

Catalano, Shannan M. 2005. "Criminal Victimization, 2004." *Bureau of Justice Statistics, National Crime Victimization Survey,* pp. 1–11.

Chambers, W. V., et al. 1994. "The Group Psychological Abuse Scale: A Measure of the Varieties of Cultic Abuse." *Cultic Studies Journal,* 11 (1): 88–117.

Chambliss, William J. 1964. "A Sociological Analysis of the Law of Vagrancy." *Social Problems,* 12 (Summer): 67–77.

Chambliss, William J. 1973. "The Saints and the Roughnecks." *Society,* 11 (December): 24–31.

Charlton, James I. 1999. *Nothing About Us Without Us: Disability, Oppression, and Empowerment.* Berkeley: University of California Press.

Charon, Joel M. 1995. *Ten Questions: A Sociological Perspective* (2nd ed.), Belmont, CA: Wadsworth.

Chasnoff, Ira J., et al. 1989. "Temporary Patterns of Cocaine Use in Pregnancy." *Journal of the American Medical Association,* 261 (March 24–31): 1741–1744.

Clark, Russell D., III. 1990. "The Impact of AIDS on Gender Differences in Willingness to Engage in Casual Sex." *Journal of Applied Social Psychology,* 20 (9): 771–782.

Clark, Russell D., III, and Elaine Hatfield. 1989. "Gender Differences in Receptivity to Sexual Offers." *Journal of Psychology and Human Sexuality,* 2 (1): 39–55.

Clark, Russell D., III, and Elaine Hatfield. 2003. "Love in the Afternoon." *Psychological Inquiry,* 14 (3&4): 227–231.

Clarke, Ronald V., and Marcus Felson (eds.). 1993. *Routine Activities Theory and Rational Choice.* New Brunswick, NJ: Transaction.

Clinard, Marshall B. 1952. *The Black Market: A Study of White Collar Crime.* New York: Rinehart.

Clinard, Marshall B. 1964. "The Theoretical Implications of Anomie and Deviant Behavior." In Marshall B. Clinard (ed.), *Anomie and Deviant Behavior: A Discussion and Critique.* New York: Free Press, pp. 1–56.

Cockerham, William C. 2003. *Sociology of Mental Disorder* (6th ed.). Upper Saddle River, NJ: Prentice Hall.

Cohen, Albert K. 1955. *Delinquent Boys: The Subculture of the Gang.* Glencoe, IL: Free Press.

Cohen, Albert K. 1959. "The Study of Social Disorganization and Deviant Behavior." In Robert K. Merton, Leonard Broom, and Leonard S. Cottrell Jr. (eds.), *Sociology Today: Problems and Prospects.* New York: Basic Books, pp. 461–484.

Cohen, Lawrence E., and Marcus Felson. 1979. "Social Change and Crime Rate Trends: A Routine Activity Approach." *American Sociological Review,* 44 (August): 588–608.

Cohen, Maimon M., Michelle J. Marinello, and Nathan Back. 1967. "Chromosomal Damage in Human Leukocytes Induced by Lysergic Acid Diethylamide." *Science,* 155 (17 March): 1417–1419.

Cohen, Stanley. 1972, 2002. *Folk Devils and Moral Panics.* 1st ed. London: MacGibbon & Kee; 3rd ed., London: Routledge.

Cohen, Stanley. 1985. *Visions of Social Control.* Cambridge, UK: Polity Press.

Cole, Stephen. 1975. "The Growth of Scientific Knowledge: Theories of Deviance as a Case Study." In Lewis A. Coser (ed.), *The Idea of Social Structure: Papers in Honor* of Robert K. Merton. New York: Harcourt Brace Jovanovich, pp. 175–220.

Coles, Claire D. 1992. "Effects of Cocaine and Alcohol Use in Pregnancy on Neonatal Growth and Neurobehavioral Status." *Neurotoxicology and Teratology,* 14 (January–February): 1–11.

Compton, R. P., et al. 2002. "Crash Risk of Alcohol Impaired Driving." In *Proceedings of the 16th International Conference of Alcohol, Drugs and Traffic Safety,* Montreal, Canada, pp. 39–44.

Conant, Eve. 2009. "Rebranding Hate in the Age of Obama." *Newsweek,* May 4, pp. 30–33.

Cooperman, Alan. 2002. "Sexual Abuse Scandal Hits Orthodox Jews." *The Washington Post,* June 29, p. A2.

Cooperman, Alan, and Lena H. Sun. 2002. "Hundreds of Priests Removed Since '60s." *The Washington Post,* June 9, pp. A1, A18.

Cose, Ellis. 2009. "A Message of Hope from a Pile of Bones." *Newsweek,* April 13, pp. 29–31.

Coser, Lewis. 1956. *The Functions of Social Conflict.* New York: Free Press.

Costello, Barbara J. 2006. "Cultural Relativism and the Study of Deviance." *Sociological Spectrum,* 26 (November–December): 581–594.

Cowell, Alan. 1994. "Israeli's Death: Atrocity or Act of War?" *The New York Times,* October 17, May 11, p. A11.

Cowley, Geoffrey. 1996. "The Biology of Beauty." *Newsweek,* June 3, pp. 61–66.

Cressey, Donald R. 1953. *Other People's Money.* Glencoe, IL: Free Press.

Cressey, Donald R. 1960. "Epidemiology and Individual Conduct." *Pacific Sociological Review,* 3 (Fall): 47–58.

Cressey, Donald R. 1988. "Poverty of Theory in Corporate Crime Research." *Advances in Criminological Theory,* 1 (1): 31–56.

Crews, Frederick. 1995. *The Memory Wars: Freud's Legacy in Dispute.* New York: New York Review of Books.

Curra, John. 2000. *The Relativity of Deviance.* Thousand Oaks, CA: Sage.

Currie, Elliott P. 1993. *Reckoning: Drugs, the Cities, and the American Future.* New York: Hill & Wang.

Daly, Kathleen, and Meda Chesney-Lind. 1988. "Feminism and Criminology." *Justice Quarterly,* 5 (December): 497–538.

Davis, Kingsley. 1937. "The Sociology of Prostitution." *American Sociological Review,* 2 (October): 744–755.

Davis, Kingsley, and Wilbert E. Moore. 1945. "Some Principles of Stratification." *American Sociological Review,* 10 (April): 242–249.

Davis, Lennard J. (ed.). 1997. *The Disability Studies Reader.* New York: Routledge.

Davison, Bill. 1967. "The Hidden Evils of LSD." *The Saturday Evening Post,* August 12, pp. 19–23.

DAWN (Drug Abuse Warning Network). 2008a. *National Estimates of Drug-Related Emergency Department Visits, 2006.* Rockville, MD: SAMHSA.

DAWN (Drug Abuse Warning Network). 2008b. *Area Profiles of Drug-Related Mortality, 2004.* Rockville, MD: SAMHSA.

DeJong, William. 1980. "The Stigma of Obesity: The Consequences of Naive Assumptions Concerning the Causes of Physical Deviance." *Journal of Health and Social Behavior,* 21 (March): 75–87.

Dion, Karen K. 1972. "Physical Attractiveness and Evaluation of Children's Transgressions." *Journal of Personal and Social Psychology,* 24: 207–213.

Dishotsky, Norman, William D. Loughman, Robert F. Mogar, and Wendell R. Lipscomb. 1971. "LSD and Genetic Damage." *Science,* 172 (April 30): 431–440.

Doherty, Edmund G. 1978. "Are Different Discharge Criteria Used for Men and Women Psychiatric Inpatients?" *Journal of Health and Social Behavior,* 19 (March): 107–116.

Dohrenwend, Bruce P., and Barbara Snell Dohrenwend. 1976. "Sex Differences and Psychiatric Disorder." *American Journal of Sociology,* 81 (May): 1447–1454.

Donadio, Claudia. 2009. "Bishop Offers Apology for Holocaust Remarks." *The New York Times,* February 22, p. A6.

Douglas, Jack D. 1976. *Investigative Social Research: Individual and Team Field Research.* Thousand Oaks, CA: Sage.

Douglas, Jack D., and Frances C. Waksler. 1982. *The Sociology of Deviance: An Introduction.* Boston: Little, Brown.

Downes, David, and Paul Rock. 2007. *Understanding Deviance: A Guide to the Sociology of Crime and Rule-Breaking* (5th ed.). Oxford, UK: Oxford University Press.

Duneier, Mitchell. 1999. *Sidewalk.* New York: Farrar, Straus & Giroux.

Dunham, H. Warren. 1965. *Community and Schizophrenia: An Epidemiological Analysis.* Detroit: Wayne State University Press.

DuPont, Robert L. 1997. *The Selfish Brain: Learning from Addiction.* Center City, MN: Hazleden.

Durkheim, Emile. 1951. *Suicide: A Study in Sociology* (trans. John A. Spaulding and George Simpson, ed. George Simpson). Glencoe, IL: Free Press (orig. pub. 1897).

Duster, Troy. 1970. *The Legislation of Morality: Law, Drugs, and Moral Judgment.* New York: Free Press.

Dworkin, Andrea. 1981. *Pornography: Men Possessing Women.* New York: Perigee.

Dworkin, Andrea. 1987. *Intercourse.* New York: Free Press.

Egan, Timothy. 1989. "Putting a Face on Corporate Crime." *The New York Times,* July 14, p. B8.

Earleywine, Mitch. 2002. *Understanding Marijuana: A New Look at the Scientific Evidence.* Oxford, UK and New York: Oxford University Press.

Edgerton, Robert B. 1969. "On the Recognition of Mental Illness." In Robert B. Edgerton (ed.), *Perspectives in Mental Illness.* New York: Holt, Rinehart & Winston, pp. 49–72.

Edgerton, Robert B. 1976. *Deviance: A Cross-Cultural Perspective.* Menlo Park, CA: Cummings.

Elias, Norbert. 1994. *The Civilizing Process* (trans. Edmund Jephcott). Oxford, UK and Cambridge, MA: Blackwell Publishers (orig. pub. 1939).

Ericson, Richard V., Patricia M. Baranek, and Janet B. L. Chan. 1991. *Representing Order: Crime, Law, and Justice in the News Media.* Toronto: University of Toronto Press.

Erikson, Kai T. 1964. "Notes on the Sociology of Deviance." In Howard S. Becker (ed.), *The Other Side: Perspectives on Deviance.* New York: Free Press, pp. 9–21.

Erikson, Kai T. 1967. "A Comment on Disguised Observation in Sociology." *Social Problems,* 14 (Spring): 366–373.

Erikson, Kai T. 1990. "Toxic Reckoning: Business Faces a New Kind of Fear." *Harvard Business Review,* 68 (January–February): 118–126.

Estrich, Susan. 1987. *Real Rape.* Cambridge, MA: Harvard University Press.

Etcoff, Nancy L. 1999. *Survival of the Prettiest: The Science of Beauty.* Garden City, NY: Doubleday.

Evans, Rhonda. 2003. *A History of the Service of Ethnic Minorities in the U.S. Armed Forces.* Santa Barbara, CA: Center for the Study of Sexual Minorities in the Military.

Falwell, Jerry, Ed Dobson, and Ed Hinson. 1996. "Wrongdoing as an Offense in the Eyes of God." In Erich Goode (ed.), *Social Deviance.* Boston: Allyn & Bacon, pp. 12–14.

FBI (Federal Bureau of Investigation). 2008. *Uniform Crime Reports: Crime in the United States.* Washington, DC: U.S. Department of Justice.

Feagin, Joe R., and Robert Parker. 1990. *Building American Cities: The Urban Real Estate Game* (2nd ed.). Englewood Cliffs, NJ: Prentice Hall.

Fears, Darryl. 2002. "Hate Crimes Against Arabs Surge, FBI Finds." *The Washington Post,* November 26, p. A2.

Felson, Richard B. 1991. "Blame Analysis: Accounting for the Behavior of Protected Groups." *The American Sociologist,* 22 (Spring): 5–23.

Ferrell, Jeff, and Mark S. Hamm (eds.). 1998. *Ethnography at the Edge: Crime, Deviance, and Field Research.* Boston: Northeastern University Press.

Fiedler, Leslie. 1978. *Freaks: Myths and Images of the Secret Self.* New York: Simon & Schuster.

Fiffer, Steve. 1999. *Three Quarters, Two Dimes, and a Nickel: A Memoir of Becoming Whole.* New York: Free Press.

Finch, Emily, and Vanessa E. Munro. 2007. "The Demon Drink and the Demonized Woman: Socio-Sexual Stereotypes and Responsibility Attribution in Rape Trials Involving Intoxicants." *Social and Legal Studies,* 16 (4): 591–614.

Fischer, Anita, Janos Marton, E. Joel Millman, and Leo Srole. 1979. "Long-Range Influences on Mental Health: The Midtown Longitudinal Study, 1954–1974." In Roberta Simmons (ed.), *Research in Community Health,* vol.1. Greenwich, CT: JAI Press, pp. 305–333.

Foucault, Michel. 1979. *Discipline and Punish: The Birth of the Prison* (trans. Alan Sheridan). New York: Vintage Books.

Foucault, Michel. 2003. *Abnormal* (ed. Valerio Marchelli and Antonella Salomoni; trans. Graham Burchell). New York: Picador.

Frank, Nathaniel. 2002. "Real Evidence on Gays in the Military." *The Washington Post,* December 3, p. A25.

Freidson, Eliot. 1966. "Disability as Deviance." In Marvin B. Sussman (ed.), *Sociology and Rehabilitation.* Washington, DC: American Sociological Association, pp. 71–99.

Freidson, Eliot. 1970. *Profession of Medicine: A Study of the Sociology of Applied Knowledge.* New York: Dodd, Mead.

Friedman, Wolfgang. 1964. *Law in a Changing Society.* Harmondsworth, UK: Penguin Books.

Friedrichs, David O. 2004. *White Collar Crime: Trusted Criminals in Contemporary Society* (2nd ed.). Belmont, CA: Wadsworth.

Gagnon, John H., and William Simon. 1973, 2005. *Sexual Conduct: The Social Sources of Human Sexuality* (1st & 2nd ed.). Chicago: Aldine; New Brunswick, NJ: Transaction Aldine.

Gallagher, Bernard J., III. 2002. *The Sociology of Mental Illness* (4th ed.). Upper Saddle River, NJ: Prentice Hall.

Gardner, Martin. 1957. *Fads and Fallacies in the Name of Science* (2nd rev. ed.). New York: Dover.

Garland, David. 1990. *Punishment and Modern Society: A Study in Social Theory.* Chicago: University of Chicago Press.

Garner, David M., et al. 1980. "Cultural Expectations of Thinness in Women." *Psychological Reports,* 47: 483–491.

George, William H., and Jeannette Norris. 1991. "Alcohol, Disinhibition, Sexual Arousal, and Deviant Sexual Behavior." *Alcohol Health and Research World,* 15 (Spring): 133–138.

Gelsthorpe, Loraine, and Alison Morris. 1988. "Feminism and Criminology in Britain." *British Journal of Criminology,* 28 (Spring): 223–240.

Gieringer, Dale. 1990. "How Many Crack Babies?" *The Drug Policy Letter,* 11 (March/April): 4–6.

Gilovich, Thomas. 1991. *How We Know What Isn't So: The Fallibility of Human Reasons in Everyday Life.* New York: Free Press.

Givens, James B. 1977. *Society and Homicide in Thirteenth-Century England.* Stanford, CA: Stanford University Press.

Glassner, Barry. 1982. "Labeling Theory." In M. Michael Rosenberg, Robert A. Stebbins, and Allan Turowitz (eds.), *The Sociology of Deviance.* New York: St. Martin's Press, pp. 71–89.

Glassner, Barry. 1999. *The Culture of Fear: Why Americans Are Afraid of the Wrong Things.* New York: Basic Books.

Glazer, Myron. 1975. "Impersonal Sex." In Laud Humphreys (ed.), *Tearoom Trade: Impersonal Sex in Public Places.* Chicago: Aldine, pp. 213–222.

Goffman, Erving. 1963. *Stigma: Notes on the Management of Spoiled Identity.* Englewood Cliffs, NJ: Prentice-Hall/Spectrum.

Goldberg, Carey. 1997. "On Adultery Issue, Many Aren't Ready to Cast the First Stone." *The New York Times,* June 9, pp. A1, A18.

Goldman, Douglas. 1955. "Treatment of Psychotic States with Chlorpromazine." *Journal of the American Medical Association,* 157 (April 19): 1274–1278.

Goodstein, Laurie. 2002. "Ousted Members Say Jehovah's Witnesses' Policy on Abuse Hides Offenses." *The New York Times,* August 11, p. 20.

Goodstein, Laurie. 2003. "Trail of Pain in Church Crisis Leads to Narly Every Diosese." *The New York Times,* August 11, p. 20.

Goldstein, Paul J. 1985. "The Drugs/Violence Nexus: A Tripartate Conceptual Framework." *Journal of Drug Issues,* 15 (Fall): 493–506.

Goldstein, Avram. 2001. *Addiction: From Biology to Drug Policy.* New York: Oxford University Press.

Goleman, Daniel. 1986. "To Expert Eyes, Streets Are Open Mental Wards." *The New York Times,* November 4, pp. C1, C3.

Goode, Erich. 1996. "The Ethics of Deception in Social Research: A Case Study." *Qualitative Sociology,* 19 (1): 11–33.

Goode, Erich. 2008a. "Moral Panic and Disproportionality: The Case of LSD Use in the Sixties." *Deviant Behavior,* 29 (6): 533–543.

Goode, Erich (ed.). 2008b. *Out of Control: Assessing the General Theory of Crime.* Stanford, CA: Stanford University Press.

Goode, Erich. 2008c. *Drugs in American Society* (7th ed.). New York: McGraw-Hill.

Goode, Erich, and Nachman Ben-Yehuda. 1994, 2009. *Moral Panics: The Social Construction of Deviance* (1st & 2nd ed.). Malden, MA & Oxford, UK: Blackwell; New York & Oxford, UK: Wiley-Blackwell.

Goode, Erich, and Angus Vail (eds.). 2008. *Extreme Deviance.* Thousand Oaks, CA: Pine Forge Press/Sage.

Goodstein, Laurie. 2009. "Catholic Order Jolted by Reports That Its Founder Led Double Life." *The New York Times,* February 4, p. A19.

Gottfredson, Michael R. and Travis Hirschi (eds.). 1987. *Positive Criminology.* Newbury Park, CA: Sage.

Gottfredson, Michael R., and Travis Hirschi. 1990. *A General Theory of Crime.* Stanford, CA: Stanford University Press.

Gouldner, Alvin W. 1968. "The Sociologist as Partisan: Sociology and the Welfare State." *The American Sociologist,* 3 (May): 103–116.

Gouldner, Alvin W. 1970. *The Coming Crisis of Western Sociology.* New York: Basic Books.

Gove, Walter R. 1972. "The Relationship Between Sex Roles, Marital Status, and Mental Illness." *Social Forces,* 51 (September): 34–44.

Gove, Walter R. 1975a. "The Labelling Theory of Mental Illness: A Reply to Scheff." *American Sociological Review,* 40 (April): 242–248.

Gove, Walter R. 1975b. "The Labelling Perspective: An Overview." In Walter R. Gove (ed.), *The Labelling of Deviance.* New York: John Wiley & Sons/Halstead/Sage, pp. 35–81.

Gove, Walter R. 1979a. "The Labelling Versus the Psychiatric Explanation of Mental Illness: A Debate That Has Become Substantially Irrelevant (Reply to Horwitz)." *Journal of Health and Social Behavior,* 20 (September): 301–304.

Gove, Walter R. 1979b. "Sex, Marital Status, and Psychiatric Treatment: A Research Note." *Social Forces,* 58 (September): 89–93.

Gove, Walter R. (ed.). 1980. *The Labelling of Deviance: Evaluating a Perspective.* Thousand Oaks, CA: Sage.

Gove, Walter R. (ed.). 1982a. *Deviance and Mental Illness.* Thousand Oaks, CA: Sage.

Gove, Walter R. 1982b. "Labelling Theory's Explanation of Mental Illness: An Update of Recent Evidence." *Deviant Behavior,* 3 (July–September): 307–327.

Gove, Walter R. 1989. "On Understanding Mental Illness and Some Insights to Be Gained from the Labelling Theory of Mental illness" (unpublished paper).

Gove, Walter R., and Terry R. Herb. 1974. "Stress and Mental Illness Among the Young: A Comparison of the Sexes." *Social Forces,* 53 (December): 256–265.

Grant, Marcus, and Jorge Litvak (eds.). 1998. *Drinking Patterns and Their Consequences.* Washington, DC: Taylor & Francis.

Grealy, Lucy. 1995. *Autobiography of a Face.* New York: HarperCollins.

Green, Jesse. 2001. "The New Gay Movement." *New York,* March 5, pp. 27–28, 82.

Greenberg, Joel. 1995. "Shared Hate: Jews and Arabs Mark Mosque Slayings." *The New York Times,* February 17, p. A3.

Greenfield, Lawrence A. 1998. *Alcohol and Crime.* Washington, DC: U.S. Department of Justice.

Grinspoon, Lester, and James B. Bakalar. 1976. *Cocaine: A Drug and Its Social Evolution.* New York: Basic Books.

Gronfein, William. 1985. "Psychotropic Drugs and the Origins of Institutionalization." *Social Problems,* 32 (June): 437–454.

Gross, Edward. 1978. "Organizational Crime: A Theoretical Perspective." In Norman Denzin (ed.), *Studies in Symbolic Interaction.* Greenwich, CT: JAI Press, pp. 55–88.

Groth, Nicholas, with H. Jean Burnham. 1979. *Men Who Rape: The Psychology of the Offender.* New York: Plenum Press.

Gruenbaum, Adolph. 1993. *Validation in the Clinical Theory of Psychoanalysis: A Study in the Philosophy of Psychoanalysis.* Madison, CT: International Universities Press.

Gurr, Ted Robert. 1989. "Historical Trends in Violent Crime: Europe and the United States." In Ted Robert Gurr (ed.), *Violence in America,* vol. I. Newbury Park, CA: Sage, pp. 21–54.

Hall, Jerome. 1952. *Theft, Law, and Society* (2nd ed.). Indianapolis, IN: Bobbs-Merrill.

Harkey, John, David L. Miles, and William Rushing. 1976. "The Relationship Between Social Class and Functional Status: A New Look at the Drift Hypothesis." *Journal of Health and Social Behavior,* 17 (September): 194–204.

Harlow, Caroline Wolf. 1987. "Robbery Victims." *Bureau of Justice Special Report,* April, pp. 1–10.

Hawkins, Richard, and Gary Tiedeman. 1975. *The Creation of Deviance: Interpersonal and Organization Determinants.* Columbus, OH: Charles E. Merrill.

Haworth, Alan, and Ronald Simpson (eds.). 2004. *Moonshine Markets: Issues in Unrecorded Alcohol Beverage Production and Consumption.* New York: Brunner-Mazel.

Heidensohn, Frances. 1968. "The Deviance of Women: A Critique and an Enquiry." *British Journal of Sociology,* 12 (2): 160–175.

Henshel, Richard L. 1990. *Thinking About Social Problems.* San Diego, CA: Harcourt Brace Jovanovich.

Hevey, David. 1992. *The Creatures Time Forgot: Photography and Disability Imagery.* London: Routledge.

Hiller, Dana V. 1981. "The Salience of Overweight in Personality Characterization." *Journal of Psychology,* 108: 233–240.

Hiller, Dana V. 1982. "Overweight as a Master Status: A Replication." *Journal of Psychology,* 110: 107–113.

Hindelang, Michael J. 1974. "Decisions of Shoplifting Victims to Invoke the Criminal Justice Process." *Social Problems,* 21 (Spring): 58–593.

Hirschi, Travis. 1969. *Causes of Delinquency.* Berkeley: University of California Press.

Hitt, Jack. 2000. "The Second Sexual Revolution." *The New York Times Magazine,* February 20, pp. 34–41.

Hirschi, Travis, and Michael R. Gottfredson (eds.). 1994. *The Generality of Deviance.* New Brunswick, NJ: Transaction.

Hockenberry, John. 1995. *Moving Violations: War Zones, Wheelchairs, and Declarations of Independence.* New York: Hyperion.

Hollinger, Richard, and Lynn Langton. 2008. *2007 National Retail Security Survey: Final Report.* Gainesville, FL: Department of Criminology, Security Research Project.

Hollingshead, August B., and Frederick C. Redlich. 1958. *Social Class and Mental Illness.* New York: John Wiley.

Horgan, Constance, Kathleen Carley Skwara, and Gail Strickler. 2001. *Substance Abuse: The Nation's Number One Health Problem.* Princeton, NJ: Robert Wood Johnson Foundation.

Horwitz, Allan V. 1990. *The Logic of Social Control.* New York: Plenum Press.

Hough, Michael. 1987. "Offenders' Choice of Target: Findings from Victim Surveys." *Journal of Quantitative Criminology,* 3 (3): 355–369.

Hubner, John, and Lindsey Gruson. 1989. *Monkey on a Stick.* New York: Harcourt, Brace, Jovanovich.

Humphreys, Laud. 1970, 1975. *Tearoom Trade: Impersonal Sex in Public Places* (1st & expanded ed.). Chicago: Aldine; New York: Aldine.

Hunt, Jennifer. 1985. "Police Accounts of Normal Force." *Urban Life,* 13 (January): 315–341.

Hunt, Morton. 1971. *The Affair: A Portrait of Extra-Marital Love in Contemporary America.* New York: New American Library/Signet.

Inciardi, James A. 1987. "Beyond Cocaine: Basuco, Crack, and Other Coca Products." *Contemporary Drug Problems,* 14 (Fall): 461–492.

Jenkins, Philip. 1996. *Pedophiles and Priests: Anatomy of a Contemporary Crisis.* New York & Oxford, UK: Oxford University Press.

Johnson, Anne, et al. 1994. *Sexual Attitudes and Lifestyles.* Oxford, UK: Blackwell Scientific Publications.

Johnson, Eric A., and Eric H. Monkkonen (eds.). 1996. *The Civilization of Crime: Violence in Town and Country Since the Middle Ages.* Urbana: University of Illinois Press.

Johnson, Ida. M. 2002. "Rape, Date and Marital." In David Levinson (ed.), *Encyclopedia of Crime and Punishment.* Thousand Oaks: Sage, pp. 1346–1352.

Johnston, Lloyd D., et al. 2005. *National Survey Results on Drug Use, 1975–2004,* vol. I, Secondary School Students. Bethesda, MD: National Institute on Drug Abuse.

Johnston, Lloyd D., et al. 2008. "2008 Data from In-School Surveys of 8th-, 10th-, and 12th-Grade Students." Ann Arbor, MI: University of Michigan News Service, December 11.

Johnston, Lloyd D., et al. 2009. *Monitoring the Future: National Results on Adolescent Drug Use, Overview of Key Findings, 2008.* Bethesda, MD: National Institute on Drug Abuse.

Jones, Edward E. 1986. "Interpreting Interpersonal Behavior: The Effects of Expectancies." *Science,* 234 (October): 41–46.

Jones, Edward E., et al. 1984. *Social Stigma: The Psychology of Marked Relationships.* New York: W.H. Freeman.

Jones, Russell A. 1977. *Self-Fulfilling Prophecies: Social, Psychological, and Physiological Effects of Expectancies.* Hillsdale, NJ: Lawrence Erlbaum.

Jones, Trevor, Brian MacLean, and Jock Young. 1986. *The Islington Crime Survey: Crime, Victimization, and Policing in Inner City London.* Aldershot, UK: Gower. November 22, pp. 20–25.

Kagay, Michael R. 1990. "Deficit Raises as Much Alarm as Illegal Drugs, Poll Finds." *The New York Times,* July 25, p. A9.

Kahneman, Daniel, Paul Slovic, and Amos Tversky (eds.). 1982. *Judgment Under Uncertainty: Heuristics and Biases.* Cambridge, UK: Cambridge University Press.

Kates, William. 2005. "Museums Answer Critics of Evolution." *The Washington Post,* December 26, pp. A22, A23.

Katz, Irwin. 1981. *Stigma: A Social Psychological Analysis.* Hillsdale, NJ: Lawrence Erlbaum.

Katz, Jack. 1988. *Seductions of Crime: Moral and Sensual Attractions of Doing Evil.* New York: Basic Books.

Kendall, R. E., et al. 1971. "Diagnostic Criteria of American and British Psychiatrists." *Archives of General Psychiatry,* 25 (August): 123–130.

Kessler, Ronald C. 1979. "Stress, Social Status, and Psychological Distress." *Journal of Health and Social Behavior,* 20 (September): 259–272.

Kessler, Ronald C., et al. 1994. "Lifetime and 12-Month Prevalence of DSM-III Psychiatric Disorders in the United States." *Archives of General Psychiatry,* 51 (1): 8–19.

Kety, Seymour S. 1974. "From Rationalization to Reason." *American Journal of Psychiatry,* 131 (September): 957–963.

Kinsey, Alfred Kinsey, Alfred C., Wardell B. Pomeroy, and Clyde E. Martin. 1948. *Sexual Behavior in the Human Male.* Philadelphia: W.B. Saunders.

Kinsey, Alfred C., Wardell B. Pomeroy, Clyde E. Martin, and Paul H. Gebhard. 1953. *Sexual Behavior in the Human Female.* Philadelphia: W.B. Saunders.

Kitcher, Philip. 1982. *Abusing Science: The Case Against Creationism.* Boston: MIT Press.

Kitsuse, John I. 1972. "Deviance, Deviant Behavior, and Deviants: Some Conceptual Problems." In William J. Filstead (ed.), *An Introduction to Deviance: Readings in the Process of Making Deviants.* Chicago: Markham, pp. 233–243.

Kitsuse, John I. 1980. "The New Conception of Deviance and Its Critics." In Walter R. Gove (ed.), *The Labelling of Deviance: Evaluating a Perspective.* Thousand Oaks, CA: Sage, pp. 381–392.

Konigsberg, Eric. 1998. "The Cheating Kind." *The New York Times Magazine,* March 8, p. 65.

Kornhauser, Ruth. 1978. *Social Sources of Delinquency: An Appraisal of Analytic Models.* Chicago: University of Chicago Press.

Kossey, Donna. 1994. *Kooks: Guide to the Outer Limit of Human Belief.* Venice, CA: Feral House.

Krauthammer, Charles. 1993. "Defining Deviancy Up." *The New York Republic,* November 22, pp. 20–25.

Krauthammer, Charles. 2002. "Why Didn't the Church Call the Cops?" *The Washington Post,* June 7, p. A27.

Kring, Ann M., Sheri L. Johnson, Gerald C. Davison, and John M. Neale. 2010. *Abnormal Psychology* (11th ed.). New York: John Wiley & Sons.

Krohn, Marvin D., and Ronald L. Akers. 1977. "An Alternative View of the Labeling Versus Psychiatric Perspectives on Societal Reaction to Mental Illness." *Social Forces,* 56 (December): 341–361.

Krugman, Paul. 2003. *The Great Unraveling: Losing Our Way in the New Century.* New York: W.W. Norton.

Ksir, Charles, Carl L. Hart, and Oakley Ray. 2006. *Drugs, Society, and Human Behavior* (11th ed.). New York: McGraw-Hill.

Kunkel, Karl R. 1999. "Reclaiming Deviance as a Unique Course from Criminology: Revisited." *Teaching Sociology,* 27 (January): 38–43.

Kurtz, Steven, et al. 2004. "Sex Work and Date Violence." *Violence Against Women,* 10: 357–385.

Lakshmi, Rama. 2002a. "Mob Attacks Indian Train: 57 Killed." *The Washington Post,* February 28, p. A13.

Lakshmi, Rama. 2002b. "Avenging Hindu Mobs Attack Muslims in India." *The Washington Post,* March 1, p. A14.

Lamy, Philip. 1996. *Millennium Rage: Survivalists, White Supremacists, and the Doomsday Prophecy.* New York: Plenum Press.

Landman, Janet T. and Robyn Dawes. 1982. "Psychotherapy Outcome: Smith and Glass' Conclusions Stand Up Under Scrutiny." *Psychological Bulletin,* 57: 504–516.

Lane, Charles. 2003. "Justices Overturn Texas Sodomy Ban." *The Washington Post,* June 27, pp. A1, A16.

Lane, Roger. 1997. *Murder in America: A History.* Columbus: Ohio State University Press.

Langlois, Judith, et al. 2000. "Maxims or Myth of Beauty: A Meta-Analytic and Theoretical Review." *Psychological Bulletin,* 126 (3): 390–423.

Laumann, Edward O., John H. Gagnon, Robert T. Michael, and Stuart Michaels. 1994. *The Social Organization of Sexuality: Sexual Practices in the United States.* Chicago: University of Chicago Press.

Lawson, Anette. 1988. *Adultery: An Analysis of Love and Betrayal.* New York: Basic Books.

Leigh, Barbara S. 1999. "Peril, Chance, Adventure: Conceptions of Risk, Alcohol Use and Risky Behavior in Young Adults." *Addiction,* 94 (3): 371–383.

Leighton, D. C., et al. 1963. *The Character of Danger: Psychiatric Symptoms in Selected Communities.* New York: Basic Books.

Lemert, Edwin M. 1951. *Social Pathology: A Systematic Approach to the Theory of Sociopathic Behavior.* New York: McGraw-Hill.

Lemert, Edwin M. 1953. "An Isolation and Closure Theory of Naïve Check Forgery." *Journal of Criminal Law, Criminology, and Police Science,* 44 (September–October): 296–307.

Lemert, Edwin M. 1958. "The Behavior of the Systematic Check Forger." *Social Problems,* 6 (Fall): 141–149.

Lemert, Edwin M. 1972. *Human Deviance, Social Problems, and Social Control* (2nd ed.). Englewood Cliffs, NJ: Prentice Hall.

Lemley, Brad. 2000. "Isn't She Lovely?" *Discover,* January, pp. 43–49.

Leonard, Eileen B. 1982. *Women, Crime, and Society: A Critique of Theoretical Criminology.* New York: Longman.

Lerner, Melvin J. 1980. *The Belief in a Just World: A Fundamental Delusion.* New York: Plenum Press.

Lerner, Michael A. 1989. "The Fire of 'Ice'," *Newsweek,* November 27, pp. 37, 38, 40.

Levine, Martin P., and Richard R. Troiden. 1988. "The Myth of Sexual Compulsivity." *Journal of Sex Research,* 25 (August): 347–363.

Levitt, Steven D. 2004. "Understanding Why Crime Fell in the 1990s: Four Factors That Explain the Decline and Six That Do Not." *Journal of Economic Perspectives,* 18 (1): 163–190.

Levitt, Steven D., and Stephen J. Dubner. 2005. *Freakonomics: A Rogue Economist Explores the Hidden Side of Everything.* New York: William Morrow.

Liazos, Alexander. 1972. "The Poverty of the Sociology of Deviance: Nuts, Sluts, and Deviated Preverts." *Social Problems,* 20 (Summer): 103–120.

Liem, Ramsay, and Joan Liem. 1978. "Social Class and Mental Health Reconsidered: The Role of Economic Stress and Economic Support." *Journal of Health and Social Behhavior,* 19 (June): 139–156.

Link, Bruce G. 1987. "Understanding Labeling Effects in the Area of Mental Disorders: An Assessment of the Effects of Expectations of Rejection." *American Sociological Review,* 52 (February): 96–112.

Link, Bruce G., and Frances T. Cullen. 1989. "The Labeling Theory of Mental Disorder: A Review of the Evidence." In James Greenly (ed.), *Mental Illness in Social Context.* Detroit: Wayne State University Press.

Link, Bruce G., Frances T. Cullen, Elmer Struening, Patrick Shrout, and Bruce P. Dohrenwend. 1989. "A Modified Labeling Theory Approach to Mental Disorders: An Empirical Assessment." *American Sociological Review,* 54 (June): 400–423.

Linton, Simi. 1998. *Claiming Disability: Knowledge and Identity.* New York: New York University Press.

Lofland, John. 1969. *Deviance and Identity.* Englewood Cliffs, NJ: Prentice-Hall.

Loftus, T. A. 1960. *Meaning and Methods of Diagnosis in Clinical Psychiatry.* Philadelphia: Lea & Febinger.

Long, Gary L., and D. S. Dorn. 1983. "Sociologists' Attitudes Toward Ethical Issues: The Management of an Impression." *Sociological and Social Research,* 67: 288–300.

Louderback, Llewellyn. 1970. *Fat Power: Whatever You Weigh Is Right.* New York: Hawthorn Books.

Lowman, John, Robert J. Menzies, and T. S. Palys (eds.). 1987. *Transcarceration: Essays in the Sociology of Social Control.* Gower, UK: Aldershot.

Lyall, Sarah. 2009. "Facing Anonymous Charges, Poet Departs Race for Post at Oxford." *The New York Times,* May 13, pp. C1, C5.

Lynch, Michael J., and W. Byron Groves. 1995. "In Defense of Comparative Criminology: A Critique of General Theory and the Rational Man." In Freda Adler and William S. Laufer (eds.), *The Legacy of Anomie Theory.* New Brunswick, NJ: Transaction, pp. 367–392.

MacAndrew, Craig, and Robert B. Edgerton. 1969. *Drunken Comportment.* Chicago: Aldine.

Macdonald, Scott, et al. 2006. "Variations of Alcohol Impairment in Different Types, Causes and Contexts of Injuries: Results of Emergency Room Studies from 16 Countries." *Accident Analysis and Prevention,* 38: 1107–1112.

Mack, John. 1995. *Abductions: Human Encounters with Aliens* (rev. ed.). New York: Bantam Books.

MacKinnon, Catherine A. 1979. *Sexual Harassment of Working Women.* New Haven, CT: Yale University Press.

Maddox, George L., Kurt W. Back, and Veronica Liederman. 1968. "Overweight as Social Deviance and Disability." *Journal of Health and Social Behavior,* 9 (December): 287–298.

Madigan, Nick. 2003. "Professor's Snub of Creationists Prompts U.S. Inquiry." *The New York Times,* February 3, p. A11.

Mairs, Nancy. 1997. *Waist-High in the World: A Life Among the Disabled.* Boston: Beacon.

Malamuth, Neil M. 1981. "Rape Proclivity Among Males." *Journal of Social Issues,* 37 (4): 138–157.

Malamuth, Neil M., Christopher L. Heavey, and Daniel Linz. 1992. "Predicting Men's Antisocial Behavior Against Women: The Interaction Model of Sexual Aggression." In Gordon C. Nagayama Hall (ed.), *Sexual Aggression: Issues in Etiology and Assessment, Treatment, and Policy.* New York: Hemisphere, pp. 63–97.

Markoff, John. 2009. "With Sensitive Software, Iranians and Others Outwit Net Censors." *The New York Times,* May 1, pp. A1, A3.

Marquis, Christopher. 2002. "Military Discharges of Gays Rise, and So Do Bias Incidents." *The New York Times,* March 14, p. A24.

Marshall, Helen, Kathy Douglass, and Desmond McDonnell. 2007. *Deviance and Social Control: Who Rules?* South Melbourne, Australia: Oxford University Press.

Martin, Dell. 1976. *Battered Wives.* San Francisco: Glide Foundation.

Marx, Karl, and Friedrich Engels. 1947. *The German Ideology,* Parts I and III. New York: International Publishers (orig. pub. 1846).

Matthews, Roger, and Jock Young (eds.). 1986. *Confronting Crime.* Thousand Oaks, CA: Sage.

Mazzetti, Mark, and Scott Shane. 2009. "Memos Spell Out Brutal C.I.A. Mode of Interrogation." *The New York Times,* April 17, pp. A1, A10.

McCaghy, Charles H. 1967. "Child Molesters: A Study of Their Career as Deviants." In Marshall B. Clinard and Richard Quinney (eds.), *Criminal Behavior Systems: A Typology.* New York: Holt, Rinehart & Winston, pp. 75–88.

McCaghy, Charles H. 1968. "Drinking and Disavowal: The Case of Child Molesters." *Social Problems,* 16 (Summer): 43–49.

McCaghy, Charles H., et al. 2006. *Deviant Behavior: Crime, Conflict, and Interest Groups.* Boston: Allyn & Bacon.

McIntosh, Mary. 1968. "The Homosexual Role." *Social Problems,* 16 (Fall): 182–192.

Meacham, Jon. 2009. "The End of Christian America." *Newsweek,* April 13, pp. 34–38.

Mechanic, David. 1989. *Mental Health and Social Policy* (3rd ed.). Englewood Cliffs, NJ: Prentice Hall.

Meier, Robert F. 1982. "Perspectives on the Concept of Social Control." *Annual Review of Sociology,* 8: 35–55.

Merton, Robert K. 1938. "Social Structure and Anomie." *American Sociological Review,* 3 (October): 672–682.

Merton, Robert K. 1948. "The Self-Fulfilling Prophecy." *Antioch Review,* 7 (Summer): 193–210.

Merton, Robert K. 1957. *Social Theory and Social Structure* (rev. & expanded ed.). Glencoe, IL: Free Press.

Messner, Steven F., and Richard Rosenfeld. 1997. *Crime and the American Dream* (2nd ed.). Belmont, CA: Wadsworth.

Michael, Robert T., John Gagnon, Edward O. Laumann, and Gina Kolata. 1994. *Sex in America: A Definitive Survey.* Boston: Little, Brown.

Miller, Jody. 2001. "Sex Tourism in Southeast Asia." In Alex Thio and Thomas C. Calhoun (eds.), *Readings in Deviant Behavior.* Boston: Allyn & Bacon, pp. 147–151.

Miller, Judith Droitcour, and Ira H. Cisin. 1980. *Highlights from the National Survey on Drug Abuse: 1979.* Rockville, MD: National Institute on Drug Abuse.

Miller, Lisa, et al. 2002. "Sins of the Fathers." *Newsweek,* March 4, pp. 43–52.

Millman, Marcia. 1975. "She Did It All for Love: A Feminist View of the Sociology of Deviance." In Marcia Millman and Rosabeth Moss Kantor (eds.), *Another Voice: Feminist Perspectives on Social Life and Social Science.* Garden City, NY: Doubleday-Anchor, pp. 251–279.

Millman, Marcia. 1980. *Such a Pretty Face: Being Fat in America.* New York: W.W. Norton.

Minton, Henry L. 2002. *Departing From Deviance: A History of Homosexual Rights and Emancipatory Science in America.* Chicago: University of Chicago Press.

Mitchell, David T., and Sharon L. Snyder (eds.). 1997. *The Body and Physical Differences: Discourses of Disability.* Ann Arbor: University of Michigan Press.

Mocan, Naci, and Erdal Tekin. 2006. "Ugly Criminals." Cambridge, MA: NBER Working Paper no.12019, January.

Monestier, Martin. 1987. *Human Oddities* (trans. Robert Campbell). Secaucus, NJ: Citadel Press.

Morin, Richard. 2006. "The Ugly Face of Crime." *The Washington Post,* February 17, p. 2.

Morin, Richard, and Alan Cooperman. 2003. "Majority Against Blessing Gay Unions." *The Washington Post,* August 14, pp. A1, A10.

Morris, Henry M. 1972. *The Remarkable Birth of Planet Earth.* San Diego: Creation-Life Publishers.

Moynihan, Daniel Patrick. 1993. "Defining Deviancy Down." *American Scholar,* 64 (Winter): 25–33.

Muecke, Marjorie. 1992. "Mother Sold Food, Daughter Sells Her Body: The Cultural Continuity of Prostitution." *Social Science and Medicine,* 35: 891–901.

Muehlenhard, Charlene L, and Melaney A. Linton. 1987. "Date Rape and Sexual Aggression in Dating Situations: Incident and Risk Factors." *Journal of Counseling Psychology,* 34 (2): 186–196.

Murphy, Jane M. 1976. "Psychiatric Labeling in Cross-Cultural Perspective." *Science,* 191 (12 March): 1019–1028.

Musto, David F. 1987, 1999. *The American Disease: Origins of Narcotic Control* (expanded ed.; 3rd ed.). New York: Oxford University Press.

Mydans, Seth, and Mark McDonald. 2009. "Novelist Given 3 Years for Insulting Thai King." *The New York Times,* January 20, p. A8.

Nettler, Gwynn. 1974. "On Telling Who's Crazy." *American Sociological Review,* 39 (December): 893–894.

Nettler, Gwynn. 1984. *Explaining Crime* (3rd ed.). New York: McGraw-Hill.

Neuspiel, D. R., et al. 1991. "Maternal Cocaine Use and Infant Behavior." *Neurotoxicology and Teratology,* 13 (March–April): 229–233.

Newman, Graeme. 1976. *Comparative Deviance: Perception in Law in Sex Cultures.* New York: Elsevier.

Newman, William M. 1973. *American Pluralism: A Study of Minority Groups and Social Theory.* New York: Harper & Row.

Numbers, Ronald L. 1992. *The Creationists: The Evolution of Scientific Creationism.* Berkeley: University of California Press.

Nyaronga, Dan, Thomas K. Greenfield, and Patricia A. McDonald. 2009. "Drinking Context and Drinking Problems Among Black, White, and Hispanic Men and Women in the 1984, 1995, and 2005 U.S. National Alcohol Surveys." *Journal of Studies on Alcohol,* 70 (January): 16–26.

O'Donnell, John A. and Richard R. Clayton. 1982. "The Stepping-Stone Hypothesis—Marijuana, Heroin, and Causality." *Chemical Dependencies: Behavioral and Biomedical Issues,* 4 (3): 229–241.

Oreskes, Michael. 1990. "Drug War Underlines Fickleness of Public." *The New York Times,* September 6, p. A22.

Park, Robert E. 1926. "The Urban Community as a Spatial Pattern and a Moral Order." In Ernest W. Burgess (ed.), *The Urban Community.* Chicago: University of Chicago Press, pp. 3–18.

Parker, Robert Nash, and Randi S. Cartmill. 1998. "Alcohol and Homicide in the United States 1934–1995—Or One Reason Why U.S. Rates of Violence May Be Going Down." *Journal of Criminal Law and Criminology,* 88 (Summer): 1369–1398.

Parks, Kathleen A., and William Fals-Stewart. 2004. "The Temporal Relationship Between College Women's Alcohol Consumption and Victimization Experiences." *Alcoholism: Clinical and Experimental Research,* 28 (April): 625–629.

Parrot, Andrea, and Steven Allen. 1984. "Acquaintance Rape: Seduction or Crime? When Sex Becomes a Crime." Paper presented at the Eastern Regional Society for the Study for the Scientific Study of Sex. April 6–8.

Parsons, Talcott. 1951. *The Social System.* New York: Free Press.

Paton-Simpson, Grant R. 1995. *"Underconsumption" of Alcohol as a Form of Deviance: Minimum Drinking Norms in New Zealand Society and the Implications of their Production and Reproduction During Social Occasions.* PhD Dissertation. Aukland, New Zealand: University of Aukland.

Parker, Robert Nash. 1995. *Alcohol and Homicide: A Deadly Combination of Two American Traditions.* Albany: State University of New York Press.

Paul, D. M. 1975. "Drugs and Aggression." *Medicine, Science, and Law,* 15 (1): 16–21.

Pearlin, Leonard I., and Joyce S. Johnson. 1977. "Marital Status, Life Strains, and Depression." *American Sociological Review,* 42 (October): 704–715.

Pernanen, Kai. 1991. Alcohol and Violence. New York: Guilford Press.

Perrin, Robin. 2005. "When Religion Becomes Deviance: Introducing Religion in Deviance and Social Problems Courses." Unpublished paper, Pepperdine University, Social Sciences Division.

Perrow, Charles. 1984. *Normal Accidents: Living with High-Risk Technologies.* New York: Basic Books.

Petrunik, Michael. 1980. "The Rise and Fall of 'Labeling Theory': The Construction and Deconstruction of a Sociological Strawman." *Canadian Journal of Sociology,* 5 (3): 213–233.

Pfohl, Stephen. 1994. *Images of Deviance and Social Control: A Sociological History* (2nd ed.). New York: McGraw-Hill.

Phillips, Derek L. 1964. "Rejection of the Mentally Ill: The Influence of Behavior and Sex." *American Sociological Review,* 29 (October): 755–763.

Piattelli-Palmarini, Massimo. 1994. *Inevitable Illusions: How Mistakes of Reason Rule Our Minds.* New York: John Wiley & Sons.

Pinker, Steven. 2009. "Why Is There Peace?" *Greater Good Magazine,* April.

Plummer, Kenneth. 1979. "Misunderstanding Labelling Perspectives." In David Downes and Paul Rock (eds.), *Deviant Interpretations.* London: Martin Robinson, pp. 85–121.

Plummer, Kenneth. 1982. "Symbolic Interactionism and Sexual Conduct: An Emergent Perspective." In Mike Brake (ed.), *Human Sexual Relations: Toward a Redefinition of Politics.* New York: Pantheon Books, pp. 223–241.

Polk, Kenneth. 1991. Review of Michael R. Gottfredson and Travis Hirschi, *A General Theory of Crime,* Stanford, CA: Stanford University Press; 1990, in *Crime and Delinquency,* 37 (2): 275–279.

Pollack, Earl, and Carol A. Taube. 1975. "Trends and Projections in State Hospital Use." In Jack Zussman and Elmer Bertsch (eds.). *The Future Role of the State Hospital.* Lexington, MA: D.C. Heath, pp. 31–55.

Polsky, Ned. 1998. *Hustlers, Beats, and Others* (expanded ed.). New York: Lyons Press.

Potter, R. H. 1999. "Deviance Down Under or How a Deviance Assignment Became a Folk Devil." In Martin D. Schwartz and Michael O. Maume (eds.), *Teaching the Sociology of Deviance.* Washington DC: American Sociological Association, pp. 52–60.

Powdermaker, Hortense. 1960. "An Anthropological Approach to the Problem of Obesity." *Bulletin of the New York Academy of Medicine,* 36: 286–295.

Powell, Michael. 2002. "A Fall from Grace." *The Washington Post,* August 4, pp. F1, F4–F5.

Powell, Michael. 2005. "Judge Rules Against Intelligent Design." *The Washington Post,* December 21, pp. A1, A20.

Priest, G. L. 1990. "The New Legal Structure of Risk Control." *Daedalus,* 119: 207–228.

Quindlen, Anna. 1990. "Hearing the Cries of Crack." *The New York Times,* October 7, p. E19.

Quinney, Richard. 1970. *The Social Reality of Crime.* Boston: Little, Brown.

Quinney, Richard. 1979. *Criminology* (2nd ed.) Boston: Little, Brown.

Rand, Michael R. 2008. "Criminal Victimization, 2007." *Bureau of Justice Statistics Bulletin,* December, 1–11.

Rand, Michael, and Shannan Catalano. 2007. "Criminal Victimization, 2006," *Bureau of Statistics Bulletin,* (December), pp. 1–11.

Rashbaum, William K. 2008. "Revelations About Governor Began in Routine Tax Inquiry." *The New York Times,* March 11, pp. A1, A18.

Ray, Joel G., et al. 2008. "Alcohol Sales and Risk of Serious Assault." *PLos Medicine,* May, pp. 1–15.

Reckless, Walter C. 1950. *The Crime Problem.* New York: Appleton-Century-Crofts.

Reiger, Darrel A., et al. 1988. "One-Month Prevalence of Mental Disorders in the United States Based on Five Epidemiological Catchment Areas Sites." *Archives of General Psychiatry,* 45 (November): 977–986.

Reinarman, Craig, and Harry G. Levine (eds.). 1997. *Crack in America: Demon Drugs and Social Justice.* Berkeley: University of California Press.

Rennison, Callie Marie, and Michael R. Rand. 2003. "Criminal Victimization, 2002." *Bureau of Justice Statistics, National Crime Victimization Survey,* August, pp. 1–12.

Reuter, Peter, and Franz Trautmann (eds.). 2009. *A Report on Global Illicit Drugs Markets, 1998–2007.* Amsterdam: European Commission.

Rhodes, William, Mary Layne, Anne-Marie Bruen, Patrick Johnston, and Lisa Becchetti. 2001. *What America's Users Spend on Illegal Drugs.* Washington, DC: Executive Office of the President, Office of National Drug Control Policy.

Richardson, Diane. 1996. "Heterosexuality and Social Theory." In Diane Richardson (ed.), *Theorising Heterosexuality.* Buckingham, UK: Open University Press, pp. 1–20.

Richardson, Gale A., and Nancy L. Day. 1994. "Detrimental Effects of Prenatal Cocaine Exposure: Illusion or Reality?" *Journal of the American Academy of Child and Adolescent Psychiatry,* 33 (January): 28–34.

Rimland, Bernard. 1969. "Psychogenesis Versus Biogenesis: The Issue and the Evidence." In Stanley C. Plog and Robert B. Edgerton (eds.), *Changing Perspectives in Mental Health.* New York: Holt, Rinehart & Winston, pp. 702–735.

Roberts, Cathy. 1989. *Women and Rape.* New York: New York University Press.

Roiphe, Katie. 1997. "Adultery's Double Standard." *The New York Times Magazine,* October 7, pp. 54–55.

Ronai, Carol Rambo. 1992. "The Reflexive Self Through Narrative: A Night in the Life of an Erotic Dancer/Researcher." In Carolyn Ellis and Michael G. Falherty (eds.), *Investigating Subjectivity: Research on Lived Experience.* Thousand Oaks, CA: Sage, pp.102–124.

Ronai, Carol Rambo, and Carolyn Ellis. 1989. "Turn-Ons for Money: Interactional Strategies of the Table Dancer." *Journal of Contemporary Ethnography,* 18 (October): 271–298.

Rosenhan, David L. 1973. "On Being Sane in Insane Places." *Science,* 179 (January 19): 250–258.

Rosenthal, Jack. 1981. "The Pornography of Fat." *The New York Times,* May 29, p. A26.

Ross, Brian. 2008. "Spitzer Quits but Other Public Figure May Be Linked to Escort Ring." *ABC News,* March 12.

Rowell, Earle Albert, and Robert Rowell. 1937. *On the Trail of Marihuana: The Weed of Madness.* Mountain View, CA: Pacific Press.

Rubington, Earl, and Martin S. Weinberg (eds.). 2007. *Deviance: The Interactionist Perspective* (10th ed.). Boston: Allyn & Bacon.

Rumbarger, John J. 1989. *Profits, Power, and Prohibition: Alcohol Reform and the Industrializing of America 1800–1930.* Albany: State University of New York Press.

Rushing, William. 1979a. "The Functional Importance of Sex Roles and Sex-Related Behavior in Societal Reactions to Residual Deviants." *Journal of Health and Social Behavior,* 20 (September): 208–217.

Rushing, William. 1979b. "Marital Status and Mental Disorder: Evidence in Favor of a Behavioral Model." *Social Forces,* 58 (December): 540–556.

Russell, Diana E. H. 1975. *The Politics of Rape: The Victim's Perspective.* New York: Stein & Day.

Ryan, William. 1976. *Blaming the Victim.* New York: Random House.

Sagarin, Edward. 1969. *Odd Man In: Societies of Deviants in America.* Chicago: Quadrangle.

SAMHSA. 2008. *Results from the 2007 National Survey on Drug Use and Health: National Findings.* Rockville, MD: Substance Abuse and Mental Health Services Administration.

Sanday, Peggy Reeves. 1981. "The Socio-cultural Context of Rape: A Cross-Cultural Study." *Journal of Social Issues,* 37 (1): 5–27.

Sanday, Peggy Reeves. 1990. *Fraternity Gang Rape: Sex, Brotherhood and Privilege on Campus.* New York: New York University Press.

Sanday, Peggy Reeves. 1996. "Rape-Prone Versus Rape-Free Campus Cultures." *Violence Against Women,* 2 (June): 191–208.

Sanders, Clinton R. 1989. *Customizing the Body: The Art and Culture of Tattooing.* Philadelphia: Temple University Press.

Scheff, Thomas J. 1966, 1984, 1999. *Being Mentally Ill: A Sociological Theory* (1st, 2nd & 3rd ed.). Chicago: Aldine; New York: Aldine de Gruyter.

Schneider, Alan. 1999. "The Academic Path to Pariah Status." *The Chronicle of Higher Education,* July 2, pp. A12–A24.

Schultes, Richard Evans, and Albert Hofmann. 1979. *Plants of the Gods: Origins of Hallucinogenic Use.* New York: Alfred van der Mark Editions.

Schur, Edwin M. 1979. *Interpreting Deviance: A Sociological Introduction.* New York: Harper & Row.

Schur, Edwin M. 1980. *The Politics of Deviance: Stigma Contests and the Users of Power.* Englewood Cliffs, NJ: Prentice-Hall.

Schur, Edwin M. 1984. *Labeling Women Deviant: Gender, Stigma, and Social Control.* New York: Random House.

Schwartz, John. 2009. "Vocal Minority Insists It Was All Smoke and Mirrors." *The New York Times,* July 14, p. D8.

Scull, Andrew. 1984. *Decarceration: Community Treatment and the Deviant—A Radical View* (2nd ed.). Cambridge, UK: Polity Press.

Scull, Andrew. 1988. "Deviance and Social Control." In Neil J. Smelser (ed.), *Handbook of Sociology.* Thousand Oaks, CA: Sage, pp. 667–693.

Scully, Diana. 1990. *Understanding Sexual Violence: A Study of Convicted Rapists.* Boston: Unwin Hyman.

Scully, Diana, and Joseph Marolla. 1985. "Riding the Bull at Gilley's: Convicted Rapists Describe the Rewards of Rape." *Social Problems,* 32 (February): 251–262.

Shackleford, Todd K., and Avi Besser. 2007. "Predicting Attitudes Toward Homosexuality: Insights from Personality Psychology." *Individual Differences Research,* 5 (2): 106–114.

Shenon, Philip. 1990. "War on Drugs Remains Top Priority, Bush Says." *The New York Times,* September 6, p. A22.

Shermer, Michael. 1997. *Why People Believe Weird Things: Pseudoscience, Superstition, and Other Confusions of Our Time.* New York: W.H. Freeman.

Short, James F., Jr. 1990. "Hazards, Risk, and Enterprise: Approaches to Law, Science, and Social Policy." *Law and Society Review,* 24 (1): 179–198.

Siegel, Larry. 2008. *Criminology: Theories, Patterns, and Typology* (10th ed.). Belmont, CA: Wadsworth Thompson.

Simon, Jesse, and Jack Zussman. 1983. "The Effect of Contextual Factors on Psychiatrists' Perception of Illness: A Case Study." *Journal of Health and Social Behavior,* 24 (2): 186–198.

Singer, Margaret, and Janja Lalich. 1995. *Cults in Our Midst.* San Francisco: Jossey-Bass.

Skolnick, Jerome H., and James J. Fyfe. 1993. *Above the Law: Police and the Excessive Use of Force.* New York: Free Press.

Slackman, Michael. 2008. "9/11 Rumors That Harden Into Conventional Wisdom." *The New York Times,* September 9, p. A16.

Slovic, Paul, Baruch Fischoff, and Sarah Lichtenstein. 1980. "Risky Assumptions." *Psychology Today,* June, pp. 44–48.

Slovic, Paul, Mark Layman, and James H. Flynn. 1991. "Risk, Perception, Trust, and Nuclear Waste: Lessons from Yucca Mountain." *Environment,* 33 (April): 28–30.

Smith, Mary Lee, Gene Glass, and Thomas Miller. 1980. *The Benefits of Psychotherapy.* Baltimore: Johns Hopkins University Press.

Spillane, Joseph F. 2000. *Cocaine: From Medical Marvel to Modern Menace in the United States, 1884–1920.* Baltimore, MD: Johns Hopkins University Press.

Spira, Alfred, et al. 1992. "AIDS and Sexual Behavior in France." *Nature,* 360 (3 December): 407–409.

Spira, Alfred, et al. 1993. *Les Comportments Sexuels en France.* Paris: La Documentation Francais.

Spitzer, Robert L. 1975. "On Pseudoscience in Science, Logic in Remission, and Psychiatric Diagnosis: A Critique of Rosenhan's 'On Being Sane in Insane Places.' " *Journal of Abnormal Psychology,* 84 (5): 442–452.

Spitzer, Robert L. 1976. "More on Pseudoscience in Science and the Case for Psychiatric Diagnosis: A Critique of D. L. Rosenhan's 'On Being Sane in Insane Places' and 'The Contextual Nature of Psychiatric Diagnosis.' " *Archives of General Psychiatry,* 33 (April): 459–470.

Srole, Leo, et al. 1962. *Mental Health in the Metropolis: The Midtown Manhattan Study.* New York: McGraw-Hill.

Stark, Rodney, and William Sims Bainbridge. 1996. *Religion, Deviance, and Social Control.* New York and London: Routledge.

Stimpson, Gerry, Marcus Grant, Marie Choquet, and Preston Garrison. 2007. *Drinking in Context: Patterns, Interventions, and Partnerships.* New York: Routledge.

Stoller, Robert J., and R. H. Geertsma. 1963. "The Consistency of Psychiatrists' Clinical Judgment." *Journal of Nervous and Mental Disease,* 137 (January): 58–66.

Stormo, Karla J., Alan R. Lang, and Werner G. K. Stritzke. 1997. "Attributions About Acquaintance Rape: The Role of Alcohol and Individual Differences." *Journal of Applied Social Psychology,* 24 (4): 279–305.

Styles, Joseph. 1979. "Outsider/Insider: Researching Gay Baths." *Urban Life,* 8 (July): 135–152.

Summers, Anne. 1981. "Hidden from History: Women Victims of Crime." In Satyanshu K. Mukerjee and Jocelynne A. Scutt (eds.), *Women in Crime.* North Sydney, Australia: George Allen/Unwin Australia, pp. 22–30.

Sumner, Colin. 1994. *The Sociology of Deviance: An Obituary.* Buckingham, UK: Open University Press.

Sutherland, Edwin H. 1939. *Principles of Criminology* (3rd ed.). Philadelphia: Lippencott.

Sutherland, Edwin H. 1940. "The White Collar Criminal." *American Sociological Review,* 5 (February): 1–12.

Sutherland, Edwin H. 1949. *White Collar Crime.* New York: Dryden.

Tannenbaum, Frank. 1938. *Crime and the Community.* New York: Ginn.

Tausig, Mark, Janet Michello, and Sree Subedi. 2004. *A Sociology of Mental Illness* (2nd ed.). Upper Saddle River, NJ: Prentice Hall.

Tedeschi, James T., and Richard B. Felson. 1994. *Violence, Aggression, and Coercive Actions.* Washington, DC: American Psychological Association.

Testa, Maria. 2004. "The Role of Substance Use in Male-to-Female Physical and Sexual Violence." *Journal of Interpersonal Violence,* 19 (December): 1494–1505.

Thoits, Peggy. 1985. "Self-Labeling Processes in Mental Illnesses: The Role of Emotional Distance." *American Journal of Sociology,* 91 (September): 221–249.

Thomas, W. I., and Florian Znanieki. 1918–1920. *The Polish Peasant in Europe and America.* Chicago: University of Chicago Press.

Thompson, Rosemarie Garland (ed.). 1996. *Freakery: Cultural Spectacles of the Extraordinary Body.* New York: New York University Press.

Thompson, Rosemarie Garland. 1997. *Extraordinary Bodies.* New York: Columbia University Press.

Torrey, E. Fuller, Anne E. Bowler, Edward H. Taylor, and Irving I. Gottesman. 1994. *Schizophrenia and Manic Depressive Disorder: The Biological Roots of Mental Illness as Revealed by the Landmark Study of Identical Twins.* New York: Basic Books.

Toufexis, Anastasia. 1991. "Innocent Victims." *Time,* May 13, pp. 56–60.

Townsend, John Marshall. 1978. *Cultural Conceptions of Mental Illness.* Chicago: University of Chicago Press.

Townsend, John Marshall. 1980. "Psychiatry Versus Societal Reaction: A Critical Analysis." *Journal of Health and Social Behavior,* 21 (September): 268–278.

Tracy, Paul E., Marvin E. Wolfgang, and Robert M. Figlio. 1990. *Delinquency in Two Birth Cohorts.* New York: Plenum Press.

Traub, Stuart H., and Craig B. Little (eds.). 1999. *Theories of Deviance* (5th ed.). Itasca, IL: Peacock.

Turk, Austin T. 1969. *Criminality and the Legal Order.* Chicago: Rand McNally.

Turner, Ronny E., and Charles Edgley. 1983. "From Witchcraft to Drugcraft: Biochemistry as Mythology." *Social Science Journal,* 20 (October): 1–12.

Turner, R. Jay, and John W. Gartrell. 1978. "Social Factors in Psychiatric Outcome: Toward a Resolution of Interpretive Controversies." *American Sociological Review,* 43 (June): 368–382.

Ullman, Sarah E, George Karabatsos, and Mary P. Koss. 1999. "Alcohol and Sexual Assault in a National Sample of College Women." *Journal of Interpersonal Violence,* 16 (June): 603–625.

Unnever, James D. 1987. Review of James M. Byrne and Robert J. Sampson (eds.), *The Social Ecology of Crime.* New York: Springer-Verlag; 1986, in *Contemporary Sociology,* 16 (November): 845–846.

van der Veen, Marjolein. 2001. "Rethinking Commodification and Prostitution." *Rethinking Marxism,* 13 (Summer): 30–51.

van Wagtendonk, Reinout. 2009. "US Waterboarding Officials Could Face Prosecution." *Radio Netherlands Worldwide Internet Archive,* March 22.

von Hentig, Hans. 1948. *The Criminal and His Victim.* New Haven, CT: Yale University Press.

Warheit, George J., Charles E. Holzer III, Roger A. Bell, and Sandra A. Avery. 1976. "Sex, Marital Status, and Mental Health: A Reappraisal." *Social Forces,* 55 (December): 459–470.

Warren, Carol A. B., and John M. Johnson. 1972. "A Critique of Labeling Theory from the Phenomenological Perspective." In Robert A. Scott and Jack D. Douglas (eds.), *Theoretical Perspectives on Deviance.* New York: Basic Books, pp. 69–92.

Warwick, Donald P. 1973. "Tearoom Trade: Means and Ends in Social Research." *The Hastings Center Studies,* 1 (1): 27–38.

Weber, Max. 1946. *From Max Weber: Essays in Sociology* (trans. & ed. Hans H. Gerth and C. Wright Mills). New York: Oxford University Press.

Weber, Max. 1963. *The Sociology of Religion* (trans. Ephraim Fischoff). Boston: Beacon Press (orig. pub. 1922).

Weil, Andrew. 1972. *The Natural Mind: A New Way of Looking at Drugs and the Higher Consiousness.* Boston: Houghton Mifflin.

Weintraub, Bernard, and Jim Rutenberg. 2003. "Gay-Themed TV Gains a Wider Audience." *The New York Times,* July 29, pp. A1, C5.

Weisburd, David, Stanton Wheeler, Elin Waring, and Nancy Bode. 1991. *Crimes of the Middle Classes: White-Collar Offenders in the Federal Courts.* New Haven, CT: Yale University Press.

Weitzer, Ronald (ed.). 2000. *Sex for Sale: Prostitution, Pornography, and the Sex Industry.* New York & London: Routledge.

Weitzer, Ronald. 2005. "New Directions in Research on Prostitution." *Crime, Law, and Social Change,* 43: 211–235.

Wellings, Kaye, Julia Field, Anne Johnson, and Jane Wadsworth. 1994. *Sexual Behavior in Britain: The National Survey of Sexual Attitudes and Lifestyles.* New York: Penguin.

Wells, Jonathan. 2000. *The Icons of Evolution.* Washington, DC: Regenery.

Wheeler, Stanton. 1960. "Sex Offenses: A Sociological Critique." *Law and Contemporary Society,* 25 (Spring): 258–278.

WHO (World Health Organization). 2005. *Alcohol Use and Sexual Risk Behaviour: A Cross-Cultural Study in Eight Countries.* Geneva, Switzerland: WHO.

Wilkinson, Gregg S. 1975. "Patient-Audience Social Status and the Social Construction of Psychiatric Disorder: Toward a Differential Frame of Referential Hypothesis." *Journal of Health and Social Behavior,* 16 (March): 28–38.

Williams, Joyce E., and Willard A. Nielson, Jr. 1979. "The Rapist Looks at His Crime." *Free Inquiry into Creative Sociology,* 7 (November): 128–132.

Williams, Terry. 1996. "Exploring the Cocaine Culture." In Carolyn D. Smith and William Kornblum (eds.), *In the Field: Readings in the Field Research Experience* (2nd ed.). Westport, CT: Praeger, pp. 27–32.

Wills, Garry. 2002. "Scandal." *The New York Review of Books,* May 23, pp. 6–9.

Wolfe, Linda. 1976. *Playing Around: Women and Extra-Marital Sex.* New York: New American Library/Signet.

Wright, James D., Peter H. Rossi, and Kathleen Daly. 1983. *Under the Gun: Weapons, Crime, and Violence in America.* New York: Aldine De Gruyter.

Wright, Richard T., and Scott Decker. 1994. *Burglars on the Job: Streetlife and Residential Break-ins.* Boston: Northeastern University Press.

Young, Robert, Helen Sweeting, and Patrick West. 2008. "A Longitudinal Study of Alcohol Use and Antisocial Behaviour in Young People." *Alcohol and Alcoholism,* 43 (October): 204–214.

Young, Stanley. 1989. " 'Zing!' Speed: The Choice of a New Generation." *Spin Magazine,* July, pp. 83–84, 124–125.

Zador, Paul L., Sheila A. Krawchuk, and Robert B. Voas. 2000. "Alcohol-Related Relative Risk of Driver Fatalities and Driver Involvement in Fatal Crashes in Relation to Driver Age and Gender." *Journal of Studies on Alcohol,* 61 (May): 387–395.

Zimring, Franklin E. 2007. *The Great American Crime Decline.* Oxford, UK & New York: Oxford University Press.

Author Index

Q

R

S

T

U

V

W

Y

Z

Subject Index

D

E

F